Artificial Neural Networks for Speech and Vision

CHAPMAN & HALL NEURAL COMPUTING SERIES

Series editors: Igor Aleksander, Imperial College, London, UK
Richard Mammone, Rutgers University, New Jersey, USA

Since the beginning of the current revival of interest in Neural Networks, the subject is reaching considerable maturity, while at the same time becoming of interest to people working in an increasing number of disciplines. This series seeks to address some of the specializations that are developing through the contributions of authoritative writers in the field. This series will address both specializations and applications of neural computing techniques to particular areas.

1. **Delay Learning in Artificial Neural Networks**
   Catherine Myers
2. **Analogue Neural VLSI: A pulse stream approach**
   Alan Murray and Lionel Tarassenko
3. **Neurons and Symbols: The stuff that mind is made of**
   Igor Aleksander and Helen Morton
4. **Artificial Neural Networks for Speech and Vision**
   Edited by Richard J. Mammone

Artificial Neural Networks for Speech and Vision

Edited by

Richard J. Mammone

Professor of Electrical and Computer Engineering
Rutgers University
New Jersey, USA.

CHAPMAN & HALL
London · Glasgow · New York · Tokyo · Melbourne · Madras

Published by Chapman & Hall, 2–6 Boundary Row, London SE1 8HN, UK

Chapman & Hall, 2–6 Boundary Row, London SE1 8HN, UK

Blackie Academic & Professional, Wester Cleddens Road, Bishopbriggs, Glasgow G64 2NZ, UK

Chapman & Hall Inc., One Penn Plaza, 41st Floor, New York NY 10119, USA

Chapman & Hall Japan, Thomson Publishing Japan, Hirakawacho Nemoto Building, 6F, 1-7-11 Hirakawa-cho, Chiyoda-ku, Tokyo 102, Japan

Chapman & Hall Australia, Thomas Nelson Australia, 102 Dodds Street, South Melbourne, Victoria 3205, Australia

Chapman & Hall India, R. Seshadri, 32 Second Main Road, CIT East, Madras 600 035, India

First edition 1994

© 1994 Richard J. Mammone

Typeset in 10/12 pts Times by Thomson Press (India) Ltd, New Delhi
Printed in Great Britain at The University Press, Cambridge

ISBN   0 412 54850 X

A catalogue record for this book is available from the British Library

Library of Congress Cataloging-in-Publication Data

Artificial neural networks for speech and vision / edited by Richard J. Mammone.
    p. cm. — (Chapman & Hall neural computing series; 4)
    Includes bibliographical references and index.
    ISBN 0-412-54850-X
    1. Neural networks (Computer science) 2. Automatic speech recognition. 3. Computer vision. I. Mammone, Richard J.
    II. Series: Chapman & Hall neural computing; 4.
    QA76.87.A7433   1993   93-32966
    006.3—dc20   CIP

Contents

PART THREE   ANN APPLICATIONS IN VISION

Contributors

A. Agarwal
Motorola, Inc., Cambridge, MA, USA

O.K. Al-Shaykh
Department of Electrical Engineering, Iowa State University, IA, USA

Francesca Albertini
Dipartimento di Matematica, Universita di Padova, Padova, Italy

Gabriele Anzellotti
Department of Mathematics, University of Trento (Povo), Italy

Benjamin B. Bederson
Bellcore, Morristown, NJ, USA

Alain Biem
ATR Auditory and Visual Perception Research Laboratories, Kyoto, Japan

Toufic Boubez
Center for Computer Aids for Industrial Productivity, Rutgers University,
Piscataway, NJ, USA

David J. Burr
Bellcore, Morristown, NJ, USA

Leon N. Cooper
Institute for Brain and Neural Systems, Brown University, Providence, RI,
USA

Trevor J. Darrell
Vision and Modeling Group, The Media Laboratory, MIT, Cambridge, MA,
USA

Bert de Vries
David Sarnoff Research Center, Princeton, NJ, USA

John Doherty
Department of Electrical Engineering, Iowa State University, IA, USA

Gerald M. Edelman
Neuroscience Institute, New York, NY, USA

K. R. Farrell
Center for Computer Aids for Industrial Productivity, Rutgers University, Piscataway, NJ, USA

Gregory Francis
Center for Adaptive Systems and Department of Cognitive and Neural Systems, Boston University, MA, USA

W. Einar Gall
Neuroscience Institute, New York, NY, USA

A. N. Gertner
AT & T Bell Laboratories, Murray Hill, NJ, USA

C. Lee Giles
Institute for Advanced Computer Studies, University of Maryland, MD, USA

Federico Girosi
Artificial Intelligence Laboratory, MIT, Cambridge, MA, USA

Allen Gorin
AT & T Bell Laboratories, Murray Hill, NJ, USA

Philip Gouin
Nestor, Inc., Providence, RI, USA

Stephen Grossberg
Center for Adaptive Systems and Department of Cognitive and Neural Systems, Boston University, MA, USA

Kurt Hornik
Vienna Center for Neural Networks, Technische Universität Wien, Austria

Biing-Hwang Juang
AT & T Bell Laboratories, Murray Hill, NJ, USA

Shigeru Katagiri
ATR Auditory and Visual Perception Research Laboratories, Kyoto, Japan

J. J. Kosowsky
Division of Applied Science, Harvard University, Cambridge, MA, USA

Gary M. Kuhn
Siemens Corporate Research, Princeton, NJ, USA

Vincent Maillot
Dept. de Mathématiques et d'Informatique, Ecole Normale Supérieure, Paris, France

R. J. Mammone
Center for Computer Aids for Industrial Productivity and Department of Electrical and Computer Engineering, Rutgers University, Piscataway, NJ, USA

Clifford B. Miller
NEC Research Institute, Princeton, NJ, USA

Ennio Mingolla
Center for Adaptive Systems and Department of Cognitive and Neural Systems, Boston University, MA, USA

Arthur Nádas
Computer Science Department, IBM T. J. Watson Research Center, Yorktown Heights, NY, USA

D. K. Naik
Center for Computer Aids for Industrial Productivity, Rutgers University, Piscataway, NJ, USA

Alex P. Pentland
Vision and Modeling Group, The Media Laboratory, MIT, Cambridge, MA, USA

Michael P. Perrone
Institute for Brain and Neural Systems, Brown University, Providence, RI, USA

David C. Plaut
Department of Psychology, Carnegie Mellon University, Pittsburgh, PA, USA

L. Y. Pratt
Department of Mathematics and Computer Science, Colorado School of Mines, Golden, CO, USA

Mazin G. Rahim
AT & T Bell Laboratories, Murray Hill, NJ, USA

George N. Reeke, Jr.
Neuroscience Institute, New York, NY, USA

Ananth Sankar
AT & T Bell Laboratories, Murry Hill, NJ, USA

Eric L. Schwartz
Department of Cognitive and Neural Systems, Boston University, MA, USA

Christopher Scofield
Nestor, Inc., Providence, RI, USA

Tim Shallice
Department of Psychology, University College, London, UK

Eduardo D. Sontag
Department of Math, Rutgers University, Piscataway, NJ, USA

Olaf Sporns
Neuroscience Institute, New York, NY, USA

Steven C. Suddarth
Air Force Office of Scientific Research/NM Bolling AFB, DC, USA

Naftali Tishby
Department of Computer Science and Center for Neural Computation, Hebrew University, Jerusalem, Israel

Giulio Tononi
Neuroscience Institute, New York, NY, USA

Richard S. Wallace
Courant Institute of Mathematical Sciences, New York University, NY, USA

Raymond L. Watrous
Siemens Corporate Research, Princeton, NJ, USA

Joseph Wilder
Center for Computer Aids for Industrial Productivity, Rutgers University, Piscataway, NJ, USA

Wen Wu
Center for Computer Aids for Industrial Productivity, Rutgers University, Piscataway, NJ, USA

A. L. Yuille
Division of Applied Science, Harvard University, Cambridge, MA, USA

Preface

Our understanding of computational models which are analogous to the neural structure of the brain has evolved rapidly over the past several years. The field has reached the point where many practical systems are becoming available for applications in speech and vision. A complementary effect has also occurred where the investigation of Artificial Neural Networks (ANNs) has evoked interesting questions and insights for researchers in the fields which deal with biological speech and vision. The purpose of this book is to integrate much of the current issues and applications of ANNs to speech and vision in a single volume. The field of ANNs has attracted interest from many diverse disciplines. The synergistic relationship among the areas of computer science, engineering, psychology, neurology, mathematics and physics has created a uniquely productive environment.

This book covers some of the latest developments in the design and training of neural networks. In addition numerous applications of ANNs in Speech and Vision are given. We refer to ANNs in the plural due to the fact that there are many different types of networks included under this heading. Probably the most popular is the Multi-Layer Perceptron (MLP) which uses the well-known back-propagation training algorithm. However, there are numerous ANNs based on dynamic and statistical models. Many of these ANNs are derived from modeling biological neurons or some physical phenomenon such as spin glasses. The various approaches to ANNs are reviewed in the first part of the book.

Some of the most promising current research on ANNs with applications in speech and vision is contained in this book. The work is reported by the best sources on the subject, the investigators themselves. The book is divided into three sections; the first section gives an overview of the general field of ANNs with several advanced topics; the second section is a compilation of the latest applications of ANNs in speech and language; and the third section is an overview of the most up-to-date ANN based vision systems.

One goal of current ANN research is to improve our understanding of neurological or physical phenomenon. There is also a great deal of interest in the use of ANNs to perform tasks which were previously the exclusive domain of biological systems. These tasks are most frequently applications involving pattern recognition of some kind. For example, to automatically recognize a written or spoken word, or to recognize a face or a defective part on an assembly line.

Some of the issues currently under investigation include the effects of noise, the temporal and spatial correlations between feature vectors, the rate of convergence of learning algorithms, and the uniqueness of the 'optimal' weights found by these algorithms. These topics are covered in the first part of the book. In addition, the first part describes new methods of enhancing the performance of ANNs to include optimal combining or fusing of multiple output decisions, transfer of learning, long-term memory retention while learning new tasks, the effects of relabeling the classes for improved learning and the use of previously learned tasks to improve future learning.

The second part of the book presents the latest developments in the use of ANNs for speech and language. The applications of ANNs in speech and language understanding have been primarily to enhance the performance of previously developed systems which recognize speakers, words and the meaning of spoken or written language. The generic problem involves the mapping from written text or acoustic waveforms to higher order symbols or the intended 'meaning'. This process typically involves the parsing of the waveform into Phoneme type segments. It is shown that this segmentation can be accomplished using ANNs. The most common speech classifier today is probably the Hidden Markov Model (HMM). Relationships between the HMM and ANNs are of fundamental interest to the speech community. The temporal correlation of input vectors can be taken advantage of by feed-forward or time-delay neural networks or by feedback neural networks such as in recurrent neural networks. Recurrent neural networks are shown to have certain advantages for speech applications. The use of alternative criteria for optimization while learning speech tasks based on Bayesian ideas is also shown to enhance the performance of neural networks for speech. The analog between the effects of language in biological and artificial neural networks is of interest to both neurological and computer oriented researchers. The use of ANNs to understand the meaning from text or speech is an exciting new application. These topics are all discussed in the second part of the book.

The third part of the book is concerned with the role of ANNs in vision. Computational models offer not only pedagogical advantages in enhancing our understanding of biological vision systems, but they also provide practical machine vision systems for government and industry. There are many neural-based vision systems currently in progress. The vision systems reported here make use of biologically motivated computational models. Thus, we see active vision concepts used where a vision system selects the next view point of an object based on cues extracted from previous views. In addition, stochastic type optimization techniques are used which are based on a Darwinian model of the nervous system. The ability to identify objects from an image regardless of the orientation and location is another goal where ANN vision systems attempt to emulate biological systems. The segmentation of image data based on time-varying imagery is an important process under investigation. The imitation of biological vision systems has led to numerous practical systems which can help automate data entry and the transmission of image data such as line drawings. These are all topics which are dealt with in the third and final section of the book devoted to ANNs in vision.

The book consists of 30 chapters divided into three parts. The first part consists of 14 chapters which start by introducing the basic principles of ANNs, and go on to discuss advanced topics on the training and use of ANNs in speech and vision. The first chapter by Burr gives an overview of the progress in ANNs over the last ten years with emphasis on Multi-Layer Perceptrons (MLP). The second chapter by Suddarth gives a brief overview of ANNs from a dynamic systems point of view. The third chapter by Yuille and Kosowsky presents a statistical view of ANNs. A comprehensive analysis of linear ANNs with respect to noise is given in Chapter 4 by Hornik. A locally recurrent elastic ANN is introduced by de Vries in Chapter 5. Higher order recurrent ANNs are described in Chapter 6 by Giles and Miller.

The idea of Radial Basis Functions (RBF) or local receptive field ANNs is combined with a wavelet basis in Chapter 7 by Boubez. An analysis of the rate of convergence for RBF ANNs is given in Chapter 8 by Girosi and Anzellotti. The question of uniqueness of the optimum weight vector of an ANN is discussed in Chapter 9 by Albertini, Sontag and Maillot. Chapter 10 by Perrone and Cooper introduces a method of improving performance when ANNs disagree. Chapter 11 by Pratt presents a method whereby information learned on one ANN can be exchanged with other ANNs. Chapter 12 by Agarwal and Mammone introduces a method of eliminating the catastrophic forgetting problem of ANNs. Chapter 13 by Wu and Mammone presents a new learning algorithm which illustrates the importance of selecting appropriate labels for learning a specific task. Chapter 14 by Naik and Mammone introduces a method whereby the learning curve trajectories of problems learned previously can be used to help accelerate the learning of similar problems in the future.

The second part of the book is on Applications in Speech and Language Understanding and contains nine chapters. Chapter 15, 'A Self-Learning Neural Tree Network for Phone Recognition', by Rahim, illustrates how to use a Neural Tree Network to recognize the basic acoustic units of speech. Chapter 16 by Nádas discusses the relationships between ANNs and Hidden Markov Models (HMM). Chapter 17 by Kuhn and Watrous gives a comparison of feed-forward and recurrent neural network sensitivities for speech recognition. Chapter 18 by Katagiri, Juang and Biem, entitled 'Discriminative Feature Extraction', describes an interesting and exciting new way to train neural networks. Chapter 19 by Plaut and Shallice examines the similarities and differences of the types of errors made by using damaged artificial and actual neural networks. Chapter 20 by Sankar and Gorin introduces a system which learns symbolic concepts such as the color 'blue' while in a conversational mode with a teacher. Chapter 21 by Gorin and Tishby formulates the language acquisition problem as an algebraic system of linear equations. An incremental or on-line learning algorithm is introduced in Chapter 22 by Farrell, Mammone and Gorin to solve the algebraic formulation of the language acquisition problem given in Chapter 21. Chapter 23 by Gertner and Gorin illustrates a realistic application of incremental learning.

The third part of the book focuses on Application of ANNs in Vision. Chapter 24 by Bederson, Wallace and Schwartz introduces a multi-resolution active vision system called Cortex I. Chapter 25 by Reeke *et al.* also introduces a vision system called NOMAD which is based on a Darwin 'survival of the fittest' learning strategy. Chapter 26 by Francis, Grossberg and Mingolla introduces a cooperative-competitive feedback neural-based vision system. Chapter 27 by Darrell and Pentland introduces a vision system for recognition of gestures. Chapter 28 by Wilder presents a face recognition system based on the neural tree network. Chapter 29 by Al-Shaykh and Doherty presents a method for space invariant image recognition. Chapter 30 by Gouin and Scofield introduces a neural network strategy for the segmentation of text information in a realistic environment.

This book is intended for people who are interested in gaining a working knowledge of the care and feeding of modern neural networks. Each chapter of this book was written to be as self-contained as possible. However, I recommend reading the first few chapters first for someone unfamiliar with ANNs.

Richard J. Mammone
Piscataway, NJ
March, 1993

Acknowledgements

I would like to thank all of the authors of this volume who so generously contributed their work. My thanks to S. Sivaprasad and Alvin Garcia for their help in typing and organizing the manuscript. Also a special thanks to Mrs Barbara Daniels for her diligent typing and help in organizing the manuscript.

I would also like to thank Chapman & Hall, particularly Eliane Wigzell, for her patience in waiting for the manuscript.

Part One

Artificial Neural Networks (ANN)

1

Artificial neural networks: A decade of progress*

DAVID J. BURR
Bellcore, Morristown, NJ 07962, USA

1.1 Introduction

The field of Artificial Neural Networks (ANN) was born in the 1940s when McCulloch and Pitts (1943) proposed a computational model based on a simple **neuron-like** logical element. Donald Hebb (1949) described a learning rule for adapting the connection strengths of these artificial neurons. The Hebb rule or **delta** rule became the basis of almost all ANN research that was to follow. After an extended period of early activity (Rosenblatt, 1962; Widrow and Hoff, 1960), only a few researchers in the USA, Europe and Asia managed to maintain financial support for their work. Since its rebirth in the early 1980s, the ANN field has experienced extremely rapid growth, attracting followers from many disciplines ranging from physics and engineering through physiology and psychology. Conferences on ANN theory and applications are now abundant, and many journals now exist.

The early part of the rebirth is generally attributed to Hopfield (1982), who stimulated many with his excellent talks on dynamics and emergent properties of ANNs. Rumelhart, Hinton and Williams (1986) developed a generalization of the delta rule which would make possible the training of powerful multi-layered learning networks. Sejnowski and Rosenberg (1986) demonstrated this with their NETtalk system, which learned to speak English from examples of letter-to-sound rules. Demonstrations of difficult ANN learning tasks in speech recognition, language development and pattern recognition soon followed.

---

* Reproduced with permission from *AVIOS'92 Conference Proceedings*; published by American Voice Input/Output Society, 1992.

Artificial Neural Networks for Speech and Vision. Edited by Richard J. Mammone. Published in 1993 by Chapman & Hall, London. ISBN 0 412 54850 X

In recent years we have seen the application of ANNs to many problems, including phoneme recognition, word spotting, talker identification, language recognition, signal separation, time series prediction and combinatorial optimization. The decade has also shown much progress in the development of new learning algorithms, structured neural networks, unsupervised learning and VLSI implementations. For overviews of the ANN field, see Lippmann (1989) or Hanson and Burr (1991).

I will first review the areas of multi-layer networks, recurrent nets, hybrid networks and elastic nets. Then I will describe recent applications in the areas of speech, language, sound localization, character recognition and sonar processing. Finally, I will draw some conclusions on progress during the decade.

1.2 Multi-layer Perceptrons and learning

Multi-layer Perceptrons (MLP) have played a central role in the rebirth of the field. Layers naturally differentiate the inputs from the outputs and the internal or **hidden** units. It is the hidden units which form complex nonlinear discrimination boundaries for classification. Cybenko (1989) proved that a single hidden layer is sufficient for forming arbitrary functions. Linsker (1988) demonstrated that the hidden units learn those values which are the principal components of the data. Learning is accomplished by minimizing the error between outputs and target values (Rumelhart *et al.*, 1986), or by maximizing an entropy measure on the outputs. Conjugate gradient methods have also been used to accelerate learning (Kramer and Sangiovanni-Vincentelli, 1989).

Instead of minimizing the error, a method called Learning Vector Quantization (LVQ) directly minimizes the number of misclassifications. LVQ techniques were originally proposed by Kohonen (1988), and related techniques have been described by Hampshire (1990) and Katagiri *et al.* (1991). (For a recent application of LVQ, see Bennani *et al.*, 1990.) Similar techniques based on vector **prototypes** include the Reduced Coulomb Energy (RCE) of Scofield (1988) and the adaptive resonance models of Carpenter and Grossberg (1987). Another alternative to gradient descent is the cascade correlation architecture of Fahlman and Lebiere (1990), which fits the error surface first with a coarse approximation and then iteratively improves the fit by selectively adding hidden neurons.

1.3 Recurrent and time delay networks

Recurent networks contain both feed-forward and feedback connections to model time-varying or dynamic patterns (Watrous, 1987; Jordan, 1986; Bengio, 1991). Recurrent networks are well suited to time sequence modeling for speech and handwriting recognition and for economic prediction. Recurrent weights can be adapted or learned just like feed-forward weights using a variation of back propagation expanded in time (Watrous *et al.*, 1988). Miyata describes a variation of a recurrent Jordan network which uses hierarchies of time resolution (Miyata, 1988) Bridle (1990) showed that recurrent networks using entropy error measures are equivalent to Hidden Markov Models (HMM) commonly used in speech recognition.

Because of the excessive data required to train fully connected MLP networks with large numbers of free parameters, networks with limited interconnections have been proposed. One particularly interesting architecture is the Time Delay Neural Network (TDNN) (Waibel *et al.*, 1989). TDNNs have been studied extensively, and generally report good results when compared to HMM systems. A recent competition (Weigend and Gershenfeld, 1992) showed that the TDNN architecture was useful for solving several different time series prediction problems.

1.4 HMMs and hybrid systems

ANNs have been integrated with conventional methods of signal processing such as Hidden Markov Models. When used for pattern classification, ANNs have an advantage over HMMs because they find optimal discrimination boundaries between classes. HMMs are naturally able to incorporate syntactic and semantic constraints into compositional search strategies via the Viterbi algorithm. Therefore, hybrid networks which combine HMMs and ANNs are an area of strong interest. One example of a hybrid is described by Leung *et al.* (1992), who combined a Viterbi search with a segment-based MLP. Austin *et al.* (1992) described another version in which N-best sentences are derived from a conventional HMM model, and an MLP is used to rescore the sentences.

Fuzzy systems are used to perform pattern classification by encoding explicit fuzzy rules to perform the task (Zadeh, 1965). In contrast, neural networks learn by adapting their weights, and rules are often difficult to infer. Hybrid systems are currently being studied which hope to benefit from fuzzy initialization using explicit rules with neural adaptation to optimize performance. There is now cooperation between neural networks and fuzzy systems conferences.

1.5 Elastic and feature mapping networks

Elastic and feature maps are very common in mammalian nervous systems for performing topographic sensory maps (speech, vision, touch) to the cortex. Maps preserve topographic neighborhood relationships from the (2D) sensor to the corresponding cortical layer. In binocular vision they give rise to the cortical columns or ocular dominance stripes (Schwartz, 1985). Researchers have attempted to simulate the cortical column production in artificial mapping models (Cowan and Friedman, 1991; Blasdel and Obermayer

1992). Willshaw and Von der Malsburg (1976) showed earlier how principles of self-organization could be used to construct brain maps, and Amari (1980) proposed a mathematical mapping model.

Computational models for elastic and feature mapping have been proposed independently by Kohonen (1982) and Burr (1981). Input pattern matches are generated by the nearest neighbor rule and then re-estimated by convolution with a neighborhood kernel function. An important property of the kernel function is that it decreases in radius with successive iterations, allowing the feature map to converge to a solution. Elastic mapping, which was once computationally expensive, is now more practical due to recent improvements in parallel processing hardware (Abidi, 1989 – personal communication).

Von der Malsburg (1988) has developed elaborate graph matching networks for topological mapping. Elastic maps have been applied to handwriting recognition (Burr, 1981) and to the traveling salesman problem (Durbin and Willshaw, 1987; Burr, 1988). Kohonen (1988) studied extensively the use of feature mapping networks for dimensionality reduction, in particular for speech recognition.

1.6 MLP applications

Neural networks outperform conventional methods for multi-sensor fusion and multi-modal recognition. Yuhas *et al.* (1990) have combined visual and acoustic cues in an MLP which reads lips while listening to speech. Bellagarda and Kanevsky (1991) have proposed using handwritten input with spoken text in a combined system. They argue that the spoken letter confusions characterized by the **E-set** sounds are better discriminated in written form. DARPA is also said to be exploring funding of research in multi-modal recognition.

Word spotting is being revisited in the light of possible telephone and database retrieval services accessible by voice. Classical HMM-Viterbi methods are robust in their integration of training over many speakers, but are sub-optimal in their scoring technique. Neural networks have been proposed to do word spotting (English and Boggess, 1992) by using time delay weights which are adapted by example.

Muthusamy and Cole (1992) have done some interesting work in spoken language recognition. Their initial experiments showed that four different languages could be recognized using a model based on segments of the utterance. They achieved 89.5% accuracy on the four languages using a large set of broad category features. Recently, they have extended the database to ten different languages.

Language translation has recently been rejuvenated by the promise of new funding from DARPA. Brown (1992) described a conventional estimation maximization approach to translation. It uses a conventional Viterbi search together with a bilingual side-by-side corpus of French and English. A conventional French–English dictionary proposes word matches while the corpus provides statistics regarding actual translations. Their algorithm reduces the translation to a best path search through a word transition lattice.

Binaural localization is an important problem with applications in microphone steering for audio teleconferencing, and in aids for the hearing impaired. Herault and Jutten (1986) proposed a signal separation algorithm based on an adaptive process for unmixing signals, but their algorithm cannot deal with time delays. Platt and Faggin (1992) described an enhanced Herault network which can unmix time-delayed signals. Unfortunately, real audio signals contain reverberation which can confuse the algorithm.

Character recognition has received attention recently since databases for handwritten characters have become available. LeCun *et al.* (1989) described a hierarchical MLP with increasing receptive field sizes for learning handwritten characters. Guyon *et al.* (1990) applied a TDNN to handwriting recognition, and Martin and Pittman (1991) used a standard MLP network for character recognition.

A novel area of application for neural networks is in sonar recognition (Gorman and Sejnowski, 1988). Roitblatt *et al.* (1992) simulated a dolphin's echo location capability using a variety of neural networks. Dolphins are known to have highly refined echo location capabilities which are difficult to mimic.

1.7 Summary

It has been possible to give only a sampling of the literal explosion of work that has occurred in the ANN field during the past decade. In summary, it appears that the field has prospered, not only by the high quality of results that have been achieved, but also by the many applications that ANNs have touched. The future holds promise of greatly improved learning speed by replacing software learning algorithms with highly parallel hardware. The merging of ANNs into existing conventional systems is a healthy trend, as it indicates an appreciation of the value added by neural networks, which are ideal for complex multi-feature discrimination tasks.

References

Amari, S. (1980) Topographic organization of neural fields. *Bulletin of Mathematical Biology*, **42**, 339–64.

Austin, S., Zavaliagkos, G., Makhoul, J. and Schwartz, R. (1992) Speech recognition using segmental neural nets. *Proc. ICASSP*, March, 1992, San Francisco, USA.

Bellagarda, J.R. and Kanevsky, D. (1991) Enhanced machine recognition of speech through the integration of handwriting side information. *J. Acoust. Soc. Am.*, **90**(4) Pt. 2, 2272.

Bengio, Y. (1991) Artificial Neural Networks and Their Application to Sequence Recognition. Ph.D. thesis, McGill University.

Bennani, Y., Fogelman-Soulie, F. and Gallinari, P. (1990) Text-dependent speaker identification using learning vector quantization. *Proc. International Neural Networks Conference*, **2**, 1087–90, July 9–13, 1990, Paris, France.

Blasdel, G. and Obermayer K. (1992) Optical and neural network analyses of orientation and ocular dominance in monkey striate cortex. *Neural Networks for Computing Conference*, April 7–10, 1992, Snowbird, USA.

Bridle, J.S. (1990) Alpha nets: A recurrent neural network architecture with a hidden Markov model interpretation. *Speech Communication*, **9**(1), 83–92.

Brown, P. (1992) A statistical approach to machine translation. *Neural Networks for Computing Conference*, April 7–10, 1992, Snowbird, USA.

Burr, D.J. (1981) A dynamic model for image registration. *Computer Graphics and Image Processing*, **15**, 102–12.

Burr, D.J. (1988) An improved elastic net method for the travelling salesman problem, *IEEE International Conference on Neural Networks*, July, 1988, San Diego, USA.

Carpenter, G.A. and Grossberg, S. (1987) ART 2: Self organization of stable category recognition codes for analog input patterns. *Applied Optics*, **26**(23), 4919–30.

Cowan, J.D. and Friedman, A.E. (1991) Single spin models for the development of ocular dominance and iso-orientation patches, in *Advances in Neural Information Processing Systems*, **3**, Morgan-Kaufmann, San Mateo, pp. 26–31.

Cybenko, G. (1989) Approximation by superpositions of a sigmoidal function. *Mathematics of Control, Signals, and Systems*, **2**(4).

Durbin, R. and Willshaw, D.J. (1987) An analogue approach to the travelling salesman problem using an elastic net method. *Nature*, **326**(6114), 689–91.

English, T.M. and Boggess, L.C. (1992) Back propagation training of a neural network for word spotting, *Proc. ICASSP*, **II**, 357–60, March 23–26, 1992, USA.

Fahlman, S.E. and Lebiere, C. (1990) The cascade-correlation learning architecture, in *Advances in Neural Information Processing Systems*, 2nd edn, (ed. D.S. Touretzky), Morgan-Kaufmann, San Mateo, pp. 524–32.

Gorman, R.P. and Sejnowski, T. (1988) Analysis of hidden units in a layered network trained to classify sonar signals. *Neural Networks*, **1**, 75–80.

Guyon, I., Albrecht, P., LeCun, Y., Denker, J. and Hubbard, W. (1990) Time delay neural network character recognizer for a touch terminal. *Proc. International Neural Networks Conference*, **1**, July 9–13, 1990, Paris, France.

Hampshire, J.B. II (1990) A novel objective function for improved phoneme recognition using time-delay neural networks. *IEEE Trans. on Neural Networks*, **1**(2).

Hanson, S.J. and Burr, D.J. (1991) What connectionist models learn: learning and representation in connectionist networks. *Behavioral and Brain Sciences*, **13**(3), 471–518. (See also *Neural Network Theory and Applications* (eds R. Mammone and Y. Zeevi), Academic Press, New York, 1991.)

Hebb, D.O. (1949) *The Organization of Behavior*, Wiley, New York.

Herault, J. and Jutten, C. (1986). Space or time adaptive signal processing by neural networks models. *AIP Conference Proceedings 151*, 207–11, Snowbird, USA.

Hopfield, J.J. (1982) Neural networks and physical systems with emergent collective computational abilities. *Proc. Nat. Acad. Sci.*, **74**, 2554–8.

Jordan, M.I. (1986) Serial Order: A Parallel Processing Approach. Center for Human Information Processing, UCSD. *Technical Report*.

Katagiri, S., Lee, C.H. and Jung, B.H. (1991) Discriminative multi-layer feed-forward networks, *Neural Networks for Signal Processing, Proc. 1991 IEEE Workshop*, September 30–October 2, 1991, Princeton, NJ, USA.

Kohonen, T. (1982) Self organized formation of topologically correct feature maps. *Biological Cybernetics*, **43**, 59–69.

Kohonen, T. (1988) The neural phonetic typewriter. *IEEE Computer Magazine*, **21**, 11–22.

Kramer, A.H. and Sangiovanni-Vincentelli, A. (1989) Efficient parallel learning algorithms for neural networks, in *Advances in Neural Information Processing Systems*, 1st edn (ed. D.S. Touretzky), Morgan-Kaufmann, San Mateo, pp. 40–8.

LeCun, Y., Jackel, L.D., Boser, B., Denker, J.S., Graf, H.P., Guyon, I., Henderson, D., Howard, R.E. and Hubbard, W. (1989) Handwritten digit recognition: Applications of neural network chips and automatic learning. *IEEE Communications Magazine*, **27**(11), 41–6.

Leung, H.C., Hetherington, I.L., and Zue, V.W. (1992) Speech recognition using stochastic segment neural networks, *Proc. ICASSP*, March 23–36, 1992, San Francisco, CA USA.

Linsker, R. (1988) Self organization in a perceptual network. *IEEE Computer Magazine*, **21**, 105–17.

Lippmann, R.P. (1989) Pattern classification using neural networks. *IEEE Communications Magazine*, **27**(11), 47–64.

Von der Malsburg, C. (1988) Pattern recognition by labeled graph matching. *Neural Networks*, **1**, 141–8.

Martin, G.L. and Pittman, J.A. (1991) Recognizing hand-printed letters and digits using back propagation learning. *Neural Computation*, **3**(3), 258–67.

McCulloch, W.S. and Pitts, W. (1943) A logical calculus of the ideas immanent in nervous activity. *Bulletin of Mathematical Biophysics*, **5**, 115–33.

Miyata, Y. (1988) The Learning and Planning of Actions. PhD thesis, Psychology Department, University of California, San Diego.

Muthusamy, Y.K. and Cole, R.A. (1992) A segment-based automatic language identification system, in *Advances in Neural Information Processing Systems*, **4**, Morgan-Kaufmann, San Mateo.

Platt, J.C. and Faggin, F. (1992) Network for the separating of sources that are superimposed and delayed, in *Advances in Neural Information Processing Systems*, **4**, Morgan-Kaufmann, San Mateo.

Roitblatt, H., Moore, W.B., Nachtigall, D.E. and Penner, R.H. (1992) Natural dolphin echo location using an integrator gateway network, in *Advances in Neural Information Processing Systems*, **3**, Morgan-Kaufmann, San Mateo, pp. 273–81.

Rosenblatt, F. (1962) *Principles of Neuro-Dynamics*, Spartan, Washington, DC.

Rumelhart, D.E., Hinton, G.E. and Williams, R. (1986) Learning internal representation by error propagation, *Nature*, **323**, 533–6.

Schwartz, E.L. (1985) On the mathematical structure of retinotopic mapping of primate striate cortex. *Science*, **227**, 1066.

Scofield, C.L. (1988) Learning internal representations in the coulomb energy network, *Proc. IEEE International Conference on Neural Networks*, I, 271–6, San Diego, CA, USA.

Sejnowski, T. and Rosenberg, C. (1986) NETtalk: A parallel network that learns to read aloud. *The Johns Hopkins University EE and CS Technical Report*.

Waibel, A., Hanazawa, T., Hinton, G., Shikano, K. and Lang, K. (1989) Phoneme recognition using time-delay neural networks. *IEEE Transactions on Acoustics, Speech and Signal Processing*, **37**, 328–39.

Watrous, R.L. (1987) Learning algorithms for connectionists networks: applied gradient methods of nonlinear optimization, *IEEE First International Conference on Neural Networks*, II, 619–27, San Diego, CA, USA.

Watrous, R.L., Ladendorf, B. and Kuhn, G.M. (1988) Complete gradient optimization for a recurrent network applied to /b/, /d/, /g/ discrimination, *115th Meeting of the Acoustical Society of America*, Seattle, WA, USA.

Weigend, A.S. and Gershenfeld, N.A. (1992) Results of the times series competition at the Santa Fe Institute, *Neural Networks for Computing Conference*, April 7–10, 1992, Snowbird, UT, USA.

Widrow, B. and Hoff, M.E. (1960) Adaptive switching circuits, *1960 WESCON Convention Record*, Part IV, 96–104.

Willshaw, D.J. and Von der Malsburg, C. (1976) How patterned neural connections can be set up by self organization. *Proc. Royal Social of London B*, **194**, 431–45.

Yuhas, B.P., Goldstein, M.H. Jr., Sejnowski, T.J. and Jenkins, R.E. (1990) Neural networks models of sensory integration for improved vowel recognition. *Proc. IEEE* **78**(10), 1658–78.

Zadeh, L.A. (1965) Fuzzy sets. *Information and Control*, **8**, 338–53.

2

Continuous computing: thoughts on Turing equivalence, programming and noise

STEVEN C. SUDDARTH
Air Force Office of Scientific Research, NM Bolling AFB, DC, USA

2.1 Introduction

Continuous computing is a topic of recent interest, drawing researchers from biology, quantum physics, dynamical systems, neural networks and even chemistry. Currently, the most practical continuous computation device, the neural network, has been of great interest because of inherent parallelism and learning capability. The range of applications for neural networks, however, is currently limited without assistance from more conventional types of computing. In fact, nearly all current applications of neural networks are carefully engineered components of larger computing systems which include other tasks such as I/O, pre- and post-processing, display, storage and even symbolic reasoning. In many applications such as speech and signal processing, temporal dynamics have greatly complicated the processes of learning and execution. Thus, many use recurrent networks which are capable of generating and using an internal state.

This chapter explores issues in extending recurrent neural systems into the domain currently occupied by more conventional von-Neumann computers. The possible advantages of such machines could be extensive. They could use inherent parallel structure to quickly perform more conventional computing tasks such as I/O, data housekeeping and display. They could conceivably mix learning, optimization and symbolic programming into a seamless whole,

Artificial Neural Networks for Speech and Vision. Edited by Richard J. Mammone. Published in 1993 by Chapman & Hall, London. ISBN 0 412 54850 X

capable of performing complex tasks with high agility. Finally, they could provide more physically and logically robust versions of existing symbolic algorithms.

The possibility of continuous-state processors brings up a number of interesting questions, like:

- Are they Turing-equivalent?
- How can they be programmed? Can we perform learning? Can we mix the two?
- What about noise? Are they robust?
- How should states be encoded?

While no major new results will be discussed in this chapter, it will provide a framework for thinking about continuous computing and the special challenges it presents.

2.2 Time and neuromorphic processing

Many non-linear learning systems, such as neural networks, can be modeled by equations like

$$\mathbf{y} = f(\mathbf{w}, \mathbf{x})$$

where the vectors $\mathbf{x}$, $\mathbf{y}$ and $\mathbf{w}$ represent inputs, outputs and adjustable parameters. Dynamical learning systems, on the other hand, could be equivalently represented by

$$[\dot{\mathbf{s}}(t), \mathbf{y}(t)] = f[\mathbf{w}(t), \mathbf{x}(t), \mathbf{s}(t), \mathbf{u}(t)]$$

where the vector-valued function $\mathbf{s}(t)$ represents an internal state, and $\mathbf{u}(t)$ represents an optional external forcing function (such as a clock signal). These systems exhibit memory and a natural ability to make temporal associations. Systems of this sort include those investigated by Freeman (1987), Baird (1990) and Pineda (1987). Systems such as this can also be modeled in discrete time using an iterated map of the form

$$[\mathbf{s}_{n+1}, \mathbf{y}_n] = f[\mathbf{w}_n, \mathbf{x}_n, \mathbf{s}_n]$$

Examples of this type of system are found in Pollack (1990), Giles et al. (1992) and Elman (1989). Such a system might merely be an iterated map, or a Poincaré section of some more complex function, as in Chua et al. (1993).

2.3 Processing with dynamical systems

Although one can process with a large variety of dynamical systems, we are particularly interested in cases where $\mathbf{s}(t)$ corresponds in some fashion to the current state of a state machine (such as a finite state automaton). This concept is illustrated in Figure 2.1. Such systems have been investigated by

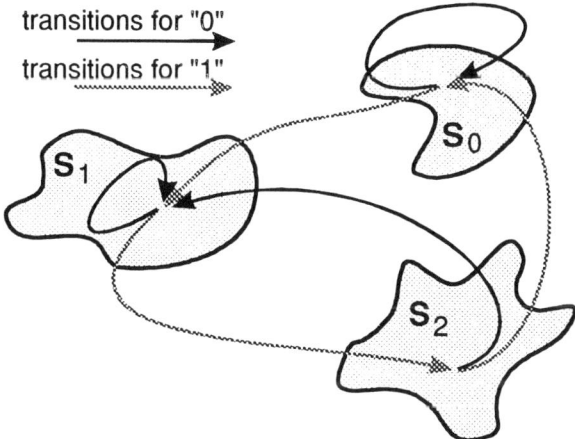

Figure 2.1 *Simple 'analog' state machine.*

Brockett (1991), Crutchfield and Young (1989), Giles *et al.* (1992), Pollack (1990), Freeman (1987) and Baird (1990). States and input values in such systems can be continuous valued and continuous in time.

Of particular interest in the systems is Turing-equivalence. Typically, analog Turing-equivalence is discussed in terms of constructing state machines with an arbitrary number of states, substituting states for tape memory. Ideally, such a dynamical system would be able to model a universal Turing machine, and would accept programming in addition to learning. Finally, theoretical results seem to indicate that such machines could have 'soft' memory, i.e. memory that degrades gracefully (decreases precision) as its capacity is exceeded.

While Turing-equivalence for such systems is important, proving that a system is Turing-equivalent merely shows that it can theoretically solve any computable problem. The proof of Turing-equivalence does not indicate that a practical system can be built to solve a specific problem. The proof of Turing-equivalence merely shows that there is some part of the system which is capable of implementing finite-state automata, and there is another part capable of implementing a memory of arbitrary size. Turing-equivalence does not indicate that good programs can be found to solve computable programs. It also says nothing about the robustness of such systems.

2.4 Programming

One method of programming involves the creation of 'designer' dynamical systems. These systems are composed of vector spaces containing subspaces or regions corresponding to the states of a single automaton. Inputs serve as forcing functions on a vector field within that space to drive state changes through the desired transitions. Let's assume that the state **s** is defined as a volume in a Euclidean space, $\mathscr{R}^n$, and that the system receives continuous vector-valued inputs which map onto an a-ary alphabet. Programming is equivalent to finding parameters **w** for a vector-valued mapping

$$m(\mathbf{s}_i, \mathbf{x}_a, \mathbf{w}) \rightarrow \mathbf{s}_j$$

for a particular set of triplets $(\mathbf{x}_a, \mathbf{s}_i, \mathbf{s}_j)$. In a continuous-time dynamical system, the problem is further complicated by the fact that these mappings must go from state to state via a set of non-intersecting manifolds. Figure 2.2 shows an example of developing the mapping for a simple up-down counter.

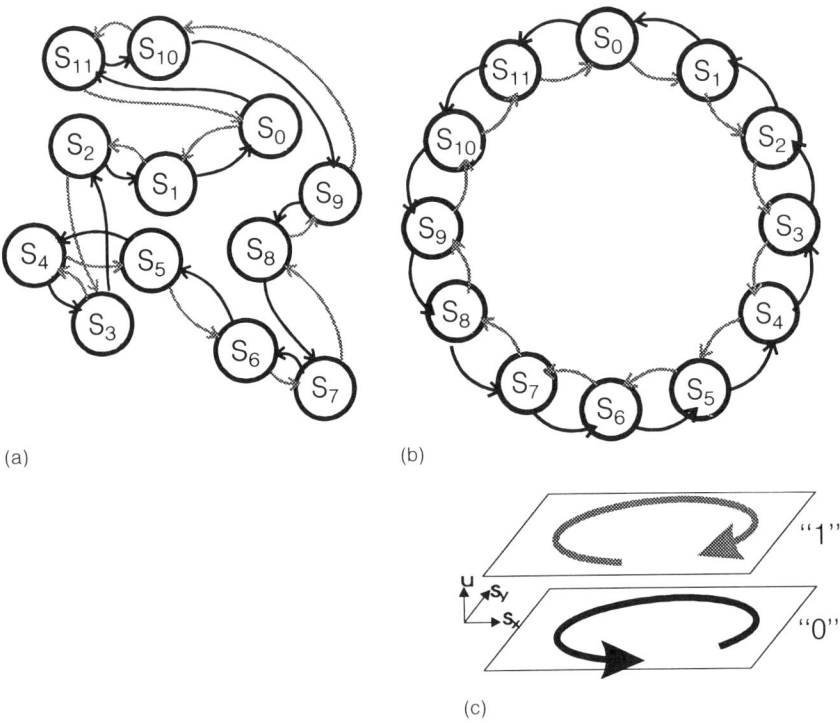

(a)

(b)

(c)

Figure 2.2 *(a) A 12-state up-down counter. Now we assume that each state will be represented by a location in a 2D state space defined by the state vector (s_x, s_y); (b) the location of the states is optimized for realization in a 3D state space; (c) the state space is developed, based upon the assumption that the input u is from $\{-1, 1\}$. The equations of motion for the state system might look like:*

$$d \begin{bmatrix} S_X \\ S_Y \end{bmatrix} = \begin{bmatrix} 0 & \omega U \\ -\omega U & 0 \end{bmatrix} \begin{bmatrix} S_X \\ S_Y \end{bmatrix}$$

While the above system would not be structurally stable, quantizing (s_x, s_y) at regular intervals would yield a structurally stable solution.

The process of finding the parameters **w** that implement the map for all i, j and a is not straightforward. Typically, this problem is solved in one of two ways:

- An optimization technique (such as recurrent back-propagation) is used to find the set of mappings that are most consistent with the required transitions. This is the technique used in Elman (1989) and Baird (1990).
- Some sort of memory stores a set of mappings $\mathbf{w}_i$ for each state $\mathbf{s}_i$ (or optionally for each clock cycle n). This is the method used by Giles *et al.* (1992) and Pollack (1990).

Thus, one must choose between optimization and the use of large memory. Optimization is not well suited to explicit programming, and is not guaranteed to find a set of mappings that is consistent for all transitions (in a low-dimensional state-space). On the other hand, memorizing mappings involves storing $O(s \cdot w)$ parameters, where w is the dimension of the parameter vector, and s is the number of states.

2.5 Noise

We can reasonably assume that power or computer memory will somehow restrict us to placing all of the states for our system within some d-dimensional volume (the state space). We can also assume that there will be some source of noise, and that noise source will corrupt state information. Let's now look at a straight-forward analysis à la Shannon.

Assume our system has a number of states S which are mapped onto a subset of A^d points defined by an alphabet of A characters in the space $\mathscr{R}^d$. For example, during each 'machine cycle', the system state could be attracted to one of the A^d points. After the next 'clock cycle', the system would be attracted to another point based upon the inputs. By assuming that the alphabet is made up of real numbers equally spaced between $-E$ and E, we can derive a state capacity (i.e. the maximum number of states that could be encoded in the space without experiencing a rapid growth in error probability). The result is an outgrowth of Shannon's famous channel capacity theorem (Shannon and Weaver, 1949; Wozencraft and Jacobs, 1965); it is given by:

$$C_s = \left(1 + \frac{E^2}{\sigma^2} \right)^{d/2}$$

where σ^2 is the noise variance for each dimension. It should be noted that the expression C_s can grow at a rate faster than 2^d for $E^2/\sigma^2 > 3$.

Using the channel capacity argument does not guarantee that one can store C_s states. It does, however, establish an upper bound. If one tries to store more than C_s states, the probability of error will approach certainty for large d. If one stores less than C_s states, one could conceivably find a code that makes the probability of error vanish for large d. There are many codes used in communications that are capable of storing slightly less than C_s states with a vanishing error probability. Therefore, if one has sufficient energy (or low enough noise), significant storage gains can be made by using analog states rather than binary. Of course, even within this capacity we can expect a finite error probability for any particular state. We must also realize that most coding methods used for communications are not based upon the need to store states in a semantically meaningful way, and the codes do not necessarily place states in an optimal fashion for encoding transitions.

It should also be noted that the channel capacity argument only considers the storage of states, and it ignores the need for volumes which form the 'tubes through state-space' corresponding to the edges of the state transition graph. An open question concerns whether a general limit can be derived for how many edges can be encoded, or if such a result must depend upon the particular state-machine implemented.

2.6 Storing programs

A Turing-equivalent machine needs a memory of arbitrary size. Traditionally, such memories have been expanded by adding dimensions to the state space (such as adding floating-gate transistor). Some, however, have been excited by claims concerning dynamical systems and their ability to store an arbitrary number of memories with a fixed dimensionality. A result of Crutchfield and Young (1989) indicates that dynamical systems, as they go through cascades of increasing period, are capable of representing strings of increasing length. This trend continues until the onset of deterministic chaos, at which time the state of the machine is best represented by a string of infinite length and complexity. In a chaotic system, there is an infinite variety of such trajectories that depend upon the initial conditions.

An example of this capability can be illustrated with a simple quadratic map defined by

$$s_{n+1} = 1 - 4(s_n - \tfrac{1}{2})^2$$

This one-dimensional map can exhibit chaotic, periodic and fixpoint behavior. Now, let's assume that the series of states s is used to encode a binary string b, defined as

$$b_n = 0 \quad s_n \in [0, 0.5]$$
$$b_n = 1 \quad s_n \in [0.5, 1]$$

At this point, we can encode any string b of infinite length by properly choosing the value of s_0. This concept is shown in Figure 2.3. The figure shows that properly choosing the initial condition to fall within a particular dashed boundary can produce the associated string of length three (the first three bits of the string b as the map iterates from its initial condition).

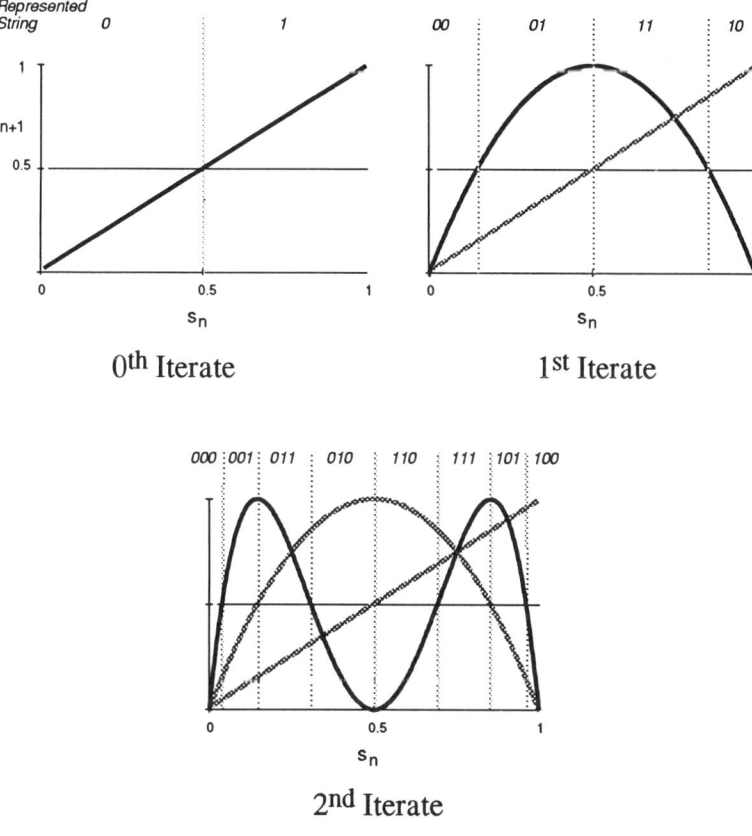

Figure 2.3 *Storing strings up to length 3 using the quadratic map.*

This argument, although mathematically sound, is certainly limited by the previous Shannon-based capacity result. For, as we make the strings longer, we must map 2^n intervals onto the interval $[0, 1]$. Therefore, as n becomes arbitrarily large, the recalled string will likely be arbitrarily wrong! For this reason, we cannot compute with infinite complexity using finite resources. However, it should be clear that continuous-state memory could encode strings longer than the number of free parameters. Given a sufficiently clever 'coding' scheme, one could reasonably expect to create a system that can 'borrow' complexity at the expense of error tolerance. The issue is to find a code that simultaneously exhibits:

- noise tolerance and graceful degradation
- sufficient intelligibility for programming
- a link to a reinforcement strategy for learning.

2.7 Summary

Hopefully, this discussion is illuminating both in terms of the potential design and capabilities of a continuous-state machine, but also in terms of the problems that must be addressed before we could reasonably expect to see such machines implemented.

These problems include arriving at a better understanding of system capacities *vis-à-vis* noise tolerance, as well as practical issues of design that are capable of encoding (programming) an arbitrary state machine design into a dynamical system in an efficient manner. This 'programming' program is further complicated in the case of the creation of a universal machine. It is the author's intent to favorably influence the work of researchers much greater than himself on these topics.

Acknowledgements

I particularly wish to thank Ray Brown, Lee Giles, Jordan Pollack, Walter Freeman, Santosh Venkatesh and Eduardo Sontag, whose comments and papers guided my thoughts.

References

Baird, B. (1990) A learning rule for CAM storage of continuous periodic sequences. *Int. Joint Conf. on Neural Networks*, **3**, 493.

Brockett, R. (1991) An estimation theoretic basis for the design of sorting and classification networks, in *Neural Networks: Theory and Applications* (eds R. Mammone and Y. Zeevi), Lawrence Erlbaum, NJ, p. 23.

Chua, L., Brown, R. and Hamilton, N. (1993) Fractals in the twist-and-flip circuit. *IEEE Trans. on Systems, Circuits and Computers* (in press).

Crutchfield, J. and Young, K. (1989) Inferring statistical complexity. *Phys. Rev. Lett.*, **63**(2), 105.

Elman, J. (1989) Finding structure in time. *Cognitive Science*, **14**, 179.

Freeman, W. (1987) Simulation of chaotic EEG patterns with a dynamic model of the olfactory system. *Biological Cybernetics*, **56**, 139.

Giles, C.L., Miller, C., Chen, D. *et al.* (1992) Learning and extracting finite state automata with second-order recurrent neural networks. *Neural Computation*, **4**, 393.

Pineda, F. (1987) Generalization of back-propagation to recurrent neural networks. *Phys. Rev. Lett.*, **18**, 2229.

Pollack, J. (1990) Language induction by phase transition in dynamical recognizers, in *Advances in Neural Information Processing Systems 3* (eds R. Lippman, J. Moody and D. Touretzky), Morgan-Kaufmann, San Mateo, p. 619.

Shannon, C. and Weaver, I. (1949) *The Mathematical Theory of Communication*, University of Illinois Press.

Wozencraft, J. and Jacobs, I. (1965) *Principles of Communication Engineering*, Wiley, Chichester.

3

Statistical physics algorithms that converge

A.L. YUILLE and J.J. KOSOWSKY
Division of Applied Science, Harvard University, Cambridge, MA 02138, USA

3.1 Statistical physics and mean field theory for optimization

In recent years there has been significant interest in adapting techniques from statistical physics, in particular mean field theory, to provide deterministic heuristic algorithms for obtaining approximate solutions to optimization problems (Hopfield and Tank, 1985; Grzywacz and Yuille, 1986; Peterson and Söderberg, 1989; Simic, 1990; Yuille, 1990; Geiger and Girosi, 1989; Rose *et al.*, 1990; Platt and Hopfield, 1986). These algorithms, some of which are known as deterministic annealing, are closely related to simulated annealing (Kirkpatrick *et al.*, 1983; Geman and Geman, 1984) and the Boltzmann machine (Kienker *et al.*, 1986). Both approaches formulate the optimization problem in terms of minimizing a cost function and defining a corresponding Gibbs distribution. Simulated annealing then proceeds by sampling the Gibbs probability distribution as the temperature is reduced to zero, while deterministic annealing attempts to track an approximation to the mean of the distribution. Although simulations have shown that mean field methods often yield effective algorithms (Durbin and Willshaw, 1987; Peterson and Söderberg, 1989; Peterson, 1990), there has been little theoretical analysis of them, and few attempts to explain how they relate to more standard optimization algorithms.

In this chapter we demonstrate connections between mean field theory methods and other approaches. It appears that a number of existing algorithms can be viewed as special cases of mean field theory of appropriate statistical physical systems. We will be specifically concerned with linear programming with barrier functions (Bayer and Lagarias, 1989), optimization

Artificial Neural Networks for Speech and Vision. Edited by Richard J. Mammone.
Published in 1993 by Chapman & Hall, London. ISBN 0 412 54850 X

by embedding the system in a continuous group (Brockett, 1988, 1989; Brockett and Wong, 1989), and interior point methods (Karmakar, 1984, 1990; Faybusovich, 1990).

As an explicit example we summarize our earlier work (Kosowsky and Yuille, 1991; Yuille and Kosowsky, 1991) on the linear assignment problem. In this previous work we defined a number of algorithms, including deterministic annealing, for solving the assignment problem. We proved their convergence, gave bounds on the convergence times, and showed relations to other optimization algorithms.

3.2 The saddle point approximation

In this chapter we will only consider optimization problems that can be formulated in terms of minimizing an energy $E[V]$ with respect to binary variables $V = \{V_{ia}\}$. We assume that V corresponds to an $N \times N$ square matrix $\{V_{ia}\}$. We impose global row constraints $\sum_a V_{ia} = 1, \forall i$ and column constraints $\sum_i V_{ia} = 1, \forall a$. Note that $\{V_{ia}\}$ now represents a permutation matrix, and thus the solution space of the original optimization problem can be embedded in the permutation group of N elements.

A specific example, that we study in more detail below, is the linear assignment problem. The energy can be written as

$$E[V] = - \sum_{ia} V_{ia} A_{ia}, \tag{1}$$

where the $\{A_{ia}\}$ are fixed weights. To obtain an intuitive, economic understanding of this problem, one can let the i's label people, the a's label objects, and set A_{ia} to be the benefit of the ath object to the ith person. The problem then consists of finding a one-to-one mapping between people and objects such that the overall benefit is maximized. This suggests an **auction algorithm** (Bertsekas, 1990), where prices of objects are introduced and each person bids for objects. Curiously this method is closely related to a mean field theory algorithm. The linear assignment problem also arises in the minimal mapping theory for long-range motion perception (Ullman, 1979).

We now introduce a Gibbs distribution (Parisi, 1988) so that the probability of any specific configuration V is given by

$$P[V] = \frac{e^{-\beta E[V]}}{Z}, \tag{2}$$

where $\beta = 1/T$ is the inverse of the temperature and the corresponding **partition function** of the system is

$$Z = \sum_V e^{-\beta E[V]}, \tag{3}$$

where the summation should be taken only over configurations that satisfy the global row and column constraints. This is known as hard constraints (Peterson and Söderberg, 1989; Simic, 1990; Yuille, 1990). Our treatment follows Peterson and Söderberg (1989).

We can write the partition function as

$$Z = \sum_V \int [dS] e^{-\beta E[S]} \left\{ \prod_{ia} \delta(S_{ia} - V_{ia}) \right\} \left\{ \prod_i \delta \left(\sum_a S_{ia} - 1 \right) \right\}, \qquad (4)$$

where the first terms in the integrand imbed the V's in a continuous space of S variables and the last term imposes the global row constraints. The global column constraint will be imposed while explicitly summing over the V's.

Writing the Dirac delta function as $\delta(x) = (1/2\pi) \int e^{i\omega x} d\omega$, we get that

$$Z = \sum_V \int_S [dS] \int_U [dU] \int_P [dP] e^{-\beta E[S]} \exp \left(\sum_{ia} U_{ia}(S_{ia} - V_{ia}) \right)$$
$$\cdot \exp \left(\sum_i P_i \left(\sum_a S_{ia} - 1 \right) \right), \qquad (5)$$

after rotating the P and U contours in the complex plane (this is known as a Wick rotation, and is justified in this case since the integrand has no poles in the complex P and U planes).

We now take the summation over V inside the integral and explicitly compute it. This yields

$$Z = \int_S [dS] \int_U [dU] \int_P [dP] \exp(-\beta E_{\text{eff}}[S, U, P]), \qquad (6)$$

where

$$E_{\text{eff}}[S, U, P] = E[S] - \frac{1}{\beta} \left\{ \sum_{ia} S_{ia} U_{ia} + \sum_i P_i \left(\sum_a S_{ia} - 1 \right) \right. $$
$$\left. + \sum_a \log \left\{ \sum_i e^{-U_{ia}} \right\} \right\}. \qquad (7)$$

The saddle point approximation says that the mean fields S, U, P are those that extremize the effective energy. In particular, the mean fields of the S will correspond to the mean fields of the V variables. In the limit as $T \to 0$, the mean fields will correspond to the lowest energy states.

The equations for the extrema are

$$\frac{\partial E_{\text{eff}}}{\partial S_{ia}} = \frac{\partial E}{\partial S_{ia}} - \frac{1}{\beta} P_i - \frac{1}{\beta} U_{ia} = 0, \qquad (8)$$

$$\frac{\partial E_{\text{eff}}}{\partial U_{ia}} = -\frac{1}{\beta} S_{ia} + \frac{1}{\beta} \frac{e^{-U_{ia}}}{\sum_j e^{-U_{ja}}} = 0, \qquad (9)$$

$$\frac{\partial E_{\text{eff}}}{\partial P_i} = \sum_a S_{ia} - 1 = 0. \tag{10}$$

Observe that the second and third relations ensure, respectively, that the global row and column constraints are satisfied.

3.2.1 Optimization methods

Once we have obtained the saddle point equations for a specific problem we must attempt to solve them. Optimization problems can be divided into two categories depending on whether these equations have single or multiple solutions.

For certain classes of problem only one solution will exist. Two prototypical algorithms will always be capable of solving the problem: (1) steepest descent in the effective energy, and (2) tracking the minimum energy solution as the temperature decreases. The first method is similar to existing neural network algorithms while the second (see section 3.3.4) is sometimes equivalent to interior point algorithms.

For more specific problems a larger variety of algorithms exist, and bounds can be given to ensure that the solution to the effective energy problem is sufficiently close to the true solution (see section 3.5).

For mean-field problems with multiple extrema we can use deterministic annealing. This involves obtaining a solution at high temperature – there will always be a unique, easily calculable solution in the limit as $T \to \infty$ – and tracking it down as T decreases. This method is not guaranteed to converge to the correct solution but gives good results empirically (Durbin and Willshaw, 1987; Peterson and Söderberg, 1989; Peterson, 1990). It can be thought of as an approximation to simulated annealing. As will be shown in section 3.3.5, there is often a critical temperature T_c for the system which gives an initial condition for the annealing.

The same saddle point method can be applied to problems where the energy depends also on a continuous variable and where only one, or none, of the global constraints are imposed. The modification is straightforward and can be seen in Geiger and Girosi (1989), Yuille (1990), Rose et al. (1990) and Ohlsson et al. (1992). A similar approach, though without using partition functions, was described by Koch and Yuille (1986).

3.3 Related algorithms

This section describes relations between mean-field methods and other related techniques. The method by which the two sets of global constraints are imposed is critically important for optimization problems. Early neural networks which attempted to impose them using energy biases were comparatively unsuccessful (Wilson and Pawley, 1988). We now describe several related methods of imposing constraints.

3.3.1 Imposing constraints by Lagrange multipliers

In the preceding statistical physics approach, the global column constraints
were imposed during the summation over the $\{V_{ia}\}$ states while the global
row constraints were imposed by inserting delta functions into the formula
for the partition function. These two methods are reflected in the saddle point
equations: in (9) the first set of global constraints is implicit, whereas in (10)
the second set is explicit.

We can therefore think of the $\{U_{ia}\}$ as a choice of coordinates that implicitly
imposes the first set of constraints. Alternatively, however, we can eliminate
the $\{U_{ia}\}$ variables and impose both sets of constraints by Lagrange multipliers.
To see this we take the log of (9) to get

$$\log S_{ia} + \log \left\{ \sum_j e^{-U_{ja}} \right\} = -U_{ia}. \tag{11}$$

Multiplying by S_{ia}/β and summing over a and i, using the global row
constraints, yields

$$\frac{1}{\beta} \sum_{ia} S_{ia} \log S_{ia} = -\frac{1}{\beta} \sum_{ia} U_{ia} S_{ia} - \frac{1}{\beta} \sum_a \log \left\{ \sum_i e^{-U_{ia}} \right\}. \tag{12}$$

Introducing Lagrange multipliers $\{P_i\}$ and $\{Q_a\}$ and substituting (12) in (7)
gives

$$E'_{\text{eff}}[S, P, Q] = E[S] + \frac{1}{\beta} \sum_{ai} S_{ai} \log S_{ai} + \sum_i P_i \left(\sum_a S_{ai} - 1 \right)$$

$$+ \sum_a Q_a \left(\sum_i S_{ai} - 1 \right). \tag{13}$$

Extremizing with respect to S, P and Q gives

$$\frac{\partial E}{\partial S_{ai}} + \frac{1}{\beta}(1 + \log S_{ai}) + Q_i + P_a = 0, \tag{14}$$

$$\sum_a S_{ai} = 1, \tag{15}$$

$$\sum_i S_{ai} = 1. \tag{16}$$

Thus the asymmetry used in imposing the constraints is illusory. Instead it
is due to the choice of coordinate $\{U_{ai}\}$.

The entropy term $(1/\beta)\sum_{ia} S_{ia} \log S_{ia}$ can be considered as a barrier function
(Bayer and Lagarias, 1989), which ensures that $S_{ia} \geqslant 0, \forall i, a$. Though its value
goes to zero as $S_{ia} \to 0$ its gradient, $1 + \log S_{ia}$, becomes arbitrarily large and
negative in this limit – which ensures that the $\{S_{ia}\}$ remain positive.

Equation (13) gives a new effective energy for the system which is related
to the previous effective energy (7). The extrema of the effective energies will

correspond even though the effective energies themselves are functions of different variables.

From this perspective deterministic annealing is very similar to barrier function methods. The difference being that the barrier is explicitly derived as an entropy term and its coefficient T, the temperature, is reduced as the algorithm proceeds.

We note that equation (13) can also be derived directly as an approximation to the free energy of the system (Yuille and Elfadel, 1992).

3.3.2 Barrier function for alternative statistical system

The more traditional barrier function, $-\sum_{ia} \log S_{ia}$, can be obtained as the entropy of an alternative statistical system.

We derived the previous effective energies (7) and (13) by considering a physical system where the states of the system correspond to all possible permutations. This corresponds to the subset of the vertices of the hypercube corresponding to those that obey the global constraints.

Alternatively, we can define a physical system whose states are those internal to the hypercube which satisfy the same global constraints. The lowest energy of this more generalized system is also found at the optimal permutation. We should point out, however, that the resulting physical system contains far more unnecessary states and hence is likely to be inferior to the original method. As we will show, however, it does correspond to several existing optimization methods.

We will obtain these results by deriving them as a special case of more general problem maximizing $E = E[x]$ subject to the constraints $\sum_j A_{ij} x_j = b_i$, $\forall i$ and $x_i \geq 0$, $\forall i$. The partition function corresponding to the Gibbs distribution is

$$Z = \int [dx] e^{-\beta E[x]} \prod_i \delta \left(\sum_j A_{ij} x_j - b_i \right) \theta(x_i), \tag{17}$$

where $\theta(x)$ is the Heaviside function. We can substitute the relations $\delta(x) = (1/2\pi) \int e^{iPx} \, dP$ and $\theta(x) = (1/2\pi) \int (1/iR) e^{iRx} \, dR$. Hence, after a Wick rotation

$$Z = \int [dx][dP][dR] e^{-\beta E[x]} \exp \left(\sum_i P_i \left(\sum_j A_{ij} x_j - b_i \right) \right)$$

$$\cdot \exp \left(-\sum_i \log R_i \exp \sum_i R_i x_i \right). \tag{18}$$

Thus, we have an effective energy

$$E_{\text{eff}}[x, P, R] = E[x] - \frac{1}{\beta} \sum_i P_i \left(\sum_j A_{ij} x_j - b_i \right)$$

$$+ \frac{1}{\beta} \sum_i \log R_i - \frac{1}{\beta} \sum_i R_i x_i. \tag{19}$$

We can eliminate the $\{R_i\}$ variables at an extrema, by solving for $\partial E_{\text{eff}}/\partial R_i = 0$, to obtain $R_i = (1/x_i)$, $\forall i$. Substituting this back into the effective energy, and dropping the constant term, gives

$$E_{\text{eff}}[x, P] = E[x] - \frac{1}{\beta} \sum_i P_i \left(\sum_j A_{ij} x_j - b_i \right) - \frac{1}{\beta} \sum_i \log x_i. \qquad (20)$$

Thus we obtain the log potential sometimes used as a barrier function. If we restrict the energy to $E[x] = \sum_i x_i c_i$ we obtain a standard method for solving linear programming problems.

For the particular case studied previously ((13)) we obtain

$$E'_{\text{eff}}[S, P, Q] = E[S] + \sum_i P_i \left(\sum_a S_{ia} - 1 \right) + \sum_a Q_a \left(\sum_i S_{ia} - 1 \right)$$

$$- \frac{1}{\beta} \sum_{ia} \log S_{ia}. \qquad (21)$$

3.3.3 The rotation group

Brockett (1988, 1989) and Brockett and Wong (1989) have recently proposed an alternative approach to solving optimization problems where the solution space is embedded in the permutation group. In this method the permutation group is embedded in the rotation group $O(N)$, instead of in the full space of $N \times N$ matrices (as in section 3.2). Then, since the rotation group is continuous, steepest descent can be performed with respect to the normal metric on this group. This gives an elegant, geometrically motivated system with relations to Symplectic geometry, Lie Groups and Hamiltonian systems. For certain problems, such as sorting lists of numbers and finding eigenvectors of matrices, it can be shown that the system converges to the correct solution.

One can obtain Brockett's formulation by the substitution

$$S_{ai} = \theta_{ai}^2, \qquad (22)$$

where the θ's are required to lie in the orthogonal group

$$\sum_a \theta_{ai} \theta_{aj} = \delta_{ij}, \qquad (23)$$

$$\sum_i \theta_{ai} \theta_{bi} = \delta_{ab}. \qquad (24)$$

It can be readily seen that the diagonal terms of (23) and (24) are sufficient to ensure that the global row and column constraints are satisfied (by setting $i = j$ in (23) and $a = b$ in (24) and using (22)). However, the offdiagonal terms in (23) and (24) impose additional restrictions not found in the statistical physics approach.

Brockett proves that for the sorting problem, steepest descent on the energy function restricted to the orthogonal group is guaranteed to converge to the correct solution from almost all starting points. From the assignment problem, however, the energy function restricted to the orthogonal has many local minima and the algorithm only converges to a 2-opt solution. Other embeddings are possible.

Brockett's method can be thought of as steepest descent projected onto the space satisfying the global constraints. This projection uses the normal metric (i.e. the metric derived from the Killing form of the orthogonal Lie algebra) rather than the metric induced on the orthogonal group from its standard imbedding in R^{n^2}. This method converges to a solution which minimizes

$$E[\theta] = \sum_{ia} A_{ia} \theta_{ia}^2 + \sum_{ij} P_{ij} \left\{ \sum_a \theta_{ai} \theta_{aj} - \delta_{ij} \right\}, \tag{25}$$

where the $\{P_{ij}\}$ are Lagrange multipliers.

This is similar to our effective energies (7) and (13) though without an entropy term and with a new choice of coordinates.

3.3.4 Temperature tracking and relations to interior point methods

Once an effective energy has been obtained there may be several practical ways for obtaining its minimum. Probably the most standard approach is to do steepest descent, or one of its more computationally efficient variations. If the effective energy has local minima then deterministic annealing is required. This involves lowering the temperature while doing steepest descent.

An alternative approach suited to problems with a single minima is to a version of deterministic annealing by writing down a differential equation to track the unique energy minimum as a function of temperature. At high temperature (small β) the solution can typically be solved for explicitly, thereby giving initial conditions for the temperature tracking differential equation.

More precisely, we use the equations

$$\frac{\partial E_{\text{eff}}[S:\beta]}{\partial S_{ia}} = 0, \quad \forall i, a, \tag{26}$$

to implicitly define a solution $S^*(\beta) = \{S_{ia}^*(\beta)\}$ as function of temperature. Differentiating (26) with respect to β gives an equation for updating $S_{ia}^*(\beta)$ as β changes:

$$\left. \frac{\partial^2 E_{\text{eff}}[S:\beta]}{\partial S_{ia} \partial \beta} \right|_{(S=S^*(\beta))} + \sum_{jb} \frac{dS_{jb}^*}{d\beta} \left. \frac{\partial^2 E_{\text{eff}}[S:\beta]}{\partial S_{ia} \partial S_{jb}} \right|_{(S=S^*(\beta))} = 0, \quad \forall i, a. \tag{27}$$

This equation can be inverted to solve for $(dS_{jb}^*)/(d\beta)$ (care must be taken to ensure that the global constraints are satisfied). Then, given $S_{(\beta=0)}^*$, one can use (27) to find the solution as temperature goes to zero.

Surprisingly, for the linear programming problem, Faybusovich (1990) has shown that this temperature tracking algorithm is equivalent to his variant of the interior point algorithm (Karmakar, 1984, 1990; Bayer and Lagarias, 1989), provided the β is re-interpreted as the time variable for the interior point algorithm. This is encouraging since interior point algorithms have been shown empirically to be effective ways of solving linear programming problems. We emphasize, however, that temperature tracking (deterministic annealing) is more general than interior point methods since it is not restricted to linear programming problems.

For problems with more than one miminum, we expect bifurcations when $\partial^2 E_{\text{eff}}/\partial S_{ia}\partial S_{jb}$ develops a zero eigenvalue. In such cases, (27) cannot be inverted and we obtain a phase transition.

3.3.5 Multiple minima – Phase transitions

For more challenging optimization problems, such as the TSP, there will be many local minima and analysis becomes difficult. For some specific problems, it can be shown (Durbin et al. 1989; Peterson and Söderberg, 1989; Yuille and Elfadel, 1992) that there are phase transitions in the solution. We should note that, strictly speaking, phase transitions cannot occur in the problems that we are considering because of their finite size, and can only occur in the limit as the size of the system goes to infinity. Nevertheless, our systems will display the essential properties of such transitions. More specifically, there will be a critical temperature T_c above which the solution to the mean field equations is constant over temperature and below which this solution is unstable. T_c can be computed analytically and gives an upper bound for the temperature in the annealing process.

We will show how to compute T_c for a special class of problems that includes the TSP and many models for texture and pattern generation (Yuille and Elfadel, 1992). The generic form is

$$E[V] = \sum_{ijab} R_{ij} d_{ab} V_{ia} V_{jb}, \tag{28}$$

with the standard global constraints.

For the TSP d_{ab} is the distance between cities. The matrix R_{ij} is shift-invariant and is given by $R_{ij} = 2\delta_{ij} - 2\delta_{i,j+1}$. (Note: this is slightly different from the usual form for the TSP but it is equivalent once the global constraints are applied.)

Using the Free energy formulation with Lagrange multipliers we obtain an effective energy

$$E_{\text{eff}}[S, P, Q] = \sum_{ijab} R_{ij} d_{ab} S_{ia} S_{jb} + T \sum_{ia} S_{ia} \log S_{ia}$$

$$+ \sum_{a} P_a \left(\sum_{i} S_{ia} - 1 \right) + \sum_{i} Q_i \left(\sum_{a} S_{ia} - 1 \right). \tag{29}$$

Extremizing this effective energy gives

$$2\sum_{jb} R_{ij}d_{ab}S_{jb} + T\{1 + \log S_{ia}\} + P_a + Q_i = 0, \tag{30}$$

subject to the row and column constraints for $\{S_{ia}\}$.

It can be seen that, using the shift-invariance of R_{ij}, there is always a trivial solution with $S_{ia} = 1/N$ (shift-invariance implies $\sum_j R_{ij}$ is a constant, independent of i) by setting $P_a = -2T\sum_b d_{ab}(1/N)$ and $Q_i = \text{const}, \forall i$.

To determine the stability of the solution we must look at the eigenvalues of the Hessian H_{ijab} of the unconstrained effective energy ($E_{\text{eff}}^{\text{unc}}[S] = \sum_{ijab} R_{ij}d_{ab}S_{ia}S_{jb} + T\sum_{ia} S_{ia}\log S_{ia}$) at $S_{ia} = 1/N, \forall i, a$. This becomes

$$H_{ijab} = 2R_{ij}d_{ab} + NT\delta_{ij}\delta_{ab}. \tag{31}$$

The stability will depend on the eigenvalues of the Hessian, though we need only consider eigenvalues whose eigenvectors respect the global constraints (i.e. eigenvectors e_{ia} such that $\sum_i e_{ia} = 0, \forall a$ and $\sum_a e_{ia} = 0, \forall i$). In other words, for stability, the Hessian must be positive definite when projected onto the subspace corresponding to the global constraints.

For high T the second term dominates and the solution $S_{ia} = 1/N, \forall i, a$ is stable. For low temperature the first term dominates and a phase transition will occur unless $R_{ij}d_{ab}$ is positive definite (in all the directions obeying the global constraints). The phase transition is desirable since we do not want $S_{ia} = 1/N, \forall i, a$ to be a stable solution as $T \to 0$. Moreover, it gives a critical temperature T_c, and initial conditions, to start the annealing.

The eigenvectors of H_{ijab} are of form $X_j^\mu Y_b^\nu$ where the $\{X_j^\mu\}$ and $\{Y_b^\nu\}$ are eigenvectors of R_{ij} and d_{ab} respectively (μ and ν label the eigenvectors and j and b their components). Since R_{ij} is shift-invariant its eigenvectors are of form $X_j^\mu = e^{(\sqrt{-1})2\pi j\mu/N}$ for $\mu = 1, \ldots, N$. In general, d_{ab} will not be shift invariant and its eigenvectors must be found for each specific problem.

3.4 Bounds on convergence

It is important to investigate the convergence of mean field theory algorithms both with temperature and with time. For example, how does the minimum of the effective energy at temperature T relate to the solution to the original problem? In this section we state three theorems, which are proven in the appendix, which quantify the changes in the energy and the effective energy along a trajectory of extrema as the temperature varies. In the next section these results will be applied to a specific problem to obtain convergence bounds.

Theorem 3.1 *The rate of change of effective energy at an extremum is given by $\beta(DE_{\text{eff}})/(D\beta) = -(E_{\text{eff}} - E)$ for any energy function $E[V]$, where D denotes the covariant derivative.*

This theorem tells us how the depth of an extrema in the effective energy changes with temperature.

Theorem 3.2 *We can write* $\beta(DE_{\text{eff}})/(D\beta) = -(1/\beta)\sum_{ai}S_{ai}\log S_{ai}$, *where the right hand side can be interpreted as the entropy of the state.*

This theorem relates the change in depth of an extrema to the entropy.

Theorems 3.1 and 3.2 can be used to obtain bounds on the convergence of the system as the temperature goes to zero.

Theorem 3.3 *Let* $E[T]$ *be the energy, not the effective energy, of a trajectory of the extrema of the effective energy (see equations (41), (42) and (43) in the appendix) as temperature* T *varies. Then, for all* T_1 *we have* $|E[T=0] - E[T=T_1]| \leqslant 3T_1N\log N$.

For a specific choice of the energy function, and assuming uniqueness of the saddle point solution, we can use Theorem 3.3 to put a bound on T_1 to ensure that the saddle point solution is arbitrarily close to the true solution. See section 3.5 for a special case.

A key point is that the bound $3TN\log N$ in Theorem 3.3 arises from our being able to bound the size of the entropy term $|\sum_{ia}S_{ia}\log S_{ia}|$, occurring in Theorem 3.2, by $N\log N$. If we used the more traditional barrier function $\sum_{ia}\log S_{ia}$, the entropy for an alternative statistical system (see section 3.3.2) such a bound would be impossible. We may then hypothesize that the entropy term $\sum_{ia}S_{ia}\log S_{ia}$ will yield better convergence properties than the standard barrier function. Moreover, as discussed in section 3.3.2, the statistical physics system that has the traditional barrier function as its entropy contains many unnecessary states.

3.5 The linear assignment problem

As an example of a specific system where analytical results can be obtained we will summarize our earlier work on the assignment problem. The proofs of these results are not straightforward, and we refer the interested reader to our technical reports (Kosowsky and Yuille, 1991; Yuille and Kosowsky, 1991).

The assignment problem has energy

$$E[V] = -\sum_{ia} V_{ia}A_{ia}, \tag{32}$$

where the $\{A_{ia}\}$ are numbers.

An effective energy can be obtained for this problem using (7). The equation for the extrema can be solved to give S and U as functions of P only.

Substituting back into the effective energy gives the P-energy:

$$E_P[P:\beta] = \frac{1}{\beta} \sum_i \log \left\{ \sum_a e^{\beta(A_{ia} - P_a)} \right\} + \sum_a P_a. \tag{33}$$

The mean field variables can be determined from the P by the relation

$$S_{ia} = \frac{e^{\beta(A_{ia} - P_a)}}{\sum_b e^{\beta(A_{ib} - P_b)}}. \tag{34}$$

3.5.1 Convergence and bounds

This section states several theorems, which can be used for putting bounds on convergence times of algorithms for linear assignment.

Theorem 3.4 *The Hessian of E_p is positive semi-definite and, for non-zero temperature $T = 1/\beta$, there is a unique minimum of E_P up to the translation $P_a \mapsto P_a + K$, $\forall a$. Imposing the constraint, $\sum_a P_a = 0$, yields a unique minimum at $\tilde{P}(\beta)$. This translation invariance does not affect the solution $\{S_{ia}^*\} = \{S_{ia}[\tilde{P}(\beta), T]\}$.*

Proof: See Kosowsky and Yuille (1991). □

Thus, there is a unique optimal solution for non-zero temperature, and we can find the minimum of E_P by steepest descent at fixed temperature. At zero temperature there may, in certain non-generic situations, be more than one optimal solution.

By using the bounds described in the previous section, and additional analysis for the specific form of the assignment energy function, one can prove the following theorem:

Theorem 3.5 *Suppose the assignment problem associated with the $N \times N$ benefit matrix $\{A_{ia}\}$ admits a unique optimal solution. Let Δ equal the difference in energy between the optimal solution and the second best solution. Then, rounding-off each of the entries of $S_{ia}[\tilde{P}, T]$ to the nearest integer yields the unique permutation matrix that solves the assignment problem whenever*

$$T < \frac{\Delta}{2N \log N}. \tag{35}$$

Proof: See Yuille and Kosowsky (1991). □

This theorem tells us that once we have found the minimum of E_P at fixed temperature we can obtain the solution to the assignment problem by rounding-off the corresponding $\{S_{ia}\}$'s to the nearest integer, provided the temperature is below the bound given above.

In practice, it is never completely clear that a steepest descent algorithm has converged. Hence we proved the following theorem:

Theorem 3.6 *Suppose that* $N \geqslant 4$ *and* $\|\nabla E_P[P:T]\| \leqslant \varepsilon$. *Then for all* i *and* a

$$|S_{ia}(P, T) - \Pi_{ia}^*| < 7.2 \frac{N^2 \log N}{\Delta}$$

$$\left\{ \varepsilon \left\{ 2 \left(\max_{i,a} A_{ia} - \min_{i,a} A_{ia} \right) + T \log \frac{N - 1 + \varepsilon}{1 - \varepsilon} \right\} + T \log N \right\}, \qquad (36)$$

where $\{\Pi_{ia}^*\}$ *is the optimal assignment.*

Proof: See Yuille and Kosowsky (1991). $\square$

This theorem shows that provided the temperature is sufficiently small we do not need to get to the minimum of E_P. Instead, we can put a threshold on $\|\nabla E_P\|$ and stop the descent as soon as this threshold is reached. This will only take a finite time since, as E_P is convex, we can put a lower bound on the rate of decrease of E_P until it reaches the threshold.

3.5.2 Algorithms

Using the results of the previous section we can formulate algorithms for solving the assignment problem, demonstrate their stability and put bounds on their convergence times.

The first algorithm involves steepest descent in the E_P energy. The steepest descent equation is:

$$\frac{dP_a}{dt} = \sum_i \frac{e^{\beta(A_{ia} - P_a(t))}}{\sum_c e^{\beta(A_{ic} - P_c(t))}} - 1. \qquad (37)$$

This equation is stable since it corresponds to steepest descent. Its convergence time can be estimated by first observing that $dE_P[P(T)]/dt = -\|\nabla E_P[P(T)]\|^2$. Recalling that the P-energy is convex, it follows that after $(E_P[P(T) = 0] - E_P[\tilde{P}(T)])/\varepsilon^2$ units of time we can descend to a point where $\|\nabla E_P[P(T)]\| < \varepsilon$. By putting a lower bound on $E_P[\tilde{P}(T)]$ and using Theorem 3.6 we see that the algorithm converges in polynomial time.

Steepest descent also has an interesting economic interpretation and can be related to Bertsekas' auction algorithm (Bertsekas, 1990). To see these connections we interpret the $\{P_a\}$ as the prices of objects labeled by a and the $\{A_{ia}\}$ as the utility of the object a to the person i. We interpret our algorithm as adjusting the prices of objects until the total demand $\sum_i S_{ia} = \sum_i (e^{\beta(A_{ia} - P_a(t))})/(\sum_c e^{\beta(A_{ic} - P_c(t))})$ for an object a is equal to its rigid supply 1. Thus we refer to our algorithm as the **invisible hand algorithm**.

This is closely related to Bertsekas' auction algorithm (Bertsekas, 1990), where the price of objects is adjusted, by a bidding process, until only one person desires each object. One can roughly think of our algorithm as a parallel continuous time version of Bertsekas' serial discrete time algorithm.

Another algorithm is the temperature tracking approach mentioned in section 3.3.4. The algorithm can be obtained by solving

$$\frac{\partial^2 E_P}{\partial P_a \partial \beta} + \sum_b \frac{\partial^2 E_P}{\partial P_a \partial P_b} \frac{dP_b}{d\beta} = 0. \tag{38}$$

Note that this equation cannot be solved directly since $\partial^2 E_P/\partial P_a \partial P_b$ has only a single zero eigenvalue, corresponding to the translation invariance $P_a \mapsto P_a + K, \forall a$. If we eliminate this invariance by imposing the constraint $\sum_a P_a = 0$, so that $\sum_a (dP_a/d\beta) = 0$, then we get a unique trajectory for the temperature tracking problem.

Theorem 3.6 tells us that we do not need to know the value of the $\{P_a(\beta = 0)\}$ precisely, provided the gradient is small enough. Then we can use Theorem 3.6 to get temperature and time bounds on the algorithm. Stability can be ensured by adding a small amount of steepest descent as a gradient restoring force.

As mentioned in section 3.2, this temperature tracking algorithm is equivalent to a version of the interior point methods (Karmakar, 1984, 1990; Bayer and Lagarias, 1989; Faybusovich, 1990).

The E_P energy can also be minimized by a variety of algorithms. First note that the minimum must obey the equation

$$\sum_i \frac{e^{\beta(A_{ia} - P_a)}}{\sum_b e^{\beta(A_{ib} - P_b)}} = 1, \forall a. \tag{39}$$

Then, we appeal to the following theorem (we thank D. Mumford for bringing this theorem to our attention):

Theorem 3.7 *(Sinkhorn) Given a strictly positive $N \times N$ matrix M, there exists a unique corresponding doubly stochastic matrix $\Theta^M = D^1 M D^2$ where D^1 and D^2 are strictly positive diagonal matrices and are themselves unique up to a scale factor. Moreover, the iterative process of alternatively normalizing the rows and column of M to each sum to 1, converges to the corresponding doubly stochastic matrix Θ^M.*

Proof: See Sinkhorn (1964). □

To apply this theorem we identify $\{M_{ia}\}$ with $\{e^{\beta A_{ia}}\}$. Then, since Θ^M is doubly stochastic, $D_{ii}^1 = 1/(\sum_{a=1}^N M_{ia} D_{aa}^2)$ and Sinkhorn's iterative procedure yields a vector $\{P_a = -1/\beta \log(D_{aa}^2)\}$ which obeys (39).

3.6 Conclusion

We have related the mean field statistical physics methods to more standard optimization techniques such as linear programming with barrier functions and interior point methods. We stress that the mean field methods are more general than these techniques, since they are more generally applicable and have proven themselves to be good heuristic algorithms for obtaining solutions to difficult optimization problems.

In addition, we have analysed the mean field approach for the special case of the linear assignment problem and obtained convergence bounds for a variety of physics-based algorithms and related them to more standard approaches.

Acknowledgements

We would like to acknowledge support from DARPA with contract AFOSR-89-0506 and to thank the Brown, Harvard and MIT Center for Intelligent Control Systems for a United States Army Research Office grant number DAAL03-86-C-0171. We would also like to thank Roger Brockett and Leonid Faybusovich for helpful conversations.

Appendix 3A: Proofs

We first prove Theorem 3.1.

Proof: We use the standard analysis to obtain an effective energy

$$E_{\text{eff}}[S, U, P] = E[S] - \sum_{ai} U_{ai} S_{ai} - \frac{1}{\beta} \sum_i \log \left\{ \sum_a e^{-\beta U_{ai}} \right\} - \sum_a P_a \left(\sum_i S_{ai} - 1 \right),$$
(40)

where we have absorbed factors of β into the definitions of U and P.

At an extremum we have

$$\frac{\partial E}{\partial S_{ai}} - U_{ai} - P_a = 0,$$
(41)

$$S_{ai} = \frac{e^{-\beta U_{ai}}}{\sum_b e^{-\beta U_{bi}}},$$
(42)

$$\sum_i S_{ai} = 0.$$
(43)

Now differentiate E_{eff} with respect to β at an extremum. We have

$$\frac{DE_{\text{eff}}}{D\beta} = \frac{\partial E_{\text{eff}}}{\partial \beta} + \sum_{ai} \frac{\partial E_{\text{eff}}}{\partial S_{ai}} \frac{dS_{ai}}{\partial \beta} + \sum_{ai} \frac{\partial E_{\text{eff}}}{\partial U_{ai}} \frac{dU_{ai}}{d\beta} + \sum_a \frac{\partial E_{\text{eff}}}{\partial P_a} \frac{dP_a}{d\beta},$$
(44)

where the last three terms on the right-hand side vanish at an extremum. Hence, from (40)

$$\frac{DE_{\text{eff}}}{D\beta} = \frac{1}{\beta^2} \sum_i \log \left\{ \sum_a e^{-\beta U_{ai}} \right\} + \frac{1}{\beta} \sum_i \sum_a \frac{U_{ai} e^{-\beta U_{ai}}}{\sum_b e^{-\beta U_{bi}}}.$$
(45)

Using (42) we can rewrite the second term on the right-hand side as $(1/\beta)\sum_{ai}U_{ai}S_{ai}$.

At an extrema $\sum_i S_{ai} = 1$ so

$$E_{\text{eff}} = E[S] - \sum_{ai}U_{ai}S_{ai} - \frac{1}{\beta}\sum_i \log\left\{\sum_a e^{-\beta U_{ai}}\right\}. \qquad (46)$$

Thus we have the result

$$\frac{DE_{\text{eff}}}{D\beta} = -\frac{1}{\beta}\{E_{\text{eff}} - E\}. \qquad (47)$$

$\square$

Now we prove Theorem 3.2.

Proof: It follows directly from (46), (13) and Theorem 3.1 that, at an extrema,

$$\beta\frac{DE_{\text{eff}}}{D\beta} = -\frac{1}{\beta}\sum_{ai}S_{ai}\log S_{ai}. \qquad (48)$$

$\square$

Now for Theorem 3.3.

Proof: The system has entropy $-\sum_{ai}S_{ai}\log S_{ai}$ and must obey the global constraints $\sum_a S_{ai} = 1$ for all i and $\sum_i S_{ai} = 1$ for all a. Extremizing the entropy, imposing the global constraints by Lagrange multipliers, shows that the entropy is bounded below by 0 and above by $\log N$ (at the state $S_{ai} = (1/N)$).

Setting $\beta = (1/T)$ and using Theorem 3.2 gives

$$\left|\frac{DE_{\text{eff}}}{DT}\right| \leqslant N\log N, \qquad (49)$$

and hence

$$|E_{\text{eff}}[T = T_1] - E_{\text{eff}}[T = 0]| \leqslant T_1 N\log N. \qquad (50)$$

From Theorem 3.1 we can immediately deduce that, for any temperature T,

$$|E_{\text{eff}}[T] - E[T]| \leqslant T_1 N\log N. \qquad (51)$$

Using the triangle inequality with (51) twice, with $T = 0$ and $T = T_1$, and (50) once we obtain

$$|E[T = 0] - E[T = T_1]| \leqslant 3T_1 N\log N. \qquad (52)$$

$\square$

References

Bayer, D.A. and Lagarias, J.C. (1989) The nonlinear geometry of linear programming. I: Affine and projective scaling trajectories. *Transactions of the AMS*, **314**(2), 499–526.

Bertsekas, D.P. (1990) The auction algorithm for assignment and other network flow problems: A tutorial, *INTERFACES*, **20**, 133–49.

Brockett, R.W. (1988) *Dynamical systems that sort lists, diagonalize matrices and solve linear programming problems*. Proceedings of the IEEE conference on Decision and control, December.

Brockett, R.W. (1989) Least squares matching problems. *Journal of Linear Algebra and its Applications*, **122/123/124**, 761–7.

Brockett, R.W. and Wong W.S. (1989) A gradient flow for the assignment problem. To appear.

Durbin, R., Szeliski, R. and Yuille, A.L. (1989) An analysis of the elastic net approach to the travelling salesman problem. *Neural Computation*, **1**, 348–58.

Durbin, R. and Willshaw, D. (1987) An analog approach to the travelling salesman problem using an elastic net method. *Nature*, **326**, 689–91.

Faybusovich, L. (1990) Interior point methods and entropy. Preprint.

Geiger, D. and Girosi, F. (1989) Parallel and deterministic algorithms from MFRs: Integration and surface reconstruction. *Artificial Intelligence Laboratory Memo 1114*, MIT, Cambridge, MA, June.

Geman, S. and Geman, D. (1984) Stochastic relaxation, Gibbs distributions and the Bayesian restoration of images. *IEEE Trans. PAMI*, **6**, 721–41.

Grzywacz, N.M. and Yuille, A.L. (1986) *Massively parallel implementations of theories of apparent motion*. AIP Conference Proceedings 151. Neural Networks for Computing (ed. J. Denker), American Institution of Physics.

Hopfield, J.J and Tank, D.W. (1985) Neural computation of decisions in optimization problems. *Biological Cybernetics*, **52**, 141–52.

Karmakar N. (1984) A new polynomial-time algorithm for linear programming. *Combinatorica*, **4**(4), 373–95.

Karmakar N. (1990) Riemannian geometry underlying interior point methods for linear programming. Preprint.

Kienker, P.K., Sejnowski, T.J., Hinton, G.E. and Schumacher, L.E. (1986) Separating figure from ground with a parallel network. *Perception*, **15**, 197–216.

Kirkpatrick, S., Gelatt, C. Jr. and Vecchi, M. (1983) Optimization by simulated annealing. *Science*, **220**, 671–80.

Koch, C.J.M. and Yuille, A.L. (1986) *Analog 'Neuronal' Networks in Early Vision*. Proceedings of the National Academy of Science, **83**, 4263–7.

Kosowsky, J.J and Yuille, A.L. (1991) The invisible hand algorithm: Solving the assignment problem with statistical physics. *Harvard Robotics Laboratory Technical Report 91–1*, Harvard University, Cambridge, MA.

Ohlsson, M., Peterson, C. and Yuille, A.L. (1992) Track finding with deformable templates – the elastic arms approach. *Computer Physics Communications*.

Parisi, G. (1988) *Statistical Field Theory*. Addison-Wesley, Reading, MA.

Peterson, C. (1990) 'Parallel distributed approaches to combinatorial optimization problems – benchmark studies on T.S.P. *Neural Computation*, **2**(3), 261–70.

Peterson, C. and Söderberg, B. (1989) A new method for mapping optimization problems onto neural networks. *Int. Jour. Neural Systems*, **1**(1), 3–22.

Platt, J. and Hopfield, J. (1986) Analog decoding using neural networks, in *Neural Networks for Computing*, American Institute of Physics Press, New York, pp. 365–9.

Rose, K., Gurewitz, E. and Fox, G. (1990) A deterministic annealing approach to clustering. *Pattern Recognition Letters*, **11**, 589–94.

Simic, P. (1990) Statistical mechanics as the underlying theory of 'elastic' and 'neural' optimization. *NETWORK: Computation in Neural Systems*, **1**(1), 1–15.

Sinkhorn, R. (1964) A relationship between arbitrary positive matrices and doubly stochastic matrices. *Ann. Math Statist.*, **35**, 876–9.

Ullman, S. (1979) *The Interpretation of Visual Motion*. MIT Press, Cambridge, MA.

Wilson, G. and Pawley, G. (1988) 'On the stability of the travelling salesman problem algorithm of Hopfield and Tank. *Biological Cybernetics*, **58**, 63–70.

Yuille, A.L. (1990) Generalized deformable models, statistical physics and matching problems. *Neural Computation*, **2**, 1–24.

Yuille, A.L. and Elfadel, I.M. (1992) *Mean-field theory and phase transitions for grayscale texture synthesis*. Proceedings 26th Conference on Information Sciences and Systems, Princeton University.

Yuille, A.L. and Kosowsky, J.J. (1991) The visible hand algorithm: Time convergence and temperature tracking. *Harvard Robotics Laboratory Technical Report 91–10*, Harvard University, Cambridge, MA.

4

Noisy linear networks

KURT HORNIK

Vienna Center for Neural Networks, Technische Universität Wien, Wiedner Hauptstraße 8–10/1071, A-1040 Wien, Austria

4.1 Introduction

Over the last few years, (bottleneck) linear neural network architectures have received a considerable amount of interest due to their importance in feature extraction. Suppose that an n-dimensional random vector x is to be compressed into a p-dimensional vector $y = c(x)$, where $p < n$, in a way that relative to some performance criterion, y contains as much information about x as possible. If the mean square error of the best linear estimate of x from y (the 'linear reconstruction error') is used as criterion and x is centered and square integrable, extraction of the first p principal components of the input covariance matrix $\sum = \mathrm{Cov}(x)$, a **linear** compression method, is optimal (Bourlard and Kamp, 1988), i.e. the error function $\mathbf{E}|x - Bc(x)|^2$ is minimized for $B = U_p T^{-1}$ and $c(x) = T U'_p x$, where the p columns of U_p are mutually perpendicular unit length eigenvectors of associated $\sum$ with the p largest eigenvalues of $\sum$, and T is an invertible $p \times p$ matrix. If, in addition, the data is Gussian, these choices also minimize the mutual information between x and y (cf. Baldi and Hornik, 1992).

In this chapter, we are concerned with situations where a linear feature extraction process is contaminated by noise. More precisely, suppose that upon presentation of an input x, the network actually computes $y = Ax + e$, where e is the processing noise. Such noise might, for example, be caused by intrinsic unreliability of the network units or external noise during transmission of the signals. We assume that e is centered with covariance matrix $\mathrm{Cov}(e) = \lambda R$ and uncorrelated with x. Here, λ is the noise level, and R describes the noise structure (if, for example, the output units are physically close, it may be unrealistic to assume that the noise components are uncorrelated). Clearly,

Artificial Neural Networks for Speech and Vision. Edited by Richard J. Mammone. Published in 1993 by Chapman & Hall, London. ISBN 0 412 54850 X

this is not the only possible noise model. For ease of exposition, we also assume that both Σ and R are strictly positive.

4.2 Linear feature extraction contaminated by noise

In this case, the optimal linear reconstruction By of x from $y = Ax + e$ is obtained with $B = B_\lambda(A) = \Sigma A'(A\Sigma A' + \lambda R)^+$, and the conditional covariance matrix $\text{Cov}(x - B_\lambda(A)y)$ of x given y equals

$$\Sigma_\lambda(A) = \Sigma - \Sigma A'(A\Sigma A' + \lambda R)^+ + A\Sigma.$$

Suppose it is desired to minimize the size of $g(\Sigma_\lambda(A))$ of this matrix, where g is a suitable **monotone** function. Of course, the natural choice is the **trace** $\text{tr}(\Sigma_\lambda(A))$, i.e. the sum of the eigenvalues of $\Sigma_\lambda(A)$, which is just the minimal mean square error in linear reconstructions of x from y. Another plausible measure is the **determinant** $\det(\Sigma_\lambda(A))$, i.e. the product of the eigenvalues of $\Sigma_\lambda(A)$; if the data is Gaussian, this quantity corresponds to the mutual information between x and y.

Note that this minimization problem no longer involves B, and thus explicit linear reconstruction of x from y is not required. Hence, the y-layer could be the network output in an unsupervised as well as a hidden layer in a supervised auto-associative realization.

In the noisy case, it is clearly necessary to constrain the weights A to some suitable compactum $\mathscr{A}$. Otherwise, the network would try to make A and thereby the signal-to-noise ratio at the y-layer as large as possible. Hence, the problem of interest really is to

$$\text{minimize } g(\Sigma_\lambda(A)) \text{ over } \mathscr{A}.$$

Unfortunately, it turns out that for $\lambda > 0$, explicit solutions of this problem are almost impossible to find, even for simple ('natural') choices of g and $\mathscr{A}$.

Let $\mathscr{A}_\lambda$ be the set of minima at noise level λ, and let us write $\lim_{\Lambda \ni \lambda \to \lambda_0} \mathscr{A}_\lambda \subseteq \mathscr{B}$ if the limits of all (convergent) sequences $A_\lambda \in \mathscr{A}_\lambda$ for $\Lambda \ni \lambda \to \lambda_0$ are in $\mathscr{B}$.

We have the following result:

Theorem 4.1 *Suppose that g is continuous and that $\mathscr{A}_0$ has an element of full rank. Then*

$$\lim_{\lambda \to 0+} \min_{\mathscr{A}} g(\Sigma_\lambda(A)) = \min_{\mathscr{A}} g(\Sigma_0(A)).$$

If, in addition, $\mathscr{A}$ contains only full rank matrices, then

$$\lim_{\lambda \to 0+} \mathscr{A}_\lambda \subseteq \mathscr{A}_0$$

Hence we find that in the low-noise case, the solutions of the noisy problems are close to the solutions of the noise-free problem (at least in the above sense). For the MSE criterion ($g = \text{tr}$), the result says that if $\mathscr{A}$ contains matrices of the form TU'_p with T and U_p as further above, then for small noise the net acts as an approximate PCA analyser. The determinant criterion is not really useful here, as for nonzero A we always have $A\Sigma_\lambda(A) = O$, and hence $\det(\Sigma_\lambda(A)) = 0$.

Now let us investigate what happens in the high-noise case, i.e. for $\lambda \to \infty$. Assume that g is differentiable at Σ with Fréchet differential $Dg(\cdot \; ; \Sigma)$. Then as $\lambda \to \infty$,

$$\Sigma_\lambda(A) = \Sigma - \lambda^{-1}\Sigma A'R^{-1}A\Sigma + O(\lambda^{-2})$$

uniformly over $\mathscr{A}$, and hence

$$g(\Sigma_\lambda(A)) = g(\Sigma) - \lambda^{-1}Dg(\Sigma A'R^{-1}A\Sigma; \Sigma) + O(\lambda^{-2})$$

uniformly over $\mathscr{A}$. From this, one can easily show the following:

Theorem 4.2 *Let g be differentiable at Σ and let $\mathscr{A}^*$ be the set of all maxima of $Dg(\Sigma A'R^{-1}A\Sigma; \Sigma)$ over $\mathscr{A}$. Then*

$$\lim_{\lambda \to \infty} \mathscr{A}_\lambda \subseteq \mathscr{A}^*.$$

Let us consider our two cases of main interest. The trace operator is linear, hence $D\,\mathrm{tr}(\Sigma A'R^{-1}A\Sigma; \Sigma) = \mathrm{tr}(\Sigma A'R^{-1}A\Sigma) = \mathrm{tr}(\Sigma^2 A'R^{-1}A)$, and the asymptotic MSE-problem is to maximize $\Phi_{\mathrm{tr}}(A) = \mathrm{tr}(\Sigma^2 A'R^{-1}A)$ over $\mathscr{A}$. The derivative of the determinant is (cf. Magnus and Neudecker, 1988, Theorem 1) $D\det(H; \Sigma) = \det(\Sigma)\mathrm{tr}(\Sigma^{-1}H)$. Hence, the asymptotic information-theoretic problem is to maximize $\Phi_{\det}(A) = \mathrm{tr}(\Sigma A'R^{-1}A)$ over $\mathscr{A}$. More generally, we could consider the problem of choosing A in a way that $y = Ax + e$ contains as much information about some centered target t as possible. In this case, it is readily seen that if $\Sigma_{te} = O$, we obtain the high-noise asymptotic problem by replacing Σ^2 by $\Sigma_{xt}\Sigma_{tx}$ in the trace case, and by replacing Σ by $\Sigma_{xt}\Sigma_{tt}^{-1}\Sigma_{tx}$ in the determinant case, respectively (here, $\Sigma_{te} = \mathbf{E}te'$, etc.). To sum up, in any case we arrive at a problem of the form

$$\text{maximize } \mathrm{tr}(MA'R^{-1}A) \text{ over } \mathscr{A}.$$

Of course, in general an explicit solution is not possible. In the sequel, we shall focus on three cases of leading interest.

We start with the case where we impose an upper bound on the Hilbert–Schmidt norm of A (i.e. on the sum of the squares of all entries of A).

Theorem 4.3 *Suppose that*

$$\mathscr{A} = \{A : \mathrm{tr}(AA') \leqslant \kappa\}.$$

Then $\mathscr{A}^*$ is the set of all matrices of the form

$$A = \sqrt{\kappa}rm',$$

where

$$m \quad \text{is a normalized principal eigenvector of} \quad M$$
$$r \quad \text{is a normalized principal eigenvector of} \quad R^{-1}.$$

(A 'principal eigenvector' is an eigenvector associated with the largest eigenvalue.) We observe that the rows of all such matrices are parallel. In particular, if $R = I_p$, than all vectors r in $\mathbb{R}^p$ are eigenvectors of R^{-1}, and we may take $r = [1/p, \ldots, 1/p]'$ to obtain an optimum with identical rows.

Corollary 4.4 *Let* $\mathscr{A} = \{A : \text{tr}(AA') \leqslant \kappa\}$. *Then for both trace and determinant criterion,*

$$\mathscr{A}^* = \{A : A = \sqrt{\kappa} r u'\}$$

where r is a normalized principal eigenvector of R^{-1} and u is a normalized principal eigenvector of Σ.

Therefore, in either case the network reacts to high noise by extracting the first principal component only.

Due to its non-locality, the above constraint is typically thought of as 'biologically implausible'. Hence, let us consider the case where we impose bounds on the length of each of the rows of A, i.e. suppose that

$$\mathscr{A} = \{A : |a_i|^2 = a_i' a_i \leqslant \kappa_i, i = 1, \ldots, p\},$$

where a_i is the ith row of A. In this case, we have not succeeded in describing $\mathscr{A}^*$ for general R. One can show that all Kuhn–Tucker points A satisfy $AM = RDA$, where $D = \text{diag}(\delta_1, \ldots, \delta_p)$ is the matrix of Lagrange multipliers. If m is an eigenvector of M with eigenvalue μ, then $\mu Am = AMm = RD\,Am$, i.e. either $Am = 0$ or Am is an eigenvector of RD with eigenvalue μ. Hence, the row space of such A is spanned by $q \leqslant p$ eigenvectors of M, but it is not clear which q the optimal A's have (and whether they are optimal).

For the special case where $R = \text{diag}(\rho_1, \ldots, \rho_p)$ is diagonal (i.e. if the noise components are uncorrelated), we have to maximize $\text{tr}(AMA'R^{-1}) = \sum_{i=1}^p \rho_i^{-1} a_i' M a_i$ over $\mathscr{A}$. In this case, it is immediate that $\mathscr{A}^* = \{A : a_i = \sqrt{\kappa_i} m_i, i = 1, \ldots, p\}$, where each m_i is a normalized principal eigenvector of M. (If the principal eigenspace has dimension greater than one, the m_i are not necessarily parallel.)

A similar analysis for this special case has been given in Linsker (1988) (for $R = I_p$ and all κ_i equal to one). Linsker's INFOMAX principal proceeds by maximizing Shannon's information rate

$$\frac{1}{2} \log \frac{\det(A\Sigma A' + \lambda R)}{\det(\lambda R)}$$

which for large λ approximately equals $\text{tr}(A\Sigma A'R^{-1})/2 = \Phi_{\text{det}}(A)/2$.

To sum up, for at least the special case of diagonal R, we find once again that in the high-noise case, the network tends to extract the first principal component only.

Finally, let

$$\mathscr{A} = \{A : AA' = I_p\}$$

be the set of all A with mutually perpendicular, unit length rows. (Of course, these constraints are also non-local.) Again, we have been unable to identify $\mathscr{A}^*$ for general R. The Kuhn–Tucker points now satisfy $AM = RLA$, where L is a lower diagonal matrix of Lagrange multipliers, and the conclusions are similar to the case where perpendicularity was not enforced. If $R = I_p$, we have to maximize $\mathrm{tr}(AMA')$ over $\mathscr{A}$, whence $\mathscr{A}^* = \{A \in \mathscr{A} : A = TU'_p, T \text{ orthogonal}\}$. In this case, the network asymptotically performs full PCA for both $\lambda \to 0$ and $\lambda \to \infty$, and thus does not adjust too well to the different noise levels (in the high noise case, full PCA is inferior to extracting the first principal component only!).

Of course, the above discussions do not say too much about moderate noise levels. It would be interesting, for example, to understand how rapidly the rows of the matrices in $\mathscr{A}_\lambda$ become parallel under the Hilbert–Schmidt constraint or whether rank degeneracies already occur for finite λ.

Thus far, nothing has been said about actually learning A. Of course, constrained gradient descent on $g(\sum_\lambda(A))$ or its sample counterpart could be employed; however, this leads to quite complicated and 'biologically implausible' algorithms. On the other hand, the local PCA algorithms that have been introduced within the last few years typically **force** the outputs components to be uncorrelated (Földiák, 1989; Rubner and Tavan, 1989; Sanger, 1989; Kung and Diamantaras, 1990; Leen, 1991; cf. also Hornik and Kuan, 1992). Hence, these algorithms may work reasonably well for small noise (because then minimizing the size of $\sum_\lambda(A)$ roughly amounts to full PCA of $\sum$), but are inappropriate for dealing with high noise (where optimal behavior is performed by reliably extracting the first principal component only).

In addition to that, we observe that these algorithms typically stop performing their tasks above certain noise levels. Consider the famous constrained-hebbian type one-unit algorithm introduced by Oja (1982) where, upon presentation of a new pattern x, $a = A'$ is modified according to

$$\Delta a \propto xy - y^2 a.$$

In the noisy case, the ODE associated with this algorithm (by suitably 'averaging over all patterns'; for further details, see, for example, Hornik and Kuan, 1992) becomes

$$\dot{a} = \sum a - (a' \sum a + \lambda)a,$$

where for notational simplicity we absorbed the scalar R into λ. The equilibria of this ODE are either zero or eigenvalues of $\sum$ with eigenvalue $a' \sum + \lambda$.

Hence, if the noise level λ is as large as the principal eigenvalue of Σ, $a = 0$ is the only equilibrium, and, as

$$\frac{1}{2}\frac{d|a|^2}{dt} = a'\dot{a} = a'\sum a(1 - a'a) - \lambda a'a \leqslant - a'\sum aa'a$$

is negative unless $a = 0$, we find that $a = 0$ is actually globally attractive. Therefore, we arrive at the rather dramatic conclusion that as soon as the noise is as large as the inputs, the Oja PCA extractor does not extract anything. As most multiunit PCA algorithms are based upon combining Oja's rule with certain decorrelation mechanisms, we *a fortiori* expect these to exhibit the same deficiency.

Our discussion shows that the currently available linear feature extraction techniques are practically incapable of dealing with too much noise at the feature layer. Ideally, such algorithms should gradually adjust to high noise by increasingly allowing the units to cooperate rather than always forcing them to compete. Developing such algorithms and deepening our understanding of the effects of unreliability in linear network architectures should be an interesting topic for future research.

Appendix 4A: Mathematical proofs

Proof of Theorem 4.1. Let $A_0 \in \mathscr{A}_0$ be full rank. Clearly,

$$g(\sum_\lambda(A_0)) \geqslant \min_{\mathscr{A}} g(\sum_\lambda(A)) \geqslant \min_{\mathscr{A}} g(\sum_0(A)) = g(\sum_0(A_0)).$$

By continuity of g and the fact that A_0 is full rank, $\lim_{\lambda \to 0+} g(\sum_\lambda(A_0)) = g(\sum_0(A))$, whence the first assertion. To prove the second one, choose $A_\lambda \in \mathscr{A}_\lambda$ for all $\lambda > 0$ in a way that $\lim_{\lambda \to 0+} A_\lambda = A_0$ exists. Then by assumption, A_0 is full rank, whence $g(\sum_\lambda(A_\lambda)) \to g(\sum_0(A_0))$, which in combination with what we just established completes the proof of the theorem.

Proof of Theorem 4.2. Let $\Phi(A) = Dg(\sum A'R^{-1}A\sum; \sum)$ and choose $A_\lambda \in \mathscr{A}_\lambda$ such that $\lim_{\lambda \to \infty} A_\lambda = A_\infty$ exists. Trivially, $\Phi(A_\infty) \leqslant \max_{\mathscr{A}} \Phi(A) := \phi$. Suppose this inequality were strict. Then we can find $\gamma > 0$ and a subsequence λ_k such that $\Phi(A_{\lambda_k}) \leqslant \phi - \gamma$ for all k. Choose $A^* \in \mathscr{A}^*$ such that $\Phi(A^*) = \phi$. Then

$$g(\sum_{\lambda_k}(A_{\lambda_k}) - g(\sum_{\lambda_k}(A^*))$$
$$= \lambda_k^{-1}(\Phi(A_{\lambda_k}) - \Phi(A^*)) + O(\lambda_k^{-2})$$
$$\geqslant \lambda_k^{-1}\gamma + O(\lambda_k^{-2})$$

implying that

$$\liminf_k \lambda_k(g(\sum_{\lambda_k}(A_{\lambda_k}) - g(\sum_{\lambda_k}(A^*))) > 0,$$

which is impossible. Hence, necessarily $\Phi(A_\infty) = \phi$, i.e. $A_\infty \in \mathscr{A}^*$.

In what follows, we shall make use of the vec operator which maps a matrix into a vector by stacking the columns of the matrix one above the other, the Kronecker product $P \otimes Q$ of two matrices P and Q which is obtained by replacing each entry π_{ij} of P with the matrix $\pi_{ij}Q$, and certain results on vec and $\otimes$ which can, for example, be found in Magnus and Neudecker (1988).

Proof of Theorem 4.3. We have

$$\mathrm{tr}(MA'R^{-1}A)$$
$$= \mathrm{vec}(A)'\mathrm{vec}(R^{-1}AM)$$
$$= \mathrm{vec}(A)'(M \otimes R^{-1})\mathrm{vec}(A)$$

and $|\mathrm{vec}(A)|^2 = \mathrm{tr}(AA') \leqslant \kappa$. Hence, $\mathscr{A}^*$ is the set of all A for which $a = \mathrm{vec}(A)$ maximizes $a'(M \otimes R^{-1})a$ over $a'a \leqslant \kappa$. By well known results from linear algebra, all such a are of the form $\sqrt{\kappa}v$, where v is a normalized principal eigenvector of the matrix $V = M \otimes R^{-1}$, and it remains to verify that v is of the form $\mathrm{vec}(rm')$. Let r and m be unit length eigenvectors of R^{-1} and M with corresponding eigenvalues λ_r and λ_m, respectively. Then

$$(M \otimes R^{-1})\mathrm{vec}(rm') = \mathrm{vec}(R^{-1}rm'M) = \lambda_r\lambda_m\mathrm{vec}(rm'),$$

and $|\mathrm{vec}(rm')|^2 = \mathrm{tr}(rm'(rm')') = \mathrm{tr}(r'rm'm) = 1$, i.e. $\mathrm{vec}(rm')$ is a unit length eigenvector of $M \otimes R^{-1}$ with eigenvalue $\lambda_r\lambda_m$. R^{-1} and M both being symmetric, it is easily seen that we can obtain all eigenvectors of $M \otimes R^{-1}$ in this way. In particular, the principal eigenvalue of $M \otimes R^{-1}$ is the product of the principal eigenvalue of M and that of R^{-1}, whence the theorem.

Kuhn–Tucker points. In the case $\mathscr{A} = \{A : a_i'a_i \leqslant \kappa_i, i = 1, \ldots, p\}$, the Lagrangian is

$$\mathrm{tr}(MA'R^{-1}A) + \sum_{i=1}^{p} \delta_i(\kappa_i - a_i'a_i)$$
$$= \mathrm{vec}(A)'(M \otimes R^{-1})\mathrm{vec}(A) + \sum_{i=1}^{p} \delta_i(\kappa_i - \mathrm{vec}(A)'(I \otimes e_ie_i')\mathrm{vec}(A)),$$

where e_i is the ith Cartesian unit vector. Hence setting the derivative with respect to $\mathrm{vec}(A)$ equal to zero, we obtain

$$(M \otimes R^{-1})\mathrm{vec}(A) = \sum_{i=1}^{p} \delta_i(I \otimes e_ie_i')\mathrm{vec}(A)$$

respectively $\mathrm{vec}(R^{-1}AM) = \sum_{i=1}^{p} \delta_i\mathrm{vec}(e_ie_i'A)$, or equivalently $R^{-1}AM = DA$. The case where in addition perpendicularity is enforced follows analogously.

References

Baldi, P. and Hornik, K. (1992) *Learning in linear networks*. Preprint.
Bourlard, H. and Kamp, Y. (1988) Auto-association by multilayer perceptrons and singular value decomposition. *Biological Cybernetics*, **59**, 291–4.

Földiák, P. (1989) Adaptive network for optimal linear feature extraction. *Proceedings of the International Joint Conference on Naural Networks*, SOS Printing, San Diego pp. I: 401–5.

Hornik, K. and Kuan, C.-M. (1992) Convergence analysis of local feature extraction algorithms. *Neural Networks*, **5** 229–40.

Kung, S.Y. and Diamantaras, K. I. (1990) A neural network learning algorithm for adaptive principal component extraction (APEX). *Proceedings of the IEEE International Conference on Acoustics, Speech, and Signal Processing ICASSP-90* IEEE, New York, pp. II: 861–4

Leen, T. (1991) Dynamics of learning in linear feature-discovery networks. *Network*, **2**, 85–105.

Linsker, R. (1988) Self-organization in a perceptual network. *Computer*, **21**, 105–17.

Magnus, J.R. and Neudecker, H. (1988) *Matrix differential calculus with applications in statistics and econometrics*. Wiley, Chichester.

Oja, E. (1982) A simplified neuron model as a principal component analyzer. *Journal of Mathematics and Biology*, **15**, 267–73.

Rubner, J. and Tavan, P. (1989) A self-organizing network for principal component analysis. *Europhysics Letters*, **10**, 693–8.

Sanger, T.D. (1989) Optimal unsupervised learning in a single-layer linear feedforward neural network. *Neural Networks*, **2**, 459–73.

5

Short-term memory structures for dynamic neural networks

BERT de VRIES
David Sarnoff Research Center, CN 5300, Princeton, NJ 08540, USA

5.1 Introduction

In this chapter a family of short-term memory network structures for sequence processing neural networks is introduced. Sequence processing (or **dynamic**) neural nets receive an M-dimensional pattern $u(t)$, where t is a time index, and produce an L-dimensional output pattern $y(t)$, Relevant information concerning $u(s)$ for $s < t$ is stored in the N network states $x(t)$. A wide variety of dynamic neural net topologies have been proposed. A partial list includes network architectures proposed by Mozer (1989), Elman (1990), Jordan (1986), fully recurrent nets by Williams and Zipser (1989), high-order recurrent nets by Giles *et al.* (1990), and several others. Each of these network topologies reflects a different design trade-off, although the sheer amount of different structures for similar tasks indicates that the field is rather experimental and *ad hoc*.

Here I develop a class of memory structures particularly for use in so-called locally recurrent, globally feedforward (LRGF) networks (Back and Tsoi, 1991). Networks of this kind are connected in a feedforward manner, i.e. there are no global loops. In contrast to static networks however, a pre-synaptic state $x_i(t)$ may pass through a **linear** filter before connecting to a higher indexed node. Thus, for LRGF networks the states evolve according to

$$x_i(t) = \sigma\left(\sum_{j<i} \sum_k w_{ijk}[g_k \cdot x_j(t)] \right) \qquad (1)$$

where $g_k(t)$ is a delay kernel (a linear filter) and $\cdot$ is the convolution operator.

Artificial Neural Networks for Speech and Vision. Edited by Richard J. Mammone. Published in 1993 by Chapman & Hall, London. ISBN 0 412 54850 X

As an example, for feedforward delay nets, $g_k(t) = \delta(t - k)$, and (1) reduces to $x_i(t) = \sigma(\sum_{j < i} \sum_k w_{ijk} x_j(t - k))$.

In the following we introduce a family of delay kernels and analyse their properties in the context of a sequence processing protocol.

5.2 Memory filters

First, we restrict the class of linear filters under consideration by two conditions.

Definition (memory filter). *A sequence (impulse response) $g(t)$ is called a memory filter if the following two conditions hold:*

1. $g(t)$ is **causal**, that is, $g(t) = 0$ for $t < 0$.
2. $g(t)$ is **normalized** in the sense that $\sum_{t=0}^{\infty} |g(t)| = 1$.

These conditions are motivated by common sense arguments. The causality condition reminds us that a memory can only store events from the past, not from the future. The normalization condition is there because we don't want an amplifier or attenuating filter: a memory filter should just delay an event.

The use of the memory filter is the following. A signal $v(t)$ is called a **memory state** (of $u(t)$) if $v(t) = \sum_k g(t - k) u(k)$ where $g(t)$ is a memory filter.

Theorem 5.1 *A memory filter is Bounded-Input-Bounded-Output (BIBO) stable*

Proof: A filter $g(t)$ is BIBO stable if $\sum_{t=-\infty}^{\infty} |g(t)| < \infty$ (Oppenheim and Schafer, 1975). This condition is trivially satisfied according to conditions 1 and 2 in the definition of the memory filter. □

The characteristics of linear filters are usually expressed in the frequency domain in terms of their magnitude and phase response. In the case of memory filters however we are more interested in temporal properties such as memory depth and resolution. There are several ways to estimate the memory depth of a filter (mean delay, rms delay, etc.). Here we choose to estimate the **depth** D of a filter as the mean delay, computed as

$$D \equiv \sum_{t=0}^{\infty} tg(t) = Z\{tg(t)\}|_{z=1} = -\left.\frac{\mathrm{d}G(z)}{\mathrm{d}z}\right|_{z=1}, \tag{2}$$

where $G(z) \equiv \sum_{t=0}^{\infty} g(t) z^{-t}$ is the z-transform of $g(t)$ (Oppenheim and Schafer, 1975).

Next, some examples of memory filters are presented.

5.2.1 The tapped delay line

An important case of a memory filter is, of course, a (non-dispersive) delay operator. A Kth order tapped delay line, the memory structure for feedforward

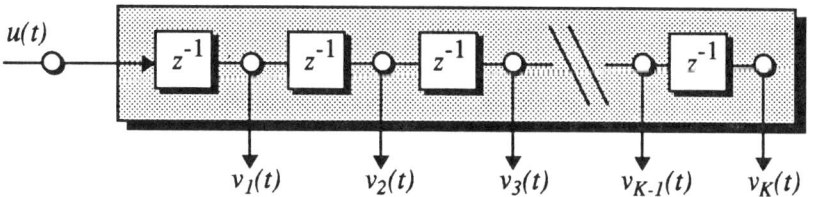

Figure 5.1 *Tapped delay line.*

delay neural nets, can be regarded as a one-input-K-output filter with impulse responses $g_k(t) = \delta(t - k)$. The transfer function in the z-domain is given by $G_k(z) = z^{-k}$.

The memory depth D of a Kth order delay line is $D = K$. The resolution R, the number of memory state variables per time step delay, is $R = 1$ (Figure 5.1).

5.2.2 The leaky integrator

The impulse response of the leaky integrator is given by

$$g(t) = (1 - \mu)\mu^{t-1}S(t - 1), \quad |\mu| < 1, \tag{3}$$

where μ is an adaptive parameter and $S(t)$ is the unit step function. In the neural net literature, leaky integrators are sometimes referred to as **context nodes** (Elman, 1990) or **memory neurons** (Poddar and Unnikrishnan, 1991).

The depth or reach of the leaky integrator is given by

$$D \equiv \sum_{t=0}^{\infty} tg(t) = \frac{1}{1 - \mu}. \tag{4}$$

For the leaky integrator the z-transform of the impulse response evaluates to

$$G(z) = \frac{1 - \mu}{z - \mu}. \tag{5}$$

The memory depth of the leaky integrator increases for increasing values of $\mu(\mu < 1)$. The case $\mu = 0$ reduces the integrator to a unit delay operator z^{-1}, whereas $\mu = 1 - \varepsilon$ with ε very small leads to a very deep memory. The cost of increasing memory depth is a reduced temporal resolution. The temporal resolution for the leaky integrator is $R = 1/D = 1 - \mu$ (Figure 5.2).

5.2.3 The gamma memory filter

The gamma memory filter consists of a cascade of K leaky integrators with the same parameter μ (Figure 5.3). The gamma filter generalizes the tapped delay line and the leaky integrator into a unified parametrized structure. The

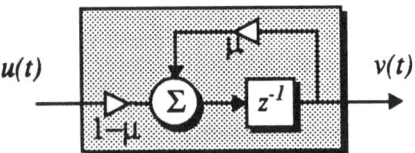

Figure 5.2 *Leaky integrator.*

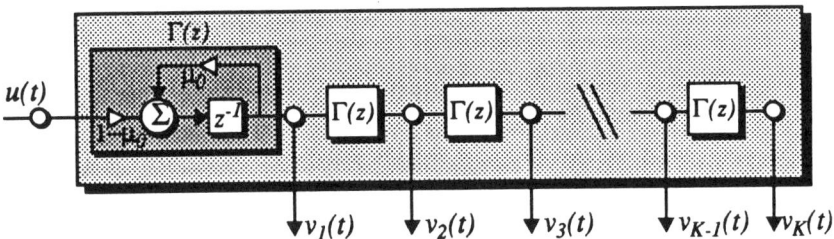

Figure 5.3 *Gamma delay line.*

transfer function to the kth tap is given by

$$G_k(z) = \frac{V_k(z)}{U(z)} = \left(\frac{1-\mu}{z-\mu}\right)^k. \tag{6}$$

The mean memory depth for a Kth order gamma memory evaluates to

$$D = -\left.\frac{dG_K(z)}{dz}\right|_{z=1} = \frac{K}{1-\mu}. \tag{7}$$

Thus, for the same μ, the depth of the gamma memory is K times larger than for the leaky integrator. Yet, the resolution for the gamma memory is similar to the leaky integrator,

$$R = \frac{K}{K/(1-\mu)} = 1 - \mu. \tag{8}$$

Note that all three memory structures (tapped delay line, leaky integrator and gamma filter) obey the relation

$$order = depth \times resolution\ (K = DR). \tag{9}$$

Gamma filters have been applied in diverse temporal processing applications. In general, the ability to control depth and resolution by two parameters (K and μ) in contrast to one parameter (K for tapped delay line and μ for leaky integrator), leads to improved temporal processing performance for neural nets with gamma memory (de Vries, 1991).

5.2.4 The time-alignment filter

Sometimes I compare the gamma filter with a homogeneous rubber band that spans the delay domain. By stretching the band (increase μ), the depth of the memory increases, but as the band remains homogeneous, the distances between the taps increase proportionally and uniformly for all taps. Thus, the resolution of the gamma filter is the same at each tap. For some applications, an adaptive **tap-dependent** resolution is needed. In particular, for speech signals, variations in speech rate create a necessity for more freedom in resolution.

The time-alignment (TA) filter provides this kind of memory structure (Figure 5.4). The backbone of the TA filter is a gamma memory structure, parametrized by μ_0, which controls the depth and resolution of the delay line. **Tap-dependent modulations** of depth and resolution are implemented by variation of the parameters μ_i, $i = 1,\ldots,K$. The connection pattern between $\tilde{u}(t)$ and $v(t)$ defines the boundaries of the tap-dependent modulations. Note that for $\mu_i = 0$, $i = 0, 1, \ldots, K$, the TA filter reduces to a tapped delay line and for $\mu_i = 0$, $i = 0, 1, \ldots, K$, the TA filter becomes a gamma filter.

The transfer function of the TA filter is given by

$$G_k(z) \equiv \frac{V_k(z)}{U(z)} = \Gamma^{k-1}(z)[(1 - \mu_k)\Gamma(z) + \mu_k]. \tag{10}$$

The memory depth at tap k is

$$D_k = -\left.\frac{\mathrm{d}G_k(z)}{\mathrm{d}z}\right|_{z=1} = \frac{k - \mu_k}{1 - \mu_0}, \tag{11}$$

and the resolution at tap k is given by

$$R_k \equiv \frac{1}{D_k - D_{k-1}} = \frac{1 - \mu_0}{1 - \mu_k + \mu_{k-1}} = \frac{1 - \mu_0}{1 - \Delta_k \mu_k}, \tag{12}$$

where $\Delta_k \mu_k \equiv \mu_k - \mu_{k-1}$.

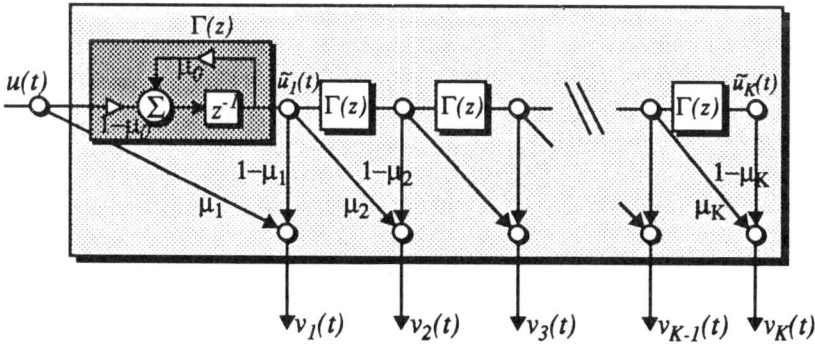

Figure 5.4 *Time-alignment memory filter.*

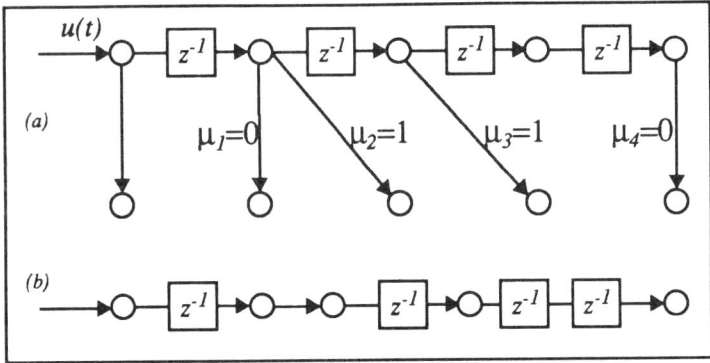

Figure 5.5 *Example of a TA filter. Structure (a) is equal to structure (b).*

A particular example which demonstrates the tap-dependent resolution is displayed in Figure 5.5. Note that the parametrization $\{\mu_0, \mu_1, \mu_2, \mu_3, \mu_4\} = \{0, 0, 1, 1, 0\}$ leads to a tapped delay line with unequal tap delays. This feature is very interesting when dealing with speech where sometimes signal values change slowly (vowels) and sometimes rapidly (consonants).

5.3 Dealing with temporal variation

The problem with speech is that apart from spectral variation, a spatial pattern recognition problem, there is also a large amount of temporal variation for one word (class). Temporal variation occurs naturally and is due to changes in speaking rate and prosodics at various levels. In a word recognition problem, we distinguish between two kinds of temporal variation: the overall **duration** of a word may vary as well as the duration of various phonemes (vowels, consonants, etc., the **phonetic duration problem**) that constitute a word will vary significantly within a word class. To compensate for or nullify temporal variation in a speech recognition task is sometimes referred to as the **time-warp** problem or **time-alignment** problem.

Neural networks have been shown to be excellent tools for static pattern recognition problems. Indeed, in speech recognition problems where temporal variation is largely reduced prior to feeding the neural nets, excellent classification results have been reported (for instance Waibel *et al.* (1988), on experiments with the time-delay neural net). At this moment, we still do not have a satisfactory model for handling **unpredictable** temporal variation with neural nets. As a result, current research leans strongly toward combining the (static) pattern matching capabilities of neural nets with the proven time-alignment properties of the dynamic time-warping algorithm (Sakoe *et al.*, 1989) and hidden Markov models (Boulard and Wellekens, 1990).

Let us analyse why neural nets do not perform well in an environment with unpredictable temporal variation. In a neural net, we store in the weight vector w some kind of average of the words that are presented during training. Thus, the weights are tuned to the average speaking rate in the training set. It is important to realize that we can never store **unpredictable** aspects of speech (such as speaking rate). We conclude that independent of whether we use a recurrent or feedforward net, for constant weights, an additive net such as $x(t) = \sigma(\sum_{j,k} w_{ijk} x_j(t-k))$ cannot be invariant to the speaking rate. By invariance I mean that $x(t)$ would not depend on the speaking rate.

To achieve a speaking rate invariant network we need to augment the net with a speaking rate dependent (set of) variable(s) $m(t)$ that modulate(s) the states $x(t)$. $m(t)$ may modulate the states $x(t)$ directly or indirectly by modulating the weights w (which makes the weights time-varying, since $w = w(m(t))$). An example of state modulation by a variable that measures the speaking rate was proposed by Sun et al. (1992). This network is entirely invariant to the speaking rate.

Here I propose an alternative model. The idea is to let the parameters μ of the time-alignment filter be **fast adaptive** so as to compensate for temporal variation. There are three time scales in this processing scheme. The slowest time scale relates to the adaptation of the weights w that store the average word prototypes. We call w the **slow weights**. The input signal $u(t)$ and states $x(t)$ (and $y(t)$) change faster. The time-alignment parameters $\mu(t)$ are adapted at an even faster time scale than the states: at every time step t, we adapt $\mu(t)$ so as to maximize a performance measure (for the sequence classification case, maximize the net output $y(t)$). The parameters $\mu(t)$ are called **fast weights**.

5.3.1 Example: keyword spotting

How this all fits together in a practical example is illustrated in Figure 5.6. The keyword spotter consists of a cascade of a time-alignment memory filter and a (static) Pattern Matching (PM) network. The pattern matching network is non-linear and parametrized by slow weights w. The slow weights w are adapted only during the training phase. A layered feedforward net or a one-layer higher order net are good choices.

The speech spectral input $u(t)$ cannot be just windowed and fed to the PM net however. The unpredictable temporal variation will sharply degrade recognition performance. Thus as a pre-processing stage we insert a **fast adaptive** time-alignment network. At every time step t (or every few time steps), the network adapts $\mu(t)$ so as to maximize $y(t)$, in other words, to obtain the best possible temporal alignment of $u(t)$ parametrized by $\mu(t)$. It is assumed here that $y(t)$ holds a measure of fit for a particular word. This scheme is very similar to a dynamic time-warping (DTW) pre-processing stage. Such an approach, DTW followed by a pattern matching network, has been proposed and performs very promisingly (Sakoe et al., 1989). The scheme that I propose is different in that *the time-warp stage is performed by an adaptive neural net*

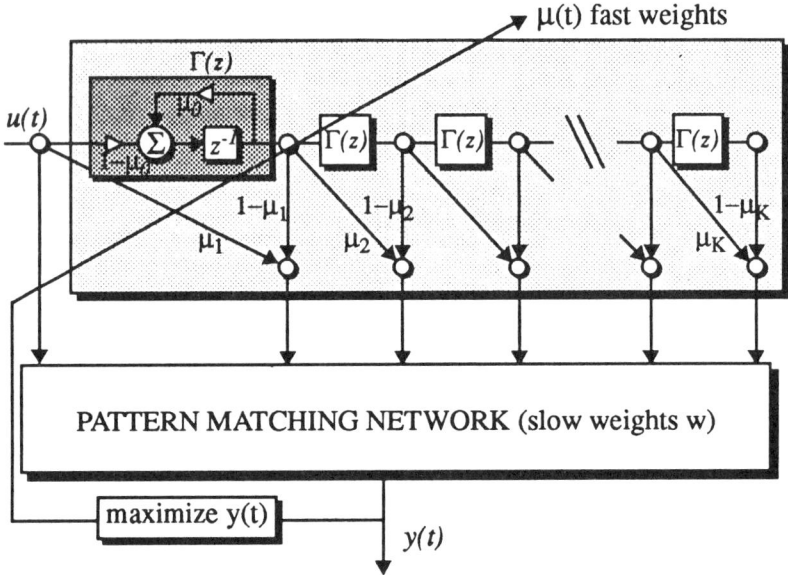

Figure 5.6 *A fast adaptive dynamic neural net architecture for word spotting.*

itself. As a result, we do not need a dynamic programming pre- or post-processing algorithm. Instead, the time-warping is implemented by a gradient descent procedure such as backpropagation. There are several interesting features regarding this architecture. Note that the amount of temporal warp allowed is easily regulated by limiting the excursions of $\mu(t)$; for instance we can require $|\mu_i(t)| \leqslant \alpha < 1$ where α holds a warping bound. Also, the **structure** of the allowed time warps can be changed by altering the connection pattern between the gamma taps and the filter outputs in the time alignment memory filter.

5.4 Conclusions

In this chapter I have introduced a class of parametrized memory filters for use in sequence processing neural networks. If these filters are used in globally feedforward networks, the total network will be guaranteed stable, since the memory filters are stable for all parametrizations. Whereas in signal processing applications it is common to analyse filters in terms of their frequency response, memory filters are 'better understood' in terms of temporal properties such as depth and resolution. An understanding of the properties of memory filters may help in the choice of an appropriate network architecture for a sequence processing task.

Acknowledgements

This research was supported by the Advanced Projects Agency of the Department of Defense and was monitored by the Air Force Office of Scientific Research under Contract No. F49620-C-0072. The United States Government is authorized to reproduce and distribute reprints for governmental purposes notwithstanding any coypright notation herein.

References

Back, A.D. and Tsoi, A.C. (1991) FIR and IIR synapses, a new neural network architecture for time series modelling. *Neural Computation*, **3**, 375–85.

Boulard, H. and Wellekens, C.J. (1990) Links between Markov models and multilayer perceptrons. *IEEE Transactions on Pattern Analysis and Machine Intelligence*, **12**(12), 1167–78.

de Vries, B. (1991) Temporal processing with neural networks – the development of the gamma model. PhD Dissertation, University of Florida.

Elman, J.L. (1990) Finding structure in time. *Cognitive Science*, **14**, 179–211.

Giles, C.L., Sun, G.Z., Chen, H.H. and Lee, Y.C. (1990) Higher order recurrent networks and grammatical inference. *Advances in Neural Information Processing*, **2**, 380.

Jordan, M.I. (1986) Attractor dynamics and parallelism in a connectionist sequential machine. *Proceedings 8th Annual Conference of Cognitive Science Society*, 531–46.

Mozer, M.C. (1989) A focused backpropagation algorithm for temporal pattern recognition, *Complex Systems*, **3**, 349–81.

Oppenheim, A.V. and Schafer, R.W. (1975) *Digital Signal Processing*. Prentice-Hall, Englewood, NJ.

Poddar, P. and Unnikrishnan, K.P. (1991) Non-linear prediction of speech signals using memory neuron networks. *Proceedings IEEE Workshop on Neural Networks for Signal Processing*, 395–404.

Sakoe, H., Isotani, R., Yoshida, K., Iso, K., and Watanabe, T. (1989) Speaker independent word recognition using dynamic programming neural networks. *Proc. ICASSP-89*, 29–33.

Sun, G.Z., Chen, H.H., Lee, Y.C. and Liu, Y.D. (1992) Time warping recurrent neural networks and trajectory classification. *IJCNN Proceedings*, Baltimore, MD, I-431-436.

Waibel, A., Hanazawa, T., Hinton, G., Shikano, K. and Lang, K. (1988) Phoneme recognition: neural networks versus hidden Markov models. *ICASSP-88*, 107–10.

Williams, R.J. and Zipser, D. (1989) A learning algorithm for continually running fully recurrent neural networks. *Neural Computation*, **1**, 270–80.

6

The effect of higher order in recurrent neural networks: experiments

C. LEE GILES* and CLIFFORD B. MILLER[†]

*Institute for Advanced Computer Studies, University of Maryland, College Park, MD, USA
[†]NEC Research Institute, 4 Independence Way, Princeton, NJ 08540, USA

6.1 Introduction

Because of their innate ability to model 'internal state' information and process temporal signals, there has been much recent interest in recurrent neural network models. Although they operate only in discrete time, such networks are naturally dynamic and thus readily extend the computational power of feed-forward neural networks. Interestingly, one of the first neural network models was recurrent (McCulloch and Pitts, 1943). The representational issues of recurrent neural networks to finite state automata was further explored by Kleene (1956) and Minsky (1967), and recently extended to cellular automata (Fogelman-Soulie et al., 1987; Goles and Martinez, 1990). Then there was much initial interest in steady-state recurrent network models (Hopfield, 1982) for optimization problems. Since then there has been much work on how recurrent neural networks are related to and learn automata (see for example Cleeremans et al., 1989; Elman, 1990; Giles et al., 1990, 1992; Horne et al., 1992; Jordan, 1986; Lucas and Damper, 1990; Mozer and Bachrach, 1990; Pollack, 1991; Sun et al., 1990; Watrous and Kuhn, 1992a).

The focus of this chapter is on the **order** of the recurrent neural network models, and how well this type of order relates to the performance of recurrent neural networks in learning temporal sequences. There could be many

Artificial Neural Networks for Speech and Vision. Edited by Richard J. Mammone. Published in 1993 by Chapman & Hall, London. ISBN 0 412 54850 X

definitions of order in neural network models. Our definition of order is the same as that of Minsky and Papert (1969), and the polynomial order of Cover (1965). (A similar but more restrictive definition is that of 'sigma-pi' units – Rumelhart *et al.*, 1986). In general, these higher order extensions have enhanced the computational power of higher-order feed-forward neural networks for specific problems usually at the cost of lower generality and higher complexity (for some examples, see Giles and Maxwell, 1987; Psaltis *et al.*, 1988). These feed-forward 'higher order' neural networks have found successful use in many models and applications, from placing *a priori* knowledge into a neural network to modeling synaptic interconnections (for example, see Guyon *et al.*, 1992; Koch and Poggio, 1992; Pao, 1989; Perantonis and Lisboa, 1992; Peretto and Niez, 1986).

It is straightforward to extend this definition of order to recurrent neural network models (Baldi and Venkatesh, 1987; Personnaz *et al.*, 1987; Guyon *et al.*, 1988; Lee *et al.*, 1986; Psaltis *et al.*, 1988). Until recently, there was little evidence that increasing the order in a dynamic recurrent network (associative memory is another issue) gave any of the computational advantages seen in higher-order feed-forward networks. Representational and experimental arguments could be made for using higher order recurrent networks to learn automata (Das *et al.*, 1992; Giles *et al.*, 1990, 1992; Pollack, 1990, 1991; Siegelmann and Sontag, 1991; Sun *et al.*, 1990; Watrous and Kuhn 1992a). In particular, Goudreau *et al.* (1992) show that for hard-threshold neurons, a single-layer first-order recurrent neural network cannot represent all finite state automata. In addition, recent experimental comparisons of grammar learning (Das *et al.*, 1992) showed that higher order made it easier to learn context-free grammars using a neural network pushdown automaton. The motivation of this work was to give an experimental comparison of order in simple recurrent neural networks.

To compare learning performance of the higher-order architectures, we chose the testbed problem of grammatical inference, in which the goal is to infer a grammar with an **inference engine**, given a sample of strings generated by the grammar. If the sample contains both positive and negative examples, then in the worst case the problem is NP-hard. (See Angluin and Smith, 1983; Fu, 1982; Miclet, 1990 for a discussion of difficulty and existing methods of solution. Also see Lang, 1992, for a very promising new method and impressive results.) For a discussion of grammars, finite state automata and languages, see a text such as Hopcroft and Ullman (1979). To determine how well the grammar has been learned, one can either extract the grammar from the inference engine which learned the grammar, or test how well the inference engine classifies previously unseen strings – the task of generalization. In this study we do both – perform generalization and extract the grammar (in the form of a finite state automaton) from the neural network. For our purposes, the inference engine is a recurrent neural network of first or second order (defined below).

6.2 Dynamic recurrent neural networks

6.2.1 Definition of recurrent neural networks

A dynamic recurrent neural network (RNN) can process temporal input sequences of arbitrary length that vary over (discrete) time. (Steady-state recurrent networks cannot handle sequences of arbitrary length.) (See Hertz *et al.*, 1991, for a discussion of dynamic recurrent network models.) A recurrent neural network consists of a set of N recurrent 'state' neurons, some serving as 'output' units and the rest as 'hidden' units, and a set of L *non*-recurrent 'input' neurons which receive signals from outside the network. Both hidden and output units feedback into themselves through a set of synchronous delay lines (see Figure 6.1). Thus, our model of an RNN can be thought of as a feed-forward network with an arbitrary (potentially infinite) number of identical layers; the weight W_{ij} of any given neural interconnect $i \rightarrow j$ has the same value on each layer.

In this simple fully-connected RNN, all state neurons are functionally equivalent and symmetrically connected; the only real distinction between output and hidden units is at time steps when certain neurons are singled out to show 'target' values. This distinction is conceptual only – in other words, *all* the state neurons always feed into the next layer (time step) with full connectivity, regardless of the designation of output neurons. One could also create additional **nonrecurrent** units to act as output on different time steps. These 'output time steps' could occur at any time during a temporal input sequence – they are defined by the problem at hand. In classification problems, output usually occurs only at the end of the sequence, or at periodic intervals. In transduction (translation) problems, one might expect outputs at most (or possibly all) time steps. We present an experimental performance comparison of the 'first-order' and 'second-order' RNN architectures in a classification problem. (See Goudreau *et al.*, 1992, and Siegelmann and Sontag, 1991 for some theoretical comparisons.)

6.2.2 The definition of 'order'

The 'order' of a neural network refers to the dimensionality of product terms in the weighted sum, which reflects the connectivity of the network. Note that all discussions of RNN's in this chapter are restricted to fully-connected RNN's; hence the connectivity is the same throughout the network at all time steps. The recurrence equation for a RNN, which defines its temporal dynamics, typically filters a weighted sum of states and/or inputs through a nonlinear 'discriminant' function. This function has the general form

$$S^{(t+1)} = F(S^{(t)}, I^{(t)}; W, \Theta) \tag{1}$$

where $S(t) \in \mathcal{R}^N$ represents the values of all state neurons (the 'state vector') at time t, $I^{(t)} \in \mathcal{R}^L$ the values of all input neurons (the 'input vector') at time t,

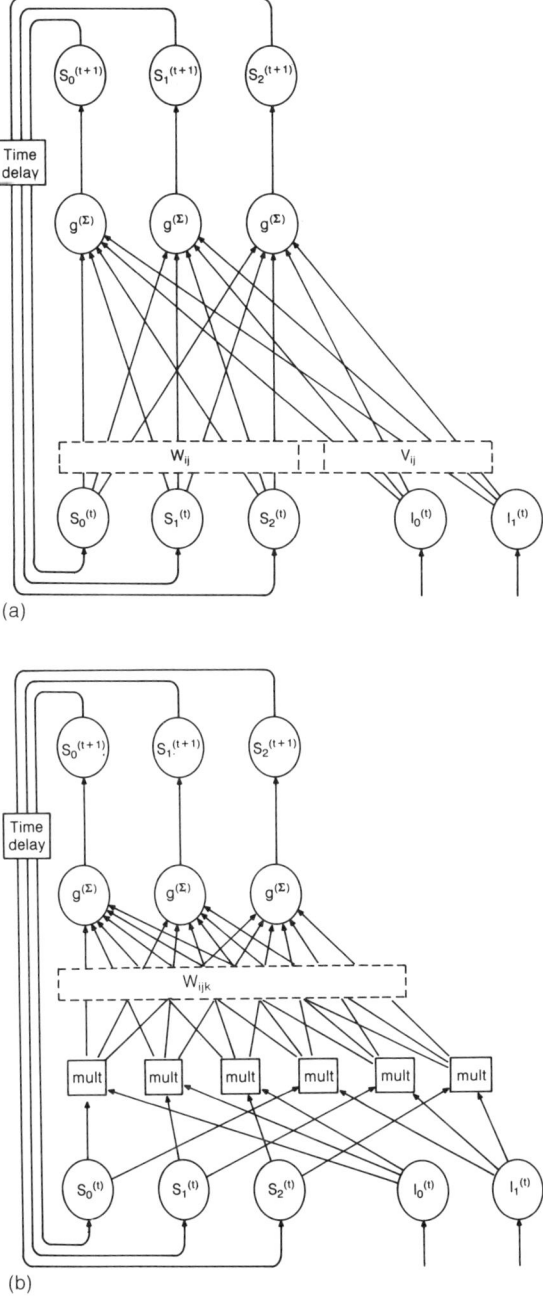

Figure 6.1 *First-order (a) and second-order (b) single layer recurrent neural networks.* $S_i^{(t)}$ *represents the value of the ith state neuron at time t, and* $I_k^{(t)}$ *represents the value of the kth input neuron at time t. Units marked* $g^{(\Sigma)}$ *represent the sigmoid function operating on the sum of all incoming connections. Blocks marked mult represent the second-order operation* $W_{ijk} \times S_j^{(t)} \times I_k^{(t)}$.

F is a vector function (usually a nonlinear mapping), **W** is a set of weight matrices defining the weighted interconnects between layers, and Θ is a set of biases on the state neurons. It is important to note that equation (1) is the standard definition of the {state; input → next-state} mapping found in the definitions of both finite state automata (Kohavi, 1978) and nonlinear systems models (Narendra and Parthasarathy, 1990). In addition, for each type of recurrent neural network we discuss, there exists **only one hidden layer** per time step. We do this in order to explore as simple a model as possible. However, a final 'output' layer, with its own set of weights, is added to the network by the input encoding (discussed below), which appends an 'end symbol' to an input sequence to designate the end of an input string. This gives additional degrees of freedom to the decision-making process and gets around the representation limitations imposed by the first order, single hidden layer model (Goudreau et al., 1992).

Inspection of the recurrence equation for each type of architecture reveals their differences. For first-order recurrent nets, we define the recurrence as

$$S_i^{(t+1)} = f(Y_i^t), \quad Y_i^t = \sum_j^N W_{ij} S_j^{(t)} + \sum_k^L V_{ik} I_k^{(t)} + \Theta_i. \tag{2}$$

In this architecture there are two independent sets of weights, one for the state neurons (**W**, size $N \times N$), and one for the input neurons (**V**, size $N \times L$). There is also a set of N biases Θ, one for each state neuron. Here f is a nonlinear **discriminant** function; in our implementation of the RNN, this function is a sigmoid, $f(x) = (1 + \exp(-x))^{-1}$, which limits the activation range of all state neurons to $0 < S_i^{(t)} < 1$.

For second order nets, our definition of the recurrence equation is

$$S_i^{(t+1)} = f(Y_i^t), \quad Y_i^t = \sum_j^N \sum_k^L W_{ijk} S_j^{(t)} I_k^{(t)} + \Theta_i. \tag{3}$$

For this type of net there is only a single set of weights **W**, but its structure is more complex than either of the two sets of weights in the first-order net, since it is in fact a 'higher-order' $N \times N \times L$ matrix. f and Θ_i are the same here as for the first-order case.

The first-order weight matrices have dimensionality $D(\mathbf{W}) = N^2$ and $D(\mathbf{V}) = NL$ elements for a total of $N^2 + NL = N(N + L)$ elements. The second-order weight matrix has $D(\mathbf{W}) = N^2 L$ elements. Hence in the limit of large N, second-order RNN's have L times as many weights as first-order RNN's.

6.2.3 Input encoding

A **string** is defined as a series of symbols $\sigma(t)$ presented to the neural network one per time step t. The symbols are taken from a finite discrete alphabet Σ. These symbols are transformed into neuron input vectors $\sigma(t) \to \mathbf{I}^{(t)}$ via a one-to-one mapping called an 'input encoding scheme'.

All results obtained in this study use 'local' or 'unary' input encoding (also referred to as 'one-hot' encoding in VLSI (Ashar *et al.*, 1992)). In this input encoding scheme, the mapping from input symbols to input-neuron activations is a direct, one-to-one mapping: when symbol σ appears in the string, input neuron σ is turned on and all others are turned off. Symbolically this can be represented as $I_k^{(t)} = \delta_{k\sigma(t)}$ (δ signifies Kronecker delta).

This kind of encoding has important consequences in the recurrence equations of the two types of RNN's studied here. If we substitute in the Kronecker delta equation for the input activations, the recurrence equations become

$$S_i^{(t+1)} = f\left(\sum_j^N W_{ij} S_j^{(t)} + V_{i\sigma(t)} + \Theta_i \right) \quad \text{[first-order]}$$

$$S_i^{(t+1)} = f\left(\sum_j^N W_{ij\sigma(t)} S_j^{(t)} + \Theta_i \right) \qquad \text{[second-order]}. \qquad (4)$$

Note that these equations can also be expressed in vector form (where dot products take the place of the sum over j):

$$S_i^{(t+1)} = f(\mathbf{W}_i \cdot \mathbf{S}^{(t)} + V_{i\sigma(t)} + \Theta_i) \quad \text{[first-order]}$$
$$S_i^{(t+1)} = f(\mathbf{W}_{i\sigma(t)} \cdot \mathbf{S}^{(t)} + \Theta_i) \qquad \text{[second-order]}. \qquad (5)$$

In equation (5), letters in boldface denote N-vectors.

These forms of the equations suggest that, when a local input encoding is used, the input has the effect of an additional, input-dependent bias in first-order RNN's, whereas in the second-order case the input acts as a selector for different banks of weights. These second-order weights enable a direct respresentation of the ordered triple of {*state, input, next-state*} that is fundamental in a discrete-time input state equation. They also make it very easy to directly encode any available *a priori* knowledge about state information (Omlin, 1992) into the network. With a first order network, such encoding requires the solution of a linear equation (Frasconi *et al.*, 1991, 1992).

6.2.4 Training a recurrent neural network

In recent years, a great variety of neural-network training algorithms have been developed (for an overview see Hertz *et al.*, 1991; Pao, 1989). Most of these algorithms apply to feed-forward networks, but simple modifications extend them to recurrent networks. The training algorithm discussed here is a feed-forward version of real-time, recurrent learning (RTRL) (Narendra and Parthasarathy, 1990; Williams and Zipser, 1989). We present a brief exposition of recurrent neural network training, followed by a description of our training algorithm.

From a mathematical perspective, a neural net can be thought of as a vector in high dimensional space. In the previous section we reviewed the dimensionality of the recurrent neural networks discussed in this paper. Although the threshold function $f(x)$ is a fixed entity in the neural network, the **parameters** of the function, i.e. the weights and biases, are adjustable. These parameters, taken together, form a vector in this high-dimensional space. The process of training a neural network is actually a search for a minimum of an energy function $E(\mathbf{W})$ defined over the parameter space. (Note that we use unsubscripted $\mathbf{W}$ to refer to both weights and biases.) The 'energy' in the case of language recognition is the average classification error made by the system. Later in this section we present the mathematical form of the energy function and a definition of its gradient in parameter space.

There are many possible definitions of 'error' in language recognition. In applying a neural network, which has real-valued outputs, to a discrete 'yes-or-no' problem, we need to define a performance criterion – namely, exactly what response do we want the neural network to use in signaling 'yes' or 'no'? There are many ways to divide the N-dimensional state-space in which the network operates. We have chosen a simple one: assign a **single neuron** to respond 'yes' with a value of 1, or 'no' with a value of 0. Note that since these are the only two responses we require of the network, in practice we can tolerate some small deviations from the 0/1 response, and so we actually require that 'yes' generate a response of $> 1 - \varepsilon$, and 'no' a response $< \varepsilon$, where $0 < \varepsilon < 0.5$. We call ε the **error tolerance**.

Our goal in error minimization is to reduce the error E on every training example to $E < \varepsilon$. In some applications one might only require that the average error be minimized, but in our case since we use real-time, on-line training, we require a definite correct answer for every input string, i.e. $E < \varepsilon$ for **every** training example.

In our training algorithm, we determine the network's response to each training example, and if the error exceeds the tolerance ε, compute a **weight update**, that is, a correction to the weights and biases that reduces the network's response error. (It is important to compare this to other methods such as batch training (Watrous and Kuhn, 1992a) or training at each time step, as in a prediction problem (Cleeremans *et al.*, 1989).) We designate the output neuron as S_0, and its value at the end of the input string as $S_0^{(f)}$ (f stands for the 'final' time step). Our performance criterion is then $E = |T - S_0^{(f)}| < \varepsilon$, where T is the **target** value for the input string, i.e. 1 for 'yes' and 0 for 'no'.

Since the network's response varies as we change the parameters (weights and biases), the error also varies. This is the justification for viewing error as a function defined over parameter space, $E(\mathbf{W})$. The task of minimizing the error reduces to finding a global minimum of this function in parameter space. We employ a variant of gradient descent to accomplish this task. Although the gradient $\nabla_w E$ may be expressed in closed form (as derived below), in practice we calculate it numerically for each input string based on the above recurrence equations.

Consider first using a Newton's method algorithm for descending the error surface to a minimum. This is accomplished by following the negative gradient in small increments.

$$\Delta \mathbf{W} = - \alpha \nabla_{\mathbf{w}} E. \tag{6}$$

Here, α is a positive constant called the 'learning rate', an experimentally adjustable parameter which defines the step size taken during gradient descent. Small values of α give slow but stable convergence on minima in parameter space; larger values may speed convergence but may also lead to instability or may overshoot small minima basins.

It turns out, however, that $E_{\text{tot}}(\mathbf{W}; \mathbf{X})$, the sum total of all individual error responses over an entire training set $\mathbf{X}$, is not in general well-behaved. This error surface is full of local minima, where the error response is very small for some input strings, but not all. During gradient descent, the trajectory of the weight vector tends to be deflected into these local minima, and if the minimum has a large attraction basin the algorithm may not be able to escape. Large attractor basins which do not contain the global minimum of E_{tot} represent networks that perform well on a majority of strings, but give a very large error for some others – clearly not optimal performance.

The problem of local minima can be overcome somewhat by using 'momentum' (Hertz *et al.*, 1991), which incorporates previous gradients into the current gradient

$$\Delta^{\tau} \mathbf{W} = - \alpha \nabla_{\mathbf{w}} E + \eta \Delta^{\tau - 1} \mathbf{W}. \tag{7}$$

We use τ as a counter of 'number of weight updates computed'. Here, $\Delta^{\tau - 1} \mathbf{W}$ signifies the weight update $\Delta \mathbf{W}$ that was computed the last time an error was made; $\Delta^{\tau} \mathbf{W}$ is the current update. The 'momentum factor', $0 < \eta < 1$, specifies the strength with which the previous update influences the current one. The net effect of the momentum is that the local gradient deflects the trajectory through parameter space, but does not completely dominate it.

The recursive definition of $\Delta^{\tau} \mathbf{W}$ can be expanded in τ to give

$$\Delta^{\tau} \mathbf{W} = - \alpha \sum_{k=0}^{\tau_0} \eta^k \nabla_{\mathbf{w}} E(\mathbf{W}^{\tau - k}), \tag{8}$$

where τ_0 is the number of weight updates made so far during training. This makes it clear that the weight update at any time τ is actually influenced by many local gradients, each evaluated at earlier points $\mathbf{W}^{\tau - k}$ along the trajectory. The result is an average or 'effective' gradient with many fewer attractor basins, making it much easier to find the global minimum basin. The larger the momentum, the greater the averaging effect.

In our training algorithm, we actually minimize the squared error, $E^2 = \frac{1}{2}(T - S_0^{(f)})^2$, over all training examples. This avoids the derivative discontinuity in the absolute value $|T - S_0^{(f)}|$ and also helps to focus on larger errors in the training set. Hence the gradient becomes

$$\nabla_{\mathbf{w}} E^2 = 2E \nabla_{\mathbf{w}} E, \tag{9}$$

$$= - (T - S_0^{(f)}) \nabla_{\mathbf{w}} S_0^{(f)}. \tag{10}$$

Since the target value T does not depend on the weights, $\nabla_{\mathbf{w}} T = 0$.

The gradient $\nabla_w S_0^{(f)}$ is the term we compute from the recurrence equations. The gradient vector has as many components as the weight vector, and each component is a partial derivative with respect to a single weight. Hence we can compute these components explicitly:

$$
\text{first-order}
\begin{cases}
\dfrac{\partial S_i^{(t+1)}}{\partial W_{lm}} = f'(Y_i^{(t)}) \cdot \left(\delta_{il} S_m^{(t)} + \sum_{j}^{N} W_{ij} \dfrac{\partial S_j^{(t)}}{\partial W_{lm}} \right) \\[3mm]
\dfrac{\partial S_i^{(t+1)}}{\partial V_{ln}} = f'(Y_i^{(t)}) \cdot \left(\delta_{il} I_n^{(t)} + \sum_{j}^{N} W_{ij} \dfrac{\partial S_j^{(t)}}{\partial V_{ln}} \right) \\[3mm]
\dfrac{\partial S_i^{(t+1)}}{\partial \Theta_l} = f'(Y_i^{(t)}) \cdot \left(\delta_{il} + \sum_{j}^{N} W_{ij} \dfrac{\partial S_j^{(t)}}{\partial \Theta_l} \right)
\end{cases}
\tag{11}
$$

$$
\text{second-order}
\begin{cases}
\dfrac{\partial S_i^{(t+1)}}{\partial W_{lmn}} = f'(Y_i^{(t)}) \cdot \left(\delta_{il} S_m^{(t)} I_n^{(t)} + \sum_{j,k}^{N,L} W_{ijk} \dfrac{\partial S_j^{(t)}}{\partial W_{lmn}} I_k^{(t)} \right) \\[3mm]
\dfrac{\partial S_i^{(t+1)}}{\partial \Theta_l} = f'(Y_i^{(t)}) \cdot \left(\delta_{il} + \sum_{j,k}^{N,L} W_{ijk} \dfrac{\partial S_j^{(t)}}{\partial \Theta_l} I_k^{(t)} \right)
\end{cases}
\tag{12}
$$

Here f' is the derivative of f, and $Y_i^{(t)}$ represents the argument of f in the original recurrence equations. We will refer to these derivatives collectively with the symbol $\nabla_w S^{(t)}$. Note that $\nabla_w S^{(0)} = 0$, since we assume that the initial state vector $S^{(0)}$ is not dependent on the weights. (To make the initial values weight dependent would assume some *a priori* knowledge about the problem to be solved.) All subsequent terms $\nabla_w S^{(t)}$ can be computed **in parallel** with $S^{(t)}$.

6.2.5 Training algorithm

We present here an outline of the training algorithm used in our experiments. We take the approach that the neural network can learn more effectively if the problem is learned piece by piece rather than wholesale. So far comparisons with other results (Watrous and Kuhn, 1992a) seem to bear this out. Thus, we divide up the learning process into several periods called 'cycles'. During each cycle we train on a small subset of the training set called the 'working set'. Typically, the working set initially contains $X_i < 100$ examples. The goal during a learning cycle is to learn all the examples in the working set with accuracy ε, or in other words so that $\forall x, E(x) < \varepsilon$. The neural net is given a finite number of epochs to learn the working set. The cycle ends when either the working set is learned or the time limit is reached. Then the neural net is tested on the whole training set (weights frozen during testing), and if $E(x) > \varepsilon$ for some examples in this set, a small number of these examples (up to X_r, the recycle-set size) are added to the working set, and a new cycle begins. Cycling continues until the entire training set is learned to within tolerance, or until the upper limit on cycles is reached.

During an epoch, the neural net may not get to train on all strings if it makes too many errors. We define low and high error **thresholds**, E_l and E_h, and count the number of times these thresholds are exceeded. If there are at least five large errors (i.e. $E > E_h$) and 30 small errors ($E > E_l$), the epoch is then terminated and the neural net instructed to begin again at the beginning of the working set. This allows the size of the working set to actually contract temporarily during learning. This often helps the network to avoid forgetting examples it has already learned as the working set grows.

A pseudocode outline of the training algorithm is presented below:

```
select initial working set
select initial weights
repeat up to MAXCYCLES cycles {
/* training phase */
    repeat up to MAXEPOCHS epochs {
        large_err_count = small_err_count = 0;
        for n = 1 to working_set_size {
            present string(n);
            evaluate error E;
            if (E > epsilon) {
                compute gradient and weight update;
                change weights;
                increment small_err_count;
                if (E > El) increment large_err_count;
            }
            if (large_err_count > = 5 and small_err_count > = 30)
                break out of for loop; /* end epoch */
        }
        if (large_err_count = =0 and small_err_count = =0)
            break out of epoch loop; /* end this cycle of training */
    }
/* testing phase */
    test_err_count=0;
    for n=1 to training_set_size {
        present string (n);
        evaluate error;
        if (E>epsilon) increment test_err_count;
    }
    if (test_err_count = =0)
        break out of cycle loop; /* training is finished */
    else
        add error strings to working set (up to Xr)
}
```

6.3 Training recurrent neural networks to infer grammars

6.3.1 Benchmark grammars

To make comparisons of the performance characteristics of different order networks, we have selected a benchmark set of problems. Recently, a set of seven small languages introduced by Tomita (1982) has become a benchmark for recurrent neural network learning (see, for example, Horne *et al.*, 1992; Pollack, 1991; Watrous and Kuhn, 1992a). These seven languages are relatively simple, and are recognized by small discrete finite state automata (DFA). In this study we have used these languages to study several properties of the first- and second-order RNN's described above.

More recently, we have been studying a more complex language represented by a much larger DFA to show how learning and generalization performance scale with the complexity of the problem. The DFA of this problem is a minimal, randomly generated 10-state machine referred to as 'Random-10' in the following discussion. We present some preliminary comparative results for this language as well.

These eight grammars generate regular languages with strings of arbitrary length over the alphabet $\Sigma = \{0, 1\}$, and can be described as follows:

$T_1 = 1^*$.

$T_2 = (10)^*$.

$T_3 =$ an even number of consecutive 1's is always followed by an even number of consecutive 0's.

$T_4 =$ any string not containing '000'.

$T_5 = [(01 | 10)(01 | 10)]^*$

$T_6 = $ Mod-3 $[(N_1 - N_0) \bmod 3 = 0]$.

$T_7 = 0^*1^*0^*1^*$.

Random-10 = randomly generated DFA; see Figure 6.2.

In this notation, (string)* represents a string repeated 0 or more times, (string-A | string-B) represents 'either string-A or string-B' (exclusive-OR), and N_0, N_1 represent the number of 0's and 1's, respectively, contained in a string. (Note that our definition of T_5 is *not* the dual parity (4 state DFA) that is usually used. We gave our own interpretation of this language. For results on this language, see Giles *et al.*, 1990, and Watrous and Kuhn, 1992a). In Figure 6.2 we show diagrams of the discrete finite state automata (DFA) that recognize these eight languages. These are the state automata that the neural networks of our study try to infer from example strings of their languages.

Except for T_6, all the Tomita languages become exponentially sparse with increasing length. That is, the fraction of positive examples of length L is exponentially smaller than the total number of examples of length L. This has the implication that with increasing length, the different states in the DFA have varying importance (and representation) in a sample of strings of that

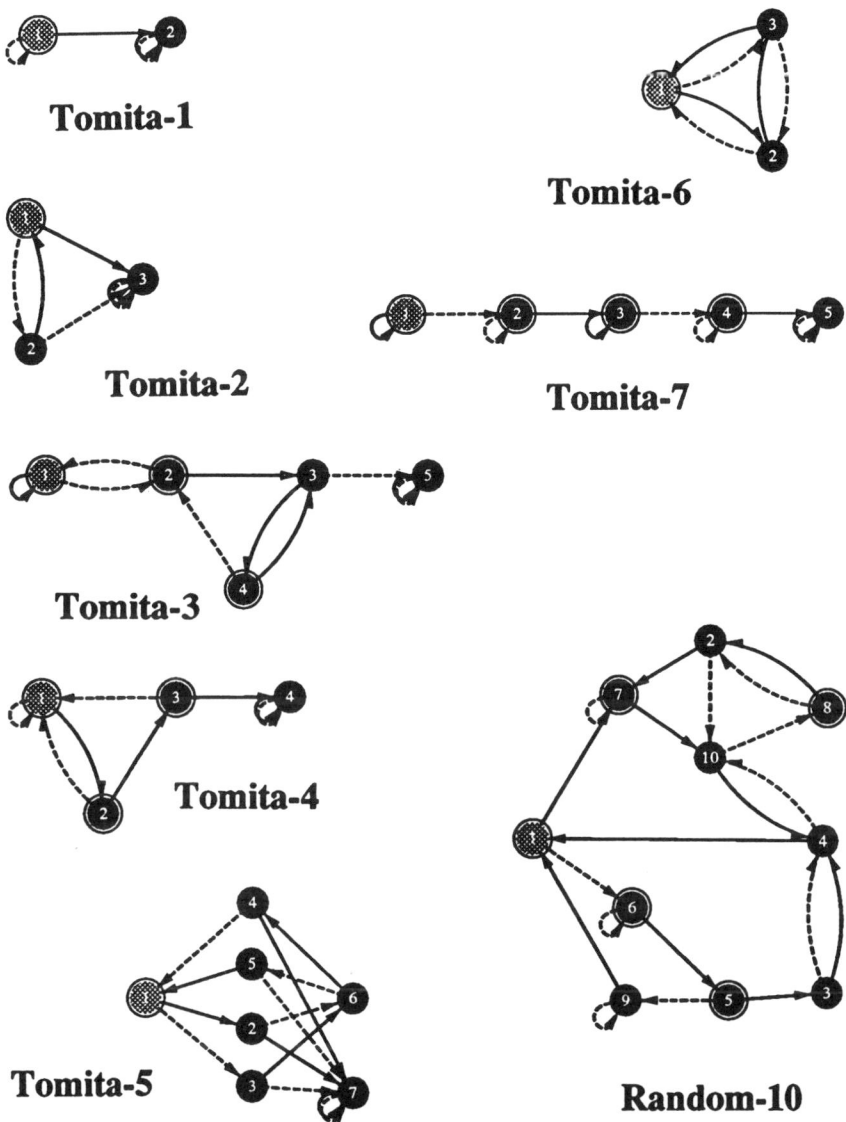

Figure 6.2 *Discrete Finite State Automata (DFA) for the seven Tomita languages and the Random-10 language described in the text. The initial state in each DFA is shaded gray and labelled 1. Final (accepting) states are drawn with an extra circle. Solid arcs indicate transitions for input symbol 0; dashed arcs, symbol 1.*

length. These effects can be balanced by choosing alphabetical training sets which have a uniform distribution over length. It has been shown empirically, via discrete methods (Lang, 1992), that a selection of examples which ranges over lengths $0, \ldots, D + 5$ should be sufficient to infer a generating DFA of depth D. (The **depth** of a DFA is the depth of a graph constructed from it with the initial state at the root.) This hypothesis is also borne out in the case of recurrent neural nets, assuming the network has a sufficient number of weights.

Languages T_1, T_2, and T_6 have depth 1; T_3, T_4, and T_5 have depth 3; T_7 and Random-10 have depth 4. Hence we use strings up to length $D + 5 = 9$ in our training sets, as discussed below.

6.3.2 Extracting DFA's from neural networks

We briefly discuss a method for extracting a DFA from a recurrent neural network after (or during) training. Essentially, the algorithm works by heuristically clustering the network's distribution in N-dimensional state space and then discretizing the space using staircase functions $S_i' = S_i - S_i$ $\mod (1/q)$, where $q \geqslant 2$ is an integer **quantization parameter**. For other methods of creating state transition diagrams (see Cleeremans *et al.*, 1989, and Watrous and Kuhn, 1992b. Also, Watrous and Kuhn (1992b) give another method for DFA extraction.) The resulting state automaton is an approximate discretized form of the neural network's dynamics and classification behavior. If the extracted DFA is equivalent to the original DFA (i.e. the one which generated the neural net's training set), the neural network has successfully inferred the grammar. We have shown previously (Omlin and Giles, 1992) that these extracted DFA's often outperform the neural network in generalization power, even when the extracted DFA is not exactly correct. For more details of the extraction process, see Giles *et al.* (1992).

6.4 Results

6.4.1 Description of experiments

We present results that compare the training and generalization performance of first- and second-order recurrent neural networks on the eight benchmark grammars described above. Training simulations were performed for first- and second-order RNN's with 3–9 neurons. For each of these 14 configurations we ran 10 training simulations with data sets generated from each of these eight grammars. Each initial weight value was chosen randomly and uniformly over the interval $[-1.0, 1.0]$. Each network was then trained on all strings of length 0–9 in the target language (1 023 total), presented in alphabetical order. (Recently work by Porat and Feldman (1991) showed enhanced learning capacity using alphabetical order in string presentation.) Training parameters were $\alpha = 0.5$, $\eta = 0.5$, $E_l = 0.2$, $E_h = 0.5$, $X_i = 50$, $X_r = 50$ (see section 6.2.5 for definitions). Training proceeded for a maximum of 10 cycles of 500 epochs each.

Each network either converged on a solution in $\leqslant 5000$ epochs or was terminated. The successfully converged networks were tested for generalization on all strings of length 10–15 (64 512 total). Additionally, we tested these networks on their DFA extraction performance. Results are presented below.

6.4.2 Convergence results

We show the number of successful convergences (out of 10 runs) for each network configuration, and for those successful runs, the average convergence time measured in epochs, in Table 6.1. The latter are also plotted graphically in Figure 6.3. For comparison, we ran two sets of runs on the Tomita languages: one which used bias terms and one which did not (all bias terms set to zero and frozen).

The general trend for both first and second order RNN's is faster convergence for larger numbers of neurons, and comparable relative convergence times for the two different orders. More complex grammars tend to require more time for convergence, though second order converges faster in most cases, especially with larger numbers of neurons. Also, the tabular data shows that first-order nets are less reliable, in terms of likelihood of convergence, particularly with small numbers of neurons, while second-order nets show no degradation of training success except at the very smallest network size, $N = 3$. This behavior is much more pronounced in the case of the Random-10 language, where first-order RNN's consistently fail to converge in the required time, while second-order RNN's start to show consistent success for larger values of N.

Successful convergence occurred less often for networks that used bias (shown in the lower half of Table 6.1). Convergence times in successful cases were somewhat longer than for networks that did not use bias. Because biased networks converge less often than non-bias networks, we will not consider bias networks in further analysis.

Figure 6.3b shows the same convergence-time data, but plotted as a function of number of weights rather than neurons. This demonstrates a more pronounced effect: the convergence time drops quickly from a high value as the number of weights are increased, but appears to approach an asymptotic limit of efficiency. It should be remembered when viewing this plot that the **CPU time** required for these simulations is proportional to N^4L^2 in the second-order case (recall that N is the number of state neurons and L the number of input neurons) and to N^4 in the first-order case (assuming large N), so although the 'convergence time' (measured in epochs) drops to a constant as the networks grow, the CPU time required to compute the solutions grows (asymptotically) as N^4L^2 or N^4. If one were to plot the 'real time' required for successful convergence, equal to the epochal time multiplied by cN^4L^2 or

Table 6.1 Convergence results for the seven Tomita languages and the Random-10 language. Data are for first- and second-order RNN's with 3 to 9 neurons: (top) without bias; (bottom) with bias [Random-10 was not run with bias]. Ten runs were generated for each architecture, size, and language. The left subcolumn for each value N shows the number of runs (out of 10) which converged within 5000 epochs. The right subcolumn shows the average number of epochs for those runs which did converge

lang	arch	n = 3		n = 4		n = 5		n = 6		n = 7		n = 8		n = 9	
T-1	F.	10	40.4	10	40.0	10	32.5	10	27.7	10	28.8	10	26.4	10	23.1
	S.	10	46.3	10	37.2	10	37.7	10	42.1	10	33.3	10	34.3	10	29.9
T-2	F.	10	203.7	10	175.2	10	162.8	10	147.2	10	134.2	10	126.8	10	113.2
	S.	10	183.3	10	113.6	10	108.0	10	101.0	10	80.7	10	85.4	10	77.7
T-3	F.	3	244.3	9	197.2	10	406.4	10	328.0	10	193.5	10	459.2	10	425.6
	S.	10	294.7	10	94.7	10	64.3	10	62.8	10	54.5	10	53.8	10	51.7
T-4	F.	9	211.1	9	103.4	10	95.5	10	93.7	10	97.0	10	83.3	10	100.6
	S.	10	133.7	10	81.5	10	70.8	10	55.1	10	54.4	10	49.0	10	46.2
T-5	F.	1	591.0	4	490.7	10	470.5	10	376.4	10	327.9	10	277.1	10	258.7
	S.	2	1728.0	10	491.9	10	289.8	10	265.2	10	213.4	10	190.5	10	158.6
T-6	F.	4	1311.5	7	445.6	7	364.4	8	344.1	7	369.6	6	346.0	10	506.2
	S.	10	95.3	10	70.3	10	64.4	10	57.8	10	54.1	10	50.1	10	49.6
T-7	F.	3	792.3	4	427.7	6	438.8	9	454.7	7	283.6	8	306.2	10	342.6
	S.	8	570.6	10	306.5	10	214.9	10	163.9	10	160.2	10	147.5	10	121.0
R-10	F.	0	—	0	—	0	—	0	—	0	—	0	—	0	—
	S.	0	—	0	—	1	377.0	3	458.3	8	556.6	9	731.8	10	202.9

		n		n		n		n		n		n		n	
T-1	F.B.	10	37.0	10	34.1	10	29.0	10	27.5	10	26.2	10	25.8	10	25.3
	S.B.	10	38.9	10	42.7	10	33.7	10	35.1	10	31.9	10	34.1	10	32.2
T-2	F.B.	10	188.1	10	167.5	10	152.6	10	143.6	10	120.9	10	119.5	10	93.6
	S.B.	10	146.7	10	150.9	10	113.7	10	113.0	10	97.0	10	81.5	10	88.2
T-3	F.B.	5	119.8	9	344.7	9	957.3	8	458.6	10	498.2	10	493.1	9	365.1
	S.B.	8	119.1	10	145.2	10	79.4	10	67.2	9	62.0	10	57.1	10	51.8
T-4	F.B.	7	180.7	10	153.0	9	105.9	9	135.8	9	91.1	10	85.2	10	91.2
	S.B.	10	211.2	10	94.2	10	100.3	10	80.5	10	71.9	10	60.4	10	58.6
T-5	F.B.	1	886.0	2	460.5	7	391.0	8	482.5	9	295.6	9	251.4	10	288.7
	S.B.	6	588.2	9	364.9	10	290.8	10	271.6	10	191.1	10	211.0	10	177.7
T-6	F.B.	0	—	5	235.0	9	275.4	9	210.8	9	362.2	7	161.1	9	211.4
	S.B	10	306.4	10	75.7	10	77.7	10	61.2	10	56.0	10	53.2	10	57.2
T-7	F.B.	0	—	5	389.8	7	890.6	3	343.3	5	338.4	7	237.0	9	493.4
	S.B.	5	880.8	10	574.7	10	265.4	9	193.2	10	176.5	10	150.2	10	197.8

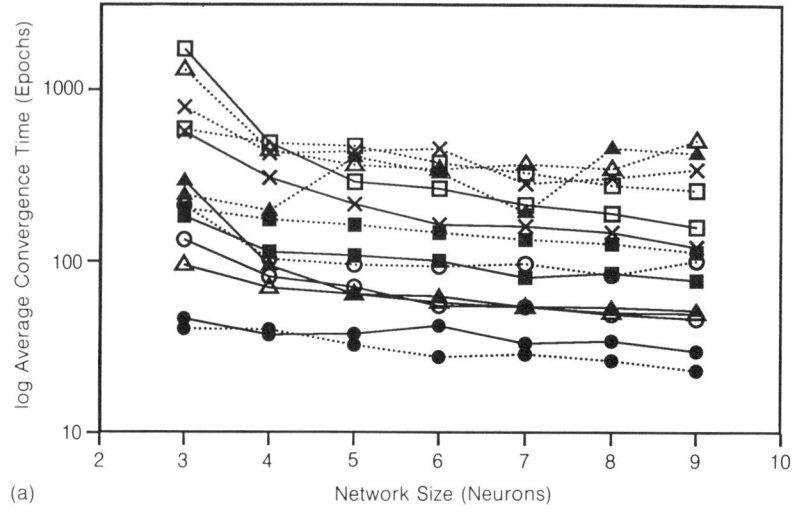

(a)

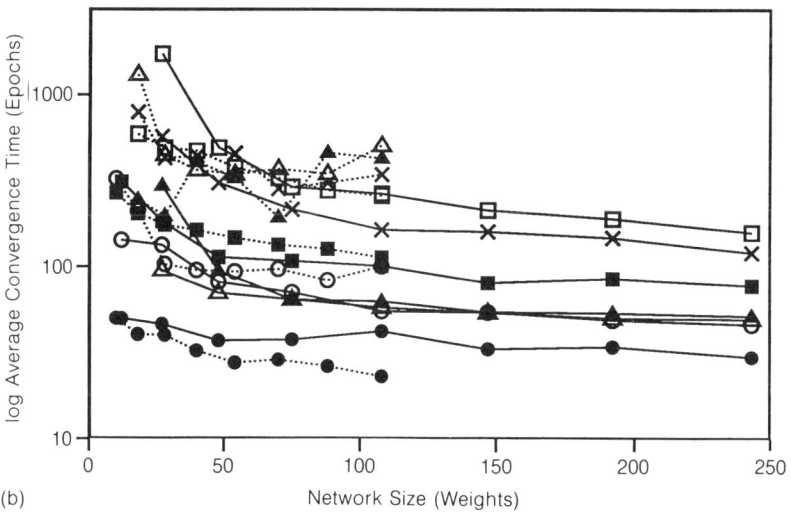

(b)

Figure 6.3 *Average convergence times (in epochs) of first- and second-order RNNs for each of Tomita's seven languages. (a) dependence on number of neurons; (b) dependence on number of weights. ——: First-order; ---: Second-order; ●: Tomita-1; ■: Tomita-2; ▲: Tomita-3; ○: Tomita-4; □: Tomita-5; △: Tomita-6; X: Tomita-7.*

cN^4 (c = the average CPU time required for one epoch), there would be a minimum in the curve located near $N \approx 5$ (for these systems at least). This is an experimentally determined 'optimal' network size.

6.4.3 Generalization results

Generalization results are shown in Table 6.2 for all converged runs. Generalization was tested for strings of length 10–15 (64 512 strings) at tolerances $\varepsilon = 0.2$ (all languages) and $\varepsilon = 0.5$ (Tomita's languages only); the

Table 6.2 *Generalization test results for first- and second-order RNN's. Tests were run only on nets that converged. The tables show the average number of errors made over the test set of all strings of length 10–15 (64 512 total) in the learned language. (Top) results for tolerance* $\varepsilon = 0.2$; *(bottom) for* $\varepsilon = 0.5$. *(Preliminary results only* ($\varepsilon = 0.2$) *for the Random-10 language.)*

lang	arch	$n = 3$	$n = 4$	$n = 5$	$n = 6$	$n = 7$	$n = 8$	$n = 9$
T_1	F.	1	3	1	2	2	3	1
T_1	S.	3	2	3	3	2	3	1
T_2	F.	6	2	2	3	4	2	2
T_2	S.	2	6	2	9	5	3	5
T_3	F.	66	85	85	181	285	251	219
T_3	S.	682	908	933	2101	1202	2191	1736
T_4	F.	38	39	117	87	87	88	496
T_4	S.	340	147	134	592	369	791	1240
T_5	F.	1048	191	207	443	263	257	345
T_5	S.	984	655	1060	815	917	635	696
T_6	F.	39	239	510	511	830	720	896
T_6	S.	8130	7602	16254	13045	8248	12192	8725
T_7	F.	170	196	285	366	711	126	717
T_7	S.	419	694	1121	1307	1292	388	889
R_{10}	F.	—	—	—	—	—	—	—
R_{10}	S.	—	—	22	18	23	26	18
T_1	F.	0	0	0	0	0	0	0
T_1	S.	0	0	0	0	0	0	0
T_2	F.	0	0	0	0	0	0	0
T_2	S.	0	0	0	0	0	0	0
T_3	F.	23	0	1	9	97	36	40
T_3	S.	27	0	0	2	0	3	22
T_4	F.	13	8	29	2	18	26	90
T_4	S.	5	0	0	19	32	94	41
T_5	F.	105	58	30	149	56	34	12
T_5	S.	429	146	261	145	150	99	125
T_6	F.	5	12	0	9	58	3	288
T_6	S.	0	0	74	10	0	30	0
T_7	F.	27	12	63	75	169	37	317
T_7	S.	95	132	245	110	274	22	58

data shown gives the average **number** of strings in the test set that gave errors $E > \varepsilon$. The minimal measure of performance of the RNN is $\varepsilon = 0.5$; as long as the network holds its classification error below this level, we consider the RNN to perform correctly. However, a typical RNN will accumulate small inaccuracies in output classification, which we call **drift**, as it processes a string, and for sufficiently long strings, this accumulating inaccuracy can eventually lead to errors $E > 0.5$, which of course is a misclassification. One way to measure the extent to which a network is drifting is to look at the number of classification errors for $E > 0.2$. A network which has very few errors at this

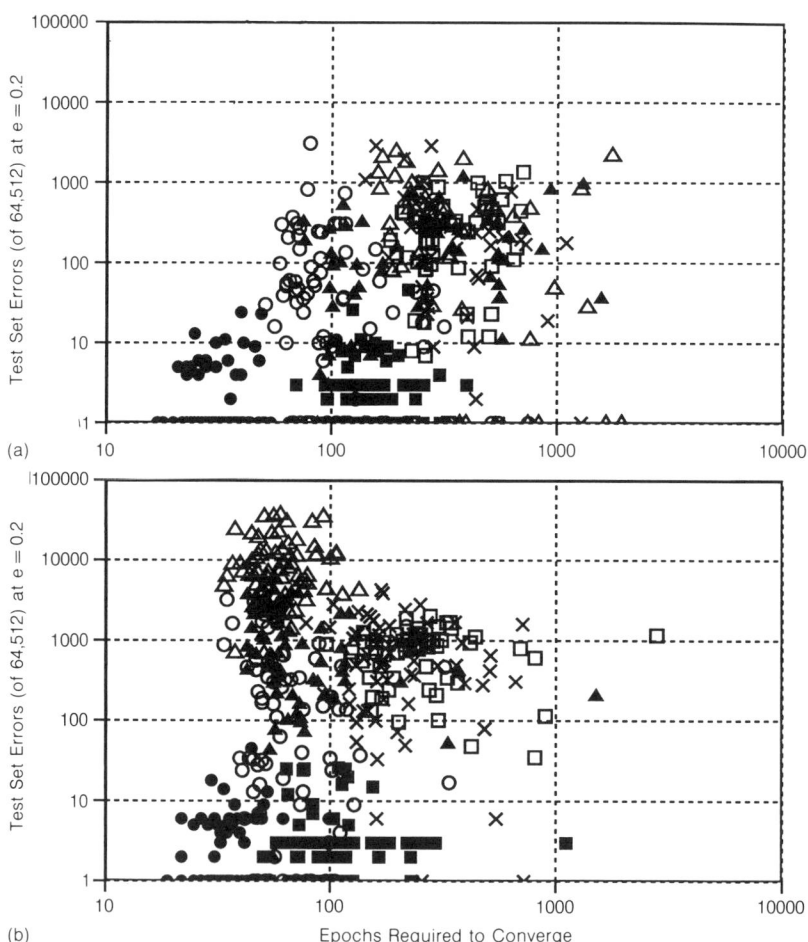

Figure 6.4 *Convergence times (in epochs) for each successful training run, correlated with the number of errors made during generalization tests for $E > 0.2$. (a) First-order, (b) second-order (see text (section 6.4.3) for further explanation).* ●: *Tomita-1;* ■: *Tomita-2;* ▲: *Tomita-3;* ○: *Tomita-4;* □: *Tomita-5;* △: *Tomita-6;* X: *Tomita-7.*

level will most likely perform extremely well for very long strings because its drift is very slight, whereas a network with more errors at $E > 0.2$ will have quicker performance degradation at longer lengths.

For $\varepsilon = 0.5$, both first- and second-order nets perform well. In all cases, the average number of errors is less than 1% of the test set. Both types of nets tested perfectly on languages T_1 and T_2; the worst performance was on T_5 and T_7. There is no consistent difference between first- and second-order RNN's at this level.

However, generalization at $\varepsilon = 0.2$ gives a different story. Except for T_1 and T_2, which show near perfect test results, both architectures show considerable drift, as indicated by the large error rates (as much as 25%) shown in the tables. Two trends are immediately apparent in this data: (1) Second-order nets have considerably more drift than first-order nets. (2) Drift generally increases with larger numbers of neurons.

These trends both seem to indicate that a larger number of weights contributes to increased drift. This effect might be counteracted by (1) training to a smaller tolerance $\varepsilon < 0.2$; (2) altering the discriminant function so it has steeper slope $[f(x) \to f(\beta x), \ \beta > 1.0]$; (3) selectively reducing the number of weights in the network (i.e. partial connectivity).

Figure 6.4 shows how convergence time and generalization performance are related. One point is plotted on this diagram for every successful training run, showing the number of epochs required to converge on one axis and the number of errors incurred on the generalization test for $\varepsilon = 0.2$ on the other axis. From this figure we can conclude that quick convergence does not imply good generalization; in fact, convergence and generalization appear not to be correlated. Additionally, most runs converge within 1000 epochs; runs that converge in time > 1000 epochs do not have any notable performance advantage over more quickly convergent runs. Thus, for these training conditions and for languages of similar complexity, it makes sense to limit training time to 1000 epochs. If training appears to require longer time, then other parameters such as learning rate and momentum should probably be adjusted.

6.4.4 Inference (DFA extraction) results

Finally, we tested all successfully converged networks for successful inference by using the DFA extraction algorithm described above (section 6.3.2). In Table 6.3 we show for each network configuration the average number of times a correct DFA was extracted from the corresponding neural network. The data are generated by running the extraction algorithm for quantization values $q = 2, \ldots, 10$ on each converged neural network, comparing the extracted DFA after Moore-minimization to the target DFA, and counting the number of matches. We compute the average number of matches for all 10 runs of each network configuration. In addition, we show the average size of the

Table 6.3 DFA extraction analysis. This table presents data for the heuristic DFA extraction procedure (described in the text) as applied to all successfully converged first- and second-order runs in this study. Each column gives data for different numbers N of neurons. The left subcolumn in each column gives the average number of successful extractions. The right subcolumn gives the average smallest unminimized size of correct extracted DFA's

lang	arch	n = 3		n = 4		n = 5		n = 6		n = 7		n = 8		n = 9	
		extr	size	extr	size	extr	size	extr	size	extr	size	extr	size	extr	size
T_1	F.	9.0	3.9	9.0	4.8	9.0	5.6	9.0	6.3	9.0	7.7	9.0	7.1	9.0	9.2
T_1	S.	9.0	3.1	9.0	3.6	9.0	5.0	9.0	5.4	9.0	7.1	9.0	7.2	9.0	8.6
T_2	F.	9.0	5.9	8.4	9.7	8.7	9.3	8.9	9.5	8.7	12.0	8.7	14.7	8.9	13.3
T_2	S.	9.0	3.5	9.0	4.3	8.9	6.0	9.0	6.6	9.0	7.8	9.0	10.1	9.0	9.9
T_3	F.	2.4	8.5	7.3	10.3	7.8	12.2	7.7	11.2	7.0	15.6	6.0	16.2	6.7	19.4
T_3	S.	7.0	9.2	8.5	7.4	8.8	8.4	6.9	9.0	7.5	10.2	4.9	11.8	4.9	12.5
T_4	F.	6.8	6.9	7.6	7.0	8.7	8.0	8.5	8.4	8.3	12.7	7.2	12.1	6.1	15.2
T_4	S.	8.5	6.3	8.7	7.9	8.7	7.5	8.6	7.8	8.2	9.3	7.8	12.7	7.3	12.3
T_5	F.	0.7	10.0	2.0	16.5	5.6	16.4	4.2	25.9	4.4	25.2	3.0	28.7	3.8	41.6
T_5	S.	0.5	15.0	2.9	13.2	2.1	14.9	1.7	23.5	2.0	16.6	1.4	30.4	1.5	24.3
T_6	F.	3.6	5.8	5.6	9.3	6.1	8.8	6.4	11.3	5.0	15.4	4.5	13.4	5.7	15.0
T_6	S.	9.0	3.1	8.8	3.2	8.4	4.5	7.8	5.4	8.4	6.6	5.8	8.9	6.3	10.5
T_7	F.	2.7	6.0	3.4	8.8	4.9	9.0	7.6	11.2	5.4	13.4	6.7	13.0	6.4	15.1
T_7	S.	6.3	7.4	8.2	7.3	7.8	7.6	8.1	8.5	7.3	9.0	8.3	10.7	8.1	10.7

smallest **unminimized** extracted DFA which minimizes to the correct target DFA.

The general trend is that the second-order architecture can extract the correct DFA with greater reliability. One notable exception to this trend is in language T_5, where first-order has the advantage, though both architectures perform relatively poorly in extracting the DFA for this language (most likely because T_5 is the largest DFA of the entire set of Tomita's grammars). On the whole, even though second-order architecture shows more drift inaccuracy, it is not enough to prevent it from inferring a correct grammar.

The data shown for the average unminimized extracted DFA size show a strong trend: the size of the state machine is always larger when extracted from a first-order net. This appears to corroborate findings of Goudreau *et al.* (1992) that indicate that first-order networks must use state-splitting to learn small regular languages. If, indeed, the first-order networks in the experiments reviewed here are using state-splitting, the extraction procedure will reveal this by producing a larger unminimized state machine. In fact, since state-splitting requires a larger fractional volume of state space to implement (assuming the same number of neurons and the same language to infer), this may well account for the higher failure rate for first-order nets in extracting correct DFA's.

6.5 Conclusions

We have shown that both first- and second-order recurrent neural networks can easily learn the grammars of Tomita using real-time recurrent learning using a full-gradient training algorithm. We also show that networks of both architectures generalize well in recognizing longer input sequences than initially trained on, and can also extract the correct DFA's that generate the languages. Our results demonstrate that these properties hold fairly consistently for numbers of neurons in the range $N = 3, \ldots, 10$.

Both architectures have comparable learning power and generalization performance for simple regular grammars, e.g. those in Tomita's benchmark. Second-order recurrent nets tend to be quicker and more reliable in converging to a good solution, particularly as the target language becomes more complex, as demonstrated by the convergence results for the Random-10 language. However, second-order RNN's tend to accumulate more inaccuracies in classification when processing long strings. Thus, we speculate, second-order recurrent nets will show poorer performance for longer input sequences. Our results demonstrate that this is indeed the case for input sequences of up to length 15. This problem with inaccuracy seems strongly correlated with larger numbers of weights. We propose a few methods to counteract this problem: (1) training to smaller tolerance; (2) using steeper threshold functions, and (3) selectively reducing the number of weights in the network.

Interestingly though, second-order nets appear more reliable for **inferring** the actual grammars, since they succeed more often in **extracting** correct DFA's. We hypothesize that the greater inference success of second-order nets is explained by the fact that first-order nets may need to use state-splitting (Goudreau *et al.*, 1992) to implement state machines, which limits the flexibility and efficiency of the internal representations that first-order nets can use.

It is generally held that for every problem that neural networks could be applied to, there is an 'optimal' size network best suited to that problem. Our results support this belief. We show that generalization on long strings is somewhat better for smaller networks of both architectures, but also that this trend is balanced by another factor – recurrent networks learn in fewer epochs the larger they are, and will altogether fail to converge on a solution if they are too small.

Finally, our initial experimental results with the more complex 'Random-10' language indicate that second-order RNN's have **significantly better scaling behavior** than first-order RNN's in terms of their ability to infer more complicated grammars (those with larger number of states). For our convergence conditions *none* of the seventy first-order training runs converged whereas over half of the second-order did. Generalization results for these 'unconverged' first-order runs indicated that these nets had learned essentially nothing and were giving random responses. Thus, on the basis of the results presented here, second-order nets appear to have significant computational advantages over simpler first-order architectures.

Acknowledgements

We would like to acknowledge the computational assistance of L.C. An, and useful discussions with D. Chen, M.W. Goudreau, K. Lang and C. Omlin.

References

Angluin, D. and Smith, C. (1983) Inductive inference: Theory and methods. *ACM Computing Surveys*, **15**(3), 237.

Ashar, P., Devadas, S. and Newton, A. (1992) *Sequential Logic Synthesis*. Kluwer, Norwell, MA.

Baldi, P. and Venkatesh, S. (1987) Number of stable points for spin-glasses and neural networks of higher orders. *Physical Review Letters*, **58**(9), 913–15.

Cleeremans, A., Servan-Schreiber, D. and McClelland, J. (1989) Finite state automata and simple recurrent networks. *Neural Computation*, **1**(3), 372.

Cover, T. (1965) Geometrical and statistical properties of systems of linear inequalities with applications in pattern recognition. *IEEE Trans. on Electronic Computers*, **14**, 815.

Das, S., Giles, C. and Sun, G. (1992) Learning context-free grammars: Limitations of a recurrent neural network with an external stack memory. *Proceedings Fourteenth Annual Conference of the Cognitive Science Society*, Morgan Kaufmann, San Mateo, CA.

Elman, J. (1990) Finding structure in time. *Cognitive Science*, **14**, 179–211.

Fogelman-Soulie, F., Robert, Y. and Tchuente, M. (eds) (1987) *Automata Networks in Computer Science, Theory and Applications*. Princeton University Press, Princeton, NJ.

Frasconi, P., Gori, M., Maggini, M. and Soda, G. (1991) A unified approach for integrating explicit knowledge and learning by example in recurrent networks. *Proceedings of the International Joint Conference on Neural Networks*, **1**, 811.

Frasconi, P., Gori, M., Maggini, M. and Soda, G. (1992) Unified integration of explicit rules and learning by example in recurrent networks. *IEEE Transactions on Knowledge and Data Engineering*. To appear.

Fu, K. (1982) *Syntactic Pattern Recognition and Applications*. Prentice-Hall, Englewood Cliffs, NJ.

Giles, C. and Maxwell, T. (1987) Learning, invariance, and generalization in high-order neural networks. *Applied Optics*, **26**(23), 4972.

Giles, C., Miller, C., Chen, D., Chen, H., Sun, G. and Lee, Y. (1992) Learning and extracting finite state automata with second-order recurrent neural networks. *Neural Computation*, **4**(3), 380.

Giles, C., Sun, G., Chen, H., Lee, Y. and Chen, D. (1990) Higher order recurrent networks & grammatical inference, in *Advances in Neural Information Processing Systems 2* (ed. D. Touretzky), Morgan Kaufmann, San Mateo, CA, pp. 380–7.

Goles, E. and Martinez, S. (1990) *Neural and Automata Networks*. Kluwer, Boston, MA.

Goudreau, M., Giles, C., Chakradhar, S. and Chen, D. (1992) First-order vs. second-order single layer recurrent neural networks. September. Submitted.

Guyon, I., Personnaz, L., Nadal, J. and Dreyfus, G. (1988) Storage and retrieval of complex sequences in neural networks. *Physical Review A*, **38**(12), 6365.

Guyon, L., Vapnik, V., Boser, B., Bottou, L., and Solla, S. (1992) Structural risk minimization for character recognition, in *Advances in Neural Information Processing Systems 4* (eds J. Moody, S. Hanson, and R. Lippmann), Morgan Kaufmann, San Mateo, CA, pp. 471–9.

Hertz, J., Krogh, A. and Palmer, R. (1991) *Introduction to the Theory of Neural Computation*. Addison-Wesley, Redwood City, CA.

Hopcroft, J. and Ullman, J. (1979) *Introduction to Automata Theory, Languages, and Computation*. Addison-Wesley, Reading, MA.

Hopfield, J. (1982) Neural networks and physical systems with emergent collective computational abilities. *Proceedings of the National Academy of Sciences – USA*, **79**, 2554.

Horne, B., Hush, D. and Abdallah, C. (1992) The state space recurrent neural network with application to regular grammatical inference. *Technical Report UNM Technical Report No. EECE 92-002*, Department of Electrical and Computer Engineering, University of New Mexico.

Jordan, M. (1986) Attractor dynamics and parallelism in a connectionist sequential machine. *Proceedings of the Ninth Annual Conference of the Cognitive Science Society*, Lawrence Erlbaum, NJ, pp. 531–46.

Kleene, S. (1956) Representation of events in nerve nets and finite automata, in *Automata Studies* (eds C. Shannon and J. McCarthy), Princeton University Press, Princeton, NJ, pp. 3–42.

Koch, C. and Poggio, T. (1992) Multiplying with synapses and neurons, in *Single Neuron Computation* (eds S.Z. T. McKenna, J. Davis), Academic Press, Boston, MA.

Kohavi, Z. (1978) *Switching and Finite Automata Theory*. McGraw-Hill, New York, NY.

Lang, K. (1992) Random dfa's can be approximately learned from sparse uniform examples. *Proceedings of the Fifth ACM Workshop on Computational Learning Theory*, Pittsburgh, PA, July.

Lee, Y., Doolen, G., Chen, H. *et al.* (1986) Machine learning using a higher order correlational network. *Physica D*, **22-D**(1-3), 276.

Lucas, S. and Damper, R. (1990) Syntactic neural networks. *Connection Science*, **2**, 199–225.

McCulloch, W.P.W.S. and Pitts, W. (1943) A logical calculus of ideas immanent in nervous activity. *Bulletin of Mathematical Biophysics*, **5**, 115–33.

Miclet, L. (1990) Grammatical inference, in *Syntactic and Structural Pattern Recognition; Theory and Applications* (eds H. Bunke and A. Sanfeliu), World Scientific, Singapore.

Minsky, M. (1967) *Computation: Finite and Infinite Machines*. Prentice-Hall, Englewood Cliffs, NJ. pp. 32–66.

Minsky, M. and Papert, S. (1969) *Perceptrons*. MIT Press, Cambridge, MA.

Mozer, M. and Bachrach, J. (1990) Discovering the structure of a reactive environment by exploration. *Neural Computation*, **2**(4) 447.

Narendra, K. and Parthasarathy, K. (1990) Identification and control of dynamical systems using neural networks. *IEEE Trans. on Neural Networks*, **1**(1), 4.

Omlin, C.G.C. (1992) Inserting rules into recurrent neural networks. *Proceedings IEEE Workshop on Neural Networks for Signal Processing*, Copenhagen, Denmark.

Omlin, C.M.C.W. and Giles, C.L. (1992) Extraction of rules from discrete-time recurrent neural networks. To be published.

Pao, Y. (1989) *Adaptive Pattern Recognition and Neural Networks*. Addison-Wesley, Reading, MA.

Perantonis, S. and Lisboa, P. (1992) Translation, rotation, and scale invariant pattern recognition by higher-order neural networks and moment classifiers. *IEEE Transactions on Neural Networks*, **3**(2), 241.

Peretto, P. and Niez, J. (1986) Long-term memory storage capacity of multiconnected neural networks. *Biological Cybernetics*, **54**, 53.

Personnaz, L., Guyon, I. and Dreyfus, G. (1987) High-order neural networks: Information storage without errors. *Europhysics Letters*, **4**, 863.

Pollack, J. (1990) Recursive distributed representations. *Journal of Artificial Intelligence*, **46**, 77.

Pollack, J. (1991) The induction of dynamical recognizers. *Machine Learning*, **7**, 227.

Porat, S. and Feldman, J. (1991) Learning automata from ordered examples. *Machine Learning*, **7**(2-3), 109.

Psaltis, D., Park, C. and Hong, J. (1988) Higher order associative memories and their optical implementations. *Neural Networks*, **1**, 149.

Rumelhart, D., Hinton, G. and Williams, R. (1986) Learning internal representations by error propagation, in *Parallel Distributed Processing*, MIT Press, Cambridge, MA.

Siegelmann, H. and Sontag, E. (1991) Turing compatibility with neural nets. *Applied Mathematics Letters*, **4**(6), 77–80.

Sun, G., Chen, H., Giles, C. *et al.* (1990) Connectionist pushdown automata that learn context-free grammars. *Proceedings of the International Joint Conference on Neural Networks*, **I**, 577–80.

Tomita, M. (1982) Dynamic construction of finite-state automata from examples using hill-climbing. *Proceedings of the Fourth Annual Cognitive Science Conference*, Ann Arbor, MI, 105.

Watrous, R. and Kuhn, G. (1992a) Induction of finite-state languages using second-order recurrent networks. *Neural Computation*, **4**(3), 406.

Watrous, R. and Kuhn, G. (1992b) Induction of finite state languages using second-order recurrent networks, in *Advances in Neural Information Processing Systems 4* (eds J. Moody, S. Hanson, and R. Lippmann), Morgan Kaufmann, San Mateo, CA, pp. 309–16.

Williams, R. and Zipser, D. (1989) A learning algorithm for continually running fully recurrent neural networks. *Neural Computation*, **1**, 270–80.

7

Receptive field partitioning for wavelet networks

TOUFIC I. BOUBEZ
Department of Biomedical Engineering, and CAIP Parallel Computing Laboratory, Rutgers University, Piscataway, NJ 08855-1390, USA

7.1 Introduction

Feed-forward multi-layer neural networks (FFNN) have recently emerged as a popular tool both for classification purposes and for approximating continuous functions (Huang and Lippmann, 1987; Rumelhart *et al.*, 1986a; Sontag, 1989; Lippmann, 1987, 1989a, 1989b). Although the problem of learning a mapping from a given set of examples is a recurring theme in several disciplines such as function approximation, pattern recognition, nonparametric regression and statistical learning, the neural networks model has fared well for certain classes of problems when compared to more traditional approaches (Hanson and Burr, 1991; Lippmann, 1989b; Ripley, 1993). In the general FFNN model, a set of computing elements called **neurons** are connected to form a network in which every neuron processes the inputs it receives and produces an output which is forwarded to one or more neurons. Each neuron is a nonlinear input-output unit with a sigmoidal transfer function, which was historically developed as a simplification of biological neuron behaviour. A sigmoidal transfer function, being differentiable, lends itself to gradient descent optimization methods. In recent papers, learning in neural networks is associated with long standing methods of classical function approximation, and the use of more general basis functions is proposed as an alternative to the sigmoid (Poggio and Girosi, 1990; Lippmann, 1989a).

While the idea of substituting basis functions for the neuron transfer function is appealing, the problem of choosing which class of functions to use becomes apparent. Several different classes of functions have been proposed, with radial basis functions (RBF) (Poggio and Girosi, 1990; Robinson *et al.*,

Artificial Neural Networks for Speech and Vision. Edited by Richard J. Mammone. Published in 1993 by Chapman & Hall, London. ISBN 0 412 54850 X

1988; Kanerva, 1984) splines (Friedman, 1991; Lane *et al.*, 1991; Rogers, 1991) and polynomials (Sanger 1990; Sanger *et al.*, 1991) being the most popular. In this chapter, a solution to this problem is inspired by biological classifiers and pattern matchers such as the visual and auditory systems. In biological systems, the building block at the lower levels is the receptor neuron, which reacts to stimuli within a relatively small neighborhood of its input space, called its **receptive field**. In many systems, these receptors are connected in a hierarchical structure to form increasingly complex receptive fields. Recent work with wavelets, a family of functions which exhibit similar properties of local support and hierarchical structure, has shown their power in modeling functions, especially those with sharp transitions and localized behavior (Strang, 1989; Daubechies, 1988; Beylkin *et al.*, 1989). We therefore propose to combine these ideas into the formation of wavelet neural networks (WNN) where the neurons in the network have wavelet-like response functions, and the connection weights are the corresponding wavelet coefficients.

In this chapter we first describe feed-forward neural networks and basis function networks as a framework for classification and function approximation. We then introduce biological sensory receptors and the idea of localized receptive fields. Wavelet-based multiresolution analysis is then presented, and used to develop the wavelet neural network model and introduce a hybrid constructive-destructive network creation algorithm. Finally, we present a preliminary implementation of the model and compare its results with some well-known neural network models.

7.2 Feed-forward neural networks

7.2.1 The general model

In the general feed-forward model, a network consists of a set of processing elements, or neurons, organized in successive layers, with the outputs of neurons in each layer fully connected by synapses of variable weights to the inputs of neurons in the next layer (Figure 7.1). Each neuron thus receives one or several inputs, and produces one output, which is forwarded to all the neurons in the next layer. This output is usually a function of the internal state of the neuron and is called the **neuron transfer function** or **activation function**. The internal state is itself a function of the inputs converging on the neuron, their respective connection weights, and a biasing input that is usually added to these. If y_i is the output of neuron i, s_i its internal state, and w_{ij} the connection weight from neuron j to neuron i, we can write

$$s_i = \sum_j w_{ij} y_j + b_i \quad j = \text{all neurons contributing to } i \qquad (1)$$

$$y_i = h(s_i) \qquad (2)$$

The neuron activation function $h(s_i)$ is usually a sigmoid (Figure 7.2) and can

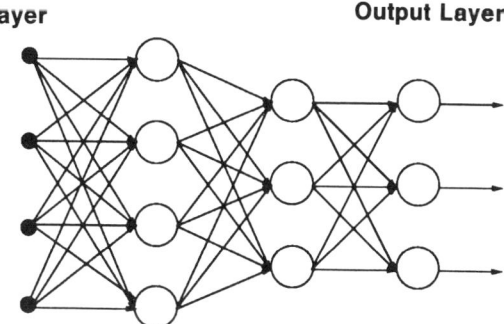

Figure 7.1 *Feed-forward neural network.*

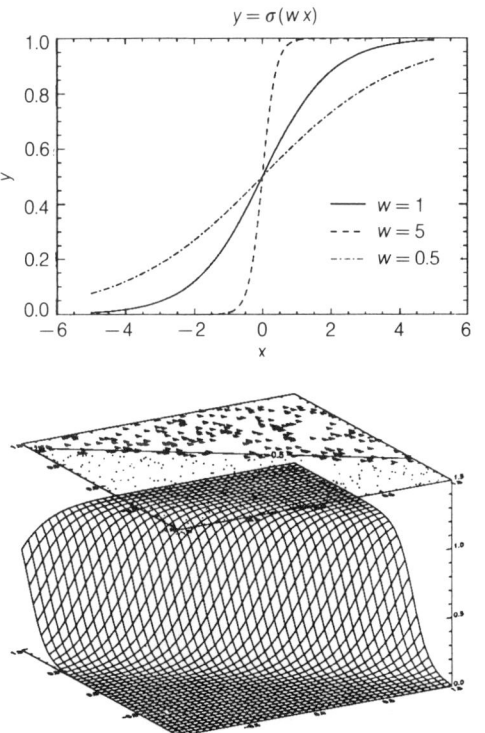

Figure 7.2 *Hyperplane classification in one and two dimensions.*

be written as

$$h(s_i) = \frac{1}{1 + e^{-s_i}} = \sigma\left(\sum_j w_{ij}y_j + b_i\right). \tag{3}$$

Neuron units in a network are grouped in layers, and the layers are customarily organized as one input layer, one or several hidden layers, and one output layer, with a one-directional flow of information from input to output. An input is presented at the input layer, propagates through the hidden layer(s) and produces an output at the output layer. A network is trained to perform a certain task by presenting it with examples and modifying the weights to produce the desired output. Since the problem of training a network, or finding the correct weights for a recognition task, is NP-complete (Judd, 1987), heuristic training methods have to be used. A popular training method is a gradient descent method called back-propagation (Rumelhart et al., 1986a, b), in which the error at the output of every layer is propagated back to the previous layer, and the weights are changed in a way to decrease that error.

7.2.2 Some shortcomings of the general model

Feed-forward networks are easy to implement, and have been shown to produce relatively good results for some classes of problems (Ripley, 1993; Hanson and Burr, 1991). There remain, however, some important problems associated with their use.

One problem involves the use of the sigmoid as a neuron activation function. In order to understand the role of the sigmoid activation, let us rewrite equations (1) and (3) in vector notation:

$$s_i = \mathbf{W}^{(i)} \cdot \mathbf{y} + b_i, \tag{4}$$

$$h(s_i) = \sigma(\mathbf{W}^{(i)} \cdot \mathbf{y} + b_i), \tag{5}$$

where $\mathbf{y}$ is the vector of inputs to neuron i, and $\mathbf{W}^{(i)}$ is row (i) of a cross-connectivity matrix $\mathbf{W}$ whose elements w_{ij} are the weights of the connections from the output of neuron j to the input of neuron i. We can now see that the sigmoid activation function effectively divides the input space of the neuron into two subspaces separated by the hyperplane whose equation is given by

$$\mathbf{W}^{(i)}\mathbf{y} + b_i = 0, \tag{6}$$

and that the sharpness of the separation is controlled by weights $\mathbf{W}^{(i)}$ (Figure 7.2). A network is trained by varying the connection weights and thus moving the hyperplanes in the input space. It can be shown that sigmoidal decomposition is a universal approximator, **if enough units are used** (Cybenko, 1989; Hornik et al., 1989; Sontag, 1989). The number of hidden units to use in the hidden layers, however, cannot be easily determined beforehand, although there are some rules of thumb (Camargo, 1990; Lippmann, 1987). The problem is compounded by the extent of the effect that each hyperplane can have on other hyperplanes (non-local effects). The guessing process is a significant bottleneck for complex data sets, and some methods have been developed to alleviate it. Constructive methods, for example, start with a small number of elements in the hidden layer and add more as they are needed. Destructive methods, on the other hand, start with a large number of elements and remove the ones that are not contributing significantly to the solution.

Another significant problem is the training method for networks of this type. Gradient descent methods are in general very susceptible to local minima and flat spots, and the back-propagation algorithm is not immune to this, as shown by several researchers (Sontag and Sussmann, 1989; Ripley, 1993). In addition, it can take several thousand epochs to adequately train a network on a reasonably-sized data set. As an example, a typical training run on the BP simulator (Rumelhart *et al.*, 1986a) for the Peterson–Barney formant frequency problem for vowel recognition, takes 18 500 training epochs to train a 25 hidden units network for a recognition score of 76% and 8430 epochs for 100 hidden units and a score of 71.6% (L.Y. Pratt, personal communication). Other researchers have also raised the issue of long training time (Lippmann, 1989b).

7.2.3 Basis function networks

Basis function networks can be considered a particular case of the general feed-forward neural network model. The premise of these networks is that the function to be approximated can be written as the expansion

$$\hat{f}(\mathbf{x}) = \sum_i \alpha_i B_i(\mathbf{x}) \tag{7}$$

where the B_i are basis functions and the α_i are the corresponding coefficients. The network structure is such that there is only one hidden layer, containing neurons whose activation functions are not sigmoid, but correspond to the chosen basis functions. The connection weights are then taken to represent the associated coefficients, and are computed, along with other function parameters, by any one of the popular learning methods. The output layer performs the summation of the weighted outputs from the hidden layer, to generate the function approximation (Figure 7.3). In keeping with the notation introduced in section 7.2.1, and denoting the input feature vector by $\mathbf{x}$, the new network equations can be written as

$$s_i = \mathbf{x}. \tag{8}$$

$$y_i = B_i(s_i) \quad \text{for the hidden layer.} \tag{9}$$

$$= \sum_j w_{ij} y_j = \hat{f} \quad \text{for an output unit.} \tag{10}$$

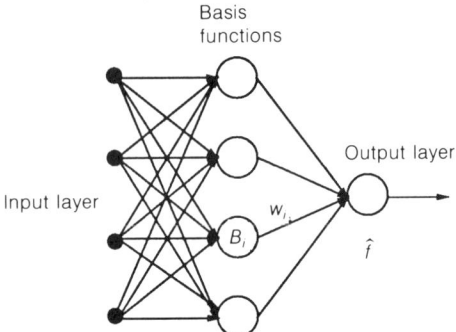

Figure 7.3 *Basis function network.*

As mentioned previously, several types of basis functions have been used, the most common being radial basis functions (RBF), splines and polynomial functions. The main problem in this approach is that of selecting an appropriate set of basis functions and their optimization parameters. In addition, as in classical function approximation, the problem of scaling with the number of output dimensions, the so-called 'curse of dimensionality', remains an important one.

7.3 Biological sensory receptors

One of the main principles governing the organization in the nervous system is the topographical layout of the sensory pathways (Kelly, 1985). Somato-topic, visuotopic and tonotopic maps construct a complete picture of the sensory inputs based on information supplied by **local** receptors. Furthermore, these sensory systems are hierarchically organized (Martin, 1985), such that larger and more complex patterns are synthesized at each level by combining and overlapping the responses of neurons at the lower levels. At the lowest level in the hierarchy, the peripheral receptor surface such as the retina or the skin, the main computing element is the receptor neuron. These receptors do not necessarily perform hyperplane classification. Instead, each receptor reacts to a specific, finite area of the sensory space, called its receptive field, in a variety of graded responses (Kandel, 1985). The first order receptors converge onto second order neurons, usually in the central nervous system, which also have a receptive field constructed from a synthesis of the first order receptive fields. This hierarchical organization can proceed onto several levels.

For example, center-surround retinal and lateral geniculate cells (Kuffler *et al.*, 1984) possess receptive fields at different scales and locations throughout the visual field, and exhibit the well-known 'Mexican-hat' activation function (Figure 7.4). These cells are connected to simple, complex and hypercomplex cortical cells (Hubel and Wiesel, 1962) in a hierarchy of overlapping receptive

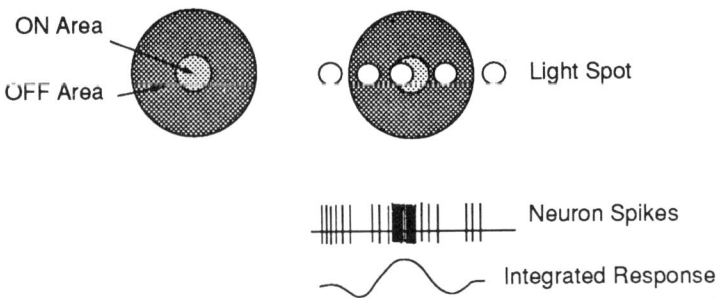

Figure 7.4 *On-center receptive field of retinal ganglion cell. Neuron firing and integrated activation function are shown as a light spot is moved across the receptive field.*

fields. In another example, the tonotopic organization of the auditory nervous system is a result of the selective reactions of distinct regions in the relay nuclei, at each level in the auditory pathways, to the different frequencies in the sound spectrum to which the ear is sensitive (Kelly, 1985).

In the next section we will introduce a class of basis functions whose localization properties and hierarchical structure, similar to biological receptors, will afford us a large degree of control over the selection and placing of the required bases in a network.

7.4 The wavelet transform

7.4.1 *The continuous wavelet transform*

Wavelets are a family of functions that, in the continuous case, take the form

$$\psi^{(a,b)}(x) = |a|^{-1/2}\psi\left(\frac{x-b}{a}\right), \tag{11}$$

where a is a dilation factor and b a translation factor on the original function $\psi(x)$, which has to be square integrable and satisfy

$$C_\psi = \int |\xi|^{-1}|\hat{\psi}(\xi)|^2\,d\xi < \infty. \tag{12}$$

By varying these parameters, the location and frequency content of the wavelet function can be controlled. The continuous wavelet transform is defined as

$$(Wf)(a,b) = \langle f, \psi^{(a,b)}\rangle, \tag{13}$$

allowing us to decompose $f(x)$ into its components at different scales of frequency and space (location) by varying a and b. The function $f(x)$ can then be reconstructed by performing the inverse operation and integrating over the transform space of a and b so that

$$f(x) = \frac{1}{C_\psi} \int\int (Wf)(a,b)\psi^{(a,b)} \frac{da\,db}{a^2}. \tag{14}$$

Wavelets thus form a basis of functions with variable local support (Daubechies, 1988; Mallat, 1989; Strang 1989), controlled by the dilation and translation factors. The Wavelet Transform maps one-dimensional functions $f(x)$ onto a two-dimensional plane of translation and dilation a and b. For discrete functions, we will wish to restrict a and b to discrete values. This is naturally achievable by setting $a = a_0^m$ with $a_0 \neq 1$, $m \in \mathbf{Z}$ and $b = nb_0$ with $b > 0$ (Kelly, 1985). The function can now be reconstructed from the discrete set of wavelet functions by

$$f = \sum_{m,n} \langle f, \psi_{m,n} \rangle \psi_{m,n}^*. \tag{15}$$

This discretization will next be used to construct a hierarchical set of **orthonormal** bases for the discrete case.

7.4.2 Multiresolution analysis

Let us now define a linear operator A_{2^j} such that $f_{2^j} = A_{2^j}f(x)$ approximates $f(x)$ to a resolution of 2^j samples per unit length, and that f_{2^j} is the best approximation of f in the corresponding vector space denoted by $\mathbf{V}_{2^j} \subset \mathbf{L}^2(\mathcal{R})$. A_{2^j} is then an orthogonal projection on $\mathbf{V}_{2^j}$. The ladder of subspaces in $\mathbf{L}^2(\mathcal{R})$

$$\forall j \in \mathbf{Z}, \quad \mathbf{V}_{2^j} \subset \mathbf{V}_{2^{j+1}}\ldots \tag{16}$$

is called a **multiresolution approximation** of $\mathbf{L}^2$ (Mallat, 1989). Clearly, then, a higher resolution space $\mathbf{V}_{2^{j+1}}$ will generally contain more information than $\mathbf{V}_{2^j}$. This difference in content is spanned by the orthogonal complement of $\mathbf{V}_{2^j}$ in $\mathbf{V}_{2^{j+1}}$, denoted by $\mathbf{O}_{2^j}$.

To properly characterize a signal $f(x)$, we now need to compute its representation at a certain resolution 2^j, called the 'smooth signal' and the difference of information between the resolutions 2^j and 2^{j+1}, called the 'detail signal'. It can be shown that in a multiresolution approximation there exists a unique function $\phi(x)$, called a scaling function, such that if we set $\phi_{2^j}(x) = 2^j\phi(2^jx)$, then $(\sqrt{2^{-j}}\phi_{2^j}(x - 2^{-j}n))_{n \in \mathbf{Z}}$ forms an orthonormal basis of $\mathbf{V}_{2^j}$. The discrete approximation of $f(x)$ at a resolution 2^j can then be represented by a set of inner products

$$A_{2^j}^d f = (\langle f(x), \phi_{2^j}(x - 2^{-j}n) \rangle)_{n \in \mathbf{Z}}. \tag{17}$$

Furthermore, if H is a discrete filter with impulse response

$$h(n) = \langle \phi_{2^{-1}}(u), \phi(u - n) \rangle \quad \forall n \in \mathbf{Z}, \tag{18}$$

then this scaling function $\phi(x)$ can be computed by

$$\hat{\phi}(\omega) = \prod_{p=1}^{+\infty} H(2^{-p}\omega). \tag{19}$$

It can also be shown that, given the conjugate filter G such that

$$G(\omega) = e^{-i\omega}\overline{H(\omega + \pi)}, \tag{20}$$

then the function whose Fourier transform is given by

$$\hat{\psi}(\omega) = G\left(\frac{\omega}{2}\right)\hat{\phi}\left(\frac{\omega}{2}\right), \tag{21}$$

is an orthogonal wavelet whose dilations and translations

$$(\sqrt{2^{-j}}\psi_{2^j}(x - 2^{-j}n))_{n \in \mathbf{Z}}, \tag{22}$$

form an orthogonal basis spanning the space $\mathbf{O}_{2^j}$ of the detail signal at resolution 2^j. By successively applying the two filters H and G, $f(x)$ can be characterized to any resolution.

7.4.3 Practical wavelet decompositions

In practice, the multiresolution decomposition of a signal $\mathbf{f}$ of length N is performed through a pyramid scheme. In the first step, at level $L = 0$, the filters H and G are applied to obtain the smooth and detail signals, respectively, of length N each. These two signals are then decimated by two, to a length of $N/2$ each, reducing them to the proper resolution. The filtering and decimation steps can be combined into one matrix operator $\mathbf{F}_0$ that takes the following form:

$$\begin{bmatrix} h_0 & h_1 & h_2 & h_3 & & & & \\ g_0 & g_1 & g_2 & g_3 & & & & \\ & & h_0 & h_1 & h_2 & h_3 & & \\ & & g_0 & g_1 & g_2 & g_3 & & \\ & & & \vdots & & & & \\ h_2 & h_3 & & & & & h_0 & h_1 \\ g_2 & g_3 & & & & & g_0 & g_1 \end{bmatrix}, \tag{23}$$

where the coefficients h_i and g_i are the H and G filter coefficients respectively. This operator produces an interlacing of smooth and detail signals that can be separated by a permutation matrix $\mathbf{P}_0$. If the next level is desired, the same procedure is applied to the smooth signal, resulting in new smooth and detail signals for this level. This procedure can be repeated down to the finest resolution level, as shown in the example below:

$$
\begin{bmatrix} f_1 \\ f_2 \\ \vdots \\ f_N \end{bmatrix}
\overset{\mathbf{F}_0}{\to}
\begin{bmatrix} s_1 \\ d_1 \\ s_2 \\ d_2 \\ \vdots \\ s_{N/2} \\ d_{N/2} \end{bmatrix}
\overset{\mathbf{P}_0}{\to}
\begin{bmatrix} s_1 \\ \vdots \\ s_{N/2} \\ d_1 \\ \vdots \\ d_{N/2} \end{bmatrix}
\overset{\mathbf{F}_1}{\to}
\begin{bmatrix} ss_1 \\ sd_1 \\ \vdots \\ ss_{N/4} \\ sd_{N/4} \\ d_1 \\ \vdots \\ d_{N/2} \vdots \end{bmatrix}
\cdots .
\tag{24}
$$

This series of steps can be combined in one operator, called the decomposition matrix $\mathbf{D}$:

$$
\mathbf{D} = (\mathbf{P}_L \mathbf{F}_L) \cdots (\mathbf{P}_1 \mathbf{F}_1)(\mathbf{P}_0 \mathbf{F}_0)
\tag{25}
$$

such that

$$
\mathbf{Df} = \mathbf{w},
\tag{26}
$$

$$
\mathbf{f} = \mathbf{D}^{-1}\mathbf{w} = \mathbf{Rw},
\tag{27}
$$

where $\mathbf{R}$ is the reconstruction matrix whose columns are the scaling and wavelet basis functions, and $\mathbf{w}$ the corresponding coefficients. It is important to note at this point that both $\mathbf{D}$ and $\mathbf{R}$ have been computed independently from $\mathbf{f}$. The basis functions can thus be computed beforehand and stored for later reference, for example during the training phase in a neural network. As an example, Figure 7.5 shows a reconstruction matrix $\mathbf{R}$ for the Daubechies (1988) D4 wavelet, while Figure 7.6 shows some columns from this reconstruction matrix, displaying D4 at different locations and levels of resolution.

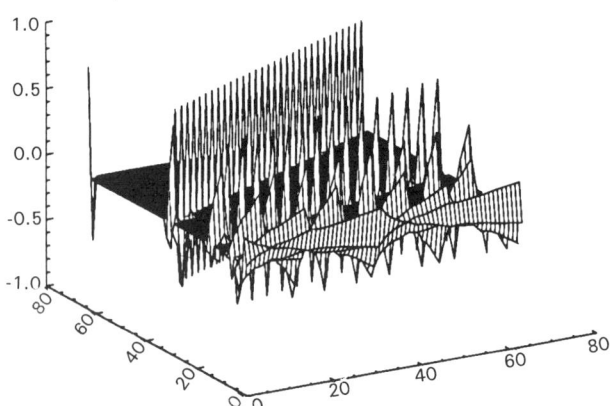

Figure 7.5 *D4 generating and wavelet functions.*

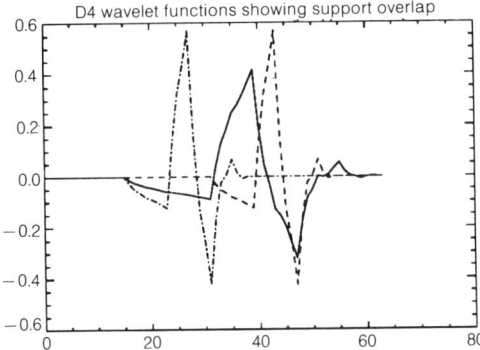

Figure 7.6 *Overlapping support for some D4 wavelet functions.*

These constructions are valid for one-dimensional wavelets. In higher dimensions, it is usually considered computationally more efficient to use outer products of one-dimensional basis functions (Lane *et al.*, 1991), even if the functions are not separable in dimensions (Sanger, 1990). This will be the method used in the examples presented later.

7.5 Wavelet neural networks (WNN)

7.5.1 A general model

By analogy with biological sensory systems, we can now construct a network of neurons whose activation functions possess wavelet-like properties of translation, dilation and **local support**. These neurons can be combined as a set of basis functions that can be used for clustering and continuous function approximation. The weights can now be thought of as the wavelet coefficients (Figure 7.7) and a gradient-descent scheme could be derived to compute them through training. The new network equations can be rewritten for this new model

$$\mathbf{s}_i = \mathbf{A}_i \mathbf{x} \tag{28}$$

$$y_i = \phi(\mathbf{s}_i, \mathbf{b}_i) \quad \text{for scaling functions}$$
$$= \psi(\mathbf{s}_i, \mathbf{b}_i) \quad \text{for wavelet functions} \tag{29}$$

In these equations, $\mathbf{A}_i$ is a diagonal matrix whose elements are the dilation parameters in each dimension, and $\mathbf{b}_i$ is a translation **vector**. The objective of training is then to optimize the values of $\mathbf{A}_i$ and $\mathbf{b}_i$. A simpler model would have one global dilation parameter a_i for each unit, so that $\mathbf{s}_i = a_i\mathbf{x}$. This general model, however, has some of the same drawbacks as the original neural networks model of sigmoidal activation functions, namely that the number of hidden units is still hard to determine, and the training time can

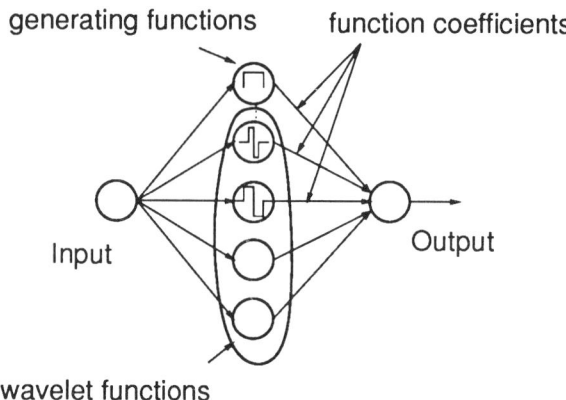

Figure 7.7 *Wavelet basis network.*

be extensive, due to the large parameter space to be explored. By taking advantage of the localized representation of sets of orthonormal wavelets and the recursive nature of their construction, several improvements can be achieved. For this, we shall make use of a recursive partitioning method to subdivide the feature space into subregions corresponding to the receptive fields of the neurons in the network. By having the activation function of a neuron correspond to a wavelet function over its receptive field, a multi-resolution approximation of the input function is obtained.

7.5.2 The receptive field partitioning model

If $\hat{f}(\mathbf{x})$ is the approximation of $f(\mathbf{x})$ over the domain of interest, traditional recursive partitioning regression can be written as

$$\text{if } \mathbf{x} \in R_m, \quad \text{then} \quad \hat{f}(\mathbf{x}) = g_m(\mathbf{x}), \tag{30}$$

where R_m are disjoint regions that partition the domain, and g_m are different approximating functions defined on each subregion. This partitioning is achieved through training by recursively splitting each subregion at every step into two other subregions according to some fitting criterion. In the Multi-variate Adaptive Regression Splines (MARS) algorithm (Friedman, 1991), for example, multivariate spline basis functions $B_m^{(q)}(x)$ are used to approximate $f(\mathbf{x})$

$$\hat{f}(\mathbf{x}) = \sum_{m=1}^{M} a_m B_m^{(q)}(\mathbf{x}) \tag{31}$$

and a lack-of-fit criterion $LOF(g(\mathbf{x}))$ is computed to select the new term to be added at every step. For Wavelet Networks, a useful algorithm can take advantage of the following:

- Different wavelet basis functions have overlapping support. In particular, for a given function at level L_i, several functions can be generated at level L_{i+1} over the same support interval (Figure 7.6). In the proposed receptive field partitioning (RFP) model, this provides a way to refine the wavelet decomposition in areas of greatest error computed by a *LOF* function. Another advantage is that the wavelet set could be grown as a tree, where the support of each parent node spans the support of all its children nodes. For example, Neural Tree Networks (NTN) (Sankar and Mammone, 1991) offer several implementation advantages over general feed-forward networks.

- As opposed to other continuously variable basis functions, a set of discrete one-dimensional wavelet basis functions over each dimension of the training domain can be constructed in advance to any resolution desired, as was described in section 7.4.3, and stored. Precomputing the functions allows for measurable speedups in training time, since a look-up table method can be used for determining the output of each hidden unit. These values can be recomputed later in the training if a resolution finer than the starting resolution is deemed necessary.

- Since an orthonormal set of bases can be constructed, each wavelet coefficient is in effect the projection $\langle f, \psi \rangle$ of the function f to be approximated onto the corresponding basis function ψ. This leads to two major gains: the wavelet coefficients can be computed without resorting to gradient descent or other optimization methods, and there is no need to retrain units whose weights have already been computed as the refining proceeds and additional wavelets are required.

- Finally, because of the local support property, only a small set of elements need be active at one time. This is especially important during training. For each training example, only wavelets whose support interval, or receptive field, includes that particular point are affected by the weight changes. We shall call this the **receptive field activation principle**. In this manner, the number of operations can be greatly reduced at every step, since typically, in a recursion of level L, only $O(L)$ elements will be active at any point.

7.5.3 The receptive field partitioning (RFP) algorithm

We can now proceed with a general algorithm to construct a WNN. To avoid the geometric explosion of the number of basis functions with the input space dimension, it is extremely important that a sparse set of basis functions be used. This sparse set is best determined by a constructive method. The object, then, is to start with the bases at the lowest level in each dimension (coarse resolution) and refine the approximation by adding units from higher resolutions as the error warrants. These units are added to partition the receptive field of the basis with the highest error. This objective is highly facilitated by the localized properties of the wavelet functions used.

The algorithm starts by generating an initial set of bases, the **seed bases**, consisting of the generating functions and the bases at the lowest (coarse) resolution, and maintains two pools of bases throughout the training. The first pool, the **main pool**, contains all the bases that are being used in the current computation and constitutes the actual neural network. The second pool, the **development pool**, contains all the bases that have not been refined yet, and is a subset of the first. Any basis that is selected for refinement gets removed from this pool and its children are added to both pools. After the score target has been reached, the network is pruned by removing nodes whose effect on the total score is minimal.

The algorithm is summarized below:

Input: Feature vectors, wavelet type (i.e. Haar, D4, etc.), score target.
Initialize:
    1. Compute the seed bases.
    2. Create the main and development pools.
    3. Compute the coefficients for the seed bases.
    4. Compute the classification score.

Main Loop:
    While (score < target-score)
        1. Compute LOF for development pool.
        2. Select basis ϕ with largest LOF and generate its sub-bases ϕ_i.
        3. Remove ϕ from development pool but keep it in the main pool.
        4. Add ϕ_i to the development and main pools.
        5. Compute the coefficients for ϕ_i.
        6. **if** (size (main_pool) is large) **then** prune.
        7. Compute the classification score.
    End While
    Prune Network
Output: Wavelet Network structure and weights (coefficients).

7.6 Results

Preliminary versions of the methods described in this chapter were implemented and tested on one-dimensional and two-dimensional test patterns. For comparison purposes, we also trained networks using the Cascade–Correlation algorithm (Fahlman and Lebiere, 1989) on the same test patterns. In the first test, a one-dimensional pattern, in the form of a set of input–output pairs, was used to train a network of Haar wavelets as basis functions, with $LOF(\psi_i) = \langle \psi_i(\mathbf{x}), \text{Error}(\mathbf{x}) \rangle$. The training was performed in 17 epochs, and the resulting network has 36 nodes. The results are shown in Figure 7.8. In this case, as the

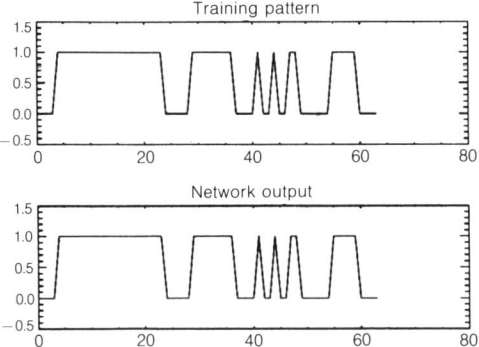

Figure 7.8 *One-dimensional training pattern and results.*

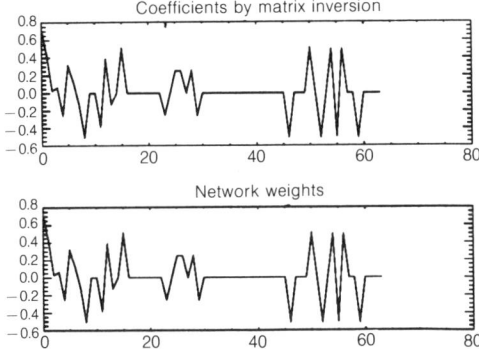

Figure 7.9 *Coefficients obtained by matrix inversion compared to those obtained by the network.*

input samples are evenly distributed, we can compute the exact wavelet coefficients by matrix inversion, and compare them to the network. We find that there are 36 non-zero coefficients and that the network has obtained the correct coefficients (Figure 7.9). The Cascade–Correlation program took an average of 1556 epochs and 16 cascaded hidden units with 170 weights to achieve the same results.

The second test consisted of a two-dimensional spiral pattern of 1024 evenly-spaced data points. In this instance outer products of the one-dimensional D4 wavelet were used as two-dimensional basis functions (Figure 7.6). The network was trained using the RFP algorithm to a target score of 0.9 (90% successful classification) and achieved it in 83 epochs using 170 weights for 170 units. Again, results and network weights compared very well with the results and non-zero coefficients obtained by matrix inversion methods (Figure 7.10). It should be noted at this point that matrix inversion

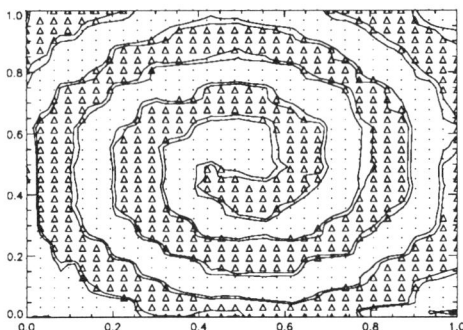

Figure 7.10 *Training results for a two-dimensional spiral pattern of evenly distributed points.*

methods involve the computation of every coefficient for the whole set of bases (1024 coefficients in this case), whereas the given algorithm will construct the set of bases with non-zero coefficients that will approximate the training pattern to a given competence level. The Cascade–Correlation program failed in several attempts to learn the pattern. This could be due, however, to a bad choice of initial parameters, although several different ones were tried.

The final test was the well-known double spiral pattern benchmark (Fahlman and Lebiere, 1989; Lang and Witbrock, 1988), which involves classifying points that fall on two interlocked spirals (Figure 7.11). Fahlman and Lebiere (1989) report that a modified version of backpropagation in use at MITRE required 150 000 to 200 000 epochs to solve the problem, and that no solutions could be found using standard backpropagation. The Cascade–Correlation algorithm required an average of 1700 epochs to learn the pattern,

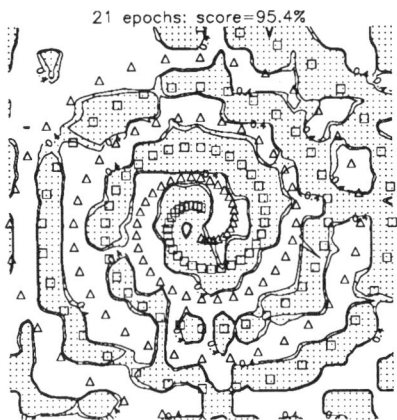

Figure 7.11 *Two-spiral benchmark pattern and results.*

with a median of 15 sigmoid units (Fahlman and Lebiere, 1989). The RFP algorithm, given a target score of 95%, achieved a score of 95.4% in 21 epochs for an un-pruned total of 202 units.

Acknowledgements

This research was supported in part by the National Science Foundation under NSF grants IRI-9116558 and ECS-9110424, and by the Computational Engineering Laboratory of the Center for Computer Aids for Industrial Productivity (CAIP). CAIP is supported by the New Jersey Commission on Science and Technology, Rutgers – the State University of New Jersey, and the CAIP Industrial members.

References

Baum, E.B. (1988) On the capabilities of multilayer perceptrons. *J. of Complexity*, **4**(3), 193–215.

Beylkin, G., Coifman, R. and Rokhlin, V. (1989) Fast wavelet transforms and numerical algorithms I. *Report No. YALEU/DCS/RR-696*, Yale University, USA.

Camargo, F.A. (1990) Learning algorithms in neural networks. *CUCS-062-90*, Computer Science Department, Columbia University.

Cybenko, G. (1989) Approximation by superpositions of a sigmoidal function. *Math. Control, Signals and Systems*, **2**, 303–14.

Daubechies, I. (1988) Orthonormal bases of compactly supported wavelets. *Comm. on Pure and Applied Math.*, **XLI**, 909–96.

Fahlman, S.E. and Lebiere, C. (1989) The Cascade–Correlation learning architecture, in *Advances in Neural Information Processing Systems 2*, (ed. D.S. Touretzky), Morgan Kaufmann, San Mateo, CA, 524–32.

Friedman, J.H. (1991) Multivariate adaptive regression splines. *The Annals of Statistics*, **19**(1), 1–141.

Hanson, S.J. and Burr, D.J. (1991) What connectionist models learn: learning and representation in connectionist networks, in *Neural Networks: Theory and Applications* (eds. R. Mammone and Y. Zeevi), Academic Press, New York, NY.

Hornik, K.M., Sinchcombe, M. and White, H. (1989) Multilayer feedforward networks are universal approximators. *Neural Networks*, **2**, 359–66.

Huang, W.Y. and Lippmann, R.P. (1987) Comparisons between neural network and conventional classifiers. *Proc. IEEE First Conference on Neural Networks*, **4**, 485–93.

Hubel, D.H. and Wiesel, T.N. (1962) Receptive fields, binocular interaction and functional architecture in the cat's visual cortex. *J. Physiology*, **160**, 106–54.

Judd, S. (1987) Learning in networks is hard. *Proc. IEEE First Conference on Neural Networks*, **4**, 685–92

Kandel, E.R. (1985) Central representation of touch, in *Principles of Neural Science* (eds. E.R. Kandel and J.H. Schwartz), Elsevier, Amsterdam.

Kanerva, P. (1984) *Self-Propagating Search: A Unified Theory of Memory*. PhD thesis, Stanford University, CA, USA.

Kelly, J.P. (1985) Principles of the functional and anatomical organization of the nervous system, in *Principles of Neural Science* (eds. E.R. Kandel and J.H. Schwartz), Elsevier, Amsterdam.

Kuffler, S.W., Nicholls, J.G. and Martin, A.R. (1984) *From Neuron to Brain: A Cellular Approach to the Function of the Nervous System*, WH Freeman, San Francisco, CA.

Lane, S.H., Flax, M.G., Handelman, D.A. and Gelfand, J.J. (1991) Multi-layer perceptrons with B-spline receptive field functions, in *Advances in Neural Information Processing Systems 3* (eds. R.L. Lippman, J.E. Moody and D.S. Touretzky), Morgan Kaufmann, San Mateo, CA.

Lang, K.J. and Witbrock, M.J. (1988) Learning to tell two spirals apart, *Proc. Connectionist Models Summer School*, Morgan Kaufmann, San Mateo, CA.

Lippmann, R.P. (1987) An introduction to neural computing. *IEEE ASSP Magazine*, April.

Lippmann, R.P. (1989a) Pattern classification using neural networks. *IEEE Comm. Magazine*, November.

Lippmann, R.P. (1989b) Review of neural networks for speech recognition. *Neural Computation*, **1**, 1–38.

Mallat, S.G. (1989) A theory for multiresolution signal decomposition: the wavelet representation. *IEEE Trans. Pattern Analysis and Machine Intelligence*, **7**(11).

Martin, J.H. (1985) Receptor physiology and submodality coding in the somatic sensory system, in *Principles of Neural Science* (eds. E.R. Kandel and J.H. Schwartz), Elsevier, Amsterdam.

Poggio, T. and Girosi, F. (1990) Regularization algorithms for learning that are equivalent to multilayer networks. *Science*, **2**(47), 978–82.

Ripley, B.D. (1993) Statistical aspects of neural networks. *Proc. Séminaire Européen do Statistique*. Chapman & Hall, London.

Robinson, A.J., Niranjan, M. and Fallside, F. (1988) Generalising the Nodes of the Error Propagation Network. *Report No. CUED/F-INFENG/TR. 25*, Cambridge University Engineering Department, UK.

Rogers, D. (1991) G/Splines: A hybrid of Friedman's multivariate adaptive regression splines (MARS) with Holland's genetic algorithm. *RIACS Tech. Rep. 91.10*, NASA Ames Research Center, CA, USA.

Rumelhart, D.E., McClelland, J.L. and the PDP Research Group (1986a), *Parallel Distributed Processing*, MIT Press, Cambridge, MA.

Rumelhart, D.E., Hinton, G.E. and Williams, R.J. (1986b) Learning representations by back-propagating errors. *Nature*, **323**, 533–6.

Sanger, T.D. (1990) Basis-function trees for approximation in high-dimensional spaces. *Proc. 1990 Connectionist Models Summer School*, Morgan Kaufmann, San Mateo, CA.

Sanger, T.D., Sutton, R.S. and Matheus, C.J. (1991) Iterative construction of sparse polynomial approximations. *NIPS Conference*, December.

Sankar, A. and Mammone, R.J. (1991) Neural tree networks, in *Neural Networks: Theory and Applications* (eds. R. Mammone and Y. Zeevi), Academic Press, London.

Sontag, E.D. (1989) Feedforward nets for interpolation and classification. *Advances in Neural Information Processing Systems 2* (ed. D.S. Touretzky), Morgan Kaufmann, San Mateo, CA, pp. 524–32.

Sontag, E.D. and Sussmann, H.J. (1989) Backpropagation can give rise to spurious local minima even for networks without hidden layers. *Complex Systems*, **3**, 91–106.

Strang, G. (1989) Wavelets and dilation equations: a brief introduction. *SIAM Review*, **31**(4), 614–27.

Widrow, B. and Winter, R.G. (1988) Neural nets for adaptive filtering and adaptive pattern recognition. *Computer*, March, 25–39.

8

Rates of convergence for radial basis functions and neural networks

FEDERICO GIROSI* and GABRIELE ANZELLOTTI[†]
*Artificial Intelligence Laboratory, MIT, 545 Technology Square #788, Cambridge, MA, 02139, USA
[†]Department of Mathematics, University of Trento, Povo (TN) 38050, Italy

8.1 Introduction

Let $\{\mathbf{x}_i\}_{i=1}^N$ be a set of random points in R^d, drawn according to some unknown distribution, and let $\{y_i\}_{i=1}^N$ be a set of values such that

$$y_i = f(\mathbf{x}_i) + \varepsilon_i, \tag{1}$$

where f is a function belonging to some normed space of functions Φ and ε_i are i.i.d. random variables with zero mean. Let us consider the problem of recovering f, or an estimate of it, from the knowledge of the **data set** $D \equiv \{(\mathbf{x}_i, y_i) \in R^d \times R\}_{i=1}^N$, that is the problem of approximating the function f from a sparse set of noisy data. This problem is very common in a variety of disciplines, and has received particular attention in the last few years, especially from people in the fields of artificial intelligence and computer science. In fact, the problem of learning to perform some task from a set of examples can be usually formulated in this way, where the examples correspond to the data set D, and the task to the unknown function f (Barron and Barron, 1988; Poggio and Girosi, 1990; Girosi, 1992; Hertz, Krogh and Palmer, 1991). A typical way to (approximately) solve this problem consists in approximating the element f of Φ by an element of A_n, some appropriate

Artificial Neural Networks for Speech and Vision. Edited by Richard J. Mammone.
Published in 1993 by Chapman & Hall, London. ISBN 0 412 54850 X

submanifold of Φ parametrized by a number n of parameters. Once the sub-manifold A_n has been selected, the approximation to f from A_n is chosen to be

$$\hat{a}_{n,N} \equiv \arg\min_{a \in A_n} Q_{\mathrm{emp}}[a], \tag{2}$$

where we have defined the **empirical risk** (Vapnik, 1982) as

$$Q_{\mathrm{emp}}[a] \equiv \sum_{i=1}^{N} (a(\mathbf{x}_i) - y_i)^2. \tag{3}$$

In the case in which the minimum of the empirical risk does not exist over the approximating subset A_n, we take $\hat{a}_{n,N}$ as an element of A_n for which the empirical risk is 'small enough'.

It would be clearly extremely important to be able to have *a priori* estimates for the **generalization error** $\| f - \hat{a}_{n,N} \|$, where $\|\cdot\|$ is some norm defined on Φ such as the sup norm, or some weighted L_p norm. A bound on the generalization error would allow us to estimate, for any fixed number of examples, the optimal number of parameters n that has to be used, and the reliability of our solution, guaranteeing that, using that number of parameters and of data points, we will never make an error larger than a certain threshold. To study this fundamental quantity, we notice that the error that we make when we approximate the unknown function f by $\hat{a}_{n,N}$ has two main sources:

1. The finite number N of data points. The empirical risk $Q_{\mathrm{emp}}[a]$ is an estimate of the distance of the approximating function a from the unknown function f. As the number of data points grows this estimate becomes more and more accurate. In fact, under very general conditions, the following equation holds in probability

$$\lim_{N \to \infty} Q_{\mathrm{emp}}[a] = Q[a] \equiv \int_{R^d} (f(\mathbf{x}) - a(\mathbf{x}))^2 P(\mathbf{x})\, d\mathbf{x} + \sigma^2, \tag{4}$$

where $P(\mathbf{x})$ is the probability distribution of the sample points and σ^2 is the variance of the noise in equation (1). Therefore the expected risk $Q[a]$ is the quantity that we would like to minimize, but we can only minimize an approximation of it, that is $Q_{\mathrm{emp}}[a]$. While the convergence of $Q_{\mathrm{emp}}[a]$ to $Q[a]$ is established under very general conditions, the convergence of the minimum of $Q_{\mathrm{emp}}[a]$ to the minimum of $Q[a]$ is a much more delicate question, and it happens under more restrictive conditions. This problem has been studied by a number of authors (Vapnik and Chervonenkis, 1971, 1981, 1991; Vapnik, 1982; Pollard, 1984), and depends critically on properties of the approximating manifold A_n (such as its **Vapnik–Chervonenkis dimension**), while it is much less dependent on the class Φ of functions we want to approximate.

2. The finite number of parameters of our approximation scheme A_n. Even in the case in which we have an infinite number of data points, that is we know exactly the expected risk $Q[a]$, we still make an error due to the fact that

we are approximating a function f, that is an infinite dimensional object, using a finite number of parameters. Supposing we have infinite data, the best approximation we could compute is (if it exists)

$$\hat{a}_n = \arg\min_{a \in A_n} Q[a], \qquad (5)$$

and our approximation error would be $E_n \equiv \| f - \hat{a}_n \|$. The manifolds A_n are always chosen in such a way that E_n goes to zero as n tends to infinity, and its rate of convergence depends on global properties of Φ, such as differentiability and the dimension d of the definition domain, and on the structure of the approximating submanifold A_n.

The main tools to analyse the first source of error come from statistics and probability theory, due to the stochastic nature of the sampling process, while the second source of error does not require any probabilistic formulation, and it is mainly analysed in the framework of functional analysis and approximation theory.

In this chapter we present some results about the rate of convergence to zero of the approximation error, under the assumption of having infinite data. We feel that once we have bounds on E_n, the tools that have been developed to analyse the minimization of the empirical risk data (Vapnik and Chervonenkis, 1971, 1981, 1991; Vapnik, 1982; Pollard, 1984; Haussler, 1989) could be used to estimate the generalization error $\| f - \hat{a}_{n,N} \|$, that is our main object of interest, and few results in this direction already exist (Barron, 1991a; Cox, 1984).

We consider the case in which a function is approximated by linear combination of translates of a given function G, that is the approximating functions have the form

$$a(x) = \sum_{\alpha=1}^{n} c_\alpha G(\mathbf{x} - \mathbf{t}_\alpha),$$

where both the coefficients c_α and the **centers** $\mathbf{t}_\alpha$ are free parameters. In the next section we review the problem of rates of convergence, together with some classical results. In section 8.3 we present a lemma, due to several authors (Jones, 1992; Barron, 1991), that shows how to construct a sequence of functions f_n which approximate certain functions in a Hilbert space with a rate of convergence $O(1/\sqrt{n})$. We will use this lemma, in section 8.4, to derive the main results about approximation by translates of a given function G. As shown in section 8.5, for appropriate choices of G the rate of convergence $O(1/\sqrt{n})$ can be obtained for certain Radial Basis Functions Schemes (Micchelli, 1986; Powell, 1987, 1990; Dyn, 1991; Poggio and Girosi, 1990; Girosi, 1992) on certain spaces of functions of Sobolev type. In section 8.6, we compare this result with other applications of the same lemma, and in section 8.7 we will draw some conclusions and sketch some open problems. For the convenience of the reader, we collect in the Appendix a few known results about Sobolev spaces and integration of Banach valued functions.

8.2 Rates of convergence

Let Φ be a normed space of functions and let A be a subset of Φ. The prototypical problem in approximation theory consists in approximating an element f of Φ by an element of A, that is looking for an element in A that has minimum distance from f. It is also natural to consider the **distance of f from A** as

$$\delta(f, A) \equiv \inf_{a \in A} \| f - a \| \qquad (6)$$

and to study this quantity for different choices of A and $f \in \Phi$. In the classical theory of approximation the set A is usually a linear k-dimensional subspace $A_k \subset \Phi$ (Lorentz, 1986) (the algebraic or the trigonometric polynomials of given degree and the splines with fixed knots are typical examples of such subspaces), while in nonlinear approximation theory it is usually a k-dimensional manifold (DeVore, 1991). Usually, one has a family of manifolds $\{A_k\}_{k=1}^{\infty}$ such that $\bigcup_k A_k$ is dense in Φ, and

$$A_1 \subset A_2 \subset \cdots \subset A_n \subset \cdots,$$

so that the quantity $\delta(f, A_k)$ is a monotonically decreasing function of k converging to zero and the approximation in A_k gets arbitrarily close to f provided one takes k sufficiently large. However, since the computational time needed to find an approximation to f in A_k is going to increase with k, it is of great interest to know the rate of convergence to zero of $\delta(f, A_k)$ as a function of k. This rate of convergence can be taken as a measure of the complexity of f with respect to the manifolds A_k, in the sense that 'simple' functions should have a fast rate of convergence.

As an example, let us consider as space Φ the space $\Lambda_{s\alpha}^d$ of the functions whose partial derivatives of order s are bounded in the uniform norm on the d-dimensional cube $I = [0, 1]^d$ and satisfy a Lipschitz condition with exponent α (Lorentz, 1986, p. 50). On the space Φ we consider the uniform norm $\| f \| = \max_I | f(x) |$. Choosing as manifold A_k the set of polynomials of degree $n - 1$ in each of the d variables, i.e. a linear space of dimension $k = n^d$, the following bound can be obtained (Lorentz, 1986):

$$\delta(f, A_k) \leqslant N \, d k^{-s + \alpha/d}, \qquad (7)$$

where N is a constant that depends of f and s.

From this example we see that the rate of convergence dramatically slows down when the dimension d increases, revealing the discouraging phenomenon known under the name of 'curse of dimensionality' (Bellman, 1961). However, for every fixed number of dimensions, arbitrary inverse-power rates of convergence can be obtained if the smoothness index s is chosen big enough (although the bound 7 becomes meaningless if both d and s are very large). This result is typical in linear approximation theory since the computation of the n-width (Lorentz, 1962; Pinkus, 1986) of the space $\Lambda_{s\alpha}^d$ shows that the best linear technique cannot improve the rate of convergence $O(k^{-(s+\alpha/d)})$ (Lorentz, 1986, p. 135).

Similar results, in both linear and nonlinear approximation theory (DeVore, 1991), hold for other spaces of functions in which smoothness is measured in a different way. We are therefore led to argue that in practical situations we can only approximate functions whose smoothness increases with the dimension. As an example we consider again the spaces $\Lambda_{s\alpha}^d$ for $s = d$. It is clear from equation (7) that in this case the rate of convergence of polynomial approximation to an $f \in \Lambda_{d\alpha}^d$ is $O(k^{-1})$ and it is in this sense 'independent on dimensionality'.

In a recent paper (1992) Jones showed how to construct a sequence of functions f_n that approximate certain functions in a Hilbert space with a rate of convergence $O(1/\sqrt{n})$. An application of this result to projection pursuit regression, neural networks and hinging hyperplane approximation has already been presented in (Jones, 1992; Barron, 1991; Breiman, 1992), where appropriate approximation schemes and spaces Φ^d of functions in R^d are described in which the complexity of approximation increases mildly with d. It is worth observing that this is obtained at the expense of the functions contained in Φ^d being more and more 'regular' when d increases.

8.3 The Maurey–Jones–Barron lemma

Our result is based on a lemma by Jones (1992) on the convergence rate of an iterative approximation scheme in Hilbert spaces. A formally similar lemma, brought to our attention by R. Dudley (1991, personal communication), is due to Maurey, and was published by Pisier in 1981. However Jones' lemma is constructive while Maurey's is not. Here we report a version of the lemma due to Barron (Barron, 1991) that contains a slight refinement of Jones' result.

Lemma 8.1 (Maurey–Jones–Barron) *If f is in the closure of the convex hull of a set $\mathscr{G}$ in a Hilbert space H with $\|g\| \leqslant b$ for each $g \in \mathscr{G}$, then for every $n \geqslant 1$ and for $c > b^2 - \|f\|^2$ there is a f_n in the convex hull of n points in $\mathscr{G}$ such that*

$$\|f - f_n\|^2 \leqslant \frac{c}{n}.$$

The interesting feature of this lemma is that the sequence $\{f_n\}_{n=0}^{\infty}$ has the following structure:

$$f_{n+1} = \alpha_n f_n + (1 - \alpha_n) g_n, \tag{8}$$

where α_n and g_n are chosen in order to 'approximately solve' the following minimization problem:

$$\inf_{\alpha_n \in [0,1], g_n \in \mathscr{G}} \| f - \alpha_n f_n - (1 - \alpha_n) g_n \|,$$

where by 'approximately solve' we mean that it is sufficient at each step to reach a distance from the infimum of order $O(1/n^2)$. The lemma is therefore constructive, providing a procedure that can achieve the prescribed rate.

To exploit this result we need to define suitable classes of functions which are the closure of the convex hull of some subset $\mathscr{G}$ of a Hilbert space H. We are therefore naturally led to study functions that can be represented as 'infinite' convex combinations of the type

$$f = \sum_{i=1}^{\infty} \alpha_i g_i \quad \alpha_i \geqslant 0, \quad g_i \in \mathscr{G}, \quad \sum_{i=1}^{\infty} \alpha_i = 1. \tag{9}$$

One way to approach the problem consists in utilizing the **integral representation** of functions. Suppose that the functions in a Hilbert space H can be represented by the integral

$$f(\mathbf{x}) = \int_{\mathscr{M}} G_{\mathbf{t}}(\mathbf{x}) \, d\alpha(\mathbf{t}) \tag{10}$$

where $d\alpha$ is some measure on the parameter set $\mathscr{M}$. If $d\alpha$ is a finite measure, the integral (10) can be seen as an infinite convex combination of the type of equation (9), and therefore the function f belongs to the closure of the convex hull of some subset of H. In the next section we formalize this idea in the special case in which the functions $G_{\mathbf{t}}(\mathbf{x})$ are the translates $G(\mathbf{x} - \mathbf{t})$ of a fixed function G, and we show how it leads to define approximation techniques whose rate of convergence in appropriate spaces of functions is $O(1/\sqrt{n})$.

8.4 Approximation by translates of a function G

Let G be a fixed function belonging to $L_2(R^d) \equiv L_2$. We define the space L_G as the set of the functions of the form

$$f = G * \lambda \tag{11}$$

where λ is any signed Radon measure whose total variation $|\lambda|_{R^d} \equiv \|\lambda\|$ is finite, and the symbol $*$ stands for the convolution operation. Assuming from now on that $\|G\|_{L_2} = 1$, the following inequality holds (Stein and Weiss, 1971):

$$\|f\|_{L_2} \leqslant \|\lambda\|,$$

showing the inclusion $L_G \subset L_2$. It is natural to approximate elements of L_G by elements of the set

$$G_n = \left\{ f \in L_2 \mid f = \sum_{i=1}^{n} \lambda_i G_{\mathbf{t}_i}, \quad \lambda_i \in R, \quad \mathbf{t}_i \in R^d \right\}, \tag{12}$$

where we indicate by $G_{\mathbf{t}}$ the function G translated by the vector $\mathbf{t}$, i.e. $G_{\mathbf{t}}(\mathbf{x}) = G(\mathbf{x} - \mathbf{t})$. Using Lemma 8.1 we can now prove the following.

Theorem 8.2 Let f be a function in L_G, so that $f = G * \lambda$, where $G \in L_2$, $\|G\|_{L_2} = 1$, and λ is a Radon signed measure of bounded total variation $\|\lambda\|$. Then f belongs to the L_2-closure of the convex hull of the set

$$A = \{sG_t | t \in R^d, \ |s| \leqslant \|\lambda\|\}$$

and there exist n coefficients c_α and n vectors $\mathbf{t}_\alpha$ such that:

$$\| f - \sum_{\alpha=1}^{n} c_\alpha G(\mathbf{x} - \mathbf{t}_\alpha) \|_{L_2}^2 \leqslant \frac{c}{n}$$

for all $c > \|\lambda\|^2 - \|f\|_{L_2}^2$.

Proof: We consider the vector-valued function

$$T : R^d \to L_2(R^d)$$

such that

$$T(\mathbf{t}) = G_\mathbf{t}.$$

The function T is continuous, hence λ-measurable, moreover one has

$$\int_{R^d} \| T(\mathbf{t}) \|_{L_2} d|\lambda|(\mathbf{t}) = \| G \|_{L_2} \int_{R^d} d|\lambda|(\mathbf{t}) = \| \lambda \| < + \infty.$$

Therefore the Bochner integral of T with respect to λ exists (see Appendix 8A):

$$\eta = \int_{R^d}^{\mathscr{B}} T(\mathbf{t}) \, d\lambda(\mathbf{t}),$$

and by Lemma (8A.2) we have

$$\eta \in \overline{\mathrm{co}\, A} \tag{13}$$

where $A = \{sG_t | t \in R^d, |s| \leqslant \|\lambda\|\}$, co A stands for the convex hull of the set A, and the bar stands for the closure in L_2. Now we shall prove that $\eta = f$. This can be done by proving that

$$F * f = F * \eta, \quad \forall F * \in (L_2)^* \tag{14}$$

where $(L_2)^*$ is the dual space of L_2, that is L_2 itself. From the properties of the Bochner integral we have

$$F * \eta = F * \int_{R^d}^{\mathscr{B}} T(\mathbf{t}) \, d\lambda(\mathbf{t}) = \int_{R^d} (F * G_\mathbf{t})) \, d\lambda(\mathbf{t}).$$

Taking this into account, the identity (14) can be written as

$$\int_{R^d} d\mathbf{x}\, \phi(\mathbf{x}) \int_{R^d} G(\mathbf{x} - \mathbf{t}) \, d\lambda(\mathbf{t}) = \int_{R^d} d\lambda(\mathbf{t}) \int_{R^d} d\mathbf{x}\, \phi(\mathbf{x}) G(\mathbf{x} - \mathbf{t}), \quad \forall \phi \in L_2.$$

Now by Fubini's theorem the two sides of this last equation are equal, and therefore $\eta = f$.

By equation (13) $f = \eta$ belongs to the L_2 closure of the convex hull of the set A, which is contained in the ball of radius $\|\lambda\|$. By the Maurey–Jones–Barron lemma we can find a set of n coefficients c_α and n vectors $\mathbf{t}_\alpha$ such that

$$\|f - \sum_{\alpha=1}^{n} c_\alpha G(\mathbf{x} - \mathbf{t}_\alpha)\|_{L_2}^2 \leqslant \frac{c}{n}$$

for all $c > C(f) = \|\lambda\|^2 - \|f\|_{L_2}^2$.   □

In Theorem 8.2 the approximation error is measured in the L_2 norm. Imposing some restrictions on the function G a similar estimate can be obtained for other norms, and in particular for the L_∞ norm. In fact, suppose that $G \in H^{s,2}$, where $H^{s,2}(R^d) \equiv H^{s,2}$ is the Sobolev space of the functions whose weak derivatives up to order s are in L_2 (see Appendix B). Then one can easily see that Theorem 8.2 can be formulated in the Hilbert space $H^{s,2}$ instead of L_2:

Theorem 8.3 *Let f be a function such that $f = G * \lambda$, where $G \in H^{s,2}$, $\|G\|_{H^{s,2}} = 1$, and λ is a Radon signed measure of bounded total variation $\|\lambda\|$. Then f belongs to the $H^{s,2}$-closure of the convex hull of the set*

$$A = \{sG_\mathbf{t} | \mathbf{t} \in R^d, \quad |s| \leqslant \|\lambda\|\}$$

and there exist n coefficients c_α and n vectors $\mathbf{t}_\alpha$ such that

$$\|f - \sum_{\alpha=1}^{n} c_\alpha G(\mathbf{x} - \mathbf{t}_\alpha)\|_{H^{s,2}}^2 \leqslant \frac{c}{n}$$

for all $c > \|\lambda\|^2 - \|f\|_{H^{s,2}}^2$.

We notice that if the condition $s > d/2$ holds, then the Sobolev embedding theorem (see Appendix B) guarantees that $H^{s,2} \subset C^0$ and that $c_1 > 0$ exists such that

$$\|\cdot\|_\infty \leqslant c_1 \|\cdot\|_{H^{s,2}}.$$

Therefore the approximating sequence $\{f_n\}$ converges uniformly, and the following corollary holds:

Corollary 8.4 *Under the conditions of Theorem (4.2), if $s > d/2$ there exists n coefficients c_α, n vectors $\mathbf{t}_\alpha$ and a constant c_1 such that*

$$\|f - \sum_{\alpha=1}^{n} c_\alpha G(\mathbf{x} - \mathbf{t}_\alpha)\|_{L_\infty}^2 \leqslant c_1 \frac{c}{n}$$

for all $c > \|\lambda\|^2 - \|f\|_{H^{s,2}}^2$.

From a practical point of view, in many cases, what is really interesting is an estimate of the error in the sup norm, instead of the L_2 or $H^{s,2}$ norm. Think, for example, of the problem of approximating the trajectory of a robot arm: it is clear that what is really needed in this case is a small L_∞ norm of the difference between the desired and the approximated trajectory, while a small L_2 norm is of little interest.

Remark: We notice that the elements of the set G_n defined by equation (12) can also be seen as points of a manifold A_k whose dimension is $k = n(d + 1)$. Therefore Theorem 8.2 can also be formulated in terms of the number of parameters k that are needed to achieve a certain error, saying that if $f \in L_G$ then

$$\delta(f, A_k) \leqslant C(f) \sqrt{\frac{d+1}{k}}.$$

If we compare this result with the typical estimates (DeVore, 1991), we notice that in this case the way the dimension affects the convergence curve is much less dramatic, corresponding to a simple scale dilation. This means that in some sense the complexity of the space L_G does not increase very much when the dimension increases. It is interesting to characterize, for several specific choices of G, the structure of L_G, and this will be done in the next section for two particular choices of G.

8.5 Examples of functions G

In this section we consider two choices for the function G and study the corresponding functions spaces L_G. We remind that for any given $G \in L_2(R^d)$ the space L_G is define as

$$L_G = \{ f \in L_2(R^d) | f = G * \lambda, \lambda \in \mathcal{M}(R^d) \}$$

where $\mathcal{M}(R^d) \equiv \mathcal{M}$ is the space of Radon signed measures of bounded total variation on R^d.

8.5.1 The Gaussian

We consider the Gaussian function $G(\mathbf{x}) = e^{-\|\mathbf{x}\|^2}$, since approximation with Gaussian basis functions is often used in practical applications (Moody and Darken, 1989; Poggio and Girosi, 1990; Poggio and Edelman, 1990; Sanner and Slotine, 1992). Clearly, $G \in L_2(R^d)$, so that the space L_G is well defined in any dimension. Due to the smoothness of the Gaussian and to its fast decay property, this space of functions is rather small. However, it contains an interesting subset of the space of band limited functions, the functions whose Fourier transform has compact support. In particular, let us define the space of functions $B_k(R^d)$

$$B_k(R^d) \equiv \{ f | \tilde{f} \in C_0^k(R^d) \}, \tag{15}$$

that is the set of functions whose Fourier transform has compact support and

k continuous derivatives. Then the following inclusion holds

$$B_k(R^d) \subset L_G, \quad \forall k > \frac{d}{2}. \tag{16}$$

In fact, if $f \in B_k(R^d)$ then we have

$$\frac{\tilde{f}(\mathbf{s})}{\tilde{G}(\mathbf{s})} = \alpha e^{\|\mathbf{s}\|^2} \tilde{f}(\mathbf{s}) \equiv \tilde{\lambda} \in C_0^k(R^d),$$

where α is a constant depending only on the dimension d. Therefore, $f = G * \lambda$ where λ is the Fourier transform of the function $\tilde{\lambda} = \tilde{f}/\tilde{G}$. Since the following inclusion holds (see Appendix B)

$$C_0^k(R^d) \subset A(R^d), \quad \forall k > \frac{d}{2},$$

where $A(R^d)$ is the space of the functions whose Fourier transform belongs to $L_1(R^d)$, then $\lambda \in L_1$ and $f \in L_G$.

We notice that the Gaussian function and its derivatives of any order belong to L_2, and therefore $G \in H^{s,2}$ for any $s > 0$. Hence we can apply Corollary 8.4 to conclude that the convergence rate $O(1/\sqrt{n})$ also holds for approximation in the sup norm.

8.5.2 Bessel–Macdonald kernels

We now consider the Bessel–Macdonald kernels, a family of functions $G_m(\mathbf{x})$ defined in terms of their Fourier transforms:

$$\tilde{G}_m(\mathbf{s}) = \frac{1}{(1 + 4\pi^2 \|\mathbf{s}\|^2)^{m/2}} \quad m > 0.$$

The functions $G_m(\mathbf{x})$ are integrable functions that decay exponentially at infinity and may have a singularity at the origin (Stein, 1970, p. 132). However, if $m > d$ they are continuous and actually differentiable of any order $q < m - d$. We want to work with continuous functions, and in what follows we will always make the assumption $m > d$. Since $\tilde{G}_m(\mathbf{s})$ is positive and radial, we also have that, by Bochner's theorem, $G_m(\mathbf{x})$ is positive definite (Micchelli, 1986), and therefore approximation by translates of $G_m(\mathbf{x})$ is a Radial Basis Functions approximation scheme. The following observations can be done regarding the functions G_m and the space L_{G_m}:

1. One has

$$G_m \in H^{s,2} \quad \text{for} \quad 0 < s < m - \frac{d}{2}.$$

Since we have made the assumption $m > d$ one can take s such that

$d/2 < s < m - d/2$. Then we can apply Corollary 8.4 to conclude that the rate of convergence $O(1/\sqrt{n})$ also holds for approximation in the sup norm.

2. Since $L_1 \subset \mathcal{M}$, the space L_{G_m} contains the space $\mathcal{L}^1_m(R^d) \equiv \mathcal{L}^1_m$ of those functions that can be written as $f = G_m * \lambda$ with $\lambda \in L_1$. For more information about the space $\mathcal{L}^1_m$, which is a special instance of the so-called **potential spaces**, the reader is referred to Stein (1970). The space $\mathcal{L}^1_m$ is related to the Sobolev space $H^{m,1}(R^d) \equiv H^{m,1}$ of the functions whose weak derivatives up to order m are in L_1 (see Appendix B). More precisely one has (Stein, 1970, p. 160)

$$H^{m,1} \subset \mathcal{L}^1_m \subset L_{G_m} \quad \text{for all } m \text{ even.}$$

Therefore, we conclude that if $m > d$ and m is even, by superposition of translates of G_m, we can approximate with a rate of convergence $O(1/\sqrt{n})$ all the functions of $H^{m,1}$, and hence all C^m functions which rapidly decrease to infinity.

3. Again for $s < m - d/2$ and $m > d$, m even, we have the following characterization of the space L_{G_m}:

$$L_{G_m} = \{f \in H^{s,2} | (I - \Delta)^{m/2} f \in \mathcal{M}\}.$$

In fact, if $f \in L_{G_m}$, i.e. $f = G_m * \lambda$ with $\lambda \in \mathcal{M}$, then $(I - \Delta)^{m/2} f = \lambda$, since G_m is the fundamental solution of the operator $(I - \Delta)^{m/2}$. On the other hand, if $f \in H^{s,2}$ and $(I - \Delta)^{m/2} f = \lambda \in \mathcal{M}$, then by taking the convolution of both sides with G_m we have $f = G_m * \lambda$.

8.6 Other approximation schemes

Other choices of integral representation lead to different approximation schemes and different spaces of functions that can be approximated with a similar convergence rate. For example, using the Fourier representation of a function (if it exists) we have

$$f(\mathbf{x}) = \int_{R^d} d\mathbf{s} \cos(\mathbf{s} \cdot \mathbf{x} + \theta(\mathbf{s})) |\tilde{f}(\mathbf{s})| \tag{17}$$

where $\theta(\mathbf{s})$ is the phase of the Fourier transform $\tilde{f}(\mathbf{s})$ of f. Jones (1992) considers the space $A(R^d)$ (Appendix B) of the functions such that their Fourier transform is in $L_1(R^d)$, and shows that they can be approximated by functions of the form

$$f_n(\mathbf{x}) = \sum_{i=1}^{n} \lambda_i \cos(\mathbf{t}_i \cdot \mathbf{x} + \theta_i) \tag{18}$$

with the rate of convergence $O(1/\sqrt{n})$.

Another result of this type has been proved by Barron (1991). He considers the set of the functions such that

$$\int_{R^d} ds \, \|s\| \, |\tilde{f}(s)| < +\infty, \tag{19}$$

that is the functions whose gradient is in $A(R^d)$, and approximates elements of this set by functions of the form

$$f_n(x) = \sum_{i=1}^{n} \lambda_i \sigma(t_i \cdot x + \theta_i),$$

where $\sigma(\cdot)$ is any sigmoidal function. Condition (19) can be rewritten as

$$\|s\| \, |\tilde{f}(s)| \in L_1(R^d). \tag{20}$$

Denoting by I_d the function

$$I_d(x) = \frac{1}{\|x\|^{d-1}},$$

and noticing that its Fourier transform is $\tilde{I}_d(s) = \|s\|^{-1}$ we can also say that the space of functions that satisfy condition equation (19) is the space of functions that can be written as

$$f = I_d * \lambda, \quad \lambda \in A(R^d). \tag{21}$$

There is a remarkable analogy between this set of functions and the function space $\mathcal{L}_m^1$ considered in section 8.5.2, i.e. the set of functions such that

$$f = G_m * \lambda, \quad \lambda \in L_1(R^d), \quad m > d. \tag{22}$$

In equation (21), the function I_d goes to zero faster and faster as d increases, while its Fourier transform remains unchanged. In equation (22), because of the constraint $m > d$, it is the **Fourier transform** of G_m that goes to zero faster and faster as d increases, while the asymptotic decay of G_m is always exponential. Moreover, in equation (22) λ has to belong to L_1, while in equation (21) it is the **Fourier transform** of λ that belongs to L_1.

Another application of Jones' lemma has been developed by Brieman (1992), who approximates a function f with a linear superposition of **hinging hyperplanes**. A pair of hinging hyperplanes is a function consisting of two hyperplanes that are continuously joined at a hinge. The approximating functions have therefore the form

$$f_n(x) = a + \Delta \cdot x + \sum_{i=1}^{n} h^+(t_i \cdot x + \theta_i)$$

where a, Δ, t_i and θ_i are free parameters, and $h^+(x)$ is the truncated linear function, that is $h^+(x) = x\theta(x)$, and $\theta(x)$ is the Heaviside function. Breiman shows that the rate of convergence $O(1/\sqrt{n})$ can be obtained if hinging hyperplanes are used to approximate functions such that

$$\int_{R^d} ds \, \|s\|^2 |\tilde{f}(\mathbf{s})| < +\infty. \tag{23}$$

The space of functions defined by this condition is similar to the one defined by Barron (equation 19), and similar considerations apply.

8.7 Conclusions

We briefly summarize the main results presented:

- Let f be a function on R^d and assume that f can be written as $f = G * \lambda$, where G is square integrable on R^d and λ is a signed Radon measure of bounded total variation. Then there is a linear superposition of n translates of G that approximates f in the L_2 norm with a rate of convergence $O(1/\sqrt{n})$.
- Let f be a function on R^d whose Fourier transform has compact support and k continuous derivatives, with $k > d/2$. Then there exists a Gaussian Radial Basis Functions expansion with n basis functions that approximates f in the L_2 norm with a rate of convergence $O(1/\sqrt{n})$. The same result holds for approximation in the sup norm.
- Let f be any function of the Sobolev space $H^{m,1}(R^d)$, with $m > d$, m even. Then there exists a Radial Basis Functions expansion, whose basis function is the Bessel–Macdonald kernel $G_m(x)$, that approximates f with a rate of convergence $O(1/\sqrt{n})$ in the norm of $H^{s,2}$, with $d/2 < s < m - d/2$. A similar rate of convergence can also be obtained for the approximation in the sup norm.

All these examples involve spaces of functions with a number of derivatives that increases with the dimension, and are consistent with the intuitive idea that spaces of functions in a high number of dimensions are very difficult to approximate, unless some constraints are imposed to prevent their 'size' from growing exponentially fast. One interesting feature of these results is that, thanks to the **constructive** nature of Jones' and Barron's lemma, an iterative procedure is provided that can achieve that rate.

The results presented in this work may be deepened and generalized in several directions, some of which will be described below:

- The condition that the basis function has to belong to a Hilbert space, say L_2, is too restrictive, and does not allow us to deal with cases in which G is a function that grows to infinity. A possible solution consists in considering semi-Hilbert spaces, in which the norm is replaced by a seminorm, and to work with the equivalence classes naturally defined by the seminorm. Since all the Radial Basis Functions theory can be formulated in terms of seminormed spaces of functions, this might allow us to apply these results to a more general set of basis functions, and not only to positive definite functions, as the Gaussian and the Bessel–Macdonald kernel, that necessarily fall off to zero.

- The results about the Bessel–Macdonald kernel G_m are not fully satisfactory, due to the fact that the shape of the function changes with the dimension (due to the constraint $m > d$). However, they might be used to prove a result about a slightly different approximation scheme, in which we taken in account also **dilates** of the basis function. In fact, it can be proved that the Bessel–Macdonald kernel has an integral representation in terms of Gaussian functions of different scales (Stein, 1970), and combining this result with the results of section 8.5.2 it should be possible to prove that functions belonging to L_{G_m} can be approximated with a rate of convergence $O(1/\sqrt{n})$, in the L_2 norm, by an approximating function of the following type

$$f_n(\mathbf{x}) = \sum_{\alpha=1}^{n} c_\alpha e^{-\|\mathbf{x} - \mathbf{t}_\alpha\|^2/\sigma_\alpha^2}$$

The necessary conditions for this result to hold, and under which it can be stated for the L_∞ norm are currently under study (Girosi, 1992a).

- It is still not clear whether the spaces of functions considered here, and by Jones (1992), Barron (1991) and Breiman (1992), are sufficiently large to include functions that could be encountered in practical cases. Moreover, the relationship between these different spaces are not well understood, and it would be important to be able to say, given a function, or a set of data, which technique is more appropriate for that particular task.

Acknowledgements

We thank Tomaso Poggio for useful discussions and for a critical reading of the manuscript.

Appendix 8A: The Bochner integral

Let $\Omega \subset R^d$ and let λ be a positive measure on Ω. For function $f : \Omega \to X$ with X a Banach space there are several available notions of measurability and integration (Dunford and Schwartz, 1958; Diestel and Uhl, 1997). In particular, for all (strongly) λ-measurable functions f such that $\int_\Omega \|f\|_X d\lambda < +\infty$ we can define the Bochner integral

$$\int_\Omega^{\mathscr{B}} f \, d\lambda. \tag{24}$$

Clearly, if λ is a Borel measure the continuous functions $f : \Omega \to X$ are (strongly) measurable. One has Lemma 8A.1 (Diestel and Uhl, 1977, p. 48).

Lemma 8A.1 *Let λ be a positive Borel measure on $\Omega \subset R^d$ and $f(\mathbf{t}):\Omega \to X$ with X a Banach space. If f is Bochner integrable with respect to λ then*

$$\frac{1}{\lambda(\Omega)}\int_\Omega^{\mathscr{B}} f(\mathbf{t})\,d\lambda(\mathbf{t}) \in \overline{\mathrm{co}\,f(E)}.$$

If one considers a signed Radon measure λ on Ω one can still define the integral of a measurable function $f:\Omega \to X$ with respect to λ as

$$\int_\Omega^{\mathscr{B}} f(\mathbf{t})\,d\lambda(\mathbf{t}) \equiv \int_\Omega^{\mathscr{B}} f(\mathbf{t})\frac{d\lambda}{d|\lambda|}(\mathbf{t})\,d|\lambda|(\mathbf{t}) \tag{25}$$

where $|\lambda|$ is the total variation of λ and $(d\lambda)/(d|\lambda|)$ denotes the Radon–Nikodym derivative of λ with respect to $|\lambda|$. From Lemma (8A.1) once can easily obtain:

Lemma 8A.2 *Let λ be a signed Radon measure on $\Omega \subset R^d$ and $f(\mathbf{t}):\Omega \to X$ with X a Banach space. If f is λ- measurable and is such that*

$$\int_\Omega \|f\|\,d|\lambda| < +\infty$$

then the Bochner integral of f with respect to λ is well defined, and

$$\frac{1}{|\lambda|(\Omega)}\int_\Omega^{\mathscr{B}} f(\mathbf{t}) \subset \overline{\mathrm{co}\,S}, \tag{26}$$

where

$$S = \{sf(\Omega) \mid s\in R, |s| \leqslant 1\}.$$

In fact, the scalar function $(d\lambda)/(d|\lambda|)(\mathbf{t})$ is measurable, the function $f(\mathbf{t})(d\lambda)/(d|\lambda|)(\mathbf{t})$ is measurable, and, moreover,

$$\int_\Omega \left\| f\frac{d\lambda}{d|\lambda|}\right\| \int_\Omega \|f\|\,d|\lambda| < +\infty.$$

Hence the integral $\int_\Omega^{\mathscr{B}} f\,d\lambda$ is well defined as the right member of (14). Then by Lemma (8A.1) applied to the function $h(\mathbf{t}) = f(\mathbf{t})(d\lambda)/(d|\lambda|)(\mathbf{t})$ one has:

$$\frac{1}{|\lambda|(\Omega)}\int_\Omega^{\mathscr{B}} f(\mathbf{t})\frac{d\lambda}{d|\lambda|}(\mathbf{t})\,d|\lambda|(\mathbf{t}) \in \overline{\mathrm{co}\,h(\Omega)}.$$

On the other hand since $|(d\lambda)/(d|\lambda|)| = 1$ one has

$$\mathrm{co}\,h(\Omega) = \mathrm{co}\,S$$

and (26) follows.

Appendix 8B: Sobolev spaces and the space A

Here we collect a few facts about certain spaces of functions frequently used in the chapter.

Sobolev spaces. For each positive integer s and $1 \leqslant p \leqslant \infty$ one defines the Sobolev space $H^{s,p}(R^d) \equiv H^{s,p}$ as the space of those L_p functions in R^d whose derivatives up to the order s are L_p functions. The space $H^{s,p}$ is a Banach space with the norm

$$\sum_{|\alpha| \leqslant s} \| D^\alpha f \|_{L_p},$$

where α is a multi-index and D^α is the derivative of order α. The space $H^{s,2}$ is a Hilbert space with respect to the scalar product

$$(u, v) = \sum_{|\alpha| \leqslant s} \int_{R^d} D^\alpha u D^\alpha v.$$

One has also the characterization

$$H^{s,2} = \{ u \in L_2 | (1 + |\omega|^2)^{s/2} \tilde{u}(\omega) \in L_2 \}$$

which can be used also to define the Sobolev spaces $H^{s,2}$ for non-integer s. One has the following result, which is a special case of the Sobolev embedding theorem (Stein, 1970):

Theorem 8B.1 *If k is a positive integer and $s > k + d/2$ then*

$$H^{s,2} \subset C^k$$

and there is a constant c_1 such that

$$\max_{|\alpha| \leq k} \sup_{x \in R^d} |D^\alpha f(x)| \leqslant c_1 \| f \|_{H^{s,2}}.$$

The Fourier algebra A. The space A of the tempered distributions whose Fourier transform is a summable function is in current use in Fourier analysis (Herz, 1968; Katznelson, 1968; Larsen, 1971). One has

$$H^{k,2} \subset A \quad \text{for} \quad k > \frac{d}{2}.$$

In fact (Barron, 1991; footnote) one may write

$$\tilde{f} = \frac{1}{(1 + |\omega|^2)^{k/2}} [\tilde{f}(1 + |\omega|^2)^{k/2}]$$

where both factors on the right side belong to L_2 if $k > d/2$. In particular it follows that $C_0^k \subset H^{k,2} \subset A$ for $k > d/2$.

It is also clear that $A \subset C_0$ where C_0 is the completion in the L_∞ norm of C_0^0, i.e. the space of continuous bounded functions that converge to zero for $\| x \| \to \infty$.

References

Barron, A.R. (1991) Universal approximation bounds for superpositions of a sigmoidal function. Technical Report 58, Department of Statistics, University of Illinois at Urbana-Champaign, Champaign, IL.

Barron, A.R. (1991a) Approximation and estimation bounds for artificial neural networks. Technical Report 59, Department of Statistics, University of Illinois at Urbana-Champaign, Champaign, IL.

Barron, A.R. and Barron R.L. (1988) Statistical learning networks: a unifying view, in *Symposium on the Interface: Statistics and Computing Science*, Reston, Virginia.

Bellman, R.E. (1961) *Adaptive Control Processes*. Princeton University Press, Princeton, N.J.

Breiman, L. (1992) Hinging hyperplanes for regression, classification, and function approximation (Submitted for publication).

Cox, D.D. (1984) Multivariate smoothing spline function. *SIAM J. Numer, Anal.*, **21**, 789–813.

DeVore, R.A. (1991) Degree of nonlinear approximation in *Approximation Theory*, **VI** (eds C.K. Chui, L.L. Schumaker and D.J. Ward), Academic Press, New York, pp. 175–201.

Diestel, J. and Uhl, J.J. (1977) Vector Measures, in *Mathematical Surveys*. American Mathematical Society, Providence, Rhode Island.

Dunford, N. and Schwartz, J. (1958) *Linear operators*. Pure and applied mathematics, 7. Interscience Publishers, New York.

Dyn, N. (1991) Interpolation and approximation by radial and related functions, in *Approximation Theory*, **VI** (eds C.K. Chui, L.L. Schumaker, and D.J. Ward), Academic Press, New York, pp. 211–34.

Girosi, F. (1992) On some extensions of radial basis functions and their applications in artificial intelligence. *Computers Math. Applic.* **24**(12), 61–80.

Girosi, F. (1992a) Rates of convergence of approximation by translates and dilates of a given function (In preparation).

Girosi, F. and Anzellotti, G. (1992) Rates of convergence of approximation by translates. A.I. Memo 1288, Artificial Intelligence Laboratory, Massachusetts Institute of Technology.

Haussler, D. (1989) Decision theoretic generalizations of the PAC model for neural net and other learning applications. Technical Report UCSC-CRL-91-02, University of California, Santa Cruz.

Hertz, J.A., Krogh, A. and Palmer R. (1991) *Introduction to the theory of neural computation*. Addison-Wesley, Redwood City, CA.

Herz, C.S. (1968) Lipschitz spaces and Bernstein's theorem on absolutely convergent Fourier transforms. *Indiana Journal of Mathematics*, 283–323.

Jones, L.K. (1992) A simple lemma on greedy approximation in Hilbert space and convergence rates for Projection Pursuit Regression and neural network training. *Annals of Statistics*, **20**(1), 608–13.

Katznelson, Y. (1968) *An introduction to harmonic analysis*. John Wiley and Sons, New York.

Larsen, R. (1971) *An introduction to the theory of multipliers*. Springer-Verlag, New York.

Lorentz, G.G. (1962) Metric entropy, widths, and superposition of functions. *Amer. Math. Monthly*, **69**, 469–85.

Lorentz, G.G. (1986) *Approximation of Functions*. Chelsea Publishing Co., New York.

Micchelli, C.A. (1986) Interpolation of scattered data: distance matrices and conditionally positive definite functions. *Constr. Approx.*, **2**, 11–22.

Moody, J. and Darken, C. (1989) Fast learning in networks of locally-tuned processing units. *Neural Computation*, **1**(2), 281–94.

Pinkus, A. (1986) *N-widths in Approximation Theory*. Springer-Verlag, New York.

Pisier, G. (1981) Remarques sur un resultat non publiè de B. Maurey. In *Seminarie d'analyse fonctionelle 1980–1981* (ed. Centre de Mathematique), Palaiseau.

Poggio, T. and Edelman, S. (1990) A network that learns to recognize 3D objects. *Nature*, **343**, 263–6.

Poggio, T. and Girosi, F. (1990) Networks for approximation and learning. *Proceedings of the IEEE*, **78**(9).

Poggio, T. and Girosi, F. (1990a) Regularization algorithms for learning that are equivalent to multilayer networks. *Science*, **247**, 978–82.

Pollard, D. (1984) *Convergence of stochastic processes*. Springer-Verlag, Berlin.

Powell, M.J.D. (1987) Radial basis functions for multivariable interpolation: a review (eds. J.C. Mason and M.G. Cox) in *Algorithms for Approximation*. Clarendon Press, Oxford.

Powell, M.J.D. (1990) The theory of radial basis functions approximation in 1990. Technical Report NA11, Department of Applied Mathematics and Theoretical Physics, Cambridge.

Sanner, R.M. and Slotine, J.-J.E. (1992) Gaussian networks for direct adaptive control. *IEEE Transactions on Neural Nets*, **3**(6), 837–63.

Stein, E.M. (1970) *Singular integrals and differentiability properties of functions*. Princeton University Press, Princeton, N.J.

Stein, E.M. and Weiss, G. (1971) *Introduction to Fourier analysis on Euclidean spaces*. Princeton mathematical series, **32**. Princeton University Press, Princeton, NJ.

Vapnik, V.N. (1982) *Estimation of Dependences Based on Empirical Data*. Springer-Verlag, Berlin.

Vapnik, V.N. and Chervonenkis A.Ya. (1971) On the uniform convergence of relative frequences of events to their probabilities. *Th. Prob. and its Applications*, **17**(2), 264–80.

Vapnik, V.N. and Chervonenkis, A.Ya. (1981) The necessary and sufficient conditions for the uniform convergence of averages to their expected values. *Teoriya Veroyatnostei i Ee Primeneniya*, **20**(3), 543–64.

Vapnik, V.N. and Chervonenkis, A.Ya (1991) The necessary and sufficient conditions for consistency in the empirical risk minimization method. *Pattern Recognition and Image Analysis*, **1**(3), 283–305.

9

Uniqueness of weights for neural networks

FRANCESCA ALBERTINI*, EDUARDO D. SONTAG* and
VINCENT MAILLOT[†]

*Department of Mathematics, Rutgers University, New Brunswick, NJ 08903, USA
[†]Département de Mathématiques et d'Informatique, Ecole Normale Supérieure, 75005 Paris, France

9.1 Introduction

In most applications dealing with learning and pattern recognition, neural nets are employed as models whose parameters, or 'weights', must be fit to training data. Gradient descent and other algorithms are used to minimize an error functional, which penalizes mismatches between the desired outputs and those that a candidate net – with a fixed architecture and varying weights – produces.

There are many numerical issues that arise naturally when using such a design approach, in particular: (1) the possibility of local minima which are not globally optimal, and (2) the possibility of multiple global minimizers. The first question was dealt with by many different authors (for instance, Brady *et al.*, 1989; Sontag and Sussman, 1989, 1991) and will not reviewed here. Regarding point (2), observe that there are obvious transformations that leave the behavior of a network invariant, such as interchanges of all incoming and outgoing weights between two neurons, that is the relabeling of neurons, or, for odd activation functions, flipping the signs of all incoming and outgoing weights at any given node. Two networks differing in such a manner give the same error on the training data. When there is a net that fits perfectly the data, all nets differing from it by one of the above transformations also attain the global minimum (zero) of the error functional.

A natural question, asked by Hecht–Nielsen (1989) is to what extent are neuron exchanges and sign flips the only transformations that generically

Artificial Neural Networks for Speech and Vision. Edited by Richard J. Mammone.
Published in 1993 by Chapman & Hall, London. ISBN 0 412 54850 X

occur? If, indeed, these are the only possible ones, then essentially all the internal structure is uniquely determined by the external behavior of the network. Moreover, the set on invariant transformations is then finite. (One may want to build additional symmetries into a network to increase representational bias, by imposing artificial conditions such as asking that certain weights be equal, which is helpful in designing networks that focus on invariances in the input patterns; see, for example, Denker *et al.*, 1987. This leads to richer transformation groups, but that is a different issue than that treated here.)

Various conditions can be given which assure that equality of behavior between two networks implies equality up to neuron relabeling and sign flips. An important consequence in those cases in which the conditions apply is that there is no possible dimensionality reduction in the parameter space, contrary to the situation in classical linear identification, where canonical forms have to be introduced to achieve parameter identifiability. (Seen more positively, the parametrizations provided by neural networks have very little redundancy.) In this short expository survey, we sketch various known facts about this issue, including recent results about recurrent nets, and we provide a new and simple proof of a uniqueness result that applies in the single-hidden layer case.

9.2 Single-hidden layer nets

Let $\sigma: \mathbb{R} \to \mathbb{R}$ be any function, and let m, n, p be positive integers. A single-hidden layer net with m inputs, p outputs, n hidden units, and activation function σ is specified by a pair of matrices B, C and a pair of vectors β, c_0, where B and C are (respectively) real matrices of sizes $n \times m$ and $p \times n$, and c_0 are (respectively) real vectors of size m and p. We denote such a net by a 5-tuple

$$\Sigma = \Sigma(B, C, \beta, c_0, \sigma),$$

omitting σ if obvious from the context. In particular, Σ has **no offsets** if $\beta = c_0 = 0$ (the terminology 'biases' or 'thresholds' is sometimes used instead of offsets).

For simplicity, we will assume from now on that $p = 1$; generalizations to the multiple-output case are not hard, but they complicate the notations. Thus, from now on, C is a row n-vector and c_0 is a constant.

Let $\sigma_n: \mathbb{R}^n \to \mathbb{R}^n$ indicate the application of σ to each coordinate of an n-vector:

$$\vec{\sigma}_n(x_1, \ldots, x_n) = (\sigma(x_1), \ldots, \sigma(x_n)).$$

(We will drop the subscript as long as its value is clear from the context.) The **behavior** of Σ is defined to be the map

$$\mathrm{beh}_\Sigma: \mathbb{R}^m \to \mathbb{R}: u \mapsto C\vec{\sigma}(Bu + \beta) + c_0.$$

In other words, the behavior of a network is a composition of the type $f \circ \vec{\sigma} \circ g$, where f and g are affine maps. Given two networks Σ and $\hat{\Sigma}$, we say that they are (input/output) **equivalent**, and denote

$$\Sigma \sim \hat{\Sigma},$$

if $\mathrm{beh}_\Sigma = \mathrm{beh}_{\hat{\Sigma}}$ (equality of functions). The question to be studied, then, is when does $\Sigma \sim \hat{\Sigma}$ imply $\Sigma = \hat{\Sigma}$?

Consider first the case in which σ is the identity. In that case, $\mathrm{beh}_\Sigma = CBu + (C\beta + c_0)$, and we see that any two nets Σ giving rise to the same products CB and $C\beta + c_0$ have the same behavior. Assume that $\Sigma \sim \hat{\Sigma}$. Under suitable minimality conditions (B, $\hat{B}$ of full row rank and C, $\hat{C}$ of full column rank), there must exist an invertible matrix T such that $\hat{C} = CT$, $\hat{B} = T^{-1}B$, and $\hat{c}_0 = C(\beta - T\hat{\beta}) + c_0$. Conversely, for any given Σ, any such T, and any $\hat{\beta}$, the above formulas define a $\hat{\Sigma}$ which is equivalent to the given one. Thus, uniqueness is very far from being satisfied. The same argument applies if σ is any linear map. Observe, as the same fact will be needed later, that without minimality assumptions nothing at all can be concluded; for instance, if B, $\hat{B}$, β, $\hat{\beta}$, c_0, $\hat{c}_0$ all vanish, one has $\Sigma \sim \hat{\Sigma}$ but there need be no relation among C and $\hat{C}$.

One might at first think that nonlinear maps σ provide uniqueness up to finitely many symmetries. But it is easy to see that far more is needed. For instance, such a property cannot hold for polynomials, nor for periodic functions, nor for the exponential function (see below). Thus one is led to the search for easily verifiable conditions on the mapping σ which imply the desired property. We formalize what is needed:

Definition The function σ satisfies the **independence property** (IP) if, for every positive integer l, nonzero real numbers $b_1, \ldots, b_l$, and real numbers $\beta_1, \ldots, \beta_l$ for which the pairs (b_i, β_i), $i = 1, \ldots, l$ satisfy

$$(b_i, \beta_i) \neq \pm (b_j, \beta_j) \quad \forall i \neq j,$$

it must hold that the functions

$$1, \sigma(b_1 x + \beta_1), \ldots, \sigma(b_l x + \beta_l)$$

are linearly independent. The function σ satisfies the **weak** independence property (WIP) if the above linear independence property is only required to hold for all pairs with $\beta_i = 0$, $i = 1, \ldots, l$. $\qquad \square$

Observe that the independence condition is:

$$c_0 + \sum_{i=1}^{l} c_i \sigma(b_i x + \beta_i) = 0 \quad \forall x \in \mathbb{R} \Rightarrow c_0 = c_1 = \cdots = c_l = 0.$$

This is the property needed for the desired uniqueness results, as we discuss next.

Recall that some sort of nontriviality hypothesis is needed. Let $\Sigma(B, C, \beta, c_0, \sigma)$ be given, and denote by B_i the transpose of the ith row of the matrix B and by c_i and β_i the ith entries of C and β, respectively. With these notations, $\text{beh}_\Sigma(u) = c_0 + \sum_{i=1}^n c_i \sigma(B_i u + \beta_i)$. As in Sussmann (1992), we say that Σ is **irreducible** if the following properties hold:

1. $c_i \neq 0$ for each $i = 1, \ldots, n$.
2. $B_i \neq 0$ for each $i = 1, \ldots, n$.
3. $(B_i, \beta_i) \neq \pm (B_j, \beta_j)$ for all $i \neq j$.

Given $\Sigma(B, C, \beta, c_0, \sigma)$, a **sign-flip** operation consists of simultaneously reversing the signs of c_i, B_i and β_i, for some i. A **node-permutation** consists of interchanging (c_j, B_j, β_j) with (c_j, B_j, β_j), for some i, j. Given two nets Σ and $\hat{\Sigma}$, we say that they are **equivalent** if $n = \hat{n}$ and (B, C, β, c_0) can be transformed into $(\hat{B}, \hat{C}, \hat{\beta}, \hat{c}_0)$ by means of a finite number of sign-flips and node-permutations. Of course, equivalent nets have the same behavior (since σ has been assumed to be odd). The next simple remark establishes the connection between the concepts just introduced. The proof is adapted from Sussmann (1992). We assume for simplicity that the function σ is odd, but it is easy to generalize this in various ways.

Lemma 9.1 *Let σ be odd and satisfy property IP. Assume that Σ and $\hat{\Sigma}$ are both irreducible, and $\Sigma \sim \hat{\Sigma}$. Then, Σ and $\hat{\Sigma}$ are equivalent. If σ only satisfies WIP, the same statement is true for nets with no offsets.*

Proof: Assume that Σ and $\hat{\Sigma}$ are as in the statement, so

$$C \vec{\sigma}(Bu + \beta) + c_0 = \hat{C} \vec{\sigma}(\hat{B}u + \hat{\beta}) + \hat{c}_0 \quad \text{for all } u \in \mathbb{R}^m. \tag{1}$$

Pick any fixed vector $\bar{u} \in \mathbb{R}^m$ such that:

- $B_i \bar{u} \neq 0$ and $\hat{B}_i \bar{u} \neq 0$ for all $i = 1, \ldots, n$,
- $(B_i \bar{u}, \beta_i) \neq \pm (B_j \bar{u}, \beta_j)$ and $(\hat{B}_i \bar{u}, \hat{\beta}_i) \neq \pm (\hat{B}_j \bar{u}, \hat{\beta}_j)$ for all $i \neq j$.

Such vectors exist, because we only need to avoid the union of the hyperplanes in $\mathbb{R}^m$ determined by each of the equations: $B_i u = 0$, $(B_i + B_j)u = 0$ for each i, j for which $\beta_i = -\beta_j$, $(B_i - B_j)u = 0$ for each i, j for which $\beta_i = \beta_j$, and the corresponding ones for $\hat{\Sigma}$.

In particular, we may consider elements $u \in \mathbb{R}^m$ of the form $u = \bar{u}x$ in equation (1). With the notations $b_i = B_i \bar{u}$ and $\hat{b}_i = \hat{B}_i \bar{u}$, we obtain the identity

$$(c_0 - \hat{c}_0) + \sum_{i=1}^n c_i \sigma(b_i x + \beta_i) - \sum_{i=2}^n \hat{c}_i \sigma(\hat{b}_i x + \hat{\beta}_i) = 0 \quad \text{for all } x \in \mathscr{R}.$$

If the functions $1, b_i x + \beta_i, \hat{b}_i x + \hat{\beta}_i, i = 1, \ldots, n$ are linearly independent, then all $c_i = 0$, contradicting irreducibility. Since property IP holds (or WIP in the case of nets with no offsets, for which all $\beta_i = \hat{\beta}_i = 0$), the only way in which linear independence can fail is if some b_i or $\hat{b}_i$ vanishes, which cannot be the case because of the choice of $\bar{u}$, or – since also by construction $(b_i, \beta_i) \neq \pm (b_j, \beta_j)$ and similarly for the $(\hat{b}_i, \hat{\beta}_i)$'s – if $(b_i, \beta_i) = \pm(\hat{b}_j, \hat{\beta}_j)$ for some i, j. Thus, using odd σ, we may relabel indices, apply if necessary a sign-flip and collect these two terms, resulting in an equation:

$$(c_0 - \hat{c}_0) + (c_1 - \varepsilon\hat{c}_1)\sigma(b_1 x + \beta_1) + \sum_{i=2}^{n} c_i\sigma(b_i x + \beta_i) - \sum_{i=2}^{n} \hat{c}_i\sigma(\hat{b}_i x + \hat{\beta}_i) = 0$$

with $\varepsilon = \pm 1$, where now no pair (b_i, β_i) or $(\hat{b}_i, \hat{\beta}_i)$ equals $\pm(b_1, \beta_1)$. We may iterate this argument until all terms have been collected, which leads to an equation such as

$$(c_0 - \hat{c}_0) + \sum_{i=1}^{n} (c_i - \varepsilon_i\hat{c}_i)\sigma(b_i x + \beta_i) = 0.$$

Once more using property IP, this implies that $c_0 = \hat{c}_0$ and $c_i = \varepsilon_i\hat{c}_i$ for all i, completing the proof. $\qquad\square$

Remark For infinitely differentiable σ, there is a slightly different argument that can be used in the above proof, instead of the choice of a direction $\bar{u}$, but which makes the stronger assumption that all derivatives of σ satisfy IP or WIP. This argument was given by Diaconis and Shahshahani (1984), which dealt with projection-pursuit algorithms in statistics, an area closely related to neural networks; we sketch the idea next. Again, we need to reduce an equation such as (1) to the scalar case. To do this, we apply a sequence of partial derivation operators $w_k \cdot \nabla$, where each w_k is chosen so as to kill one direction at a time among the vectors B_i, while the rest of the directions provide a nonzero inner product. After this procedure, there results a scalar linear dependence involving a derivative of σ instead of σ itself. $\qquad\square$

Our goal is then to explore easily verifiable and weak conditions for IP and WIP to hold.

9.2.1 The WIP property

Characterizing WIP is especially easy, and very classical: for odd analytic functions σ, property WIP holds if and only if σ is not a polynomial.

Lemma 9.2 If σ is a polynomial, WIP does not hold. Conversely, if σ is odd and infinitely differentiable, and if there are an infinite number of nonzero derivatives $q_k = \sigma^{(k)}(0)$, then σ satisfies property IP.

Proof: If σ is a polynomial of degree r, the functions $\sigma(b_i x)$ are all polynomials of degree r, and hence are linearly dependent, for any choice of distinct and positive numbers b_i, $i = 1, \ldots, r + 2$. For the converse, we need to see that $c_0 + \sum_{i=1}^{l} c_i\sigma(b_i x) \equiv 0$ implies that $c_0 = c_1 = \cdots = c_l = 0$, assuming that all the

b_i are nonzero and have different absolute values. Since σ is odd, $\sigma(0) = 0$, so $c_0 = 0$. Furthermore, we may assume after sign-flips if necessary, that all $b_i > 0$. Taking derivatives of various orders, and evaluating at $x = 0$, one obtains $q_k \sum_{i=1}^{l} c_i b_i^k = 0$ for all k. Let $C = (c_1, \ldots, c_l)$. Picking l nonzero derivatives q_{k_j}, $j = 1, \ldots, l$, it results that $CM = 0$, where M is the generalized Vandermonde matrix with entries $b_i^{k_j}$. It is a classical fact that such a matrix is nonsingular (Descartes' rule of signs), so $C = 0$ as desired.   □

Thus the conditions in Lemma 9.1 are satisfied for many interesting nonlinearities, for the case of nets with no offset. Nets with no offsets appear naturally in signal processing and control applications, as there it is often the case that one requires that the zero input signal causes no effect, corresponding to equilibrium initial states for a controller or filter.

Even stronger results can be proved if constraints are imposed on the matrix B. For instance, one may require that the successive rows of B have the form $(d_1, \ldots, d_k, 0, \ldots, 0)$, $(0, d_1, \ldots, d_k, 0, \ldots, 0)$, $(0, 0, d_1, \ldots, d_k, 0, \ldots, 0), \ldots$. Such a constraint is natural if one is dealing with a composition

$$f \circ \sigma \circ g,$$

where f, g are finite impulse response filters, and the inputs u are thought of as time signals. (The d_i's are the coefficients of the filter g; the coefficients defining f are the entries of C.) If any d_i is nonzero, then all rows of B are nonzero, and it holds automatically that $B_i \neq \pm B_j$ for all $i \neq j$; essentially, due to the regularity of B, one is dealing here with a case closer to that of one neuron $(n = 1)$ than general n. The uniqueness result in this context is essentially what was proved by Boyd and Chua (1983). (Actually, they dealt with more general time-invariant linear systems than FIR filters, as well as a continuous-time version, and later (1985) the authors generalized their work to other structures containing one scalar nonlinearity. That work was in turn motivated by the older work by Smith and Rugh, 1974, and Harper and Rugh, 1976, which dealt with interconnections of linear systems and memory free non-linearities.)

9.2.2 The IP property

It appears to be harder to obtain elegant characterization of the stronger property IP. For obvious examples of functions not satisfying IP, take $\sigma(x) = e^x$, any periodic function, or any polynomial. One case is relatively simple: the one concerning dependence equations in which all $b_i = 1$ in the definition of the property IP. Now the only condition left is that the elements β_i must be all distinct. Given an equation

$$c_0 + \sum_{i=1}^{l} c_i \sigma(x + \beta_i) \equiv 0, \tag{2}$$

taking Fourier transforms results in the desired conclusion that all c_i must vanish, as long as σ is not identically zero (a.e.). Of course, many functions do not admit Fourier transforms, but observe that any linear combination of functions satisfying a nontrivial identity as above again satisfies a similar identity (with larger l). Thus, for instance, if there is a nonzero linear combination of translates of σ which is integrable, then σ itself cannot satisfy such an equation. An example is any 'squashing' function (σ is measurable, nondecreasing and bounded), in which case $\sigma(x + 1) - \sigma(x - 1)$ is in L^1.

The most interesting case, for neural network applications, is $\sigma(x) = \tanh(x)$, or equivalently after a linear transformation, the standard sigmoid $1/(1 + e^{-x})$. (It is more convenient to work with $\tanh(x)$, as it is odd.) For this function σ, consider first again the case when $b_i = 1$ and equation (2). From this equation, with a change of variables $z = e^{-2x}$, we obtain

$$\hat{c}_0 + \sum_{i=1}^{l} \frac{\hat{c}_i}{q_i + z} \equiv 0, \tag{3}$$

where $\hat{c}_0 = c_0 - \sum c_i$, $\hat{c}_i = 2c_i q_i$, and $q_i = e^{2\beta i}$. Taking the limit as $z \to +\infty$, we have that $\hat{c}_0 = 0$. We may consider the identity (3) over the complexes (analytic continuation), and take residues at the various $z = -q_i$; from here one concludes the desired linear independence.

In place of the residue argument, we may instead use a formula due to Cauchy, which shows the stronger fact that from the values of the right-hand side of (3) at any l points $z_1, \ldots, z_l$ one can retrieve the c_i's uniquely: let M be the matrix with entries $M_{ij} = 1/(q_i + z_j)$, then (Davis, 1963, Section 11.3):

$$\det M = \frac{\prod_{i>j}(z_i - z_j)(q_i - q_j)}{\prod_{i,j}(q_i + z_j)} \neq 0.$$

Thus $(\hat{c}_1, \ldots, \hat{c}_l)M = 0$ once more implies that all $\hat{c}_i = 0$.

The reduction of questions about tanh-nets to questions about rational functions, by means of the transformation $z = e^{-2x}$, formed the basis of the approach taken by Sontag and Sussmann (1989) to study local minima of gradient descent (see also the recent work of Williamson and Helmke, 1992, which carries this much further into deeper questions of approximation theory). A similar reduction can be done whenever the b_i are rational numbers, but the above proof works only under the assumption that all the b_i are equal. However, for the particular function $\sigma = \tanh$, the full property IP, with no further restrictions on the b_i's, was established by Sussmann (1992) using a very different argument. We now wish to show that a residue type of argument works in general, and in the process we extend considerably the class of functions to which it applies.

Theorem 9.3 *Assume that σ is a real-analytic function, and it extends to an analytic function $\sigma: \mathbb{C} \to \mathbb{C}$ defined on a subset $D \subseteq \mathbb{C}$ of the form:*

$$D = \frac{\{z \,\|\, \mathrm{Im}\, z \,\| \leq \lambda\}}{\{z_0, \bar{z}_0\}}$$

for some $\lambda > 0$, where $\operatorname{Im} z_0 = \lambda$ and z_0 and $\bar{z}_0$ are singularities, i.e. there is a sequence $z_n \to z_0$ so that $|\sigma(z_n)| \to \infty$, and similarly for $\bar{z}_0$. Then, σ satisfies property IP.

Proof: Assume that

$$c_0 + c_1\sigma(b_1 z + \beta_1) + \cdots + c_r\sigma(b_r z + \beta_r) \equiv 0 \tag{4}$$

is an equation of linear dependence, with r as small as possible. Thus $c_i \neq 0$ for all $i = 1, \ldots, r$. Without loss of generality, we may assume that $|b_1| \geqslant b_i$ for all $i > 1$. After a change of variables $b_1 z + \beta_1 \to z$, we have that $(b_1, \beta_1) = (1, 0)$, $(b_i, \beta_i) \neq \pm(1, 0)$ for all $i \geqslant 2$, and $b_i \leqslant 1$ for all i. Thus, by the assumptions on singularities, $b_i z_0 + \beta_i$ is not a singularity of σ, for all $i \geqslant 2$. Dividing the expression in (4) by $\sigma(z)$ and taking limits as $z \to z_0$, we obtain $c_1 = 0$, a contradiction. $\qquad\square$

A typical example of a σ satisfying the hypotheses of the theorem is that of a σ having a meromorphic extension which has a unique pole of minimal positive real part. Most rational functions satisfy this, as well as the main example in neural networks research, $\sigma(x) = \tanh(x)$. In this case, the set of poles is the set $\{(k\pi/2)i, \ k \text{ odd}\}$ and one can take $z_0 = (\pi/2)i$. Another interesting example for neural nets is that of $\arctan(x)$. In this case, integrating $1/(1 + z^2)$, one can find a branch defined on the complement of $\{\operatorname{Re} z = 0, |\operatorname{Im} z| \geqslant 1\}$.

Remark C. Fefferman (personal communication) has recently been able to extend this argument to 'multiple hidden layer' nets, for the special case of the nonlinearity $\tanh(x)$.

9.3 Recurrent nets

A **recurrent net** with m inputs, p outputs, dimension n, and activation function σ is specified by a triple of matrices A, B, C and a pair of vectors β, c_0, where A, B and C are (respectively) real matrices of sizes $n \times n$, $n \times m$ and $p \times n$, and β and c_0 are (respectively) real vectors of size m and p. We use the notation.

$$\Sigma = \Sigma(A, B, C, \beta, c_0, \sigma),$$

again omitting σ if obvious from the context. Because this is natural in control applications, and since the only results to be described are for that case, we assume that Σ has **no offsets** (i.e. $\beta = c_0 = 0$), and write just $\Sigma(A, B, C, \sigma)$.

We will interpret the above data (A, B, C) as defining a controlled and observed dynamical system evolving in $\mathbb{R}^n$ (in the standard sense of control theory; see, for example, Sontag, 1990) by means of a differential equation

$$\dot{x} = \vec{\sigma}(Ax + Bu), \quad y = Cx \tag{5}$$

in continuous-time (dot indicates time derivative), or a difference equation

$$x^+ = \vec{\sigma}(Ax + Bu), \quad y = Cx \tag{6}$$

in discrete-time ('+' indicates a unit time shift). Other systems models are possible; for instance, 'Hopfield nets' have dynamics of the form

$$\dot{x} = -Dx + \vec{\sigma}(Ax + Bu) \tag{7}$$

(with D a diagonal matrix and often A symmetric); results analogous to those to be described can be obtained for these more general models as well.

Depending on the interpretation (5) or (6), one defines an appropriate behavior beh_Σ, mapping suitable spaces of input functions into spaces of output functions, again in the standard sense of control theory (Sontag, 1990). For instance, in continuous time, one proceeds as follows: for any measurable essentially bounded $u(\cdot):[0, T] \to \mathbb{R}^m$, we denote by $\phi(t, \xi, u)$ the solution at time t of (5) with initial state $x(0) = \xi$; this is defined at least on a small enough interval $[0, \varepsilon)$, $\varepsilon > 0$. (The maps σ of interest in neural network theory tend to be mostly globally Lipschitz, in which case $\varepsilon = T$). For each input, we let $\text{beh}_\Sigma(u)$ be the output function corresponding to the initial state $x(0) = 0$, that is,

$$\text{beh}_\Sigma(u)(t) := C(\phi(t, 0, u)),$$

defined at least on some interval $[0, \varepsilon)$. Given recurrent nets Σ and $\hat{\Sigma}$ (necessarily with the same numbers of input and output channels, i.e. with $p = \hat{p}$ and $m = \hat{m}$), we again say that Σ and $\hat{\Sigma}$ are equivalent (in discrete or continuous time, depending on the context) if it holds that $\text{beh}_\Sigma = \text{beh}_{\hat{\Sigma}}$; as before, we denote $\Sigma \sim \hat{\Sigma}$. (To be more precise, in continuous-time, we require that for each u the domains of definitions of $\text{beh}_\Sigma(u)$ and $\text{beh}_{\hat{\Sigma}}(u)$ coincide, and their values be equal for all t in the common domain.)

Next we summarize the main results from Albertini and Sontag (1992a, b) on weight uniqueness for recurrent networks.

9.3.1 Continuous-time

We assume from now on that σ is infinitely differentiable, and that it satisfies the following assumptions:

$$\sigma(0) = 0, \quad \sigma'(0) \neq 0, \quad \sigma''(0) = 0, \quad \sigma^{(q)}(0) \neq 0 \quad \text{for some } q > 2. \tag{$*$}$$

We let $\mathscr{S}(n, m, p)$ denote the set of all recurrent nets $\Sigma(A, B, C, \sigma)$ with fixed n, m, p. Two nets Σ and $\hat{\Sigma}$ in $S(n, m, p)$ are **sign-permutation equivalent** if there exists a nonsingular matrix T such that

$$T^{-1}AT = \hat{A}, \quad T^{-1}B = \hat{B}, \quad CT = \hat{C}$$

and T has the special form

$$T = PD,$$

where P is a permutation matrix and $D = \operatorname{diag}(\lambda_1, \ldots, \lambda_n)$, with each $\lambda_i = \pm 1$. The nets Σ and $\hat{\Sigma}$ are just **permutation equivalent** if the above holds with $D = I$, i.e. T is a permutation matrix.

Let $\mathbf{B}^{n,m}$ be the class of $n \times m$ real matrices B for which

1. $b_{i,j} \neq 0$ for all i, j,
2. for each $i = j$, there exists some k such that $|b_{i,k}| \neq |b_{j,k}|$.

For any choice of positive integers n, m, p, we denote by $S^c_{n,m,p}$ the set of all triples of matrices (A, B, C), $A \in R^{n \times n}$, $B \in R^{n \times m}$, $C \in R^{p \times n}$ which are 'canonical' (observable and controllable, as in Sontag, 1990, section 5.5). This is a generic set of triples, in the sense that the entries of the ones that do not satisfy the property are zeroes of certain nontrivial multivariable polynomials.

Finally, we let

$$\mathscr{S}(n, m, p) = \{\Sigma(A, B, C, \sigma) | B \in \mathbf{B}^{n,m} \text{ and } (A, B, C) \in S^c_{n,m,p}\}.$$

Then (in Albertini and Sontag, 1992a) the following result was proved:

Theorem 9.4 *Assume that σ is odd and satisfies property* (∗). *For any two $\Sigma, \hat{\Sigma}$, $\Sigma \sim \hat{\Sigma}$ if and only if Σ and $\hat{\Sigma}$ are sign-permutation equivalent.*

If we simply modify the definition of $\mathbf{B}^{n,m}$ to consist now of matrices for which (1) holds and (2) is replaced by

2′. for each $i \neq j$, there exists some k such that $b_{i,k} \neq b_{j,k}$,

and defining $\mathscr{S}$ as above, but with this new $\mathbf{B}^{n,m}$, the above reference also proved:

Theorem 9.5 *Assume that σ is not odd and satisfies property* (∗). *For any two $\Sigma, \hat{\Sigma}, \Sigma \sim \hat{\Sigma}$ if and only if Σ and $\hat{\Sigma}$ are permutation equivalent.*

Albertini and Sontag (1992a) explain how in fact the assumption that both nets have the same activation function σ is basically redundant, as the equality of activation functions can be derived from the equality of behavior. Many more results are given there, for other continuous-time models.

9.3.2 Discrete-time

Similar results hold for discrete-time recurrent nets. These are dealt with in detail by Albertini and Sontag (1992a). Proofs are technically different than in the continuous case, but the results are analogous. More precisely, we assume that σ not only satisfies (∗), but also the following extra condition, which appeared above in the context of single-hidden layer nets with no offsets: $\sigma^{(k)}(0) \neq 0$ for infinitely many integers k. Then the same theorems as before hold, provided that we redefine

$$\hat{S}(n, m, p) = \{(A, B, C) | (A, B, C) \in \mathscr{S}(n, m, p), c_{ij} \neq 0 \; \forall i, j\}.$$

Acknowledgements

This research was supported in part by US Air Force Grant AFOSR-91-0343. F. Albertini is currently also at Universita' di Padova, Dipartimento di Matematica, 35100 Padova, Italy.

References

Albertini, F. and Sontag, E.D. (1992a) For neural networks, function determines form. *Neural Networks* (to appear). (Summary in For neural networks, function determines form. *Proc. IEEE Conf. Decision and Control, Tucson, December 1992.* IEEE Publications, pp. 26–31.

Albertini, F. and Sontag, E.D. (1992b) Identifiability of discrete-time neural networks. Preprint.

Boyd, S. and Chua, L.O. (1983) Uniquences of a basic nonlinear structure. *IEEE Trans. Circuits and Systems*, **30**, 648–51.

Boyd, S. and Chua, L.O. (1985) Uniqueness of circuits and systems containing one nonlinearity. *IEEE Trans. Automatic Control*, **30**, 674–81.

Brady, M., Raghavan, R. and Slawny, J. (1989) Backpropagation fails to separate where perceptrons succeed. *IEEE Trans. Circuits and Systems*, **36**, 665–74.

Davis, P.J. (1963) *Interpolation and Approximation.* Blaisdell, New York.

Denker, J., Schwartz, D., Wittner, B., Solla, S.A., Howard, R., Jackel, L. and Hopfield, J. (1987) Automatic learning, rule extraction and generalization. *Complex Systems*, **1**, 877–922.

Diaconis, P. and Shahshahani, M. (1984) On nonlinear functions of linear combinations. *SIAM J. Sci. Stat. Comput.*, **5**, 175–91.

Harper, T.R. and Rugh, W.J. (1976) Structural features of factorable Volterra systems. *IEEE Trans. Automatic Control*, **21**, 822–32.

Hecht-Nielsen, R. (1989) Theory of the backpropagation neural network. *Proceedings Int. Joint Conf. on Neural Networks*, Washington, DC, IEEE Publications, NY, pp. 593–605.

Smith, W.W. and Rugh, W.J. (1974) On the structure of a class of nonlinear systems. *IEEE Trans. Automatic Control*, **19**, 701–6.

Sontag, E.D. (1990) *Mathematical Control Theory: Deterministic Finite Dimensional Systems*, Springer, New York.

Sontag, E.D. and Sussmann, H.J. (1989) Backpropagation can give rise to spurious local minima even for networks without hidden layers. *Complex Systems*, **3**, 91–106.

Sontag, E.D. and Sussmann, H.J. (1991) Backpropagation separates where perceptions do. *Neural Networks*, **4**, 243–9.

Sussmann, H.J. (1992) Uniqueness of the weights for minimal feedforward nets with a given input-output map. *Neural Networks*, **5**, 589–93.

Williamson, R.C. and Helmke, U. (1992) Existence and uniqueness results for neural network approximations. Preprint.

10

When networks disagree: Ensemble methods for hybrid neural networks

MICHAEL P. PERRONE and LEON N. COOPER
Physics Department, Neuroscience Department, Institute for Brain and Neural Systems, Box 1843, Brown University, Providence, RI 02912, USA

10.1 Introduction

Hybrid or multi-neural network systems have frequently been employed to improve results in classification and regression problems (Cooper, 1991; Reilly *et al.*, 1988, 1987; Scofield *et al.*, 1991; Baxt, 1992; Bridle and Cox, 1991; Buntine and Weigend, 1992; Hansen and Salamon, 1990; Intrator *et al.*, 1992; Jacobs *et al.*, 1991; Lincoln and Skrzypek, 1990; Neal, 1992a,b; Pearlmutter and Rosenfeld, 1991; Wolpert, 1990; Xu *et al.*, 1992, 1990). Among the key issues are how to design the architecture of the networks; how the results of the various networks should be combined to give the best estimate of the optimal result; and how to make best use of a limited data set. In what follows, we address the issues of optimal combination and efficient data usage in the framework of ensemble averaging.

In this chapter we are concerned with using the information contained in a set of regression estimates of a function to construct a better estimate. The statistical resampling techniques of jackknifing, bootstrapping and cross-validation have proven useful for generating improved regression estimates through bias reduction (Efron, 1982; Miller, 1974; Stone, 1974; Gray and Schucany, 1972; Härdle, 1990; Wahba, 1990, for review). We show that these ideas can be fruitfully extended to neural networks by using the ensemble methods presented. The basic idea behind these resampling techniques is to improve one's estimate of a given statistic θ, by combining multiple estimates

Artificial Neural Networks for Speech and Vision. Edited by Richard J. Mammone. Published in 1993 by Chapman & Hall, London. ISBN 0 412 54850 X

of θ generated by subsampling or resampling of a finite data set. The jackknife method involves removing a single data point from a data set, constructing an estimate of θ with the remaining data, testing the estimate on the removed data point and repeating for every data point in the set. One can then, for example, generate an estimate of θ's variance using the results from the estimate on all of the removed data points. This method has been generalized to include removing subsets of points. The bootstrap method involves generating new data sets from one original data set by sampling randomly with replacement. These new data sets can then be used to generate multiple estimates for θ. In cross-validation, the original data is divided into two sets: one which is used to generate the estimate of θ, and the other which is used to test this estimate. Cross-validation is widely used neural network training to avoid over-fitting. The jackknife and bootstrapping methods are not commonly used in neural network training due to the large computational overhead.

These resampling techniques can be used to generate multiple distinct networks from a single training set. For example, resampling in neural net training frequently takes the form of repeated on-line stochastic gradient descent of randomly initialized nets. However, unlike the combination process in parametric estimation, which usually takes the form of a simple average in parameter space, the parameters in a neural network take the form of neuronal weights which generally have many different local minima. Therefore, we cannot simply average the weights of a population of neural networks and expect to improve network performance. Because of this, one typically generates a large population of resampled nets, chooses the one with the best performance and discards the rest. This process is very inefficient. Here we present ensemble methods which avoid this inefficiency, and avoid the local minima problem by averaging in functional space not parameter space. In addition, we show that the ensemble methods actually benefit from the existence of local minima, and that with the ensemble framework, the statistical resampling techniques have very natural extensions. All of these aspects combined provide a general theoretical framework for network averaging, which in practice generates significant improvement on real-world problems.

10.2 Basic Ensemble Method

In this section we present the Basic Ensemble Method (BEM), which combines a population of regression estimates to estimate a function $f(x)$ defined by $f(x) = E[y|x]$.

Suppose that that we have two finite data sets whose elements are all independent and identically distributed random variables: a training data set $\mathcal{A} = \{(x_m, y_m)\}$ and a cross-validatory data set $\mathcal{CV} = \{(x_l, y_l)\}$. Further, suppose that we have used $\mathcal{A}$ to generate a set of functions, $\mathcal{F} = f_i(x)$, each element of which approximates $f(x)$.[1] We would like to find the best approximation to $f(x)$ using $\mathcal{F}$.

One common choice is to use the **naive estimator**, $f_{\text{naive}}(x)$, which minimizes the mean square error relative to $f(x)$,[2]

$$\text{MSE}[f_i] = E_{\mathscr{C}\mathscr{V}}[(y_m - f_i(x_m))^2],$$

thus

$$f_{\text{naive}}(x) = \arg\min_i \{\text{MSE}[f_i]\}.$$

This choice is unsatisfactory for two reasons: First, in selecting only one network from the population of networks represented by $\mathcal{F}$, we are discarding useful information that is stored in the discarded networks; second, since the $\mathscr{C}\mathscr{V}$ data set is random, there is a certain probability that some other network from the population will perform better than the naive estimate on some other previously unseen data set sampled from the same distribution. A more reliable estimate of the performance on previously unseen data is the average of the performances over the population $\mathcal{F}$. Below, we will see how we can avoid both of these problems by using the BEM estimator, $f_{\text{BEM}}(x)$, and thereby generate an improved regression estimate.

Define the **misfit** of function $f_i(x)$, the deviation from the true solution, as $m_i(x) \equiv f(x) - f_i(x)$. The mean square error can now be written in terms of $m_i(x)$ as

$$\text{MSE}[f_i] = E[m_i^2].$$

The average mean square error is therefore

$$\overline{\text{MSE}} = \frac{1}{N} \sum_{i=1}^{i=N} E[m_i^2].$$

Define the BEM regression function $f_{\text{BEM}}(x)$, as

$$f_{\text{BEM}}(x) \equiv \frac{1}{N} \sum_{i=1}^{i=N} f_i(x) = f(x) - \frac{1}{N} \sum_{i=1}^{i=N} m_i(x).$$

If we now assume that the $m_i(x)$ are mutually independent with zero mean,[3]

---

[1] For our purposes, it does not matter how $\mathcal{F}$ was generated. In practice we will use a set of backpropagation networks trained on the $\mathscr{A}$ data set, but started with different random weight configurations. This replication procedure is standard practice when trying to optimize neural networks.

[2] Here, and in all of what follows, the expected value is taken over the cross-validatory set $\mathscr{C}\mathscr{V}$.

[3] We relax these assumption in section 10.4, where we present the Generalized Ensemble Method.

we can calculate the mean square error of $f_{BEM}(x)$ as

$$MSE[f_{BEM}] = E\left[\left(\frac{1}{N}\sum_{i=1}^{i=N} m_i\right)^2\right]$$

$$= \frac{1}{N^2}E\left[\sum_{i=1}^{i=N} m_i^2\right] + \frac{1}{N^2}E\left[\sum_{i \neq j} m_i m_j\right]$$

$$= \frac{1}{N^2}E\left[\sum_{i=1}^{i=N} m_i^2\right] + \frac{1}{N^2}\sum_{i \neq j} E[m_i]E[m_j]$$

$$= \frac{1}{N^2}E\left[\sum_{i=1}^{i=N} m_i^2\right], \tag{1}$$

which implies that

$$MSE[f_{BEM}] = \frac{1}{N}\overline{MSE}. \tag{2}$$

This is a powerful result because it tells us that by averaging regression estimates, we can reduce our mean square error by a factor of N when compared to the population performance. By increasing the population size, we can in principle make the estimation error arbitrarily small! In practice, however, as N gets large our assumptions on the misfits, $m_i(x)$, eventually break down (see section 10.5).

Consider the individual elements of the population $\mathscr{F}$. These estimators will more or less follow the true regression function. If we think of the misfits functions as random noise functions added to the true regression function and these noise functions are uncorrelated with zero mean, then the averaging of the individual estimates is like averaging over the noise. In this sense, the ensemble method is smoothing in functional space and can be thought of as a regularizer with a smoothness assumption on the true regression function.

An additional benefit of the ensemble method's ability to combine multiple regression estimates is that the regression estimates can come from many different sources. This fact allows for great flexibility in the application of the ensemble method. For example, the networks can have different architectures or be trained by different training algorithms or be trained on different data sets. This last option – training on different data sets – has important ramifications. One standard method for avoiding over-fitting during training is to use a cross-validatory hold-out set.[4] The problem is that since the network is never trained on the hold-out data the network may be missing valuable information about the distribution of the data particularly if the total data set is small. This will always be the case for a single network using a cross-

---

[4] The cross-validatory hold-out set is a subset of the total data available to us and is used to determine when to stop training. The hold-out data is not used to train.

validatory stopping rule. However, this is not a problem for the ensemble estimator. When constructing our population $\mathscr{F}$, we can train each network on the entire training set and let the smoothing property of the ensemble process remove any over-fitting or we can train each network in the population with a different split of training and hold-out data. In this way, the population as a whole will see the entire data set while each network has avoided over-fitting by using a cross-validatory stopping rule. Thus the ensemble estimator will see the entire data set while the naive estimator will not. In general, with this framework we can now easily extend the statistical jackknife, bootstrap and cross-validation techniques (Efron, 1982; Miller, 1974; Stone, 1974) to find better regression functions.

10.3 Intuitive illustrations

In this section, we present two toy examples which illustrate the averaging principle which is at the heart of the ensemble methods presented in this chapter.

For our first example, consider the classification problem depicted in Figure 10.1. Regions A and B represent the training data for two distinct classes which are Gaussianly distributed. If we train a perceptron on this data, we find that hyperplanes, 1, 2, and 3 all give perfect classification performance for the training data; however, only hyperplane 2 will give optimal generalization performance. Thus, if we had to choose a naive estimator from this population of three perceptrons, we would be more likely than not to choose a hyperplane with poor generalization performance. For this problem, it is clear that the BEM estimator (i.e. averaging over the three hyperplanes) is more reliable.

For our second example, suppose that we want to approximate the Gaussian distribution shown in Figure 10.2a and we are given two estimates shown in Figure 10.2b. If we must choose either one or the other of these estimates we will incur a certain mean square error; however, if we average these two functional estimates we can dramatically reduce the mean square error. In Figure10.2c, we represent the ensemble average of the two estimates

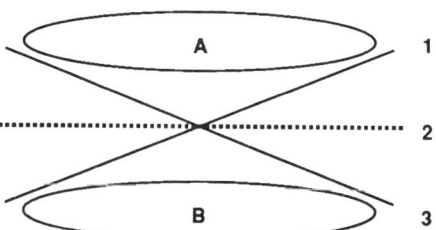

Figure 10.1 *Toy classification problem. Hyperplanes 1 and 3 solve the classification problem for the training data, but hyperplane 2 is the optimal solution. Hyperplane 2 is the average of hyperplanes 1 and 3.*

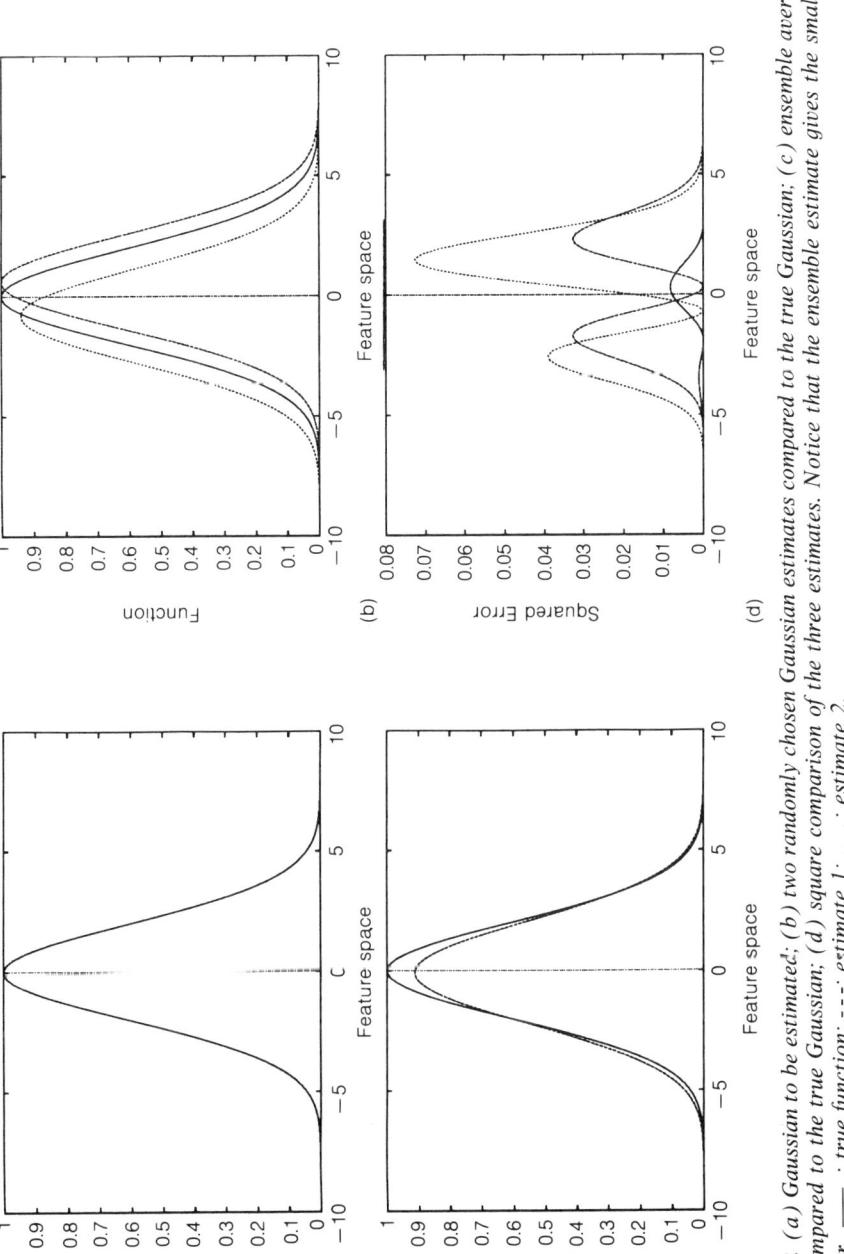

Figure 10.2 (a) Gaussian to be estimated; (b) two randomly chosen Gaussian estimates compared to the true Gaussian; (c) ensemble average estimate compared to the true Gaussian; (d) square comparison of the three estimates. Notice that the ensemble estimate gives the smallest square error. ———— : true function; – – – : estimate 1; ..... : estimate 2.

from Figure 10.2b. Comparing Figure 10.2b to Figure 10.2c, it is clear that the ensemble estimate is much better than either of the individual estimates. In Figure 10.2d, we compare the square error of each of the estimates.

We can push this simple example a little further to demonstrate a weakness of the Basic Ensemble Method and the need for a more general approach. Suppose that $x \sim \mathcal{N}(0, \sigma^2)$ and we are given $\mathscr{D} \equiv \{x_i\}_{i=1}^{i=N}$ and σ. We can estimate the true Gaussian by estimating its mean with

$$\mu \equiv \frac{1}{N} \sum_{j=1}^{j=N} x_j,$$

or we can use a modification of the jackknife method (Gray and Schucany, 1972) to construct a population of estimates from which we can construct an ensemble estimator. Define the ensemble estimate as

$$g_{\text{ensemble}}(x) \equiv \frac{1}{N} \sum_{j=1}^{j=N} g(x; \mu_{(-i)}),$$

where

$$\mu_{(-i)} \equiv \frac{1}{N-1} \sum_{j \neq i} x_j$$

and

$$g(x; \alpha) \equiv \frac{1}{\sqrt{2\pi\sigma^2}} e^{-(x-\alpha)^2/\sigma^2}.$$

We can now explicitly compare these two estimates using the mean integrated square error (MISE) of the estimates,

$$\text{MISE}[g(x; \alpha)] \equiv E_{\mathscr{D}}\left[\int_{-\infty}^{+\infty} (g(x; \alpha) - g(x; 0))^2 \, dx \right].$$

Calculating $\text{MISE}[g(x; \mu)]$ and $\text{MISE}[g_{\text{ensemble}}(x)]$ in this special case, it is easy to show that

$$\text{MISE}[g(x; \mu)] < \text{MISE}[g_{\text{ensemble}}(x)].$$

Comparing this result with equation (2), there seems to be a contradiction: the ensemble average is performing worse on average! The reason the ensemble performs worse on average is that two of the main assumptions from section 10.2 are wrong: The misfit functions from the population are not uncorrelated nor are they in general zero mean. Since these assumptions do not hold in general, we present an alternative formulation of the ensemble method in which these assumptions are not made (see section 10.4).

The above example helps to illustrate two important aspects of neural network regression which should be considered when performing ensemble averages: For neural networks, the existence of multiple local minima prohibits the simple parameter averaging we performed when we approximated

$g(x; \mu)$ in the example above. And in general, we do not know whether the function we are trying to estimate is representable by a given neural network as we assumed was true in the example above.

10.4 Generalized Ensemble Method

In this section we extend the results of section 10.2 to a generalized ensemble technique which always generates a regression estimate which is as low or lower than both the best individual regressor, $f_{\text{naive}}(x)$, and the basic ensemble regressor, $f_{\text{BEM}}(x)$, and which avoids overfitting the data. In fact, it is the best possible of any linear combination of the elements of the population $\mathcal{F}$.

Define the Generalized Ensemble Method estimator, $f_{\text{GEM}}(x)$, as

$$f_{\text{GEM}}(x) \equiv \sum_{i=1}^{i=N} \alpha_i f_i(x) = f(x) + \sum_{i=1}^{i=N} \alpha_i m_i(x),$$

where the α_i's are real and satisfy the constraint that $\sum \alpha_i = 1$. We want to choose the α_i's so as to minimize the MSE with respect to the target function $f(x)$. If again we define $m_i(x) \equiv f(x) - f_i(x)$ and in addition define the symmetric correlation matrix $C_{ij} \equiv E[m_i(x)m_j(x)]$ then we find that we must minimize

$$\text{MSE}[f_{\text{GEM}}] = \sum_{i,j} \alpha_i \alpha_j C_{ij}. \tag{3}$$

We now use the method of Lagrange multipliers to solve for α_k. We want α_k such that $\forall k$

$$\partial_{\alpha_k} \left[\sum_{i,j} \alpha_i \alpha_j C_{ij} - 2\lambda \left(\sum_i \alpha_i - 1 \right) \right] = 0.$$

This equation simplifies to the condition that

$$\sum_k \alpha_k C_{kj} = \lambda.$$

If we impose the constraint, $\sum \alpha_i = 1$, we find that

$$\alpha_i = \frac{\sum_j C_{ij}^{-1}}{\sum_k \sum_j C_{kj}^{-1}}. \tag{4}$$

If the $m_i(x)$'s are uncorrelated and zero mean, $C_{ij} = 0 \ \forall i \neq j$ and the optimal α_i's have the simple form

$$\alpha_i = \frac{\sigma_i^{-2}}{\sum_j \sigma_j^{-2}},$$

where $\sigma_i^2 \equiv C_{ii}$, which corresponds to the intuitive choice of weighting the f_i's by the inverse of their respective variances and normalizing. Combining equations (3) and (4), we find that the optimal MSE is given by

$$\text{MSE}[f_{\text{GEM}}] = \left[\sum_{ij} C_{ij}^{-1} \right]^{-1}. \tag{5}$$

The results in this section depend on two assumptions: the rows and columns of C are linearly independent and we have a reliable estimate of C. In certain cases where we have nearly duplicate networks in the population $\mathcal{F}$, we will have nearly linearly dependent rows and columns in C, which will make the inversion process very unstable and our estimate of C^{-1} will be unreliable. In these cases, we can use heuristic techniques to sub-sample the population $\mathcal{F}$ to assure that C has full rank (see section 10.6). In practice, the increased stability produced by removing near degeneracies outweighs any information lost by discarding nets. Since the C we calculate is the sample correlation matrix not the true correlation matrix, C is a random variable as are $\text{MSE}[f_{\text{GEM}}]$ and the optimal α_i's. Thus noise in the estimate of C can lead to bad estimates of the optimal α_i's. If needed, we can get a less biased estimate of C^{-1} by using a jackknife procedure (Gray and Schucany, 1972) on the data used to generate C.

Note also that the BEM estimator and the naive estimator are both special cases of the GEM estimator, and therefore $\text{MSE}[f_{\text{GEM}}]$ will always be less than or equal to $\text{MSE}[f_{\text{BEM}}]$ and $\text{MSE}[f_{\text{naive}}]$. An explicit demonstration of this fact can be seen by comparing the respective MSE's under the assumption that the $m_i(x)$'s are uncorrelated and zero mean. In that case, comparing equations (1) and (5), we have

$$\text{MSE}[f_{\text{BEM}}] = \frac{1}{N^2} \sum_i \sigma_i^2 \geqslant \left[\sum_i \sigma_i^{-2} \right]^{-1} = \text{MSE}[f_{\text{GEM}}],$$

with equality only when all of the σ_i are identical. This relation is easily proven using the fact that $a/b + b/a \geqslant 2 \ \forall a, b > 0$. Similarly, we can write

$$\text{MSE}[f_{\text{naive}}] = \sigma_{\text{min}}^2 \geqslant \left[\sum_i \sigma_i^{-2} \right]^{-1} = \text{MSE}[f_{\text{GEM}}].$$

Thus we see that the GEM estimator provides the best estimate of $f(x)$ in the mean square error sense.

10.5 Experimental results

In this section, we report on an application of the Generalized Ensemble Method to the NIST OCR database. The characters were hand-segmented, hand-labeled and preprocessed into 120 dimensional feature vectors by convolution with simple kernels. The database was divided into three types (numbers, uppercase characters and lowercase characters) and each of these types was divided into independent training, testing and cross-validatory sets with sizes listed in Table 10.1.

Table 10.1 *Database divisions*

Data set	Training set	CV set	Testing set	Classes
Numbers	13241	13241	4767	10
Uppercase	11912	11912	7078	26
Lowercase	12971	12970	6835	26

We trained a population of 10 single hidden unit layer backpropagation networks for a variety of different hidden unit layer sizes for each type of data. Each network was initialized with a different random configuration of weights. Training was stopped using a cross-validatory stopping criterion. For simplicity, we calculated the weights for the GEM estimator under the assumption that the misfits were uncorrelated and zero mean.

Straight classification results are shown in Figures 10.3, 10.5 and 10.7. In these plots, the classification performance of the GEM estimator (labeled 'Ensemble'), the naive estimator (labeled 'Best Individual') and the average estimator from the population (labeled 'Individual') are plotted versus the number of hidden units in each individual network. Error bars are included for the average estimator from the population. In all of these plots there is an increase in performance as the number of hidden units increases. Notice, however, that in all of these results the ensemble estimator was not only better than the population average but it was also as good as or better than the naive estimator in every case.

Typically for character recoginition problems, it is worse for the network to make an error than it is for the network to reject a pattern. This weighted cost

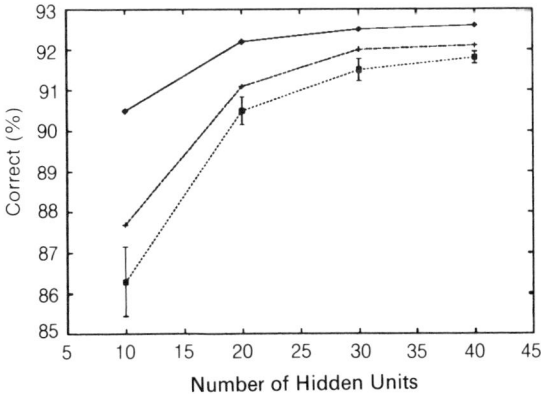

Figure 10.3 *Upper case percentages.* ◆ : *ensemble*; + : *best individual*; ■ : *individual*.

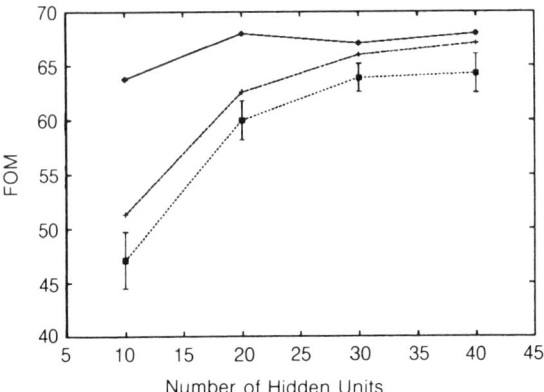

Figure 10.4 *Upper case FOM.* ◆ *: ensemble;* + *: best individual;* ■ *: individual.*

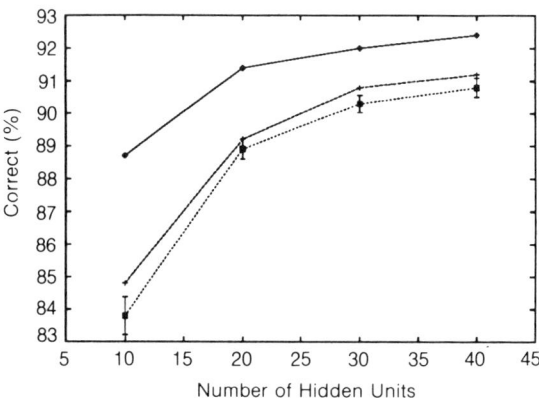

Figure 10.5 *Lower case percentage.* ◆ *: ensemble;* + *: best individual;* ■ *: individual.*

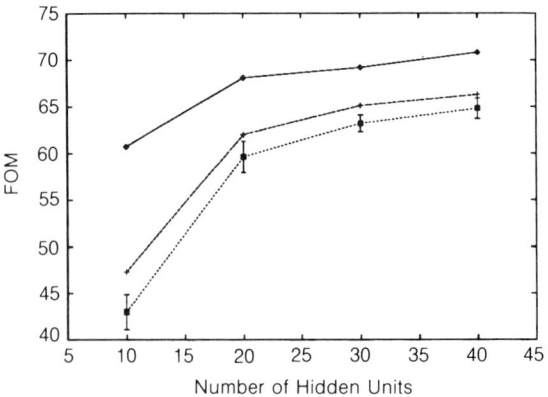

Figure 10.6 *Lower case FOM.* ◆ *: ensemble;* + *: best individual;* ■ *: individual.*

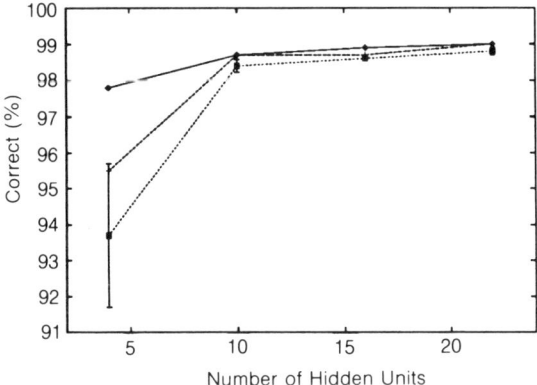

Figure 10.7 *Numbers percentage.* ♦ *: ensemble;* + *: best individual;* ■ *: individual.*

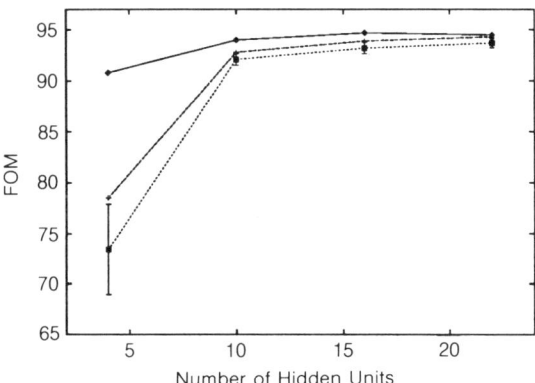

Figure 10.8 *Numbers FOM.* ♦ *: ensemble;* + *: best individual;* ■ *: individual.*

can be taken into account by calculating a Figure of Merit (FOM) instead of a straight performance measure. We define our FOM as follows:

$$\text{FOM} \equiv \%\,\text{Correct} - \%\,\text{Rejected} - 10(\%\,\text{Error}).$$

In our simulations we found an optimal rejection threshold for each network based on the cross-validatory set. FOM results are shown in Figures 10.4, 10.6 and 10.8. Again, notice that in all of these results, just as in the straight classification results, the ensemble estimator was not only better than the population average but it was also better than the naive estimator.

These results for a difficult, real-world problem show that the GEM estimator is significantly and dramatically better than standard techniques.

It is important to consider how many networks are necessary for the ensemble methods presented in this paper to be useful. If we take the BEM result seriously (equation 2), we should expect that increasing the number of networks in the population can only improve the BEM estimator. However as stated in section 10.2, eventually our assumptions on the misfits breakdown and equation (2) is no longer valid. This fact is clearly demonstrated in Figure 10.9, where we show the FOM performance saturate as the number of nets in the population increases. In the figure, we see that saturation in this example occurs after only six or eight nets are in the ensemble population. This is a very interesting result because it gives us a measure of how many distinct[5] nets are in our population. This knowledge is very useful when sub-sampling a given population. This result also suggests a very important observation: Although the number of local minima in parameter space is extremely large, the number of distinct local minima in functional space is actually quite small!

We can make another important observation if we compare Figure 10.9 with Figure 10.4. Consider the value of the FOM on the test data for an ensemble of 4 networks (Figure 10.9). Compare this value to population average FOM for nets with 40 hidden units (Figure 10.4). These values are not

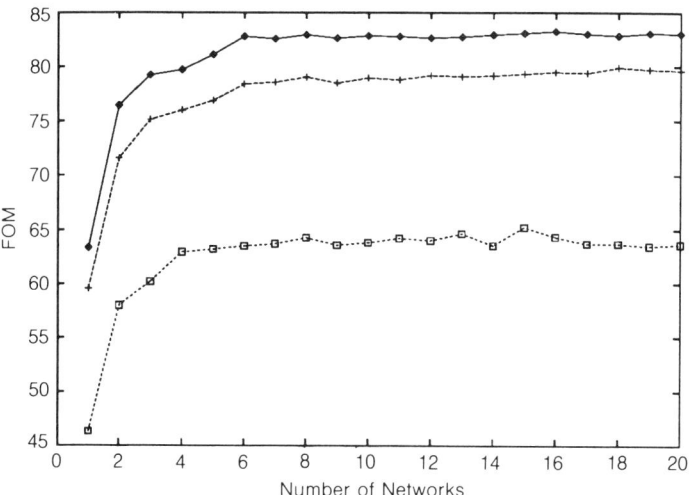

Figure 10.9 *Ensemble FOM versus the number of nets in the ensemble. Ensemble FOM graphs for the upper case training, cross-validatory and testing data are shown. Each net in the populations had 10 hidden units. The graphs are for a single randomly chosen ordering of 20 previously trained nets. No effort was made to optimally choose the order in which the nets were added to the ensemble. Improved ordering gives improved results.* ◆: *train FOM;* +: *CV FOM;* □: *test FOM.*

---

[5] By 'distinct', we mean that the misfits of two nets are weakly correlated. It is, of course, arguable what should be considered weakly correlated. For the purposes of this chapter, networks are distinct if the related correlation matrix, C, has a robust inverse.

significantly different; however, training a population of large nets to find the best estimator is computationally much more expensive than training and averaging a population of small nets. In addition, small networks are more desirable since they are less prone to over-fitting than large networks.[6]

It is also interesting to note that there is a striking improvement for an ensemble size of only two.

10.6 Improving BEM and GEM

One simple extension of the ensemble methods presented in this chapter is to consider the BEM and GEM estimators of all of the possible populations which are subsets of the original network population $\mathscr{F}$.[7] All the information we need to perform subset selection is contained in the correlation matrix, C, which only has to be calculated once.

In principal, the GEM estimator for $\mathscr{F}$ will be a better estimator than the GEM estimator for any subset of $\mathscr{F}$, however, in practice, we must be careful to assure that the correlation matrix is not ill-conditioned. If, for example, two networks in the population are very similar, two of the rows of C will be nearly collinear. This collinearity will make inverting the correlation matrix very error prone and will lead to very poor results. Thus in the case of the GEM estimator it is important to remove all duplicate (or nearly duplicate) networks from the population $\mathscr{F}$. Removing duplicates can be easily done by examining the correlation matrix. One can remove all networks for which the dot product of its row in the correlation matrix with any other row in the correlation matrix is above some threshold. This threshold can be chosen to allow a number of nets equal to the number of distinct networks in the population, as described in section 10.5.

An alternative approach (Wolpert, 1990), which avoids the potential singularities in C, is to allow a perceptron to learn the appropriate averaging weights. Of course, this approach will be prone to local minima and noise due to stochastic gradient descent, just as the original population $\mathscr{F}$ was; thus we can train a population of perceptrons to combine the networks from $\mathscr{F}$ and then average over this new population. A further extension is to use a nonlinear network (Jacobs et al., 1991; Reilly et al., 1987; Wolpert, 1990) to learn how to combine the networks with weights that vary over the feature space, and then to average an ensemble of such networks. This extension is reasonable since networks will, in general perform better in certain regions of the feature space than in others.

---

[6] Of course we cannot make the individual nets too small or they will not have sufficient complexity.

[7] This approach is essentially the naive estimator for the population of BEM and GEM estimators. Averaging over the population of BEM or GEM estimators will not improve performance.

In the case of the BEM estimator, we know that as the population size grows our assumptions on the misfits, $m_i(x)$, are not longer valid. When our assumptions break down, adding more nets to the population is a waste of resources, since it will not improve the performance, and if the nets we add have particularly poor performance, we can actually lower the performance of the BEM estimator. Thus, it would be ideal if we could find the optimal subset of the population $\mathscr{F}$ over which to average. We could try all the $2^N - 1$ possible non-empty subsets of $\mathscr{F}$, but for large N this search becomes unmanageable. Instead, we can order the elements of the population according to increasing mean square error[8], and generate a set of N BEM estimates by adding successively the ordered elements of $\mathscr{F}$. We can then choose the best estimate. The BEM estimator is then guaranteed to be at least as good as the naive estimator.

We can further refine this process by considering the difference between the mean square error for the BEM estimator for a population of N elements and the mean square error for the BEM estimator for the same population plus a new net. From this comparison, we find that we should add the new net to the population if the following inequality is satisfied:

$$(2N + 1)\,\mathrm{MSE}[\hat{f}_N] > 2 \sum_{i \neq \mathrm{new}} E[m_{\mathrm{new}}m_i] + \mathbf{E}[m_{\mathrm{new}}^2],$$

where $\mathrm{MSE}[\hat{f}_N]$ is the mean square error for the BEM estimator for the population of N and m_{new} is the misfit for the new function to be added to the population. The information to make this decision is readily available from the correlation matrix C. Now, if a network does not satisfy this criterion, we can swap it with the next untested network in the ordered sequence.

10.7 Conclusions

We have developed a general mathematical framework for improving regression estimates. In particular, we have shown that by averaging in functional space, we can construct neural networks which are guaranteed to have improved performance.

An important strength of the ensemble method is that it does not depend on the algorithm used to generate the set of regressors, and therefore can be used with any set of networks. This observation implies that we are not constrained in our choice of networks, and can use nets of arbitrary complexity and architecture. Thus the ensemble methods described in this chapter are completely general in that they are applicable to a wide class of problems, including neural networks and any other technique which attempts to minimize the mean square error.

---

[8] The first element in this sequence will be the naive estimator.

One striking aspect of network averaging is the manner in which it deals with local minima. Most neural network algorithms achieve sub-optimal peformance specifically due to the existence of an overwhelming number of sub-optimal local minima. If we take a set of neural networks which have converged to local minima and apply averaging we can construct an improved estimate. One way to understand this fact is to consider that, in general, networks which have fallen into different local minima will perform poorly in different regions of feature space, and thus their error terms will not be strongly correlated. It is this lack of correlation which drives the averaging method. Thus, the averaging method has the remarkable property that it can efficiently utilize the local minima that other techniques try to avoid.

It should also be noted that since the ensemble methods are performing averaging in functional space, they have the desirable property of inherently performing smoothing in functional space. This property will help avoid any potential over-fitting during training.

In addition, since the ensemble method relies on multiple functionally independent networks, it is ideally suited for parallel computation during both training and testing.

We are working to generalize this method to take into account confidence measures and various nonlinear combinations of estimators in a population.

Acknowledgements

We would like to thank the members of the Brown University Institute for Brain and Neural Systems, in particular Nathan Intrator for many useful discussions. We would also like to thank Nestor Inc. for making the NIST OCR database available to us.

Research was supported by the Office of Naval Research, the Army Research Office, and the National Science Foundation.

References

Baxt, W.G. (1992) Improving the accuracy of an artifical neural network using multiple differently trained networks. *Neural Computation*, **4**(5).

Bridle, J.S. and Cox, S.J. (1991) RecNorm: simultaneous normalization and classification applied to speech recognition, in *Advances in Neural Information Processing Systems 3*.

Buntine, W.L. and Weigend, A.S. (1992) Bayesian back-propagation. *Complex Systems*, **5**, 603–43.

Cooper, L.N. (1991) Hybrid neural network architectures: Equilibrium systems that pay attention, in *Neural Networks: Theory and Applications* (eds R.J. Mammone and Y. Zeevi), Academic Press, New York, pp. 81–96.

Efron, B. (1982) *The Jackknife, the Bootstrap and Other Resampling Plans*. SIAM, Philadelphia, PA.

Gray, H.L. and Schucany, W.R. (1972) *The Generalized Jackknife Statistic*. Dekker, New York, NY.

Hansen, L.K. and Salamon, P. (1990) Neural network ensembles. *IEEE Transactions on Pattern Analysis and Machine Intelligence*, **12**(10), 993–1000.

Härdle, W. (1990) *Applied Nonparametric Regression*. University of Cambridge Press, New York, NY.

Intrator, N., Reisfeld, D. and Yeshurun, Y. (1992) Face recognition using a hybrid supervised/unsupervised neural network. Preprint.

Jacobs, R.A., Jordan, M.I., Nowlan, S.J. and Hinton, G.E. (1991) Adaptive mixtures of local experts. *Neural Computation*, **3**(2).

Lincoln, W.P. and Skrzypek, J. (1990) Synergy of clustering multiple back propagation networks, in *Advances in Neural Information Processing Systems 2*.

Miller, R.G. (1974), The jackknife – a review. *Biometrika*, **61**(1), 1–16.

Neal, R.M. (1992a) Bayesian learning via stochastic dynamics, in *Advances in Neural Information Processing Systems*, (eds. J.E. Moody, S.J. Hanson and R.P. Lippmann) Morgan Kaufmann, San Mateo, CA.

Neal, R.M. (1992b) Bayesian mixture modeling by Monte Carlo simulation. *Technical report crg-tr-91-2*, University of Toronto.

Pearlmutter, B.A. and Rosenfeld, R. (1991) Chaitin-kolmogorov complexity and generalization in neural networks, in *Advances in Neural Information Processing Systems 3*.

Reilly, D.L., Scofield, C.L., Cooper, L.N. and Elbaum, C. (1988) Gensep: A multiple neural network learning system with modifiable network topology, in *Abstracts of the First Annual International Neural Network Society Meeting*.

Reilly, R.L., Scofield, C.L., Elbaum, C., and Cooper, L.N. (1987) Learning system architectures composed of multiple learning modules. *Proc. IEEE First Int. Conf. on Neural Networks*, Volume 2.

Scofield, C., Kenton, L. and Chang, J. (1991) Multiple neural net architectures for character recognition. *Proc. Compcon, San Francisco, CA*, 487–91.

Stone, M. (1974) Cross-validatory choice and assessment of statistical predictions (with discussion). *J. Roy. Stat. Soc. Ser. B*, **36**, 111–47.

Wahba, G. (1990) *Spline Models for Observational Data*. SIAM, Philadelphia. PN.

Wolpert, D.H. (1990) Stacked generalization. *Technical report LA-UR-90-3460*, Complex Systems Group, Los Alamos, NM.

Xu, L., Krzyzak, A. and Suen, C.Y. (1990) Associative switch for combining classifiers. *Technical report x9011*, Department of Computer Science, Concordia University, Montreal, Canada.

Xu, L., Krzyzak, A. and Suen, C.Y. (1992) Methods of combining multiple classifiers and their applications to handwriting recognition. *IEEE Transactions on Systems, Man, and Cybernetics*, **22**(3).

11

Non-literal transfer among neural network learners

L.Y. PRATT

Department of Mathematics and Computer Science, Colorado School of Mines, Golden, CO 80401, USA

11.1 Introduction

Neural networks have generated considerable interest in recent years in both applied and research communities (cf. Rumelhart *et al.*, 1987b; McClelland and Rumelhart 1988; Moody *et al.*, 1992). A neural network task of particular interest is that of **classifier induction** – the problem of building a classification algorithm given a set of training examples illustrating its input and output. For example, a commonly studied classification problem is to map speech signals into identifiers for the individual sounds that make up words (phonemes). Training data would consist of a set of examples of ⟨speech signal, phoneme⟩ pairs. A neural network that had been trained on such a set of examples could then, in principle, map an arbitrary speech signal to the correct phoneme, even if the exact speech signal to be tested hadn't been in the set of training examples. Inputs to a classifier are called **features** – an output identifies the input to be a member of one of a set of **classes**.

Neural networks are often praised for the fact that the only expertise required in their construction is that required to gather and pre-process the training data. However, in practice, in order to attain reasonable performance, additional information is often manually inserted via changes to network topology, node activation functions and other parameters. Since this procedure may be cumbersome and time-consuming, several studies, both in neural networks and the related area of symbolic machine learning, have explored how to automate the process of incorporating information that supplements the training data.

Artificial Neural Networks for Speech and Vision. Edited by Richard J. Mammone. Published in 1993 by Chapman & Hall, London. ISBN 0 412 54850 X

This chapter describes how a new source of supplemental information may be utilized by an automated procedure to speed neural network learning. This source of information consists of the weights from networks that have been trained on tasks that are related to the one at hand. Section 11.2 first describes the foundations of this approach in symbolic (non-neural network) machine learning, and in prior efforts to insert knowledge into neural networks. Then section 11.3 describes the Discriminability-Based Transfer (DBT) algorithm for modifying neural network weights as they're transferred from a source to a target task. Then sections 11.4 and 11.5 report experimental methodology and results that support the use of the DBT method. Finally, section 11.6 summarizes and discusses the implications of these results for future work.

11.2 Motivation and related work

11.2.1 Symbolic machine learning

Some symbolic machine learning studies have explored how training data can be supplemented by using **domain knowledge**: rules describing aspects of the problem at hand. For example, a rule for a 'chair recognition' classifier might express that all chairs have seats, and that some are made of wood. Several systems include both an Explanation-Based Learning (EBL) (Mitchell *et al.*, 1985) component that facilitates the use of domain knowledge, as well as an **inductive** component, which learns from training data (i.e. examples of chairs). These components communicate in two directions: an EBL theory is used to focus the use of the training data, and the inductive learner is capable of generating new rules in the language of the domain theory [OCCAM (Pazzani, 1989), GEMINI (Danyluk, 1989), IOU (Mooney and Ourston, 1989)]. Several systems also transfer knowledge in a single direction, using domain knowledge to provide input to a process that creates new features for inductive learning [STABB (Utgoff, 1986), Zenith (Fawcett and Utgoff, 1991), CINDI (Callan and Utgoff, 1991)].

11.2.2 Benefits to supplementing training data with extra information

These approaches have demonstrated the following improvements to symbolic learning:

- **Faster learning:** prior knowledge may be used to bias search through concept space by initializing an incremental learner near a solution, or by introducing constraints which limit search.
- **Reduced number of training examples:** domain knowledge can substitute for a subset of training examples, thereby eliminating their necessity.
- **Improved performance:** inserted theories may supplement an incomplete or incorrect set of training examples to boost classification accuracy.

These benefits may also be realizable within the field of neural networks.

11.2.3 Inserting knowledge into neural networks

Neural network inductive learners such as back-propagation (Rumelhart *et al.*, 1987a) can also benefit from domain knowledge. As mentioned in section 11.1, this information is often incorporated manually, by preprocessing and selecting features, and by choosing an appropriate network topology, objective function, and node activation function. Until recently, however, the question of how to automatically incorporate knowledge expressed in a formal langauge has not been explored.

Recently, Towell *et al.* (1990) have described the KBANN algorithm, which is a first step in the direction of automating the utilization of explicit forms of knowledge to supplement neural network training data. KBANN uses a domain theory to determine network topology and to pre-set some network weights. There are, however, two potential limitations to the KBANN approach:

1. Domain knowledge for a problem may be difficult to acquire – this **knowledge engineering bottleneck** (Hayes-Roth, 1983) is a commonly cited problem.
2. Important aspects of learning may not be readily expressible in the language of propositional logic rules that is required as input to KBANN.

11.2.4 The transfer paradigm

In this chapter, we propose using a source of domain information that, although it is often readily available, has been exploited only rarely in neural network research. We propose using a classifier that has already been trained to solve a task which is related to the one at hand. Such an approach avoids the two problems listed above: as classifiers are constructed for more and more

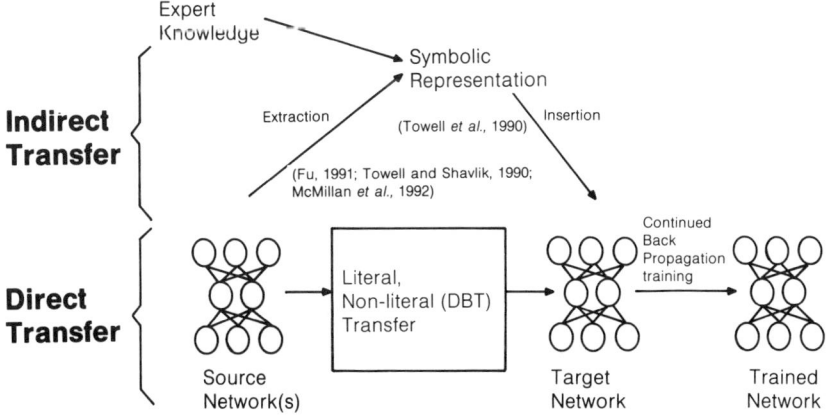

Figure 11.1 *General framework for network transfer (see text for discussion).*

problems, it is reasonable to expect to be able to build on previous results instead of starting from scratch with every training run. Furthermore, we avoid the representational shift required by systems that insist on the use of logical rules.

We will use the word **transfer** to refer to the process of using a learned classifier, or parts thereof, to bias a new learning procedure. **Indirect** transfer is that which requires an intervening shift in representation (such as to a propositional domain theory); **direct** transfer translates the same representational formalism (such as neural network weights) from a **source** (pre-trained) learner to the **target** problem. Figure 11.1 shows the relationship of transfer to other work on inserting and extracting symbolic knowledge to and from neural networks. It is described in more detail below.

11.2.5 Literal transfer (from subnetworks)

For iterative learning methods like back-propagation, one simple method of direct transfer is to copy the results of learning (which for neural networks are the values of trained weights) to use as the initial conditions of the target learner. We'll call this **literal** transfer. Previously, literal from multiple source neural networks, each of which form a subproblem of a target problem, has been explored (Waibel *et al.*, 1989; Pratt and Kamm, 1991; Pratt *et al.* 1991, Pratt, 1992). In this paradigm, source networks are responsible for subsets of the output classes, and may receive specialized input features for the class subset. Such a decomposition of training can lead to substantially increased learning speed.

11.2.6 Transfer between populations

Another important transfer paradigm, to be explored in this chapter, is when the input features and output classes between source and target learners are identical, but the mapping to be learned changes. Such a shift in mapping is fairly commonly encountered. A speech recognition system may, for example, be trained on British English speech, but we may have an application for recognizing American English speech. The two tasks are closely related, so utilizing parts of a pre-trained classifier makes sense (section 11.6 will discuss the concept of 'related task' in more depth). In general, the availability of a transfer technique allows training time to be amortized over several related applications.

11.2.7 Literal transfer: a baseline for between-population transfer

As is the case when input features and/or output classes of the source and target classifiers are different (as in the sub-network transfer studies mentioned above), the simplest approach to transfer between systems with the same input features and output classes is simply to use the trained source classifier on the target task. For an iterative learning method, literal transfer may also be used to initialize the target network, which is then trained further on the target training data (as shown on the right of Figure 11.1). Previous exploration of this approach has studied the degree to which literally transferred source weights can interfere with target task learning; for several problems, it has been shown that the degree of interference is so large that it's better not to use any information from the source (cf. Martin, 1988; McCloskey and Cohen, 1989; Tenorio and Lee, 1989).

This chapter demonstrates that it is indeed possible to improve on literal transfer by modifying the source network weights before they're used to initialize further training on examples representing the target task. We introduce an algorithm for non-literal transfer called Discriminability-Based Transfer (DBT). DBT adjusts the retentiveness of decision region boundaries coded by source network weights so that more useful boundaries move less during target training, and boundaries that are less relevant to the target task are freed to change position. We show in section 11.5 that DBT can give superior learning speed over literal transfer, over just using source weights on the target task, and over a baseline condition, where target network weights are initialized randomly (the usual approach to neural network training). We present evidence from a variety of domains that supports the claim that DBT is superior to these methods.

11.3 Discriminability-Based Transfer (DBT) algorithm

In this chapter, we present results for a specific formulation of transfer. We consider a classifier that is a single-layer feedforward neural network, trained using back-propagation. There is a single source network, which has the same input features and output classes as the target problem, but a different (but related) target concept. Our goal is to learn quickly on the target task, and not necessarily to retain performance on the source task. We also restricted the design of the algorithm to solve this problem so that it changed only the initial conditions to the back-propagation algorithm. This was done to retain as much similarity as possible with standard usage of back-propagation, which has been widely successful.

As discussed above, in literal transfer, network weights are just copied from source to target. However, given the ability to analyse the transferred weights as well as the differences between source and target network tasks, more complex manipulations of the weights can improve their ability to be utilized during further training on the target data. Our approach is based on interpreting neural network weights as defining hyperplane decision regions in feature space. The weights and bias leading to each hidden unit define an inequality which separates all possible input vectors into two sets, for which the hidden unit's activation is > 0.5 and < 0.5, respectively. In section 11.3.1

we describe this interpretation of neural network weights in terms of hyperplanes in feature space. We then turn to how the intuition gained from this representation can lead us to understand what can go wrong with literal transfer.

11.3.1 Geometric understanding of neural network representation

Geometrical interpretation of training data

Training data for a classifier induction task are repesented as a list of ⟨input, target⟩ patterns. If there are only two values in the input vector, then this data can be plotted in two-dimensional **feature space** by labeling points specified by an input value with the corresponding target value. For example, Figure 11.2 shows how the training data shown in Table 11.1 would be plotted.

Figure 11.2 can be interpreted as meaning that when a testing data pattern is input to a classifier that has been trained on the set of training data shown, it should be classified into the target category of the nearest training data item.

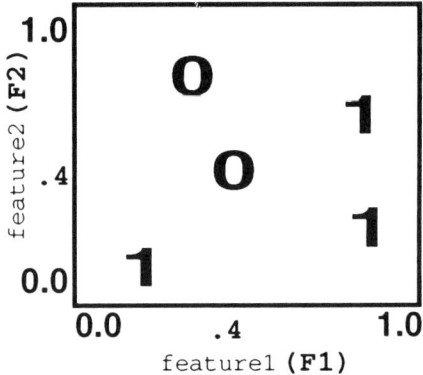

Figure 11.2 *Set of training data plotted in feature space.*

Table 11.1 *Training data and HU activations*

Input	Target
0.1, 0.1	1
0.3, 0.8	0
0.4, 0.4	0
0.8, 0.5	1
0.8, 0.2	1

For example, a testing data item whose input features are 0.0, 0.1 should probably be mapped to class 1.

Geometrical interpretation of hidden units in a classifier

Consider a single-hidden-layer back-propagation network that is fully connected in the input-to-hidden (IH) and hidden-to-output (HO) layers, and trained for a classification task. Each output unit represents a different class. Let the input-to-hidden or output unit j be $I_j = \sum_i w_{ij} y_i$, where y_i is the activation of incoming unit i, and w_{ij} is the weight between units i and j. Following common practice, assume that the bias is represented as one of the weights w_{ij}, connected to an input unit that has a constant activation of 1. Also, let the activation function be the sigmoidal: $y_i = 1/(1 + e^{-I_j})$ where y_i is the activation of neuron i, and I_i is its input.

For large positive I_j, the sigmoid function is close to 1; it is near 0 for large negative I_j. As I_j approaches 0, y_j approaches 0.5. Because of the shape of the sigmoid, many I_j values yield y_j close to 0 or 1, however, and so a simplified way of understanding y_j is to ask whether it is less than or greater than 0.5. $y_j = 0.5$ when $I_j = \sum_i w_{ij} y_i = 0$. We can plot the equation of this line for each hidden unit in feature space along with the training data, as illustrated in Figure 11.3. Table 11.2, discussed below, shows HU activations in this network for the training data.

In the network of Figure 11.3, hidden unit 1 (HU1) has activation $=0.5$ when $1.0F1 + 0.0F2 + 0.6 = 0$. Similarly, HU2 has activation $=0.5$ when $1.0F1 + 1.0F2 + 0.4 = 0$. In general, networks have more than two input features, so hidden units can be represented as $n-1$-dimensional hyperplanes separating data in η-space.

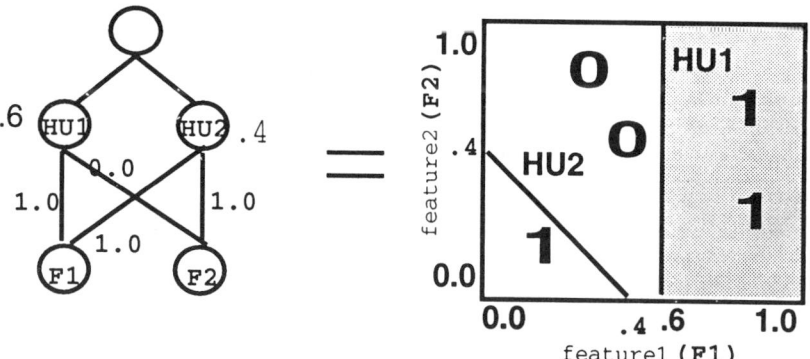

Figure 11.3 *Small feed-forward network and the corresponding hyperplane interpretation for its hidden units. Values shown beside arcs are weights, and beside nodes are biases.*

Table 11.2 *Training data and HU activations. The hyperplane formed by HU1 separates the space of training data inputs for which that hidden unit will have activation > 0.5 from those for which it will have activation < 0.5. As shown in the rightmost two columns of this table, HU1 will have high activation on training items p3 and p4 but not on p0, p1, or p2.*

Label	Input	Target	HU1 activation	HU2 activation
p0	0.1, 0.1	1	$< 0.5 (\approx 0)$	$< 0.5 (\approx 0)$
p1	0.3, 0.8	0	$< 0.5 (\approx 0)$	$> 0.5 (\approx 1)$
p2	0.4, 0.4	0	$< 0.5 (\approx 0)$	$> 0.5 (\approx 1)$
p3	0.8, 0.5	1	$> 0.5 (\approx 1)$	$> 0.5 (\approx 1)$
p4	0.8, 0.2	1	$> 0.5 (\approx 1)$	$> 0.5 (\approx 1)$

Note that the position of a hyperplane is not determined by the absolute magnitudes of the weights (including bias) leading to the associated hidden unit, but by their ratio. Thus the same hyperplanes shown in Figure 11.3 could have been generated by a network other than the one shown, by multiplying a hidden unit's incoming weights (including bias) by a constant value.

Criterion for successful classification

For many classifier induction tasks[1], a necessary condition for a properly trained classifier is that, as in Figure 11.3, hidden unit hyperplanes are arranged in such a way that no region created by hyperplanes contains training data targets of different classes.

To understand this necessity, recall that hidden unit activations tend towards 0 or 1. Separation is a necessary condition because input activations that cause the same hidden unit activation vector will, by definition of feed-forward, cause identical output unit activation vectors. Therefore, for two different input vectors with different target classes, hidden units must have different activation vectors if the network is to produce a proper classification, where the two vectors produce different output classes. In our simplified model, these two vectors must be on different sides of at least one hyperplane, so that it activates > 0.5 for one and < 0.5 for the other. This differing HU vector can then lead to a differing output vector. For example, hidden unit activations for the network of Figure 11.3 were shown in Table 11.2.

Separating training data of different target classes by hyperplanes is not a sufficient condition for correct classification because it is also necessary that the hidden-to-output weights, which are not represented by these diagrams, have the proper values. It also may be true that for a given set of training data

---

[1] See Sontag (1989) for exceptions. The consequence of this simplification is that it may appear that more hidden units are necessary to solve a problem than are strictly required.

and a given positioning of the input-to-hidden hyperplanes, no hidden-to-output weight vector exists that will properly separate the data. This is because the hidden-to-output layer must implement a linear separation on its input domain, which may not be possible.

The left-hand image in Figure 11.4 plots a trained network's output activation against its two input features, for a simple problem constructed using a Gaussian distribution. On the right is shown the equivalent contour plot (lines of equal height are shown dashed) and the hyperplanes used to separate this problem. From this image it can be seen that the actual contour of the network's decision surface roughly follows a smoothed conjunction of IH hyperplane positions. This gives evidence that IH hyperplane positions provide a good indication of the network's overall behavior (including HO weights). Further evidence to this effect is provided by studies (Dewan and Sontag, 1990) showing that trained networks often have large weight magnitudes. Large IH magnitudes tend to lead to large positive or large negative I_j for hidden units j. As described above, this tends to make hidden units have near-binary (close to 0 or 1) activations.

Many researchers (cf. Widrow and Winter, 1988; Hanson and Burr, 1987; Fahlman, 1990; Cohn et al., 1990) have used static versions of the graphical display technique described in this section. Unlike several other techniques,

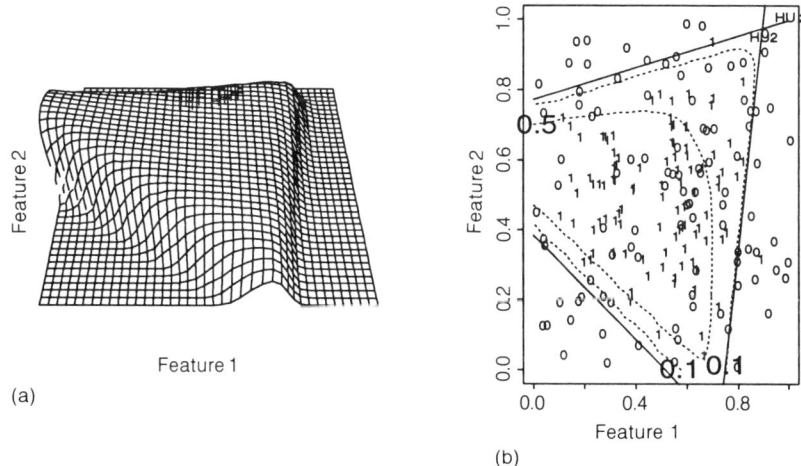

(a)

(b)

Figure 11.4 *Output activation contour and corresponding hidden units for Gaussian distribution problem. (a) A 3D plot, where height corresponds to the entire network's output value for various points of feature space; (b) the IH planes in the network, along with the 0.5- and 0.1-level contours of the 3D plot. As can be seen, these contours follow the general shape formed by IH hyperplanes, indicating that IH hyperplanes provide an approximate representation of the network's decision regions. Note that the network shown does not classify the training data with 100% accuracy – neither hyperplanes nor contours separate all 0s from all 1s.*

such as Hinton Diagrams (Hinton *et al.*, 1984), and some sophisticated graphical interface packages (e.g. Wejchert and Tesauro, 1990), this method does not only illustrate the value of weights but also provides a means for displaying the relationship of the weights to the training examples that they are meant to classify. We now return to the question of how to use this geometrical intuition to help to understand transfer.

11.3.2 What can go wrong with literal transfer?

To understand the need for a more sophisticated method than literal transfer, consider the case when only a subset of the source network input-to-hidden (IH) layer hyperplanes are relevant to the target problem, as illustrated by the fabricated task shown in Figure 11.5. Here only two of the hyperplanes used to solve the source problem are relevant for the target task; the remaining two will need to move to separate 0s from 1s in the target data.

We have observed that, during target task back-propagation learning, some hyperplanes initialized by literal transfer from a source network don't shift out of their initial positions, despite the fact that they don't help to separate the target training data. The weights defining such hyperplanes often have

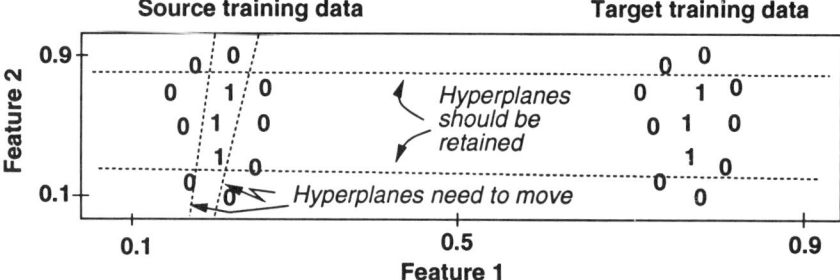

Figure 11.5 *Problem illustrating the need for DBT. The source and target tasks are identical, except that the target task has been shifted slightly along one axis, as represented by the training data shown here. Because of this shift, two of the source network hyperplanes are helpful in separating class-0 from class-1 data in the target task, and two are not.*

Figure 11.6 *Snapshots of hidden unit hyperplane positions, showing how a too-high magnitude hyperplane (HU1) from literal transfer can slow down learning. This demonstration was created by copying HU2 and HU3's initial positions from their final positions in a trained network. They had average weight magnitudes of 4.93 and 4.99, respectively. HU1 was given a position that did not separate the training data. Its magnitude was 5.83. Note how HU1 (near the bottom of the figure) seems fixed in place. Its high magnitude causes learning to be slow (taking about 3100 epochs to converge), compared to a randomly initialized network on this problem (which takes 600 epochs).*

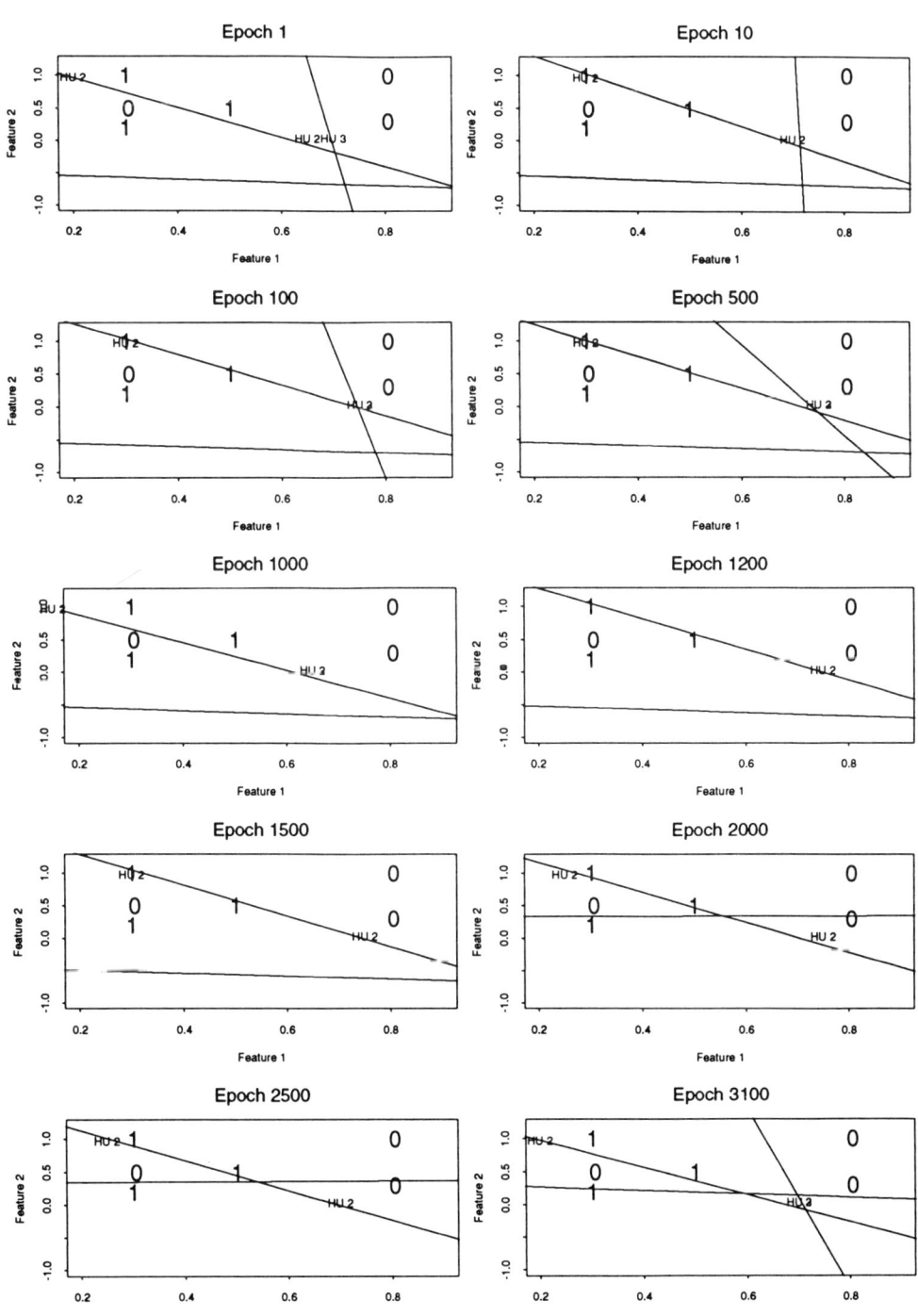

Input:
  Source network weights
  Target training data
  Parameters: c (cutoff factor), s (scaleup factor)
Output:
  Initial weights for target network, assuming same topology as source
    network
Method:
  For each source network hidden unit i
    Compare the hyperplane defined by incoming weights to i to the target
      training data, calculating IM_{ti} ($\varepsilon[0,1]$), (the "discriminability" of that
      hyperplane. "t" indicates target training data; "i" indicates the hyper-
      plane whose discriminability on that data is measured)
      Rescale IM_{ti} values so that largest has value s. Put result in s_i.
  For iM_{ti}'s that are less than c
    If highest magnitude ratio between weights defining hyperplane i is
      > 100.0, reset weights for that hyperplane randomly
    Else uniformly scale down hyperplane to have low-valued weights
      (maximum magnitude of 0.5), but in the same position as before.
    For each remaining IH hidden unit i
      For each weight w_{ji}^t defining hyperplane i in target network
      Let $w_{ji}^t =$ source weight $w_{ji} \times s_i$
  Set hidden-to-output target network weights randomly in $[-0.5, 0.5]$

Figure 11.7 *Discriminability-Based Transfer (DBT) algorithm.*

high magnitudes (Dewan and Sontag, 1990). Figure 11.6 shows a simulation
of such a situation, where a hyperplane that has a high magnitude, as if it came
from a source network, causes learning to be slowed down because it doesn't
move into place.

This effect can be understood by analysis of the backpropagation input-to-
hidden layer weight update equation (Rumelhart *et al.*, 1987a):

$$\Delta w_{ij} = \eta y_j (1 - y_j) \left[\sum_k \delta_k w_{jk} \right] x_i. \tag{1}$$

Here, η is the learning rate, j indexes hidden units, i indexes input units, k
indexes output units, x_i is the activation of input unit i, y_j is the activation of
hidden unit j and w_{ij} is the weight from input unit i to hidden unit j. δ_k is
a weighted error from higher layers. Note that Δw_{ij} does not depend directly
on the magnitudes of input-to-hidden (IH) weights w_{ij} and so larger weights
will be changed relatively slower. Furthermore, high-magnitude IH weights
tend to lead to high-magnitude inputs to hidden neurons. This leads to y_j
being close to 0 or 1, which lowers $y_j(1 - y_j)$, which reduces Δw_{ij}, which makes

the hyperplane partially determined by w_{ij} move slower (see Pratt *et al.*, 1991, for experimental evidence of this effect).

Although these input-to-hidden equation factors aren't the only ones affecting the rate of hyperplane movement (error from the output layer and input activations are also factors), we do expect that, all other things being equal, large weight magnitudes lead to slower hyperplane movement, which is problematic for source hyperplanes that are in less useful positions for the target task.

To address this problem, it is necessary to rescale hyperplanes so that useful ones are defined by high-magnitude weights and inappropriate hyperplanes use low magnitudes. This approach is the one used by the DBT algorithm, shown in Figure 11.7, and which is described below.

11.3.3 DBT I/O

DBT takes as input the weights defining the source classifier, and the target training data. Two parameters to DBT, called c and s, must also be determined in advance. They are discussed in more detail below. DBT outputs initial weights for subsequent back-propagation training on the target task. It attempts to determine these initial weights so that they speed up target learning compared to networks initialized with literal or random weights.

11.3.4 Evaluating hyperplanes with IM

DBT first evaluates the information (or **discriminability**) measure of each individual source network hyperplane on the target data, using the following multi-class metric, borrowed from decision tree induction techniques (Quinlan, 1986; Mingers, 1989):

$$\mathrm{IM} = \frac{1}{N}(\sum\sum x_{ij}\log x_{ij} - \sum x_{i.}\log x_{i.} - \sum x_{.j}\log x_{.j} + N\log N).$$

Here, N is the number of patterns, i is either 0 or 1, depending on the side of a hyperplane on which an example falls, j indexes over all classes, x_{ij} is the count of class j patterns on side i of the hyperplane, $x_{i.}$ is the count of all patterns on side i and $x_{.j}$ is the total number of patterns in class j.

IM is a measure of the information gained by knowing the value of an attribute (side of a hyperplane boundary) for the purpose of classification. The higher the IM of an attribute, the greater the uniformity of class data in the subsets of feature space it creates. As an example, Figure 11.8 shows the training data for a fabricated two-feature, two-class problem and a possible configuration of the hyperplanes formed by each hidden unit at the end of training. Hyperplane $h1$'s higher IM corresponds to the fact that it separates the two classes better than $h2$.

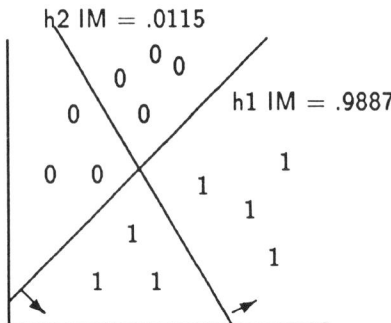

Figure 11.8 *Hyperplanes and their IM. Arrows indicate regions of feature space where hidden units have activations > 0.5.*

11.3.5 Modifying weights to be proportional to IM

DBT modifies the weights defining each source hyperplane to be proportional to the IM value, according to the input parameter, s. DBT is based on the idea that the best initial target magnitude M_t for a hyperplane is $M_t = s \times M_s \times IM_t$, where s ('scaleup') is a constant of proportionality, M_s is the magnitude of a source network hyperplane, and IM_t is the discriminability of the hyperplane on the target training data.

We assume that this simple relationship holds over some range of IM_t values. A second parameter, c, determines a cut-off in this relationship – source hyperplanes with $IM_t < c$ receive magnitudes based on a different function: magnitudes are very low, so that they are effectively equivalent to hyperplanes in a randomly initialized network. If the largest ratio between weight magnitudes defining a hyperplane with $IM_t < c$ is < 100.0, then those weights are scaled down uniformly to very low magnitudes, but with the same hyperplane position. In empirical trials, we observed that hyperplanes defined by some large and some small weights did not correctly move into position, so if a hyperplane has $IM_t < c$ and it has a largest weight magnitude ratio $>= 100.0$, then that hyperplane's weights are simply randomized in $[-0.5, 0.5]$.

To determine s and c for a particular source and target task, we trained DBT several times on the target task, for a small number of epochs with different s and c values. Assuming that the average TSS (total sum of squared error over all classes and all training patterns) over a few epochs is indicative of asymptotic performance, we chose the s and c values that yielded the best average TSS after a few epochs. We used local hill climbing in average TSS space to decide how to move in s, c space.

11.3.6 HO layer weights

DBT randomizes the weights in the network's hidden-to-output layer. At first, it seemed useful to set hidden-to-output (HO) weights based on source weights. However, we found experimentally that, since HO representations strongly depend on proper IH representations, and since the transfer algorithm creates only approximately positioned IH hyperplanes, it is better to set HO weights to low random values to achieve maximum flexibility.

11.4 Training methodology

We now describe the methodology used for a series of experiments to test the effectiveness of the DBT algorithm.

Since networks initialized using DBT are trained using standard back-propagation, the values of the learning rate (η) and momentum (α) parameters to that algorithm must be determined, as well as the DBT parameters s and c. We have developed local empirical search algorithms for automatic selection of η, α, s, and c based on results from learning on the training set. The IMBS algorithm described in Ramachandran and Pratt (1992) was used to determine proper hidden unit counts.

To establish its generality, DBT was compared to both random target network initialization and literal transfer on a variety of tasks with different characteristics. These tasks are summarized below:

1. **Peterson–Barney vowel recognition:** a 10-vowel task, which was originally described in Peterson and Barney (1952), and was recently recreated by Watrous (1991). This data consists of the formant values F1 and F2 for each of two repetitions of each of ten vowels by 76 speakers (1520 utterances). The vowels were pronounced in isolated words consisting of the consonant 'h', followed by a vowel, followed by 'd'. Source networks were trained on female-only speech, the target task was to recognize speech from males only. Our hypothesis was that by using a female-trained network as an initial bias, learning speed on the male-only network could be improved. 24 hidden units were used, with $\eta = 0.85$, $\alpha = 0.1$. The target task had 636 patterns.

2. **3-class Peterson–Barney subset:** a simplification of the full Peterson–Barney task, where only 3 of the 10 vowels need be separated. Again, source networks were trained on only female speakers, and the target task was to recognize male speech. Three hidden units were used, with $\eta = 0.3$, $\alpha = 0.000005$. The target task had 192 patterns.

3. **Transfer from all Peterson–Barney females to one male:** a simplification of the full Peterson–Barney task, where only the source networks for female speakers for all classes were transferred to target network for only a single male speaker. 24 hidden units were used, with $\eta = 1.1$, $\alpha = 0.75$. The target task had 20 patterns.

4. **Heart disease diagnosis for Switzerland patients, transfer to Hungary:** using a 14-attribute set of diagnosis information, we trained networks on a heart disease diagnosis problem (Detrano et al., 1989; Gennari et al., 1989). We used networks trained on two different source problems, represented by data from a hospital in Hungary. The target problem was to train a network

to perform the diagnosis task on Swiss patients. Seven hidden units were used, with $\eta = 1.1$, $\alpha = 0.55$. The target task had 1230 patterns.

5. **Heart disease diagnosis for Switzerland patients, transfer to VA hospital:** this task has the same characteristics as transfer from Hungarian patients, but this time the source patients were at a VA hospital in Long Beach, California.

6. **DNA promoter problem:** the DNA promoter recognition task described in Towell et al., (1990). It is linearly separable. An artificial transfer situation was created by using a source network trained on an arbitrarily chosen, and non-representative, 26-pattern subset of the 106 available positive and negative examples. The target task was the entire 106 patterns. One hidden unit was used, with $\eta = 1.05$, $\alpha = 0.7$.

7. **Chess endgame problem:** this classification task is to determine whether White or Black will win a chess game, based on a feature set describing an endgame position in which the pawn is in location a7 and it is white's turn to move (Shapiro, 1988; Holte et al., 1989; Shavlik et al., 1991). We constructed a transfer scenario from this problem by extracting from the training data all examples in which, if white's pawn were promoted, the king would be attacked in some way. Networks trained on this subproblem were used as transfer sources to a target problem for the full endgame task. 12 hidden units were used, with $\eta = 0.65$, $\alpha = 0.05$. The target task had 591 patterns.

Source networks were trained to a large number of epochs using different automatically determined η and α values. The different source networks were trained for each problem, each starting from different initial conditions. From each set of target training data, ten different 90%/10% holdout conditions were generated (Weiss and Kulikowski, 1991). Training was done on a partition of the data consisting of 90%; then generalization (testing) curves were obtained by testing on the remaining 10%, for 10 different such splits. For each holdout, 10 different initial conditions were used for target training. For random trials, each of these was a different set of initial random weights. For literal trials, these were each literal weights from a different one of the 10 source networks. For DBT trials, each initial condition used the results of applying the DBT transfer algorithm to a different source network. This resulted in 100 different training runs for each condition and each problem.

By averaging the 100 scores at each epoch, we obtained a DBT, literal and random initialization learning curve for target training on each of the seven tasks described above.

For purposes of comparison, we also tested the source networks directly on the target tasks, without any training on the target data. This yielded 10 different numbers (one for each holdout condition) for each of the seven tasks. For each task, the 10 numbers were averaged together.

11.5 Results

Empirical results for neural networks are often reported in terms of relative performance levels obtained on a set of test data (cf. Weiss and Kulikowski, 1991). Since our goal was to establish that the DBT method improves not the performance of the final network, but the learning algorithms' speed in achieving that level, a more complicated analysis of test data learning curve shapes was required. Previous authors' approaches to this problem have involved choosing a stopping criterion (such as 99.5% performance, *cf.* Shavlik *et al.*, 1991), and measuring the number of training epochs to reach that point. Such an approach was problematic for our benchmarks, because many were more difficult problems, and so were never able to reach such a high performance score. Furthermore, this measure doesn't capture the shape of the curve leading to the 99.5% level, as illustrated in Figure 11.9.

One solution that may seem suggested by Figure 11.9 is to simply take the area under the learning curves, but this retains the problem of 99.5% being an arbitrary criterion – would the relative areas have been the same if, say, 80% had been used as the criterion instead?

To address these issues, we used as a stopping point the epoch at which the curves reflect populations that do not have statistically significantly different results. To understand how this was done, recall that each of our curves reflects an average of 100 different runs – 10 for each different holdout condition for each of 10 different initial conditions. Therefore, at each epoch, two populations of 100 numbers can be compared. We performed a one-sided T-test to compare curves at each epoch, and considered the curves to be significantly different if the T-test reflected at least 99.0% confidence that the numbers came from different populations. We then determined the number of epochs for which the method to be tested was statistically significantly different from the baseline method of random initialization.

The problems on which DBT was evaluated were designed to represent an applied situation in which there may be limited computing resources available.

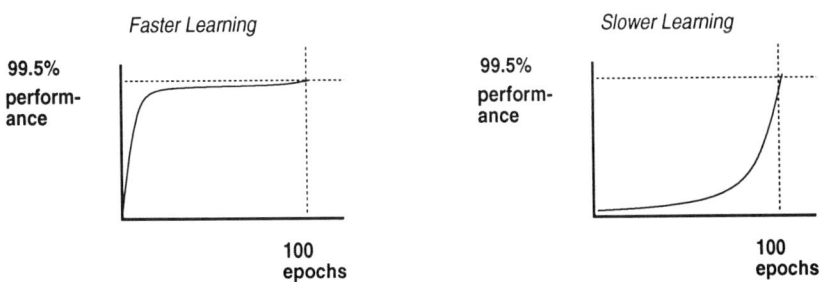

Figure 11.9 *An illustration of how a fixed criterion may not capture learning speed. Though both of these curves reach the 99.5% performance level point at the same time, they are different shapes before that time.*

The number of epochs of statistically significant superiority could thereby be potentially used to estimate the probability that, if training was stopped early, the resulting performance would be statistically superior.

Although this approach makes the choice of stopping criterion more objective, the issue remains that the shape of the curves before achieving that criterion performance level has been lost. Therefore, we also measured the point (in terms of percent of epochs before the stopping criterion) at which curves reached 66%, 95% and 98% of the highest curves' level at the stopping point. This approach to comparing curve shapes allows for same-method, different-task comparisons (since we measure the same quantities for every task), and for same-task, different-method comparisons (since we can compare multiple methods to the random initialization baseline to see which does relatively better).

Using these measures, we compared DBT-trained networks to those that had been randomly initialized. To gather evidence in support of DBT over literal transfer, we also compared networks initialized via literal transfer to randomly initialized networks.

Our primary results are as follows:

DBT vs. Random

- As expected, final performance levels for DBT and randomly initialized networks were not statistically significantly different.
- DBT demonstrated some number of significantly better epochs over random networks for 6/7 of the tasks studied. In no epoch was a randomly initialized network significantly better than one initialized via DBT.
- Curve shape, DBT vs. random:
  - DBT networks converged up to 25 times faster to the 66% level than random nets.
  - DBT networks converged up to 32 times faster to the 95% level than random nets.

Table 11.3 *Performance of source networks on target tasks. Random network scores at the end of target training are shown for comparison.*

Task	Average source score on target data	Randomization of last performance
PB	0.51	0.86 ± 0.01
PB123	0.70	0.90 ± 0.02
PB-onemale	0.68	0.95 ± 0.00
Heart-HS	0.42	0.99 ± 0.00
Heart-VAS	0.72	0.99 ± 0.00
DNA	0.75	0.89 ± 0.02
Chess	0.86	0.97 ± 0.01

  -DBT networks converged up to 43 times faster to the 98% level than random nets.

Literal vs. Random

- For 4/7 tasks, literal networks were asymptotically *inferior* to random networks.
- The number of epochs of statistically significant literal superiority over random, averaged over our seven benchmark tasks, was 108, compared to 134 for DBT vs. random. Literal networks were statistically significantly *inferior* to random networks for an average of 208 epochs.
- Curve shape, literal vs. random:
  - Literal networks converged up to 59 times faster to the 66% level than random networks.
  - At the 95% level, one literal network never reached this point; the remaining literal networks were up to 59 times faster than random networks to this criterion.
  - At the 98% level, 2 literal networks never reached this point; the remaining literal networks were up to 77 times faster to reach this point than random networks.

These results are broken down by task in Tables 11.4 and 11.5. Figure 11.10 gives notes explaining how to read these tables.

Using source networks on target tasks, without target training

Table 11.3 shows the average score of source networks, as tested on the target training data. For comparison, scores of randomly initialized target networks at the end of training are shown. These results show that using the source network on the target task is not a good idea – they do not achieve the same performance scores as randomly initialized networks.

11.6 Discussion

In summary, these results support the hypothesis that DBT gives substantial and significant learning speed improvement over randomly initialized networks on a diversity of tasks. If random initialization had been used instead of DBT, learning would have been measurably slower according to all criteria studied on 6/7 tasks, and would have had a similar speed on the remaining task.

These results also support the hypothesis that the complexity of DBT is justified compared to literal transfer. Unlike DBT, literal initialization led to a majority of networks that gave asymptotically worse performance than randomly initialized networks. On the remaining tasks, the literal condition was faster to converge on average in some situations, perhaps based on a strong similarity between source and target problems.

Table 11.4 *Results of DBT comparisons to randomly initialized networks.*

Task	DBT Last Perf	Rand Last Perf	Eps sig. DBT sp'y	Eps of norm crve	% Conv. time to 66% of random			% Conv. time to 95% of random			% Conv. time to 98% of random		
					DBT	Rand	ratio	DBT	Rand	ratio	DBT	Rand	ratio
PB	0.85 ± 0.01	0.86 ± 0.01	26	26	3.85	26.92	1:7	3.85	80.77	1:21	3.85	88.46	1:23
PB123	0.91 ± 0.02	0.90 ± 0.02	185	185	0.54	8.65	1:16	1.08	34.05	1:32	1.08	45.95	1:43
PB-onemale	0.89 ± 0.06	0.95 ± 0.00	391	415	1.20	29.40	1:25	2.65	74.22	1:28	3.13	77.11	1:25
Heart-HS	0.99 ± 0.00	0.99 ± 0.00	194	254	0.39	0.39	1:1	0.39	0.39	1:1	1.18	1.97	1:2
Heart-VAS	0.99 ± 0.00	0.99 ± 0.00	5	6	16.67	16.67	1:1	16.67	16.67	1:1	16.67	50.00	1:3
DNA	0.89 ± 0.02	0.89 ± 0.02	0*	0*	1.00	1.00	1:1	5.00	4.00	1.3:1	8.00	6.00	1.3:1
Chess	0.98 ± 0.01	0.97 ± 0.01	140	140	2.14	11.43	1:5	14.29	35.00	1:2	23.57	55.71	1:2
Mean			134										

Table 11.5 *Results of literal comparisons to randomly initialized networks.*

Task	Literal Last Perf	Rand Last Perf	Epchs of 1sig /rsig	Epchs of norm crve	% Conv. time to 66% of rand			% Conv. time to 95% of rand			% Conv. time to 98% of rand		
					Lit	Rand	ratio	Lit	Rand	ratio	Lit	Rand	ratio
PB	0.84 ± 0.01	0.86 ± 0.01	24/0	24	4.17	25.00	1:6	8.33	83.33	1:10	8.33	91.67	1:11
PB123	0.90 ± 0.02	0.90 ± 0.02	107/0	116	0.86	12.93	1:15	0.86	50.86	1:59	0.86	66.38	1:77
PB-onemale	0.80 ± 0.06	0.95 ± 0.00	254/516*	1000*	0.30	17.60	1:59	∞	53.70	∞:1	∞	64.90	∞:1
Heart-HS	0.99 ± 0.00	0.99 ± 0.00	2/531†	700†	0.14	0.14	1:1	0.14	0.14	1:1	3.00	1.00	3:1
Heart-VAS	0.97 ± 0.00	0.99 ± 0.00	0/398†	400†	0.25	0.25	1:1	0.25	0.25	1:1	34.50	1.50	23:1
DNA	0.87 ± 0.03	0.89 ± 0.02	0/11†	26†	3.85	3.85	1:1	42.31	19.23	2:1	∞	23.08	∞:1
Chess	0.98 ± 0.01	0.97 ± 0.01	367/0	373	0.27	4.29	1:16	4.56	14.48	1:3	7.77	27.35	1:4
Mean			108/ 208										

- First two columns show score at end of epochs for which tasks were trained, along with the 99.0% confidence interval.
- The column 'Eps sig. DBT sp'y' shows for how many epochs DBT or literal transfer was found to be statistically significantly superior to a random network (99.9% confidence).
- The column 'Eps of norm crve' shows the number of epochs used to generate a 'normalized' curve, from which measures reflecting curve shape during epochs of significance (to be shown in remaining columns) were derived. The number in this column was determined by taking all epochs starting at epoch 1, up to and including the last epoch for which a significant difference was detected. Discrepancies between values in this and the previous column represent 'false convergence' – where the test condition (DBT or literal) and random networks seemed to have reached a point of no significant difference, but they later diverged again.
- Columns to the right of the fourth give the percentage of normalized epochs required for DBT and random networks to reach different criteria, along with the ratio of these times. Each criterion is expressed in terms of percent of highest random score at the end of the normalized epochs.
- Amount of speedup to different criteria on the normalized curve are shown: 66%, 95%, 98%. Most ratios are rounded to the nearest whole number.
  66% criterion is related to the point that an exponential curve begins to flatten out.
  95% criterion shows % convergence time differences near to top performance score. Note that there is no speedup to the 95% level for the Heart-HS and Heart-VAS for DBT tasks compared to randomly initialized networks. 98% criterion addresses this problem – at this level the DBT curves for the Heart-HS and Heart-VAS tasks show speedup compared to randomly initialized networks.
- * in Table 11.4 indicates that there were no epochs of significance. Remaining entries are for entire curve, though there was no significance there.
- Column 3 of Table 11.5 indicates that random networks were often significantly superior to literally initialized networks. The two entries in each row of this column show the number of epochs for which the literal network was significantly better than the random network, followed by the number of epochs that the random network was significantly better than the literal network.
- * in Table 11.5 indicates that, for the PB-onemale task, curves crossed during learning, from literal being superior to random being superior, and at the end of training, random remained asymptotically superior. Remaining measures are over entire curve. Note that ∞ entries in this row indicate that the literal network never reached the indicated criterion.
- † indicates that the literal network was significantly inferior to the random network at the end of training; normalization period was the entire learning session. Note that, despite this fact, the Heart literal networks did get to within 98% of the random score, albeit slower. The DNA networks didn't reach the 98% criterion, but did get to 95% of the random score.

Figure 11.10 *Notes on reading results tables.*

Finally, we've shown that, for the tasks studied, DBT was superior to simply using the source network on the target task.

11.6.1 Future directions

Several potential future directions for this work are outlined below.

Performance improvement via transfer

An initial goal for transfer was to improve network performance as well as learning speed. Studies like Kolen and Pollack (1990) showed that asymptotic back-propagation performance was very sensitive to initial conditions, so it made sense to believe that, by changing these conditions, performance could be improved over randomly initialized networks.

However, we were surprised by the fact that random networks that we trained gave very good asymptotic performance – there were very few local minima (which would have caused asymptotic performance to be substantially lower for random networks than for others) observed during training. We can speculate that some aspect of our careful training methodology for choosing α and η led to this good performance.

Upon consideration of these results, it seems that, if the target training data adequately represents the target concept, then little is to be gained by transfer over random initialization in terms of asymptotic performance. Even random networks will eventually learn the target concept.

Nonetheless, it should still be possible to develop transfer methods that demonstrate asymptotic performance improvement over randomly initialized target networks. This could be done by incorporating a stronger bias from the source network. Recall that the goal of our transfer methodology was only to fit the target training data as well as possible. All parameters (η, α, #HU, s, c) were chosen based on the target training data. There was no effort to retain source weights when they were irrelevant to the target training data, but when they might have been nonetheless relevant to the generalization performance on the target task (which may not have been adequately represented by the target data).

To improve performance via transfer requires some means of forcing the network to use source weights, even when they're incompatible with the target training data. Probably the simplest such technique is to limit the number of epochs on which the target data is trained. However, this approach requires reliable knowledge of the relevance (and perhaps also the **degree** of relevance) of the source to the target task.

Quantifying relevance of source to target task

The seven tasks described in section 11.4 were chosen because, based on our knowledge of the domains from which they were drawn, it appeared that there were at least two closely related tasks between which transfer might be possible. In a practical situation, obtaining a source network might be expensive, so it might be helpful to develop methods for assessing source/target task relevance before source training is performed or source weights are available. This might be done using formal domain knowledge about task similarities and differences.

An alternative approach is to analyse source and target training data and source weights, if available, to ascertain relevance. Since DBT attempts to retain hyperplanes with high IM values, simply measuring the IM of source network hyperplanes on target training data can give a rough determination of relevance. For the seven tasks studied, we observed some correlation between IM and eventual DBT superiority over randomly initialized networks. These results are not significant, however, since they were only over the seven tasks studied. Even with a more extensive body of test results, however, the correlation between IM and eventual performance will remain an approximate predictor of DBT success until methods are developed to estimate final back-propagation performance, given initial conditions.

Further paradigms for DBT

The DBT algorithm allows information about the target data to be merged with weights from the source classifier. Such a procedure is applicable in contexts other than transfer, such as in active learning schemes (where new training data is obtained by querying the environment (cf. Cohn *et al.*, 1990), and in pedagogical training methods (where training data is segregated into stages to speed learning). DBT may also be used as a postprocessor to a method such as KBANN, to adapt a knowledge source to the training data prior to learning. In these contexts, DBT acts as a catalyst – allowing faster learning by preprocessing weights according to new training data.

11.7 Conclusion

This chapter has described the problem of transfer of information between neural networks for inductive learning. Transfer can improve learning on tasks related to those for which classifiers have previously been trained. We have presented the results of empirical tests that demonstrate that the DBT algorithm gives a substantial amount of learning speed-up over random initialization. Furthermore, the use of the DBT algorithm has been justified via comparison to more straightforward approaches, such as literal transfer, and simply using the source network on the target task.

This study demonstrates transfer's feasibility; we believe that the continued development of sophisticated transfer techniques should lead to powerful autonomous learning systems that are able to build on their own results.

Acknowledgments

This work was partially supported by DOE#DE-FG02-91ER 61129, through subcontract #097P753 from the University of Wisconsin.

Thanks to Mike Mozer, Aaron Gordon, and Alan Rock for reviewing drafts of this chapter, and to Jack Mostow, Haym Hirsh, Casimir Kulikowski, Mick Noordewier, and Steve Hanson for continuing input into this research program. Haym Hirsh, John Smith, David Loewenstern, Vince Sgro and Paul Hoeper gave helpful suggestions on papers on which this chapter was based. Tom Fawcett helped with many of the symbolic referencees. Alex Waibel suggested the application of transfer to speaker-dependent tasks. The heart disease data was collected by: Matthias Pfister, MD, of University Hospital in Zurich, Switzerland; Andras Janosi, MD, of Hungarian Institute of Cardiology, Budapest; and Robert Detrano, MD, of the VA Medical Center, Long Beach and Cleveland Clinic Foundation. We used software distributed with McClelland and Rumelhart (1988) for many of our simulations.

References

Atlas, L.E., Connor, J., Park, D. *et al.* (1990a) A performance comparison of trained multi-layer perceptrons and trained classification trees. *IEEE International Conference on Systems, Man, and Cybernetics, Cambridge, Massachusetts*, November 14–17.

Atlas, L., Cole, R., Muthasamy, Y. *et al.* (1990b) A performance comparison of trained multi-layer perceptrons and trained classification trees, in *Advances in Neural Information Processing Systems 2* (ed. D.S. Touretzky), Morgan Kaufmann, San Mateo, CA, pp. 622–9.

Atlas, L., Cole, R., Muthusamy, Y. *et al.* (1990c) Performance comparisons between backpropagation networks and classification trees on three real-world applications. *Proceedings of the IEEE*, **78**(10), 1614–19.

Callan, J.P. and Utgoff, P.E. (1991) Constructive induction on domain information. *Proceedings of the Ninth National Conference on Artificial Intelligence (AAAI-91)*, Anaheim, CA, pp. 614–19.

Cohn, D., Atlas, L.E., Ladner, R. *et al.* (1990) Training connectionist networks with queries and selective sampling, in *Advances in Neural Information Processing Systems 2* (ed. D.S. Touretzky), Morgan Kaufmann, San Mateo, CA, pp. 566–73.

Cole, R.A., Muthusamy, Y.K., Atlas, L. *et al.* (1990) Speaker-independent vowel recognition: Comparison of backpropagation and trained classification trees. *Proceedings Twenty-Third Annual Hawaii International Conference on System Sciences, Kilua-Kona, Hawaii*, January 2–5, pp. 132–141.

Danyluk, A.P. (1989) Finding new rules for incomplete theories: explicit biases for induction with contextual information. *Proceedings Sixth International Workshop on Machine Learning*, Cornell University, pp. 34–6, June.

Detrano, R., Jansosi, A., Steinbrunn, W. *et al.* (1989) International application of a new probability algorithm for the diagnosis of coronary artery disease. *American Journal of Cardiology*, **64**, 304–10.

Dewan, H.M., and Sontag, E. (1990) Using extrapolation to speed up the back-propagation algorithm. *Proceedings International Joint Conference on Neural Networks*, Washington, DC, volume 1, pp. 613–16.

Dietterich, T.G., Hild, H. and Bakiri, G. (1990) A comparative study of ID3 and back-propagation for English text-to-speech mapping. *Technical Report (unnumbered)*, Department of Computer Science, Oregon State University.

Fahlman, S. (1990) The cascade-correlation learning architecture. *Technical Report CMU-CS-90-100*, Carnegie Mellon Computer Science Department.

Fawcett, T.E. and Utgoff, P.E. (1991) A hybrid method for feature generation. *Proceedings of the Eighth International Workshop on Machine Learning*, Evanson, IL, 137–41.

Fisher, D.H. and McKusick, K.B. (1989) An empirical comparison of ID3 and back-propagation. *Proceedings of the Eleventh International Joint Conference on Artificial Intelligence*, Detroit, MI, pp. 788–93.

Fu, L. (1991) Rule learning by searching on adapted nets. *Proceedings Ninth National Conference on Artificial Intelligence (AAAI-91)*, Anaheim, CA, pp. 590–5.

Gennari, J.H., Langley, P. and Fisher, D. (1989) Models of incremental concept formation. *Artificial Intelligence*, **40**, 11–61.

Hanson, S.J. and Burr, D.J. (1987) Knowledge Representation in Connectionist Networks. *Technical report*, Bell Communications Research, Morristown, New Jersey.

Hayes-Roth, B. (1983) The blackboard architecture: A general framework for problem solving? *Report HPP-88-30*, Department of Computer Science, Stanford University.

Hertz, J.A., Palmer, R.G. and Krogh, A.S. (1991) *Introduction to the Theory of Neural Computation*. Addison-Wesley, Redwood City, CA.

Hinton, G.E., Sejnowski, T.J. and Ackley, D.H. (1984) Boltzmann machines: constraint satisfaction networks that learn. *Technical Report CMU-CS-84-119*, Carnegie-Mellon University.

Holte, R.C., Acker, L.E. and Porter, B.W. (1989) Concept learning and the problem of small disjuncts. *Proceedings International Joint Conference on Artificial Intelligence*, Morgan Kaufmann, San Mateo, CA, pp. 813–18.

Kolen, J.F. and Pollack, J. (1990) Scenes from exclusive-or: Back propagation is sensitive to initial conditions. *Proceedings Twelfth Annual Conference of the Cognitive Science Society*, Cambridge, MA, p. 868.

Maren, A.J., Harston, C.T. and Pap, R.M. (1990) *Handbook of Neural Computing Applications*. Academic Press, New York, NY.

Martin, G. (1988) The effects of old learning on new in Hopfield and Backprop-agation nets. *Technical Report ACA-HI-019*, Microelectronics and Computer Technology Corporation (MCC).

McClelland, J.L. and Rumelhart, D.E. (1988) *Explorations in Parallel Distributed Processing: A Handbook of Models, Programs, and Exercises*. MIT Press, Cambridge, MA

McCloskey, M. and Cohen, N.J. (1989) Catastrophic interference in connectionist networks: the sequential learning problem. *The Psychology of Learning and Motivation*, **24**.

McMillan, C., Mozer, M. and Smolensky, P. (1992) Rule induction through integrated symbolic and subsymbolic processing, in *Advances in Neural Information Processing Systems 4*, (eds. J.E. Moody, S.J. Hanson and R.P. Lippmann), Morgan Kaufmann, San Mateo, CA, pp. 969–76.

Mingers, J. (1989) An empirical comparison of selection measures for decision-tree induction. *Machine Learning*, **3**(4), 319–42.

Mitchell, T.M., Keller, R.M. and Kedar-Cabelli, S.T. (1985) Explanation-based generalization: A unifying view. *Technical Report ML-TR-2*, Rutgers University Department of Computer Science.

Moody, J.E., Hanson, J. and Lippmann R.P. (eds) (1992) *Advances in Neural Information Processing Systems 4*. Morgan Kaufmann, San Mateo, CA.

Mooney, R. and Ourston D. (1989) Induction over the unexplained: Integrated learning of concepts with both explainable and conventional aspects. *Proceedings Sixth International Workshop on Machine Learning*, Cornell University, June, pp. 5–7.

Mooney, R.J., Shavlik, J.W., Towell, G.G. and Gove, A. (1989) An experimental comparison of symbolic and connectionist learning algorithms. *Proceedings Eleventh International Joint Conference on Artificial Intelligence*, August, pp. 775–80.

Pazzani, M.J. (1989) Detecting and correcting errors of omission after explanation-based learning. *Proceedings Eleventh International Joint Conference on Artificial Intelligence*, August, pp. 713–17.

Peterson and Barney. (1952) Control methods used in a study of the vowels. *J. Acoust Soc. Am.*, **24**(2), 175–84.

Pratt, L.Y. (1990) Neural networks and decision tree induction: Exploring the relationship between two research areas, 1990. Handout at NIPS-90 workshop.

Pratt, L.Y. (1992) Experiments in the transfer of knowledge between neural networks, in *Computational Learning Theory and Natural Learning Systems, Constraints and Prospects.* (eds. S. Hanson, G. Drastal, and R. Rivest), MIT Press, Cambridge, MA.

Pratt, L.Y. and Kamm, C.A. (1991) Improving a phoneme classification neural network through problem decomposition. *Proceedings International Joint Conference on Neural Networks (IJCNN-91)*, Seattle, WA, pp. 821–6.

Pratt, L.Y., Mostow, J. and Kamm, C.A. (1991) Direct transfer of learned information among neural networks. *Proceedings Ninth National Conference on Artificial Intelligence (AAAI-91)*, Anaheim, CA, pp. 584–9.

Quinlan J.R. (1986) Induction of Decision Trees. *Machine Learning*, **1**, 81–106.

Ramachandran, S. and Pratt, L. (1992) Discriminability based skeletonisation, in *Advances in Neural Information Processing Systems 4* (eds. J.E. Moody, S.J. Hanson and R.P. Lippmann), Morgan Kaufmann, San Mateo, CA.

Rumelhart, D.E., Hinton, G.E. and Williams, R.J. (1987a) Learning internal representations by error propagation, in *Parallel Distributed Processing: Explorations in the Microstructure of Cognition* (eds. D.E. Rumelhart and J.L. McClelland), MIT Press: Bradford Books, Cambridge, MA.

Rumelhart, D.E., McClelland, J.L. and the PDP Research Group (eds.) (1987b) *Parallel Distributed Processing: Explorations in the Microstructure of Cognition*, volume 1. MIT Press: Bradford Books, Cambridge, MA.

Rutenberg, M.R. (1992) PAPNET: A neural net based cytological screening system, in *Advances in Neural Information Processing Systems 4*, Morgan Kaufmann, San Mateo, CA.

Shapiro, A.D. (1988) *Structure Induction in Expert Systems*. Addison-Wesley, New York, USA.

Shavlik, J.W., Mooney, R.J. and Towell, G.G. (1991) Symbolic and neural net learning algorithms: An experimental comparison. *Machine Learning*, **6**(2), 111–43.

Sontag, E. (1989) Sigmoids distinguish more efficiently than heavisides. *Neural Computation*, **1**, 470–2.

Tenorio, M.F. and Lee, W.T. (1989) Self-organizing neural network for optimum supervised learning. *Technical Report TR-EE-89-30*, Purdue University, School of Electrical Engineering.

Thrun, S.B., Bala, J., Bloedorn, E. *et al.* (1991) The monk's problems: A performance comparison of different learning algorithms. *Technical Report CMU-CS-91-197*, Carnegie Mellon University.

Towell, G.G. and Shavlik, J.W. (1992) Interpretation of artificial neural networks: Mapping knowledge-based neural networks into rules, in *Advances in Neural Information Processing Systems 4*, Morgan Kaufmann, San Mateo, CA, pp. 977–84.

Towell, G.G., Shavlik, J.W. and Noordewier, M.O. (1990) Refinement of approximate domain theories by knowledge-based neural networks. *Proceedings of AAAI-90*, Morgan Kaufmann, San Mateo, CA, pp. 861–6.

Utgoff, P.E. (1986) Shift of bias for inductive concept learning, in *Machine Learning: An Artificial Intelligence Approach* (eds. G. Carbonell, R.S. Michalski and T.M. Mitchell), Morgan Kaufmann, San Mateo, CA, pp. 107–48.

Waibel, A., Sawai, H. and Shikano, K. (1989) Modularity and scaling in large phonemic neural networks. *IEEE Transactions on Acoustics, Speech, and Signal Processing*, **37**(12), 1888–98.

Watrous, R.L. (1991) Current status of Peterson–Barney vowel formant data. *Journal of the Acoustical Society of America*, **89**(3), March.

Weber, B. (1990) The scary 64. *The New York Times*, October 30.

Weiss, S.M. and Kulikowski, C.A. (1991) *Computer Systems that Learn*. Morgan Kaufmann, San Mateo, CA.

Wejchert, J. and Tesauro, G. (1990) Neural network visualization, in *Advances in Neural Information Processing Systems 2* (ed. D.S. Touretzky), Morgan Kaufmann, San Mateo, CA.

Widrow, B. and Winter, R. (1988) Neural nets for adaptive filtering and adaptive pattern recognition. *IEEE Computer*, pp. 25–39, March.

12

Long-term memory for neural networks

ANSHU AGARWAL* and RICHARD J. MAMMONE[†]
*Motorola, Inc., Cambridge, MA, USA
[†]Center for Computer Aids for Industrial Productivity, Rutgers University, Piscataway, New Jersey 08855, USA

12.1 Introduction

Connectionist networks are usually trained **concurrently**, i.e. all of the training data is presented at one time. In contrast, human learning is **sequential**, i.e.. learning consists of various data sets presented at different times. Humans have the ability to retain knowledge learned previously while assimilating additional information. Unfortunately, traditional neural networks do not exhibit this retention of old knowledge. This phenomenon of forgetting prior knowledge is referred to as **interference** (Sloman and Rumelhart, 1991), **catastrophic forgetting** (or simply **forgetting**) (McCloskey and Cohen, 1989) or **blurring of old memories** (Hintan and Plaut, 1987). Another closely related problem is one of Retroactive Interference (RI), where learning a different task may interfere with tasks learned earlier. This problem is discussed by McCloskey and Cohen (1989).

Sutton (1986) has proved that gradient descent algorithms such as the back-propagation algorithm are particularly vulnerable to forgetting. We introduce a simple method which will allow neural networks to learn from new examples of tasks while not forgetting or violating data learned previously.

12.1.1 Gradient descent algorithms

A brief review of gradient-based learning will be given to help formulate the problem of forgetting. Gradient descent algorithms iteratively update a weight

Artificial Neural Networks for Speech and Vision. Edited by Richard J. Mammone. Published in 1993 by Chapman & Hall, London. ISBN 0 412 54850 X vector **w** such that an error $\mathscr{E}(\cdot)$ is reduced at each step, i.e.

$$\mathscr{E}(\mathbf{w} + \Delta\mathbf{w}) < \mathscr{E}(\mathbf{w}). \tag{1}$$

The error metric can be expanded using the Taylor series approximation to give

$$\mathscr{E}(\mathbf{w}) + \Delta\mathbf{w}\,\frac{\partial\mathscr{E}(\mathbf{w})}{\partial\mathbf{w}} + \mathcal{O}(\cdot\mathbf{w}^2) \leqslant \mathscr{E}(\mathbf{w}). \tag{2}$$

Thus, equation (1) is equivalent to the condition

$$\Delta\mathbf{w}\,\frac{\partial\mathscr{E}(\mathbf{w})}{\partial\mathbf{w}} \leqslant \mathbf{0}, \tag{3}$$

when the higher order terms in equation (2) are neglected. Thus we see that to reduce the error, the weight vector should be changed in the opposite direction to the gradient. Gradient-descent algorithms select $\Delta\mathbf{w}$ such that

$$\Delta\mathbf{w} = -\mu\,\frac{\partial\mathscr{E}}{\partial\mathbf{w}} \tag{4}$$

where μ is called the learning parameter. The Widrow–Hoff or Least Mean Squares (LMS) algorithm and backpropagation algorithm are examples of gradient-descent algorithms (Rumelhart and McClelland, 1986; Werbos, 1974).

The error function in neural networks is usually made up of non-convex surfaces. In gradient descent algorithms, larger changes are made to the weights when the error function is steep. Conversely, if the gradient is small, it indicates a gentle slope and a larger step size μ should be used. Sutton (1986) argued that gradient descent algorithms cannot differentiate between weights and nodes that are unused or of less importance. For example, in Figure 12.1

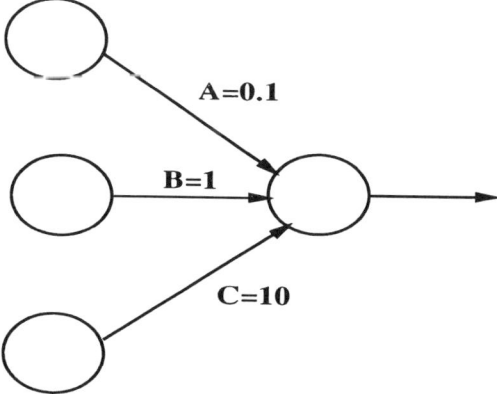

Figure 12.1 *Magnitudes of different weights differ thus changing the gradient along different dimensions.*

(Sutton, 1986) weight C is ten times larger than B and 100 times larger than A. Hence, the gradient due to C would be larger, and hence C changes more. A small change in C can affect the performance dramatically. Thus, when the network is trained on a new data set, the largest weights will affect the gradient most, and hence dominate the update correction. Thus gradient descent algorithms forget old data inherently.

Alternatively, we can view neural networks as **distributed knowledge representations** of knowledge. Information about a pattern or a set of patterns are not obtained from one unit, but from the collective action of many units. Since neurons are shared between patterns, and since the representations are learned by incremental weight changes, storing information about one pattern necessarily affects the representation of patterns stored earlier. But distributed representations provide powerful generalization and offer elegant associative memories. Thus the challenge is to reduce interference without sacrificing the quality of generalization.

12.2 Earlier approaches to the eliminating interference

12.2.1 Fast and slow weights

Hinton and Plaut (1987) suggested the use of two connections between each node instead of one. The first weight was a 'fast weight' which would be updated more often than the other 'slow weight'. Thus the fast weight vector encodes recently acquired information, while the slow weight vector primarily encodes information learned previously. The goal of the two weight vector approaches was not to eliminate interference, but to speed up the relearning process. That is, after training on a new data set, the old information can be 'deblurred' at a faster rate then before, and only a subset of the old set is needed to do this. The fast weights slowly decay to zero, and in the limit all of the information is transferred to the long-term memory. Hinton and Plaut (1987) selected 100 random input vectors of dimension 10 and mapped them into an arbitrary vector of dimension 10. The network had 100 hidden units. After the network was trained on these patterns, five new random associations were selected and the network was trained on these. This learning was found to interfere with the old learning, but when trained on only a part of the original training set, the performance improved on the entire original set. The retraining was faster than the original training. This method required a longer total training time for better performance, since the simulations would succeed only if given sufficient time to allow the decay of the fast weights.

The faster relearning can be explained using Figure 12.2 (Hetherington, 1990). We can see that the gradient is significantly smaller in one direction than the other. The weights are assumed to be randomly initialized to point A. After training on the old data, the weight moves along the valley to point B. When trained on the new set, the weight moves to point C which has the

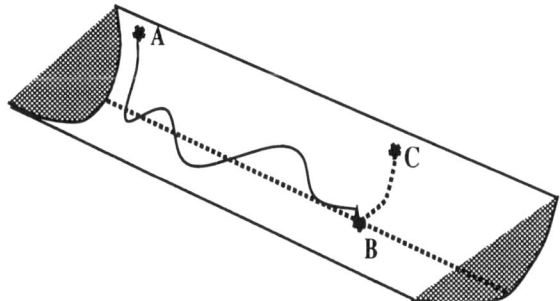

Figure 12.2 *Faster learning explanation. Point A denotes initial position of weight; point B is reached after training on old set; point C is reached after training on new set. Though the magnitude of errors at A and C are the same, C is closer to B, hence relearning is faster.*

same error value as A. But we can see that it is far closer to point B than A is. Thus relearning is faster. The figure also illustrates that the criterion of mean square error is not a good measure of interference or retention.

12.2.2 Retraining and overlapped data sets

Hetherington (1990) constructed a network repeating the Arithmetic learning experiment conducted by McCloskey and Cohen (1989). They confirmed that interference occurred when sequential training was used on two different data sets. However, they argued that learning in humans was not strictly sequential – children are tested and retrained on old rules and information while they are taught new ideas. To simulate this, Hetherington performed a series of simulations.

In the first experiment, he trained the network on the 'one's problem' and then the 'two's problem'. Then, a network was retrained on a new set which contained both the one's and the three's problem. He showed that the network learned the one's problem faster than the three's problem, even though they were problems of equal complexity. Thus, he argued, the network had not entirely forgotten the one's problem, and there were savings in relearning the one's problem. The next experiment he carried out in five stages. Each stage had a new data set included and a part of the old set removed, i.e. new data was phased in while old data was phased out. The first stage had only the 'one's problems'. The 'two's problem' was introduced in the second, and so on until the last stage, which consisted of the five's problem. He showed that except for brief periods of slight disruption, the one's problem was not significantly forgotten.

Thus he argued that McCloskey and Cohen's (1989) simulations using strictly blocking sets of data were unrealistic, and the degree of forgetting was dependent upon how much overlap there is on the retraining.

12.2.3 Episodic gating

Sloman and Rumelhart (1991) have tried to alleviate the interference problem by using a different network architecture and by using what they call **hints**. They argued that if the input vectors were mutually orthogonal, there would be no interference. But this, they argue, goes against the principles of distributed processing. Thus they proposed representational and architectural constraints which help decorrelate the patterns which are within the same domain from there outside that domain. For decorrelating patterns in the same context, they used Willshaw's network (1981). This network assumes that the number of active units in the input is far less than the total number of features available. Each output is connected to each input by either '0' or '1' weight value. Output unit activations a_i are updated according to

$$a_i = \begin{cases} 1, & \text{if } \sum_{j=1}^{n_1} w_{ij}a_j > = m_1 \\ 0, & \text{if } \sum_{j=1}^{n_1} w_{ij}a_j < m_1 \end{cases}, \tag{5}$$

in which weight w_{ij} is assigned a value of '1' if a connection exists between the input and output and is '0' otherwise. The integer m_1 is the number of inputs with value '1'. Thus each output is activated via a connection between it and the input. Since weights are only added, never removed, old knowledge is never lost. But interference occurs if there are too many inputs, since there is a greater possibility of activating outputs that should not be activated.

To reduce intercontext interference they used the episodic memory model proposed by Tulving (1972). It is known that human memory attaches a context to knowledge, thus information is recalled with respect to the situation or 'episode', hence this model is called 'episodic'. Sloman and Rumelhart (1991) applied **episodic gating** to the Willshaw network (1981) i.e. they added units that determine whether a set of connections are valid in a given context. Thus the learning is done in two stages, the first where the information is learned and the next where the context is learned. But these episodic units, being neural networks themselves exhibit forgetting and slowly forget older contexts. They used this network on the Barnes and Underwood (1959) data and it showed significant improvement in performance.

12.2.4 A new approach to providing retention

An obvious way to eliminate interference would be to retrain the network on a composite data set consisting of the old and the new patterns. McCloskey and Cohen (1989) suggested that this might be the only alternative. But this method is computationally intensive, and makes no use whatsoever of the earlier training results. Moreover, frequently, the old data may not be available. In some important applications like the detection of explosives in airline baggage, learning needs to be **online** and the training set is always increasing. This is also true in the case of adaptive language acquisition (Gorin and Levinson, 1989), the addition of new words to our vocabulary and new contexts increase the data set. In such cases retraining concurrently would be impossible.

The previous work stated suggests that the problem of interference is inherent in connectionist networks. It has been mentioned that the basic training algorithm needs to be modified (Sloman and Rumelhart, 1991; Hetherington 1990). Since the multilayer perceptrons have gained wide acceptance, it would be useful to explore alternate retraining algorithms that alleviate this problem of interference. Among the concepts stated until now, the most important one would be the idea of **context** or **constraints**. In this chapter we show that online learning, when done with constraints, reduces the interference problem. We also explore a new training algorithm, which is a modification of the steepest descent method but does not suffer from interference. This algorithm can be used to retrain both the traditional multilayer perceptrons (MLP) and the Neural Tree Network (NTN) (Mammone, 1992) architectures. We also show that this algorithm is computationally less complex and has a better rate of convergence, and thus is suitable for online applications. The NTN, by its construction, provides all the advantages of a distributed network and because of its tree structure, provides a hierarchical generalization of similar patterns that is, lower nodes of a tree contain a super set of its preceding nodes (Rahim, 1992). We also present computer simulations where the new method is applied to various problems such as: vowel classification, explosive detection and adaptive language acquisition. The simulations show good performance.

12.3 Hyperplane perturbation

The weight vector of each perceptron can be represented as a hyperplane in feature space. Each hyperplane divides the data into subsets. The placement of a hyperplane is not unique as shown in Figure 12.3. Hence, a pattern (on which the neural network has not been trained but is known to belong to one of the two categories) may be misclassified due to a small misalignment of hyperplane. This misalignment occurs because the training set is not a complete representative of all the regularities that should be represented by the neural network. When the patterns that are misclassified are close to the boundaries of a hyperplane then a simple translation or rotation (Figure 12.4) or both can correctly reclassify the misclassified data set. The extent to which each hyperplane can be translated or rotated depends on the orientation of hyperplane. If the hyperplane is perturbed so that the nearest patterns are not misclassified, then it would appear that previously observed patterns will not be misclassified by the perturbed hyperplane.

Parameters like degree of translation, axis of rotation and angle of rotation are required to constrain the translation or rotation of the hyperplane. These parameters are not fixed for a particular task as they depend on the orientation

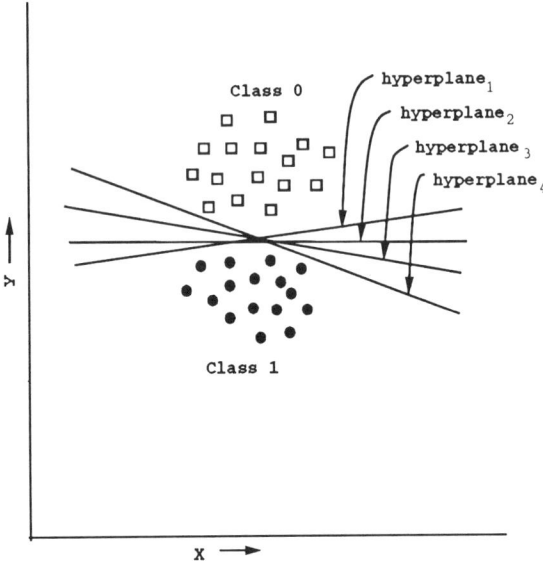

Figure 12.3 *Multiple hyperplanes solving the same problem.*

of the previously positioned hyperplanes in feature space. Therefore, an adaptive approach is described which would accomplish the task of hyperplane perturbation. Such an online training algorithm will be presented in the next section.

12.4 The Row Action Projection (RAP) algorithm

The RAP algorithm (Mammone, 1992) was originally developed by Kaczmarz (1937) and rediscovered by others (Hesman, 1980). The algorithm was developed to solve a set of linear equations

$$y = \mathbf{X}\mathbf{w}. \tag{6}$$

This system of equations can be solved by the Least Squares (LS) method, the pseudo-inverse, or the maximum likelihood approach (Mammone, 1992), but these methods are all block methods. The block methods can be prohibitive in terms of computation and memory requirements for large training data sets. Therefore, the RAP algorithm suggests itself as it operates on the rows of the feature vector matrix $\mathbf{X}$. Matrix inversion methods based on column operators such as the Greville method (Ben-Israel and Greville, 1974) and Sherman-Morrison formula (Press *et al.*, 1986) would involve more computations per iteration, whereas RAP involves only one scalar product per iteration. The RAP method can perform an operation for each sample as it is acquired, while column based methods still require a block of data to be stored

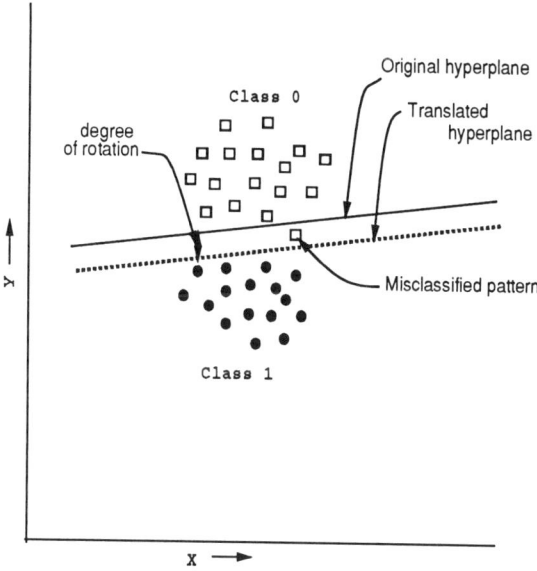

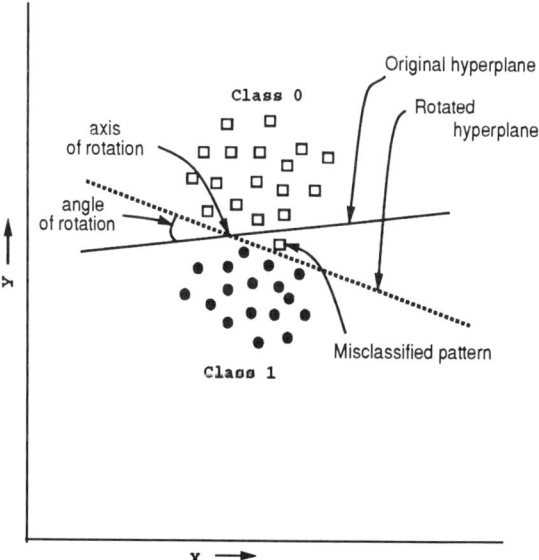

Figure 12.4 *Simple translation and rotation.*

for each operation. In addition, RAP has the characteristic of providing least squares estimates for both inconsistent and rank-deficient matrices.

The RAP method can be illustrated by writing out the set of equations for a discrete linear system.

$$y_1 = x_{11}w_1 + x_{12}w_2 + \cdots + x_{1N}w_N$$
$$y_2 = x_{21}w_1 + x_{22}w_2 + \cdots + x_{2N}w_N$$
$$\cdots \qquad \cdots \tag{7}$$
$$y_M = x_{M1}w_1 + x_{M2}w_2 + \cdots + x_{MN}w_N.$$

The locus of points that satisfy equation (7) is a hyperplane in an N-dimensional space whose surface normal is the vector $\hat{\mathbf{x}}_i$. The perpendicular distance of the hyperplane from the origin is proportional to y_i, as shown in Figure 12.5 ($N = 2$ in this case). The basic idea of RAP is to start with an initial guess for the weight vector $\mathbf{w}^0$. The initial point $\mathbf{w}^0$ is successively projected onto the hyperplanes until convergence to the solution is reached as shown in Figure 12.5. The projection is obtained from x_0 to the hyperplane by moving along the unit normal to the hyperplane. The general RAP method is given by

$$\mathbf{w}^{i+1} = \mathbf{w}^i + \mu \frac{e_j}{\|\mathbf{x}_j\|_2^2}\mathbf{x}_j,$$
$$e_j = y_j - \mathbf{x}_j\mathbf{w}^i, \tag{8}$$

where μ is step-size parameter which is bounded, i.e. $0 < \mu < 2$.

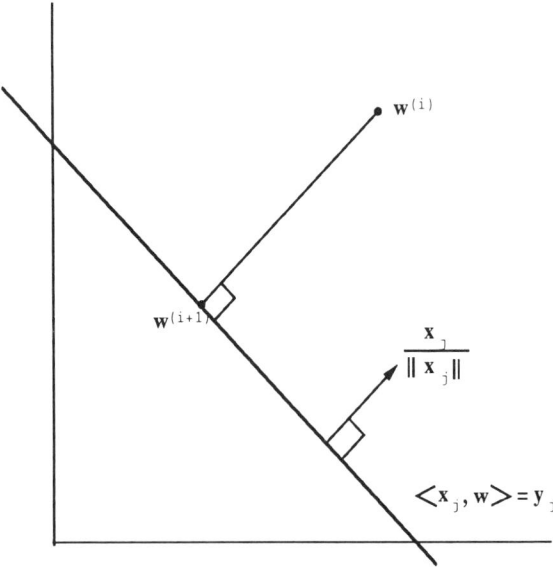

Figure 12.5 *Geometrical interpretation of RAP.*

It has also been shown that the RAP method converges asymptotically to the pseudo-inverse solution for the case of rank-deficient matrices.

12.5 Hyperplane perturbation using RAP

Thus we see that hyperplane perturbation can correct for the misclassifications that occur close to the hyperplane boundaries. In this section we discuss the requirement of imposing constraints from the original training data set. RAP is used to retrain the neural network. The initial estimate of the weight vector is chosen to be the weight vector obtained by training on the initial data. Constraints based on the closest points are imposed on the allowable amount of perturbation of the hyperplane from the original position.

12.5.1 Selection of constraints

The selection of constraints is a crucial step for the online training method. The constraints are based on the original feature vectors. The constraints should be such that they represent the training data and require minimum memory. The constraints should also allow the information to be quickly retrieved for online training. We have considered three ways of representing the training data.

(1) An arbitrary subset of feature vectors can be retained for later training. The values for each class would be of the order of the dimension of the feature space. A sufficient number selected at random can be prohibitive for many applications.

(2) Another approach for representing previously trained patterns is to denote the previously learned partitions of feature space by convex hulls. However this is prohibitive in terms of memory and processing time. If N points fall on the convex hull, it requires N^2 operations to retrieve the patterns from the convex hull (Sedgewick, 1990). In addition, the convex hull is inefficient as it considers all the points equally, whereas the information far from the hyperplane to be perturbed is not of much use in constraining its movement (Figure 12.6).

The convex hull approach can be efficient only if the patterns are clustered together and the number of patterns falling on the hull is a small number.

(3) The approach that we have used is to form a cluster of the points which are the nearest neighbors to the hyperplane. The closest point, the centroid and the variance of the cluster are stored. The set of closest neighbors (CN) are represented by their centroid and variance. These parameters are calculated during training. The CNs have the minimum perpendicular distance d from the hyperplane where,

$$d = \frac{\mathbf{w} \cdot \mathbf{x}}{\|\mathbf{w}\|_2}.$$

(9)

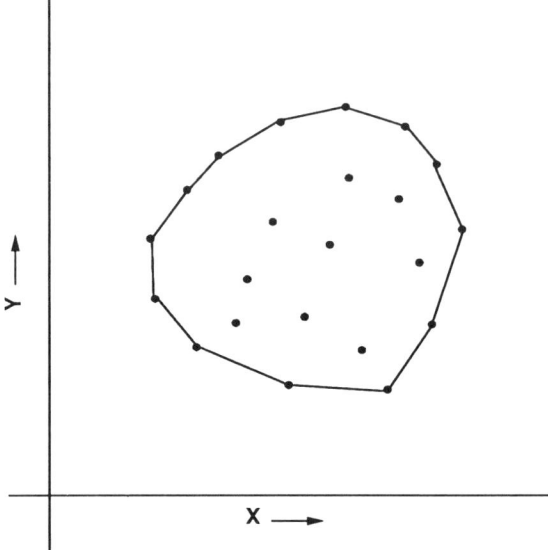

Figure 12.6 *Convex hull.*

The pattern which has minimum distance d corresponds to the closest pattern $\mathbf{x}_{CN}$.

If the dimensionality of the space is N then it has been found (Wilder, personal communication) that $3N$ patterns are sufficient for generalization. These $3N$ patterns are used to calculate the centroid and the variance of the CNs. The criteria for selecting the closest patterns depends on the problem. However, we have considered only those patterns where d is bounded such that

$$d_{\min} < d < \frac{d_{\max}}{2}.$$

Only those patterns which satisfy this criterion are considered as the M closest patterns. The centroid c_0 of these M patterns is then

$$\mathbf{c}_0 = \frac{\sum_{i=0}^{M} \mathbf{x}_i}{\mathbf{M}}. \tag{10}$$

The radius r_0 of the cluster formed by M closest patterns is the difference in the perpendicular distance of the centroid $\mathbf{c}_0$ and the closest pattern $\mathbf{x}_{CN}$ from the hyperplane

$$r_0 = \frac{\mathbf{w} \cdot \mathbf{c}_0 - \mathbf{w} \cdot \mathbf{x}_{CN}}{\| \mathbf{w} \|_2'}. \tag{11}$$

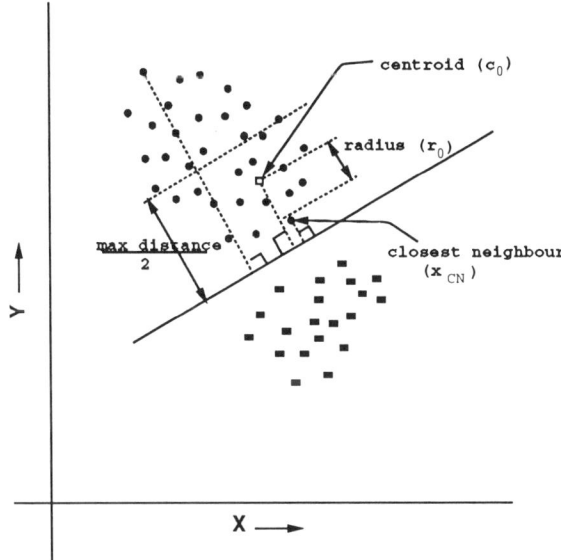

Figure 12.7 *Geometrical interpretation of chosen parameters.*

This choice of r_0 ensures that no point will be closer to the hyperplane than x_{CN}. Figure 12.7 illustrates the use of the centroid and variance for compactly modeling the CNs.

12.6 Application of new algorithm to NTN

The Online Training Method (OTM) can be applied to NTNs or MLPs. In this section we shall first review the NTN and then discuss how OTM can be used to improve the performance. The OTM can also be used and this is described in Agarwal (1993).

12.6.1 Neural Tree Network

The NTN is a hybrid pattern classifier that combines the principles of neural networks and decision trees (Sankar and Mammone, 1993). The MLP architecture has problems associated with local minima due to multiple layers. However, the NTN architecture has a lower probability of being trapped in local minima due to the use of single layered perceptron. A disadvantage of the MLP is that the number of perceptrons in the network architecture must be specified before learning. The architecture is found by trial and error. This results in extending the training time. The training algorithm for the NTN grows the appropriate network architecture. Thus the tree is grown during learning, rather being specified *a priori*, as in the MLP.

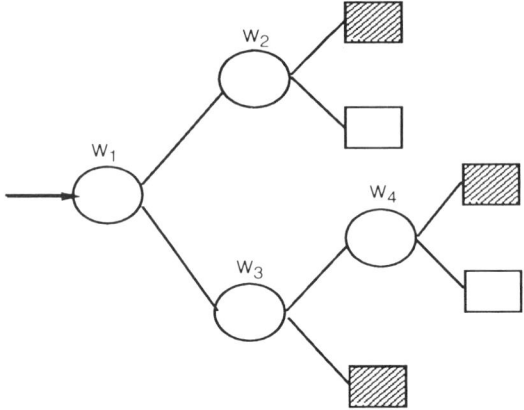

Figure 12.8 *Architecture of a binary N T N.* ▨: *class 1;* □: *class 2 (class 1 and 2 = leaf node);* ○: *node (SLP).*

Decision-trees (Werbos, 1974) also grow a network. However, decision-tree training algorithms use an exhaustive search strategy which is less efficient than the NTN training. The most widely used decision-tree learning algorithm allows only orthogonal splits of feature space. The NTN uses a gradient-descent based algorithm which uses the L_1 norm of error and is more efficient computationally than an exhaustive search. In addition, the NTN allows splits in feature space which are not perpendicular to the co-ordinates.

The NTN uses a tree architecture which is implemented sequentially. Each node of the tree is a single layer perceptron. The tree consists of a root node which is trained on all the feature vectors. Each subsequent node is trained on a subset of feature vectors. The number of branches of the tree is determined by the number of splits. The single layer perceptrons used in successive nodes split the data set until all feature vectors are correctly classified. The output of each leaf node corresponds to a particular class.

Figure 12.8 indicates an example of tree architecture.

12.6.2 *Learning algorithm for NTN*

The NTN successively divides the training set into mutually exclusive subsets, assigning each subset to a child node. Each successive division adds another level to the tree. A perfect 100% classification is obtained on the training data, since in the limit each feature vector can be isolated by using one hyperplane for each point.

The learning algorithm is recursive, and each node of the NTN is trained independently of the others. We shall consider the learning of a particular node t. The connection weights between the input nodes and the root node are randomly initialized. In the case of NTN, various labeling strategies can be followed. It has been found that the winner-takes-all strategy is the simplest, and gives good generalization. According to this strategy, the number of perceptrons in a node are equal to the number of possible classes at a node. Suppose the number of classes is m where $m \geqslant 2$. Each perceptron is used to find a hyperplane that separates the feature space into two subsets. The perceptron computes a nonlinear function of the dot product of its inputs and its weights as in back-propagation. The output of each perceptron is given by

$$y = f\left(\sum_i w_i \cdot x_i \right), \tag{12}$$

where x_i is the ith input; w_i is the ith weight and f is a non-linear function. The non-linear function used here is the logistic or sigmoidal function

$$f(x) = \frac{1}{1 + e^{-x}}. \tag{13}$$

The optimality criterion desired in training the NTN is to minimize the number of misclassifications or error. The standard back-propagation training techniques used to train MLPs minimize the L_2 norm of the magnitude of the error. The L_2 norm gives more weight to large errors than to small errors, thus the solution tends to have many errors of equal magnitude. The number of errors can thus be large, but each error will be small. The L_1 norm is more robust, that is it provides estimates with a few number of errors although they may be large. The total number of errors is usually lower with the L_1 norm than with the L_2 norm. Therefore, minimizing the L_1 norm results in better partitioning of feature space. The NTN training algorithm trains each perceptron by using a gradient-descent technique to minimize L_1 norm of the errors.

The L_1 norm of the error for pattern j is defined as

$$E_j = |t_j - y_j|, \tag{14}$$

where t_j is the jth target output and y_j is the actual output of the perceptron. The derivative of E_j with respect to the weight w_i from the ith input x_i is given by

$$\frac{\partial E_j}{\partial w_i} = -\operatorname{sgn}(t_j - y_j) f'(\mathbf{w} \cdot \mathbf{x}) x_i, \tag{15}$$

where the sgn $(\cdot)$ indicates the signum of the value within parentheses.

The weights of the perceptron are updated only if its output and target are not the same. The update rule for the perceptron when the jth pattern is presented to the network is given by

$$w_i^{n+1} = w_i^n + \eta \frac{\partial E_j}{\partial w_i}, \tag{16}$$

where $0 < \eta < 1$ is the gain term, w_i is the ith weight and n is the iteration number. Substituting the derivative of the L_1 norm of the error from (15) into (16), we obtain

$$w_i^{n+1} = w_i^n - \eta y_j (1 - y_j) \operatorname{sgn}(t_j - y_j) x_i. \tag{17}$$

The function $\operatorname{sgn}(t_j - y_j)$ is not defined when $t_j = y_j$. However, this does not affect the algorithm, since no updates are made when the output agrees with the target.

The weights are updated until the norm of error converges. After convergence, the output of the single layer pereptron is found. The output with the highest value is chosen to be the winner. All training vectors which indicate a maximum value on the same output are used to train the child node. Then this child node is trained, and the process is continued recursively until all the patterns are classified correctly.

In some cases when the number of patterns belonging to one particular class is much greater than the other class at a particular node, then the hyperplane might not split the data. In this case, the error gradient is weighted by the ratio of the number of patterns in the class which are not in the output class to the total number of patterns at a node. Alternately, virtual data might be generated to equate the lower number of points to the greater number. The virtual data is generated by adding Gaussian random number with small variance to the feature vector.

12.6.3 Algorithm for an NTN

Each node in an NTN is a single layer perceptron, therefore the task of hyperplane perturbation is relatively simple.

Each node of the tree has as many perceptrons as the number of classes. For the two class problem only one perceptron is required. The new method requires the weight vector, the closest point $\mathbf{x}_{cN}$, the centroid $\mathbf{c}_0$ and the radius r_0 for each peceptron. Additional virtual patterns can be generated by adding Gaussian noise to the centroid $\mathbf{c}_0$ with variance r_0^2. Then the online data is intermixed with the virtual data.

For ease of presentation we shall consider a two class problem throughout the discussion. The new algorithm is the same for any class problem. First, the node which misclassifies the new data is found. This is done by using the standard **backtracking** (Sedgewick, 1990) algorithm for a tree search. The leaf node where the pattern is misclassified is located. The parent of this node is selected for RAP perturbation.

The conventional RAP algorithm is modified in the following way: the iterations are not cycled over all of the patterns but only those patterns which are misclassified. The output of the node can be any value because there is no non-linear squashing function used. The patterns selected as constraints are those where the error is of the same sign as the target output.

If the error over all the patterns is less than a pre-determined threshold, then all the patterns have been correctly classified, otherwise the tree is backtracked and the same procedure is repeated for the grandparent node. This process is continued until the new data is correctly classified or the root node is reached. In the latter case, the problem cannot be solved by hyperplane perturbation and the online data requires an additional hyperplane to separate the data.

Pseudo code for re-training of NTN
begin:
1. Find the misclassified feature vectors.
2. Backtrack the tree from the leaf node to the parent node.
3. Generate virtual pattens by using a Gaussian noise generator.
4. Adjust the weight vector by the modified RAP method using the closest points as constraints.
5. Find the error in the classification.
   if the error is less than the pre-determined threshold
then:
STOP (New data is correctly classified).
else:
1. Restore the original weights for this node.
2. Move a level back in the tree.
3. Repeat the same procedure.
   if the error is less than the threshold
then
STOP (New data is correctly classified).
else:
1. STOP if the root node is reached.
2. Restore the original weights to the node.
3. New data cannot be correctly classified without growing an extra node.
end.

12.7 Simulation results

An online training algorithm is applied to various problems. A two class problem is used to demonstrate the new algorithm. The problem was solved using the OTM in the NTN as well as the MLP. The OTM is also applied to vowel recognition, language acquisition and explosive detection problems in the following sections.

12.7.1 Two class problem

The performance of the OTM for a two class problem is shown in Figures 12.9 and 12.10. Figure 12.9 demonstrates the original position of the

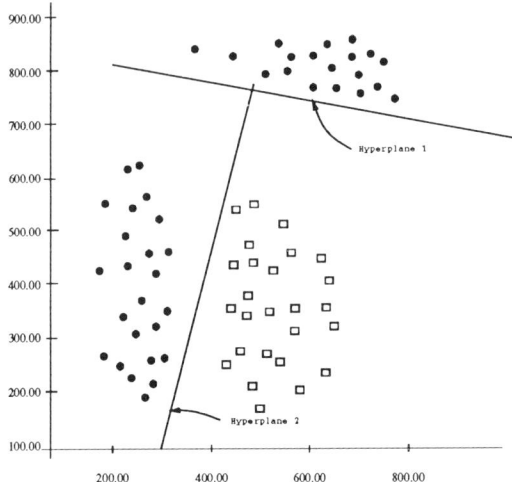

Figure 12.9 *Position of hyperplanes after initial training.*

hyperplanes in feature space after conventional training. Figure 12.10a shows that some of the new data set is misclassified by the originally trained NTN. Figure 12.10b illustrates the perturbation of one of the hyperplanes to correctly classify the new data set without disrupting the performance on the original data.

This experiment took 25 iterations of RAP to properly classify the additional patterns. It was also done using an MLP and it took 12 RAP iterations. However, each RAP iteration does not correspond to a single neuron, but to one hidden neuron and all output neurons. Thus the computational time required by each iteration in the MLP is more than the computational time required by each iteration of the perturbation in NTN.

The rate of convergence is found to be dependent on the step size μ, which is shown in Figure 12.11. It was observed that the minimum number of iterations were required if we chose a step size of 1.5 and step size higher than 2.0 resulted in unstable performance.

Table 12.1 *Performance table*

Step size	Traditional NTN #epochs	New NTN #iterations	Traditional MLP #epochs	New MLP #epochs
0.5	1500	69	2000	40
0.6	1400	50	1400	25
0.9	900	25	1100	12

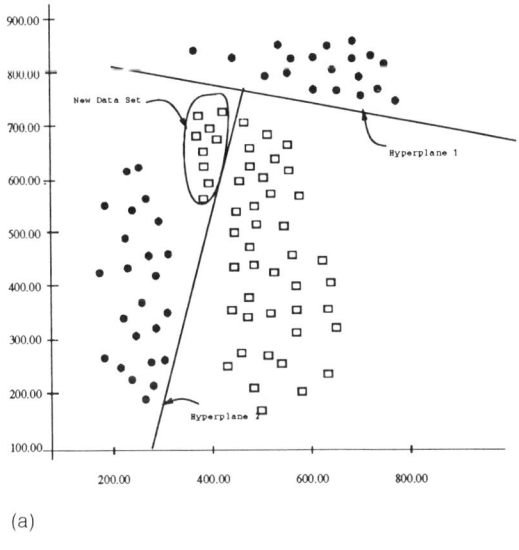

(a)

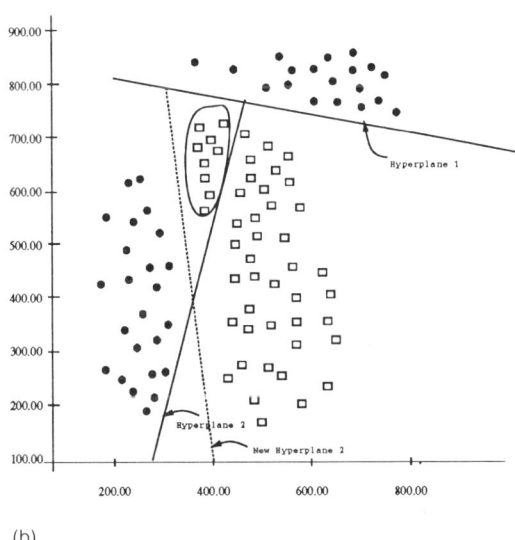

(b)

Figure 12.10 *(a) New data set misclassified; (b) position after retraining.*

Table 12.1 shows the performance of the OTM. The number of iterations taken is dependent on the step size parameter for both RAP and MLP. The performance is compared with the traditional training method and the OTM for both architectures. The number of iterations is given in terms of RAP for both MLP and NTN. The RAP iteration for an NTN is about $(1/N \cdot \#\text{iteration}$

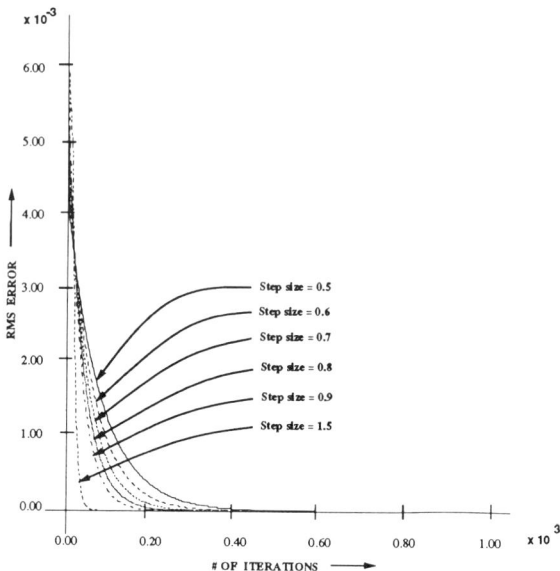

Figure 12.11 *Error* versus *number of iterations for various step sizes.*

of MLP), where N is the total number of neurons in the MLP. For the traditional NTN the number of epochs listed are for a particular node, which is responsible for classifying correctly the new data set.

12.7.2 Vowel recognition problem

Simulation results are presented in this section for a speaker-independent vowel recognition task. The training set consists of 528 feature vectors representing 11 vowel sounds obtained from four male speakers and four female speakers. The problem is to train the system on this data and then test it on an independent set of 462 feature vectors obtained from a different set of four male speakers and three female speakers. For both the training and testing set, each vowel is repeated six times by each speaker. The features are 10 log area parameters calculated using six 512 sample Hamming windowed segments from the steady part of the vowel. Details of this data set can be obtained from Robinson (1989). This particular database represents a difficult problem and the best performance of classifiers used previously is about 55%.

We trained a traditional NTN algorithm with 100% training accuracy. The tree obtained was a five level tree. The test set was divided into two subsets of 261 patterns each and it was re-trained on one subset of 261 patterns and then tested on the next subset. This gave a recognition accuracy around 70% with the same size tree.

12.7.3 Language acquisition problem

In this section, we present simulation results on the department store call manager problem as given by Gorin and Levinson (1989). The database consists of a total of 50 sentences, 40 sentences for training and 10 sentences for testing. The vocabulary consisted of 130 words. This data set was generated on the guidelines of inward call manager database (AT & T Bell labs). The dimension of the feature vector corresponds to the number of words in the vocabulary. Each entry in the pattern vector is either one (i.e. word is present in the sentence) or a zero (i.e. word is not present).

This is a three-class problem which directs a telephone caller to the furniture, clothing or hardware department. The tree obtained after the original training was one level because the data set is linearly separable. On the test set it misclassified the sentence

do you sell shoes (as furniture).

This misclassification was corrected by the new algorithm in only five iterations of the OTM.

12.7.4 Explosive detection problem

The OTM was applied to online training of a neural network used for the detection of explosives in airline baggage. Fifteen explosives and ten benign materials were used. The features were extracted from the X-ray spectrum of all these materials. Ths tree was trained on all these materials as a two class problem with the decision being whether the explosive is there or not. It gave 100% performance on the test set, but the need of re-training was seen when:

1. The explosive is mixed with some benign material.
2. A new explosive is found.
3. The explosive is masked by an absorber.

The new algorithm corrected nearly all three types of the misclassifications. It correctly classified 100% of the limited testing set used for this experiment.

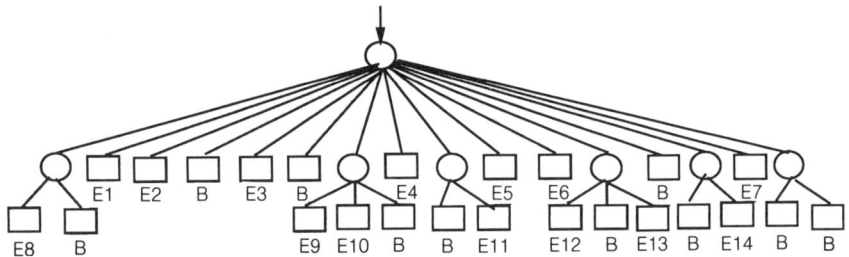

Figure 12.12 *NTN for explosive detection (15 explosives, 10 benign substances).* ○: *node;* □: *leaf; E: explosive; B: benign.*

The perturbation algorithm should retrain 100% on all those materials which can be correctly classified without growing an extra node. Figure 12.12 shows the tree structure after training on 15 explosives and 10 benign materials. The explosive materials used were common ones – TNT, dynamite, picratol. The benign materials used were also common – cotton, wood, talcum.

12.8 Conclusions and further work

The OTM overcomes the limitation of catastrophic forgetting in NNs. This characteristic provides long-term memory for neural networks. It is more efficient than total retraining and is not computationally expensive. It can frequently retrain on **all** the patterns that can be classified without adding extra nodes to the network. The algorithm used converges quickly to the solution as compared to back-propagation. In addition, since the gradient calculation is not required, RAP is computationally less complex than the back-propagation algorithm. Thus the OTM also makes it feasible to perform online training.

In cases when the online data cannot be classified correctly by a simple hyperplane perturbation, then a new hyperplane should be grown. The situation where this will be required is shown in Figure 12.13.

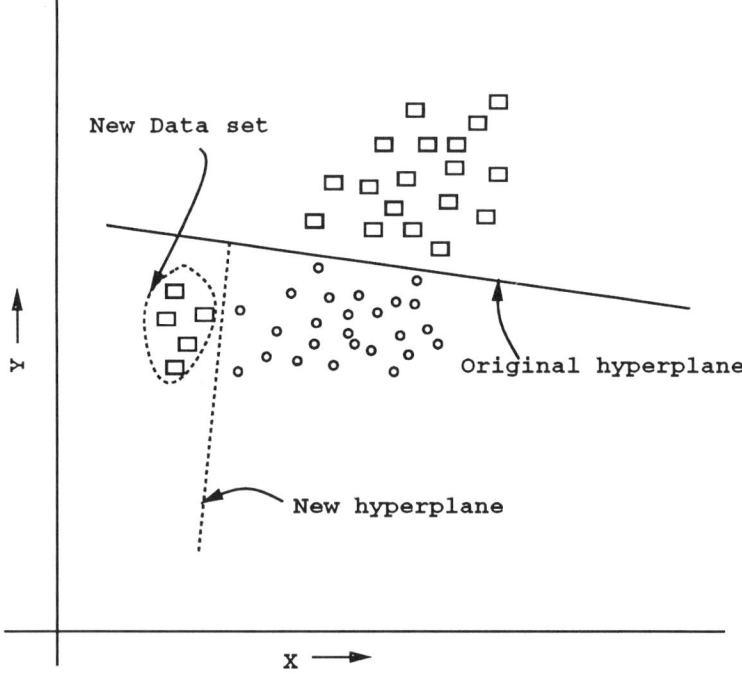

Figure 12.13 *Problem cannot be solved by perturbation.*

The present algorithm does not automatically handle this situation. Further work is to detect this situation and then grow a new node automatically.

Another possible extension would be the selection of constraints because this is an important decision in the hyperplane perturbation algorithm. If the constraints use the total set of the original data then the forgetting problem is eliminated. The most efficient representation of the previously learned data is still an open question. This chapter illustrates that the mean and variance of the closest points provided a good representation of the previously learned data. However, many other representations can be examined.

In addition, sometimes the training data is not a good representative of the old data set. In problems like the vowel recognition problem used here we can allow certain errors in the training set to improve the performance on the test set. This will provide a combined performance which is better. Therefore, there is a trade-off between overcoming forgetting and the performance. This trade-off should be studied to learn more without forgetting much of previous knowledge. However, with language acquisition problems no sentence can be forgotten to learn a new sentence. In cases like this, the trade-off does not apply.

References

Agarwal, A. (1993) *Retention in Neural Networks: To Overcome Catastrophic Forgetting Problem*. MS Thesis, Rutgers University.

Barnes, J.M. and Underwood, B.J. (1959) Fate of first-list associations in transfer theory. *Journal of Experimental Psychology*, **58**, 97–105.

Barto, A.G., Sutton, R.S. and Anterson, C.W. (1983) Neuronlike Adaptive Elements That Can Solve Difficult Learning Control Problems. *IEEE Trans. on Systems, Man and Cybernetics*, **13**(5), 834–46.

Ben-Israel, A. and Greville, T. (1974) *Generalized Inverses: Theory and Applications*. Wiley, New York.

Briemann, L., Friedman, J.H., Olshen, R.A. and Stone, C.J. (1984) Classification and regression trees. *Wadsworth International Group*, Belmont, CA.

Che, C.W., Rahim, M. and Flanagan, J.L. (1992) Robust speech recognition in a multimedia teleconferencing environment. *Journal of Acoustical Society of America*, **92**(4), pt. 2, 2476.

Cybenko, G. (1989) Approximation by superposition of a sigmoidal function. *Math. Control Signals Syst.*, **2**, 303–14.

Duda, R.O. and Hart, P.E. (1973) *Pattern Classification and Scene Analysis*. Wiley, New York.

Flanagan, J.L. (1972) *Speech Analysis Synthesis and Perception*. Springer-Verlag, Berlin.

Gorin, A.L. and Levinson, S.E. (1989) Adaptive acquisition of language. *AT&T Bell Labs Technical Memorandum*.

Herman, G.T. (1980) *Image Reconstruction from Projections: The Fundamentals of Computerized Tomography*. Academic Press, New York.

Hetherington, P.A. (1990) The Sequential Learning Problem in Connectionist Networks. *MA Thesis* Department of Psychology, McGill University, Montreal, Canada.

Hinton, G.E. and Plaut, D.C. (1987) Using Fast Weights to Deblur Old Memories. *Proceedings 9th Annual Conference of Cognitive Science Society*, 177–86.

Kaczmarz, S. (1937) Angenaherta auflosung von systemem linearer gleochugen. *Bull. Acd. Polon. Sciences et Letters*, **A35**, 355–7.

Kortge, C.A. (1990) Episodic Memory in Connectionist Networks. *Proceedings Twelfth Annual Conference of Cognitive Science Society*, pp. 764–1.

Lang, K., Waibel, A. and Hinton, G. (1990) A time delay neural network architecture for isolated word recognition. *Neural Networks*, 3(1), 23–43.

Lippmann, R.P. (1989) Review of neural networks for speech recognition. *Neural Computation*, **1**, 1–38.

Lippmann, R.P. (1989) Pattern classification using neural networks. *IEEE Communications Magazine*, 47–64.

Mammone, R.J. (1992) *Computational Methods of Signal Recovery and Recognition*. Wiley, New York, NY.

Mammone, R.J. and Zeevi, Y. (1991) *Neural Networks Theory and Applications*. Academic Press, New York, NY.

Martin, G. (1988) The effects of old learning on new Hopfield and backpropagation nets. *Technical Report ACA-HI-019*, Microelectronics and Computer Technology Corporation (MCC).

McCloskey, M. and Cohen, N.J. (1989) Catastrophic interference in connectionist networks: The sequential learning problem. *The Psychology of Learning and Motivation*, **24**, 109–65.

Nilsson, N.J. (1965) *Learning Machines*. McGraw Hill, New York.

Paik, J.K. and Katsaggelos, A.K. (1992) Image restoration using a modified Hopfield network. *IEEE Trans. Signal Processing*, **40**(2).

Paliwal, K. (1990) Neural Net Classifiers For Robust Speech Recognition Under Noisy Environments. *Proceedings ICASSP*.

Pratt, L.Y. (1992) Transfer of information among inductive learners. *Proceedings AAAI*.

Pratt, L.Y. (1992) Transfer of knowledge between neural networks. *PhD Thesis*, Rutgers University, Piscataway, NJ.

Press, W.H., Flannery, B.P., Teukolsky, S.A. and Vetterling, W.T. (1986) *Numerical Recipes in C*. Cambridge University Press, New York.

Quinlan, J.R. (1986) Introduction to decision trees. *Machine Learning*, **1**, 81–106.

Rabiner, L. and Schafer, R. (1978) *Digital Processing of Speech Signals*. Prentice Hall, Englewood Cliffs, NJ.

Rahim, M.G. (1992) *A neural tree architecture for phoeneme classification with experiments on the TIMIT Database*. IEEE ICASSP.

Ratcliff, R. (1990) Connectionist models of recognition memory: Constraints imposed by learning and forgetting functions. *Psychological Review*, **97**(2), 285–308.

Robinson, A. (1989) Dynamic Error Propagation Networks. *PhD thesis*, Cambridge University Engineering Department.

Rosenblatt, F. (1962) The perceptron: a probabilistic model for information storage and organization in the brain. *Psychological Review*, **65**, 386–408.

Rumelhart, D.E. and McClelland, J.L. (1986) *Parallel Distributed Processing*. MIT Press, Cambridge, MA.

Sankar, A. and Mammone, R.J. (1993) Growing and pruning neural tree networks. *IEEE Transactions on Computers* (to appear) **42**(3).

Sedgewick, R. (1990) *Algorithms in C*, Addison-Wesley, pp. 359–71.

Sloman, S.A. and Rumelhart, D.E. (1991) Reducing interference in distributed memories through episodic gating, in *Essays in Honor of W.K. Estes* (eds. A. Healy, S. Kosslyn and R. Shiffrin), L. Erlbaum, Hillsdale, NJ.

Werbos, P. (1974) *Beyond Regression: New Tools for Prediction and Analysis in the*

Sutton, R.S. (1986) Two problems with backpropagation and other steepest-descent learning procedures for networks. *Eighth Annual Conference of the Cognitive Science Society*, pp. 823–31.

Tanabe, K. (1971) Projection method for solving a singular system of linear equations and its applications. *Numerical Mathematics*, **17**, 203–14.

Tulving, E. (1972) Episodic and semantic memory. *Organization of Memory*, Academic Press, New York.

Waibel, A. (1989) Modular construction of time delay neural networks for speech recognition. *Neural Computation*, **1**.

Werbos, P. (1974) *Beyond Regression: New Tools for Prediction and Analysis in the Behavioural Sciences*. PhD Thesis, Harvard University.

Widrow, B. and Hoff, M.E. (1960) Adaptive switching circuits. *WESCON Convention Record*, Part IV, 96–104.

Widrow, B. and Stearns, S.D. (1985) *Adaptive Signal Processing*, Prentice-Hall, Englewood Cliffs, NJ.

Willshaw, D. (1981) Holography, associative memory and inductive generalization, in *Parallel Models of Associative Memory* (eds. G.E. Hinton and J.A. Anderson), L. Erlbaum, Hillsdale, NJ.

13

The Relabeling Exchange Method (REM) for training neural networks

WEN WU and RICHARD J. MAMMONE
*Center for Computer Aids for Industrial Productivity, Rutgers, the State University,
Frelinghuysen Road, P.O. Box 1390, Piscataway, NJ 08855-1390, USA*

13.1 Introduction

Supervised learning algorithms attempt to 'learn' the best mapping $f(\cdot)$ of a set of M feature vectors $\{\vec{x}_j^i\}$, $j = 1 \ldots M$ to a set of N class labels $\{y_i\}$, $i = 1 \ldots N$.[1] That is, given a set of M labeled vectors $\{\vec{x}_j\}$, we wish to find the function $f(\cdot)$ such that $f(\vec{x}_j^i) = y_i$. An exact mapping may not be possible or desirable (i.e. over learning the training data), in which case a mapping which is optimal in some sense is usually sought. The optimality criterion may be the least square error. The learning problem can then be formulated as a constrained optimization problem of the form

$$\begin{aligned}
\text{minimize:} \quad & \textstyle\sum_j \varepsilon_j^2 \\
\text{subject to:} \quad & y_i = f(\vec{x}_j^i) + \varepsilon_i \quad i = 1 \ldots N \\
& \qquad\qquad\qquad\quad j = 1 \ldots M.
\end{aligned}$$

Generally, the class labels y_i are arbitrarily assigned to the feature vectors $\vec{x}_j^i$ of each class i. Thus for a multiclass pattern recognition problem with N distinct classes, N consecutive numbers are typically assigned. These numbers will be called the literal labels. The ordering of the literal labels can be chosen in $N!$ ways. Some of the label assignments may allow an exact mapping $f(\cdot)$, but it will be shown that others will not. Several methods of finding optimal

---

[1] The superscript i in $\vec{x}_j^i$ denotes the class, i, to which the vector belongs.

Artificial Neural Networks for Speech and Vision. Edited by Richard J. Mammone.
Published in 1993 by Chapman & Hall, London. ISBN 0 412 54850 X

label assignments while training will be presented. It has been found that a good strategy for choosing labels is to assign labels such that they are close in some sense when the corresponding feature vectors are close. A commonly used label assignment strategy is called local labeling, where each label is a binary number of N bits, with one bit for each class. Each binary label consists of all zeros except for a '1' in the kth bit position for the kth class (Sankar and Mammone, 1990). This labeling scheme is attractive, since the labels are equally spaced. However, this scheme is not optimal in general.

It would appear that to encode N classes, the number of minimum bits should be $B = [\log_2 N]$. The use of N bits to represent N classes, as in local encoding introduces $N - B$ bits more than the apparent minimum required. This redundancy in local encoding is costly in terms of the number of nodes needed to solve a particular problem.

In this chapter we investigate the label assignment problem and propose a method to improve the performance by relabeling the feature vectors during training. The approach of relabeling the outputs to improve performance appears to be new. Previously, the structure of the feature vectors has been investigated without regard to the labels (Duda and Hart, 1973; Fisher, 1950; Kittler and Young, 1973). A number of techniques have been developed to analyse and reduce the number of dimensions of the input feature vector. There are linear transformations, for example, the Karhunen–Loeve Transformation (KLT) (Kittler and Young, 1973), the Discrete Cosine Transformation (DCT) (Ahmed et al., 1974) and Gram–Schmidt methods (Fu, 1976), etc. as well as nonlinear methods such as decision trees (Breiman et al., 1984), which have been used to study the structure of feature space. There appears to be little work available concerning the strategy of selecting the output labels, i.e. the encoding strategy. A large number of outputs (fanout) for each neuron requires an increased computation complexity of the final network architecture. It is particularly true for neural tree networks (Sankar and Mammone, 1990), since the fanout increases geometrically for each level of the tree descending from the root.

The fact that local labeling is not always good for training can be illustrated with an example. In Figure 13.1, two feature vectors are shown which belong to two different classes. Consider the case where the two feature vectors are highly correlated or 'close', i.e. $\vec{x}_1 \approx \vec{x}_2$. Since the vectors are close, it is desirable for their corresponding labels to be close. However, because the two vectors belong to different classes, the local encoding scheme will assign codes (labels) that vary by two bits. Consider bit y_1 (the first bit of the class label) in Figure 13.1. Local encoding requires the mappings $x_1 \rightarrow (y_1 = 1)$ and $x_2 \rightarrow (y_1 = 0)$, even though $\vec{x}_1 \approx \vec{x}_2$. This creates an unnecessary contradiction for the training algorithm. It has also been found that the network generalization obtained with local encoding is typically not as good as other labeling schemes. This can be seen by an example. Figure 13.2 shows the generalization map of a four-class problem. As a result of local labeling, each hyperplane

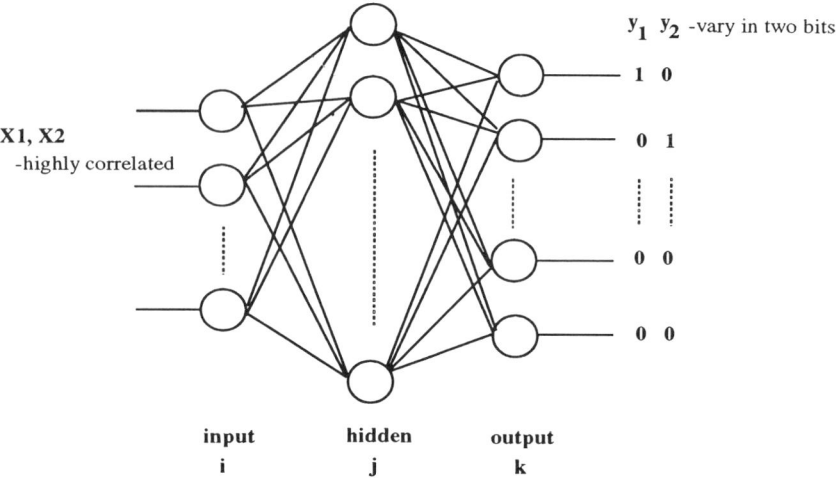

Figure 13.1 *Contradiction of local labeling.*

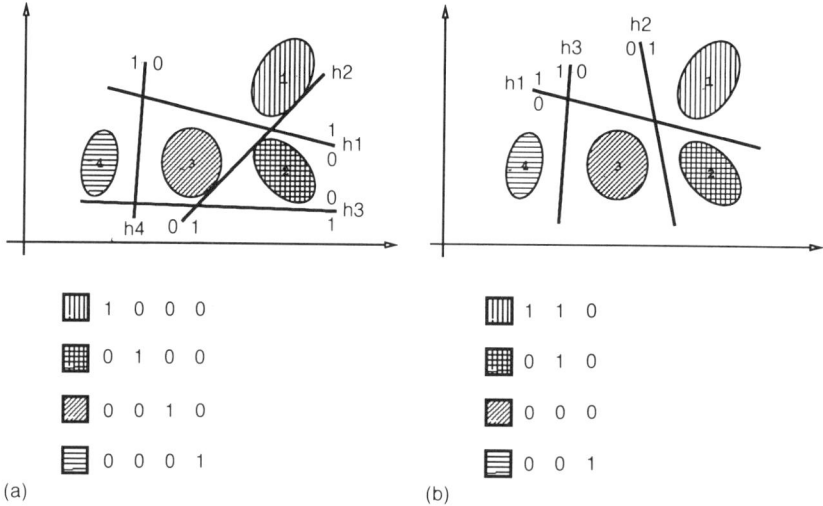

Figure 13.2 *Geometry of hyperplanes that yield from (a) local labels, and (b) ideal labels.*

should separate one class from all the other classes. From the figure, it can be seen that separation of class 2 from the rest is difficult. The resulting hyperplane will be the hyperplane h2 which gives very poor generalization (because a point which is close to either class 1 or 3 will be classified as class 2). This figure also shows that separation of class 3 from the remaining classes with one hyperplane is impossible. The hyperplane h3 found by the gradient training algorithm is unable to separate any of the classes. The ideal label assignment and hyperplanes are shown in Figure 13.2. The optimal assignment requires less output bits and gives better generalization than local encoding.

The fact that neural networks have a prefered labeling assignment is similar to the reading disability called dyslexia (Hinshelwood, 1917; Ellis, 1984; Aaron, 1989; Critchley 1981; Ellis and Miles, 1981). Thus we might say that the neural networks are dyslexic in the sense that they are sensitive to the lexical coding scheme used.

In this chapter, we shall first analyse how labels interfere with the training of a neural network. Several relabeling strategies have been investigated which are based on: (1) the simulated annealing algorithm; (2) the genetic algorithm; and (3) a heuristic algorithm called the Relabeling Exchange Method (REM). These methods are presented in section 13.3, and the performance of each method is discussed. The effects of relabeling are discussed in section 13.4. A comparison with neural networks where relabeling was not applied is also given. The conclusion and summary are given in section 13.5.

13.2 Relabeling for supervised learning

Supervised learning of a neural network can be viewed as fitting a set of M data points $\{\vec{x}_j^i\}$ to a set of N labels $\{y_i\}$ such that

$$y_i = f(\vec{x}_j^i), \quad i = 1 \ldots N, \quad j = 1 \ldots M, \tag{1}$$

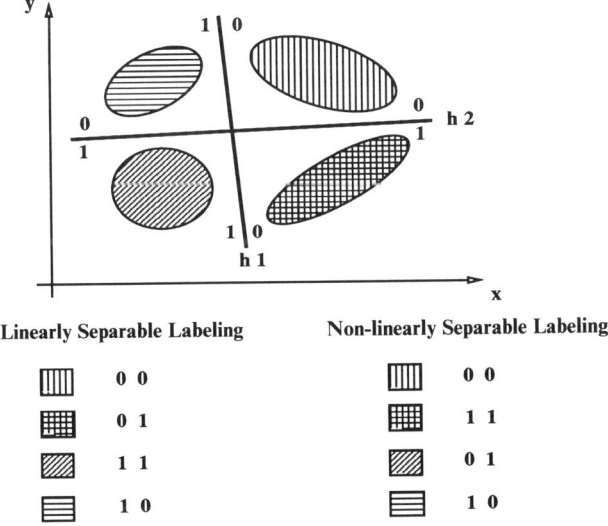

Figure 13.3 *Example of non-linearly separable labeling for linearly separable problem (after Sarkar and Mammone, 1990).*

where $\{\vec{x}_j^i\}$ is the set of feature vectors, and y_i is the label assignment to the ith class. For a given neural network structure, the parametric form of $f(\cdot)$ is fixed. The parameters or weights of the function $f(\cdot)$ are found by training. For the multilayer perceptron (MLP), for example, the form of $f(\cdot)$ is usually a composition of excitation functions $g(\cdot)$ (Cybenko, 1989). Thus

$$y_i^{(k)} = f^{(k)}(\vec{x}_i) = g\left(\sum_h w_{kh} g\left(\sum_j w_{hj} x_{ij}\right)\right), \tag{2}$$

where $y^{(k)}$ is the kth bit of the label y_i, w_{kh} are the weights from the hth hidden node to kth output node, and w_{hj} are the weights from the jth input node to hth hidden node. It is shown in Figure 13.4 that generally there are n transitions for the kth output of a MLP and n hidden units. Thus, if the assigned label requires a certain output node to change from 0 to 1 (or from 1 to 0) more than n times, a MLP with only n hidden nodes cannot satisfy the output labels. This is why the XOR problem requires two hidden nodes. For most practical problems, the degree of non-linearity is usually not known *a priori*, thus the number of hidden nodes is found by trial and error. Previous work (Gorman and Sejnowski, 1988; Mirchandani and Cao, 1989) which addressed the selection of the number of hidden nodes apparently did not consider the option of changing the initial labels. Labels are generally assigned in an arbitrary manner. This assignment can introduce additional non-linearities in the mapping function $f(\cdot)$, which require additional hidden nodes. For example, consider the first bit of the non-linearly separable labeling scheme given in Figure 13.3 (Sankar and Mammone, 1990) – it is essentially an XOR problem. This non-linearity is not intrinsic to the problem itself, but is due to the particular assignment of the labels. The number of hidden nodes needed in a MLP (or the number of levels in a NTN) depends on the degree of non-linearity of the problem. In this chapter, we shall show that after relabeling, the number of hidden nodes of a MLP (or the number of levels in a NTN) can be reduced by selecting appropriate labels.

The mapping function $f(\cdot)$ can be approximated by a Taylor series expansion which yields a high order polynomial $P_n(\cdot)$. A smooth polynomial $P_n(\vec{x})$ cannot easily fit the labels which are selected such that they change very quickly with $\vec{x}$ (see Figure 13.5). This is a problem which is common to most parameter estimation problems. A smooth function $f(\cdot)$ cannot easily map the independent variables x_i to the dependent variable y_i if they are assigned in a non-smooth manner. That is, the labeling scheme should be such that for feature vectors which are close together

$$\|\vec{x}' - \vec{x}\| < \varepsilon$$

the labels should be close

$$|y' - y| < \varepsilon \|P_n'(\vec{x})\|. \tag{3}$$

If this condition is not met, then the labels selected will generally be difficult

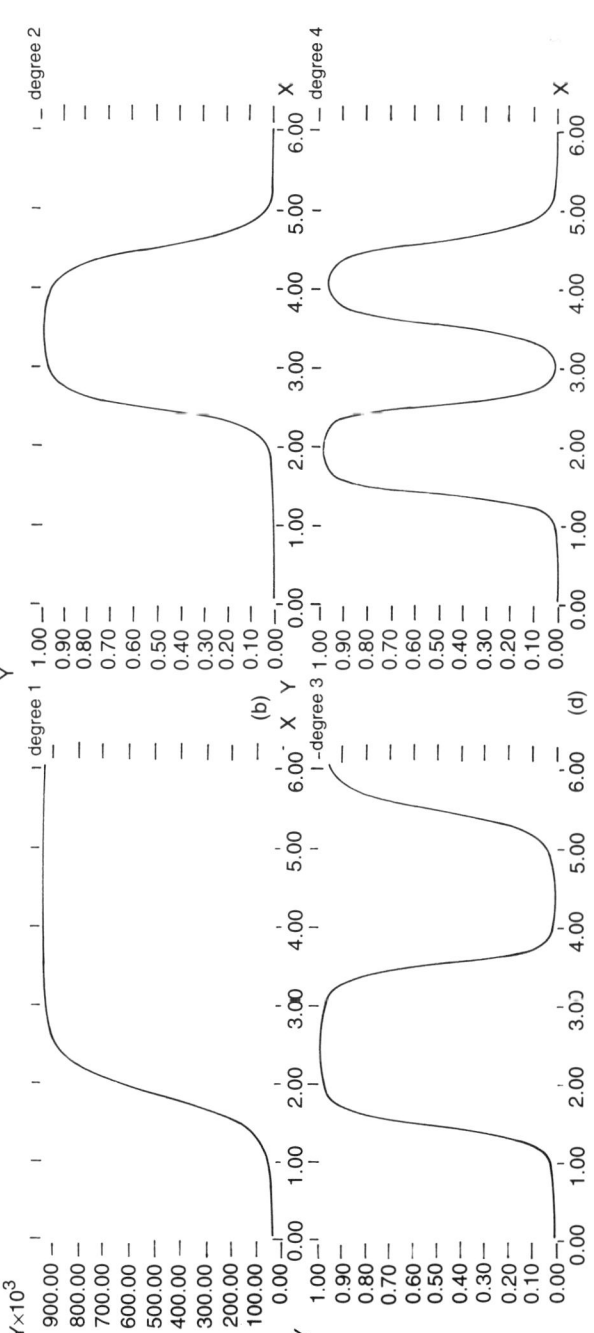

Figure 13.4 *Output of MLP with (a) 0, (b) 2, (c) 3, and (d) 4 hidden units.*

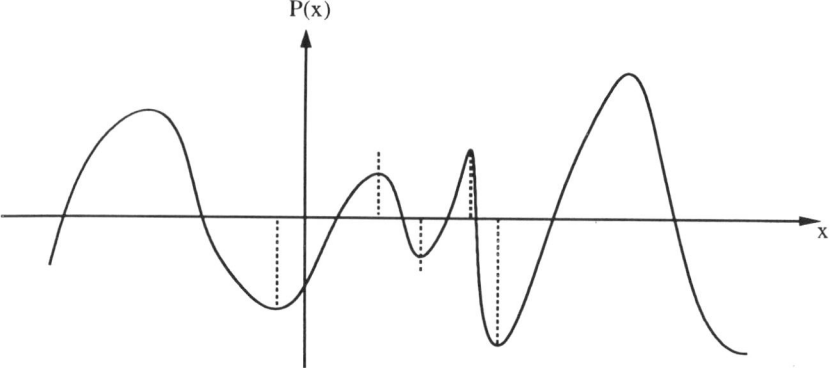

Figure 13.5 *Generally, polynomials cannot fit labels that vary quickly with x.*

to learn. The root mean square (**rms**) error of the output of the polynomial will typically be large at points where the labels change abruptly. An acceptable level of **rms** error is usually selected *a priori* to determine the order of the polynomial fit. In general, there are many label assignments which will give this acceptable **rms** error. Thus an exhaustive search of all possible labeling strategies is not required.

Another problem encountered in selecting an appropriate labeling scheme is that of selecting linearly separable labels. The problem of a non-linearly separable code was discussed previously (Sankar and Mammone, 1990) as an example of an inappropriate labeling scheme. This problem is shown in Figure 13.3. It is obvious that if the non-linearly separable code is chosen, a MLP with two hidden nodes (or an NTN with two tree levels) will be needed to solve the problem, while only a Single Layer Perceptron (SLP) is needed if the linearly separable code is chosen. Thus we shall investigate relabeling strategies which attempt to provide smooth labeling schemes which do require additional nodes to decode.

There are two types of relabeling problems corresponding to the two steps of relabeling. The closed set relabeling problem is: given a fixed set of N distinct numbers $L = \{l_1, l_2, \ldots, l_N\}$, choose labels y_i such that

$$y_i \in L = \{l_1, l_2, \ldots, l_N\}, \quad y_i \neq y_j, \quad \text{if } i \neq j.$$

Note that the number of possible assignments of the labels is $O(N!)$. We wish to find a permutation of the labels which yields an acceptable low value of the root mean square (**rms**) training error.

The second problem is the open set problem, where l_i comes from a set of candidate labels L' which has more elements (N') than the number of classes (N). We now wish to select a subset and an optimal ordering of the subset of the candidate labels which will give an acceptable value of the **rms** training error. Thus we select:

$$y_l \in L = \{l_1, l_2, \quad , l_N\} \subset \{I_{\cdot 1}, I_{\cdot 2}, \ldots, I_{\cdot N'}\} \quad y_i \neq y_j, \quad \text{if } i \neq j.$$

The total number of possible labeling schemes is $O(N' \binom{N}{N'})$.

The open set relabeling problem can be formulated as a constrained optimization problem of the form

$$\text{minimize:} \quad E = \sum_i (y_i - f(\vec{x}_i))^2 \tag{4}$$

$$\text{subject to:} \quad y_i \in \{l_1, l_2, \ldots, l_N\} \subset \{L_1, L_2, \ldots, L_{N'}\},$$

where

$$N' > N \text{ and } y_i \neq y_j, \quad \text{if} \quad i \neq j.$$

If the labels are represented as binary numbers, then the problem becomes

$$\text{minimize:} \quad E = \sum_{i,k} (y_i^{(k)} - f(\vec{x}_i)^{(k)})^2 \tag{5}$$

$$\text{subject to:} \quad y_i = 2^{b-1} y_i^{(b)} + 2^{b-2} y_i^{(b-1)} + \cdots + y_i^{(1)},$$

$$\text{and} \quad y_i \in \{a_1, a_2, \ldots, a_N\} \subset \{b_1, b_2, \ldots, b_{N'}\},$$

$$\text{with} \quad N' > N \quad \text{and} \quad y_i \neq y_j, \quad \text{if} \quad i \neq j.$$

The binary representation restricts the larger set to the integer set $\{0, \ldots, 2^b - 1\}$, where b (the number of bits needed to represent the N classes) is between $[\log_2 N]$ and $N - 1$. It might appear that only $[\log_2 N]$ bits are needed to represent N classes. This is not always true. It has been shown (Mirchandani and Cao, 1989), that in d-dimensional space, the maximum number of regions that are linearly separable using H hyperplanes is given by

$$M(H, d) = \sum_{k=0}^{d} \binom{H}{k}$$

where

$$\binom{H}{k} = 0, \quad \text{if } H < k.$$

For example, in two dimensional space, three hyperplanes can linearly separate at most seven regions (Figure 13.6). Thus, depending on the geometry of the problem in feature space, three hyperplanes may not be enough. A worst case scenario is when the classes are all lined up as shown in Figure 13.7. In this case, six hyperplanes are needed to linearly separate the classes. The number of bits required is not known a priori. There are two approaches one can use to find this number: (1) start from $[\log_2 N]$ and increase 1 bit at a time up to $N - 1$; and (2) start from $N - 1$ and decrease 1 bit at a time down to $[\log_2 N]$.

Since the number of total labeling increases factorially with N and N', an exhaustive search is infeasible for large N. This is a combinatorial optimization problem which is NP-complete. Various heuristic algorithms have been

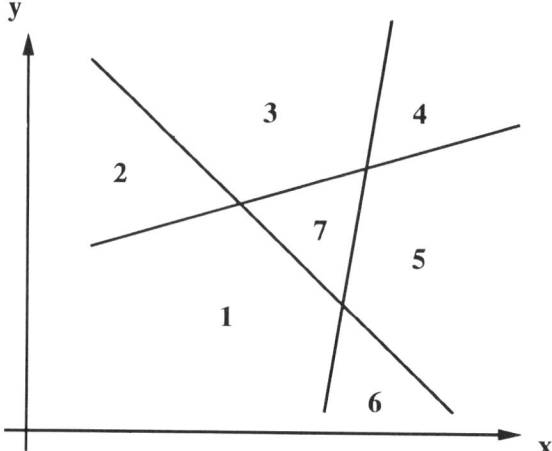

Figure 13.6 *In 2D-space, three hyperplanes can linearly separate at most seven regions.*

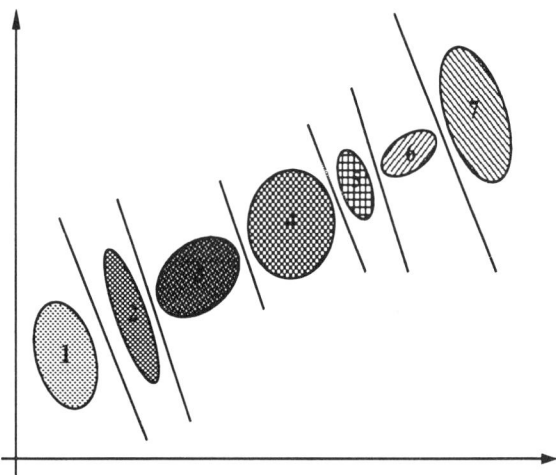

Figure 13.7 *The worst case: N linearly separable classes need N-1 hyperplanes.*

presented for combinatorial optimization problems of this kind, of which the simulated annealing algorithm (Kirkpatrick *et al.*, 1983) and the genetic algorithm (Goldberg, 1988) are two efficient methods. In the next section we shall explore the solution to the relabeling problem by these methods and a heuristic algorithm.

13.3 Relabeling algorithms and simulations

The Simulated Annealing (SA) algorithm (Kirkpatrick *et al.*, 1983) and the Genetic Algorithm (GA) (Goldberg, 1988) are reviewed in this section in the context of solving the relabeling problem. The simulated annealing algorithm has been found to be an efficient method for finding extrema of a cost function for a multi-dimensional problem. It was first introduced by Metropolis *et al.* (1953) as a model for a collection of atoms in equilibrium at a given temperature. The concept is based on the fact that molecules move more freely at higher temperatures. As the temperature decreases, the molecules settle into a regular crystalline pattern, which is a state of minimum energy. This behavior is well described in statistical mechanics. The transition population from state 1 to state 2 is proportional to $e^{-(E_2 - E_1)/k_B T}$, where E_1 and E_2 are the energies of the two states, k_B is the Boltzmann constant, and T the temperature. When the temperature is high, there are a considerable number of transitions of molecules from a low energy state to a high energy state. As the temperature decreases, most of the transitions are from high energy states to low energy states, until finally the lowest energy state is reached. In a similar fashion, the simulated annealing algorithm simulates this process to reach a minimum of the cost function or energy function. A temperature factor α is used such that

$$T(t + 1) = \alpha T(t), \quad 0 < \alpha < 1. \tag{6}$$

The temperature parameter T is decreased as the number of iterations increase. The probability of 'hill climbing' is given by

$$e^{-(E_2 - E_1)/T}, \tag{7}$$

where E_1 and E_2 are the values of the cost function before and after an iteration of SA. This algorithm has been proved to be efficient in solving many combinatorial optimization problems such as the Traveling Salesman Problem (TSP) (Lin and Kernighan, 1971), the physical layout design of circuits (Soukup, 1981) and global wiring (Vecchi and Kirkpatrick, 1983).

The SA method is used here to solve the relabeling problem in the following way. A random number generator is used to generate a set of N distinct numbers. The neural network is trained to learn the mapping on this set of labels. The **rms** error over all the training data is calculated. If it is not at or below the desired level, a different ordering of the labels is selected, and the network is trained again. The training error is compared with the one before. It is determined by equation (7) whether the change is acceptable or not. This procedure is followed until the temperature or the **rms** error reaches a predetermined level. The labels found which correspond to the least **rms** training error are selected as the final labels.

The SA algorithm for relabeling is computationally expensive. This is due to the fact that the value of the cost function of the relabeling problem can only be evaluated by training the neural network. Future work will be directed at reducing this computational load. This is the driving motivation of developing the heuristic algorithm given in the next section.

The GA method was also investigated. Genetic algorithms are random search algorithms based on the mechanics of the natural selection process and genetic reproduction. At each step of the search, the values of the cost function (called the fitness function) are calculated for several candidate values of the variables. The 'fittest' ones are more likely to be reproduced (using a random number generator) as the 'parents' for crossover to generate new candidates so that the 'children' will have characteristics of the fittest 'parents'. Occasionally, new candidates are tried randomly which is similar to natural 'mutations'. There is an extensive discussion of genetic algorithms given by Goldberg (1988). In the case of relabeling, it was found computationally unattractive and did not give labels which obtained an acceptable value of the **rms** training error.

The heuristic method, called REM, is obtained by evaluating the neural network's error metric at the ith iteration

$$E = \sum_{i,k} (y_i^{(k)} - f(\vec{x}_i)^{(k)})^2. \tag{8}$$

The estimated gradient $\Delta y_i^{(k)}$ of the error metric for the kth bit with respect to the label $y_i^{(k)}$ is

$$\Delta y_i^{(k)} \propto y_i^{(k)} - f(\vec{x}_i)^{(k)}. \tag{9}$$

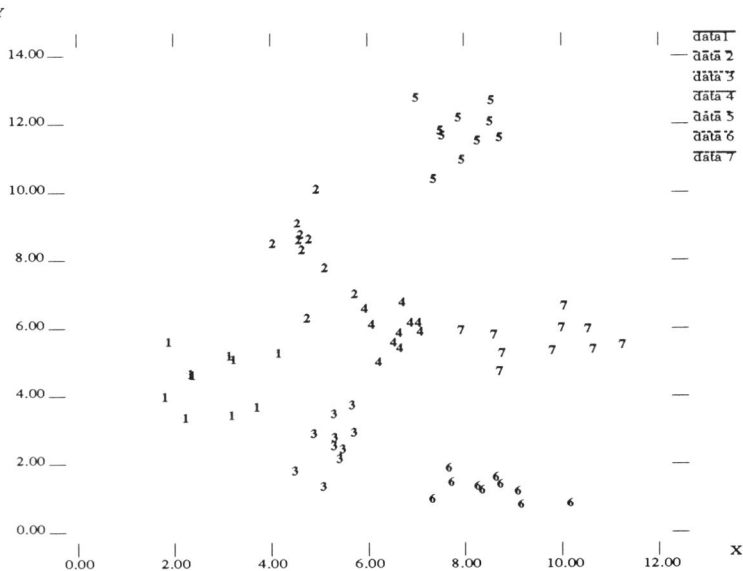

Figure 13.8 *Two-dimensional feature vectors for the seven class problem.*

The gradient of the kth bit $\Delta y_i^{(k)}$ for each label is calculated. The pair of labels which yield the maximum and minimum values are exchanged. The resulting error E given by equation (8) is calculated. This operation is performed on a bit by bit basis until the least **rms** training error is reached. The exchange of the pair of labels guarantees a set of distinct labels consisting of only those present in the set. This new method finds acceptable sets of labels with much less computational load than the SA method.

REM was used on two data sets. One is an artificial two dimensional seven class problem which is shown in Figure 13.8. The other is Detering's data (Sankar and Mammone, 1990), which consists of spectral data of 11 steady state vowels. For both data sets, the preliminary results of REM are attractive. This is discussed further in the next section.

13.4 Numerical results

In the section, we investigate REM using both NTN and MLP neural networks. The resulting generalization maps of the seven class problem are shown in Figure 13.9 for the NTN and Figures 13.10 and 13.11 for the MLP.

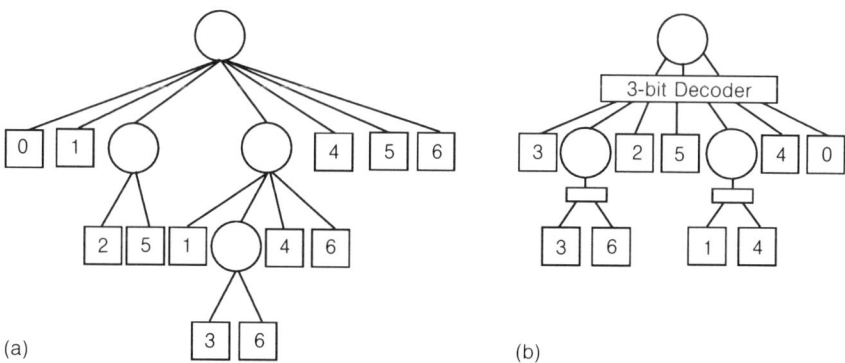

(a)   (b)

Figure 13.9 *Tree structure of the seven class problem using (a) local labeling (no. of levels = 3, no. of nodes = 4, no. of bits in total = 15, testing rate = 95.71%), and (b) relabeling (no. of levels = 2, no. of nodes = 3, no. of bits in total = 5, testing rate = 96.29%).*

No. of Hidden Nodes		0(SLP)	2	3	4	5	6	7
Without	Training Error	0.160	0.106	0.053	0.003	0.002	0.001	0.001
Relabeling	Testing Rate (%)	51.14	40.43	60.14	94.43	95.86	95.14	96.00
With	Training Error	0.007	0.023	0.001	0.001	0.001	0.001	0.001
Relabeling	Testing Rate (%)	93.43	87.29	95.71	96.14	96.00	97.14	97.00

Figure 13.10 *Solution of the seven class problem using MLP with or without relabeling using three bits.*

No. of Hidden Nodes		0(SLP)	2	3	4	5	6	7
Without	Training Error	0.160	0.106	0.053	0.003	0.002	0.001	0.001
Relabeling	Testing Rate (%)	51.14	40.43	60.14	94.43	95.86	95.14	96.00
With	Training Error	0.001	0.008	0.002	0.001	0.001	0.001	0.001
Relabeling	Testing Rate (%)	97.14	94.14	96.86	96.43	96.57	97.29	96.86

Figure 13.11 *Solution of the seven class problem using MLP with or without relabeling using four bits.*

The REM NTN tree is shorter by one level than that obtained by local encoding. Only five output bits were used. Thus, the memory required to store the weights for the REM tree is one third of that required to store the weights from the corresponding locally encoded tree. The longest retrieval time is two thirds of that required by the locally encoded NTN tree. The REM NTN tree also gives better generalization than local encoding NTN.

For the locally encoded MLP, it is shown that without relabeling, seven hidden nodes are needed to solve the problem. The REM MLP yields a single layer perceptron with better generalization than the locally encoded MLP. It should be noted that the number of output bits is critical. This is the problem of choosing the larger set from which the subset of N labels is selected (the open set problem). The labels are searched by first using three bit codes for the labels and increasing the number of bits by one to see if a smaller network structure results. It was found that four bits were optimal. This can be seen from the generalization map in Figure 13.12.

In the case of a single layer perceptron (SLP), the number of bits used for labeling is equal to the number of hyperplanes required to separate the seven classes. In Figure 13.12a three bits (i.e. three hyperplanes) are used, and it is illustrated that the hyperplanes are placed so as to separate the seven classes with good generalization. This is a result of REM training. Several sets of 'good' labels were found experimentally. All of them give rise to the same hyperplanes. Thus the optimal labels give the optimal hyperplanes. From the generalization map of Figure 13.12, we see that three hyperplanes can accomplish much of the classification task, but not all of it. It is obvious that four hyperplanes can do better then three, as shown in Figure 13.12. This is exactly the result given by REM training with the larger set $\{0, \ldots, 2^4 - 1\}$.

Similar results were obtained using Detering's vowel data. Figure 13.13 shows the results of REM training, together with that of arbitrary labeling. This demonstrates the REM solution for the closed set problem. For difficult problems such as Detering's vowel recognition, the open set problem has to be solved.

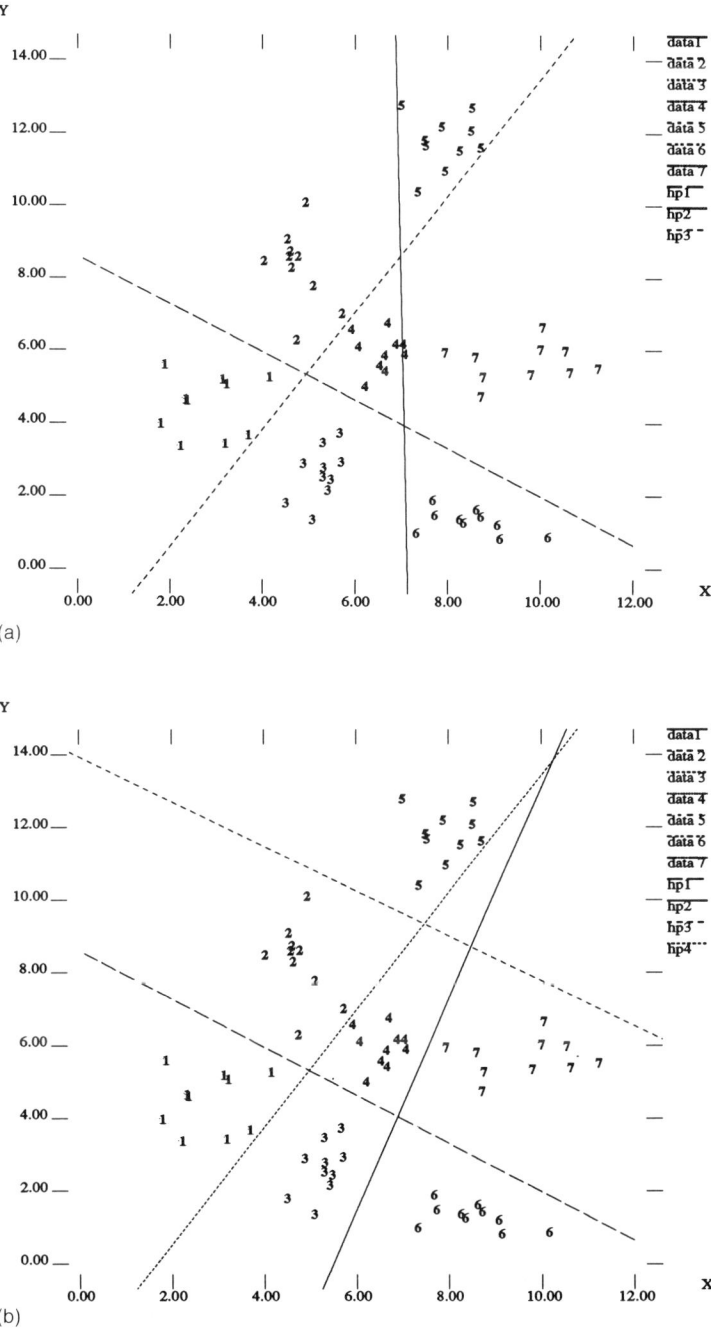

Figure 13.12 *Solution using MLP with relabeling (a) using three bits, (b) using four bits.*

No. of Hidden Nodes		2	3	4	5	6	11	22
Without	Training Error	0.141	0.115	0.103	0.097	0.076	0.025	0.005
Relabeling	Testing Rate (%)	26.41	34.20	34.85	30.52	28.35	36.36	44.59
With	Training Error	0.127	0.102	0.077	0.071	0.047	0.007	0.001
Relabeling	Testing Rate (%)	23.16	36.80	41.77	34.42	44.16	34.85	47.62

Figure 13.13 *Solution of Detering's data using MLP with or without relabeling using four bits.*

13.5 Summary

A new training algorithm for neural networks, called REM, has been introduced which adjusts the labels of the data so as to minimize the training error. It has been shown that reduction in **rms** error can be obtained by simply changing the label assignment. The REM training is also shown to give better generalization than the local encoding scheme which is widely used. This is consistent with the assertion that smaller networks generalize better (Rumelhart, 1988). For both the MLP and the NTN, a reduction in the complexity of their architectures was observed by relabeling. REM learning requires significant computation time and more efficient computation techniques are being explored. An advantage of the heuristic search method used in REM is that it can be applied to most types of neural networks. REM learning can usually be implemented as a modification to standard training algorithms.

References

Aaron, P.G. (1989) *Dyslexia and Hyperlexia.* Kluwer, Dordrecht.

Ahmed, N., Natarajan, T. and Rao, K.R. (1974) Discrete cosine transforms. *IEEE Trans. Comp.*, **23**, 90–3.

Breiman, L., Friedman, J., Olshen, R. and Stone, C. (1984) *Classification and Regression Trees.* Wadsworth International Group, Belmont, CA.

Critchley, M. (1981) Dyslexia: An Overview, in *Dyslexia Research and its Applications to Education.* Wiley, New York, NY.

Cybenko, G. (1989) Approximation by superposition of a sigmoidal function. *Math. Control Signals Syst.*, **2**, 303–14.

Duda, R.O. and Hart, P.E. (1973) *Pattern Classification and Scene Analysis.* Wiley, New York, NY.

Ellis, A.W. (1984) *Reading, Writing and Dyslexia: A Cognitive Analysis.* Lawrence Erlbaum, Hillsdale, NJ.

Ellis, N.C. and Miles, T.R. (1981) A lexical encoding deficiency I: Experimental evidence, in *Dyslexia Research and its Applications to Education*, Wiley, New York, NY.

Fisher, R.A. (1950) The use of multiple measurements in taxonomic problems. *Ann. Eugenics*, **7**(II), 179–88. (Also in *Contributions to Mathematical Statistics*, Wiley, New York.)

Fu, K.S. (1976) *Digital Pattern Recognition*. Springer-Verlag, Berlin.

Goldberg, D. (1988) *Genetic Algorithms in Machine Learning, Optimization, and Search*. Addison-Wesley, Reading, MA.

Gorman, R.P. and Sejnowski, T.J. (1988) Analysis of hidden units in a layered network. *Neural Networks*, **1**, 75–89.

Hinshelwood, J. (1917) *Congenital Word Blindness*. H.K. Lewis, London.

Kirkpatrick, S., Gelatt, C.D. Jr. and Vecchi, M.P. (1983) Optimization by simulated annealing. *Science*, **220**, 671–80.

Kittler, J. and Young, P.C. (1973) A new approach to feature selection based on the Karhunen–Loeve expansion. *Pattern Recognition*, **5**, 335–52.

Lin, S. and Kernighan, B.W. (1971) An effective heuristic algorithm for the traveling-salesman problem. *Bell Syst. Tech. J.*, **50**, 498–516.

Metropolis, N., Rosenbluth, A., Rosenbluth, M. *et al.* (1953) Equation of state calculations by fast computing machines. *J. Chem. Phys.*, **21**, 1087.

Mirchandani, G. and Cao, W. (1989) On hidden nodes for neural network. *IEEE Trans. on Circuits and Systems*, **36**(5), 661–4.

Rumelhart, D.E. (1988) Learning and generalization. *IEEE International Conference on Neural Networks*, San Diego, CA.

Sankar, A. and Mammone, R.J. (1990) Neural tree networks, in *Neural Networks, Theory and Applications* (eds R.J. Mammone and Y. Zeevi), Academic Press, pp. 281–302.

Soukup, J. (1981) Circuit layout. *Proc. IEEE*, **69**, 1281.

Vecchi, M.P. and Kirkpatrick, S. (1983) Global wiring by simulated annealing. *IEEE Trans. on Computer Aided Design*, **2**(4), 215–22.

'Learning by learning' in neural networks

D.K. NAIK and RICHARD J. MAMMONE

Center for Computer Aids for Industrial Productivity, Rutgers University, Piscataway, NJ 08855, USA

14.1 Introduction

Learning theories in artificial neural networks have been applied to learning numerous specific real world recognition tasks. However, the use of knowledge gained from past experience to improve learning in related tasks has not received significant attention. It appears that learning in artificial neural networks could employ the models proposed in the psychological studies of human learning to improve learning in artificial neural networks.

Multi-layer perceptrons (MLP) have been widely employed for learning nonlinearly separable tasks. An MLP with a single hidden layer and a sigmoidal nonlinearity can arbitrarily approximate any mapping from an input dimensional space to an output space. Training of MLPs to yield such a mapping can be carried out efficiently by the back-propagation algorithm (Werbos, 1974; Rumelhart and McClelland, 1986).

The back-propagation learning algorithm is an iterative gradient descent technique that minimizes the L_2 norm of the error between the desired outputs indicated by the labels and the actual outputs computed by the elements in the feed-forward network. The error is given by

$$E = \frac{1}{2} \sum_{i=0}^{N-1} (d_i - y_i)^2, \tag{1}$$

where N is the number of neurons at the output layer, d_i is the desired output at the output neuron i, and y_i is the output computed by the MLP for neuron i. The gradient descent method is initialized with an arbitrarily selected weight

Artificial Neural Networks for Speech and Vision. Edited by Richard J. Mammone. Published in 1993 by Chapman & Hall, London. ISBN 0 412 54850 X

vector w_0. This vector is updated using the following rule:

$$w^{n+1} = w^n - \eta \frac{\partial E}{\delta w^n}, \tag{2}$$

where n is the iteration number and η is the learning rate parameter.

Hence for a given task, back-propagation can be employed to learn the task using the weight update rule suggested above.

In this chapter we introduce a new method for training neural networks. The method uses an additional observing neural network called a Meta-Neural Network (MNN) to direct the training of each perceptron of a conventional neural network. The MNN provides the conventional or primary neural network with a step size and selects a direction vector which is optimal in a specific context. The strategy is derived from previous training sessions for similar problems. The combination of the MNN with a conventional neural network is shown to improve learning rates for several similar tasks. The Meta-Neural Network is also shown to help solve the problem of sensitivity to initial weight vectors.

Computer simulations demonstrate the improvement in the learning rate of the composite neural network on different tasks, when it has been trained on tasks belonging to a similar domain. In addition, it is shown that learning strategies acquired from training on a subset of data can be used to accelerate training for the entire data set. It is demonstrated that an artificial neural network system can exhibit the characteristics of **learning by learning** and thus accelerate the learning of tasks encountered later.

'Learning by learning' is achieved by modifying the basic gradient descent update and intergrating it with theories proposed in psychological studies on **learning by learning**. In section 14.3 we review this important concept. Section 14.4 explains how a neural network can be made to learn by learning. In section 14.5 the numerical results are presented followed by conclusion and future investigations in section 14.6.

14.2 Learning by learning with neural networks

14.2.1 The psychological concept

The process of learning a particular task which then affects the performance of learning subsequent tasks is called **transfer of learning**. A progressive improvement in performance is a form of transfer, known as **learning to learn** (Ellis, 1965). Several experiments have been carried out in psychology to verify that animals and humans learn by learning (Ward, 1937; Harlow, 1949; Marx, 1944).

One such experiment was conducted by Ward (1937). Subjects were provided with successive lists of nonsense syllables. One list was given to each subject to learn each day. Ward's results indicate that the subjects required 38 trials to completely master the first list. After learning six lists, the subjects required only 20 trials, and after 15 lists, they required only 14 trials. Ward observed that the learning was rapid during the first six lists and more gradual later. It was clear from this experiment that the subjects **learned how to learn** the material even though it consisted of nonsense syllables.

Such a learning methodology could be efficiently employed to learn strategies in artificial neural networks. For example, we can transfer some learning strategy that has been acquired by a neural network to a different neural network that has to learn a related task. Using such transfer of learning we can improve the learning speed and performance of a neural network on various related tasks. By using transfer of learning we could train a network on a small subset of the training data to **shape** the network to train more efficiently on the larger set of data.

14.2.2 Prior efforts

'Previous work has either explicitly or implicitly dealt with the concept of transfer of learning. The concept of **shaping** in psychology in the form of progressive training was employed for artificial neural networks by Wieland and Leighton (1988). They used progressive training to bias a neural network to learn more complex tasks. Kehoe (1988) developed a layered neural network model for learning to learn. Kehoe used stimuli and reinforcement as parameters for the neural network. He studied the psychological effect on animals by simulating the learning to learn ability in animal models. The results are not so much relevant to artificial neural network models as they deal more with a stimulus that can be reinforced. Further details of this model can be found in Kehoe (1988) and the references therein.

Pratt *et al.* (1991) use transfer of learning to improve learning efficiency and the generalization of artificial neural networks. Inductive learners employed in machine learning tasks incorporate symbolic information in the training process. Pratt (1992) used a trained learner to transfer information to new learning tasks.

The concept of transfer of learning was implicitly employed by using a second neural network to enchance the learning process of the primary neural network for recurrent networks by Pineda (1987), Almeida (1987) and Lapedes and Farber (1986).

14.2.3 Learning to learn using meta-nets

We introduce a different approach to transfer of learning. Learning by learning is achieved by remembering successful training strategies on problems which have been learned previously. Hence, with this approach, the dynamics of the **way** a problem is learned is remembered. Learning by learning in artificial neural networks is achieved by using an additional observing neural

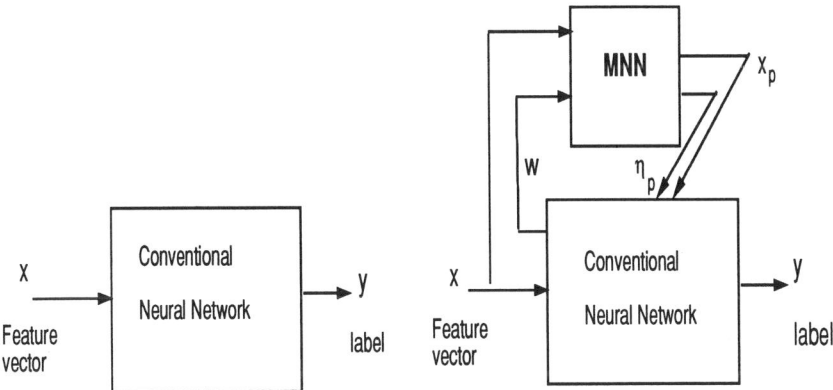

Figure 14.1 *Comparison of the original system and that using MNNs.*

network called Meta-Neural Network (MNN) to direct the training of each neuron in a previous neural network. Thus the MNN acts as an observer neural network which remembers the way problems have been solved previously by the conventional neural network. The unique feature of this approach is that we can use the MNN to train a conventional neural network over multiple related tasks or different subsets of the training data for the same tasks.

This scheme could also accelerate training in the case of large training data sets. For example, we could use a small subset of the training data for the source network and train the MNN to learn the trajectories on this small subset. The MNN can then be used to accelerate the training of the conventional neural network for the entire set of data by directing the conventional neural network to learn the problem with improved performance at the cost of training the MNN.

A block diagram comparing the original system and the system using MNNs is shown in Figure 14.1. The transfer of learning is accomplished by **encoding** the trajectory information in the MNNs. The use of MNNs to direct conventional networks yields improved learning rates on problems that are different, but analogous to problems previously **observed** by the MNN.

14.3 The meta-network approach

The model proposed here for learning by learning uses an additional observing neural network called Meta-Neural Network (MNN) to direct the training of the conventional MLP neural network. The MNN provides the conventional neural network with a **step size** and a **direction vector** which are optimal in the sense that they are based on successful training strategies learned from problems solved previously.

The MNN operates in two modes, the **observing mode** and the **guiding mode**. In the observing mode the MNN observes and learns the training of a multi-layer perceptron on several tasks. In the guiding mode, the MNN directs each hidden node of a MLP based on the information it learned when in the observing mode. In this chapter the MNN is also a multi-layer perceptron.

The approach taken consists of the following steps. In the **observing** mode,

- an MLP is trained using the back-propagation algorithm for a particular task using several initial weight vectors. Each initial weight vector will produce an optimal solution. These optima are normally obtained by training until the error has reached an acceptable minimum.
- The resulting optimal weights are stored along with the initial weights. This is **analogous** to learning a problem from different initial conditions.
- The initial and final (optimal) weight vectors are used to train the MNN to produce an optimum step size and a direction vector.

In the **guiding** mode the MNN is used to assist the conventional neural network to accelerate learning rate on problems that are similar to those previously observed by the MNN.

The block diagram of the MNN-MLP configuration is illustrated in Figure 14.2.

At this point we can note that the **transfer of learning** in this case takes place by encoding the previously learned trajectories into the MNN (Naik and Mammone, 1992).

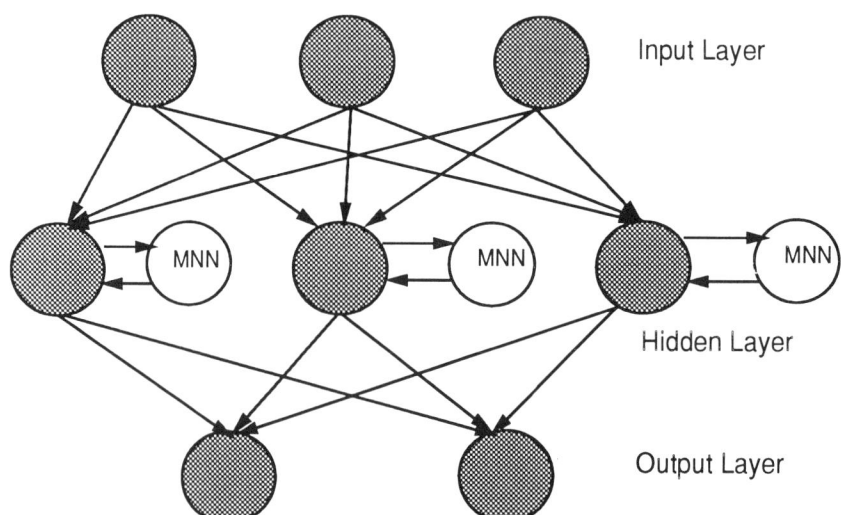

Figure 14.2 *MNN-MLP configuration.*

14.3.1 Analysis in the observing and guiding modes

The delta weight update is restated here for convenience,

$$w^{n+1} = w^n - \eta \frac{\delta E}{\delta w^n} + \alpha \Delta w^n, \tag{3}$$

where α is the momentum term, η is the learning rate, n is the iteration number and w is the weight vector.

This delta rule is used to train the conventional neural network using several initial weight vectors, which are randomly selected. The set of initial starting weight vectors and the resulting optimal weights vectors obtained by back-propagation are given by set $S = \{W_{0_i}, W_{opt_i}\}$, where i is the ith trial. The set S of weight vectors is then used to train the MNN. The conventional MLP is enhanced with the MNN. The enhanced MLP can now be retrained much faster with the MNN. This accelerated training rate is achieved by modifying the BP update rule to modify the training of the conventional MLP using a vector geometry approach.

The approach taken here implements the update equation (3), at every iteration, by **cycling** through all the feature vectors in the training set and selecting the best input vector X_i for the next iteration of the conventional neural network. This vector provides a direction vector X_p, whose resultant with the weight vector in the current iteration yields an updated weight vector which is nearest to the known optimum. The optimum magnitude to move in this optimum direction of the vector is thus found to yield the optimum step size $\hat{\eta}$.

Hence, at every iteration an MNN needs to be trained to yield the step size and the direction vector, collectively called the **selected gradient**, by taking X_p and W_i as the input feature of the MNN, where i is the current iteration.

The MNN training process can be divided into two steps:

- The first step is to select the best input vector X_i for the next iteration of back-propagation of the conventional MLP neural network.
- The second stage is to select the step size for this iteration.

The approach used is to cycle through all the pattern vectors X_k and select a vector X_p that is most similar to the known optimum direction. This is accomplished by **maximizing the cosine** of the angle

$$\cos \theta_k = \frac{(W_{opt} - W_i)}{|(W_{opt} - W_i)|} \cdot \frac{X_k}{|X_k|}, \tag{4}$$

where k cycles through all the pattern vectors, and X_p is selected such that $\cos \theta_k$ is maximum.

We also note that the expression for the optimum step size in this optimum direction X_p is given by

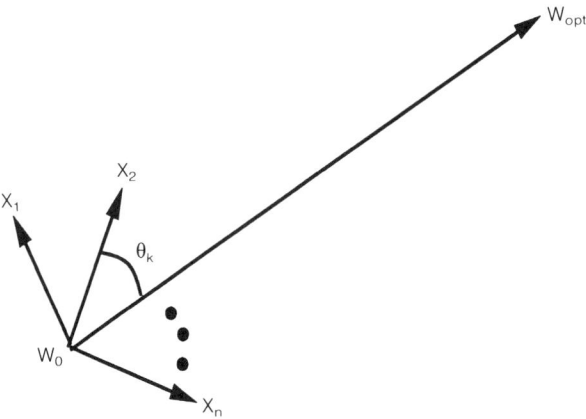

Figure 14.3 *Finding the optimum direction. W = weight vectors, X = feature vectors.*

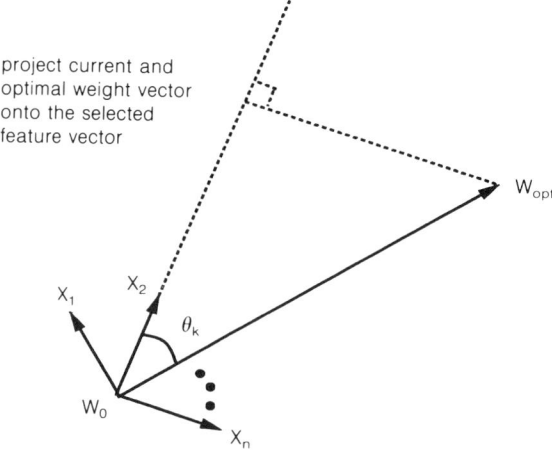

Figure 14.4 *Finding the optimum step size. W = weight vectors, X = feature vectors.*

$$\hat{\eta}_p = (W_{\text{opt}} - W_i) \cdot \frac{X_p}{|X_p|}. \tag{5}$$

The vector X_p at step size $\hat{\eta}_p$ is used to find vector W_{i+1} which has the minimum angle with the optimum vector. The expression above provides the optimum step size $\hat{\eta}_p$ and along with the optimum vector X_p is used to modify the gradient descent equation for the back-propagation as follows:

$$w^{n+1} = w^n - \eta \frac{\delta E}{\delta w^n} + \alpha \Delta w^n + \hat{\eta}_p X_p. \tag{6}$$

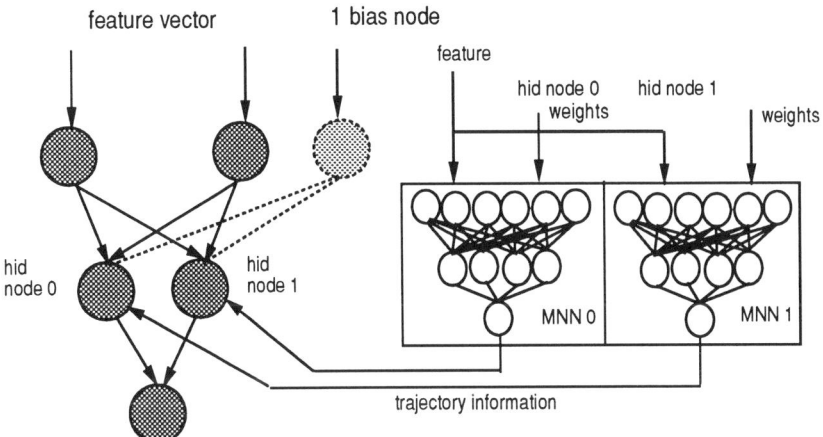

Figure 14.5 *Every hidden node is augmented by an MNN.*

Figures 14.3 and 14.4 illustrate the geometry of the approach used to find X_p and $\hat{\eta}_p$.

We can also see from Figures 14.3 and 14.4 that the optimum vector X_p is also the one which maximizes the absolute value of $\hat{\eta}_p$. The above process is repeated over all the weight vectors in the set S. At every iteration of the conventional neural network, the weight vector, the feature vectors and the corresponding $\hat{\eta}$ found in equation (5) are stored. This forms the training set for the MNN. Its is important to note that **every hidden node** of the conventional MLP be observed by an MNN, as illustrated in Figure 14.5.

Therefore, we would need to train an MNN for each hidden node. Thus the MNN is in fact a collection of neural networks, each of which encodes the trajectory information of **each hidden node** of the conventional neural network. The feature vectors are available to the layer between the input and the hidden nodes and hence, only the hyperplanes formed by the input-hidden (IH) layer are used.

After the MNN is trained by observing some sample problems, the same update rule given by equation (6) is used to train future problems. However, in the guiding mode, the step size and the direction vector are now provided to the conventional neural network by the MNN.

14.3.2 Implementation

The implementation of the above algorithm leads to further simplifications in the model. The plots of the step sizes evaluated using equation (5) for a hidden node are shown in Figure 14.6. We note that the value of $\hat{\eta}_p$ is larger at the start and reduces to very small values after first few iterations. This indicates that the vector X_p and the step size $\hat{\eta}_p$ at every iteration of the conventional

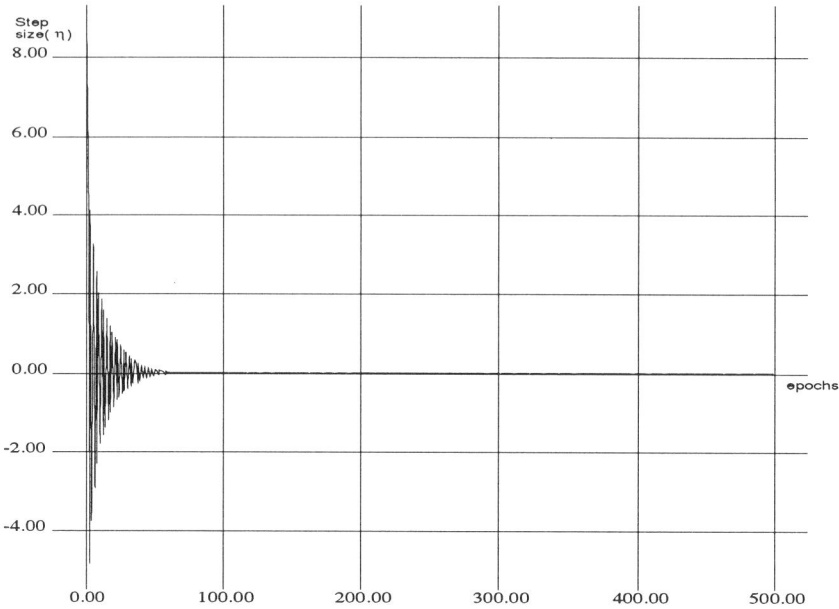

Figure 14.6 *Trajectory of output step size for a hidden node used in training on the XOR problem.*

MLP are such that they accelerate the MLP within the first few iterations. Thus step sizes generated after the first few epochs do not significantly affect learning speed.

This fact provides an important result to make the MNN training process computationally less expensive by switching off the MNN after exactly N iterations, where N is the number of feature vectors. To utilize this result efficiently we implement a strategy which limits the training data generated to train the MNN. Once a vector X_p is chosen at an epoch as the optimum vector, it is not selected again as an optimum vector for the epochs that follow. Hence at a subsequent epoch, the optimal vector is chosen only from $N - m$ feature vectors, where N is the total number of feature vectors, and m is the number of feature vectors chosen in the previous epochs. Hence, the training data for the MNN is generated for only N epochs, and the rest of the training is accomplished by conventional back-propagation as the augmented term is now zero, i.e. MNNs are switched off.

This enhanced neural network model learns to output an **optimum gradient vector** to **guide** the conventional neural network, and hence achieve good generalization over multiple problems that are similar in some sense. For example, an MNN trained to encode the trajectories of a 4 bit nonlinear Boolean function can be used to improve the learning of a more difficult 4 bit parity problem.

The MNN also generalizes to prevent a conventional MLP training process from network paralysis. If the training process gets stuck due to larger errors using the conventional MLP, then the information provided by the MNNs helps avoid network paralysis and drives the network to convergence. Hence, the enhanced model is less sensitive to initial conditions.

14.4 Numerical simulations

The new method for training multi-layer perceptrons developed in the previous sections was applied to various problems for which the results are provided in this section. All the simulations presented use the MLP configuration with an arbitrary number of hidden nodes depending upon the problem.

The next subsection provides the performance curves for an illustrative two class problem which is similar to the XOR problem. The performance of the new model is tested over several variations of the step size and momentum factor for an MLP. The new model is also shown to be insensitive to the choice of initial weights, where a normal MLP training by back-propagation would get trapped. In the second subsection, a superset of the two class problem is chosen and the improvement in the learning rate of the MNN-MLP configuration, where the MNN is trained on the two class problem, is presented. The third subsection illustrates how an MNN-MLP configuration, where the MNN was trained on a simple nonlinear Boolean function, improves the

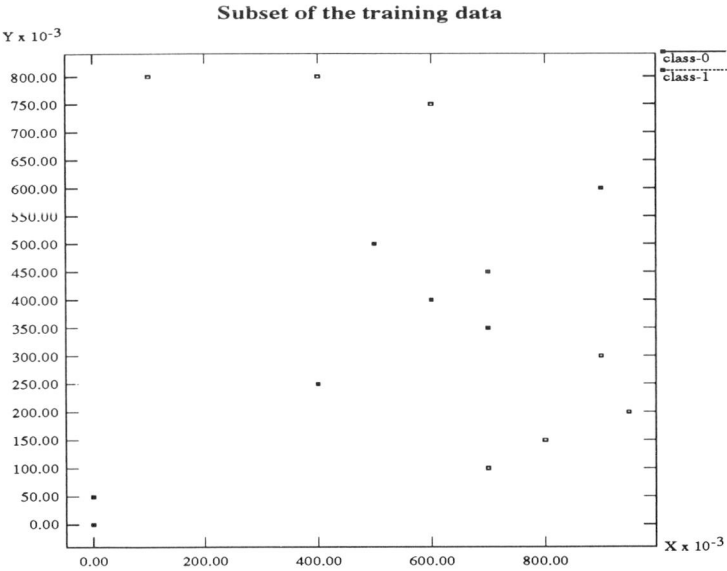

Figure 14.7 *Illustrative two class problem.*

learning rate of a more difficult parity problem and a simpler nonlinear Boolean function.

14.4.1 Insensitivity to initial choice of weights

Consider the illustrative two class problem shown in Figure 14.7. The MLP is sensitive to the choice of initial weights and tends to get stuck for large error values, making the gradient descent extremely slow. The choice of step size, number of hidden nodes and the momentum factor is also *ad hoc*. The composite MNN-MLP network is less sensitive to choice of initial weights. The configuration is found to be immune to the choice of initial weights for this particular problem.

The MNN was trained on trajectories obtained from ten runs of the MLP for which two hidden nodes were used. The weights were initialized in the range of ± 0.05, and the runs were performed using arbitrary step sizes in the range of 0.2 to 0.5 and momentum factor from 0.3 to 0.8. The composite network was then tested on several values of the step sizes and momentum factors. Three trials of initialization of weights were performed for every combination. Out of 50 random trials of initialization for training, the MLP failed to converge for nine trials. The training was successful on all nine trials, when trained with the new model. Two sample trials are illustrated in Figures 14.8 and 14.9.

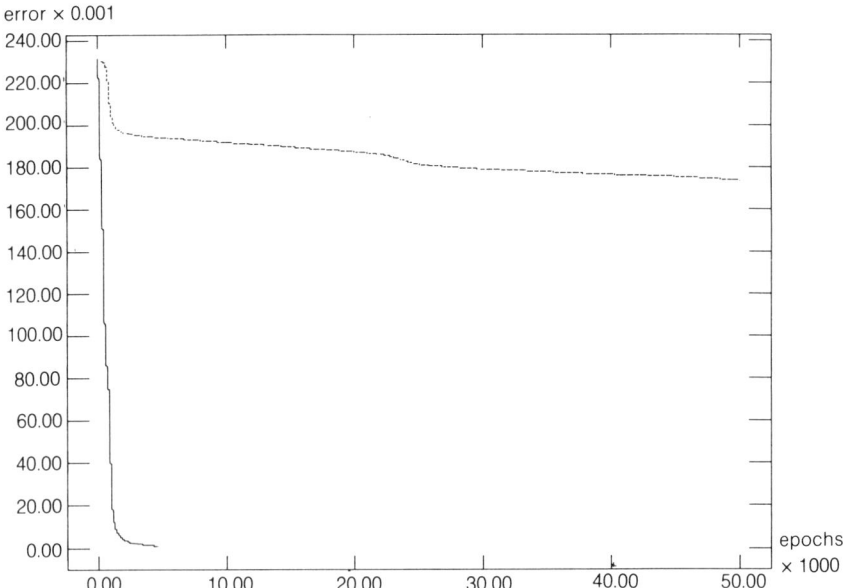

Figure 14.8 *Learning curve with and without MNN at $\eta = 0.1$ and $\alpha = 0.2$.* ——— : *with MNN; --- : without MNN.*

error × 0.001

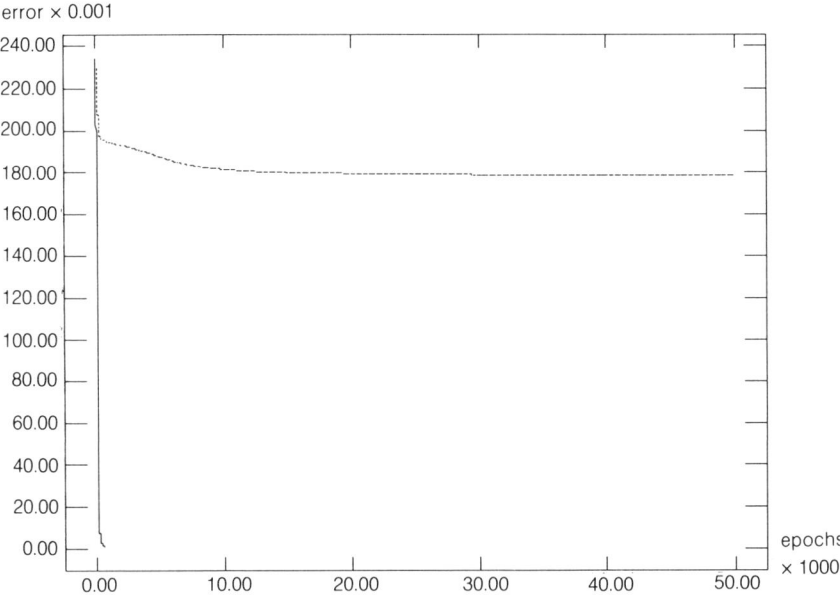

Figure 14.9 *Learning curve with and without MNN at $\eta = 0.3$ and $\alpha = 0.6$. ——— : with MNN; - - - : without MNN.*

14.4.2 Performance on a larger two class problem

A larger two class problem which is a superset of the illustrative two class problem chosen in the previous section is shown in Figure 14.10. The MNN trained on the smaller problem given in the previous section was used to improve the learning of superset problem in Figure 14.10. Since the number of feature vectors is much larger, a smaller learning rate was used to allow smoother gradient descent. The initial weights were chosen in the same range of ± 0.05, and the learning was performed with step sizes of 0.01 and 0.05 and momentum factors of 0.0 and 0.05. The number of epochs were observed when the total mean square error had converged to 1%.

Average speed-up for training superset (186 exemplars) was 6.72 (from Table 14.1). MNN was trained on 15 randomly selected exemplars shown in Figure 14.7.

Furthermore, points inconsistent with the data the MNN was trained on were added to the data set, illustrated as circled points in Figure 14.11. For $\eta = 0.01$, error was observed when the network converged to 2% within MSE and within 1% for $\eta = 0.05$, as shown in Table 14.2.

Simulations were also carried out to learn the same problem with different initial conditions. Speed-up on the same problem with different initial conditions was 16.2 for 50 random trials.

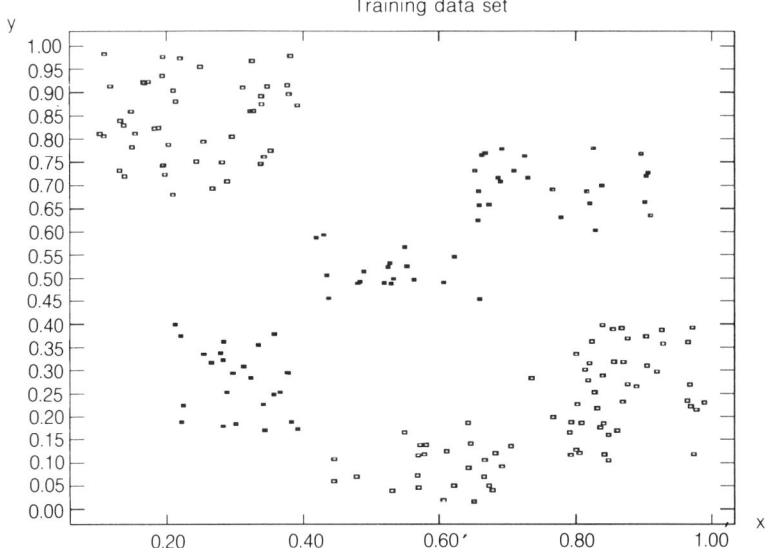

Figure 14.10 *Data set used for the two class problem.*

Table 14.1 *Performance comparison of MLP and MNN-MLP on the superset*

η, α	MLP (epochs)	MNN-MLP (epochs)
0.01, 0.00	5200	714
0.01, 0.05	4685	604
0.05, 0.05	1177	142

14.4.3 *Learning by learning for related problems*

To illustrate **learning by learning** for problems of a related domain, we chose a nonlinear Boolean problem (f_1) to train the MNN. The resulting MNN was then used to direct the conventional neural network to learn the nonlinear Boolean function (f_2) and the 4-bit parity problem.

MNN were trained on $f_1 = (a \vee b) \oplus (c \wedge d)$ and the performance was tested on $f_2 = (a \vee b) \oplus (c \oplus d)$. This successfully trained 16 out of 21 trials, and a speed-up of 1.63 was obtained.

MNN trained on f_1 was tested on a 4-bit problem $(a \oplus b) \oplus (c \oplus d)$. Four-bit parity was found difficult to train with four hidden nodes in an MLP. Out of 20 random trials at step sizes of (0.3 and 0.5) and a momentum factor of (0.1

Superset with critical features added

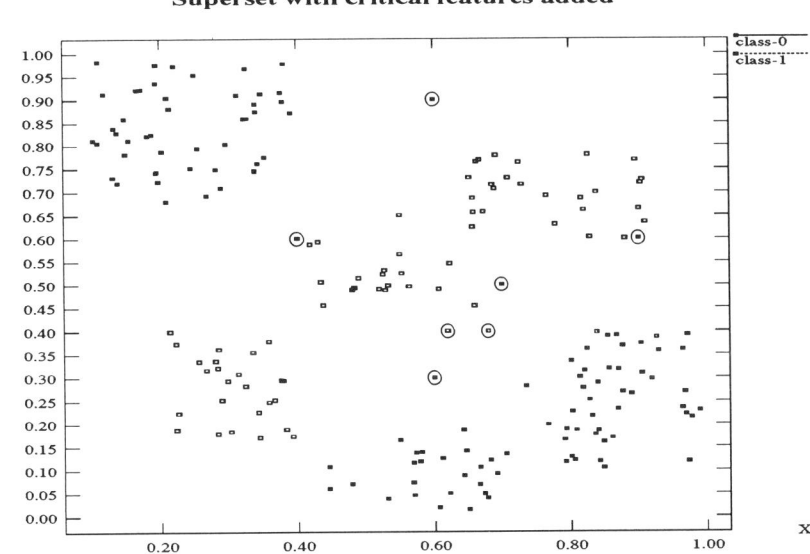

Figure 14.11 *Modified data set used for the two class problem.*

Table 14.2 *Performance comparison of MLP and MNN-MLP on the modified superset*

η, α	MLP (epochs)	MNN-MLP (epochs)
0.01, 0.00	6000	1000
0.01, 0.05	6600	900
0.05, 0.00	6000	2900
0.05, 0.05	5800	2700

and 0.3), the MLP was successful for only five trials. The new model was successful in training to within 1% MSE for 16 of these trials.

14.5 Conclusion and future work

A new approach to enhance neural network learning called the Meta-Neural Network (MNN) is introduced. The MNN has been shown to increase the learning rates for equivalent generalization on large data problems, where the MNN had been trained on only a small subset of the data. This was shown by training the MNN on a small subset of the large set of training data for a two class problem. The composite MNN-MLP configuration was then used to train on the large data set. The composite network showed significant speed-up over the conventional MLP.

The MNN also showed increased learning rates for related tasks. This was demonstrated by using an MNN trained on a four-input nonlinear Boolean function (f_1) to assist the learning of a four-input parity problem and a related four input Boolean function (f_2). The MNN was observed to be less immune to the initial choice of network parameters. This was demonstrated by training the composite network on those initial choice of weights for which a normal back-propagation algorithm became trapped at a minimum. Encouraging statistics were also obtained in case of the difficult problems such as the four-bit parity problem. A four-bit parity problem was found to be difficult to train using four hidden nodes with the choice of parameters reported. The MNN learning was found to be much faster for this problem.

Future work will investigate the issues in finding a measure similarity between related tasks. Applicability of the algorithm to other classification algorithms like Neural Tree Networks (Sankar and Mammone, 1990) will also be considered.

References

Almeida, L.B. (1987) A learning rule for asynchronous perceptrons with feedback in a combinatorial environment. *International Joint Conference on Neural Networks*, p. 199, June.

Ellis, H. (1965) *Transfer of Learning*. MacMillan, New York, NY.

Harlow, H.F. (1949) Formation of learning sets. *Psychological Review*, **56**, 51–65.

Kehoe, J. (1988) A layered network model of associative learning: Learning to learn and configuration. *Psychological Review*, **95**(4), 411–33.

Lapedes, A. and Farber, R.M. (1986) A self-optimizing, nonsymmetrical neural network for content addressable memory and pattern recognition. *Physica D*, **22**, 247.

Marx, M.H. (1944) The effects of cumulative training upon retroactive inhibition and transfer. *Comp. Pyschol. Monographs* (94).

Naik, D.K. and Mammone, R.J. (1992) Meta-neural networks that learn by learning. *Proceedings IEEE International Conference on Neural Networks*.

Pineda, F.J. (1987) Generalization of backpropagation to recurrent neural networks. *Phys. Rev. Letters*, **59**, 2229.

Pratt, L. (1992) Transfer of information among inductive learners. *Proceedings Tenth National Conference on Artificial Intelligence*, January.

Pratt, L., Mostow, J. and Kamm, C. (1991) Direct transfer of learned information among neural networks. *Proceedings Ninth National Conference on Artificial Intelligence*, Anaheim, CA.

Rumelhart, D.E. and McClelland, J.L. (1986) *Parallel and Distributed Processing, Vol. 1*. MIT Press, Cambridge, MA.

Sankar, A. and Mammone, R. (1990) A fast learning algorithm for tree neural networks. *Proceedings Conference on Information Sciences and Systems*, March.

Ward, L.B. (1937) Reminiscence and rote learning. *Pyschol. Monographs*, **49**(220).

Werbos, P. (1974) *Beyond Regression: New Tools for Prediction and Analysis in the Behavioral Sciences*. PhD thesis, Harvard University.

Wieland, A. and Leighton, R. (1988) Shaping schedules as a method for accelerated learning. *Abstracts of the First Intl. Neural Networking Conference*, 231.

Part Two
ANN Applications in Speech and Language Understanding

15

A self-learning neural tree network for phone recognition

MAZIN G. RAHIM
AT&T Bell Laboratories, Murray Hill, NJ, USA

15.1 Introduction

There are two issues to be considered when applying neural networks (Lippmann, 1987) for the recognition of speech features. The first issue is that conventional neural networks tend not to take advantage of the non-uniform correlation that exists among speech sounds. Instead, all sounds are considered equally confused. However, it is well known that the human ear can perceive certain sounds more distinctly than others (e.g. /aa/ & /b/ *vs* /p/ & /b/). The second issue is that conventional neural networks require the network architecture to be specified prior to training. The architecture is typically found through trial and error. This results in an added computational complexity and a sub-optimal recognition performance.

To accommodate the varying complexity of different classification problems, Sankar and Mammone (1991) and Stromberg *et al.* (1991) proposed combining the concept of decision trees (Breiman *et al.*, 1984) with feed-forward neural networks to form a Neural Tree Network (NTN). At each node of the tree, a neuron is employed to perform a non-linear decision. The authors evaluated their implementations on a vowel classification task and demonstrated an improvement in performance over classical decision tree methods (e.g. CART). Their recognition performance is comparable to that of conventional neural networks, but with a significant reduction in computational complexity.

When performing more complex classification tasks (e.g. >30 classes, $>20\,000$ training data, etc.), NTNs generally grow into less efficient structures, especially if the classes are highly overlapped (e.g. phonemes). Sankar and

Artificial Neural Networks for Speech and Vision. Edited by Richard J. Mammone.
Published in 1993 by Chapman & Hall, London. ISBN 0 412 54850 X

Mammone (1991), report a pruning algorithm to reduce the size of the network by improving its performance on the evaluation data. This procedure, however, requires the tree to fully grow, which may not be possible if the problem is too complex.

This chapter presents a new and a more generalized self-learning approach towards designing a NTN. The Self-Learning NTN (SL-NTN) provides an 'optimal' trade-off between computational complexity and recognition performance. It also provides insight towards the interrelationship among the applied patterns. The SL-NTN grows an efficient tree architecture through analysis of the relative 'confusion' among the applied classes. Therefore, classes which are easily separable are processed at low levels of the tree, whereas those which are highly overlapped in feature space are processed at high levels of the tree.

The design, training and operation of the SL-NTN are described in this chapter. Experimental results are presented on the TIMIT database (Lamel *et al.*, 1986) for recognition of 36 English phonemes (Rahim, 1992), and 61 English phones (Rahim, 1993).

15.2 SL-NTN: Self-Learning Neural Tree Network

A schematic diagram of an NTN is shown in Figure 15.1. At each node of the tree, a neural network is trained to classify the input data into one of several sets of classes. These sets are determined by a clustering algorithm, which splits the classes according to their relative confusion with each other. The NTN is self-learning since no external knowledge regarding the nature of the classes is required, thus, it is referred to as the Self-Learning NTN (SL-NTN). The SL-NTN establishes the intra-class correlation independently, and splits the classes in such a way so as to maximize the recognition performance while reducing the computational complexity.

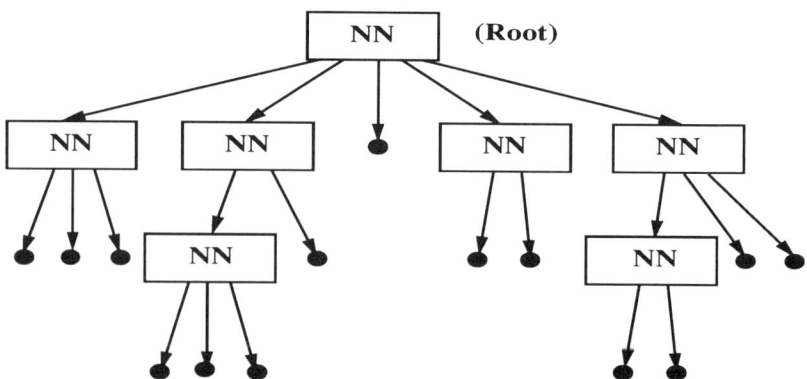

Figure 15.1 *Schematic diagram of an NTN.*

In this section, we describe in more detail the determination of the appropriate sets of classes at each node (design), the training of the SL-NTN to perform the actual classification (training), and the operation of the resulting SL-NTN (operation).

15.2.1 Design

The *first step* in designing the SL-NTN requires an estimate of the correlation among the applied classes (intra-class correlation). This estimate is utilized in the clustering algorithm to allow a split into multiple branches at each node of the tree. The intra-class correlation is obtained by training a conventional neural network at the root level of the tree to classify the input patterns into their appropriate classes. The neural network 'learns' to map each input feature vector into one of several classes. Following the training phase, the percentages of patterns confused among the different classes (i.e. confusion matrix) provide the intra-phone correlation.

The *second step* in designing the tree involves the application of the clustering algorithm. The intention is to cluster the input patterns into two or more sets of classes, imposing maximal inter-set correlation and minimal intra-set correlation. The number of sets formed by the clustering algorithm, at any node of the tree, is determined by an error threshold T.

A flow diagram of the clustering algorithm is shown in Figure 15.2. At the root node of the tree, we assume that there is a set, Ω, of N classes:

$$\Omega = \{S_1, S_2, \ldots, S_i, \ldots, S_N\}, \tag{1}$$

where S_i is the ith class. If m_{ij} represents the ijth element of the confusion matrix. D

$$D = \{m_{ij}\} \quad \forall 1 \leqslant i, j \leqslant N, \tag{2}$$

then the average distance $\bar{d}(S_i, S_j)$ between classes S_i and S_j is defined as the percentage of their patterns confused with each other:

$$\bar{d}(S_i, S_j) = \tfrac{1}{2}(m_{ij} + m_{ji}). \tag{3}$$

Similarly, if cluster (set) C has K classes, for example, then the distance between class S_i and cluster C is defined as

$$\bar{d}(S_i, C) = \frac{1}{2K} \sum_{k=1}^{K} (m_{ik} + m_{ki}). \tag{4}$$

The clustering algorithm aims to divide the classes into M 'least' confused clusters keeping the intra-cluster distance below the error threshold T. Forming M clusters requires

$$C_1 \cup C_2 \cup .. \cup C_M = \Omega, \tag{5}$$

$$C_1 \cap C_2 \cap .. \cap C_M = \emptyset. \tag{6}$$

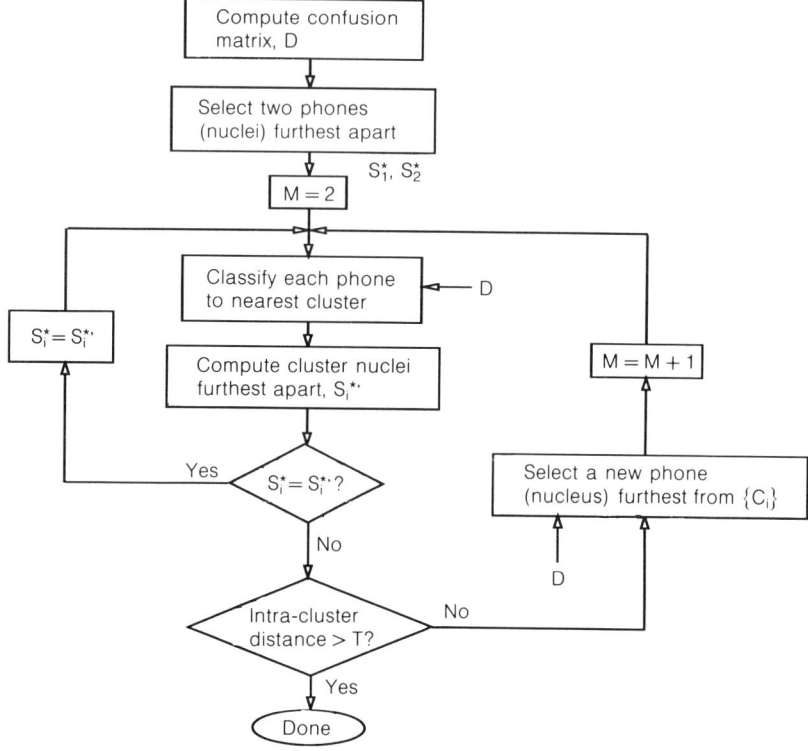

Figure 15.2 *Flow diagram of the clustering algorithm.*

The clustering algorithm proceeds as follows:

1. Identify two classes (i.e. $M = 2$) of the set Ω which are furthest apart according to the confusion matrix D:

$$(S_1^*, S_2^*) = \arg \min_{i=1,N;j>i} \bar{d}(S_i, S_j), \tag{7}$$

where S_1^* and S_2^* are referred to as the 'nuclei', and

$$S_1^* \in C_1, \tag{8}$$

$$S_2^* \in C_2. \tag{9}$$

2. Cluster the remaining classes into either C_1 or C_2. Classes with minimum distance (i.e. maximum confusion) to either C_1 or C_2 are selected first:

DO

$$(i^*, j^*) = \arg \max_{j=1,M;i=1,N;S_i \notin C_j} \bar{d}(S_i, C_j) \tag{10}$$

$$C_{j^*} = C_{j^*} \cup S_{i^*} \tag{11}$$

UNTIL

$$C_1 \cup C_2 \cup .. \cup C_M = \Omega. \tag{12}$$

3. Form further clusters by defining new nuclei

$$S_{M+1}^* = \arg \min_{j=1,M; i=1,N; S_i \neq S_j^*} \bar{d}(S_i, C_j), \tag{13}$$

and repeating Step 2.

Every time a new cluster is created, two conditions are verified:

1. The intra-cluster distance

$$G = \sum_{i,j=1,M; i \neq j} \bar{d}(C_i, C_j) \tag{14}$$

is minimum, given the required number of clusters and the confusion matrix D. Otherwise, an iterative procedure is performed in which $(M-1)$ of the nuclei are fixed, and a search is carried out to find a new nucleus that satisfies the above condition.

2. The condition where $G < T$ is always satisfied. Otherwise, the clustering algorithm is terminated.

Clearly, the value of T determines the number of sets, M, formed by the clustering algorithm. For example, if T is set to 0, a binary SL-NTN is produced. A simplified diagram of such an implementation is shown in Figure 15.3. At each node of the tree, only two clusters are available and a 2-way decision is made. Input patterns (carried by the data bus) can be accessed by

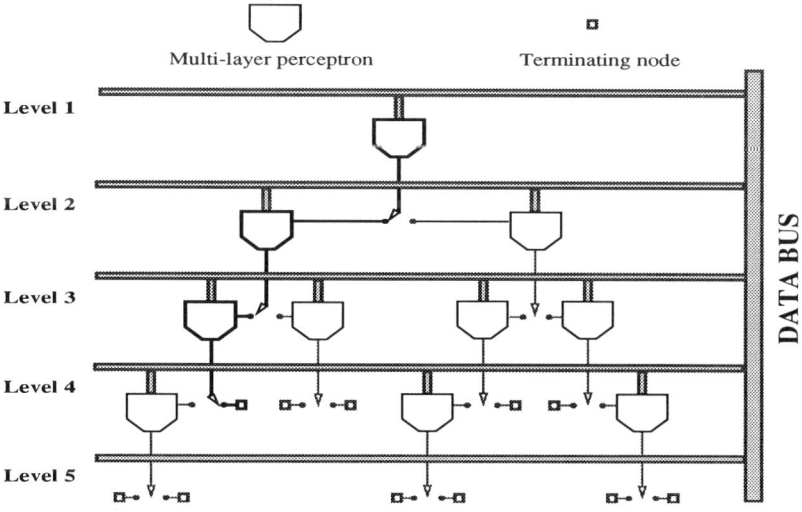

Figure 15.3 *Simplified diagram of a binary SL-NTN.*

all tree nodes. Note that as $T \rightarrow \infty$, the number of clusters approaches the number of available classes N.

Fuzzy clustering

In phoneme classification, as well as other pattern classification problems, it may not be possible to repeatedly divide classes into a multiple number of sets while maintaining a low confusion error (i.e. low value of G). It is likely that at some nodes of the tree a number of classes may be confused with more than one set. To alleviate this problem, a type of 'fuzzy' clustering is introduced in which highly confused classes are shared among several clusters. Generally, classes are shared if grouping them into separable clusters would result in a confusion error exceeding a threshold α. In a binary case, to share classes between two clusters, C_1 and C_2, we relax the condition in equation (6) to $C_1 \cap C_2 = H$, where $H = \varnothing$, or it may contain several classes. The clustering algorithm is, therefore, modified to include an additional constraint:

$$\text{if } \overline{d}(S_i, C_j) > \alpha, \quad 1 \leqslant j \leqslant M \tag{15}$$

$$C_j = C_j \cap S_i, \tag{16}$$

where α is typically 2–5%.

The building process of the SL-NTN continues by assigning a neural network for each cluster and repeating the two design steps until all classes are divided appropriately. The next stage is to train each individual neural network to perform an M-way classification.

15.2.2 Training

Upon designing the SL-NTN, the task at each node of the tree is decomposed into an M-set problem. The number of sets M varies between 2 and N, depending on the number of clusters generated by the clustering algorithm at the individual nodes. Therefore, a neural network can now be trained to perform an M-way classification requiring M output neurons. Since the intra-set (intra-cluster) correlation is minimized by the clustering algorithm, neural networks of the SL-NTN are now expected to be trained with minimal confusion error. Shared classes at any level of the tree which are mutual to several sets are omitted during training, as the decision on which set they belong to is unimportant.

Two constraints are imposed when training the designed SL-NTN: (1) the number of hidden neurons of the tree's neural networks are set equal to that used while building the tree; and (2) the 'optimal' weighting coefficients from the input layer to the hidden layer, obtained while building the tree, are used to initialize the SL-NTN prior to training. Initializing the variables of the tree in this manner helps to speed-up convergence.

15.2.3 *Operation*

Typically, for an N-class problem using a binary SL-NTN, the tree grows to $\log_2 N$ levels. The number of levels may further increase by one or two if 'fuzzy' clustering is introduced.

During operation of the SL-NTN, the input pattern is initially applied to the neural network at the root level of the tree. The appropriate neural network at the next higher level is then activated and the pattern is applied to its input layer. The pattern propagates through the tree until it is classified as one of the classes (Figure 15.3).

15.3 Experimental results

Two experiments have been conducted using the TIMIT database. The first involves 36 English phonemes (silences and diphthongs were not included). The second involves all 61 phones in the database (i.e. phonemes, silences and diphthongs).

15.3.1 *Experiment 1*

A binary implementation of a SL-NTN is tested on the 36 English phonemes of the TIMIT database. Each manually segmented phoneme is represented by 12 cepstral coefficients $c_i(t)$; 12 cepstral derivatives $\Delta c_i(t)$; 1 energy coefficient $e(t)$; 1 energy derivative $\Delta e(t)$. $c_i(t)$ are obtained through a 12th order Hamming-windowed LPC analysis performed on the middle 30 ms segment of the phoneme (Markel and Gray, 1976):

$$c_1(t) = -a_1(t) \tag{17}$$

$$c_i(t) = \frac{-1}{i}\left(\sum_{n=1}^{i-1}[(i-n)c_{i-n}(t)a_n(t)] + ia_i(t)\right) \quad i \leqslant 12, \tag{18}$$

where $a_i(t)$ are the LPC coefficients.

$\Delta c_i(t)$ are approximated by a first-order polynomial applied over a 5-frame window, at a frame rate of a 100 frame/s (Furui, 1981):

$$\frac{\delta c_i(t)}{\delta t} \approx \Delta c_i(t) = \frac{\sum_{k=-2}^{2} kc_i(t+k)}{\sum_{-2}^{2} k^2}. \tag{19}$$

$e(t)$ is computed by taking the logarithm of the average frame energy, and $\Delta e(t)$ is computed in a similar way to $\Delta c_i(t)$.

Therefore, each pattern is represented by a 26-dimensional feature vector and is labeled as one of 36 phonemes. Training data consisted of 33 000 patterns extracted from 462 speakers, and evaluation data consisted of 16 000 patterns from 168 different speakers. All speakers provided by the TIMIT database have been used for this experiment.

For both building and training the SL-NTN, neural networks at each node of the tree are selected with 5 hidden neurons. When no sharing of phonemes is allowed, the SL-NTN is found to grow to seven levels utilizing 35 networks. This implementation scored 53.9% correct classification on the test database. For comparison, a conventional neural network is evaluated on the same database, and best performance of 52.4% has been achieved when using 130 hidden neurons. This suggests that the SL-NTN results in a reduction in computational complexity by a factor exceeding 8. In addition, as the neural network at each tree node has five hidden neurons and two outputs, then the overall tree structure can be implemented in hardware with as little as seven neurons plus a look-up table to store all the weights.

When sharing of phonemes is considered, the SL-NTN grows to 8 levels utilizing 83 networks. The classification performance of this structure is improved to 58.6% with minimal increase in computational complexity. Results show that in addition to advantages in computational complexity and recognition performance, the SL-NTN provides important correlation between the phonemes. Figure 15.4 shows the distribution of the phonemes when no sharing is permitted. One observation is that the parent network performs a separation between two sets of sounds; namely (1) vowels, glides, semi-vowels and nasals, and (2) fricatives, affricates and stop consonants. Subsequent networks are found to classify phonemes according to place of articulation (e.g. alveolar fricatives), or manner of articulation (e.g. nasals). The SL-NTN also provides information on the pairs of phonemes which are highly confused (e.g. /g/ & /k/).

15.3.2 Experiment 2

The aim of this experiment is to test the SL-NTN when used for recognition of the 61 TIMIT phones. Speakers are considered from two different accentual regions; New-England and Northern. This represents 114 training speakers and 37 different testing speakers.

Spectrum analysis is performed as follows:

1. Each manually segmented phone is represented by 12 cepstral coefficients $c_i(t)$; 12 cepstral derivatives $\Delta c_i(t)$; 1 energy coefficient $e(t)$; 1 energy derivative $\Delta e(t)$. The 26-dimensional feature vector is computed as in Experiment 1.
2. To allow greater robustness; both $c_i(t)$ and $\Delta c_i(t)$ are multiplied by a bandpass lifter (Juang, et al., 1987):

$$w_i(t) = 1 + 6 \sin \frac{i\pi}{12}, \quad 1 \leqslant i \leqslant 12. \tag{20}$$

The above lifter has been well established in speech recognition work. It is used to attenuate the low quefrencies to reduce the sensitivity to spectral

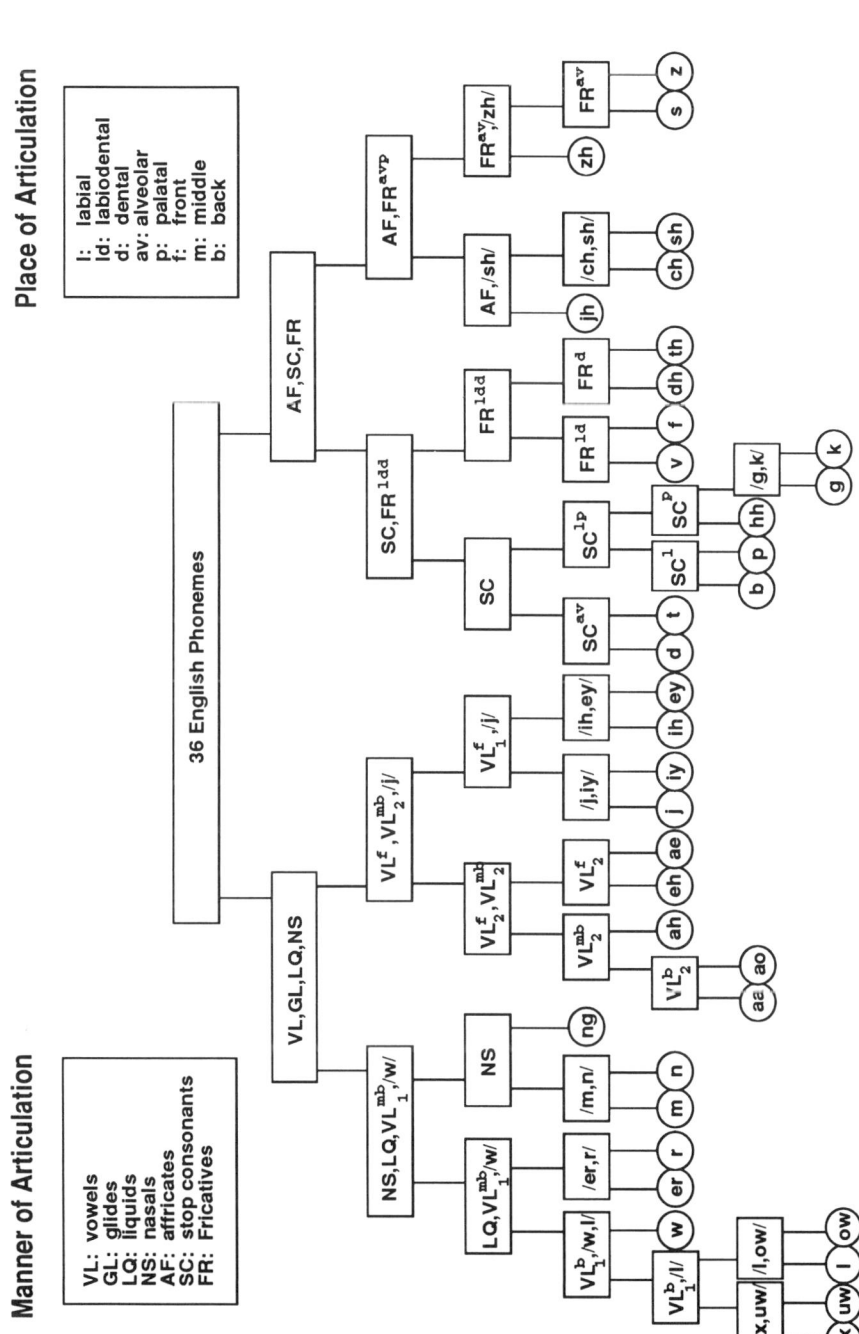

Figure 15.4 *Binary SL-NTN showing the phoneme distribution.*

tilt differences while it attenuates high quefrencies to minimize effects due to glottal excitation and formant bandwidth mismatches.

3. A scaling factor is applied to the components to equalize their variance:

$$O(t) = \{w_i(t)c_i(t), \alpha w_i(t)\Delta c_i(t), \beta e(t), \gamma \Delta e(t)\}. \tag{21}$$

4. Previous studies carried out by the author, as well as by other researchers (Burr, 1992), show that applying a Discreate Cosine Transform (DCT) (Ahmed and Rao, 1975) to the feature vectors $O(t)$, and using a 16-dimensional DCT vector, as opposed to using the 26-dimensional vector

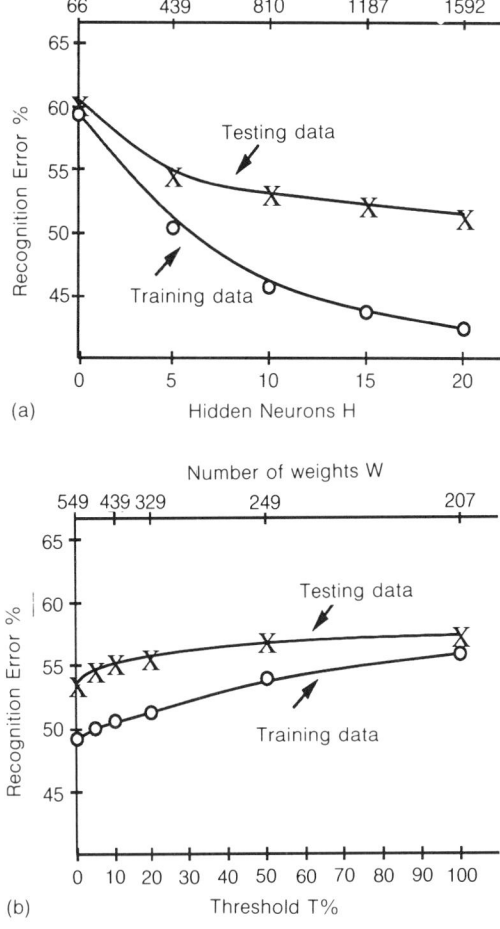

Figure 15.5 *Percentage recognition error of the SL-NTN and the number of weights W when (a) varying H and setting T = 5%, and (b) varying T and setting H = 5.*

$O(t)$, causes no degradation in the recognition performance. Therefore, each phone is represented by a vector $dct(t)(= DCT[O(t)])$.

Applying the above strategy resulted in about 43 000 patterns for training and about 14 000 for testing (the number of patterns **per** phone ranged between 10 for /eng/ to 2000 for /ix/).

Two criteria are used to evaluate the performance of the SL-NTN: percentage of recognition error; and computational complexity. The former is defined as the number of misclassified patterns, where as the latter is measured in terms of the average number of weights W activated during the recognition phase. Two factors contribute to the value of W: (1) the error threshold T, and (2) the number of hidden neurons H, of each neural network. Figure 15.5a shows the precentage recoginition error of the SL-NTN when varying H from 0 to 20, and setting T to 5%. Figure 15.5b shows the recognition error when setting H, for each neural network, to 5, and varying the threshold T from 0% to 100%.

The plots demonstrate that increasing the value of H for each network results in a reduction in the recognition error, but at the expense of increasing W (increasing H from 5 to 20 reduces the error by 2.5% and increases W by a factor of about 4). Also, the recognition error seems to increase with increasing T, but with a reduction in W (increasing T from 5% to 100% increases the error by 2.5% but reduces W by a factor of over 2).

Further experiments conducted using a binary SL-NTN (i.e. $T = 0\%$) indicate that introducing 'fuzzy' clustering results in a 1% reduction in error at the expense of increasing W by a factor of 1.2. For comparison, a conventional neural network with 100 hidden neurons (i.e. $W = 7861$) is found to produce a 54% recognition error. This indicates that the SL-NTN reduces the computational complexity by a factor exceeding 10. Generally, our experiments suggest that if a conventional neural network requires $V \times V$ weights to obtain a specific percentage accuracy, then the SL-NTN would need to activate approximately $V \cdot \log_2 V$ weights to achieve a similar accuracy.

Table 15.1 *Recognition performance on board phonemic sets as defined by the TIMIT database*

Phonemic set	Training (%)	Testing (%)
Silence and short bursts	91.3	89.9
Fricatives	78.5	77.2
Stop consonants	68.1	69.6
Vowels and diphthongs	83.3	82.9
Semi-vowels and liquids	68.9	67.5
Affricates	52.0	38.6
Nasals	56.0	55.4
Average	78.0	77.5

Table 15.2 *Recognition performance on phonemic sets obtained at the root level*

Dominant set	Training (%)	Testing (%)
Silence and short bursts	82.4	83.9
Stop cons., affr. & fric.	91.8	92.1
High voicing	82.4	83.9
Low voicing and nasals	87.1	85.7
Average	83.0	82.6

An important observation, which confirms previous findings in Experiment 1, suggests that the SL-NTN provides intra-set correlations which exist in the human auditory system. For example, when setting $T = 5\%$ and $H = 5$, the neural network at the root node produces a separation into four sets of phones: (a) silence and short bursts, (b) high voicing, (c) low voicing and nasals, and (d) affricates, fricatives and stop consonants. On the other hand, phones which are highly confused, even to the human ear (e.g. /s/ & /z/), are found to be grouped together at top levels of the tree. Generally, phones at lower levels of the tree are grouped according to their manner of articulation, whereas those at higher levels of the tree are grouped according to their place of articulation. Recognition results demonstrating the performance of the SL-NTN on broad phonemic sets, as defined by the TIMIT database, and on dominant phonemic sets obtained at the root level are presented in Tables 15.1 and 15.2.

15.4 Summary

A self-learning approach to designing neural tree networks is presented in this paper. The SL-NTN has been applied for recognition of speech sounds (phones). Results show that the SL-NTN provides (1) 'optimal' trade-off between computational complexity and recognition performance, and (2) insight towards the correlation among the phones which is known to exist in the human auditory system. The ability of the SL-NTN to perform recognition on unlabeled speech data is currently being explored.

References

Ahmed N. and Rao, H.R. (1975) *Orthogonal Transforms for Digital Signal Processing.* Springer-Verlag, Berlin.

Breiman, L., Friedman, J.H., Olshen, R.A. and Stone, C.J. (1984) *Classification and Regression Trees.* The Wadsworth Statistics-Probability Series, Wadsworth Inc.

Burr, D.J. (1992) *Comparison of Gaussian and Neural Network Classifiers on Vowel Recognition using the Discrete Cosine Transform.* IEEE ICASSP-92, San Francisco, CA.

Furui S. (1981) Cepstrum analysis technique for automatic speaker verification. *IEEE Trans. Acoust., Speech, Signal Processing*, **29**, 254–72 April.

Juang, B.H., Rabiner, L.R. and Wilpon J.G. (1987) On the use of bandpass lifering in speech recognition. *IEEE Trans. Acoust., Speech, Signal Processing*, **35**(7), 947–54.

Lamel, L.F., Kessel, R.H. and Seneff, S. (1986) *Speech Database Development: Design and Analysis of the Acoustic-Phonetic Corpus.* Proc. Speech Recognition Workshop (DARPA).

Lippmann, R.P. (1987) An introduction to computing with neural nets. *IEEE ASSP Magazine*, **4**(2), 4–22, April.

Markel, J.D. and Gray, A.H. (1976) *Linear Prediction of Speech.* Springer-Verlag, New York.

Rahim, M.G. (1992) *A Neural Tree Architecture for Phoneme Classification with Experiments on the TIMIT Database.* IEEE ICASSP-92, San Francisco, CA.

Rahim, M.G. (1993) *A Self-Learning Neural Tree Network for Recognition of Speech Features.* IEEE ICASSP-93, Minnesota, MN.

Sankar, A. and Mammone, R. (1991) *Speaker Independent Vowel Recognition Using Neural Tree Networks.* IJCNN, Seattle, MA, July.

Stromberg, J.-E., Zrida, J. and Isaksson, A. (1991) *Neural Trees: Using Neural Trees in a Tree Classifier Structure.* IEEE ICASSP-91, Toronto, Canada, pp. 137–40.

16

Some relationships between ANNs and HMMs

ARTHUR NÁDAS

Continuous Speech Recognition Group, Computer Science Department,
IBM Research Division, T.J. Watson Research Center, POB 704, Yorktown
Heights NY 10598, USA

16.1 Introduction

Hidden Markov Models (HMM) and feed-forward Artificial Neural Networks (ANN) are two complimentary tools commonly used in speech recognition and other pattern recognition and artificial intelligence problems such as handwriting recognition, image classification, machine translation, and so forth. There seems to be some agreement in the engineering community that in practice 'HMMs are better at time warping and ANNs are better at discrimination' (Bridle, 1992). There have been a number of hybrid ANN–HMM models proposed, especially in speech recognition (Franzini *et al.*, 1991).

HMMs are parametric probability distributions of the observable features, i.e. they are generative models. ANNs are parametric deterministic functions defined on the space of observable features, and their usual definition involves no probabilistic or statistical modeling. The function values of ANNs can be many things, but the most common uses are in (1) classification, where the function values are interpreted as probabilities of classes or probability distributions over the classes of interest, and in (2) regression (prediction of real or real vector values from another), where the ANN function values are in some feature space.

Because they are generative models, HMMs can be trained by statistical estimation procedures such as Maximum Likelihood (ML) estimation, Bayes estimation, etc. In particular, ML and Bayes estimation can often be ac-

Artificial Neural Networks for Speech and Vision. Edited by Richard J. Mammone. Published in 1993 by Chapman & Hall, London. ISBN 0 412 54850 X

complished in practice by the Baum–Welch algorithm (Baum and Petrie, 1966; Baum and Egon, 1967; Baum and Sell, 1968; Baum *et al.*, 1970; Baum, 1972; Ferguson, 1980).[1] It can be accomplished even more often[2] by Expectation–Maximization (EM) algorithm (Dempster *et al.*, 1977; Meilijson, 1989; Titterington, 1984). In contrast, ANNs on their own cannot be trained by these statistical methods because there is no probabilistic likelihood defined. ANNs are usually trained by some gradient following algorithm which is designed to minimize some measure of dissimilarity between predicted and observed function values.

In this chapter we consider models where a likelihood function is defined so that statistical training based on the likelihood function becomes possible; the structure of the likelihood can then be used in designing the training algorithm.[3] Two models are explored. These models relate HMMs and ANNs by either (1) structurally embedding ANNs into HMMs or (2) discovering ANNs as naturally occurring forms in HMMs. In section 16.2 the general idea of using ANNs as parts of HMMs is discussed as an alternate approach to correlation models for the output of HMMs. These correlation models were studied by Brown *et al.* (1986). After a study of the correlation models, section 16.2 continues with a generalization of the standard HMM, which is made by embedding regression type ANNs into the output structure of an HMM. These models are related to one in the work of Esther Levin (1990). In section 16.3 a generative model for the classification problem is considered. This model was introduced by Nádas (1991). The conditional class probabilities (functions on the feature space) turn out to have the form of ANNs. Both models (1) and (2) generative, and will be seen to be trainable by an EM algorithm.

16.2 HMMs that are defined by ANNs

In this section, ANNs are used as ingredients of an HMM model. The models are discussed in the speech recognition context in which this idea appeared.

---

[1] Also known as the Forward-Backward (FB) algorithm (Bakis, 1976; Brown *et al.*, 1990; Bahl *et al.*, 1974, 1983; Bahl and Jelinek, 1975; Jelinek, 1969, 1975, 1976, 1985; Baker, 1975) and for expository papers along the methods used by Ferguson (1980), see Positz (1988), Juang and Rabiner (1991), Paul (1990) and Rabiner and Juang (1989).

[2] The EM algorithm is considered by some writers (Ferguson, 1980) to be an application of the Baum–Welch re-estimation algorithm, but this view is not universal. In support of this view one may note that in the statistical literature, except for HMMs, the problems having the EM algorithm in their solution appear all to assume iid random variables for data. A case can also be made (Dempster *et al.*, 1977) for the converse view (favored here), that the Baum–Welch algorthm is an example of the EM algorthm albeit the most elaborate example extant. In support of this view, one may point to the many non-HMM type hidden variables models to which the EM algorithm is applicable.

[3] There are many statistical methods not based on relevant likelihood, e.g. least squares. We regard these as deterministic curve fitting methods. It is interesting to note that certain ANN classifiers trained by (say) least squares will in fact approximate the optimal Bayes classifiers.

The standard HMM models assume that the outputs are mutually independent given the path. We first develop a generalization so as to allow for statistical dependence of outputs along a path (Brown *et al.*, 1986) by introducing frame-to-frame correlations in a jointly Gaussian model. This is followed by the alternate ANN approach to the same problem. Both approaches produce models that use multivariate Gaussian distribution for the conditional distribution of a feature vector given the past. Both approaches induce dependence between the feature vectors, even conditionally given the state sequence (path). The first model, which we dub 'HMMC', achieves this by a second moment approach: by including frame-to-frame correlations that are transition dependent. The second model, based on ANNs, achieves the same end through a first moment approach: by embedding nonlinear conditional expectations that are transition dependent.

16.2.1 HMM with time correlated output

Summary

The usual hidden Markov models of speech recognition do not account for correlation between adjacent feature vectors given a state sequence. We model such correlations and examine the algorithms for computing the likelihood of the observed data and for training the model.

HMMC is a mathematical model which generalizes the standard hidden Markov models so as to account for correlation between speech information in adjacent (in time) frames associated with a given path. The time correlation of adjacent frames is explicitly modeled and all parameters are estimable by a re-estimation (EM) algorithm.

Explicit formulae will be given for the computation of the conditional probabilities of hidden states and hidden transitions given the observable data. In the usual hidden Markov model the key algorithm for practical computation of such probabilities consists of the Baum–Welch Forward and Backward (FB) recursions. While the usual FB is incorrect for use with HMMC, analogous recursions will be given, based on first order Markov assumptions for the conditional distribution of the observable data given the unobservable state sequence. In going through these derivations it becomes clear that further analogues of these recursions also exist for second, third and higher order Markovian assumptions. These recursions do not require any specific distributional forms for the conditional distributions of the observables; it is only the Markov property of the sequence that is required.

The model

Let S_t with values s_t be the random hidden state at time t and let a_t be the arc traversed by the hidden source from time $t-1$ to time t. Denote by X_t the feature vector at the same time. An arc a_t is a collection of state transitions $i_{t-1}j_t$ which are 'tied' in the sense that the conditional distribution of X_t given $s_{t-1} = i$ and $s_t = j$ are the same for any pair ij in the collection called arc a. Denote by μ_a and Σ_a the mean vector and covariance matrix respectively of X_t given that the arc is a. Further, let $D_a = \text{diag}(\Sigma_A^{1/2})$ be the diagonal matrix of standard deviations given the arc a so that $\Sigma_a = D_a R_a D_a$ where R_a is the associated correlation matrix.

Let Ξ be a matrix of cross correlations between the elements of X_{t-1} and the next (in time) vector X_t. Then the cross covariance matrix between X_{t-1} and X_t is $D_{a_{t-1}} \Xi D_{a_t}$.

For a segment of speech having N frames, let

$$s_0, s_1, \ldots, s_t, \ldots, s_N \tag{1}$$

denote the unobserved state sequence, and let

$$a_{i_1}, \ldots, a_{i_t}, \ldots, a_{i_N} \tag{2}$$

be the sequence of arcs traversed. Let $X_1, \ldots, X_N$ be the corresponding spectral vectors. Then the conditional probability density given the state sequence for the entire frame is

$$p(x_1^N | s_1^N) = p_{i_0 i_1}(x_1) \prod_{t=2}^{N} p_{i_{t-2} i_{t-1} i_t}(x_t | x_{t-1}) \tag{3}$$

where, writing

$$\phi(x | \mu, \Sigma) \tag{4}$$

for the multivariate Gaussian density with mean vector μ and covariance matrix Σ, one has $p_{ij}(x) = n(x | \mu_a, \Sigma_a)$ and

$$p_{ijk}(x_{t+1} | x_t) = \phi(x_{t+1} | \eta_{ab}(x_t), \Gamma_{ab}), \tag{5}$$

where the states ijk determine the arcs $a = a(i,j), b = b(j,k)$. Here the η are the regression functions

$$E_{ab}(X_{t+1} | X_t = x_t) = \eta_{ab}(x_t) = \mu_b + D_b \Xi R_a^{-1} D_a^{-1}(x_t - \mu_a) \tag{6}$$

and the Γ are the conditional covariance matrices

$$\text{Cov}_{ab}(X_{t+1} | X_t = x_t) = \Gamma_{ab} = \Sigma_b - D_b \Xi R_a^{-1} \Xi D_b. \tag{7}$$

Observe that Ξ, the one-step cross-correlation matrix, is the same for all arcs. It is meant to account for time correlation due to the inertia of the articulator mechanism, the homeostatic tendencies of the human nervous system, as well as the homemade correlation introduced during signal processing by the overlapping ('sliding') of the window.

This tying $\Xi_{ab} = \Xi$ for all pairs of arcs a, b, leads to certain difficulties in the training algorithm but it is of considerable practical interest.

The EM algorithm for HMMC

Let $\delta(EVENT)$ be one or zero as the *EVENT* occurs or not. The complete data (pooling observable vectors and unobservable state variables) sufficient statistics are

$$\sum_{t=1}^{N} \delta(a_t = a), \quad \sum_{t=1}^{N} \delta(a_t = a)X_t, \tag{8}$$

and

$$\sum_{t=1}^{N} \delta(a_t = a)X_t X_t^{(T)}, \quad \sum_{t=2}^{N} \delta(a_{t-1} = a)\delta(X_{t-1}X_t^{(T)} \tag{9}$$

where (T) denotes transposition. Let $p_t(ij) = \text{Prob}(S_{t-1} = i, S_t = j | X_1^N)$ and

$$p_t(ijk) = \text{Prob}(S_{t-2} = i, S_{t-1} = j, S_t = k | X_1^N) \tag{10}$$

be the conditional probabilities of pairs and triples of hidden states respectively given all the observable data $X_t^{(T)}$. The re-estimation step of the EM algorithm is defined through the computations of the conditional expectations of the complete data sufficient statistics given the observable data:

$$\sum_{t=1}^{N} p_t(i), \quad \sum_{t=1}^{N} p_t(ij), \quad \sum_{t=1}^{N} p_t(ij)X_t, \tag{11}$$

and

$$\sum_{t=1}^{N} p_t(ij)X_t X_t^{(T)}, \quad \sum_{t=2}^{N} p_t(ijk)X_{t-1}X_t^{(T)} \tag{12}$$

which define, in the usual way, the re-estimates of μ_a and $\Sigma_a \equiv D_a R_a D_a$ for $a = ij$ as

$$\mu_{ij} = \frac{1}{N}\sum_{t=1}^{N} x_t p_t(ij) \tag{13}$$

and

$$\Sigma_{ij} + \mu_{ij}\mu_{ij}^{(T)} = \frac{1}{N}\sum_{t=1}^{N} X_t X_t^{(T)} p_t(ij). \tag{14}$$

In the general model (no tying such as $\Xi_{ab} = \Xi$) this completes the EM algorithm except for the recursive computation of $p_t(ijk)$. In the case of tying, this completes the E-step and partially completes the M-step of the EM algorithm. 'Partially' because we have not enforced the tying constraints, i.e. have not yet extracted the common cross-correlation matrix. We do not discuss the constrained numerical maximization here, but see Dempster (1972) and Feinberg and Meyer (1985) for estimation of covariance matrices of this type.

A heuristic re-estimate of the one-step cross-correlation matrix Ξ is given by

$$\Xi = \frac{1}{N} \sum_{t=1}^{N} \sum_{ijk} D_{ij}^{-1}(X_{t-1}X_t^{(T)} - \mu_{ij}\mu_{jk}^{(T)})D_{jk}^{-1}p_t(ijk), \tag{15}$$

a form suggested in analogy with the assumed relations among the parameters of the model. Unfortunately, this estimate may fail to produce positive definite estimates of the conditional covariance matrices; see Appendix 16A for alternative parametrizations to get around this difficulty.

In any case, the pivotal quantity required for the computation of the re-estimates is $p_t(ijk)$, the conditional probability of a triple of time adjacent states given all the observable data; its computation is discussed next.

The recursions

These arguments are entirely analogous to the arguments that lead to FB, to wit: one fully exploits both the Markov property of the marginal distribution of the unseen source and the Markov property of the conditional distribution of the observable process. The major difference is that in our case one must deal with triples of states (pairs of arcs) instead of just pairs of states (singleton arcs).

Let $\phi(x_1^N)$ denote the marginal (or mixture, or unconditional) density of the observable sequence

$$\phi(x_1^N) = \sum_{s_1,s_2,\ldots,s_N} \left(\prod_{t=1}^{N} P_{s_{t-1}s_t}\right) p(x_1^N|s_1^N) \tag{16}$$

where the summation is over all possible state sequences and where $p_{ij} = \text{Prob}(S_t = j|S_{t-1} = i)$. This quantity is a factor in both the numerator and the denominator of each re-estimation formula, hence it suffices to compute the joint probability element

$$\gamma_t(ijk) = p_t(x_1^N)\phi(x_1^N) = \text{Prob}(S_{t-2}^t = ijk \ \& \ X_1^N \varepsilon(x + dx)_1^N) \tag{17}$$

which is denoted by

$$p(x_1^N, S_{t-2}^t = ijk) \tag{18}$$

for convenience. The other required conditional state probabilities $p_t(i)$ and $p_t(ij)$ are just sums of this.

Using the Markov property of both S and X one has

$$\gamma_t(ijk) \equiv p(x_1^N, S_{t-2}^t = ijk) \equiv p(x_{1t}, S_{t-2}^t = ijk)p(x_{t+1}^N|x_1^t, S_{t-2}^t) \tag{19}$$

which is

$$p(x_1^t, S_{t-2}^t = ijk)p(x_{t+1}^N|x_t, S_{t-1}^t = jk), \tag{20}$$

that is

$$p(x_1^{t-1}, S_{t-2}^{t-1} = ij)p_{jk}\phi_{ijk}(x_t|x_{t-1})p(x_{t+1}^N|x_1^t, S_{t-1}^t = jk). \tag{21}$$

In analogy with FB, denote this factorization as

$$\gamma_t(ijk) = \alpha_{t-1}(ij)p_{jk}\phi_{ijk}(x_t|x_{t-1})\beta_t(jk), \tag{22}$$

and note that α and β each depend on two adjacent states. Just as in FB, it is these two factors α and β that are recursively computable.

The recursion for $\alpha_t(jk)$ is

$$\alpha_t(jk) = \sum_{h=1}^{k} \alpha_{t-1}(hj)p_{jk}\phi_{hjk}(x_t|x_{t-1}). \tag{23}$$

This recursion is obtained in a straightforward way using the law of total probability, as well as both Markovian assumptions as follows:

$$p(x_1^t, S_{t-1} = jk) = \sum_{h=1}^{k} p(x_1^t, S_{t-2}^t = hjk). \tag{24}$$

Continuing the equality, one finds

$$\sum_{h=1}^{k} p(x_1^{t-1}, S_{t-2}^{t-1} = hj)p(x_t, S_t = k|x_1^{t-1}, S_{t-2}^{t-1} = hj), \tag{25}$$

which is the same as

$$\sum_{h=1}^{k} \alpha_{t-1}(hj)p(x_t, S_t = k|x_{t-1}, S_{t-2}^{t-1} = hj), \tag{26}$$

that is

$$\sum_{h=1}^{k} \alpha_{t-1}(hj)p(x_t|x_{t-1}, S_{t-2}^t = hjk)p_{jk}. \tag{27}$$

The recursion for $\beta_t(jk)$ is

$$\beta_t(jk) = \sum_{h=1}^{k} \beta_{t+1}(kh)p_{kh}\phi_{jkh}(x_{t+1}|x_t). \tag{28}$$

This is obtained as follows:

$$\beta_t(jk)p(x_t, S_{t-1}^t = jk) = p(x_t^N, S_{t-1}^t = jk) = \sum_{h=1}^{k} p(x_t^N, S_{t-1}^{t+1} = jkh). \tag{29}$$

which is

$$\sum_{h=1}^{k} p(x_{t+1}^N, S_t^{t+1} = kh)p(x_t, S_{t-1} = j|x_{t+1}^N, S_t^{t+1} = kh). \tag{30}$$

Continuing the equality, one has

$$\sum_{h=1}^{k} \beta_{t+1}(kh)p(x_{t+1}, S_t^{t+1} = kh)p(x_t, S_{t-1}|x_{t+1}, S_t^{t+1} = kh), \tag{31}$$

which is the same as

$$\sum_{h=1}^{k} \beta_{t+1}(kh) p(x_t^{t+1}, S_{t-1}^{t+1} = jkh). \tag{32}$$

Thus

$$\beta_t(jk) = \sum_{h=1}^{k} \beta_{t+1}(kh) \frac{p(x_t^{t+1}, S_{t-1}^{t+1} = jkh)}{p(x_t, S_{t-1}^{t} = jk)}, \tag{33}$$

which yields the recursion.

16.2.2 HMMs with imbedded ANNs

Summary

The following is a description of what is essentially a nonparametric (= many parameters) approach to the problem. For practical purposes, the multivariate Gaussian assumption for the **conditional** distribution of a feature vector corresponding to a time-slice given the path and given previous vectors will be retained. However, these conditionally Gaussian vectors will be connected with highly nonlinear regressions so that the joint distribution of output vectors given a path will be modeled in a much more flexible way than is possible with a Gaussian process, which is incapable of any but linear regressions. Put another way, this construction is able to produce non-Gaussian joint distributions for the vector sequence in spite of its use of multivariate Gaussian conditional distributions for the individual time-slices.

Let $S = \{S_t | t = 1, \ldots, T\}$ be a finite Markov chain and let X be a probabilistic function of it; $X = \{X_t | t = 1, \ldots, T'\}$ It is possible to have $T \neq T'$ by means of 'null transitions'; this will be ignored here. Assume that (S, X) are jointly distributed random processes such that the conditional probability of the output X given a path $S = s$ has the form

$$p(x|s) = \prod_{t=1}^{T} p_{s_{t-1}s_t} q_{s_{t-1}s_t}(x_t | x_{t-k}^{t-1}) \tag{34}$$

where $x_t \in \mathbb{R}^n$, p_{ij} are transition probabilities, where

$$x_a^b = x_a, x_{a+1}, \ldots, x_{b-1}, x_b, \tag{35}$$

and where $q_{ij}(x | x_{t-k}^{t-1})$ is an n-dimensional probability density. In other words, the chain is a first order Markov chain while the output is a kth order Markovian vector process when conditioned on the chain, and depends on the chain only through one step transitions. Denote the conditional regression functions given the chain (= conditional expectation of the next output vector given the past) by

$$\mu_{ij}(x_{t-k}^{t-1}) = E(X_t | S_{t-1}^t = ij, X_{t-k}^{t-1} = x_{t-k}^{t-1})$$

$$= \int_{\mathbb{R}^d} x q_{ij}(x | x_{t-k}^{t-1}) \, dx. \tag{36}$$

Construction

There are many ways to introduce neural nets into this model. A very general way is to take

$$q_{ij}(x_{t-k}^{t-1}) = f_{ij\theta_{ij}}(x_{t-k}^t) \tag{37}$$

where $f_{ij\theta_{ij}}$ is a separate ANN for each ij, an ANN which is constrained to be a density in x_t having weight parameters θ_{ij}. The joint density of the observables is then

$$\sum_{s_1^T} \prod_t p_{s_{t-1}s_t} f_{s_{t-1}s_t\theta s_{t-1}s_t}(x_{t-k}^t). \tag{38}$$

Regarded as a function $L(\theta)$ of the model parameters θ, this is the likelihood function whose maximum would furnish the MLE. However, such a maximization in a practical speech recognition problem is likely to be too hard because of difficulties in enforcing the probabilistic constraints. Hence consider the following simplifications.

ANN choice of parametric model

Model each q_{ij} by choosing a member of a parametric family

$$\mathbb{P} = \{p_\lambda | \lambda \in \Lambda\} \tag{39}$$

where the parameter is chosen by a neural function of the past. For example, $p_\lambda(x_t)$ can be taken as a multivariate Gaussian density whose mean vector and covariance matrix constitute the parameter λ. Now let

$$f_{ij\theta_{ij}} : \mathbb{R}^{nk} \to \Lambda \tag{40}$$

be a neural net function that chooses λ based on the last k vectors. The function may be specific to the transition being taken by the chain and it has weight parameters θ_{ij} specific to the transition also. Let θ denote the collection of all weight parameters. Then the likelihood function has the form

$$L(\theta) = p(x|s) = \prod_{t=1}^{T} p_{s_{t-1}s_t} p_{f s_{t-1}s_t\theta s_{1}s_t}(x_{t-k}^{t-1}). \tag{41}$$

For a sufficiently simple $\mathbb{P}$, maximization of this likelihood appears feasible. For example, there may be no constraints at all on the optimization as in the case where λ is an m dimensional location parameter and $\Lambda = \mathbb{R}^m$ or the constraints are simple enough to be incorporated into the network structure.

The following model allows the use of simpler, decision-directed[4] training methods.

ANN regression model

Conditioned on the path and the past observations, define

$$X_t = \mu_{s_{t-1}s_t}(x_{t-k}^{t-1}) + \varepsilon_t, \tag{42}$$

where the $\{\varepsilon_t\}$ is a sequence of multivariate Gaussian error vectors with mean zero and common (tied) covariance matrix Σ. (Tying is not necessary when sufficient data is available.) Note that for nonlinear μ this cannot be a Gaussian process given the path. Rather than to model the densities by neural nets, model the regression functions by neural nets. Regressions are vector valued functions with no constraints whatever.

Let

$$\mu_{ij}(x_{t-k}^{t-1}) = f_{\theta_{ij}}(x_{t-k}^{t-1}), \tag{43}$$

where $f_{\theta_{ij}}$ is a neural net with weight parameters θ_{ij} mapping the previous k vectors into a vector at the current time. For simplicity, put $f_{ij\theta_{ij}} = f_{\theta_{ij}}$, i.e. the neural nets have a common structure but their parameter depends on the transition ij.

Training algorithm

In principle, one can attempt to train by maximum likelihood, i.e. to estimate $\theta = \{\theta_{ij}\}$ by $\tilde{\theta} = \arg\max_{\theta'} L(\theta')$, but this may be very hard. In the neural regression model, however, it is possible to simplify the training procedure by using decision directed training as follows:

Step 0. Initialize $\theta = \theta^0$.

Step 1. Classification step. Find a most probable state sequence (path) $\{s_t\}$ by dynamic programming ('Viterbi Alignment'). This is a path s that maximizes $p(x|s)$.

Step 2. Re-sorting step. For each transition ij such that $s_{t-1}^t = ij$, collect observed vector strings $\{x_{t_v-k}^{t_v}\}_{v=1}^{N_{ij}}$. Denote by S_{ij} the corresponding times t when $s_{t-1}^t = ij$.

Step 3. Re-estimation step. For each transition ij estimate the parameters θ_{ij} which specify the conditional expectations $f_{\theta_{ij}}$. This is done by training the neural net $f_{\theta_{ij}}$ on the N_{ij} (input,output) pairs (x_{t-k}^{t-1}, x_t) using minimum mean squared error in the norm of the covariance matrix Σ. This is the Mahalanobis

---

[4] Decision directed training means iteration of a classification step followed by a re-estimation step. The model for one class is re-estimated based only on data which is guessed to have come from the class. Depending on the problem, this heuristic can produce a reasonable estimate or it can be worthless.

metric defined by Σ. In the case of linear regression ($=$ a perceptron whose 'sigmoid' function is the identity), this is a well known procedure referred to as 'weighted least squares' estimation where the weights are the reciprocals of the characteristic values of the covariance matrix. For our case, neural net regression, the following sub-algorithm is proposed.

Step 3.1 Initialize Σ (for example, by setting it to be the identity).

Step 3.2 For each transition ij estimate θ_{ij} by minimzing θ_{ij}

$$\sum_{t \in S_{ij}} (x_t - f_{\theta_{ij}}(x_{t-k}^{t-1}))' \Sigma^{-1} (x_t - f_{\theta_{ij}}(x_{t-k}^{t-1}))$$

$$= \sum_{k=1}^{n} \lambda_k^{-1} \sum_{t \in T_{ij}} (u_k'(x_t - f_{\theta_{ij}}(x_{t-k}^{t-1})))^2, \tag{44}$$

where the λ_k and the u_k are characteristic values and corresponding characteristic vectors of Σ (u' is the transpose of x).

Step 3.3 Re-estimate Σ as the mean squared deviation from the fitted regressions (neural net regressions) averaged over all transitions ij, i.e., as the sample covariance matrix of the T residual error vectors

$$\frac{1}{T} \sum_{ij} \sum_{t \in S_{ij}} (x_t - f_{\theta_{ij}}(x_{t-k}^{t-1}))(x_t - f_{\theta_{ij}}(x_{t-k}^{t-1}))'. \tag{45}$$

Step 3.4 Go to Step 3.2 or Step 4.
Step 4. Go to Step 1 or quit.

A particularly simple version of this model assumes that Σ is the identity matrix. In this special case an alternative (and equivalent) algorithm is to replace Step 1 and Step 3 by

Step 1' Find a minimum mean squared error path $\{s_t\}$, i.e., solve

$$\min_{s_1^T} \sum_t \| x_t - f_{\theta_{t-1}^t}(x_{t-k}^{t-1}) \|^2 \tag{46}$$

by dynamic programming.

Step 3' Re-estimate θ_{ij} by maximizing

$$\sum_{t \in T_{ij}} \| x_t - f_{\theta_{ij}}(x_{t-k}^{t-1}) \|^2. \tag{47}$$

Levin (1990) has reported the use of this mean squared error criterion with $k = 1$ in an experiment on spoken digit recognition (0–9 and *oh*).

16.3 ANNs that are defined by HMMs

Background

This section is based on the development in Nádas (1991). Consider classification of points $x \in \mathbb{R}^d$ (feature vecrtors) by using continuous functions of x for the probabilities of classes. For binary classification this means any continuous function $\mathbb{R}^d \to [0, 1]$, and for n-ary classification any continuous function from $\mathbb{R}^d$ to the $n - 1$ dimensional simplex $[0, 1]^n$. The focus here is on binary classification.

Cybenko (1989) has shown that any continuous function defined on a compact set in $\mathbb{R}^d$ can be uniformly approximated by a two-layer ANN f_C,

$$f_C(x) = \sum_{j=1}^{k} \alpha_j \sigma \left(\sum_{i=1}^{d} w_{ij} x_j + \omega_{0j} \right), \tag{48}$$

where k is a sufficiently large integer, $\sigma: \mathbb{R} \to [0, 1]$ is a sigmoid and the α_i, w_{ij} are constants. Barron (1991a) has given a bound relating k to the precision of the approximation when the target function is known. When the function is known at only N arguments, Barron (1991b) shows that taking $k = O(\sqrt{N})$ results in an approximation error of order $O(N^{-1} \log N)$.

A different class $\mathbb{C}$ of approximating functions will be introduced. Unlike (48), these functions are based on a probabilistic description of the classification process and hence enjoy certain properties which will be exploited. A function $f \in \mathbb{C} f: \mathbb{R}^d \to [0, 1]$ is defined as a conditional expectation

$$f(x) \equiv E[H(Y)|X = x] \tag{49}$$

where H is the Heaviside (unit step) function

$$H(y) = \begin{cases} 0 & \text{if } y < 0 \\ 1 & \text{if } y \geq 0 \end{cases} \tag{50}$$

and Y is jointly distributed with X. If Y were a linear function of X then U would be a perceptron, in fact a 'threshold logic unit'. We shall construct Y by adding noise to a linear function of X; one of a finite set of linear functions. This construction produces a joint distribution for (X, Y) in which

$$f(x) = \sum_{j=1}^{k} \pi_j(x) \sigma \left(\sum_{i=1}^{d} w_{ij} x_i + w_{0j} \right). \tag{51}$$

The π_j will be defined as the probability of a hidden state variable J given $X = x$, based on a probability model (mixture model) described below. The sigmoid σ will be the cumulative distribution function of the standardized noise variable ($=$ the standard normal (Gaussian) integral in our application). The form in (51) differs from f_C in (48) only in that the real constants α_j are replaced by the functions $\pi_j(x)$ (see (63)). It seems clear that $f \in \mathbb{C}$ are, in general, not ANNs, as they are in the degenerate case where the π_j are constant in x. This special case corresponds to a certain statistical independence in the model. Conversely, an ANN with one or more negative α_j cannot be in $\mathbb{C}$, so neither class contains the other.

The choice of the form of the joint distribution of (X, Y) will now be completed so as to also allow the construction of an EM algorithm estimating its parameters. The EM algorithm for learning the distribution P thus becomes an indirect but simple training algorithm for $f \in \mathbb{C}$.

A probabilistic version of the classification problem is this: given a completely specified joint distribution P of the random pair (X, I) with $X \in \mathbb{R}^d$ and $I \in \{1, \ldots, n\}$, find a classifier function $\Psi: \mathbb{R}^d \to \{1, \ldots, n\}$ which minimizes the probability of misclassification $P(\Psi(X) \neq I)$. The well known solution is to let $\Psi(x)$ be the least (say) positive integer which achieves $\max_{1 \leq i \leq n} P(I = i | X = x)$.

Binary classification

Let $n = 2$ so $I = i \in \{1, 2\}$ so that $Z \equiv I - 1$ is just a random bit. The probability element for (X, Z) has the form

$$g(x)p(z|x) \tag{52}$$

where g is a density on $\mathbb{R}^d$ for fixed x, $p(z|x)$ is a probability on $\{0, 1\}$. In the terminology of the EM algorithm, a sample from the distribution of the observable pair (X, Z) is the incomplete data and $g(x)p(z|x)$ is the incomplete data model. When this is parametrized as $g(x|\theta)p(z|x, \theta)$ then the corresponding incomplete data likelihood function is

$$L(\theta) = \sum_{t=1}^{T} \log g(x_t|\theta) + \log p(z_t|x_t, \theta). \tag{53}$$

To model the generation of the data and to construct an EM algorithm, consider the following[5] complete data model. The idea is to make local models of the joint distribution of the feature vector X and a noisy locally linear function Y whose only purpose is to define the classifying bit Z. Locality is achieved through the use of a mixing variable $J \in \{1, \ldots, k\}$ with $P(J = j) = \alpha_j$. Let

$$(X, Y, J) X \in \mathbb{R}^d, \quad Y \in \mathbb{R}, \quad J \in \{1, \ldots, k\} \tag{54}$$

denote the complete data. Conditionally on $J = j$ the density of (X, Y) is $d + 1$-dimensional Gaussian with mean vector

$$\begin{pmatrix} \mu_j \\ v_j \end{pmatrix} = \begin{pmatrix} \mu_{1j} \\ \vdots \\ \mu_{dj} \\ v_j \end{pmatrix} \tag{55}$$

and covariance matrix

$$\Gamma_j = \begin{pmatrix} \Gamma_{11j} & \Gamma_{12j} \\ \Gamma_{21j} & \Gamma_{22j} \end{pmatrix} \tag{56}$$

---

[5] There are uncountably many complete data models consistent with this incomplete data model; the choice here is one which leads to both (a) the possibility of probabilistic approximation of the actual distribution of (X, I) and (b) the possibility of its ML estimation by the EM algorithm.

where Γ_{11j} is a $d \times d$ covariance matrix for the feature vector when $J = j$, Γ_{22j} is the (scalar) variance of Y and Γ_{12j} is a $d \times 1$ matrix of covariances given $J = j$. Observe that X has a Gaussian mixture distribution describing the feature space with density

$$g(x) = \sum_{j=1}^{k} \alpha_j g_j(x) \tag{57}$$

where g_j is a multivariate Gaussian density having mean vector μ_j and covariance matrix Γ_{11j}. Also note that Y is the noisy signed distance to a hyperplane determined by the coefficients of the random linear function $E(Y|X,J)$. (Actually, the Gaussian assumption is not necessary; any tractable d-dimensional kernel will do here. The conditional distribution of Y given both $X = x$ and $J = j$ can also be replaced by any tractable non-Gaussian distribution, but the latter must have a location parameter which is linear in x. The $d + 1$-dimensional Gaussian assumption automatically satisfies this condition.)

Without loss of generality, one can parametrize Γ_j as follows:

$$\Gamma_{12j} = \Gamma'_{21j} = \Gamma_{11j}\beta_j \tag{58}$$

where β_j are the regression coefficients of the regression of Y on X given $J = j$,

$$E[Y|X = x, J = j] = v_j + \beta_j(x - \mu_j). \tag{59}$$

The variance of Y given $J = j$ is

$$\Gamma_{22j} = \gamma_j^2 + \beta'_j\Sigma\beta_j \tag{60}$$

where γ_j^2 is the conditional variance of Y given not only $J = j$, but also $X = x$ (residual variance). Now put

$$Z = H(Y) \tag{61}$$

where H is the function defined in (50). Then

$$E(Z|X = x) = \sum_{j=1}^{k} P(J = j|X = x)P(Z = 1|X = x, J = j)$$

$$= \sum_{j=1}^{k} \pi_j(x)P(Y > 0|X = x, J = j)$$

$$= \sum_{j=1}^{k} \pi_j(x)\Phi\left(\frac{1}{\gamma_j}\left\{v_j + \sum_{l=1}^{d} \beta_{lj}(x_l - \mu_{lj})\right\}\right). \tag{62}$$

The $\pi_j(x) \equiv P(J = j|X = x)$ are given by

$$\pi_j(x) = \frac{\alpha_j g_j(x)}{\sum_{l=1}^{k} \times \alpha_l g_l(x)} \tag{63}$$

where α_j are the mixing probabilities and g_j are the Gaussian densities with means μ_j and covariance matrices Γ_{11j}. Here Φ is the standard normal integral. Setting $w_{1j} = \beta_{1j}/\gamma_j$ and $w_{0j} = (v_j - \sum_{i=1}^{d} \beta_{ij}\mu_i)/\gamma_j$, and choosing the sigmoid to be the standard Gaussian CDF

$$\sigma(y) = \Phi(y) \equiv \int_{-\infty}^{y} \phi(u)du \tag{64}$$

with $\phi(u) = e^{-1/2u^2}/\sqrt{2\pi}$, one sees that (51) is precisely the conditional expectation

$$f(x) = E(Z \mid X = x) \equiv P(Z = 1 \mid X = x). \tag{65}$$

The training algorithm

Let θ denote a vector whose components form a list of all the unknown parameters of the distribution

$$\theta = ((\alpha_j, \mu_j, v_j, \Gamma_j) \mid j = 1, \ldots, k). \tag{66}$$

The E-STEP in the usual Gaussian mixture problem estimates all the unobservable complete data sufficient statistics. These are unobservable because J, the mixture index, is hidden. Our problem is similar, but differs from this in that in addition to the unavailability of J, the r.v. Y is also hidden except for its sign. Then the conditional expectations required here are based on less information than in the usual mixture problem. Let $\delta(A)$ be 1 or zero as A occurs or not. In our setup the complete data sufficient statistics are

$$N_j = \sum_{t=1}^{T} \delta(J_t = j)$$

$$SX_j = \sum_{t=1}^{T} \delta(J_t = j)X_t$$

$$SXX'_j = \sum_{t=1}^{T} \delta(J_t = j)X_t X'_j$$

$$SYX'_j = \sum_{t=1}^{T} \delta(J_t = j)Y_j X'_t$$

$$SYY_j = \sum_{t=1}^{T} \delta(J_t = j)Y_t^2$$

$$SY_j \sum_{t=1}^{T} \delta(J_t = j)Y_t. \tag{67}$$

The corresponding conditional expectations are

$$\overline{N}_j = \sum_{t=1}^{T} p_j(X_t, Z_t)$$

$$\overline{SX}_j = \sum_{t=1}^{T} p_j(X_t, Z_t) X_t$$

$$\overline{SXX'}_j = \sum_{t=1}^{T} p_j(X_t, Z_t) X_t X'_t$$

$$\overline{SYX'}_j = \sum_{t=1}^{T} p_j(X_t, Z_t) \overline{Y}_t(j) X'_t$$

$$\overline{SYY}_j = \sum_{t=1}^{T} p_j(X_t, Z_t) \overline{Y_t^2}(j)$$

$$\overline{SY}_j = \sum_{t=1}^{T} p_j(X_t, Z_t) \overline{Y}_t(j) \tag{68}$$

where

$$p_j(X_t, Z_t) = P(J_t = j \,|\, X_t, Z_t; \theta),$$

$$\overline{Y}_t(j) = E(\delta(J_t = j) Y_t \,|\, X_t, Z_t; \theta),$$

$$\overline{Y_t^2}(j) = E(\delta(J_t = j) Y_t^2 \,|\, J_t = j, X_t, Z_t; \theta), \tag{69}$$

with $\theta = \theta^{(r-1)}$. It is easily checked that $p_j(x, 1)$ is given by

$$\frac{\pi_j(x) \Phi\left(w_{0j} + \sum_{l=1}^{d} w_{lj} x_l \right)}{\sum_{i=1}^{k} \pi_i(x) \Phi\left(w_{0i} + \sum_{l=1}^{d} w_{li} x_l \right)} \tag{70}$$

and, similarly, $p_j(x, 0)$ is given by

$$\frac{\pi_j(x) \Phi\left(-w_{0j} - \sum_{l=1}^{d} w_{lj} x_l \right)}{\sum_{j=1}^{k} \pi_i(x) \Phi\left(-w_{0i} - \sum_{l=1}^{d} w_{li} x_l \right)}. \tag{71}$$

We still need to define $\overline{Y}(j)$, $\overline{Y}_{(j)}^2$, and $\overline{XY}(j)$. Since $E(XY \,|\, X, Z) = X E(Y \,|\, X, Z)$, only the first two are needed. One has for $r = 1, 2$:

$$E(\delta(J = j) Y^r \,|\, X = x, Z = z) = p_j(x, z) E(Y^r \,|\, X = x, Z = z, J = j). \tag{72}$$

The last expectation may be evaluated as follows. Writing

$$\xi_j = \xi_j(x) = v_j + \sum_{l=1}^{d} \beta_{lj}(x_l - \mu_{lj}) \tag{73}$$

one finds, for example,

$$E(Y^r | X = x, Y > 0, J = j) = E\left((\xi_j(x) + \gamma_j Y_{01})^r | Y_{01} > -\frac{\xi_j(x)}{\gamma_j} \right) \quad (74)$$

where Y_{01} is a standard scalar Gaussian r.v. with mean zero and variance one; its two conditional moments can be obtained as follows.

For real m, real a and for positive γ we need

$$E(Y | Y > a) \quad \text{and} \quad E(Y^2 | Y > a) \quad (75)$$

when Y is a scalar Gaussian random variable with mean m and variance γ^2. Writing

$$Y = m + \gamma Y_0 \quad (76)$$

where Y_0 has mean zero and variance one, one obtains

$$E(Y | Y > a) = m + \gamma E(Y_0 | Y_0 > b) \quad (77)$$

and

$$E(Y^2 | Y > a) = m^2 + 2m\gamma E(Y_0 | Y_0 > b) + \gamma^2 E(Y_0^2 | Y_0 > b) \quad (78)$$

where $b = (a - m)/\gamma$. The two conditional expected moments of Y_0 can be shown to be, writing $\phi(t) = \Phi'(t)$:

$$E(Y_0 | Y_0 > b) = \frac{\phi(b)}{1 - \Phi(b)} \quad (79)$$

which is just the reciprocal of Mill's ratio (known also by actuaries as the standard normal hazard (= force of mortality)), and $E(Y_0^2 | Y_0 > b)$ is given by

$$\frac{\frac{1}{2} - \text{sgn}(b)[\Phi(|b|) - \frac{1}{2} - |b|\phi(b)]}{1 - \Phi(b)}, \quad (80)$$

a less familiar but still easily computed expression.

Similarly $E(Y | Y < a)$ is given by

$$E(Y | Y < a) = m + \gamma E(Y_0 | Y_0 < b) \quad (81)$$

with

$$E(Y_0 | Y_0 < b) = -\frac{\phi(b)}{\Phi(b)} \quad (82)$$

and $E(Y^2 | Y < a)$ given by

$$m^2 + 2m\gamma E(Y_0 | Y_0 < b) + \gamma^2 E(Y_0^2 | Y_0 < b) \quad (83)$$

with $E(Y_0^2 | Y_0 < b)$ given by

$$\frac{\frac{1}{2} + \text{sgn}(b)[\Phi(|b|) - \frac{1}{2} - |b|\phi(b)]}{\Phi(b)}. \quad (84)$$

The M-STEP of training is simple. Assemble the results of the E-STEP to form estimates of the k mean vectors and the k covariance matrices of the model and extract the required regression coefficients β_j and residual variances γ_j^2. Compute the neural net weights and thresholds w_{ij} after the last iteration.

The n-class problem

For $n > 2$ the previous approach can be extended provided a bitstring encoding Z of the class index I is introduced. Corresponding to a random feature vector X, let $Z \in \{0, 1\}^m$ be a one-to-one encoding of the class index, I, as a bitstring. For the sake of concreteness, the reader may wish to regard Z as the binary expansion of the class index I, and in this case m is the least integer $m \geqslant \log_2 n$. The more popular encoding consists of encoding the event $I = i$ as the bitstring which is all zeros except in the ith position where it is one; in this case $m = n$. It is obvious that from the probabilistic point of view it does not matter which one-to-one encoding one chooses. Contrast this with the statistical point of view, i.e. the typical practical situation wherein the joint distribution of (X, I) is not specified completely; in this case one has some training data

$$\{(x_t, i_t)|t = 1, \ldots, N\} \tag{85}$$

to work with instead. Assume that the training data is a random sample from the distribution of (X, I). The usual statistical approach, which (for lack of a better idea) is also adopted here, is to estimate the joint distribution P by a distribution P^T and thereafter ignore the error of the estimate. Since some functions are easier to estimate than others, it is no longer clear that different encodings are equally as good. The encoding issue is not pursued here, it is simply assumed that some encoding is specified. It is likely that ultimately some problem-dependent encoding will be preferred to either of the two simple encodings mentioned above; an encoding chosen to optimize the performance of the trained classifier.

Note that in the special case where the likelihood function is unimodal the nature of the EM algorithm guarantees that the maximum likelihood estimate will not depend on the particular code chosen. The reason for this is that a choice of the code can be regarded as a choice of complete data model consistent with the given incomplete data model and therefore EM will maximize the same incomplete likelihood in every case. Unimodality assures that a change of complete data models (or even a change of initialization) will not affect the result. Note that even in this case the choice of encoding has an effect, not on the result but on the rate of convergence of the EM iteration.

Suppose that the bitstring encoding $Z \in \{0, 1\}^m$ is given and (X, Z) has some joint distribution. Define the complete data model by

$$(X, Y, J) X \in \mathbb{R}^d, \quad Y \in \mathbb{R}^m, \quad J \in \{1, \ldots, k\}, \tag{86}$$

and set $Z_i = U(Y_i)$ $i = 1, \ldots, m$. In this case conditionally on $J = j$ the density of (X, Y) is chosen to be $d + m$-dimensional Gaussian. For convenience in computing $P(I = i | X = x) \equiv P(Z = z | X = x)$ let the conditional covariance matrix of Y given both $X = x$ and $J = j$ to be diagonal. Then $P(Z = z | X = x)$ is given by

$$\sum_{j=1}^{k} \pi_j(x) \prod_{i=1}^{m} p_{ij}(x)^{z_i} (1 - p_{ij}(x))^{1 - z_i} \tag{87}$$

where

$$p_{ij}(x) = P(Y_i > 0 | X = x, J = j). \tag{88}$$

The EM algorithm is again applicable; the only new object is the conditional covariance between components of Y given both X and J. While this is zero by construction, enforcing this constraint in the M-step requires some care.

Clearly, the bitstring encoding required here makes this model less attractive than it is in the binary case. An alternative approach for multiple classes is to model the input space with a mixture as we have done and then to model the probability of each class by logistic regression. The drawback here is the lack of an EM-like algorithm for training the model.

Appendix 16.A: Alternative parametrizations and constraints in HMMC

16.A1 Summary

In this appendix, two related problems will be examined in a somewhat informal way:

1. The possible lack of positive definiteness of unconstrained estimates of covariance matrices encountered in tying cross correlation coefficients between time adjacent vectors.
2. The possible lack of consistent probabilistic model due to unconstrained estimates of the parameters when parametrizing HMMC by 'single arc modeling'.

Three parametrizations of HMMC conditional on the state (or arc) sequence will be considered:

- (P1) The standard parametrization (using joint rather than conditional moments or other methods) of a vector valued stochastic process which is (i) Markovian of order one with respect to the vector sequence, (ii) Gaussian having a density and, (iii) has full degrees of freedom. This would be our choice were it not for limitations of space, time and data.
- (P2) The parametrizations induced by tying (with respect to variations of the given arc sequence) some or all correlation coefficients of the 'vector

bivariate' joint distributions of time adjacent vectors. This choice of tying is motivated in part by cognizance of the inertia of the articulatory mechanism.

- (P3) The parametrization implied by 'single arc modeling' wherein the conditional mean vector of the current vector given the previous vector (but not the previous arc) is specified as a linear function of the previous vector (a constant vector and a constant matrix is associated with the current arc) and where the conditional covariance matrix for the current vector given the previous vector (but not the previous arc) is also associated with the current arc. This choice of parametrization is motivated by the simple form of the joint density expressed as a product of the conditional (given the past) densities of the individual vectors.

16.A2 On positive definite estimates

Before discussing the various constraints in some detail, consider two relatively easy sets, S1 and S2, of modeling assumptions that easily avoid the positive definiteness trouble without dropping the tying of cross-correlations, i.e. without an explosion of the storage required to do HMMC:

- S1 is this: assume that both the covariance matrix of a feature vector and also the cross-correlation matrix are diagonal. This is the same as having separate models for each of the d (say) coordinates of the feature vector, hence the only constraint on cross-correlations is that each of the d numbers lie between negative one and one. Such a model should secure much of the benefit due to the introduction of correlation in time (cross-correlations).
- S2 is this: assume all prototypes have the same correlation (but not the same covariance) structure. Then the required $2d$ by $2d$ covariance matrices (up to $N2 = \text{num\_arcs}**2$ many of them) will have a common correlation matrix. One still has to make this positive definite, but this constraint is much simpler than the N2 such constraints in the first version of HMMC.

Both S1 and S2 are more restrictive than one might like. Both of them share the following estimation problem with the general HMMC and all statistical models that have tied parameters: how to combine several estimates of a parameter to form a single estimate. A clean way to estimate (in S1 or S2 or in the general HMMC) is to optimize subject to the constraints that are inherent in the parametrization of the model, i.e. the parametrization of the joint distribution of all the frames of speech modeled. A constrained optimization may be difficult, but one can use the usual heuristic: in S1 and S2 estimate tied parameters by the weighted average of estimates coming from each pair of arcs which actually occurred in the data.

The issue of constraints on the estimated statistical parameters of a model is the main topic of this appendix.

16.A3 On alternative parametrizations

Our setup is this: given a state sequences $s = s_0, s_1, \ldots, s_N$ the conditional distribution of the sequence X of observable vectors $X_1, \ldots, X_N$ is Markovian with density

$$\phi_s(x) \equiv \phi_{s_1,\ldots,s_N}(x_1) \prod_{t=2}^{N} \phi_{s_1,\ldots,s_N}(x_t | x_{t-1}). \tag{89}$$

The state sequence determines the conditional joint distribution of the observables but nothing said so far shows how this is arranged. Assume that the conditional joint distribution is Gaussian, that it has a density on N times d dimensional space, and its parameters (mean vector and covariance matrix) are determined by the state squence s.

P1: The standard unconstrained (no tying) parametrization

For a vector of dimension d this means that the distribution is uniquely specified by a $N \times d$ long mean vector μ and a N times d by N times d covariance matrix Σ assumed positive definite. These may be partitioned into N d-dimensional subvectors

$$\mu = \begin{vmatrix} \mu_1 \\ \vdots \\ \mu_N \end{vmatrix} \tag{90}$$

and $N^2 d$ by d submatrices

$$\Sigma = \begin{vmatrix} \Sigma_{11} \ \Sigma_{12}, \ldots, \Sigma_{1N} \\ \Sigma_{21} \ \Sigma_{22}, \ldots, \Sigma_{2N} \\ \cdots \\ \cdots \\ \Sigma_{N1} \ \Sigma_{N2}, \ldots, \Sigma_{NN} \end{vmatrix}. \tag{91}$$

Let A be the inverse of Σ and partition it in a similar way. Let

$$\Sigma_{ii|j} = \Sigma_{ii} - \Sigma_{ij}\Sigma_{jj}^{-1}\Sigma_{ji}. \tag{92}$$

When writing out (1) in detail, the Markov assumption now shows that $A_{ij} = 0$ for $|i - j| > 1$, i.e. it shows that A is a block tridiagonal matrix

$$\Sigma^{-1} = A = \begin{vmatrix} A_{11} A_{12}, \ 0, \ldots, 0 \\ A_{21} A_{22}, A_{23}, \ldots, 0 \\ 0 \quad A_{32}, A_{33}, \ldots, 0 \\ \cdots \\ \cdots \\ 0 \quad , 0 \quad , 0, \ldots, A_{NN} \end{vmatrix} \tag{93}$$

where O is a d by d matrix of zeros,

$$A_{tt} = \Sigma_{tt|t-1} + \Sigma_{tt}^{-1}\Sigma_{t,t+1}\Sigma_{t+1,t+1|t}^{-1}\Sigma_{t+1,1}\Sigma_{tt}^{-1} \tag{94}$$

and

$$A_{t-1,t} = \Sigma_{t-1,t-1}^{-1}\Sigma_{t-1,t}\Sigma_{tt|t-1}^{-1}. \tag{95}$$

(See Dempster, 1972, on matrices with fixed zeros in the inverse.)

The pair $\theta = (\mu, \Sigma)$ is the standard parametrization of the multivariate Gaussian density. The constraints satisfied by θ are these: μ is an arbitrary real vector of length Nd and Σ is the inverse of an arbitrary positive definite block tridiagonal symmetric matrix.[6] These are precisely the minimum conditions that any estimate $\hat{\theta} = \hat{\theta}(X)$ of θ based on X must satisfy. The set of θ that satisfy these constraints is the 'parameter space', and the minimum condition on an estimator is that it falls in the parameter space. With this parametrization one rarely worries about the constraints because they are automatically satisfied by the usual moment estimators. The usual moment estimators are these: (U1) the sample mean and the sample covariance in the case of ordinary sampling from a Gaussian density, (U2) the EM type re-estimates of μ and Σ when the state sequences are not known, and (U3) Viterbi style re-estimates which use (U1) on labeled data. The worst violation of constraints possible in these cases is that Σ is nonnegative definite but not strictly positive definite. Various heuristics have been invented to deal with this such as tying some of the covariance matrices so that the pooled estimate of their common value is not singular; this heuristic is used in the case when Σ is assumed block diagonal as in the usual model which has zero cross-correlation between time adjacent feature vectors.

Tying means, among other things, to replace the original parameter space with another of lower dimension. Depending on the nature of the tying, the constraints which define the parameter space may become simpler or more complicated. For example, if the X sequence is assumed covariance stationary then only two submatrices Σ_{11}, Σ_{12} define all of Σ, via a common covariance matrix for the diagonal elements and a common cross-covariance matrix for the off diagonal elements Σ_{ij} for $j = i + 1$. In the case of $|i - j| > 1$ the cross-covariances are functions of the one step covariances

$$\Sigma = \begin{vmatrix} \Sigma_{11} & \Sigma_{12}, \ldots, \Sigma_{1N} \\ \Sigma_{21} & \Sigma_{11}, \ldots, \Sigma_{2N} \\ & \cdots \\ & \cdots \\ \Sigma_{N1} & \Sigma_{N2}, \ldots, \Sigma_{11} \end{vmatrix}. \tag{96}$$

---

[6] Note that the off diagonal elements Σ_{ij} of Σ in (3) for which $|i-j| \geq 2$ can be regarded as functions of the submatrices on the three main diagonals. This can be seen by degree of freedom considerations or by the representation (7) of the overall joint distribution in terms of its vector bivariate distributions.

In this case

$$\Sigma^{-1} = A = \begin{vmatrix} A_{11} & A_{12} & ,O_{13},\ldots,O_{1N} \\ A_{21} & A_{11} & ,A_{12},\ldots,O_{2N} \\ O_{31} & A_{21} & ,A_{11},\ldots,O_{2N} \\ & \cdots & \\ & \cdots & \\ O_{N1} & ,O_{N2} & ,O_{N3},\ldots,A_{11} \end{vmatrix}. \tag{97}$$

So far it has not been said how the density $\phi_{s_1,\ldots,s_N}(x_t|x_{t-1})$ depends on the state sequence $s_1,\ldots,s_N$. We now complete the description of the standard parametrization by relating the time indexed parameters that appear in the partitioning to the state sequence which conditions the distribution. Rewriting (1) as

$$\phi_s(x) \equiv \phi_{s_1,\ldots,s_N}(x_1) \prod_{t=2}^{N} \frac{\phi_{s_1,\ldots,s_N}(x_{t-1},x_t)}{\phi_{s_1,\ldots,s_N}(x_{t-1})} \tag{98}$$

it is clear that the overall joint density is defined by the collection of vector bivariate joint distribution of pairs of vectors (x_{t-1},x_t) and it is therefore sufficient to specify how these depend on the state sequence. One must exercise some care, however, to ensure that the result yields a unique consistent definition of the overall joint distribution. It will not do, for example, to define two different marginal distributions for X_7 (say) by independent definitions of the vector bivariate joint distributions of (X_6, X_7) on the one hand and (X_7, X_8) on the other. Here is how to do it in a consistent way:

$$\phi_{s_1,\ldots,s_N}(x_{t-1},x_t) = \phi_{s_{t-2}s_{t-1}s_t}(x_{t-1},x_t) = \phi_{a(t-1),a(t)}(x_{t-1},x_t) \tag{99}$$

where $a(t)$ is the arc determined by an 'arc mapping function' (or 'transition tying function') T which associates with each state transition (S_{t-1}, s_t) an 'arc' $a = a(t) = T(s_{t-1}, s_t)$ which serves as an index into a list of **distinct** marginal distributions of the vectors X_t and pairs $(a, b) = (a(t-1), a(t)) = T(s_{t-2}s_{t-1}, s_t)$ of which serve as an index into a list of **distinct** vector bivariate distributions of $(X_{t-1}X_t)$. Now for a given arc let $\mu(a), \Sigma(a, a)$ denote the conditional mean and covariance matrix of X_t given that the arc ending at time t is a, and for a pair of time adjacent arcs (a, b) let $\Sigma(a, b)$ be the cross-covariance matrix between elements of X_{t-1} and X_t given the arcs were (a, b). Then the joint distribution of (X_{t-1}, X_t) has mean vector

$$\mu = \begin{vmatrix} \mu(a) \\ \mu(b) \end{vmatrix} \tag{100}$$

and covariance matrix

$$\Sigma = \begin{vmatrix} \Sigma(a, a) & \Sigma(a, b) \\ \Sigma(b, a) & \Sigma(b, b) \end{vmatrix}. \tag{101}$$

It is easy to see that the constraint that the Nd by Nd matrix Σ is positive definite, can be replaced by the simpler one: every $2d$ by $2d$ covariance matrix must be positive definite. In terms of the $\Sigma(a, a)$ and $\Sigma(b, b)$ only this in turn is equivalent to the constraints that $\Sigma(a, a)$ is positive definite and $\Sigma(a, a|b)$ (or $\Sigma(b, b|a)$) is positive definite, where

$$\Sigma(a, a|b) \equiv \Sigma(a, a) - \Sigma(a, b)\Sigma(b, b)^{-1}\Sigma(b, a) \qquad (102)$$

is the conditional (or 'partial') covariance matrix of X_t, given that $X_{t-1} = x_{t-1}$ and that $T(s_{t-2}, s_{t-1,t}) = (a, b)$. The corresponding conditional mean vector is

$$v(x_{t-1}, a, b) = \mu(b) - \Sigma(b, a)\Sigma(a, a)^{-1}(x_{t-1} - \mu(a)). \qquad (103)$$

The above definition of the overall joint conditional distribution of Nd dimensional vectors, given the state sequence, is consistent. This is so because all one has to do is make sure that if an arc a had a given mean vector and covariance matrix in the definition of one vector bivariate distribution for the pair of arcs (a, b), then the same arc a had the identical mean vector and covariance matrix when it appeared in the context of other arcs such as $(a, c), (c, a), (b, a), (a, a), \ldots$.

P2: Parametrizing by tying correlations

The assumption of stationary covariances is too restrictive for the problem, it doesn't allow the output distribution to vary with the arc sequence except via the variation of the mean vectors. However, a model which has stationary correlations (instead of covariances) is free of this defect, and yet preserves much of the simplicity of the covariance stationary model; this is the model (S2). A model with significantly greater degrees of freedom is obtained by giving up stationarity of within-frame correlations but retaining the stationarity of cross-frame correlations, as in the original parametrization of HMMC. A possible drawback of this approach is that the resulting parametrization is more complicated, ergo the estimates are more difficult to constrain to the parameter space, as will be seen. There is some experimental evidence that this added degree of freedom may not result in a large improvement in modeling, but such a conclusion requires more systematic experimental work.

Let's first reparametrize the general model in terms of correlation coefficients. Let

$$D = \begin{vmatrix} D_{11} \, O_{12} \, , O_{13}, \ldots, O_{1N} \\ O_{21} \, D_{22} \, , O_{21}, \ldots, O_{2N} \\ O_{31} \, O_{21} \, , D_{33}, \ldots, O_{2N} \\ \ldots \\ \ldots \\ O_{N1} \, , O_{N2} \, , O_{N3}, \ldots, D_{NN} \end{vmatrix} \qquad (104)$$

be a block diagonal matrix which is actually a diagonal matrix, i.e. the tth diagonal block is diagonal matrix having the standard deviations of the components of X_t as its diagonal elements. Denote the matrix of first order correlations by

$$
R = \begin{vmatrix}
R_{11} \ R_{12} \ , R_{13}, \ldots, R_{1N} \\
R_{21} \ R_{22} \ , R_{21}, \ldots, R_{2N} \\
R_{31} \ R_{21} \ , R_{33}, \ldots, R_{2N} \\
\cdots \\
\cdots \\
R_{N1}, R_{N2}, R_{N3}, \ldots, R_{NN}
\end{vmatrix}
\tag{105}
$$

where the R_{ij} are d by d submatrices. The relationship between these parameters is

$$
\Sigma \equiv DRD.
\tag{106}
$$

The new parameter $\theta = (\mu, D, R)$ satisfies the following constraints: (1) μ is a real vector as before; (2) D is diagonal with positive diagonal elements; and (3) R is positive definite with each diagonal element equal to unity. This is equivalent to the standard parametrization in that one has the same degrees of freedom, only the constraints are slightly different.

Let's now tie all one step cross-correlations: put

$$
\Xi = R_{12} = R_{23} = , \ldots, R_{N-1,N}
\tag{107}
$$

so that (T denotes transpose)

$$
\Xi^T = R_{21} = R_{32} = , \ldots, R_{N,N-1}.
\tag{108}
$$

Then the partial (conditional) correlations are

$$
R(a, a \mid b) = R(a, a) - R(a, b)R(b, b)^{-1}R(b, a)
$$
$$
= R(a, a) - \Xi^T R(b, b)^{-1} \Xi
\tag{109}
$$

if the arc pair is (a, b) while Ξ and Ξ^T are interchanged if the arc pair is (b, a). In this parametrization the positive definiteness of Σ is equivalent to

(1) All standard deviations are positive, and
(2) All conditional correlation matrices defined by arc pairs (a, b) are positive definite.

Thus tying between-frame cross-correlation matrices to a common value Ξ reduces degrees of freedom, but involves many constraints on the common value, constraints defined by the within-frame correlation matrices $R(a, a)$ that are not tied. In words: the constraints are that Ξ should be small with respect to each $R(a, a)$ in the metric of each and every $R(b, b)$. Guaranteeing these constraints during estimation is possible but not simple. Ignoring the constraints (as one often does in these problems) leads to the failure of some estimates of $R(a, a|b)$ to be positive definite, even when the model is correct.

Suppose one goes further by also tying the $R(a, a)$ to a common value, then it is easy to enforce the single matrix constraint that results, hence the suggestion S2. In particular, if one takes $R(a, a) = I$, the d-dimensional identity and assume $\Xi = \Xi^T$ then (14) becomes

$$
R = \begin{vmatrix}
I & \Xi & \Xi^2, \ldots, \Xi^{N-1} \\
\Xi & I & \Xi, \ldots, \Xi^{N-2} \\
 & & \cdots \\
 & & \cdots \\
\Xi^{N-1} & \Xi^{N-2} & \Xi^{N-3}, \ldots, I
\end{vmatrix} \tag{110}
$$

which has the form of the correlation matrix in the case of scalar X_t.

P3: Single arc dependent parametrizations

Using (7) one can write (1) as

$$
\phi(x_1, \ldots, x_N) \equiv \phi_{a(1)}(x_1) \prod_{t=2}^{N} \phi_{a(t-1), a(t)}(x_t | x_{t-1}). \tag{111}
$$

It is tempting to try to parametrize the problem by removing the dependence of the parametrization at time t on the preceding arc, i.e. to write

$$
\phi(x_1, \ldots, x_N) \equiv \phi_{a(1)}(x_1) \prod_{t=2}^{N} \phi_{a(t)}(x_t | x_{t-1}). \tag{112}
$$

This can be done by specifying a triple for each arc (a)

$$
m(a), \quad C(a), \quad \Gamma(a) \tag{113}
$$

which in turn define the conditional mean of the current vector

$$
v(x | a) \equiv E_a(X_{t+1} | X_t = x) = m(a) + C(a)x \tag{114}
$$

as a linear function of the previous vector, and which define the conditional covariance matrix of the current vector given the previous one as the constant matrix $\Gamma(a)$. Such a parametrization would have the advantage that the parameters would be neatly partitioned among the distinct arcs with no requirement for storing information associated with pairs of arcs. The linearity of the regression and the constancy (as a function of the previous vector X_{t-1}) of the conditional covariances at each time and the Gaussian form of each factor in (19) will in fact guarantee a joint Gaussian density for the overall distribution provided the consistency requirement is satisfied.

This parameterization has the disadvantage that if the parameters in fact define a consistent model then they must obey some rather complicated and very likely unplanned constraints. They are unplanned in the sense that the marginal distributions determined by the different arcs obey strong linear and quadratic equalities in their mean vectors and covariance matrices, respectively. They are complicated because, on the one hand, the marginal distribution of X_t corresponding to $a = a(t)$ can only be determined by an iterative computation that reaches back to time one and, on the other hand, this marginal distribution must reappear every time arc a is encountered in any context whatever. In other words, one must enforce constraints that correspond to **strings** of arcs of all lengths. It is unlikely that this plethora of consistency constraints are automatically satisfied by either the maximum likelihood estimates (Viterbi style) or MMI estimates (hillclimbing the MMI objective instead of re-estimation). As to using the EM algorithm, it is not clear how to reconcile the unconstrained moment estimates so as to satisfy, in analogy with the weighted averaging in S2, the constraints of this parameterization. All of this suggests that the M-step of the EM algorithm requires numerical optimization.

References

Bahl, L.R. and Jelinek, F. (1975) Decoding for channels with insertions, deletions, and substitutions, with applications to speech recognition. *IEEE Trans. Info. Theory*, **21**, 404–11.

Bahl, L.R., Cocke, J., Jelinek, F. and Raviv, J. (1974) Optimal decoding of linear codes for minimizing symbol error rate. *IEEE Trans. Info. Theory*, **5**, 284–7.

Bahl, L.R., Jelinek, F. and Mercer, R.L. (1983) A maximum likelihood approach to continuous speech recognition. *IEEE Trans. Pattern Anal. Machine Intell.*, **5**, 179–90.

Baker, J.K. (1975) The DRAGON system – An overview. *IEEE Trans. Acoust. Speech and Sig. Proc.*, **23**, 24–9.

Bakis, R. (1976) *Continuous speech recognition via centisecond acoustic states.* 91st meeting of the Acoustical Society of America.

Barron, A.R. (1991a) *Approximation bounds for superpositions of a sigmoidal function.* Proc. IEEE Internat. Symp. Inform. Theory, **85**.

Barron, A.R. (1991b) *Approximation and estimation bounds for artificial neural networks.* Proc. 4th Workshop on Computational Learning Theory, Morgan Kaufmann, Palo Alto.

Baum, L.E. (1972) An inequality and associated maximization technique in statistical estimation for probabilistic functions of Markov processes. *Inequalities*, **3**, 1–8.

Baum, L.E. and Egon, J.A. (1967) An inequality with applications to statistical estimation for probabilistic functions of a Markov process and to a model for ecology. *Bull. Amer. Math. Soc.* **73**, 360–3.

Baum, L.E. and Petrie, T. (1966) Statistical inference for probabilistic functions of finite state Markov chains. *Ann. Math. Statist.* **37**, 1559–63.

Baum, L.E. and Sell, G.R. (1968) Growth transformations for functions on manifolds. *Pac. J. Math.*, **27**, 211–27.

Baum, L.E., Petrie, T., Soules, G. and Weiss, N. (1970) A maximization technique occurring in the statistical analysis of probabilistic functions of Markov chains. *Ann. Math. Statist.*, **41**, 164–71.

Bridle, J.S. (1992) *Neural networks or hidden Markov models for automatic speech recognition: is there a choice?* NATO ASI Series, **F75**, 225–36.

Brown, P.F., Cocke, J., Della Pietra, S.A. *et al.* (1990) A statistical approach to machine translation. *Computational Linguistics*, **16**.

Brown, P.F., Mercer, R.L., Nádas, A. and Nahamoo, D. (1986) A hidden Markov model with correlated output and its training. IBM Patent Disclosure, *Y0886-0391*.

Cybenko, G. (1989) Approximation by superpositions of a sigmoidal function. *Math. Control, Signals, Systems*, **2**, 303–14.

Dempster, A.P. (1972) Covariance selection. *Biometrics*, **28**, 157–75.

Dempster, A.P., Laird, N.M. and Rubin, D.B. (1977) Maximum likelihood estimation from incomplete data via the EM algorithm. *J. Roy Statist. Soc. B*, **39**(1), 1–38.

Feinberg, S.E. and Meyer, M.M. (1985) Iterative Proportional Fitting. *Encyclopedia of Statistical Sciences*, **4**, 275–9.

Ferguson, J.D. (Ed.) (1980) *Hidden Markov Models for Speech*. IDA-CRD, Princeton, NJ.

Franzini, M., Waibel, A., Lee, K.F. (1991) *Continuous speech recognition with the connectionist Viterbi training procedure*. Proc. IWANN91, 355–60.

Jelinek, F. (1969) A fast sequential decoding algorithm using a stack. *IBM J. Res. Develop.*, 675–85

Jelinek, F. (1975) The design of a linguistic statistical decoder for the recognition of continuous speech. *IEEE Trans. Info. Theory*, **21**, 250–6.

Jelinek, F. (1976) Continuous speech recognition by statistical methods. *Proc. IEEE*, **64**, 532–56.

Jelinek, F. (1985) The development of an experimental discrete dictation recognizer. *Proc. IEEE*, 1616–24.

Juang, B.H. and Rabiner, L.R. (1991) Hidden Markov models for speech recognition. *Technometrics*, **33**, 251–72.

Levin, E. (1990) *Word recognition using hidden control neural architecture*. Proc. ICASSP90, **1**, 433–6.

Meilijson, I. (1989) A fast improvement to the EM algorithm on its own terms. *J. Roy. Statist. Soc. B*, **51**, 127–38.

Nádas, A. (1991) *Classification by EM-trained dynamic artificial neural nets based on hidden perceptrons*. Proc. Interface '91, pp 285–8

Paul, D.B. (1990) Speech recognition using hidden Markov models. *The Lincoln Laboratory Journal*, 41–62.

Poritz, A.B. (1988) *Hidden Markov models: a guided tour*. Proc. IEEE Int. Conf. Acoustic, Speech and Signal Processing, 7–13.

Rabiner, L.R. and Juang, B.H. (1989) *A Tutorial on Hidden Markov Models and Selected Applications in Speech Recognition*. Proceedings of the IEEE, 257–86.

Richard, M.D. and Lippmann, R.P. (1991) Neural network classifiers estimate Bayesian, *Neural Computation*, **3**, 461–83.

Titterington D.M. (1984) Recursive parameter estimation using recursive data. *J. Roy. Statist. Soc. B*, **46**(2), 257–67.

17

Comparison of feed-forward and recurrent sensitivities in speech recognition

GARY M. KUHN and RAYMOND L. WATROUS
Siemens Corporate Research, Princeton, NJ, USA

17.1 Introduction

In earlier work, we defined and calculated the sensitivity of each output unit of a feed-forward network to each input feature in its training set at each point in time. This calculation suggested the need for a change in architecture, and led to a subsequent **joint** optimization of the network and its input features.

Now we define and calculate the sensitivity of a **recurrent** network to each input feature in the same training set at the same points in time. This calculation makes it possible to quantify the extent to which the two types of networks have similar sensitivities to their inputs.

17.2 The networks

In Kuhn and Herzberg (1991) our feed-forward network was a 'time-delay neural network' with one hidden layer:

$$y_k(t) = S\left(w_{\theta k} + \sum_{j=1}^{9} \sum_{l=}^{1,3,5} w_{jkl} S\left[w_{\theta j} + \sum_{i=1}^{17} \sum_{d=1}^{4} w_{ijd} y_i(t-l-d)\right]\right),$$

where $y_k(t)$ is the output for class k at time t, S is the symmetric sigmoid $y = 2(1 + e^{-x})^{-1} - 1$, $S(\cdot) = y_k(t)$, $S[\cdot] = y_j(t-l)$ is the output of hidden unit j at time $t-l$, $y_i(t-l-d)$ is the output of input unit i at time $t-l-d$, l is a time-**lag** from hidden to output unit, d is a time-**delay** from input to hidden unit, and $w_{\theta j}$ and $w_{\theta k}$ are bias values.

Artificial Neural Networks for Speech and Vision. Edited by Richard J. Mammone.
Published in 1993 by Chapman & Hall, London. ISBN 0 412 54850 X

The recurrent network was identical to the feed-forward network except that it also had output self-loops with unit time delay:

$$y_k(t) = S\left(w_{kk}y_k(t-1) + w_{\theta k} + \sum_{j,l} w_{jkl} S\left[w_{\theta j} + \sum_{i,d} w_{ijd}y_i(t-l-d) \right] \right).$$

The feed-forward network was trained to discriminate the spoken letter names 'b', 'd', 'e' and 'v', and achieved 88.5% accuracy on test examples. The recurrent network was trained on the same task and achieved 89.6% accuracy on the same test examples (Kuhn and Herzberg, 1991).

17.3 Feed-forward sensitivity

Kuhn (1992) defined and calculated the sensitivity of each output unit of the feed-forward network to each input feature observed in the network's training set at each point in time. This sensitivity was time-dependent, to avoid integrating over times in the input when sensitivities might have opposite sign.

The feed-forward sensitivity $s_i^k(t)$ of output unit k to input i at time t was defined as

$$s_i^k(t) = \sum_\tau \frac{\partial y_k(t+\tau)}{\partial y_i(t)}$$

where

$$\frac{\partial y_k(t+\tau)}{\partial y_i(t)} = \frac{\partial y_k(t+\tau)}{\partial x_k(t+\tau)} \sum_{l+d=\tau} \frac{\partial x_k(t+l+d)}{\partial y_i(t)}$$

and

$$\frac{\partial x_k(t+l+d)}{\partial y_i(t)} = \sum_j w_{jkl} \frac{\partial y_j(t+d)}{\partial x_j(t+d)} w_{ijd}$$

yielding

$$s_i^k(t) = \sum_\tau \frac{\partial y_k(t+\tau)}{\partial x_k(t+\tau)} \sum_{l+d=\tau} \sum_j w_{jkl} \frac{\partial y_j(t+d)}{\partial x_j(t+d)} w_{ijd}.$$

It is easy to confuse sensitivity $s_i^k(t)$ with the derivative of the output of unit k at time t with respect to feature i. Note that the derivative requires a sum over those earlier times whose feature i **affects** output k at time t, while the sensitivity requires a sum over all later times $t+\tau$ which output k **is affected by** feature i at time t.

The sensitivity is also similar to the gradient of the system error at unit k with respect to the weight from feature i. But the sensitivity omits the first factor of the error gradient, the derivative of the error with respect to unit k's output, and it substitutes w_{ijd} for the last factor of the error gradient, namely for $y_i(t-l-d)$.

To compare sensitivities when the feed-forward network was responding as desired with those when it was not, we ordered the training examples by how well they were discriminated (Kuhn, 1992). At the well-discriminated end of the ordered list of training examples, we found that there was little residual sensitivity: the network responses were locally robust to perturbations of the inputs, and the responses were correct.

At the poorly-discriminated end of the ordered list of training examples the network actually mis-classified the last 10% of the training examples. Here we could also have found little residual sensitivity, which would have meant that the network responses were once again locally robust to perturbations of the inputs, but this time, the responses would have been wrong. Instead, what we found was (1) there was much more residual sensitivity for the poorly-discriminated training examples, (2) some input features had a net negative bias of their sensitivity while others had a net positive bias, and (3) the total absolute sensitivity, i.e. the magnitude of the sensitivity, differed markedly from feature to feature.

The residual sensitivity for the poorly-discriminated training examples was both bad news and good news. It was bad news because we always wanted robust, state-to-state jumps in the outputs of our network, but we sometimes got volatile and weak ramping of the outputs. On the other hand, the residual sensitivity was also good news, because it indicated that there was still more slope to be exploited by the training algorithm.

17.4 Feature optimizing

The biases and magnitudes of the sensitivities suggested that a global one-to-one affine transformation should be applied independently to each feature. The recognizer was augmented to implement this transformation, by adding what we can think of as a new optimizing layer with a 1-element localized receptive field. Figure 17.1 shows both the original and the augmented recognizer.

Writing the original inputs-to-hidden transformation as:

$$y_j(t) = S\left[w_{\theta j} + \sum_{i,d} w_{ijd}(0 + 1 y_i(t - d)) \right]$$

the augmented transformation becomes:

$$y_j(t) = S\left[\hat{w}_{\theta j} + \sum_{i,d} \hat{w}_{ijd}(w_{\theta i} + w_{ii} y_i(t - d)) \right].$$

We can set the linear part of the original transformation equal to the linear part of the augmented transformation

$$w_{\theta j} + \sum_{i,d} w_{ijd} y_i(t - d) = \hat{w}_{\theta j} + \sum_{i,d} \hat{w}_{ijd}(w_{\theta i} + w_{ii} y_i(t - d))$$

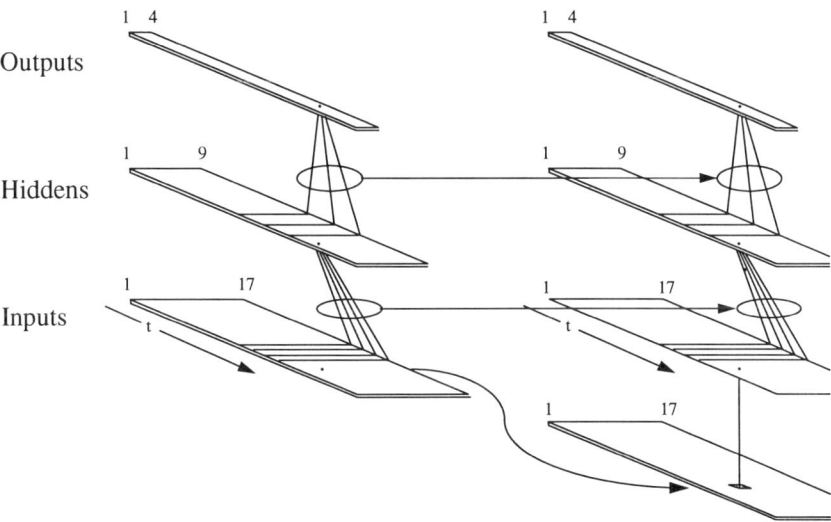

Figure 17.1 *Original and augmented recognizer.*

and then set the original weights $w_{\theta j}$ and w_{ijd} equal to the corresponding quantities from the augmented system

$$w_{\theta j} = \hat{w}_{\theta j} + \sum_{i,d} \hat{w}_{ijd} w_{\theta i}, \quad w_{ijd} = \hat{w}_{ijd} w_{ii}.$$

Does this equivalence mean that the 1-to-1 affine transformation of the inputs was useless? It does not. Any number of pairs of multipliers can produce the same (dot) product, but not all pairs will train the first member of the pair (the weight) equally easily, because training is proportional to the second member of the pair. By allowing global changes to individual components in the input, additional **paths** through weight space can open up to perhaps previously unreachable solutions. This can improve the trainability of the network, as well as the interpretability of the features. It is true however, that after training we could fold the feature optimizing weights back into the input-to-hidden weights of an architecture like that of the original classifier.

With the added layers, the network can concentrate the scale and offset of an input feature at a single location, via the 1-to-1 affine transformation, rather than having to distribute that scale and offset across all the connections and units that follow an input unit. For example, if weight decay is imposed on our optimized-to-hidden and hidden-to-output weights, more of the input scaling can be forced into the 1-to-1 affine transformation.

As it turned out, further joint optimization of the augmented feed-forward network did increase discrimination of the test examples to 89.6%, while further optimization of the original network for the same additional number of iterations yielded no increase.

17.5 Forward calculation of recurrent sensitivity

The recurrent network has self-loops with unit delay on its output units. Because of this added recursive structure, a change in the input to unit k at any time will affect all further outputs of that same unit. Therefore the recurrent sensitivity is

$$s_i^k(t) = \sum_\tau \frac{\partial y_k(t+\tau, \ldots, T)}{\partial x_k(t+\tau)} \sum_{l+d=\tau} \sum_j w_{jkl} \frac{\partial y_j(t+d)}{\partial x_j(t+d)} w_{ijd}$$

where the difference between the feed-forward and recurrent sensitivities is that the factor $(\partial y_k(t+\tau))/(\partial x_k(t+\tau))$ has become $(\partial y_k(t+\tau, \ldots, T))/(\partial x_k(t+\tau))$. Since we have $y_k(t+\tau, \ldots, T) = y_k(t+\tau) + \cdots + y_k(T)$, it follows that

$$\frac{\partial y_k(t+\tau, \ldots, T)}{\partial x_k(t+\tau)} = \frac{\partial y_k(t+\tau)}{\partial x_k(t+\tau)} \frac{\partial}{\partial y_k(t+\tau)} (y_k(t+\tau) + \cdots + y_k(T))$$

$$= \frac{\partial y_k(t+\tau)}{\partial x_k(t+\tau)} \left(1 + \frac{\partial y_k(t+\tau+1)}{\partial y_k(t+\tau)} + \cdots + \prod_{n=t+\tau}^{T-1} \frac{\partial y_k(n+1)}{\partial y_k(n)} \right)$$

$$= \frac{\partial y_k(t+\tau)}{\partial x_k(t+\tau)} \left(1 + \sum_{m=1}^{T-t-\tau} w_{kk}^m \prod_{n=t+\tau}^{t+\tau+m-1} \frac{\partial y_k(n+1)}{\partial x_k(n+1)} \right),$$

where the first term is the only term that exists in the feed-forward case.

17.6 Backward calculation of recurrent sensitivity

The forward calculation of recurrent sensitivity can either be carried out in its entirety, or it can be truncated, or it can be ignored in favor of the following **backward** calculation of recurrent sensitivity.

We use the familiar chain rule to expand:

$$\frac{\partial y_k(t+\tau)}{\partial y_i(t)} = \frac{\partial y_k(t+\tau)}{\partial x_k(t+\tau)} \frac{\partial x_k(t+\tau)}{\partial y_i(t)}$$

and

$$\frac{\partial x_k(t+\tau)}{\partial y_i(t)} = \sum_{m,\beta} w_{mk\beta} \frac{\partial y_m(t+\tau-\beta)}{\partial y_i(t)}.$$

Thus

$$s_i^k(t) = \sum_{\tau \geq 0} \frac{\partial y_k(t+\tau)}{\partial x_k(t+\tau)} \sum_{m,\beta} w_{mk\beta} \frac{\partial y_m(t+\tau-\beta)}{\partial y_i(t)}.$$

If we compare with the gradient of a mean square error objective function:

$$\phi(w) = \frac{1}{2} \sum_{n=1}^{T} \sum_{k=1}^{O} (\operatorname{tar} g_k(n) - y_k(n))^2$$

where

$$\nabla \phi(w) = \sum_{n=1}^{T} \sum_{k=1}^{O} (\operatorname{tar} g_k(n) - y_k(n)) \frac{\partial y_k(n)}{\partial x_k(n)} \sum_{m,\beta} w_{mk\beta} \frac{\partial y_m(n-\beta)}{\partial w_{ij\lambda}},$$

we see that the computation of the output-input sensitivities can be organized very similarly to the back-propagation-in-time algorithm. That algorithm may be modified by injecting an error of 1 only for the selected output unit at each time step, and by extending the back-propagation one more step to compute the partials with respect to the inputs; the sensitivities may be read off directly from the backpropagation data structure.

17.7 Simulations

To apply these definitions, we made two new training runs on our speech data, and then calculated both the feed-forward and recurrent sensitivities in the backward direction, using the GRADSIM simulator (Watrous, 1992).

The speech data are divided into a training set of 672 utterances and a test set of 96 utterances. Both the feed-forward and the recurrent network were optimized using a conjugate gradient algorithm until the MSE was reduced to 0.008; at this point, discrimination of the training set was 90.0% for the feed-forward network and 91.5% for the recurrent network.

However, discrimination of the test set was only 78.1% for the feed-forward network and only 82.3% for the recurrent network. This is worse than the 88.5% and 89.6% previously reported on the same data (Kuhn and Herzberg, 1991). We point out that in the simulations reported here, as opposed to those reported by Kuhn and Herzberg (1991), the networks actually used the logistic non-linearity $y = (1 + e^{-x})^{-1}$ rather than the symmetric sigmoid, and the training runs did not include either a perodic cross-validation step or an alternation between global stochastic search and local gradient search.

After training, the feedback weights w_{kk} for the spoken letter names 'b', 'd', 'e' and 'v' were, respectively, 4.2, 2.9, 0.4 and 1.2, indicating that the recurrent network did weight previous time more heavily for the relatively dynamic voiced stop-consonants 'b' and 'd'.

Figure 17.2–5 show, respectively, feed-forward sensitivities on the best discriminated training examples, feed-forward sensitivities on poorly-dis-criminated training examples, recurrent sensitivities on the same best-dis-criminated training examples and recurrent sensitivities on the same poorly-discriminated training examples. Training example discriminability was measured using the feed-forward network. The measure was the smallest error for an incorrect class divided by the error for the correct class.

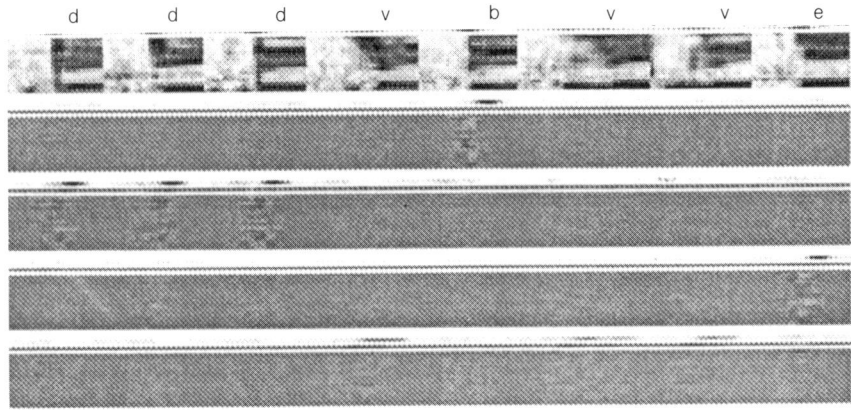

Figure 17.2 *Features and feed-forward sensitivities for best-discriminated training examples.*

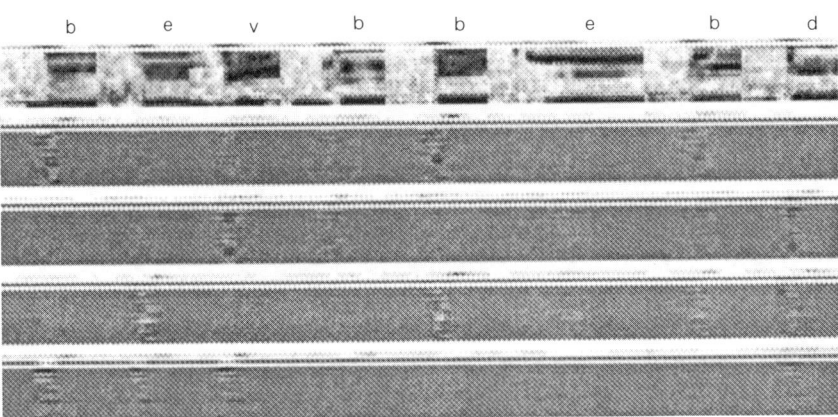

Figure 17.3 *Features and feed-forward sensitivities for poorly-discriminated training examples.*

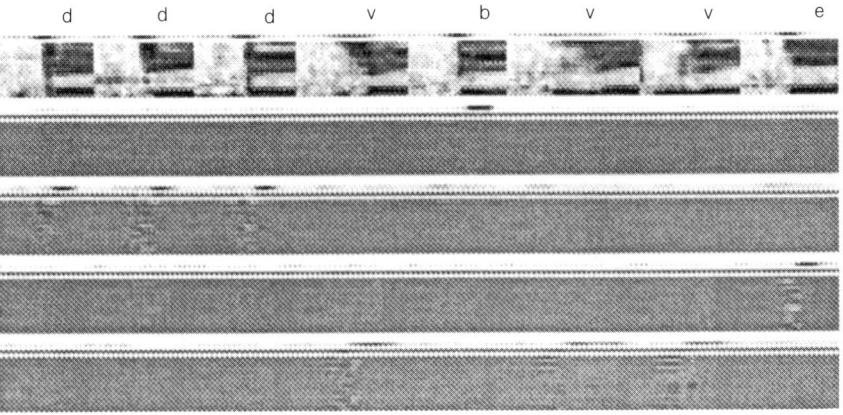

Figure 17.4 *Features and recurrent sensitivities for the same training examples as in Figure 17.2.*

b   e   v   b   b   e   b   d

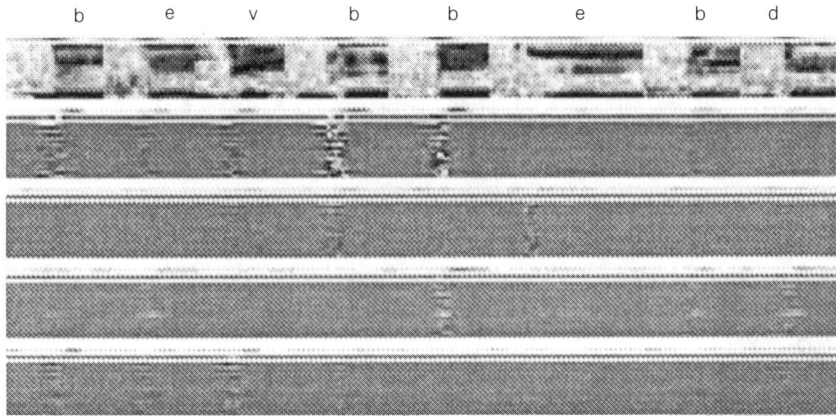

Figure 17.5 *Features and recurrent sensitivities for the same training examples as in Figure 17.3.*

More specifically, Figure 17.2 shows the 8 best-discriminated utterances and Figure 17.3 shows the last four correctly discriminated and the first for mis-discriminated utterances, both for the feed-forward network. Figures 17.4 and 17.5 show the same well-discriminated and poorly-discriminated utterances, respectively, for the recurrent network.

There are five panels in each of the four figures. In the top panel there are 17 speech features as a function of time. From bottom to top, the features are 16 filter bank energies ordered from low frequency to high (Kuhn, 1992), and one event signal (Kuhn *et al.*, 1990) turning on and off above the filter energies. In panels 2–5, we see quantities relating to the 'b', 'd', 'e' and 'v' output units. These quantities, from bottom to top in each panel, are the sensitivity of the indicated unit to each of the filter bank energies, the sensitivity of the indicated unit to the event signal, and the response of the unit. The display of the sensitivities ranges from white, for large negative values, to medium grey, for zero values, to black, for large positive values.

In Figure 17.2, the feed-forward sensitivities for the well-discriminated examples, the overall sensitivity values are fairly uniform and close to zero. Slightly lighter or darker regions are evident in some areas, especially when the output unit corresponds to the token being uttered. The recurrent sensitivities for the well-discriminated utterances, in Figure 17.4, are in general quite similar to those of the feed-forward network. There is, however, less sensitivity of the recurrent b-unit for the 'b', and increased sensitivity of the recurrent v- and e-units in response to the final 'e'.

In contrast, there are many more extreme sensitivity values in the poorly-discriminated examples. Again, the feed-forward and recurrent sensitivities are similar. For example, both want a weaker second formant if the e-unit is to increase its response (incorrectly) to the third 'b'. Some recurrent sensitivities are however more salient, particularly those of the b-unit.

Note, finally, the alternation of the sign of the sensitivities across channels and panels at the same time. This alternation suggests that the network is trying to balance the residual sensitivities.

17.8 Discussion

We have touched on several topics that we now go over again, one by one.

The definition of the speech event signal is found in (Kuhn *et al.*, 1990), where the delayed event signal was first used as both the target signal during training, and as the hypothesized target signal during recognition.

The small improvement reported for the 1-to-1 affine transformation in Kuhn (1992) is similar to the small improvement reported for the 'autonorm layer' in Seidel *et al.* (1992), where the better the data was normalized prior to being input to the network, the less benefit there was to using the 1-to-1 affine transformation.

We looked for a revealing ordering of the sensitivity data and chose an ordering by discriminability. Other revealing orderings could be examined, such as those favored by projection pursuit (Friedman and Tukey, 1974).

The use of residuals in system identification, of which residual sensitivity is only one example, is discussed in generous detail by Draper and Smith (1981, Ch.3).

A thoughtful discussion that includes approaches to training large, fixed size networks by alternating between global random search and local gradient search, is found in Barron and Barron (1988).

We believe that the sensitivity analysis permitted us to find a better architecture for joint optimization **both** of the data representation **and** of the effective parameters of the classifier. This approach of joint optimization can be juxtaposed to an approach where one emphasizes the difference between optimizing data representations and optimizing the class of approximating functions, as in Geman *et al.* (1992).

17.9 Conclusion

To recapitulate, we have a feed-forward network and a recurrent network. Each has been trained to discriminate the speech sounds 'b', 'd', 'e' and 'v' using the same set of training data. The recurrent network performs slightly better on test data.

We have already defined and calculated the sensitivity of the outputs of the feed-forward network at each time to each input feature in the training set. This calculation suggested the need for a change in architecture and led to a subsequent **joint** optimization of the network and its input features.

We have now defined and calculated the sensitivity of the recurrent network at each time to each input feature in the training set. This calculation makes it possible to quantify the extent to which the two types of networks have similar sensitivites to their inputs.

Acknowledgements

We thank colleagues F. Block, R. Cohn, R. Mammone, C. Olano, V. Poor and M. Williamson for helpful discussions.

References

Barron, A.R. and Barron, R.L. (1988) Statistical Learning Networks: A Unifying View. *Computing Science and Statistics: Proc. 20th Symposium on the Interface*, pp. 192–203.

Draper, N.R. and Smith, H. (1981) *Applied Regression Analysis*. Wiley, New York, NY, pp. 141–92.

Friedman, J. and Tukey, J. (1974) A projection pursuit algorithm for exploratory data analysis. *IEEE Trans. Computers*, **23**, 881–90.

Geman, S., Bienenstock, E. and Doursat, R. (1992) Neural networks and the bias/variance dilemma. *Neural Computation*, **4**, 1–58.

Kuhn, G.M. (1992) Joint optimization of classifier and feature space in speech recognition. *IJCNN' 92*, **IV**, 709–14.

Kuhn, G.M. and Herzberg, N.P. (1991) Some variations on training of recurrent networks, in *Neural Networks: Theory and Applications*, (eds. R. Mammone and Y. Zeevi), Academic Press, New York, NJ, pp. 233–44.

Kuhn, G.M., Watrous, R.L. and Ladendorf, B. (1990) Connected recognition with a recurrent network. *Speech Communication*, **9**, 41–9.

Seidel, F., Becks, K.H., Block, F. *et al.* (1992) B-Quark tagging using neural networks and comparison with a classical method. *Second Intl. Workshop on Software Engineering, Artificial Intelligence and Expert Systems for High Energy and Nuclear Physics*, La Londe-Les-Maures, France, January 13–18.

Watrous, R.L. (1992) GRADSIM: A connectionist network simulator using gradient optimization techniques. *Siemens Internal Report*, November 17.

18

Discriminative feature extraction

SHIGERU KATAGIRI*, BIING-HWANG JUANG**, and
ALAIN BIEM*
*ATR Auditory and Visual Perception Research Laboratories, **AT&T Bell
Laboratories

18.1 Introduction

For clarity of discussion, we assume that pattern recognition consists of two stages, feature extraction and classification. Feature extraction is usually executed based on knowledge specific to a given task or criterion that is not directly linked to the final classification goal. On the other hand, classification is generally performed by using statistical pattern classification of the resulting features. In this chapter, we present a method which integrates the two stages so as to systematically perform the entire recognition process in a manner consistent with accurate classification.

The recent advent of Minimum Classification Error formalization (MCE)/ Generalized Probabilistic Descent method (GPD) provided a new theoretical ground for discriminative pattern classification that unifies both the feature extraction and classification stages (Katagiri *et al.*, 1990, 1991a; Juang and Katagiri, 1992a, b). The usefulness of MCE/GPD has been demonstrated in many experiments. However, the full potential of this new framework has not yet been revealed. The most important philosophy of MCE/GPD was to formalize the overall procedure in a given task in a **smooth** (at least first differentiable) functional form suited to the use of a practical gradient-based search algorithm. This concept is worth applying to many procedures besides classification. Our focus in this chapter is to overcome the above-mentioned gap between feature extraction and classification by embedding a feature extraction process in an MCE/GPD-based classifier design. We call this

Artificial Neural Networks for Speech and Vision. Edited by Richard J. Mammone.
Published in 1993 by Chapman & Hall, London. ISBN 0 412 54850 X

discrimination-oriented feature extraction Discriminative Feature Extraction (DFE). This chapter is intended to introduce this novel approach to pattern recognition.

18.2 MCE/GPD-based discriminative learning

18.2.1 Discriminant function approach: background of MCE/GPD

Here, we consider an M-class classification task $\{C_j\}_{j=1}^M$. A classifier consists of a set of trainable parameters Λ. Given a set of design pairs, a pattern sample $\mathbf{x}_n$ and its class $C_k (n = 1, \ldots, N$ and $k = 1, \ldots, M)$, we aim at designing an optimal Λ. We also assume that an individual sample is already represented as a K-dimensional feature vector.

Bayes decision theory provides a fundamental guideline to design. This approach is based on the Bayes decision rule

$$C(\mathbf{x}) = C_i \quad \text{if} \quad P_\Lambda(C_i|\mathbf{x}) = \max_j P_\Lambda(C_j|\mathbf{x}) \tag{1}$$

where $\mathbf{x}$ is an arbitrary sample, $\mathbf{x} \in \mathcal{R}^K$, $C(\cdot)$ denotes a classification operation, and it is assumed that the true *a posteriori* probability has the parametrized form $P_\Lambda(C_j|\mathbf{x})$ and the precise value of Λ is known. An actual design procedure is to estimate the *a posteriori* probabilities or conditional probabilities. The above decision rule, if it can be used, represents the best classification situation, i.e. the Bayes minimum risk. Perfect execution of equation (1) guarantees realization of the Bayes minimum risk, and this rule can thus be considered a principle for statistical classifier design. However, the truth is that this approach suffers from the serious difficulty that the nature of the sample distributions, such as the form of the density function, is rarely known and it is then almost impossible to estimate desired probabilities in equation (1).

An alternative to the Bayes decision approach is represented in the following functional form classifier:

$$C: \mathcal{R}^K \to \{C_j\}_{j=1}^M. \tag{2}$$

In this most general case, the decision rule is embedded in a functional form. This formalization is less practical, however. Thus, the classifier is usually reduced to a more practical version which is associated with the following decision rule:

$$C(\mathbf{x}) = C_i \quad \text{if} \quad g_i(\mathbf{x}; \Lambda) = \max_j g_j(\mathbf{x}; \Lambda), \tag{3}$$

where $g_j(\mathbf{x}; \Lambda)$ is referred to as a discriminant function and the classifier function $C(\cdot)$ is expressed in an operational form. The classification based on equation (3) and discriminant function designs is referred to as the discriminant function approach. This approach does not require assumptions about the form of the sample distributions. This allows one to execute the classification in a manner more flexible than the Bayesian approach. Any reasonable measure such as a distance can be used as the discriminant function. The computation of these measures is usually simple. Thus, this approach is quite practical. Recall that there are many well-studied examples. A classical linear discriminant function has long been used. The resurgence of discriminative learning by modern artificial neural networks is still fresh in memory. However, even this attractive approach is not perfect. In particular, there was a big gap between actual design of discriminant functions and realization of the Bayes minimum risk. One solution to this serious difficulty is MCE/GPD.

In this section we review the background of MCE/GPD. Design of discriminant functions is usually characterized by two factors: (1) learning objective, and (2) optimization of Λ (minimum search of the objective).

The ultimate way is perhaps to find the minimum of an error count objective by using simulated annealing. This objective can be represented as the average of discountinous 2-state functions, each enumerating error one for misclassification, and zero for correct classification. Given an infinite run of adjustments, simulated annealing can find with probability one the minimum state of the objective, which corresponds to an optimal set of Λ. This property makes the method attractive, but the infinite training it requires is never realistic, and even practical implementations of the annealing process converge extremely slowly. Moreover, a simple execution of this method in a real situation where only a finite number of design samples are available means that even with an infinite training run, simulated annealing is still prone to the training robustness problem. Therefore, a more practical design method is required.

Thus, a main concern in developing MCE/GPD was to create a method satisfying the following conditions: (1) directly attaining the Bayes minimum risk; (2) learning efficiently; and (3) being highly practical. The key to the MCE/GPD solution was to embed the entire process of classification in a smooth functional form and design an at least locally optimal state of classifier parameters through gradient descent-based adaptive training. MCE and GPD are closely related to each other, and it is thus rather difficult to draw a boundary between both. In this paper, we specifically introduce them in the following catagorization: MCE is a theoretical framework for discriminative learning aiming at minimum classification error (Juang and Katagiri, 1992a, b); GPD is a practical, adaptive learning procedure suitable for discriminating various kinds of patterns in the sense of MCE (Katagiri et al., 1990, 1991a).

18.2.2 Minimum classification error formalization

Let us consider the situation that $\mathbf{x}_n$ is selected from the given design samples. We assume $\mathbf{x}_n \in C_k$. MCE formalization consists of three steps. The first step defines a discriminant function $g_j(\mathbf{x}_n; \Lambda)$ which represents the degree to which $\mathbf{x}_n$ belongs to C_j. As cited before, any reasonable measure can be used to define the function. Specifically, we assume that $g_j(\mathbf{x}_n; \Lambda)$ is a distance measure. The second step is the heart of MCE. A smooth misclassification measure is introduced here to simulate the operation in equation (3), i.e. comparison/decision among the competing classes. Among many possibilities,

$$d_k(\mathbf{x}_n; \Lambda) = g_k(\mathbf{x}_n; \Lambda) - \left[\frac{1}{M-1} \sum_{j, j \neq k} \{g_j(\mathbf{x}_n; \Lambda)\}^{-\mu} \right]^{-1/\mu} \tag{4}$$

is a typical definition, where the classification is expressed by decision on a scalar value, and μ is a positive number. $d_k(\mathbf{x}_n; \Lambda) > 0$ implies misclassification, and $d_k(\mathbf{x}_n; \Lambda) \leqslant 0$ means correct classification. Note here that varying the value of μ allows one to realize various decisions. The third step completes MCE by embedding the misclassification measure in a loss

$$\ell_k(\mathbf{x}_n; \Lambda) = \ell_k(d_k(\mathbf{x}_n; \Lambda)), \tag{5}$$

where $\ell_k(\ )$ is a monotonically-increasing smooth function. The loss is introduced to evaluate a classification result.

We focus on a smooth classification error count loss

$$\ell_k(\mathbf{x}_n; \Lambda) = \frac{1}{1 + e^{-\alpha(d_k(\mathbf{x}_n; \Lambda) + \beta)}}, \quad \alpha > 0, \tag{6}$$

where α and β are real numbers. It is now clearer that MCE can directly attain the minimum classification error situation. As a first step, let us assume that the discriminant function is selected so as to have the correct form of the *a posteriori* probability $P_\Lambda(C_i|\mathbf{x})$. The Bayes minimum risk is then expressed as

$$\mathcal{E} = \sum_{k=1}^{M} \int_{\mathcal{X}_k} P_\Lambda(\mathbf{x}, C_k) 1(\mathbf{x} \in C_k) \, d\mathbf{x}, \tag{7}$$

where

$$1(\mathcal{A}) = \begin{cases} 1, & \text{if } \mathcal{A} \text{ is true} \\ 0, & \text{otherwise,} \end{cases}$$

$$\mathcal{X}_k = \{\mathbf{x} \in \mathcal{X} \mid P_\Lambda(C_k|\mathbf{x}) \neq \max_j P_\Lambda(C_j|\mathbf{x})\},$$

and

$$\mathcal{X} \text{ is the entire observation space.}$$

This can be approximated by the misclassification measure and the loss as follows:

$$\mathcal{E} = \sum_{k=1}^{M} \int_{\mathcal{X}_k} P_\Lambda(\mathbf{x}, C_k) 1(\mathbf{x} \in C_k) 1\left(P_\Lambda(C_k|\mathbf{x}) \neq \max_i P_\Lambda(C_i|\mathbf{x}) \right) d\mathbf{x} \tag{8}$$

$$\simeq \sum_{k=1}^{M} \int_{\mathcal{X}_k} P_\Lambda(\mathbf{x}, C_k) 1(\mathbf{x} \in C_k) \ell_k(d_k(\mathbf{x}; \Lambda)) \, d\mathbf{x}.$$

An important point here is the fact that the approximation accuracy of equation (8) can be arbitrarily increased by varying the smoothing constants in the MCE functions such as the loss. That is to say, MCE possesses the capability to approximate the Bayes minimum risk with arbitrarily high accuracy, in the extreme case of this discriminant function approach. This result proves that MCE potentially bridges the gap between the discriminant function approach and the Bayes minimum risk.

The smoothness of MCE has turned out to be extremely useful in various stages of analysis. In fact, the previous discussion already shows that the use of L_p-norm form greatly increases the generality of the classification rule formalism. In addition, the effect of smoothness on training robustness should be addressed. To describe this point, we consider an empirical classification error rate

$$L(\Lambda) = \frac{1}{N} \sum_{n=1}^{N} \sum_{k=1}^{M} \ell_k(\mathbf{x}_n; \Lambda) 1(\mathbf{x}_n \in C_k). \tag{9}$$

Since sample distributions are unknown, this sample average-form, empirical error is only one measurable objective in a real situation. If the loss is a real error count, i.e. a piecewise linear 2-step function, this error rate has the shape of a piecewise linear, multi-step surface. As the number of samples increases, the surface becomes smoother and goes to a continuous, curved surface. On the other hand, the use of a smooth loss makes the surface of this error rate smoother, even if the number of samples is not increased. This effect is equivalent to perturbing and increasing the effective size of design samples. If this perturbation is properly done around the original locations of given samples, the resultant situation can increase the robustness. Interestingly, it was demonstrated that the smoothness did not drastically change the shape of the empirical error based on piecewise 2-value losses, i.e. it seems that the perturbation was locally effective. Therefore, it is probably true that this smoothness has a certain contribution to classifier robustness. This effect is evidently worth further investigating, and especially the relation between the loss smoothness and the sample finiteness (scatter property) should be an interesting topic.

18.2.3 Generalized probabilistic descent method

As suggested by the name, GPD is a modern, extended version of the classical probabilistic descent method (Amari, 1967). GPD gives a rigorous form, suited for gradient search-based design, for classifying **dynamic** (variable-durational) patterns by various kinds of system structures.

We have assumed that the pattern sample is a fixed dimensional vector. However, many kinds of natural patterns such as speech signals are actually dynamic. For instance, it is obvious that segments of the same phoneme class can have different durations. A proper classification of these dynamic patterns requires a significant extension of the traditional classification methods. In fact, even the modern artificial neural networks can hardly overcome this difficulty, and as a result many hybrid structures incorporating hidden Markov models (HMM) or Dynamic Time Warping (DTW) based on Dynamic Programming (DP) have been reported (Howell, 1988; Sakoe *et al.*, 1989; Iwamida *et al.*, 1990; Kimber *et al.*, 1990; Yu *et al.*, 1990; Gao *et al.*, 1990; Katagiri and Lee, 1990). Let us assume in the remaining part of this section that all samples' $\mathbf{x}_n$'s are dynamic. Moreover, let us assume that a DTW distance classifier assigning a dynamic reference pattern, denoted by $\mathbf{r}$, to each competing class is prepared to classify these dynamic patterns; $\mathbf{r}_k \subset \Lambda$ and $\mathbf{r}_k \in C_k$. These reference patterns are designed through the pursuit of the minimum classification error situation. Measuring different durational patterns requires the normalization of duration. As widely seen in speech recognition, DTW uses a discriminant function

$$g_k(\mathbf{x}_n; \Lambda) = \min_{\theta} \{D_\theta(\mathbf{x}_n, \mathbf{r}_k)\}, \tag{10}$$

where $D_\theta(\mathbf{x}, \mathbf{r}_k)$ is a **path distance** accumulated along the θth best (smallest distance) path selected by the DP-matching between $\mathbf{x}_n$ and $\mathbf{r}_k$ among all the possible Θ paths. The operation searching the best normalization path associated with the minimum accumulated distance is obviously discontinuous in Λ. This is an impediment in the gradient descent method. A GPD solution to this problem is to replace the best path search operation (minimum distance search operation) by a smooth search function based on L_p-norm form

$$g_k(\mathbf{x}_n; \Lambda) = \left[\sum_{\theta=1}^{\Theta} \{D_\theta(\mathbf{x}_n, \mathbf{r}_k)\}^{-\xi} \right]^{-1/\xi}, \tag{11}$$

where ξ is a positive constant. Notice that equation (11) closely approximates equation (10), when ξ goes to infinity.

Similarly, the idea of smooth search operation is utilized to define a discriminant function

$$g_k(\mathbf{x}_n; \Lambda) = \left[\sum_{b=1}^{B_k} \{D(\mathbf{x}_n, \mathbf{r}_k^b)\}^{-\zeta} \right]^{-1/\zeta}, \tag{12}$$

where

$$D(\mathbf{x}_n, \mathbf{r}_k^b) = \left[\sum_{\theta=1}^{\Theta} \{D_\theta(\mathbf{x}_n, \mathbf{r}_k^b)\}^{-\xi} \right]^{-1/\xi},$$

$D(\mathbf{x}_n, \mathbf{r}_k^b)$ is a **reference distance** between $\mathbf{x}_n$ and the bth best C_k reference $\mathbf{r}_k^b$, and B_k is the number of C_k references, for a classifier in which multiple reference patterns are assigned to each class. When ζ goes to infinity, equation (12) approximates a discriminant function which represents the corresponding class by the smallest reference distance of the class. Note that the idea of a smooth operation, underlying equations (11) and (12), is conceptually the same with that in equation (4), i.e. the smooth comparison among the competing classes.

The entire process of classifying multi-class dynamic patterns is now formalized in a smooth functional form suited for gradient search. Consequently, one can design a distance classifier having at least a locally-minimum classification error situation, by using a smooth loss, e.g. equation (6). There are several versions of gradient search algorithms. The selection here is flexible. One major motivation for GPD is to be able to accomplish adaptive learning. It is highly desirable that a classifier always learns to refine itself given a new sample. It is probably even more desirable to be able to adaptively accomplish minimization of the expected classification error. The following probabilistic descent theorem provided a rigorous mathematical ground which satisfies these requirements (Amari, 1967).

[Probabilistic Descent Theorem]
Given $\mathbf{x} \in C_k$, *if the classifier parameter adjustment* $\delta\Lambda(\mathbf{x}, C_k, \Lambda)$ *is specified as*

$$\delta\Lambda(\mathbf{x}, C_k, \Lambda) = -\varepsilon \mathbf{U} \nabla \ell_k(\mathbf{x}; \Lambda) \tag{13}$$

where $\mathbf{U}$ *is a positive-definite matrix and* ε *is a small positive real number, then*

$$E[\delta L(\Lambda)] \leqslant 0, \tag{14}$$

where

$$L(\Lambda) = \sum_{k=1}^{M} \int P_\Lambda(\mathbf{x}, C_k) 1(\mathbf{x} \in C_k) \ell_k(\mathbf{x}; \Lambda) \, d\mathbf{x}. \tag{15}$$

Furthermore, if an infinite sequence of random observations $\mathbf{x}_t$ *is presented for training and the parameter adjustment rule of (13) is utilized with a corresponding step size sequence* ε_t *which satisfies*

(i)
$$\sum_{t=1}^{\infty} \varepsilon_t \to \infty; \quad \text{and} \tag{16}$$

(ii)
$$\sum_{t=1}^{\infty} \varepsilon_t^2 < \infty, \tag{17}$$

then the parameter sequence Λ_t *according to*

$$\Lambda_{t+1} = \Lambda_t + \delta\Lambda(\mathbf{x}_t, C_k, \Lambda_t) \tag{18}$$

converges with probability one to a Λ^* *which results in a local minimum of* $L(\Lambda)$.

The above smooth formalization and the probabilistic descent theorem thus complete the adaptive discriminative training for classifying dynamic patterns by the distance classifiers.

We have used a distance measure as our discriminant function. However, a probability measure is most likely a more useful discriminant function. To this end, Chou *et al.* (1992) and Rainton and Sagayama (1992) provide a detailed description of the method to design an HMM classifer, which is considered most useful for classifying dynamic patterns at present, in the MCE framework.

Notice that a fixed-dimensional vector is merely a special case of a dynamic pattern, and that no specific assumptions of the patterns were made in the previous discussion. It is thus evident that MCE/GPD can be applied to an extremely wide range of pattern classification.

18.2.4 *Relations with other classification/training methods*

We briefly refer to the relations between MCE/GPD and other training methods. The readers may notice that the probabilistic descent theorem shows the convergence principle of an adaptive form of Error Back-Propagation. In fact, a multi-layer feed-forward network, which is conventionally designed with minimum squared error criterion and Error Back-Propagation, can be designed in a manner more consistent with classification by using MCE/GPD.

There are several attempts to pursue the minimum classification error situation, e.g. a distance classifier using a traditional, piecewise linear error rate function (Ando and Ozeki, 1991) and a multi-layer perceptron using the Classification Figure of Merit (Hampshire and Waibel, 1990). MCE/GPD is quite different from these in terms of both development philosophy and resulting formalization. On the other hand, Learning Vector Quantization (LVQ) to is a design method aiming at misclassification reduction, though it was intuitively developed, particularly without explicit measurement of error counts (Kohonen, 1986, 1990; McDermott, 1990). Interestingly, LVQ can be formalized as a simplified implementation, specially prepared for a multi-reference Euclidian distance classifier, of MCE/GPD. The detailed relation with LVQ is shown in Katagiri *et al.* (1990, 1991b). It is worth pointing out here that using LVQ is a useful implementation of MCE/GPD.

18.2.5 *Applications*

MCE/GPD has been vigorously applied to speech pattern classification, and its promising capability has clearly been demonstrated.

Applications to a multi-layer feed-forward network, particularly likelihood network and distance network, are described in detail in Katagiri *et al.* (1991b), where the effectiveness of MCE/GPD was observed on the Fisher iris task. Let us introduce here a corollary-like generalization of results in Katagiri *et al.* (1991b), i.e. a mixture-distribution continuous HMM classifier can be formalized in a generalized form by assigning Markov states to an output node of a three-layer likelihood network.

Application to speech pattern classification was started in a somewhat limited way, using a DTW classifier (Chang and Juang, 1990; Chang *et al.*, 1991). A limited implementation in a hybrid form was proposed in Chen and Chen (1991) too. Full application to DTW systems was performed in Chang and Juang (1992) and Komori and Katagiri (1992a). In particular, the former studied the smoother case of the minimum search operation of equation (12), and demonstrated the effectiveness of using multiple normalization paths. Application to HMM systems was specially formalized as segment GPD and showed great promise (Chou *et al.*, 1992). Successful results for HMM classifiers were also observed in Rainton and Sagayama (1992). It should be noted that these HMM applications showed an important departure from a rather simple classification of isolated-mode speech utterances, i.e. they provided a training meachanism for applying MCE/GPD to classification of arbitrary speech segments such as subwords, words, and phrases. This extended idea has proved to be useful in a DTW classifier too (McDermott and Katagiri, 1992). Furthermore (Sugiyama and Kurinami, 1992), where speaker mapping was trained based on MCE, showed a new direction of the application. Ohkura *et al.* (1992) showed the MCE/GPD superiority in a noisy speech classification. Application of MCE/ GPD is still in the beginning stage, however results so far all clearly demonstrate its promising capability.

18.3 Task formalization using smooth functions

We have considered in this chapter that the pattern recognition process consists of feature extraction and pattern classification. However, a real pattern recognition process is more complex. For example, in speech pattern recognition, the classification process should closely relate to a language process which may decide *a priori* probabilities. Moreover, although a simple speech classification scheme assumes that a sample (i.e. a speech segment) is extracted beforehand from continuous utterances, a real speech recognizer needs to include this segmentation process. It is certainly desirable that MCE/GPD can handle all these real situations properly; doing so may be a real goal of the MCE/GPD approach. MCE/GPD actually possesses a great potential which allows one to design recognizers that are even more general than in the above application studies. A recent study on minimum spotting error learning is showing signs of success in this new, advanced application (Komori and Katagiri, 1992b).

Our simple 2-stage definition of pattern recognition suggests a straightforward extension of MCE/GPD application, i.e. an MCE/GPD design for both feature extraction and classification (Biem and Katagiri, 1992). Here the original sample is passed to the feature-extraction and classification stages in a consistent manner, directly aimed at the (locally) minimum classification error objective. We call this extended use of MCE/GPD Discriminative Feature Extraction (DFE).

DFE is essentially equivalent to MCE/GPD. Therefore, we don't need any new, specific formalization. One may embed a feature extraction process, conditioned by the given task and available resources, in the MCE/GPD functional form. MCE/GPD is mainly based on statistics, far from heuristics. However, expertise specific to a task is certainly useful in this mathematical approach. For example, applying DFE to acoustical speech utterances directly would be rather foolhardy, or rather, it would be more realistic to employ a power spectrum, which is prepared based on speech science knowledge, as input to the recognizer. Implementation of this new concept is thus task-dependent. DFE applications for speech recognition are described in detail in the next section.

18.4 Discriminative feature extraction for speech recognition

18.4.1 Various realizations

Mainly based on knowledge of hearing and speech perception, speech is usually represented, for the purpose of recognition, as a sequence of short-time power spectra or related parameter vectors. This kind of extraction (i.e. power spectrum sequence) is certainly a proper base for an effective DFE application.

A short-time power spectrum is generally computed by using FFT or autoregressive modeling. This is sometimes computed with a band-pass filter bank. Frequency scaling is usually linear, or Bark scale, or Mel scale. Spectrum intensity is often scaled logarithmically. The idea of weighting too is widely used to control feature sensitivity. As is well known, there are many conventional realizations of such sequences. However, most of these realizations are based on analysis of human capability, and thus are not necessarily directly applicable to statistically-designed machine recognition.

DFE attempts to accomplish extractions from the standpoint of minimizing misclassifications. In place of the Bark scale, a new frequency scaling could be found. A linear representation based on autoregressive modeling too could be extended to a discriminative non-linear version. From among many possibilities, we specifically focus in this paper on cepstrum region design of power spectrum.

18.4.2 Application to lifter design

A short-time logarithmic power spectrum pattern is converted to a cepstrum vector through the Inverse Fourier Transform. In this conversion, frequency is mapped to quefrency, which corresponds to time. Let us consider a cepstrum pattern sequence as the recognizer input. It is well known that phoneme class identity, which is useful for speech recognition, locally exists in the low quefrency region. Therefore, a conventional speech recognizer selectively uses this narrow region cepstrum components as a feature for classification, by using a time window called a lifter. Notice that liftering (applying a lifter to a cepstrum vector) performs the feature extraction. A

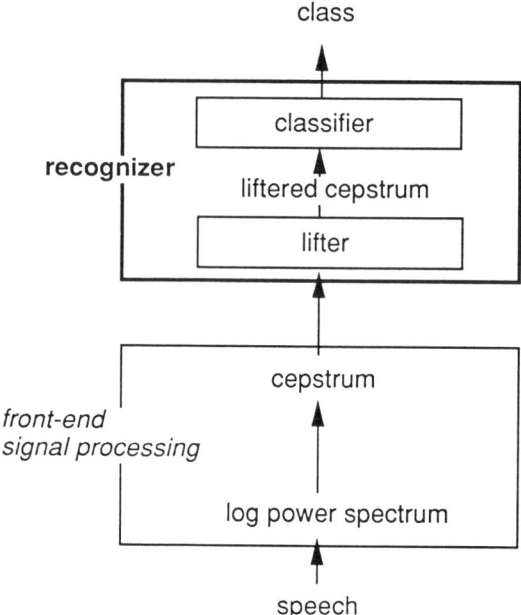

Figure 18.1 *Speech recognition using cepstrum.*

liftered cepstrum sequence is the pattern to be classified. Figure 18.1 illustrates this recognition process, i.e. the recognizer structure consisting of a lifter and a post-end classifier.

A liftered cepstrum sequence pattern may represent (phoneme) class identity more properly than an unliftered cepstrum pattern. The question here is how to design a good lifter. Conventionally, the duration of lifter is chosen so as to suppress the cepstrum components due to glottal source. Usual lifter shapes are those of lag or time windows, e.g. Hamming window, whose properties have been extensively analysed in spectrum estimation theory. In a somewhat advanced case, a lifter is designed over design samples so that cepstrum components relevant to classification can be emphasized (Tohkura, 1987). However, clearly, these lifters, designed independently of the minimum classification error situation, are not guaranteed to be optimal.

DFE consistently designs both the lifter and the post-end classifier within the MCE/GPD framework. An arbitrary system structure can be used for the post-end classifier. By way of example, we use a multi-layer feed-forward network. Our recognizer is illustrated in Figure 18.2. To simplify analysis of the lifter design, each node of the bottom lifter layer has only a vertical connection. The discriminant function here is each of the network outputs. MCE/GPD is then implemented accordingly.

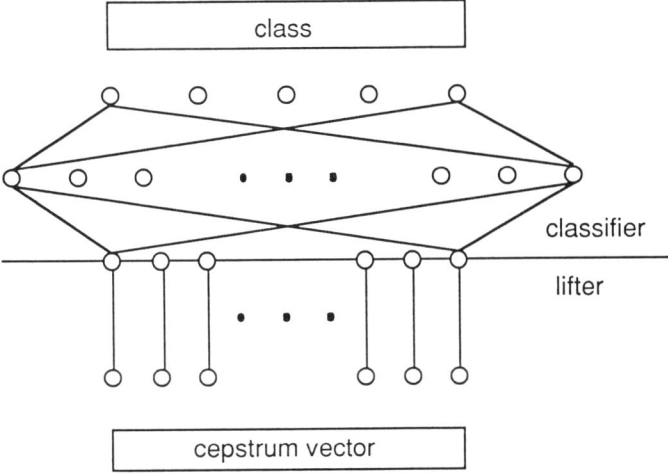

Figure 18.2 *Four-layer feed-forward network recognizer including a lifter.*

As a preliminary evaluation, we conducted experiments on the task of classifying Japanese five-category vowels. We used speech data of 100 phonetically-balanced sentences, spoken by five speakers (three males and two females) and recorded at 12 kHz sampling rate. The recognizer input was just a fixed-dimensional cepstrum vector which corresponds to a single time-windowed vowel segment; i.e. our sample was not a dynamic pattern. Each sample was prepared as follows: (1) a center segment of vowel was extracted by using a 42 ms Hamming window from the database; (2) the extracted speech signal was then converted to a 256-point cepstrum vector by using FFT/IFFT. We collected 3500 samples in total; half for design and half for training.

The recognizer was investigated with different settings for experimental conditions such as recognizer size, and produced the highest accuracy, 96.8% on design data and 88.7% on testing data. For comparison, we also evaluated the conventional use of a rectangular lifter: the rectangular lifter was realized on the lowest lifter layer by assigning two constants, 1 and 0, to the connection weights: only the post-end classifier was trained. This conventional way could not excel DFE in recognition accuracy. Although different lifter lengths were carefully tried, only 89.1% and 87.3% were attained on design and testing data, respectively.

A lifter example of the DFE design is shown in Figure 18.3. This lifter clearly suppresses cepstrum components in a high quefrency region which is usually occupied by information irrelevant to phoneme classification. The lifter also suppresses extremely-low quefrency components, which probably correspond to speaker identity. It is likely that DFE successfully distinguished

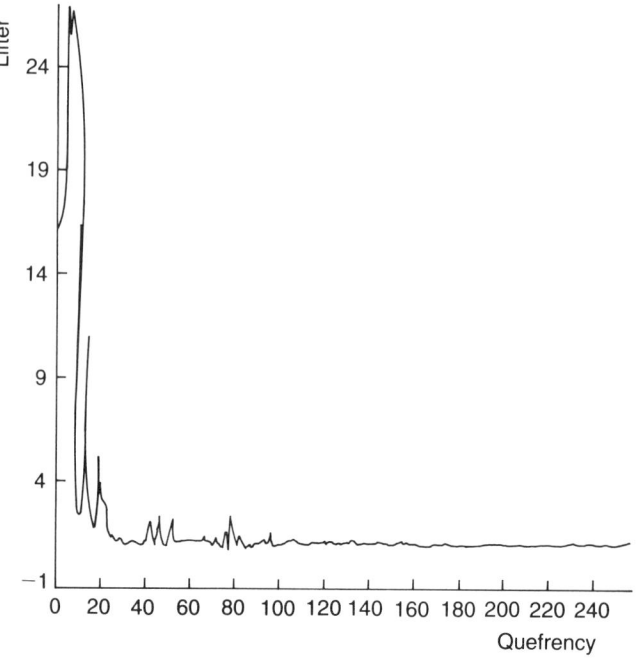

Figure 18.3 *Lifter example of the Discriminative Feature Extraction design.*

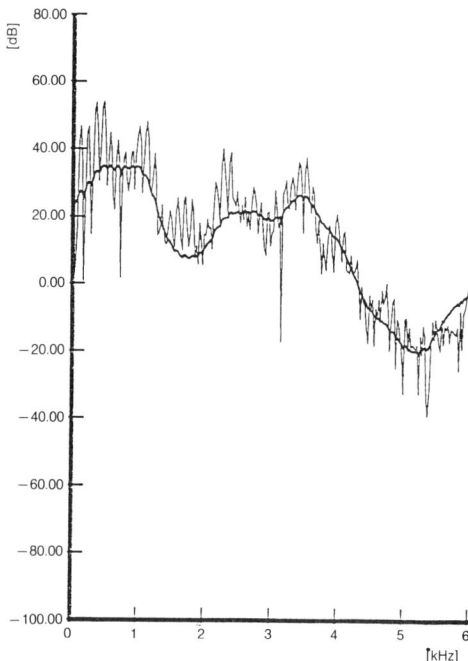

Figure 18.4 *Logarithmic power spectra of a single input cepstrum example: one calculated without the lifter (thin curve) and one calculated using the lifter in Figure 18.3 (thick line).*

vowel class identity from other features such as speaker identity. Observing the spectrum domain helps understand the results. Figure 18.4 shows two logarithmic power spectra of a single input: one was calculated without liftering, meaning that this corresponds to the input cepstrum vector, and one was calculated by using the lifter in Figure 18.3. The smoothed, liftered spectrum removes the harmonic structure due to vocal source excitation, and brings out the spectrum envelope, which mainly corresponds to the phoneme class identity.

The experimental results in the above paragraph indicate the fundamental possibility that our new design method can be superior to conventional methods. The DFE learning method is an automatic and efficient way of extracting possible feature parameters.

The results over the testing samples may need further analysis. The difference in the DFE results between design and testing data should be studied from the viewpoint of training robustness. The fact that the lifter in Figure 18.3 is not so smooth must relate to this big drop. Similar to highly-discriminative, nonlinear artificial neural networks, the smoothness of feature extraction should be carefully studied in our approach too.

18.5 Summary

In this chapter, we have summarized the new discriminative learning theory called MCE/GPD and also introduced Discriminative Feature Extraction as one of its extended applications. A motivation underlying the proposed method is to formalize the entire task at hand in a smooth functional form and efficiently find a practical solution on this form. Our approach provides a straightforward and sound basis for the realization of long standing minimum classification error pattern recognition problem.

Acknowledgements

The authors would like to thank Erik McDermott and Takashi Komori for their insightful discussions and patient support in accomplishing this study.

References

Amari, S. (1967) A theory of adaptive pattern classifiers. *IEEE, Trans. on EC*, **16**(3), 299–307.

Ando A. and Ozeki, K. (1991) A clustering algorithm to minimize recognition error function. *Trans of IEICE (A)*, **74-A**(3), 360–7 (in Japanese).

Biem, A. and Katagiri, S. (1992) Cepstrum liftering based on minimum classification error. *Tech. Report SP92-26*, pp. 17–24.

Chang, P.-C. and Juang, B.-H. (1990) Design of discriminant functions for distortion sequences in dynamic pattern matching for speech recognition. *J. Acoust. Soc. Am.*, *Suppl. 1*, **88**, S102.

Chang, P.-C. and Juang, B.-H. (1992) Discriminative template training for dynamic programming speech recognition. *Proc. ICASSP92*, **1**, pp. 493–6.

Chang, P.-C., Chen, S.-H. and Juang, B.-H. (1991) *Discriminative Analysis of Distortion Sequences in Speech Recognition. Proc. ICASSP91*, **1**, pp. 549–52.

Chen, W.-Y and Chen, S.-H. (1991) Word recognition based on the combination of a sequential neural network and the GPDM discriminative training algorithm. *Neural Networks for Signal Processing*, 376–84.

Chou, W., Juang, B.-H. and Lee, C.-H. (1992) Segmental GPD training of HMM based speech recognition. *Proc. ICASSP92*, **1**, pp. 473–6.

Gao, Y.-Q., Huang, T.-Y. and Chen, D.-W. (1990) HMM-based warping in neural networks. *Proc. ICASSP90*, **1**, pp. 501–4.

Hampshire, J. and Waibel, A. (1990) A novel objective function for improved phoneme recognition using time-delay neural networks. *Trans. Neural Networks*, **1**(2), 216–28.

Howell, D. (1988) The multi-layer perceptron as a discriminative post processor for hidden Markov networks. *FASE, Proc. of 7th FASE Symposium Speech*, pp. 1389–96.

Iwamida, H., Katagiri, S., McDermott, E. and Tohkura Y. (1990) A hybrid speech recognition system using HMMs with an LVQ-trained codebook. *J. Acoust. Soc. Jpn (e)*, **11**(5), 277–86.

Juang, B.-H. and Katagiri S. (1992a) Discrimination learning for minimum error classification. *IEEE Trans. on SP*.

Juang, B.-H. and Katagiri, S. (1992b) Discriminative training. *J Acoust. Soc. Jpn (E)*, **13**(A), 333–9.

Katagiri, S. and Lee, C.-H. (1990) *A New HMM/LVQ Hybrid Algorithm for Speech Recognition.* Proc. GLOBECOM90, **2**, pp. 1032–6.

Katagiri, S., Lee, C.-H. and Juang, B.-H. (1990) A generalized probabilistic descent method. *ASJ, Proc. of Fall Meeting*, **1**, 141–2.

Katagiri, S., Lee, C.-H. and Juang B.-H. (1991a) New discriminative training algorithms based on the generalized probabilistic descent method. *IEEE, Neural Networks for Signal Processing*, 299–308.

Katagiri, S., Lee, C.-H. and Juang, B.-H. (1991b) Discriminative multi-layer feed-forward networks, *Neural Networks for Signal Processing*, 11–20.

Kimber D., Bush, M. and Tajchman, G. (1990) Speaker-independent vowel classification using hidden Markov models and LVQ2. *Proc. ICASSP90*, **1**, pp. 497–500.

Kohonen, T. (1986) Learning vector quantization for pattern recognition. Helsinki University of Technology, *Report TKK-F-A601*.

Kohonen, T. (1990) The self-organizing map. *Proc. IEEE*, **78**(9), 1464–80.

Komori, T. and Katagiri, S. (1992a) Application of a generalized probabilistic descent method of dynamic time warping based speech recognition. *Proc. ICASSP92*, **1**, pp. 497–500.

Komori, T. and Katagiri, S. (1992b) GPD training for spotting, *ASJ, Proc. Fall Meeting*, **1**, pp. 195–6.

McDermott, E. (1990) LVQ3 for phoneme recognition. *Proc. of Spring Meeting*, **1**, pp. 151–2.

McDermott, E. and Katagiri S. (1992) Prototype-based discriminative training for various speech units. *Proc. ICASSP92*, **1**, pp. 417–20.

Ohkura, K., Rainton, D. and Sugiyama, M. (1992) Noise-robust HMMs based on minimum error classification. *ASJ, Proc. Fall Meeting*, **1**, pp. 73–4 (in Japanese).

Rainton, D. and Sagayama, S. (1992) Minimum error classificatioin training of HMMs – implementational details and experimental results. *Tech. Report SP91-107*, pp. 39–46.

Sakoe, H., Isotani, R., Yoshida, K. and Watanabe, T. (1989) Speaker independent word recognition using dynamic programming neural networks. *IEEE Proc. ICASSP89*, **1**, pp. 29–32.

Sugiyama, M. and Kurinami, K. (1992) Minimal classification error optimization for a speaker mapping neural networks. *Neural Networks for Signal Processing II*, pp. 233–42.

Tohkura, Y. (1987) A weighted cepstral distance measure for speech recognition. *Trans. on ASSP*, **35**(10), 301–9.

Yu, G., Russell, W., Schwartz, R., and Makhoul, J. (1990) Discrimination analysis and supervised vector quantization for continuous speech recognition. *Proc. ICASSP90*, **2**, pp. 685–8.

19

Word reading in damaged connectionist networks: computational and neuropsychological implications

DAVID C. PLAUT* and TIM SHALLICE†

*Department of Psychology, Carnegie Mellon University, Pittsburgh, PA 15213-3890, USA
†Department of Psychology, University College, London WC1E 6BT, UK

19.1 Introduction

Connectionist networks are also called **neural** networks because of their abstract structural similarity to groups of neurons. Based on this similarity, many researchers believe that computation in these networks reflects important properties of neural computation. One piece of evidence often put forward in support of this claim is that, like brains, connectionist networks tend to degrade gracefully with damage. That is, if some proportion of units and/or connections are removed from a network, performance on a task is typically only partially impaired rather than completely abolished. Most demonstrations of graceful degradation in networks have used only very general measures of performance, such as total error on a task. However, the argument that connectionist computation is fundamentally similar to neural computation would be far more compelling if the **way** in which connectionist networks degraded under damage – their patterns of impaired performance – mirrored the patterns of impaired behavior observed in patients with neurological damage. To the extent that this held, a detailed investigation

Artificial Neural Networks for Speech and Vision. Edited by Richard J. Mammone. Published in 1993 by Chapman & Hall, London. ISBN 0 412 54850 X

of the behavior of damaged connectionist networks would provide insight into both normal and impaired human cognition.

A complementary motivation for studying the effects of damage in networks is to extend our understanding of the nature of computation in the networks themselves. Here again, our concern is not just with the development of a network that accomplishes a task, but with understanding **how** the network accomplishes the task – the nature of its representations and processes. In most connectionist research, the adequacy of a network is evaluated by testing how well its performance generalizes to novel external input drawn from the same distribution as the training examples. In a similar way, damage to a network has the effect of generating unfamiliar activity in the remaining portions of the network. However, damage can affect internal representations in ways that cannot be directly mimicked by manipulations of the external input. Thus, the behavior of the network under damage may provide a more general, and for some purposes, more informative, indication of the nature of the representations and processes the network develops during training.

In studying patients with brain damage, the field of cognitive neuropsychology attempts to relate their patterns of impaired and preserved abilities to models of normal cognitive functioning, with the intent both of explaining the behavior of the patients in terms of the effects of damage in the model, and of informing the model based on the observed behavior of patients (Coltheart, 1985; Ellis and Young, 1988). In an analogous fashion, this chapter presents an approach that might be called 'connectionist neuropsychology', in which analyses of the effects of damage in connectionist networks are used both to provide a comprehensive, detailed account of the cognitive deficits of a particular class of brain-injured patients, and to clarify the nature of the representations and processes that develop in the networks themselves through learning. To illustrate this approach, we will focus on acquired reading disorder known as 'deep dyslexia', in which patients can pronounce a written word only via its meaning, and occasionally make errors in this process. The chapter begins with a summary of these patients' characteristics and a brief description of a preliminary connectionist model. Following this, results are presented from a systematic investigation of the major design decisions that entered into developing the model, relating to the task definition, the network architecture, the training procedure, and the testing procedure. In the interest of space, some results will only be summarized here; details may be found in Plaut and Shallice (1993). The particular emphasis of this chapter will be on results, not described in that paper, that illustrate how studying damaged networks can lead to computational insights that might not arise so clearly within other methodologies. Specifically, results presented here point out some inherent difficulties with distributed output representations, and clarify differences in the computational properties of back-propagation networks and deterministic Boltzmann Machines trained with contrastive Hebbian learning.

19.1.1 Deep dyslexia

Brain damage can produce selective impairments in a wide range of cognitive domains, including high-level vision, attention, speech and language, learning and memory, planning and motor control. The class of impairments which perhaps have received the greatest theoretical attention over the last decade or so are those that involve word reading, the so called 'acquired dyslexias'. Of these, deep dyslexia is among the most perplexing (Coltheart *et al.*, 1980). Deep dyslexic patients can only read via meaning, as evidenced by their almost complete inability to read meaningless pronounceable letter strings (e.g. MAVE). However, they also have some problems reading words – which have semantics – suggesting that the process by which words access their meanings is also impaired in these patients. The nature of this additional impairment is reflected in the errors that deep dyslexic patients typically make in oral reading – in particular, the occurrence of **semantic** errors (e.g. CAT ⇒ 'dog'). However, what makes deep dyslexia such a theoretical challenge is that virtually all patients who make semantic errors also exhibit a peculiar combination of other symptoms. Central among these are other types of errors: **visual** (e.g. CAT ⇒ 'cot'), mixed **visual-and-semantic** (e.g. CAT ⇒ 'rat'), **derivational** (e.g. WALKED ⇒ 'walk'), and **visual-then-semantic** (e.g. SYMPATHY ⇒ 'orchestra', presumably via **symphony**). These patients also produce some responses that are completely unrelated to the stimulus (e.g. CAT ⇒ 'mug'). Furthermore, their ability to read a word correctly strongly depends on its part-of speech (nouns > adjectives > verbs > function words) and its concreteness or imageability (concrete, highly imageable words > abstract, less imageable words). Strangely, the effects of concreteness – a semantic variable – interact with visual similarity in errors, such that abstract words are more likely than concrete words to produce visual errors, and the resulting responses tend to be more concrete than the stimulus (e.g. SCANDAL ⇒ 'sandals'). Of these effects, the derivational errors and part-of-speech effects may be secondary to other characteristics (Funnell, 1987), but any account of the disorder needs to explain all the other apparently independent symptoms.

19.1.2. A preliminary connectionist model

Hinton and Shallice (1991) (hereafter H&S) put forward a connectionist account of why semantic, visual and mixed visual-and-semantic errors co-occur when the process that derives the meanings of words is damaged. Based on previous work by Hinton and Sejnowski (1986) with Boltzmann Machines, they trained a recurrent back-propagation network to map from the written form (i.e. orthography) of 40 three- or four-letter words to a simplified representation of their semantics, described in terms of 68 pre-determined semantic features. The architecture of the network, shown in

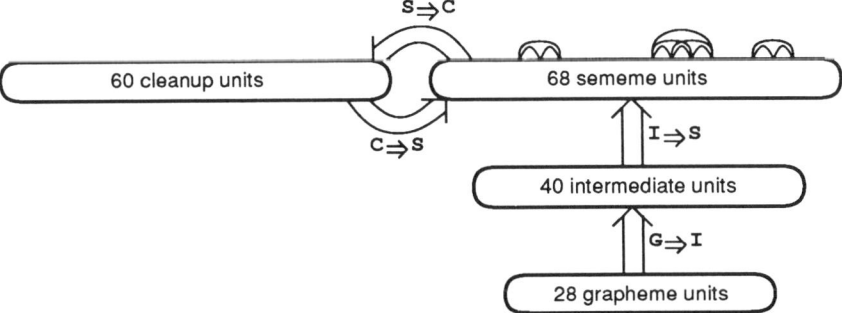

Figure 19.1 *Network architecture used by Hinton and Shallice. Arrows represent sets of connections that were lesioned in the study – they are labeled by the initials of the source and destination layers (e.g. $G \Rightarrow I$ for grapheme-to-intermediate connections). Only the randomly selected 25% of the possible connections in each of these sets were initially included in the network.*

Figure 19.1, consists of two pathways: a **direct** pathway, from **grapheme** units to **sememe** units via **intermediate** units, that generates initial semantic activity; and a **clean-up** pathway, from the sememes to **clean-up** units and back to the sememes, that iteratively refines these initial semantics into the exact semantics of the presented word. Thus, in solving the task, the network learns to make the pattern of semantic features for each word into an **attractor** in the 68-dimensional space of possible semantic representations. After training, H&S systematically lesioned the network by removing proportions of units or connections, or by adding noise to the weights, and found that the damaged network occasionally settled into a pattern of semantic activity that satisfied response criteria for a word other than the one presented. These error responses were more often semantically similar to the stimulus (i.e. from the same category) and/or visually similar to the stimulus (i.e. overlapped in at least one letter) than would be expected by chance. While the network showed a greater tendency to produce visual errors with damage near the input layer and semantic errors with damage near the output layer, both types of error occurred for almost all sites of damage.

The occurrence of semantic errors in the model is straightforward to explain. Damage to the direct pathway corrupts the initial semantic activity caused by a word. If this corrupted pattern now happens to fall within the basin of a neighboring attractor, the operation of the clean-up pathway would cause the network to settle into the semantics of a related word. Similarly, damage to the clean-up pathway alters the layout of the basins themselves, such that the normal initial semantic pattern generated by a word might fall within a neighboring attractor.

Damage to the direct pathway would also be expected to lead to visual errors, since this pathway must rely on visual distinctions among words to generate initial semantic activity that falls within the appropriate attractor basin. What is less obvious, both in patients and in the network, is why damage within semantics should lead to visual errors. H&S provide an account in terms of the nature of the attractors that develop in mapping between two arbitrarily related domains. Connectionist networks have difficulty learning to produce quite different outputs from very similar inputs, and yet, often, visually similar words have unrelated meanings (e.g. CAT and COT). In an attractor network, visually similar words are free to generate similar initial semantic patterns as long as these patterns each fall somewhere within the correct basins of attraction. As a result, in this region of semantic space, neighboring attractors correspond to **visually** similar words (see Figure 19.2). Semantic damage distorts these basins, occasionally causing the normal initial semantic pattern of a word to be captured within the basin of a visually similar word. Essentially, the layout of attractor basins must be sensitive to both visual and semantic similarity, and so these metrics are reflected in the types of errors that occur as a result of damage.

H&S's simulation provides a unified account of the nature and co-occurrence of semantic, visual, and mixed visual-and-semantic errors in deep dyslexia. By contrast, most previous explanations (e.g. Morton and Patterson, 1980) have had to resort to proposing separate, independent lesions – one producing semantic errors and the other producing visual errors. Thus, these accounts provide no principled explanation of why virtually all patients who make semantic errors also make visual errors (i.e. why patients who have

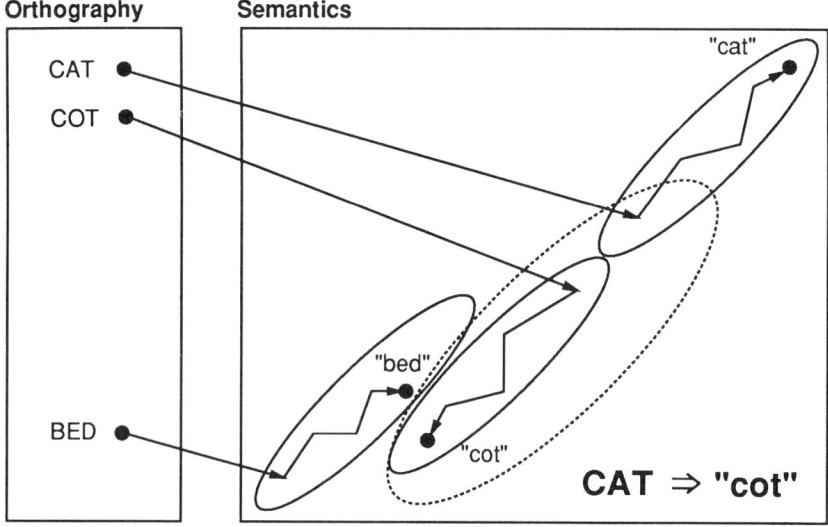

Figure 19.2 *How semantic damage can cause visual errors.* ○ : *normal basins of attraction;* ⟨⟩ : *a basin after damage.*

one lesion almost always have the other). H&S demonstrated that this co-occurrence of error types is a natural consequence of the effects of single lesions in a network that maps between visual and semantic representations of words.

Although encouraging, H & S's work is limited in two important ways. The first is that only a few of the many characteristics of deep dyslexic patients were simulated. To constitute an adequate account of these patients, the approach would have to be extended to encompass the remaining major characteristics as well – particularly, the other error types and the effects of concreteness/imageability. The second limitation is that, although H&S attribute their results to general properties of distributed representations and attractors, they investigated only a single type of network that inevitably had many specific features. They implicitly assumed that these specific features did not significantly contribute to the overall behavior of the network under damage. Clearly, it would be impossible to evaluate and improve on every aspect of the H&S model. In the following sections, each of the major design decisions that went into developing the model are systematically explored: the definition of the task of reading via meaning, the specification of a network architecture, the use of a particular training procedure, and the application of a testing procedure for evaluating the network's behavior under damage. The first issue we address is the testing procedure since its results are used in later sections.

19.2 The testing procedure

Most data on deep dyslexic reading comes from tasks in which the patient produces a verbal response to a visually presented word. Since the output of the H&S model to a letter string consists of a pattern of semantic activity, some **external** procedure is needed to convert this pattern into an explicit response so that it can be compared with the oral reading responses of deep dyslexic patients. The procedure H&S used compares the semantic activity produced by the network with the correct semantics of all known words, selecting the closest-matching word as long as the match is sufficiently good (the **proximity** criterion) and sufficiently better than any other match (the **gap** criterion). The rationale for these criteria is that semantic activity that is too unfamiliar or ambiguous would be unable to drive an output system effectively. In this way H&S's use of response criteria differs from approaches that simply take the best-matching known output as the response regardless of the quality of the match (Patterson *et al.*, 1990; Sejnowski and Rosenberg, 1987).

However, these response criteria were inadequately motivated and were only indirectly verified as appropriate. In particular, while it may be reasonable that semantics which failed the criteria could not drive an output system, no evidence was given that semantics which satisfied the criteria could succeed in generating a response. Furthermore, the criteria are insensitive to the relative semantic and phonological discriminability of words and so may be inadvertently biased towards producing certain effects. Finally, a best-match procedure is a rather powerful operation, requiring considerable knowledge about the words on which the network has been trained. If too much of the difficulty of a problem is solved by the assumed mechanisms for generating the input or interpreting the output, the role of the network itself becomes less interesting (Lachter and Bever, 1988; Pinker and Prince, 1988). This is especially ironic as a best-match (categorization) process is exactly the sort of operation at which connectionist networks are supposed to excel (Hinton and Anderson 1981; Hopfield, 1982).

Thus, it would be a significant advance over the use of response criteria to extend the H&S model to derive an explicit phonological response on the basis of semantic activity. However, it turns out that developing such a network involves overcoming difficulties which are fairly general to connectionist networks and have arisen in a number of contexts (Nystrom and McClelland, 1991; Rumelhart and McClelland 1982; Seidenberg and McClelland, 1989). In the present domain, the problem is that the damaged network produces phonological responses which are inappropriate 'blends' of the pronunciations of known words. In this section, we illustrate this problem and demonstrate a method for overcoming it, allowing us to replicate H&S's results using networks that map from orthography to phonology via semantics.

19.2.1 Phonological blends

The problems that occur in implementing an effective output system are best illustrated by describing what happens when the most straightforward procedure is used. Specifically, we develop an output network analogous to the input network, but which takes as input the semantic representation of a word and produces a phonological representation of the word. This network is then combined with an input network that maps from orthography to semantics (essentially identical to the H&S model), resulting in a much larger network that maps from orthography to phonology via semantics.

The input to the network consists of the 40 semantic representations that served as output in the H&S model. A phonological output representation was defined in terms of 33 position-specific **phoneme** units (see Plaut and Shallice, 1993, for details). For each word, exactly one unit in each of three positions is active, possibly including a unit in the third position that explicitly represents the absence of a third phoneme. This representation allows the units that represent alternative phonemes in the same position to compete in a 'winner-take-all' fashion.

To minimize the number of independent assumptions in the complete network, the architecture of the output network was designed to be as similar as possible to that of the H&S input network. The sememe (input) units were connected to a group of 40 intermediate units, which were in turn connected to the 33 phoneme units. A group of 60 clean-up units was interconnected with the phoneme units. As in the original H&S network, only a random fourth of the possible connections in each of these pathways was included. In addition, the competing phoneme units for each position were fully interconnected. The resulting network had a total of 2410 connections.

The output network was trained in exactly the same manner as the H&S network, using 'back-propagation through time' (Rumelhart *et al.*, 1986; Williams and Peng, 1990). After about 1500 sweeps through the set of words, the network successfully activated each phoneme unit to within 0.1 of its correct state for each word over the last three of eight iterations. This output network was then combined with an input network, identical to the one H&S used, that had been similarly trained to generate semantics from graphemic input. The sememe units of the input network replaced the input units of the output network. The resulting network, shown in Figure 19.3, had a total of 6110 connections. This combined network was trained further by fixing the weights of the input network and running the entire network for 14 iterations on each input, allowing the output network to adapt. This additional training was required to ensure that the output network operated correctly when receiving input from the input network (which need not be correct

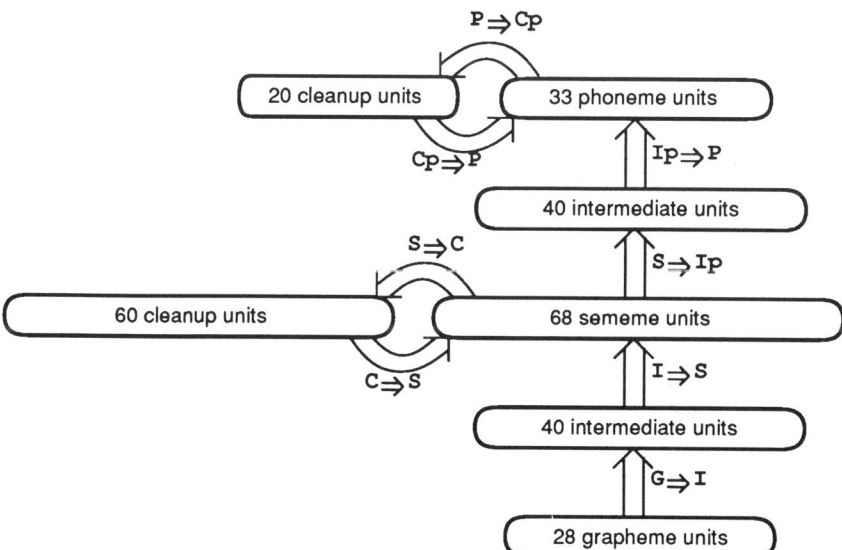

Figure 19.3 *Architecture of a network that maps from orthography to phonology via semantics. Notice that the names of sets of connections involving the intermediate and clean-up units in the phonological output network are subscripted with a p to differentiate them from the corresponding sets of connections in the input network.*

until iteration 6) instead of being clamped throughout its operation. Fixing the weights of the input network ensured that it continued to generate the correct semantics of each word. After an additional 34 sweeps through the training set, the combined network succeeded in producing the correct phonemes of each word given its graphemes as input.

Because damage will impair the ability of the network to derive the correct pronunciations of words, we need some way of deciding whether corrupted phonological activity constitutes a well-formed pronunciation. Given our phonological representation, a natural criterion is to require that exactly one phoneme unit be active in each of the three positions in order to produce a response. Since units have real-valued outputs which are rarely 0 or 1, we need a more precise definition of 'active' and 'inactive'. The criterion we use is that the most active phoneme at each position is included in the response if its likelihood, relative to the competing phonemes at that position, exceeds a **phonological response criterion** of 0.6.[1] If, at each position, exactly one phoneme satisfies this criterion, the concatenation of these phonemes is produced as the response; otherwise, the phonological activity is considered ill-formed and the network fails to respond. It is important to point out that this type of criterion is quite different from the H&S criteria, which ensure that an output is semantically familiar (i.e near the meaning of a known word). The criterion we employ does not rely on any knowledge of the particular words the network had been trained on – it considers only the **form** of the output representation.

Each of the four main sets of connections in the input network was subjected to 'lesions' by choosing at random and removing a proportion of connections. A wide range of severities was investigated: 0.05, 0.1, 0.15, 0.2, 0.25, 0.3, 0.4, 0.5 and 0.7. Twenty instances of each location and severity of lesion were carried out, and correct, omission and error responses were accumulated according to the above procedure. An error response was categorized as visually similar if it shared at least one letter in the same position with the stimulus, and was categorized as semantically similar if it belonged to the same semantic category as the stimulus.[2] In addition, the nature of the output representation and criterion creates a new type of 'blend' error consisting of a literal paraphasia – a phonologically reasonable output that does not correspond to a word known to the network. Thus, each error

---

[1] More formally, if y_i is the output of phoneme unit i, and d_i is its smallest difference from 0 or 1 (i.e., $d_i = y_i$ if $y_i \leqslant 0.5$ and $1 - y_i$ otherwise), then the network produces a response if, for every position p, $\prod_{i \in p} d_i > 0.6$ and exactly one $y_i > 0.5$. The product is the probability of the most likely binary output vector at the position when the states of the phoneme units are interpreted as independent probabilities. Thus, the response procedure is closely related to the maximum-likelihood interpretation of the cross-entropy error function used to train the network (Hinton, 1989b).

[2] In addition to visual and semantic similarity, errors can now be phonologically similar – that is, have overlapping phonemes. Since visual and phonological similarity are highly correlated, for the present purposes we will consider such errors to be visual (see Plaut and Shallice, 1993, for more detailed discussion).

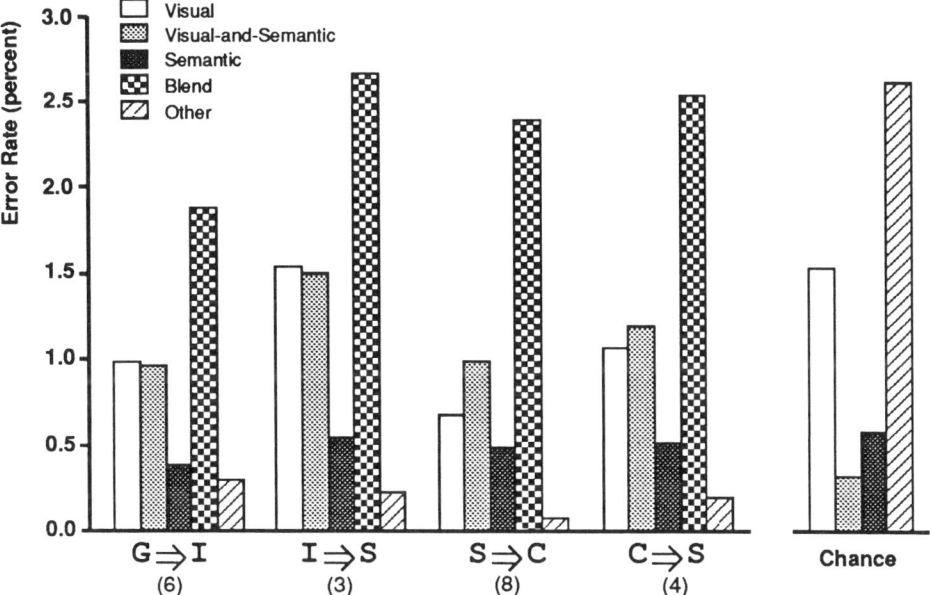

Figure 19.4 *Error rates produced by lesions to each main set of connections in the input network. 'Chance' is the distribution of error types if responses were chosen randomly from the word set. Its absolute height is set arbitrarily – only the relative rates are informative. Results are averaged over lesion densities which produced an overall correct response rate between approximately 20% and 30%. The number of lesion severities included in the calculation of error rates is indicated in parentheses below the label for each lesion location.*

response produced by the damaged network can be classified as visual, visual-and-semantic, semantic, blend or **other** (unrelated).

Figure 19.4 presents the average rates of each error type for each lesion location. The most striking aspect of the results is the high rate of blends These errors stand in sharp contrast to the behavior of deep dyslexics, who very rarely produce nonword responses in oral reading (see Coltheart *et al.*, 1980, Appendix 2). Table 19.1 presents some typical examples of blend errors produced by the network under various lesions. The semantic activity produced by each input is characterized by its proximity (i.e. normalized dot-product) with the semantics of the two nearest known words. It is informative to compare the phonology of these words with the response of the network. Semantic activity that is near two words often produces a phonological output that is a mixture of the words' phonemes (e.g. PIG $(+ RAM) \Rightarrow$ /pag/), which is why these errors are called 'blends'. Occasionally, new phonemes are introduced under the pressure of mixed semantics (e.g. DOG $(+ CAT) \Rightarrow$ /lag/). Interestingly, semantics that would easily satisfy H&S's criteria for a correct response may still be sufficiently corrupted for

Table 19.1 *Examples of nonword 'blend' errors produced by the network*

Input	Response	Nearest word[a]	Semantics[b]				Lesion
			Best	*prox*	Next	*prox*	
RIB	/r u d/	MUD	RIB	0.79	GUT	0.65	G⇒I(0.15)
DOG	/l a g/	LOG	DOG	0.88*	CAT	0.79	G⇒I(0.20)
PIG	/p a g/	PIG	PIG	0.86	RAM	0.82	G⇒I(0.25)
LIP	/r a b/	RAM	RIB	0.71	LIP	0.67	G⇒I(0.50)
HOCK	/h u k/	HOCK	HOCK	0.88*	RUM	0.76	I⇒S(0.05)
RUM	/h aw m/	HAM	HAM	0.66	PORK	0.63	I⇒S(0.25)
CUP	/k a g/	CAN	CUP	0.78	CAN	0.76	I⇒S(0.40)
RAT	/r a g/	RAM	RAT	0.97*	DOG	0.73	C⇒S(0.05)
HAM	/h u m/	RUM	BUN	0.77	HAM	0.73	C⇒S(0.25)
LEG	/p o g/	LOG	POP	0.70	LEG	0.64	C⇒S(0.50)
CAN	/k u n/	CAN	CAN	0.96*	MUG	0.80	S⇒C(0.15)
DUNE	/dy o n/	DUNE	TOR	0.81	DUNE	0.81	S⇒C(0.20)
COW	/k u g/	MUG	COW	0.90*	PIG	0.80	S⇒C(0.20)

[a] Nearest word is the word whose phonological representation has the closest proximity to the phonological output of the network.

[b] Semantics lists the best and next-best words whose semantic representations have the closest proximity *prox* to the semantic activity produced by the network. Semantics that satisfy the Hinton & Shallice response criteria are marked with an asterisk.

the output system to produce a blend (e.g HOCK (*prox* 0.88, *gap* 0.12) ⇒ /h u k/. On the other hand, semantics that are quite far from any known word may still produce a response, albeit incorrect (e.g. RUM(*prox* 0.66) ⇒ /hawm/). Clearly, the current output system behaves quite differently from what the H&S criteria assume about a response system.

19.2.2 An explanation for blends

In attempting to understand why blends occur, it is important to keep in mind that **any** pattern of activity that the network settles into is an attractor that has developed in the course of training.[3] We know that the network develops appropriate attractors for the 40 words since it produces correct responses when presented with their semantics. However, in the course of training the network develops other, spurious attractors. These attractors tend to be patterns that are combinations of trained patterns because, when the phonology of a word is trained as a response, other phonological patterns are also reinforced to the extent that they overlap with the trained pattern.

---

[3] Actually, it would be more accurate to say that training has produced the **potential** for this pattern to be an attractor given some input.

The existence of spurious attractors is a well-known property of associative networks (Hopfield, 1982) and is one way of characterizing their limited storage capacity. The existence of these additional attractors is not a problem during normal operation because inputs that would settle into them are never presented. In fact, they are not a problem for any test of generalization involving novel input that is sufficiently similar to familiar input (i.e. near in feature space or drawn from the same distribution) so as to fall into the same attractor basins. However, damage to the input network often generates semantic activity which is quite unlike any of the inputs on which the output network has been trained. When this semantic activity consists of a mixture of the semantic features of two words (e.g. PIG and RAM), rather than fall into the attractor for one or the other of these words (either producing a correct response or a conventional error), the network occasionally settles into a spurious attractor for a combination of the phonemes of the two words (e.g. /pag/), resulting in a blend.

Viewed another way, blends are the result of the natural tendency of connectionist networks to give similar outputs to similar inputs. This property is one of the major attractions of these networks because it enables them to generalize appropriately in many tasks when presented with novel input which is similar to trained input. However, what constitutes an appropriate generalization depends on the task. Consider Seidenberg and McClelland's (1989) model of word pronunciation, which maps from the orthography to the phonology of single-syllable words. The model generalizes to pronounce nonwords by combining the common pronunciations of subsets of its letters, producing a phonological output that is different from that of any known word. Thus, in this task a blend at the level of phonemes is the **correct** response to a novel input, and lexicalization (i.e. producing the exact pronunciation of a similar word) would be inappropriate. In fact, one of the problems with the Seidenberg and McClelland model is that, in response to a nonword, the model occasionally produces an inappropriate blend **at the level of phonemic features**. For example, when presented with the letter string VOST the network produces a blend of the vowel pronunciations of LOST and POST rather than choosing one or the other (J. McClelland, personal communication).[4] Thus, the problem of blends occurs when a network is not sufficiently constrained at the appropriate level of structure in the output: for the Seidenberg and McClelland task this is the phonemic level; for our task it is the lexical level (see also Rumelhart and McClelland, 1986, and Sejnowski and Rosenberg 1987).

---

[4] In general, the model often produces nonword pronunciations that differ from what normal subjects would consider the correct pronunciation (Besner *et al.*, 1990, but see Seidenberg and McClelland, 1990), suggesting that it has not sufficiently learned the appropriate regularities both between and within the phonemes of word pronunciations.

19.2.3 Eliminating blends

One way to eliminate blends would be to present the network with all possible patterns of semantic activity and explicitly train it to produce no response except to those patterns that correspond to known words. Such a procedure is unacceptable for both empirical and computational reasons: it involves presenting the network with far more information than is available to readers, and it would be intractable to train the network on a large fraction of the exponential number of possible semantic patterns. A better approach is to present only known words, but alter the training procedure in such a way that the network develops much larger and stronger basins of attraction for these words.[5] In this way, initial phonological patterns that are a mixture of the phonemes of two words will be much more likely to fall into the attractor of one or the other of the words, rather than into a spurious attractor for a blend. Developing strong attractors for known words is equivalent to having a strong 'lexical bias' in the responses of the network.

In the original architecture with 25% connectivity density, the probability that any clean-up unit would receive connections from three particular phonemes, or receive connections from two and send to a third, is only $0.25^3 = 0.016$. Hence it is unlikely that individual clean-up units can effectively bind together the phonemes of each word – these units must work together to appropriately constrain the phoneme units. To allow clean-up units to more directly constrain combinations of phonemes, a slightly different architecture will be used from the previous one. Rather than use 60 clean-up units which are each interconnected with a random fourth of the phoneme units, only 20 clean-up units will be used, but these will be fully interconnected with all of the phoneme units. The resulting network has only about 330 more connections. Notice that, with only 20 clean-up units, the network cannot devote a single unit to each word. Nonetheless, each of these units can have a more powerful influence on phonological activity than could less-densely connected units.

Our training strategy will be to develop each output network incrementally. First, the phoneme and clean-up units will be trained on noisy versions of the pronunciations of words in order to develop strong attractors for these patterns, independent of any input from semantics. This phonological clean-up pathway will then be fixed, and a direct pathway from semantics to

---

[5] The relationship between the strength of an attractor and the size of its basin of attraction is somewhat subtle. Given unlimited settling time in an undamaged network, attractors with larger basins are stronger in the sense that they pull more distant patterns to them. However, attractors with 'deeper' basins (i.e. those representing activity patterns that better satisfy the constraints imposed by the input and weights) are more robust with limited settling time (as in our networks) or under damage, and are in this sense stronger than attractors with larger, more shallow basins. A later section describes simulations using contrastive Hebbian learning in a deterministic Boltzmann Machine, in which strong attractors develop naturally so that no specific training techniques are required to eliminate phonological blends under damage.

phonology will be trained, first separately, then with the phonological clean-up added, and finally with its input generated by the input network.

This training procedure differs from the standard approach in two main ways: the use of noisy input and incremental training. In generating noisy input for an example, the activity of each input unit will be moved from 0.0 or 1.0 towards 0.5 by the absolute value of a random number drawn from a Gaussian distribution with mean 0.0 and fixed standard deviation. The target states for the output units are unchanged. Training on noisy input amounts to enforcing a particular kind of generalization: inputs which are **near** known patterns must give identical responses. Thus the basin of attraction for each trained pattern must be at least large enough to include the patterns that can be generated from it with the amount of noise used during training. An additional effect of training on noisy input is that there is a pressure for weights to remain small so that the effect of the noise on the rest of the network is minimized. This influence, much like 'weight decay' (Hinton, 1989b), causes the knowledge of the task to be more evenly distributed across all of the connections, making the network more uniformly robust to lesions (Farah and McClelland, 1991).

Incremental training has two main advantages. First, it reduces the computational demands of training, since the time to train a connectionist network with back-propagation scales much worse than linearly in the size of the network (Plaut and Hinton, 1987). Second, and more important for our purposes, training parts of the network separately encourages each part to accomplish as much of the task as possible, without relying on the strengths of the other parts. Specifically, when training the complete network, if the direct pathway can generate reasonable phonology from even noisy semantics, there is less pressure on the phonological clean-up pathway to develop strong attractors for the correct patterns. Training them separately forces them each to compensate for the noise **independently** so that their combination is more robust.

The phonological clean-up pathway of the output network was trained to produce the correct phonemes of each word during the last three of six iterations when presented with these phonemes corrupted by Gaussian noise with a standard deviation of 0.25. Because the phoneme units are both the input and output units for this stage of training, the phonemes cannot be presented by clamping the states of these units. Rather, these units were given an external input throughout the six iterations which, in the absence of other inputs, would produce the specified corrupted activity level. This technique is known as **soft clamping**. The direct pathway was trained to produce the phonemes of each word from the semantics of each word, corrupted by Gaussian noise with standard deviation 0.1. The input units were clamped in the normal way. Each pathway was trained to activate the phoneme units to within 0.2 of their correct values for a given input. After very extensive training they accomplished this in general, but the amount of noise added to their inputs made it impossible to guarantee this performance on any given trial. For this reason, training was halted when each pathway met the stopping criteria over ten successive sweeps through the training set.

The separately trained clean-up and direct pathways were then combined into a single, complete output network. This is straightforward because the two pathways have non-overlapping sets of connections, except for the biases of the phoneme units. For these, the biases from the clean-up pathway were used. The network was then given additional training on noisy input, during which only the weights in the direct pathway were allowed to change. In this way the direct pathway adjusted its mapping to more effectively use the fixed phonological clean-up in generating correct word pronunciations.

Finally, the output network was attached to the replication of the H&S input network and given a final tuning to ensure that the output network operated appropriately when its input was generated over time by an actual input network, rather than being clamped. The weights of the input network were not allowed to change, so that they continued to derive the correct semantics for each word. After this final training, which took 42 additional training sweeps, the extended network correctly derived the semantics and phonology of each word from its orthography.

Using the same random number generator seeds, the input portion of the extended network was subjected to the identical lesions as were applied to the original network. Additional lesions were applied to the semantic units themselves, and to each set of connections in the output network. For each lesion, correct, omission, and error responses were accumulated, and errors were classified according to their visual and semantic similarity to the stimulus. Figure 19.5 shows the distribution of error rates for all lesions of the extended network. Comparing with the results for the first extended network (Figure 19.4), lesions to the input network still produce distributions of visual, semantic, and mixed visual-and-semantic errors, as well as **other** (unrelated) errors, but the rates of blend errors have been dramatically reduced by the training strategy. Notice that one result of the stronger phonological attractors for word pronunciations is that the relative rates of **other** errors have increased. When a lesion results in initial phonological activity that is highly corrupted, the new output system may still succeed in cleaning it up into a familiar response, even in cases where it bears no relation to the correct response.

Interestingly, a number of the **other** errors are actually of the visual-then-semantic type found in deep dyslexia (e.g. BOG $\Rightarrow$ (dog) $\Rightarrow$ 'rat'). This type of error occurs when a lesion results in a semantic representation close to that of a word visually related to the stimulus, which is then mapped by the output system onto the phonology of a semantic neighbor of this visually related word. Thus, it is the **normal** operation of the output system that produces the semantic part of the visual-then-semantic error.

Lesions to the direct pathway of the output network ($S \Rightarrow Ip$ and $Ip \Rightarrow P$)

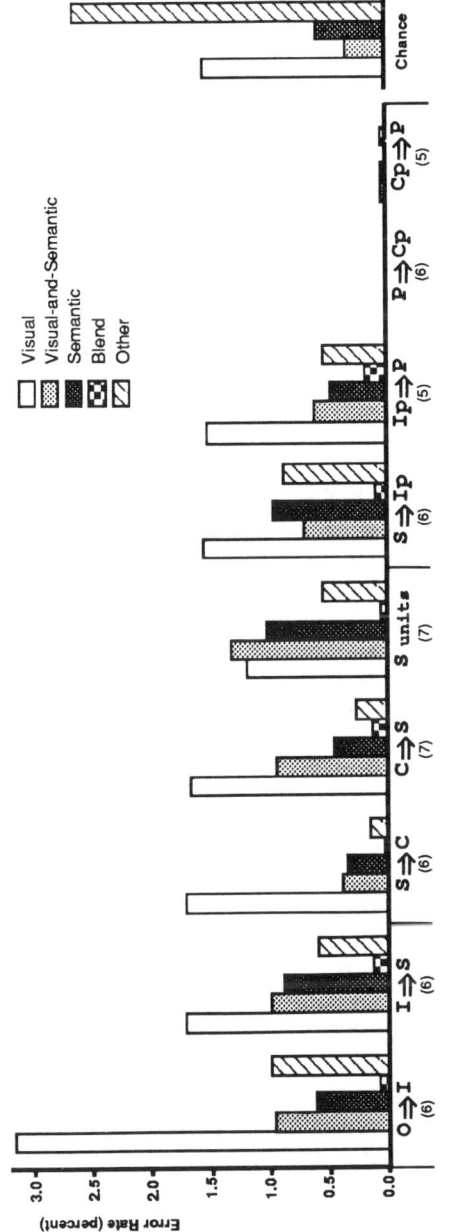

Figure 19.5 *Error distributions for the extended back-propagation network.*

produce error patterns much like input lesions, although there is a slightly greater bias towards semantic errors relative to visual errors. However, most striking is the extremely low error rate for lesions within the phonological clean-up pathway (P $\Rightarrow$ Cp and Cp $\Rightarrow$ P). Although many words can still be read correctly with impaired clean-up – average correct performance after these lesions is 50.3% – it is very rare that phonology will be cleaned up into the pronunciation of another word. This result provides direct support for H&S's claim that attractors are critical for producing error responses.

One issue is whether the pattern of errors could have arisen by chance – that is, if error responses were related to stimuli only randomly. If the distribution of error types for a given lesion location occurred by chance, the ratios of their rates with the rate of **other** errors would appproximate the corresponding ratios for the 'Chance' error distribution. However, except for phonological clean-up lesions, the rates of visual, mixed visual-and-semantic, and semantic errors, relative to the rates of **other** errors, are greater for all lesion locations than predicted by chance. Specifically, the ratios with **other** error are larger than the chance value by at least a factor of 3.3 for visual errors, 11.7 for visual-and-semantic errors, and 2.9 for semantic errors. Thus, lesions anywhere along a pathway from orthography to phonology via semantics produce qualitatively similar patterns of errors. In this way, H&S's results appear to generalize to lesions all along a route from orthography to phonology via semantics.

19.3 The network architecture

The second design decision we will consider is the relevance of network architecture, by which we mean a specification of the number of units and their interconnectivity. H&S provide only a general justification for the network architecture they chose. Hidden units are needed because the problem of mapping orthography to semantics is not linearly separable. Recurrent connections are required to allow the network to develop semantic attractors, whose existence constitutes the major theoretical claim of the work. The choices of numbers of intermediate and clean-up units, restrictions on connections among sememe units, and connectivity density were an attempt to give the network sufficient flexibility to solve the task and build strong semantic attractors, while keeping the size of the network manageable. Some aspects of the design, particularly the selective use of intra-sememe connections, were rather inelegant and *ad hoc*.

Accordingly, we carried out a systematic comparison of the effects of damage in a range of network architectures designed to allow comparisons between basic aspects of the H&S network (see Figure 19.6). Versions of each of these networks were subjected to a full range of lesion locations and severities, and evaluated both using the response criteria and using an output system. The results demonstrate that the qualitative error pattern after damage is

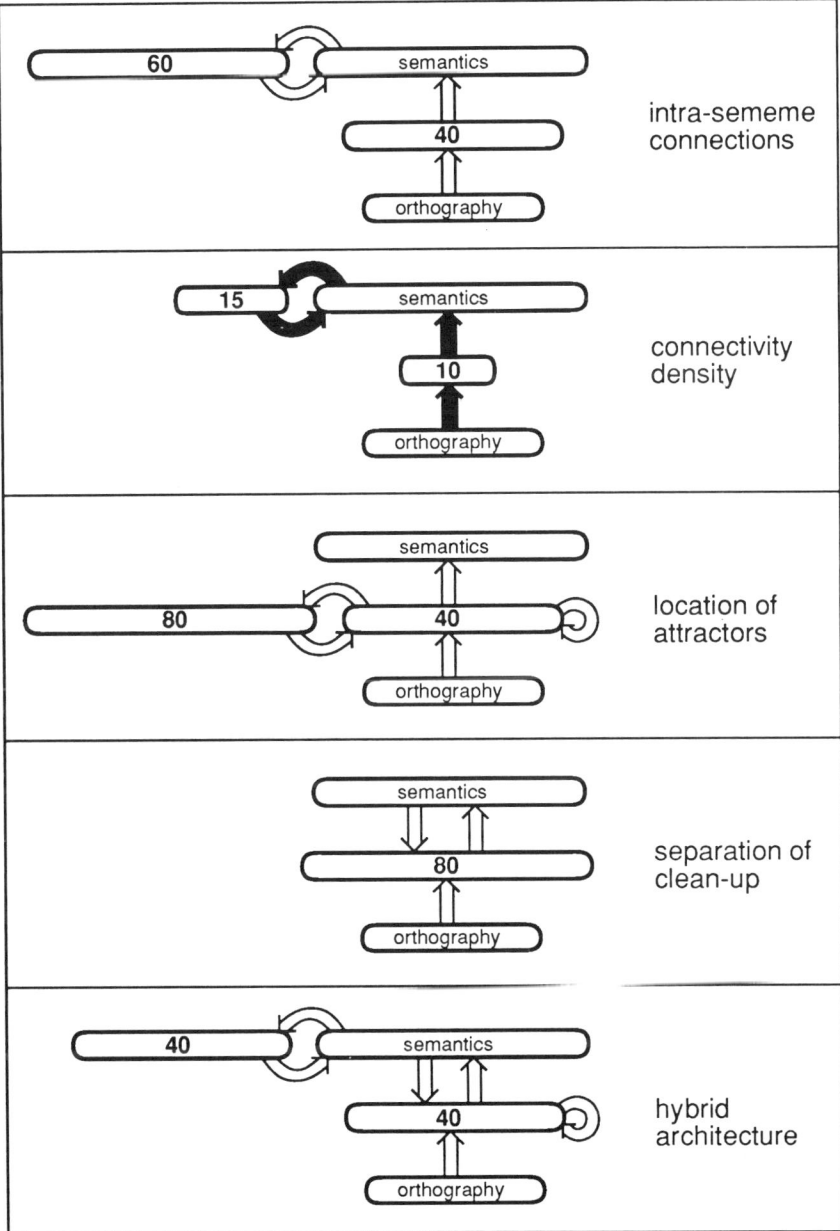

Figure 19.6 *Five alternative network architectures for mapping orthography to semantics, and the issues they are designed to address.*

surprisingly insensitive to architectural details, as long as attractors continue to operate downstream from the lesion (see Plaut and Shallice, 1993, for details). When lesions are at or beyond the level at which attractors operate, the network produces very few explicit error responses, even though correct performance may be reasonable. In this way, the results in these conditions mirror those shown for lesions of the phonological clean-up pathway just described (Figure 19.5). More critically for the present purposes, however, is that the similarity of error patterns produced by such a wide variety of architectures makes it highly unlikely that the basic results depend on any idiosyncratic characteristics of the H&S network.

19.4 The training procedure

Although back-propagation is quite a powerful training procedure, it uses information in ways that seem neurophysiologically implausible – a straight-forward implementation of the procedure would require error signals to travel backward through synapses and axons (Crick, 1989; Grossberg, 1987). As such, it seems unlikely that back-propagation *per se* is what underlies human learning, and thus its use in modeling the **results** of human learning is somewhat suspect.

Proponents of the use of back-propagation in cognitive modeling have replied to this argument in two ways. The first is to demonstrate how the procedure might be implemented in a neurophysiologically plausible way. The more common reply, and the one adopted by H&S, is to argue that back-propagation is only one of a number of procedures for performing gradient descent learning in connectionist networks. As such, it is viewed merely as a programming technique for developing a network that performs a task, and is not intended to reflect any aspect of human learning *per se*. The implicit claim is that back-propagation develops representations that exhibit the same properties as would those developed by a more plausible procedure, but that it does so much more efficiently. However, this claim is rarely substantiated by a demonstration of the similarity between systems developed with alternative procedures.[6]

In this section, we replicate the main results obtained thus far with back-propagation, within the more plausible learning framework of Contrastive Hebbian Learning (CHL) in a Deterministic Boltzmann Machine (DBM) (Peterson and Anderson, 1987; Hinton, 1989a). In this framework, weights are changed in proportion to the difference in the product of unit states after settling when both inputs and outputs are clamped (the **positive** phase), and when settling after only the inputs are clamped (the **negative** phase). CHL

---

[6] Terry Sejnowski (personal communication) has successfully re-implemented NETtalk (Sejnowski and Rosenberg, 1987) as a stochastic Boltzmann Machine. However, he made no direct comparisons of the representations that the two procedures developed.

is somewhat more biologically plausible than back-propagation because information about the correct states of output units is used in the same way as information about the input – that is, by propagating weighted unit activities, rather than passing error derivatives backward across connections. We also develop a closely-related stochastic GRAIN network (McClelland 1990, 1991) and compare it with the deterministic one.

19.4.1 Deterministic Boltzmann Machine

Figure 19.7 depicts the architecture of the DBM for mapping among the orthography, semantics, and phonology. All sets of connections are bidirectional and have full connectivity, except that no unit is connected to itself. In total, the network has 11273 connections – about twice the number of connections in one of the back-propagation networks. This extra capacity is justified because CHL is not as efficient as back-propagation in using a small number of weights to solve a task.

To help the DBM learn the structure in the task (i.e. to reproduce the co-occurrences of unit states), the network was trained on three subtasks, each corresponding to a separate negative phase: (1) generate semantics and phonology from orthography; (2) generate orthography and phonology from semantics; and (3) generate semantics and orthography from phonology. Although only the first subtask is strictly required for reading via meaning,

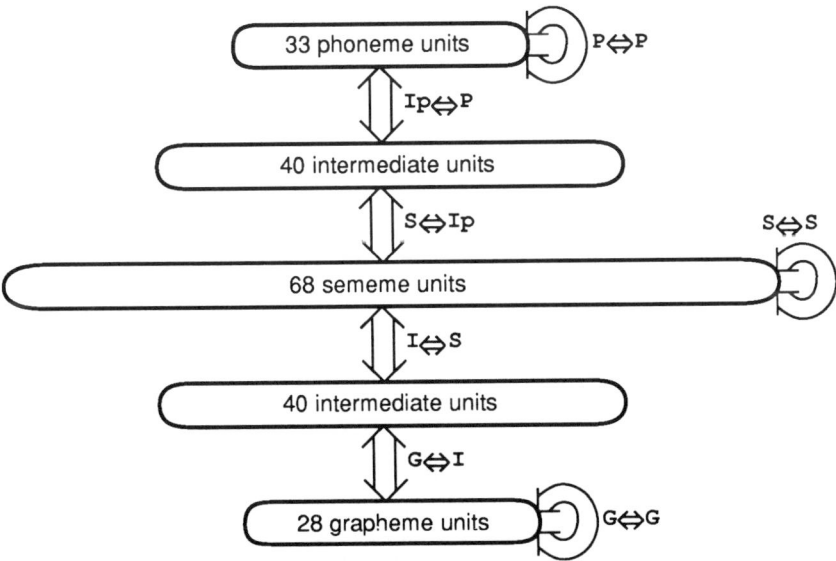

Figure 19.7 *DBM architecture for mapping among orthography, semantics and phonology.*

training on the other subtasks ensures that the network learns to model orthographic structure and its relationship to semantics in the same way as for phonological structure.[7] Also, learning the task in both directions should result in stronger and more robust attractors. The positive phase involved clamping the grapheme, sememe, and phoneme units appropriately, and computing states for the two layers of intermediate units. In order to balance the three negative phases, the products of unit states in the positive phase are multiplied by three before being added into the pending weight changes. After slightly more than 2100 sweeps through the word set, the state of each grapheme, sememe, and phoneme unit was within 0.2 of its correct states during each of the three negative phases.

After training, each of the sets of connections in the DBM were subjected to 20 instances of lesions over the standard range of severity. We also subjected the semantic units to lesions of the same range of severity, in which the appropriate proportion of semantic units is selected at random and removed from the network. Since we are primarily concerned with the task of generating semantics and phonology from orthography, we only considered behavior in the negative phase in which the grapheme units are clamped. For each lesion, correct, omission, and error response were accumulated according to the same criteria as used for the back-propagation networks.

An interesting characteristic of the DBM is that it tends to settle into unit states that are very close to ± 1, even under damage. This results in very clean phonological output when it responds. Only 9.2% of omissions fail because of the criterion of a minimum slot response probability of 0.6 for responses. Thus, the phonological output criterion could be eliminated entirely without substantially altering the results with the DBM.

Figure 19.8 presents the distribution of error types for each lesion location of the DBM. Comparing with results for input lesions to the back-propagation network (shown in Figure 19.5), the DBM is producing about 4–8 times higher error rates. However, the distribution of error types is quite similar for the two networks. Both show a high proportion of visual errors for lesions to input pathways. Furthermore, like the back-propagation network, the DBM shows very low rates of blend responses. This is interesting because, unlike in the development of the back-propagation output network, no special effort was made to prevent blends in the design or training of the DBM. Their absence appears to be a natural and encouraging consequence of the nature of the attractors developed by the DBM.

The error pattern for central lesions (S⇔S and S units) is quite similar to the pattern for input lesions. Lesioning the semantic units produces a higher

[7] Our use of a training procedure that involves learning to produce semantics from phonology in addition to producing phonology from semantics is in no way intended to imply a theoretical claim that input and output phonology are identical – it is solely a way of helping the network to learn the appropriate relationships between semantic and phonological representations.

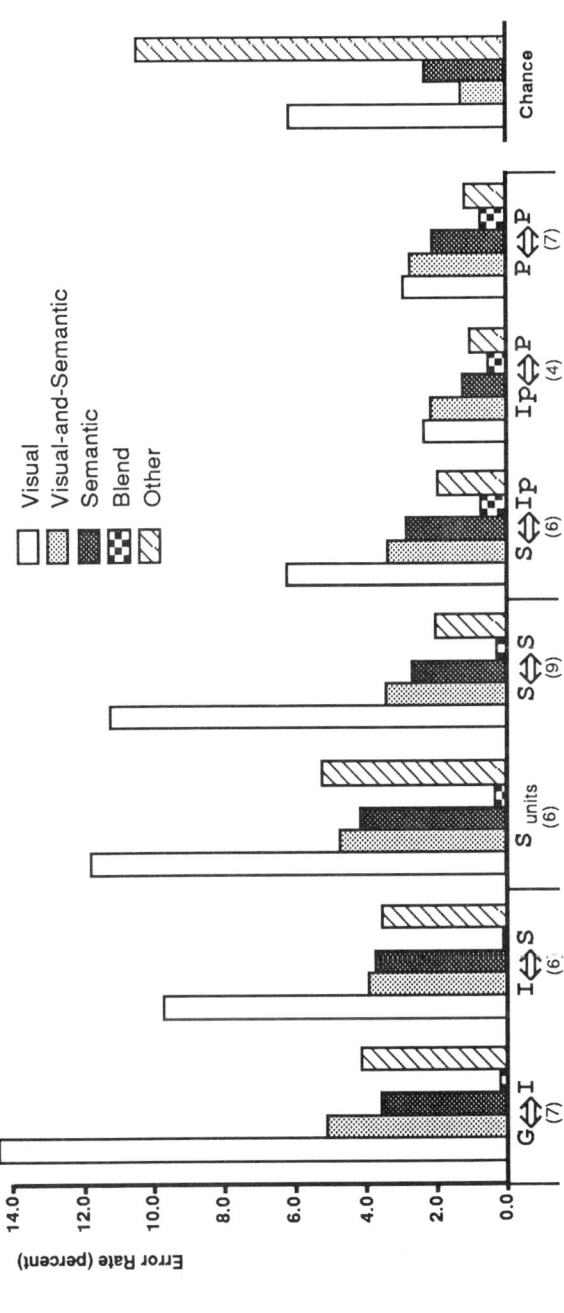

Figure 19.8 *Error rates produced by lesions to each main set of connections, as well as to the semantic units, in the DBM. Results are averaged over severities that resulted in correct performance between 10–80%.*

overall error rate (25.6%) than lesioning the connections among them (19.6%), but the largest increase is among **other** errors. Also, in the DBM these lesions don't produce the same strong bias towards semantic similarity in errors as they do in the back-propagation network.

The pattern of error rates for output lesions to the DBM is quite different from that for the back-propagation network. The error rates for lesions to the direct pathway of the DBM (S⇔Ip and Ip⇔P) are lower than for input lesions, and less biased towards visual errors. In addition, the DBM produces far fewer **other** errors than the back-propagation network. Perhaps more striking, phonological clean-up lesions in the DBM (P⇔P) still produce significant error rates, fairly evenly distributed across type, while the analogous lesions in the back-propagation network (P⇔Cp and Cp⇔P) produce virtually no error responses. With phonological clean-up damage, the DBM can use the bidirectional interactions with the intermediate units as a residual source of clean-up.

All lesion locations in the DBM show a mixture of error types, and their ratios with the **other** error rates are higher than for randomly chosen error responses. Thus, the DBM replicates the main H&S results.

19.4.2 GRAIN network

The effectiveness of noise in facilitating the development of strong attractors in the back-propagation output network suggests that it might have further benefits within the DBM framework. McClelland (1990, 1991) has recently developed a stochastic elaboration of DBMs, called GRAIN networks (for Gradual Random Adaptive Interactive Nonlinear), that use real-valued stochastic units.[8] Although the principles of GRAIN networks can be embodied in a wide range of specific network formalisms, the type of GRAIN network we will investigate is identical to a DBM except that normally distributed noise ($\mu = 0.0$, $\sigma = 0.1$) is added to the input of each unit at each time step. The influence of noise is more widespread in a GRAIN network than in the back-propagation networks, because noise is applied to every unit in the network throughout settling.

A GRAIN network with the same architecture as the DBM was trained on the same task using CHL. Because the units in a GRAIN network are stochastic, the units never completely reach a fixedpoint in state space, but randomly fluctuate around it. However, if the amount of noise is small relative to the weights, the network will rarely jump out of a minimum as a result of the noise alone. In this case, all of the variation in unit states is

---

[8] Actually, GRAIN networks were developed as an elaboration of the Interactive Activation and Competition framework (McClelland and Rumelhart, 1981; Rumelhart and McClelland, 1982) in response to the need for intrinsic variability, as reflected by empirical limitations of the original model (Massaro, 1988). However, the processing dynamics in a DBM are a special case of those in the LAC framework.

caused by independent noise with zero mean, and so the expected value of the product of two unit states is the product of the states the units would have without noise.[9] For this reason, the final unit states at the end of settling are computed without noise before being used in the weight update rule. After 3500 sweeps through the training set, the GRAIN network could reliably generate any two of the orthography, semantics, or phonology of a word when given the third.

The GRAIN network was subjected to the same set of lesions as the DBM, and correct, omission, and error responses were accumulated. The input to units remained noisy during the gathering of data on impaired performance. Figure 19.9 presents the distribution of error types for each lesion location of the GRAIN network. The pattern of errors is quite similar to that of the DBM. The major difference is that the GRAIN network has significantly higher rates of semantic errors than the DBM for almost all lesion locations. This makes sense in the following way. The amount of variation in input due to noise that a unit experiences increases as a function of its number of connections. Consider the input a unit j receives along a connection from unit i. Because the input to unit i has noise with zero mean added to it, its input to j can be thought of as a random variable with mean equal to what $s_i w_{ij}$ would be without noise (call it $s_i' w_{ij}$) and some variance dependent on the amount of noise. The summed input to j (before noise is added) is thus the sum of samples of a set of random variables. This sum is also a random variable, with mean equal to the sum of the means of the variables (i.e. $\sum_i s_i' w_{ij}$), and variance equal to the sum of their variances. Thus the mean of the summed input to a unit correctly approximates the true mean in a noiseless network, but the variance increases linearly with its number of connections. In the GRAIN network, semantic units have far more connections (149) than intermediate units (102) or phonological units (74), and so they are more drastically affected by the intrinsic noise in the states of other units. They must interact more effectively to compensate for this variability, resulting in stronger attractors at this level and thus more semantic errors under damage.

Nonetheless, it is surprising that the GRAIN network and the DBM are so similar in the nature of the attractors they develop, as reflected in their behavior under damage. One explanation may come from the behavior of the DBM during learning. The mathematical justification for the learning procedure (Hinton, 1989a) assumes that only rarely will small changes to the weights cause the network to settle into a different minimum. However, in practice this appears to be more the rule than the exception. As the weights

---

[9] Fluctuations in the states of two connected units due to noise will tend to be slightly correlated due to the weight between them, so that the product of their states without noise only approximates the expected value of their product with noise.

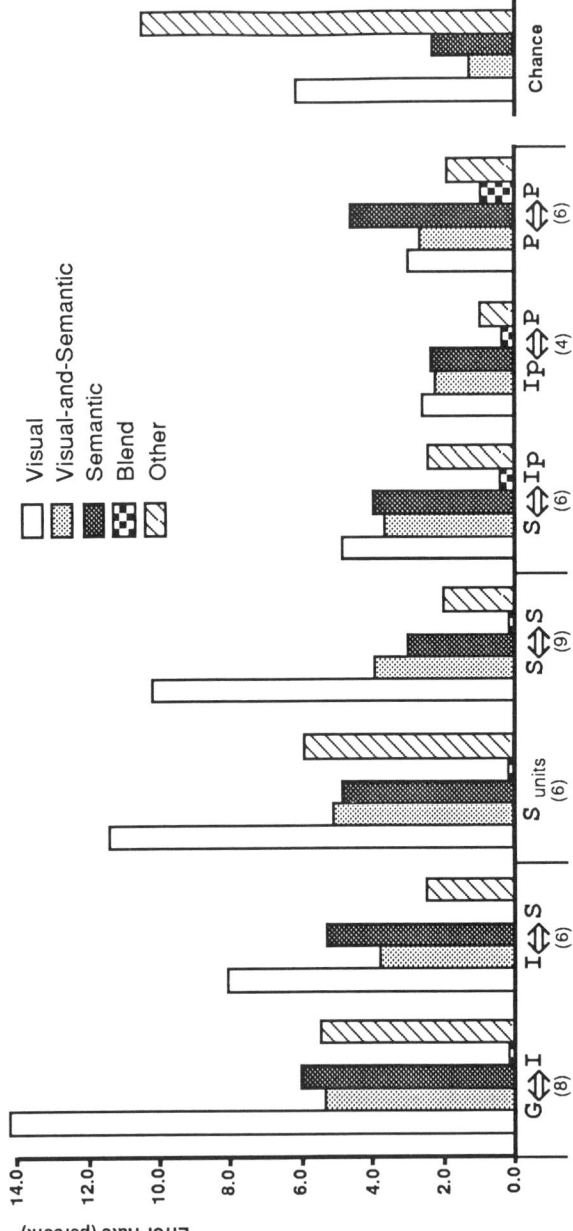

Figure 19.9 Error rates produced by lesions to each main set of connections in the GRAIN network.

slowly change, the network samples among a large number of minima during the negative phase(s), raising their energy to the degree to which they differ from the minima of each corresponding positive phase. As the network improves on the task, fewer and fewer of these minima remain sufficiently good for the network to settle into them. Eventually the network consistently reaches the single minimum that is most similar to the positive phase minimum, and reduces the difference until the training criteria are met. This type of variability **over weight changes** in settling to minima appears to have similar effects as the variability of unit states during a single settling in a GRAIN network. Both processes force the network to explore, and hence shape appropriately, a much larger amount of the energy surface in state space than will ultimately be traversed when the network has learned. Hence, one possible explanation for why the GRAIN network is no more robust to damage than the DBM is that in both networks the attractors have been strengthened by pressure from variability, albeit from different sources.

Both the DBM and GRAIN network serve to validate the claim that the nature of the attractors developed using back-propagation have properties that are similar to those developed using these alternative, more biologically plausible formalisms.

19.5 The task domain

The final aspect of the H&S model that we investigate is the definition of the task of reading via meaning. A rather severe limitation of the H&S model is that it was trained on only 40 words, allowing only a very coarse approximation to the range of visual and semantic similarity among words in a patient's vocabulary. More critically, a distinction among words known to have a significant effect on reading in deep dyslexia – concreteness or imageability – could not be addressed using the original H&S word set because it contains only concrete nouns. In this section, we summarize our work in extending the H&S approach to account for effects of concreteness and their interactions with visual errors (see Plaut and Shallice, 1991, 1993 for details).

To examine the effect of concreteness on visual errors, a set of 20 concrete and 20 abstract words were chosen such that each pair of words differed by a single letter (e.g. ROPE, ROLE). Following Jones (1985), Gentner (1981), and others, we develop a semantic representation in which concrete words have 'richer' representations, in terms of number of active features, than do abstract words. Specifically, out of 98 possible semantic features, concrete words have an average of 18.2 features, while abstract words have an average of only 4.7 features. A back-propagation network was trained to map ortho-graphy to phonology via these representations, in the same manner as for the back-propagation simulations described in section 19.2.

Because abstract words have far fewer features, they are less able to engage the semantic clean-up mechanism effectively, and must rely more heavily on the direct pathway where visual influences are strongest. As a result, lesions to the direct pathway of the input network reproduce the effects of concreteness and their interaction with visual errors found in deep dyslexia: better correct performance for concrete over abstract words, a tendency for error responses to be more concrete than stimuli, and a higher proportion of visual errors in response to abstract compared with concrete words.

Surprisingly, severe lesions to the clean-up pathway produce the **opposite** effect, with abstract words now being read better than concrete words, and concrete words producing more visual errors than do the abstract words. This reversal arises because, under this type of lesion, the processing of most concrete words is impaired but many abstract words can be read solely by the direct pathway.

In fact, there is a single known exception to the advantage for concrete words shown by deep dyslexic patients: patient CAV with **concrete word dyslexia** (Warrington, 1981). CAV failed to read concrete words like MILK and TREE but succeeded at highly abstract words such as APPLAUSE, EVIDENCE, and INFERIOR. Overall, abstract words were more likely to be correctly read than concrete (55% *vs.* 36%). In complementary fashion, 63% of his visual error responses were more abstract than the stimulus. Furthermore, the hypothesis of severe clean-up damage is consistent with other aspects of his performance. His reading disorder was quite severe initially, and he also showed an advantage for abstract words in picture-word matching with auditory presentation, suggesting modality-independent damage at the level of the semantic system.

Overall, the network successfully extends the H&S approach to account for the effects of concreteness in deep dyslexia, and also offers the possibility of explaining the single, enigmatic case of concrete word dyslexia. Thus, together with extrapolations based on previous theorizing (e.g. Funnell, 1987), the connectionist approach offers a comprehensive, principled account of the full range of symptoms found in deep dyslexia.

19.6 Conclusions

Hinton and Shallice (1991) offer a connectionist account in which the central aspects of deep dyslexia – the existence of semantic errors and their co-occurrence with visual and mixed visual-and-semantic errors – arise naturally as a result of damage to a network that builds attractors in mapping orthography to semantics. While the approach has the advantage over traditional models of being far more computationally explicit, it has the limitation that there is little understanding of the underlying principles of the model which give rise to its behavior under damage. The current research involves a set of connectionist simulation experiments aimed both at developing our understanding of these principles, and at extending the empirical adequacy of the approach on the basis of this understanding. The results demonstrate the usefulness of a connectionist approach to understanding deep dyslexia in particular, and the viability of connectionist neuropsychology in general.

Furthermore, studying the breakdown of behavior in damaged networks sheds light on their normal computational characteristics. Implementing an output system that successfully pronounces a set of words from their semantics was relatively straightforward – the limitations of the system became apparent only under damage. The tendency for distributed output representations to lead to blends under damage clarifies the need for stronger attractors that encode constraints at the appropriate level of structure in the output. The fact that contrastive Hebbian learning in a deterministic Boltzmann Machine and in a GRAIN network produces such attractors naturally, perhaps as a result of variability over weight changes, is a significant advantage of that framework.

Connectionist networks would appear *a priori* to be an appropriate formalism within which to develop computational models of neuropsychological disorders. Although the specific relationship between these networks and neurobiology is far from clear (Sejnowski *et al.*, 1989; Smolensky 1988), the belief that representation and computation in these networks resembles neural computation at some level remains one of their strongest attractions. As the present research illustrates, the fact that the behavior of connectionist networks after damage resembles that of neurological patients supports the claim that the apparent similarity is, in fact, substantial.

Acknowledgment

We would like to thank Marlene Behrmann for commenting on an earlier draft. All of the simulations described in this chapter were run on a Silicon Graphics Iris-4D/240S using an extended version of the Xerion simulator developed by Tony Plate. This research was supported by grant 87-2-36 from the Alfred P. Sloan Foundation.

References

Besner, D., Twilley, L., McCann, R.S. and Seergobin, K. (1990) On the connection between connectionism and data: Are a few words necessary? *Psychological Review*, **97**(3), 432–46.

Coltheart, M. (1985) Cognitive neuropsychology and the study of reading, in *Attention and Performance XI*, (eds. M.I. Posner and O.S.M. Marin), Lawrence Erlbaum, Hillsdale, NJ, pp. 3–37.

Coltheart, M., Patterson, K.E. and Marshall, J.C. (eds.) (1980) *Deep Dyslexia*. Routledge & Kegan Paul, London.

Crick, F.H.C. (1989) The recent excitement about neural networks. *Nature*, **337**, 129–32.

Ellis, A.W. and Young, A.W. (1988) *Human Cognitive Neuropsychology*. Lawrence Erlbaum, Hillsdale, NJ.

Farah, M.J. and McClelland, J.L. (1991) A computational model of semantic memory impairment: Modality-specificity and emergent category-specificity. *Journal of Experimental Psychology: General*, **120**(4), 339–57.

Funnell, E. (1987) Morphological errors in acquired dyslexia: A case of mistaken identity. *Quarterly Journal of Experimental Psychology*, **39A**, 497–539.

Gentner, D. (1981) Some interesting differences between verbs and nouns. *Cognition and Brain Theory*, **4**(2), 161–78.

Grossberg, S. (1987) From interactive activation to adaptive resonance. *Cognitive Science*, **11**, 23–63.

Hinton, G.E. (1989a) Deterministic Boltzmann learning performs steepest descent in weight-space. *Neural Computation*, **1**(1), 143–50.

Hinton, G.E. (1989b) Connectionist learning procedures. *Artificial Intelligence*, **40**, 185–234.

Hinton, G.E. and Anderson, J.A. (eds.) (1981) *Parallel Models of Associative Memory*. Lawrence Erlbaum, Hillsdale, NJ.

Hinton, G.E. and Sejnowski, T.J. (1986) Learning and relearning in Boltzmann machines, in *Parallel Distributed Processing: Explorations in the Microstructure of Cognition. Volume 1: Foundations* (eds. D.E. Rumelhart, J.L. McClelland and the PDP research group), MIT Press, Cambridge, MA, pp. 282–317.

Hinton, G.E. and Shallice, T. (1991) Lesioning an attractor network: Investigations of acquired dyslexia. *Psychological Review*, **98**(1), 74–95.

Hopfield, J.J. (1982) Neural networks and physical systems with emergent collective computational abilities. *Proceedings National Academy of Science, USA*, **79**, 2554–8.

Jones, G.V. (1985) Deep dyslexia, imageability, and ease of predication. *Brain and Language*, **24**, 1–19.

Lachter, J. and Bever, T. (1988) The relation between linguistic structure and theories of language learning: A constructive critique of some connectionist learning models. *Cognition*, **28**, 195–247.

Massaro, D.W. (1988) Some criticisms of connectionist models of human performance. *Journal of Memory and Language*, **27**, 213–34.

McClelland, J.L. (1990) The GRAIN model: A framework for modeling the dynamics of information processing, in *Attention and Performance XIV* (eds. D.E. Meyer and S. Kornblum), Lawrence Erlbaum, Hillsdale, NJ.

McClelland, J.L. (1991) Stochastic interactive processes and the effect of context on perception. *Cognitive Psychology*, **23**, 1–44.

McClelland, J.L. and Rumelhart, D.E. (1981) An interactive activation model of context effects in letter perception: Part 1. An account of basic findings. *Psychological Review*, **88**(5), 375–407.

Morton, J. and Patterson, K. (1980) A new attempt at an interpretation, Or, an attempt at a new interpretation, in *Deep Dyslexia* (eds. M. Coltheart, K.E. Patterson, and J.C. Marshall), Routledge & Kegan Paul, London, pp. 91–118.

Nystrom, L.E. and McClelland, J.L. (1991) Blend errors during cued recall. *Proceedings 13th Annual Conference of the Cognitive Science Society*, Lawrence Erlbaum, Hillsdale, NJ, pp. 185–90.

Patterson, K.E., Seidenberg, M.S. and McClelland, J.L. (1990) Connections and disconnections: Acquired dyslexia in a computational model of reading processes, in *Parallel Distributed Processing: Implications for Psychology and Neuroscience* (ed. R.G.M. Morris), Oxford University Press, London.

Peterson, C. and Anderson, J.R. (1987) A mean field theory learning algorithm for neural nets. *Complex Systems*, **1**, 995–1019.

Pinker, S. and Prince, A. (1988) On language and connectionism: Analysis of a parallel distributed processing model of language acquisition. *Cognition*, **28**, 73–193.

Plaut, D.C. and Hinton, G.E. (1987) Learning sets of filters using backpropagation. *Computer Speech and Language*, **2**, 35–61.

Plaut, D.C. and Shallice, T. (1991) Effects of abstractness in a connectionist model of deep dyslexia. *Proceedings 13th Annual Conference of the Cognitive Science Society*, Lawrence Erlbaum, Hillsdale, NJ, pp. 73–8.

Plaut, D.C. and Shallice, T. (1993) Deep dyslexia: A case study of connectionist neuropsychology. *Cognitive Neuropsychology* (In press).

Rumelhart, D.E., Hinton, G.E. and Williams, R.J. (1986) Learning representations by back-propagating errors. *Nature*, **323**(9), 533–6.

Rumelhart, D.E. and McClelland, J.L. (1982) An interactive activation model of context effects in letter perception: Part 2, the contextual enhancement effect and some tests and extensions of the model. *Psychological Review*, **89**, 60–94.

Rumelhart, D.E. and McClelland, J.L. (1986) On learning the past tenses of English verbs, in *Parallel Distributed Processing: Explorations in the Microstructure of Cognition. Volume 2: Psychological and Biological Models* (eds. J.L. McClelland, D.E. Rumelhart and the PDP research group), MIT Press, Cambridge, MA, 216–71.

Seidenberg, M. and McClelland, J.L. (1989) A distributed, developmental model of word recognition and naming. *Psychological Review*, **96**, 523–68.

Seidenberg, M.S. and McClelland, J.L. (1990) More words but still no lexicon: Reply to Besner et al. (1990). *Psychological Review*, **97**(3), 477–82.

Sejnowski, T.J., Koch, C. and Churchland, P.S. (1989) Computational neuroscience. *Science*, **241**, 1299–306.

Sejnowski, T.J. and Rosenberg, C.R. (1987) Parallel networks that learn to pronounce English text. *Complex Systems*, **1**, 145–68.

Smolensky, P. (1988) On the proper treatment of connectionism. *Behavioral and Brain Sciences*, **11**, 1–74.

Warrington, E.K. (1981) Concrete word dyslexia. *British Journal of Psychology*, **72**, 175–96.

Williams, R.J. and Peng, J. (1990) An efficient gradient-based algorithm for on-line training of recurrent network trajectories. *Neural Computation*, **2**(4), 490–501.

20

Adaptive language acquisition in a multi-sensory device

ANANTH SANKAR and ALLEN GORIN
AT&T Bell Laboratories, 600 Mountain Avenue, Murray Hill, NJ 07974, USA

20.1 Introduction

In our research on adaptive language acquisition, we have been investigating connectionist systems that learn the mapping from a message to a meaningful machine action through interaction with a complex environment. Previously, the only input to these systems has been the message. However, in many devices of interest, the action also depends on the state of the world, thereby motivating the study of systems with multi-sensory input. In this work, we describe and evaluate a device which acquires language through interaction with an environment which provides both keyboard and visual input. In particular, the machine action is to focus its attention, by directing its eyeball toward one of many blocks of different colors and shapes, in response to a message such as 'Look at the red square'. The attention focus is controlled by minimizing a time-varying potential function that correlates the message and visual input. This correlation is factored through color and shape **sensory primitive nodes** in an **information-theoretic connectionist network**, allowing the machine to generalize between different objects having the same color or shape. The system runs in a **conversational mode** where the user can provide clarifying messages and error feedback, until the system responds correctly. During the course of performing its task, a vocabulary of 431 words was acquired from 11 users in over 1000 unconstrained natural language conversations. The average number of inputs for the machine to respond correctly was only 1.4 sentences, and it retained 98% of what it was taught.

Artificial Neural Networks for Speech and Vision. Edited by Richard J. Mammone.
Published in 1993 by Chapman & Hall, London. ISBN 0 412 54850 X

We conclude by discussing several directions for future research based on this work, including both blocks-world extensions and other applications.

We begin by reviewing the motivations for our research on adaptive language acquisition. At present, automatic speech recognition technology is based upon constructing models of the various levels of linguistic structure assumed to compose spoken language. These models are either constructed manually or automatically trained by example. A major impediment is the cost, or even the feasibility, of producing models of sufficient fidelity to enable the desired level of performance.

An alternative proposed by Gorin *et al.* (1991a) is to build a device that acquires the necessary linguistic skills **during the course of performing its task**. We briefly review the basic principles and mechanisms of that work. A **first principle** in Gorin *et al.* (1991a) is that the primary function of language is to communicate meaning, with the consequence that language acquisition involves gaining the capability of decoding that meaning. This is in contrast to much of the research on automated language acquisition, which focuses on discovering syntactic structure, often to the exclusion of meaning. The mechanism studied in Gorin *et al.* (1991a) is a connectionist network with information-theoretic weights that learns the mapping from an input message to a meaningful machine response.

A **second principle** is that language is acquired by interaction with a complex environment. The interaction involves feedback as to the appropriateness of a machine response to a particular input stimulus. Governing learning via such feedback is an example of **reinforcement learning** (Barto and Anandan, 1985; Kaelbling, 1990), and can be contrasted with **learning by example** (Rumelhart and McClelland, 1986; Duda and Hart, 1973). When reinforcement feedback is provided judging the appropriateness of a machine's action during the course of performing its task, we have called this **learning by doing**, and the feedback a **semantic-level error signal**.

Figure 20.1 shows a mechanism inspired by these two principles, which is a connectionist network embedded in a feedback control loop. In Gorin *et al.* (1991a), the environment is a human user who provides both an input message and a semantic-level error signal as to the appropriateness of the machine's response. The machine learns to respond correctly by strengthening or weakening its weights based on the error signal. In Gorin *et al.* (1991a), a multi-layer network was employed where the input layer corresponded to a growing list of vocabulary word nodes v_m, an intermediate layer corresponded to a growing list of phrase nodes $v_m v_n$, and the output layer corresponded to the possible machine actions c_k, as shown in Figure 20.2. The output of the word detector nodes o_m are indicative of the probability that the word v_m was present in the input message. The connection weights w_{mk} were defined to be the **mutual information** $I(c_k, v_m)$ between the words and the actions. There is a bias term $w_k = \log P(c_k)$ associated with each output, where $P(c_k)$ is the probability of the device performing action c_k. This definition of

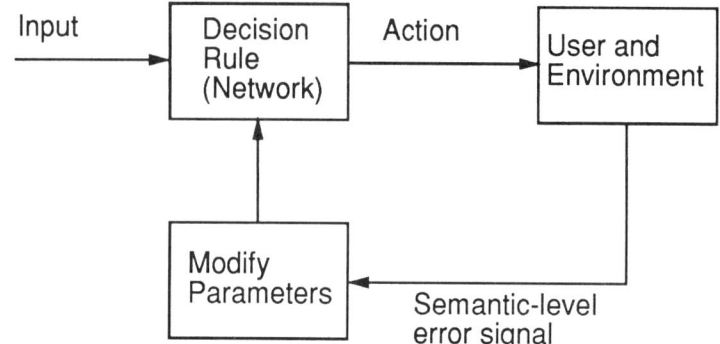

Figure 20.1 *Adaptive language acquisition.*

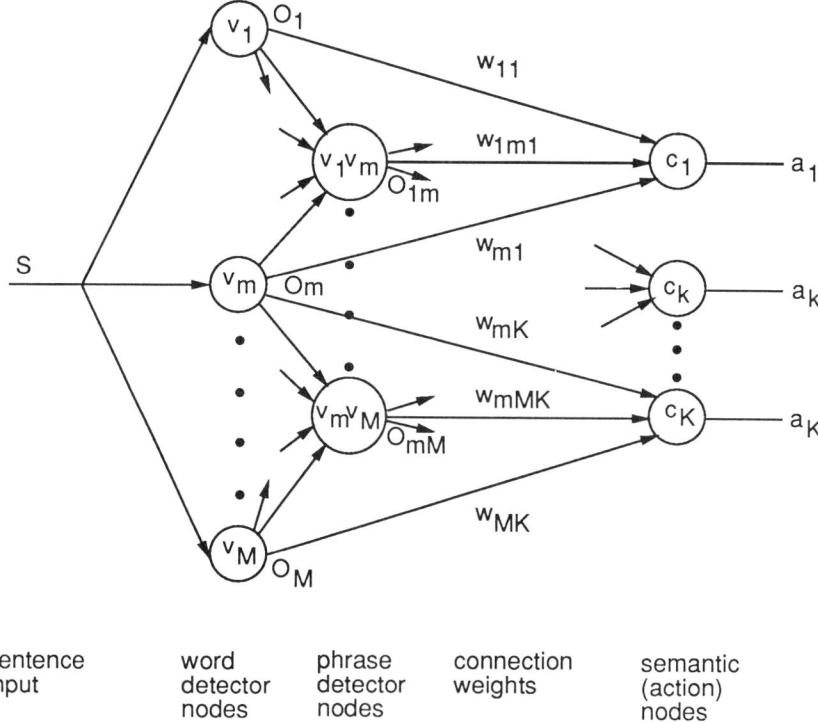

Figure 20.2 *Multi-layer network for language acquisition.*

the weights and bias is intuitive and exhibits rapid learning as demonstrated by the experiments in Gorin *et al.* (1991a,b), Miller and Gorin (1992) and Gertner and Gorin (1993), and in this chapter. The weights and biases can be estimated by smoothed relative frequency methods, which is a naturally sequential computation (Gorin *et al*, 1991a). The outputs of the network a_k are computed by $a_k = \sum_m o_m w_{mk} + w_k$. The device performs that action c_k for which the output a_k is maximum.

The utility of these principles was first studied for a text-based 3-action task that is described in detail in Gorin *et al.* (1991a), and for spoken input in Gorin *et al.* (1991b). However, as a task grows in size and complexity, it is reasonable to question the capability of the machine to learn these complex mappings. While there does, indeed, exist a body of theory addressing such questions (Cybenko, 1989; Baum, 1989), the results tend to be asymptotic in nature, requiring large numbers of examples for learning to occur. In contrast, a striking feature of human language acquisition is our ability to make sweeping generalizations from small numbers of observations. Thus, though a homogeneous network, such as that shown in Figure 20.2, might, given sufficient data, be capable of learning the associations between messages and meaningful responses for complex tasks, we are not satisfied with such asymptotic results. An alternative is to investigate how one might reflect our knowledge of device and language structure in a network architecture, to provide improved generalization capability when learning such complex mappings. A **third principle**, then, is that a language acquisition device should be well-matched with its environment and input/output periphery, as measured by its ability to rapidly adapt and generalize. This principle was exploited in Miller and Gorin (1992) for a data retrieval task where the output-periphery structure was reflected in the network architecture by factoring the action space of the device into two independent subactions through the use of a product of subnetworks. In Gertner and Gorin (1993), the environmental structure in the input language was reflected in the network architecture via a layer of subnetworks corresponding to linguistic nontermi-nals. One of the major contributions of this chapter, detailed in section 20.4, is a method to reflect the input-periphery structure of a multi-sensory device in a network architecture by constructing a network from component sensory primitive subnetworks.

In all the previous work (Gorin *et al.*, 1991a, 1991b; Miller and Gorin, 1992; Gertner and Gorin, 1993), the **environment** consisted of only a user who produced the input message and a semantic-level error signal. In many devices of interest, however, the machine response to the message also depends on the **state of the world**. This leads us to consider systems with **multi-sensory input**, i.e. input from both a user and other sources.

For example, consider an autonomous robot operating in a complex environment. A possible request to the robot might be expressed by the user as 'Give me that pen'. An appropriate response to this message depends both on which pen is indicated by 'that pen' (perhaps by the user pointing to the pen), and where the pen is located. This information is available through visual input, so that the device should be able to sense the world visually to perform its task.

Another example where the device action depends on the message and the state of the world is in the context of a voice-controlled telephone. Suppose the user commands the telephone to handle a call with the sentence, 'Please pick up that new call'. The appropriate response depends on the state of the environment, for example, whether there is a current call active, in which case it should put it on hold and pick up the new call. In any case, the first step is for the telephone to focus its attention on which call appearance corresponds to 'that call'.

In another example of a system where the device action is also affected by the state of the world, consider a voice-controlled computing environment. A typical user request to such a device might be 'Please bring up the window where I was working on the paper for the Acoustical Society'. The appropriate response in this case depends on which files are being edited in which windows and also whether the window is iconified or not. For example, if the appropriate window is iconified, it must be opened. On the other hand, if the window is open but hidden behind another open window, the computer might raise the editor window or lower the obstructing window. Again, the first step in executing such a request is for the machine to focus its attention on the appropriate window and file.

Yet another example of a device whose action depends on both the message and the state of the world is in the context of a database query system. A possible user-request might be 'Please give me a list of all the freshmen taking History-101'. The appropriate response to this request depends on the entries in the database corresponding to the year of each student and also the subjects taken. These database entries will change over time, so that the appropriate machine response needs to change as well. In our conclusions in section 20.7, we will explore in more detail potential applications of our principles and mechanisms to several such problems.

In this chapter, in particular, we investigate a **visual focus of attention task** in a blocks-world where the machine receives both a message and visual input. As a motivating example, consider a very young child lying in its crib. The child is able to look around the room, and focus its attention on various people, such as its mother and father. The most rudimentary demonstration of language acquisition is when the child looks at the correct parent in response to a prompt such as 'Where's Mummy?'. Motivated by this human scenario, we investigate an artificial system that **learns** to focus its attention on one of many blocks of different colors and shapes in response to typed messages. In this rudimentary blocks-world scenario, each block is characterized by only two features – color and shape. However, the principles and mechanisms described in this chapter extend to any number and type of features. Figure 20.3 shows an example of a blocks-world, where the eyeball is shown responding correctly to the input message, 'Look at the red square'.

Figure 20.4 shows a block diagram of the system. This is an elaboration on the basic mechanism shown in Figure 20.1. The input to the device at

MESSAGE: LOOK AT THE RED SQUARE

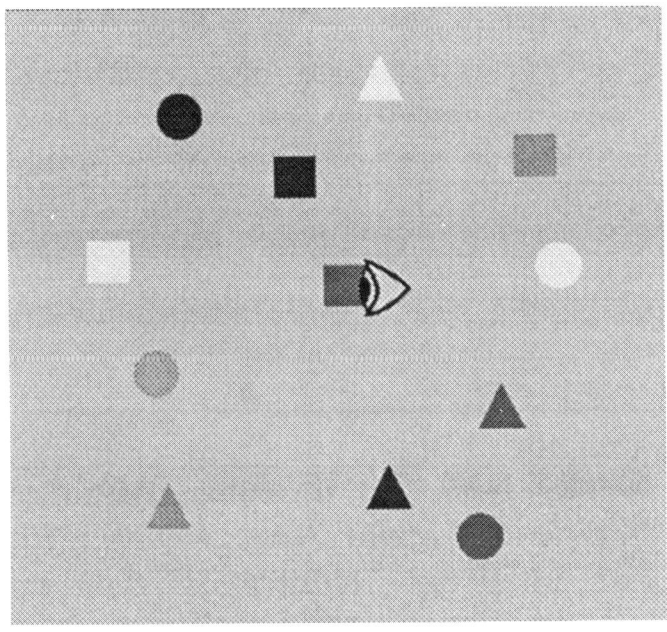

Figure 20.3 *A blocks-world example. The eyeball focuses its attention on a red square in response to the input message shown.*

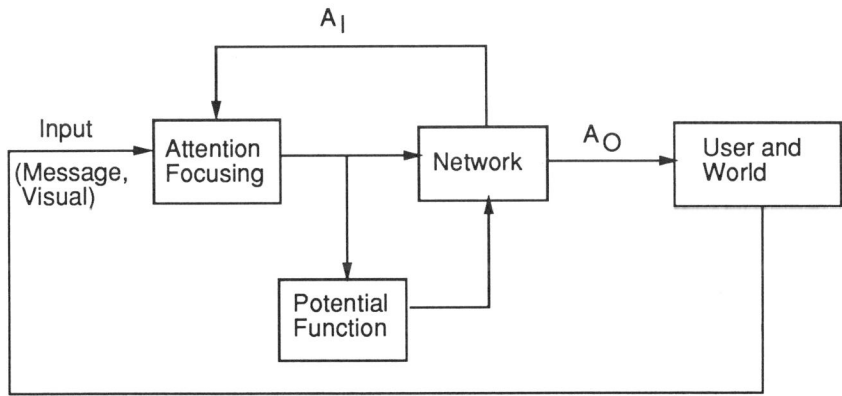

Figure 20.4 *Language acquisition for visual focus of attention.*

any time could be just the visual input, or both a message and the visual input. The visual input is filtered through an attention focusing mechanism. Depending on the current and past input, the network changes its focus of attention, causing the visual input to the device to be changed. Thus, the network provides feedback to control the position of the device's eyeball, which in turn changes the state of the visual input. This feedback is shown in the figure as A_I, which can be interpreted as an internal decision corresponding to the focus of attention of the eyeball. The presence of such feedback has been noted in research on human eye movements also (Gaarder, 1975).

The network moves the eyeball by minimizing a **time-varying potential function** which is described in section 20.3. This function is defined in the set of possible eyeball positions and its minimum corresponds to the optimum eyeball position where the message and visual input are most strongly associated. The machine responds, at any time, by moving the eyeball towards this position. As explained above, moving the eyeball causes the visual input to change. This changes the shape of the potential function, so that at the next time instant, a new minimum may emerge.

The internal decision A_I is to be distinguished from A_O, which is an **external observable action**. We may view A_O as providing evidence of the internal decision A_I. The user provides feedback with respect to A_O by typing a message, which may include a semantic-level error signal as to the appropriateness of A_O. This external user-provided feedback is to be distinguished from the internal network-provided feedback described above, both of which are used by the potential function to control the eyeball position.

In the present work, A_O and A_I are identical because the task we are investigating is just the focus of attention. We note that A_O could be more complex such as **manipulating a particular object**. In particular, A_O might be an action such as **picking up a red block**.

The message input for the device consists of typed sentences. This might be extended to spoken input, as in Gorin *et al.* (1991b). We assume that the visual input is pre-processed and that the individual objects are segmented. To extend these methods to an image of a real scene, we would use segmentation methods as described, for example, in Fu and Mui (1981) and Haralick and Shapiro (1985). We further assume that the system can distinguish between colors and shapes on the basis of their features. In the present system, the colors and shapes of objects are available to the network as tokens from a graphics program that simulates the blocks-world. The graphics program provides complete information about the shape, color and position of objects to the program simulating the language acquisition device. For an image of a real scene, we would use clustering as a pre-processing step to form different color and shape clusters, as was done for speech in Gorin *et al.* (1991b).

The input periphery of the device has structure in that there is both message and visual input. The device can also sense two visual features corresponding to color and shape. Following our third principle, we exploit this structure in the visual input-periphery of the device through the introduction of **sensory primitive subnets** corresponding to the different visual features that can be sensed. The associations between the words and the visual input is factored through the sensory primitive nodes. This enables generalization between different objects that have the same visual features. Thus, once the system learns the meaning of the word, 'red', in the context of one red object, it can generalize this knowledge to all red objects.

The system runs in a **conversational mode** where the user can provide clarifying messages and error feedback, until the system responds correctly. For example, consider the following conversation:

user:	types 'Look at the scarlet circle'
machine:	moves eyeball toward a green circle
user:	types 'No, scarlet is like red'
machine:	moves eyeball toward a red circle
user:	types 'Good'

In this example, the machine initially responds incorrectly, but corrects itself in its second response, which is rewarded by the user. The machine learns on the basis of this reinforcement by strengthening the associations between the words in this conversation and the visual input from the red circle. The sensory primitive nodes enable immediate generalization of the word 'scarlet' to any red object, regardless of shape.

The utility of these principles and mechanisms is demonstrated and evaluated in an experiment involving different users interacting with the system. The task of the device was to direct its eyeball toward the appropriate object in response to user typed commands. The task and experiments are described in detail in section 20.6. Initially, the system knows **nothing** about the language for its task, or about the different visual features. There is no vocabulary, no semantic associations, and no sensory primitive nodes. However, the words 'Good' and 'No' are pre-fabricated error signals connoting reward and punishment, respectively. As the device is presented with different visual scenes, it builds new sensory primitive nodes corresponding to the visual features it senses. Meaning is acquired by building the sensory associations between the message and visual input. The above-mentioned mechanisms are used, namely a structured connectionist network embedded in a feedback control system, which adjusts the associations between the message and visual input based on reinforcement as to the appropriateness of the machine's response. We collected over 1000 typed conversations from 11 users who interacted with the system over a three month period. It was found that the average conversation length was only 1.4 sentences, and the device retained 98% of what it was taught.

20.2 Background

Much of the research on automated language acquisition has focused on the discovery of syntax or grammar (Fu and Booth, 1975a,b), often to the exclusion of meaning. In those experimental systems which do exploit semantic information for language understanding, the standard approach has been to encode meaning symbolically, as for example in Anderson (1977). Here the system learns the mapping from the sentence to this symbolic representation on the basis of training examples, where each example is a sentence, a symbolic representation of the sentence meaning, and an indication of the main proposition of the sentence. The problem of natural language understanding is, therefore, reduced to that of translating the input message into this symbolic representation of meaning. In contrast, a different approach was presented in Gorin *et al.* (1991a), where the machine's understanding of an input message was evaluated on the basis of whether the machine **responded in an expected and appropriate manner** over a wide range of scenarios. An information-theoretic connectionist network was proposed that **learned** the mapping from the input message to a meaningful machine response. The network learned through **reinforcement-feedback** received from the environment as to the appropriateness of the machine's response to an input message. The work presented in this chapter builds on those ideas. (We will not repeat the motivating arguments for this approach to language understanding, instead referring the interested reader to Gorin *et al.*, 1991a).

Traditional rule-based Artificial Intelligence (AI) techniques for language understanding have generally ignored the problem of how the meaning of the basic units or symbols are initially acquired, usually manually programming such meaning into the system. Recent work by Harnad (1990) on the 'symbol grounding problem' suggests that the meaning of symbols must be grounded in the sensory projections of objects, and in the feature detectors that pick out the invariant features of object and event categories from their sensory projections. It is further suggested in Harnad (1990) that connectionist systems may be apt for **learning** these invariant features. The crucial difference, in our opinion, between this approach and that of rule-based AI is that the meaning of the symbols are learned rather than preprogrammed. Whereas connectionist systems can learn the associations between different sensory inputs, rule-based AI methods rely on an expert to hand-carve these associations through a set or rules. Learning is more cost effective than having experts pre-program many rules into the system, and it also has the potential to learn rules that an expert may be ignorant of. Furthermore, learning and adaptation is a crucial component of intelligence. It is thus a viable approach for machine language acquisition.

In this chapter we study an adaptive language acquisition system that learns to respond appropriately in the presence of both message and visual input. In particular, a blocks-world scenario is considered where the machine action is to move its eyeball toward a block of the appropriate color and shape in response to the message and visual input. Words acquire meaning through their associations with the visual input. These associations are learned by the machine in the course of performing its task.

The reasons we chose the blocks-world to investigate language acquisition in a multisensory device were its simplicity and anthropomorphic appeal. One of the most famous AI programs for language understanding is SHRDLU written by Winograd (1972, 1980), Boden (1977), which could respond to input text by manipulating blocks using a robot arm in a simulated blocks-world. SHRDLU could also answer questions about its world and its actions. However, in SHRDLU, the mapping from an input message to a robot response was hand-carved by the programmer. This is in contrast to the work presented in this chapter where the mapping is **learned**. The focus of attention task we have chosen in this work is much simpler than the range of things SHRDLU can do in its blocks-world. We chose to evaluate our principles initially on the focus of attention problem because it seems to be the most basic task in a blocks-world. However, as noted in section 20.1, more complicated actions can be learned if the sensory-motor periphery of the device is made more sophisticated.

There has also been much connectionist work on natural language processing. In Jain (1991), a modular recurrent connectionist network is used to learn to parse sentences. A system that learns to paraphrase script-based stories is presented in Miikkulainen and Dyer (1989, 1991). This is also a modular network. In other work, connectionist networks have been applied to learning to assign case roles to constituents in input sentences (McClelland and Kawamoto, 1986). More recently, modular connectionist networks have also been used to learn the mapping from input sentences to an output event description, consisting of a set of thematic roles and their fillers (St. John and McClelland, 1990). In all this work, the networks have been trained by example using the backpropagation algorithm (Rumelhart and McClelland, 1986). During training, the network is explicitly provided with the input sentence, and the required output. However, none of this work has addressed the problem of learning to **understand** in our sense of mapping input messages to machine action. Recently there has been some interesting work on forming internal representations which ground the meaning of words in input received from a visual modality (Cottrell *et al.*, 1990). In this work, a modular network learns to associate word labels with images and also to describe a simple movie in simple sentences. We share our motivations with this work in that the meaning of words is learned by forming associations between different sensory inputs. However, in our system, the network learns the inter-sensory associations on the basis of feedback received as to the appropriateness of its response, i.e. focusing attention. This is in contrast to Cottrell *et al.* (1990), where the network is trained either by self-supervision or by supervision with the task being to associate the word and visual inputs.

It is appropriate, at this point, to mention work on eye movements in psycho-physics. The literature here is vast, and can be found, for example, in Gaarder (1975), Yarbus (1967), Bach-Y-Rita *et al.* (1971) and Ditchburn (1973). When examining a scene, the eye executes large jumps to move from one point of fixation to another and smaller jumps while fixating. It has been noted that these eye movements can be modeled as a feedback process, with the brain analysing the current input to decide where to move the eye in the next instant (Gaarder, 1975). This is related to the feedback mechanism shown in Figure 20.4, which controls the focus of attention for the system described in this chapter. However, we make no claims as to the biological validity of the actual implementation we have used.

The learning approach used by the system presented in this chapter can be characterized as a **reinforcement learning** method. Reinforcement learning (Barto and Anandan, 1985; Kaelbling, 1990) can be contrasted to **learning by example** (Rumelhart and McClelland, 1986; Duda and Hart, 1973) in that it is not necessary to provide the system with explicit labeled examples. Rather, the system learns on the basis of reinforcement received from the environment which measures the appropriateness of the machine response to an input stimulus. The reinforcement signal takes on two values depending on whether the system responded correctly or incorrectly. In the case where there are only two possible device outputs, reinforcement learning is identical to learning by example, since the correct output can be derived from the reinforcement signal.

The multi-sensory nature of the environment is perceived via a structured input periphery. According to our third principle, reflecting such structure in the network architecture will result in improved learning and generalization. There has been previous work in such structured connectionist networks (Jacobs and Jordan, 1991; Nowlan and Hinton, 1991). In this work, the task structure is such that there is more than one independent task. The network is divided into modules and it learns to assign these tasks to different modules. However, during training, the network is told which task it must solve for each input pattern, and learning proceeds by example. Structured networks were investigated for adaptive language acquisition in Miller and Gorin (1992) and Gertner and Gorin (1993). In the former, the task structure is similar to that of Jacobs and Jordan (1991) and Nowlan and Hinton (1991). An important distinction in Miller and Gorin (1992) is that the supervision during learning is provided at the level of the observable machine action, which is composed of many independent subactions, and the assignment of subactions to the network modules is learned automatically. The subactions are, however, hidden from the observer. This can be contrasted to Jacobs and Jordan (1991) and Nowlan and Hinton (1991), where the network is capable of executing a set of independent tasks and the supervision during learning is at the level of these independent tasks. Another distinction is that a reinforcement learning mechanism is used in Miller and Gorin (1992) and Gertner and Gorin (1993), rather than learning by example as in Jacobs and Jordan (1991) and Nowlan and Hinton (1991). In Gertner and Gorin (1993), structure in the input language was exploited for an airline reservation system by building internal network nodes corresponding to linguistic non-terminals.

In the work presented in this chapter, the structure inherent in the multi-sensory input periphery of the system is exploited through the use of an intermediate layer of sensory primitive nodes, leading to improved generalization for such networks.

20.3 A feedback mechanism for visual focus of attention

Recall the block diagram of the system shown in Figure 20.4. As mentioned before, there is an internal focus of attention decision A_I, which changes the visual input to the system, and an external observable action A_O. The user evaluates the appropriateness of A_O and provides a semantic-level error signal to the device. The device learns on the basis of this signal. In this paper, A_O and A_I are identical, since the task we consider is that of focus of attention.

The focus of attention action A_I (and in this work, A_O), is controlled by a **time-varying potential function**, which has a value $P_i(x_i, y_i, t)$ at time t for each object i, located at the Cartesian coordinates (x_i, y_i). The eyeball is moved toward that object which has the minimum value of P_i. The time dependence of this function stems from the time dependence of both the message and the visual input. Time-dependent energy functions have also been explored for speech recognition by neural networks in Tank and Hopfield (1987) and Unnikrishnan *et al.* (1991), where the network states follow trajectories in time which locate minima in the energy functions which correspond to recognized words. Another example of time-dependent potential functions is in robot obstacle avoidance (Khatib, 1986). A potential field around each obstacle repels the robot, and in the case of moving obstacles, this is a time-varying potential field (Khatib, 1986).

Motivated by our example of a child learning to associate words with people in its field of view, we build into the device the following innate characteristics. A **first property** is that the device is attracted to bright, moving objects, with movement being more attractive. This property is essentially an innate curiosity. A **second property** is that the device becomes bored after looking at an object for a while, and then moves on to another object. This allows the eyeball to explore the scene. A **third property** is that the eyeball is attracted to objects whose visual input is strongly associated with the message input. Thus the device response maximizes the inter-sensory associations. Finally, the device is repelled from objects that the user deems to be inappropriate. The user conveys this information to the machine by typing 'No' as the first word of a new sentence. We now describe the implementation of these properties in detail:

1. The eyeball is attracted to bright and moving objects, where movement is more attractive than brightness. Thus, the user can catch the machine's attention by moving an object, at the same time providing a message, such as 'Thus is a blue ball', to teach the machine about that object. This

property is implemented via a function $A_i(t)$, given by

$$A_i(t) = \frac{(m_i(t) + v_i^\alpha(t))}{\sqrt{d_i(t)^2 + \varepsilon}}, \tag{1}$$

where, at time $t, m_i(t)$ and $v_i(t)$ are the intensity and speed of object $i, d_i(t)$ is the distance between object i and the eyeball position, $(x(t), y(t))$, and ε is a positive constant. $v_i(t)$ is raised to a constant power α, which can be adjusted to make speed or movement more attractive than intensity. The distance term $d_i(t)$ in the denominator reflects the fact that the device is more strongly attracted to objects that are close to the center of its field of view.

2. The device becomes bored after looking at an object for a while, and then moves on to a different object. This causes the eyeball to explore the scene as part of its innate behavior. The boredom property is implemented via the function B_i, given by

$$B_i = \exp\left(-\lambda_2 \sum_{\tau = t - T_0}^{t} e^{-\lambda_1 d_i(\tau)} \right), \tag{2}$$

where T_0 is a time window, and λ_1 and λ_2 are constants which affect the rate at which the device gets bored of an object. This function can be understood by imagining that the eyeball has been positioned at object i for T seconds. Since, during this time T the eyeball is close to object i, d_i would be small or close to 0. Thus, from equation (2), we see that

$$B_i \approx e^{-\lambda_2 T}. \tag{3}$$

This shows that B_i decays exponentially with T, the time for which the eyeball is focused on object i, causing it to lose interest in that object.

3. The device is attracted to objects whose visual input is strongly associated with the message input. The device acquires language by learning these associations. This property is implemented via a function U_i, which is a measure of the strength of the association between the message input and the visual input from object i. We postpone the discussion of this function to section 20.4.

4. Finally the device is repelled from objects that are determined to be inappropriate by the user. This is implemented via a function E_i, which is an encoding of the semantic-level error signal and is given as follows. Normally E_i is equal to zero. However, suppose the machine focuses its attention on object i in response to a message and the user decides that the response is inappropriate. The user then starts his next message input with the word 'No', a prefabricated error signal indicating that object i is incorrect. E_i is then set to a large positive number.

We can now combine the various properties described above into a potential function, whose value at time t and the position (x_i, y_i) of object i

is given by

$$P_i(x_i, y_i, t) = -A_i B_i U_i + E_i, \qquad (4)$$

where A_i and B_i reflect the device's response to the visual input, U_i its response to a message, and E_i is an encoding of the semantic-level error signal. The eyeball is moved toward the object that has the smallest value of P_i. In other words, this is the object that exerts the maximum attraction on the eyeball. This object is given by

$$i_{\min} = \arg \min_i P_i. \qquad (5)$$

The eyeball is moved toward the position $(x_{i_{\min}}, y_{i_{\min}})$ with a step size that decreases with the distance, $d_{i_{\min}}$, between the eyeball and the object, $i_{\min}$. This step size is given by

$$\Delta = 1 - e^{-\lambda_4 d_{i_{\min}}}. \qquad (6)$$

The above properties were based on our intuitions about human behavior. We do not make any claims as to the biological validity of the actual implementations described above.

20.4 Network structure

In section 20.1 we proposed a third principle for language acquisition, namely that the device architecture must reflect structure present in the environment or input/output periphery of the system in order for better learning and generalization. This principle has been explored in related work to exploit structure in the task or **output periphery** of the system (Miller and Gorin, 1992). Here, a data retrieval task was investigated where the system retrieves facts about 20 attributes of the 50 states in the USA. This was done by dividing the network into two independent subnetworks, one for the states and the other for the attributes. The outputs of each network were then combined to generate the final response of the device. Another study of this third principle is in Gertner and Gorin (1993), where the **environmental structure** in the input message was exploited for an airline information retrieval task where the device provides information about flights between two cities. The structure in the input message was reflected through the introduction of an intermediate layer of nodes corresponding to linguistic nonterminals. The outputs of these nodes were used to decide whether a particular city was an arrival or a departure city. In this work, we investigate how to reflect the structure of the device's input periphery, stemming from multi-sensory input, in the network architecture.

The input periphery of our system has structure in that there is both message and visual input. Furthermore, the device can sense two visual features – color and shape. We do not exploit structure in the message itself, although this

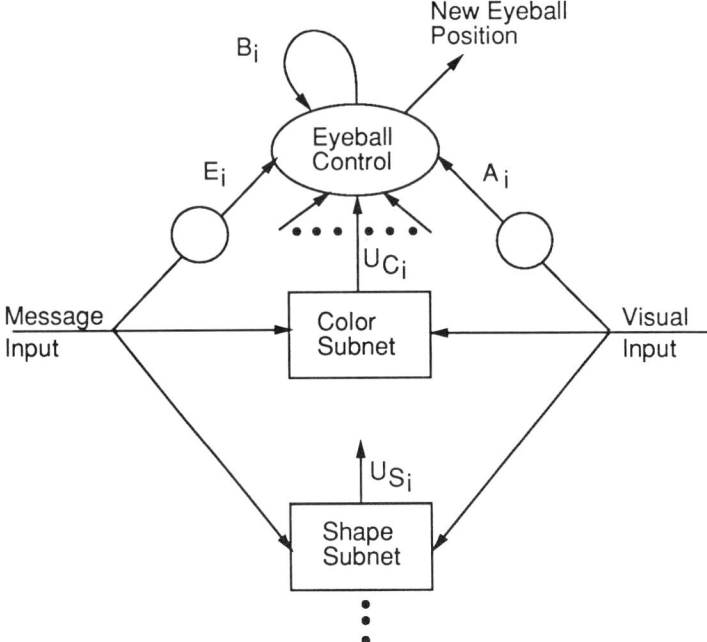

Figure 20.5 *Network architecture.*

could be done as in Gertner and Gorin (1993). The visual input structure is reflected in the network through the introduction of **sensory primitive nodes** corresponding to color and shape. These are organized into two independent subnetworks, as shown in Figure 20.5. This is similar to the structure of the network described in Miller and Gorin (1992). This method can be extended in a straightforward manner if the number of input features is greater than two, by simply adding one new subnetwork for each new feature. For example, if the features corresponded to color, shape and size we would have three subnetworks.

In Figure 20.5, A_i, B_i and E_i refer to the component functions in the potential function of equation (4). The outputs U_{C_i} and U_{S_i} are measures of the strength of the associations between the message input and the visual input corresponding to the color and shape, respectively, of object i. The term U_i in equation (4) is now given by adding U_{C_i} and U_{S_i}:

$$U_i = U_{C_i} + U_{S_i}. \tag{7}$$

Figure 20.6 shows the details of the color subnetwork. The shape subnetwork is similar. The first layer nodes are the vocabulary word detector nodes v_m, as in Figure 20.2. There are no phrase detector nodes in this system, such as those in Figure 20.2. The next layer of nodes are the color

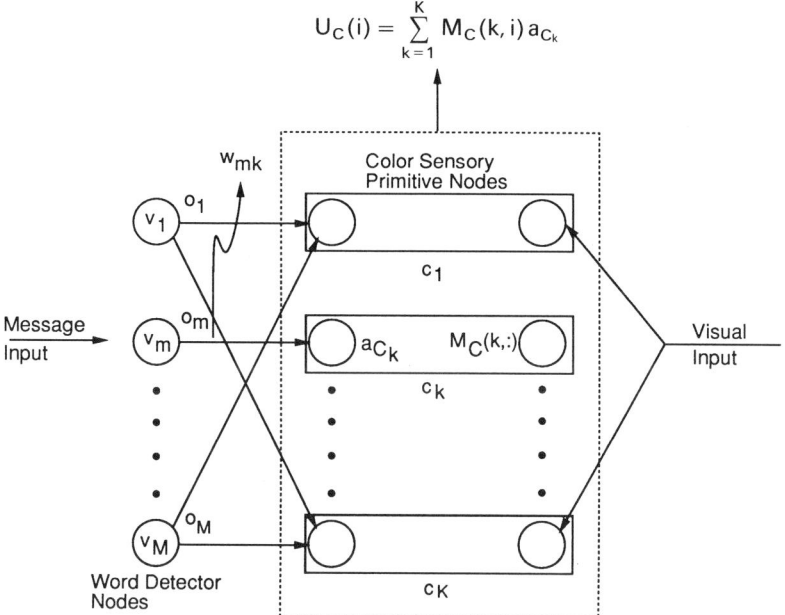

$$U_C(i) = \sum_{k=1}^{K} M_C(k,i) a_{C_k}$$

Figure 20.6 *Color subnetwork.*

sensory primitive nodes c_k. Initially, the subnetwork has no word or color sensory primitive nodes. As new words and colors are experienced, the device builds the color subnetwork by adding new word and color sensory primitive nodes.

If a word v_m in the *l*th sentence $S(l)$ is not a vocabulary word, then a new word detector node is grown. The outputs of the word detector nodes $o_m(l)$ are then given by

$$o_m(l) = \begin{cases} 1 & \text{if } v_m \in S(l) \\ 0 & \text{otherwise} \end{cases}. \tag{8}$$

Thus, $o_m(l)$ detects the presence of the word v_m in the sentence $S(l)$.

The weight between the word v_m and the color sensory primitive c_k is the mutual information $I(c_k, v_m)$, given by

$$w_{mk} = I(c_k, v_m) = \log \frac{P(c_k|v_m)}{P(c_k)}, \tag{9}$$

where $P(c_k|v_m)$ is the probability that the appropriate color is c_k, given that the input word is v_m. Each sensory primitive node also has a bias term associated with it, given by

$$w_k = \log P(c_k), \tag{10}$$

where $P(c_k)$ is simply the probability of the appropriate color being c_k. As shown in Gorin et al. (1991a), the weight and bias terms can be updated sequentially by smoothed relative frequency methods.

The output of the color sensory primitive node due to the lth sentence $S(l)$ is given by

$$a_{C_k}(l) = f\left(\sum_{m=1}^{M} o_m w_{mk} + w_k\right), \tag{11}$$

where M is the number of vocabulary words, w_{mk} and w_k are the weights and the bias of sensory primitive node k, which are defined in equations (9) and (10), and $f(\cdot)$ is the sigmoid function given by

$$f(x) = \frac{1}{1 + e^{-x}}. \tag{12}$$

As described in section 20.5, the sentences, $S(l)$ are grouped into conversations where, within a conversation, the user's goal for the machine response is assumed to be constant. The outputs $a_{C_k}(m)$ after the mth sentence in the conversation are linearly combined with the outputs in response to the previous sentences to produce a resultant output given by

$$A_{C_k}(m) = \gamma(m)a_{C_k}(m) + (1 - \gamma(m))A_{C_k}(m - 1), \tag{13}$$

where $\gamma(m)$ is a smoothing factor. In our implementation we choose $\gamma(m) = 1/m$.

The output of the color sensory primitive node c_k due to the visual input from object i is given by

$$M_C(k, i) = \begin{cases} 1 & \text{if color of object } i = \text{color } k \\ 0 & \text{otherwise} \end{cases}. \tag{14}$$

This function simply detects the color k in object i. The outputs due to the message, given by equation (13) and due to the visual input, given by equation (14) are combined to give the output U_{C_i} as follows:

$$U_{C_i} = \sum_{k=1}^{K} M_C(k, i)A_{C_k}. \tag{15}$$

Thus the output U_{C_i} is large when the color of object i is that connoted by the message. The output U_{C_i} can be interpreted as the output of a familiar construct called the Sigma-Pi node (Rumelhart and McClelland, 1986), where the outputs $M_C(k, i)$ and A_{C_k} are multiplied before being input into the Sigma-Pi node. It can be seen from equation (15) and equation (4) that the function $U_C(i)$, decreases the value of $P_i(x_i, y_i, t)$ if the color of object i is that connoted by the message input. This is exactly what is needed, since the eyeball is moved toward the object with the minimum value of P_i.

20.5 Conversation segmentation

The human-machine interaction is implemented as a control system with a semantic-level error feedback. The user may interact with the machine by either typing messages to the machine, or by changing the state of the blocks-world, which is implemented as a graphics simulation. The user can, at any time, change the state of the blocks-world by adding, removing, or changing the position of blocks, using a software package (Blewett et al., 1991) that underlies the graphics simulation.

20.5.1 Two conversation types

The interaction can be thought of as a sequence of conversations between the user and the machine. There are two distinct types of conversations that the user can have with the device. Firstly, the user may explicitly teach the machine about an object. This is done by attracting the eyeball to an object by moving the object, at the same time providing a message such as 'This is a blue ball' to teach the machine about that object. Secondly, the user can request the machine to perform some action, by typing a message such as 'Look at the red square', and then providing further information, possibly with semantic-level error feedback, until the device responds correctly. In what follows, these two types of conversations will be referred to as Type I and Type II conversations, respectively. As noted above, a Type I conversation is always started by the user moving an object, whereas a Type II conversation is started simply by typing a sentence. We now give examples of a Type I and a Type II conversation:

Example 1: A Type I conversation

> user: attracts the machine's attention by moving the red circle
> machine: moves eyeball toward the red circle
> user: types 'This is a red circle'

Example 2: A Type II conversation

> user: types 'Look at the scarlet circle'
> machine: moves eyeball toward a green circle
> user: types 'No, scarlet is like red'
> machine: moves eyeball toward a red circle
> user: types 'Good'

Of course, the problem is to detect whether a conversation is a Type I or Type II conversation, and then to take appropriate action. It is possible to do this in a principled manner. For example, we could postulate that the device strengthens associations between visual and message input when such inputs occur in close proximity in time and when the device has responded correctly. The correctness of the device's response could be measured, for example, either by a positive reinforcement from the user or by a high confidence in the device's response. The device's confidence in its response could be measured by the depth of the potential well corresponding to its response. However, in this rudimentary experiment, we use a rule-based conversation segmenter as presented below.

20.5.2 Segmenting the conversations

The important issues to consider in the segmentation problem are to detect the beginning and end of a conversation, to decide whether the conversation is Type I or Type II, and when to update the weights of the network. We now present an algorithm that addresses these issues.

Type I conversation
Recall the Type I conversation shown in Example 1. A Type I conversation is always started by the user moving an object to attract the machine's attention to it. When the machine detects this motion, the next sentence typed within a short time period is assumed to describe the object that was moved by the user. This sentence **is not used** in computing U_i in equation (15), and hence does not affect the eyeball position through the potential function. The weights between the words in the sentence and the color and shape sensory primitives corresponding to the object that was moved are updated according to the smoothed relative frequency method presented in Gorin *et al.* (1991a). The conversation ends with this weight update, and the system waits for a new conversation to start.

Type II conversation
Recall the Type II conversation shown in Example 2. If the system is not currently in a conversation, then a Type II conversation is started by the user typing a new sentence. The machine treats this sentence as a command and responds according to the potential function described before. The machine then waits for the user to respond. The user could either reward the machine, punish it, or do neither. These cases are treated separately below.

   The user rewards the machine by typing 'Good' as the first word of a new sentence. This is a hard-wired reward signal, indicating a correct machine response. The machine then updates its weights based on all the words in the conversation and the sensory primitive corresponding to the correct object. The conversation is said to have **converged** with a correct machine response. The conversation ends with the weight update and the machine waits for a new conversation to start.

   The user punishes the machine by typing 'No' as the first word of a new sentence. This is a hard-wired punishment signal, indicating an incorrect machine response. The user can also provide more information as in the second sentence of Example 2. The punishment signal has the effect of repelling the eyeball from the incorrect object as described in section 20.3.

If the user starts a new sentence with neither a reward nor a punishment signal, the conversation is ended and the new sentence is considered to be the first sentence of a new Type II conversation. In this case, both for evaluation and to guide the learning algorithm, it is necessary to decide whether or not the machine's response to the previous conversation was correct. Since the user did not explicitly provide this information, the machine decides for itself based on an **internal confidence model**. We used a simple confidence measure given as follows. Recall from equation (5) that the eyeball is moved toward the object $i_{\min}$ that corresponds to the minimum value of the potential function P_i. Let $P^n < 0$ denote the nth lowest value of P_i. The values P^1 and P^2 are computed. If the ratio P^1/P^2 is large, then the machine is confident in its action. Thus

if $\dfrac{P^1}{P^2} > C$ then confident, and response treated as correct

else   diffident, and response treated as incorrect.

where C is a confidence threshold. Thus, if the machine is confident, the previous conversation is treated as **convergent**, and the weights are updated. However, if the machine is diffident, then the response is treated as incorrect, and the previous conversation is said to be **divergent**. It is possible to learn from incorrect responses by weakening the corresponding associations. However, in this chapter we do not investigate such learning, leaving it as a subject for future work. One must be careful in setting the value of the parameter C. If C is too small, then some conversations that actually ended with an **incorrect response** may be treated as **convergent** and incorrect weight updates made. On the other hand, if C is too large, then some conversations which ended in **correct responses** may be treated as **divergent**. Clearly, the first problem is more serious, since incorrect learning would occur. Thus we conservatively set the threshold to prevent incorrect learning. It is possible to adapt the threshold C based on the ratio P^1/P^2, and the semantic-level error signal. However, we do not address this issue here, leaving it as a subject for future work.

Finally, if the user does not type a new sentence for a very long time, then the machine ends the conversation and waits for a new conversation to start. The conversation is treated as divergent, and the machine does not update its weights.

We have presented a method to segment the user interactions into conversations. As seen above, a Type I conversation is, by definition, one sentence long. However, a Type II conversation continues until the machine responds correctly or the user starts a new conversation. If we disregard the case where the user prematurely ends a Type II conversation without a reward or punishment signal, then we can analyse the convergence properties of such a conversation as shown below.

Convergence of Type II conversation

We consider the probability that a Type II conversation converges within m steps. A naive convergence model can be derived as follows. Let P_e be the probability of error in the response to the first sentence. Let us hypothesize that the next sentence will comprise an independent paraphrasing of the request, so that the probability of error is again P_e. The probability of an incorrect response to each of the first M sentences is P_e^M. Thus the probability of converging within the first M sentences is given by

$$P(m \leqslant M) = 1 - P_e^M. \tag{16}$$

We can rearrange this equation as

$$1 - P(m \leqslant M) = P_e^M, \tag{17}$$

which shows that the probability of converging within M sentences approaches 1 **exponentially fast**, as M is increased. We verify this result experimentally in section 20.6.2.

Segmenting the user interaction into conversations is a very difficult problem, since the user is allowed considerable freedom in interacting with the system. In our experiment, the users were only instructed as to the two kinds of conversations that they could have and also about the prefabricated error signals, 'No' and 'Good'. However, the users did not always follow these instructions. The algorithm presented is a simple one that appears to work well in practice. However, it has its drawbacks in that the reward and punishment signals are predetermined. A principled way of approaching this problem is to learn when a message in a given context implies a negation or affirmation of the machine's response. Prosody might play an important role here for human beings. This is hard to reflect in text input. However, it can be exploited in the case of spoken input systems such as Gorin *et al.* (1991b). Another problem with the present algorithm is the preset confidence threshold. As already mentioned, this could be adapted based on the semantic-level error signal.

20.6 Experimental results

We performed an experimental evaluation in which 11 users interacted with the system over a three month period. The users were instructed as to the two kinds of conversations that they could have with the system, and the use of the prefabricated error signals, 'No' and 'Good'. The users were also able to change the state of the blocks-world at any time using a graphics program (Blewett *et al.*, 1991). The system initially has **no** vocabulary, except for the prefabricated error messages, 'No' and 'Good'. There were initially

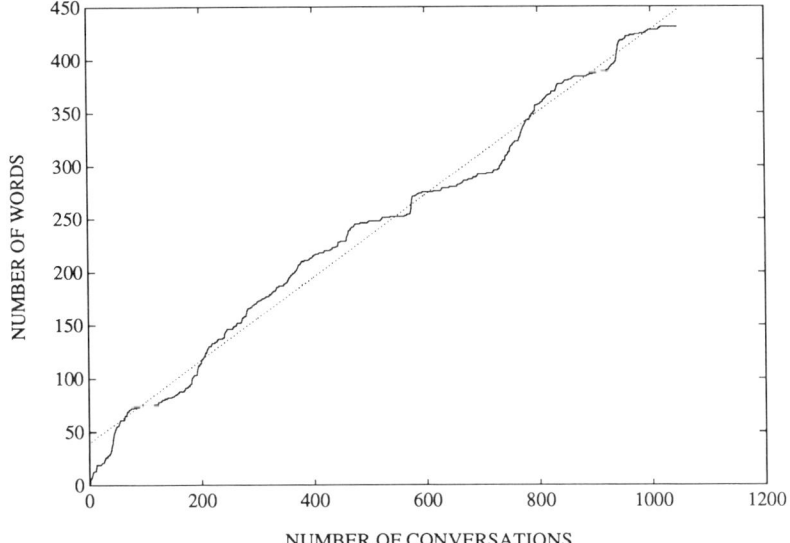

Figure 20.7 *Vocabulary growth.* ⋯⋯: *a linear regression.*

also no sensory primitive nodes. Over the course of the interactions, the system acquired a vocabulary of 431 words from 1434 typed sentences. The sentences were **unconstrained** in both grammar and vocabulary. The system also acquired three shape sensory primitive and four color sensory primitive nodes. In this rudimentary experiment, we presented the machine with only a small number of shapes and colors. However, the principles and mechanisms scale up as demonstrated, for example, in the experiments of Miller and Gorin (1992). Following the method described in section 20.5, the 1434 sentences were segmented into 1045 conversations. We now describe some quantitative analyses to evaluate the performance of the system.

20.6.1 Vocabulary

In Figure 20.7, we plot the number of vocabulary words against the number of conversations. We see that the vocabulary continually increases and shows no signs of leveling off, even for the rudimentary task considered in this chapter. This is because the users were constantly attempting to both teach the machine and test it through the use of novel, and sometimes highly imaginative words.

We also measured the frequency of the rank-ordered words. The nth most frequently occurring word has rank n and its frequency $f(n)$ is the number of times it occurs. It has been shown that $f(n)$ is inversely proportional to n for vocabularies drawn from natural texts such as novels. In other words,

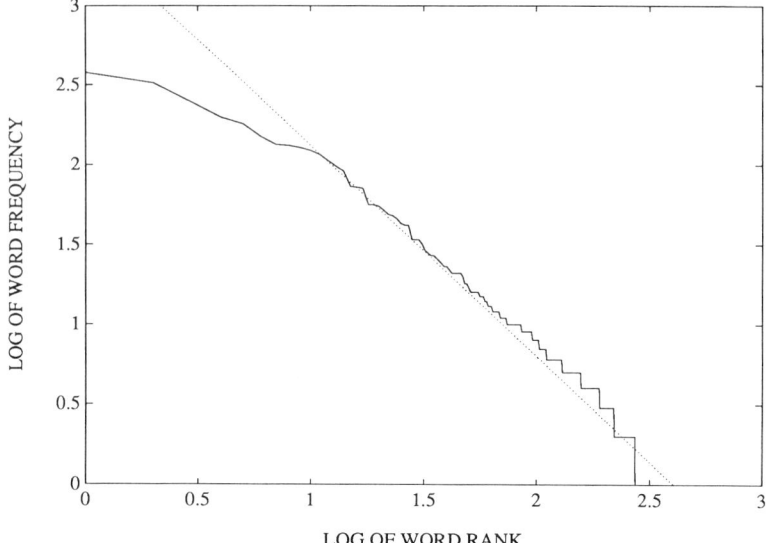

Figure 20.8 *Rank-frequency plot.* ·······: *a linear regression.*

for natural text, most words occur infrequently. This result is known as Zipf's Law (Pierce, 1961). We plot $f(n)$ against n on a log–log graph in Figure 20.8. The linear behavior of the plot shows the conformation of the vocabulary with Zipf's Law. This is a motivation for us to study algorithms that learn from few observations. The information-theoretic network performs well under these conditions, as shown in results of section 20.6.2. Similar results were also reported in Gorin *et al.* (1991a, b), Miller and Gorin (1992) and Gertner and Gorin (1993).

On looking at the individual words, we found that the semantically meaningful words for this task were spread out over all word frequencies, many of them occurring only a few times, and a few like 'Red', 'Green', 'Circle' and 'Square' occurring many times. The decision as to whether a word was semantically meaningful was made based on our knowledge of the task. Table 20.1 shows the 10 most frequent words along with their frequencies. The semantically meaningful words are capitalized. Similarly, Table 20.2 shows the 150th to the 160th ranking words.

20.6.2 *Convergence and conversation length*

The segmentation algorithm described in section 20.5 was used to partition the 1434 sentences into 1045 conversations. 122 of these were Type I conversations, which we removed from the following analysis, since they are

Table 20.1 *Ten most frequent words. Semantically meaningful words are capitalized*

Rank	Word	Frequency
1	is	377
2	a	325
3	to	245
4	go	198
5	RED	180
6	now	150
7	this	134
8	GREEN	132
9	BLUE	128
10	where	123

Table 20.2 *Words with ranks from 150 to 160. Semantically meaningful words are capitalized*

Rank	Word	Frequency
150	TRIANGULAR	5
151	my	5
152	PARALLEL	5
153	SPHEROID	5
154	PARALLELOGRAM	5
155	DOT	5
156	correct	5
157	really	4
158	know	4
159	which	4
160	wrong	4

always one sentence long. Thus we are left with 923 Type II conversations. Of these, the segmentation algorithm labeled 694 as convergent, giving a convergence rate of 75%. Recall that a convergent conversation is one where the device responds correctly after one or more sentence inputs. These 694 convergent conversations included both, those where the machine was rewarded by the user, and where the machine used its internal confidence model to decide that the conversation was convergent. We found that in all cases where the device used its internal confidence model, the conversation was actually convergent. Since the segmentation algorithm we used is only a heuristic one, we also looked at the 229 divergent conversations to discover the cause of divergence.

On manually evaluating the 229 divergent conversations, we found that the machine had actually responded correctly in 177 cases, giving a convergence rate of 94%. However, these 177 conversations were treated as divergent by the segmentation algorithm. We found that, out of the 177 conversations, 54 diverged because the user waited too long before typing a sentence, and 36 because the user moved an object, causing a conversation to end prematurely. The remaining 87 conversations diverged because the user did not reward a correct response by the machine. These figures indicate that the segmentation algorithm needs to be improved. As suggested earlier, an adaptive threshold for the internal confidence measure is one approach to improving the algorithm.

The average number of sentences and their standard deviations for the Type II conversations are shown in Table 20.3. We see that the average conversation length is only 1.4 sentences with a standard deviation of only 0.8. This indicates that, on average, the users were satisfied with the machine's response within 1 to 2 sentences. Since from section 20.6.1, we know that most words, including many semantically meaningful words, occur only a few times, the small average conversation length indicates that the learning algorithm is very fast.

We now verify the exponential convergence model given in equation (17) for Type II conversations. The maximum conversation length in the 694 Type II convergent conversations was five sentences. Thus, in order to calculate the probability of convergence within k sentences, for $k \leqslant 5$ we included in the universe the 694 Type II convergent conversations and all divergent conversations of length greater than or equal to five sentences. There were only five divergent conversations with 5 sentences or more, giving a total of 699 conversations in the universe on the basis of which to calculate $P(m \leqslant k)$, the probability of converging within k sentences.

Table 20.4 shows $P(m \leqslant k)$ for $k = 1$ to 5. In Figure 20.9, we plot

Table 20.3 *Conversation lengths*

Mean Length	Standard Deviation
1.38	0.85

Table 20.4 *Convergence probabilities*

Conversation length, k	1	2	3	4	5
Probability of convergence, $P(k)$, within k sentences	0.691	0.883	0.959	0.988	0.994

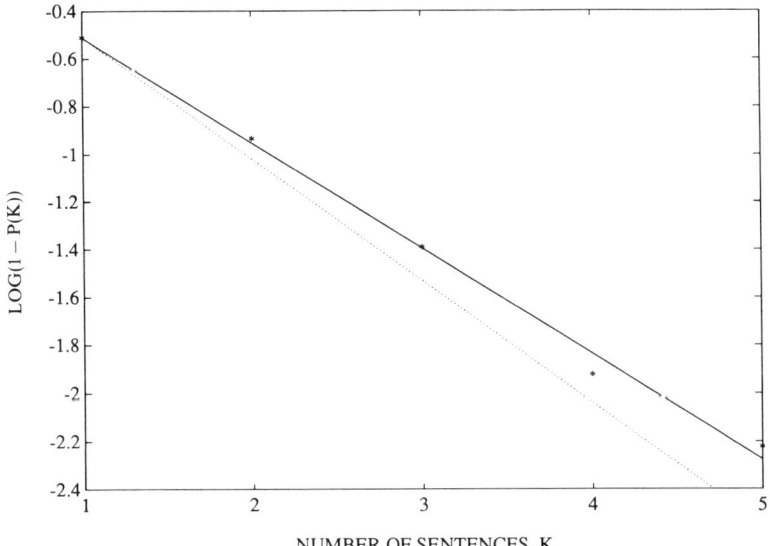

Figure 20.9 *This plot verifies the exponential convergence model of equation (17).* ———: *a linear regression;* ······: *a theoretical plot.*

$\log P(k) = \log(1 - P(m \leqslant k))$ against k. The linear behavior of the plot verifies that $P(m \leqslant k)$ exponentially approaches 1, as predicted by the model in equation (17). The dotted line in Figure 20.9 shows the theoretical plot predicted by equation (17), assuming that the probability of error P_e is just the probability of error after the first sentence. The deviation between the experimental plot and that predicted by the model of equation (17) is possibly due to the simplicity of the model. However, it is interesting to note that the deviation is not large.

20.6.3 Retention

The retention of the final system was measured by evaluating its responses to the first sentences of each conversation where the machine responded correctly in the original interaction. The object corresponding to the machine response in the original interaction provides a label against which to match the machine response during testing. Thus, this is a measure of the system's performance on a subset of the training set. The 122 Type I conversations were excluded. This is because the user does not induce a machine response in these conversations, and as such, no response is expected. Thus, out of the 816 convergent conversations, we have 694 Type II conversations, and hence 694 labeled sentences on which to test the system's retention.

The retention experiment was carried out by generating a new blocks-world scene that contained all possible shape and color combinations. This was so that the machine had at least one correct eyeball position for any of the labeled sentences. However, the scene used for testing was completely different from any of the scenes during the original interaction. The 694 sentences were then presented to the network and its response compared to the correct label. The network responded correctly according to the labels in 629 cases.

We analysed the 65 errors to determine why the machine performed incorrectly. It was found that in six cases, the labels were incorrect. This could either have been a mistake on the part of the user or a deliberate attempt to test the robustness of the machine under incorrect supervision. However, in these six cases, we found that the machine responded correctly. In 43 cases, the message required the machine to identify only one feature of the object, but the label had **both** the features corresponding to what the machine actually did during the original interaction. Thus for a sentence such as 'Look at the circle', the machine might have focused its attention on a **red circle** during the original interaction, resulting in the label being **red circle**. However, during testing, the machine focused its attention on a circle of another color. Though this is a correct response, it does not match the label and hence was counted as an error. Similarly, in four cases, the message did not require the machine to make any particular response. For example, the user might have typed 'You are doing very well', to which no particular response is expected. Thus the machine made only 12 errors on the 694 sentences showing that it remembered 98% of what it was taught.

20.7 Summary and future work

In this chapter we have described a multi-sensory system that adaptively acquires language through interaction with a complex environment. Multi-sensory devices are critical for rapid learning and generalization in the situation that the machine response to a message also depends on the state of the world. In particular, we studied a visual focus of attention task where the machine receives both message and visual input from its environment. This is in contrast to previous work where only message input was considered. Experimental evaluations based on 1434 typed sentences from 11 users showed that, in most cases, a correct response was achieved with one to two sentences, even if the response to the first sentence was incorrect. This demonstrates the error-recovery capability of the dialogue feedback control mechanism. The system retained 98% of what it was taught. We now detail some possible directions for future work.

20.7.1 Spoken language

In this chapter we have considered text input. We also assumed that the necessary visual preprocessing was done to provide color and shape tokens for each object. One direction of work is to incorporate spoken input as in Gorin *et al.* (1991b), and also the necessary visual preprocessing for noisy visual input. In Gorin *et al.* (1991b), an acoustic distortion metric is considered for clustering the input speech. An improvement on this method for both the speech and visual input channels would be to incorporate a perceptual distortion metric that is modified based on semantic/sensory associations. Thus, though the words 'Lake' and 'Rake' are acoustically similar, their associations to other sensory inputs would be quite different, resulting in a large distortion between them.

20.7.2 Focused learning

The learning algorithm we used is fast and intuitively appealing. However, no contextual information is used when updating the weights between the words and the sensory primitive nodes. For example, suppose the network is presented with the phrase 'big red ball', where it is the first occurrence of the word 'big'. If the network already has an explanation for 'red ball', in the sense of strong associations of 'red' and 'ball' to the respective color and shape subnetworks, then we would like to use this contextual information to learn **only a little** about the associations of the word 'big' in the color and shape subnetworks. In the current learning algorithm, no contextual information is used, causing the network to initially learn false associations of the word 'big', then unlearning these associations as it encounters further examples. Even though many repeated presentations of 'big' in the context of other words will cause it to have zero-valued associations (and thus be semantically null) with respect to the shape and color subnetworks, we feel that using contextual information would result in much faster learning. In Tishby and Gorin (1993), an algebraic learning method was studied where context is included. A method to incrementally solve the algebraic problem formulation posed in Tishby and Gorin (1993) is presented in Farrell *et al.* (1993). However, in these algebraic methods the intuitive appeal of the information-theoretic weights is lost. We are working on other approaches to **focus** learning on individual words using contextual information that also preserves the information-theoretic interpretation of the weights. In the context of structured tasks such as the one considered in this paper, we can also focus learning by postulating a **mutual exclusivity** between different sensory primitives. Thus if the word 'Circle' is strongly associated with the shape subnet, then it should be weakly associated with the color subnet. Furthermore, in the phrase 'red circle', since 'circle' is associated with the shape network, we would expect 'red' to be only weakly associated with the shape subnet. This idea is related to Clark's Principle of Contrast (Clark, 1987), which argues that no two words will have the same meaning in all situations.

20.7.3 *Extensions to the blocks-world*

In this chapter, devices with a rudimentary repertoire of actions have been investigated. In the focus of attention task described in this paper, the device is **capable** of more complex tasks. For example, on viewing the device response, the user can distinguish between the machine **moving to an object** or **staying at an object**. However, the device presented in this chapter cannot **learn** the difference between these responses since it cannot **sense** the effect of these different actions. Such complex actions can be included by enhancing the sensory periphery of the network. For example, the machine can learn to distinguish between 'Go to the square' and 'Stay at the square' if it can sense the effect of moving its eyeball. This proprioceptive sense would measure the tension in the eyeball muscles, enabling the device to distinguish between being in motion versus stationary.

Another possible extension is to use the network to acquire non-terminals such as nouns and adjectives via their sensory associations. For example, nouns are strongly associated to the objects in a scene, whereas adjectives are strongly associated to descriptive attributes. The strength of these associations is thus a reflection of whether a word is a noun or an adjective. Once such non-terminals are acquired, they can be used to form intermediate layers of nodes in networks such as that described in Gertner and Gorin (1993). Such nodes reflect the structure in the input language and hence improve generalization.

20.7.4 *Voice-controlled telephone*

Consider a telephone that can respond to voice commands. We may view the individual call appearances as the objects in the device's world. The attributes of these objects include whether it is an incoming or outgoing call, whether the call is connected, the telephone number making the call, the name of the person making the call, or the time elapsed during the call. A possible natural language command to the telephone might be 'Please get me John on the line'. The appropriate response is to make a call to the person named John, and perhaps leave a message for him if he is currently unavailable. To perform this task, the telephone must have learned the associations between 'John' and the appropriate telephone number. This is analogous to the inter-sensory associations of the blocks-world system described in this chapter. It must have further learned to associate 'Please get me' to the action of initiating an outgoing call. Another example command is 'Please pick up that new call'. The appropriate response depends on the state of the environment, for example, whether there is a current call active, in which case it should put it on hold and pick up the new call. Again, an attribute that is relevant to this response is the fact that there is a call currently connected.

20.7.5 Voice-controlled computing environments

In the context of a computer where operations may be performed on windows or icons, we may view these windows and icons as the objects in the blocks-world. The attributes of these objects might be which machine they are logged on to, the working directory, the number of hours or days the window has been active, the jobs or processes that are active in the windows, and properties of these jobs such as whether they are stopped, or running in the foreground or the background. An example command to the computer might be 'Please bring up the window where I was working on the paper for the Acoustical Society'. The correct response would be for the machine to display the appropriate window. To do this, the computer must have learned the associations between the message and the attribute value corresponding to the process which is editing the document. Alternately, the user might say 'I want to talk to my brother in California', to which the appropriate response is to initiate a talk process with the correct electronic mail address. In this case, the computer must have learned the association between 'brother' and the attribute value corresponding to his address. The associations between the messages and the attributes is similar to the inter-sensory associations in the blocks-world system.

20.7.6 Database applications

The principles and mechanisms studied in this paper for a blocks-world scenario can be extended and applied to a general database problem. Consider a relational database (Codd, 1970; Ullman, 1988), and an example STUDENT relation or table shown in Table 20.5. Suppose we want to query the system for all students who are freshmen with a natural language request such as 'Please give me a list of all the freshmen.' One way to learn this is to associate 'freshmen' with the rows in the table corresponding to freshmen, i.e. the first and fourth rows. This is essentially the approach taken in Miller and Gorin (1992) for a data retrieval task where the system can answer questions about 20 attributes of a the 50 states in the USA. However, if the database is changed over time, so that the first and fourth rows are no longer freshmen students, then the system would respond incorrectly, and would have to

Table 20.5 *A STUDENT relation in a relational database*

Name	I.D.	Sex	Age	Year
Smith	86227	Male	18	1
Bajaj	86178	Female	20	2
Chen	86185	Female	23	3
Jones	86201	Male	19	1
Mathur	86210	Female	22	4

relearn the proper associations. On the other hand, if the system had access to (could sense) the student-year attribute values, then it could learn to associate 'freshmen' with a particular student-year value. In this case, better generalization is achieved, since the system is robust with respect to changes in the database. Thus, better generalization will be achieved for this task, if the system **has access** to the attribute values that are relevant to the task. Such 'access' to the different attribute values is similar to the multi-sensory input of the visual focus of attention system.

Acknowledgements

We thank Steve Levinson for his suggestion of exploring multi-sensory devices. We are grateful to Doug Blewett for his help in setting up the graphics simulation. We thank Mark Jones for dicussions involving the application of this work to a voice-controlled telephone, Mukesh Dalal for discussions on the database application, Doug Blewett and Juergen Schroeter for discussions on the applications to computing environments, and Jan van Santen for discussions relating to the work on eye movements in psycho-physics. We are grateful to Mike Brown, Julia Hirschberg, Gernot Kubin, Laura Miller and Fernando Pereira for their comments and suggestions on an earlier draft of this chapter. We also thank the various users who participated in the experimental evaluation by interacting with the system.

References

Anderson, J. (1977) Induction of augmented transition networks. *Cognitive Science*, **1**, 125–57.

Bach-Y-Rita, P., Collins, C.C. and Hyde, J.E. (eds.) (1971) *The Control of Eye Movements*. Academic Press, London.

Barto, A. and Anandan, P. (1985) Pattern recognizing stochastic learning automata. *IEEE Transactions on Systems, Man, and Cybernetics*, **15**(3), 360–75.

Baum, E. (1989) What size net gives valid generalization? *Neural Computation*, **1**(1), 151–60.

Blewett, D., Anderson, S., Kilduff, M. and Udovic, S. (1991) Xtent Release 2.1: a messaging protocol and specification language for X Toolkit based applications. *AT&T Bell Laboratories Technical Memorandum*, unpublished, October.

Boden, M.A. (1977) *Artificial Intelligence and Natural Man*. Basic Books, London.

Clark, E. (1987) The principle of contrast: A constraint on language acquisition, in *Mechanisms of Language Acquisition* (ed. B. MacWhinney), Lawrence Erlbaum, Hillsdale, NJ.

Codd, E. (1970) A relational model for large shared data banks. *Communications of ACM*, **13**(6), 377–87.

Cottrell, G., Bartell, B. and Haupt, C. (1990) *Grounding Meaning in Perception*. German Workshop on Artificial Intelligence (GWAI).

Cybenko, G. (1989) Approximation by superposition of a sigmoidal function. *Mathematics of Control, Signals and Systems*, **2**, 303–14.

Ditchburn, R. (1973) *Eye-Movements and Visual Perception*. Clarendon Press, Oxford.

Duda, R. and Hart, P. (1973) *Pattern Classification and Scene Analysis*. Wiley, New York, NY.

Farrell, K., Mammone, R. and Gorin, A. (1993) Adaptive language acquisition using incremental learning. *Proceedings of ICAAAP*, **1**, 501–4.

Fu, K. and Booth, T. (1975a) Grammatical inference: Introduction and survey – part 1. *IEEE Transactions on Systems, Man, and Cybernetics*, **5**(1), 95–111.

Fu, K. and Booth, T. (1975b) Grammatical inference: Introduction and survey – part 2. *IEEE Transactions on Systems, Man, and Cybernetics*, **5**(4), 409–23.

Fu, K. and Mui, J. (1981) A survey on image segmentation. *Pattern Recognition*, **13**, 3–16.

Gaarder, K.R. (1975) *Eye Movements, Vision, and Behavior*. Wiley, New York, NY.

Gertner, A. and Gorin, A. (1993) Adaptive language acquisition for an airline information subsystem, in *Neural Networks for Speech and Vision Applications* (ed. R. Mammone), Chapman & Hall, London.

Gorin, A., Levinson, S., Gertner, A. and Goldman, E. (1991a) Adaptive acquisition of language. *Computer Speech and Language*, **5**, 101–32.

Gorin, A., Levinson, S. and Gertner, A. (1991b) Adaptive acquisition of spoken language. *Proceedings IEEE International Conference on Acoustics, Speech, and Signal Processing*, **2**, pp. 805–8.

Haralick, R. and Shapiro, L. (1985) Image segmentation techniques. *Computer, Vision, Graphics and Image Processing*, **29**, 100–32.

Harnad, S. (1990) The symbol grounding problem. *Physica D*, **42**, 335–46.

Jacobs, R.A. and Jordan, M.I. (1991) A competitive modular connectionist architecture, in *Advances in Neural Information Processing Systems 3* (eds. R.P. Lippmann, J.E. Moody and D.S. Tourctzky), Morgan Kaufmann, San Mateo, CA, pp. 767–73.

Jain, A. (1991) Parsing complex sentences with structured connectionist networks. *Neural Computation*, **3**, 110–20.

Kaelbling, L. (1990) Learning in embedded sytems. *PhD thesis*, Stanford University, CA.

Khatib, O. (1986) Real-time obstacle avoidance for manipulators and mobile robots. *International Journal of Robotics Research*, **5**(1), 90–8.

McClelland, J. and Kawamoto, A. (1986) Mechanisms of sentence processing: Assigning roles to constituents of sentences, in *Parallel Distributed Processing: Explorations in the Microstructure of Cognition, Vol. 2* (eds. J. McClelland, D. Rumelhart and the PDP Research Group), The MIT Press, Cambridge, MA.

Miikkulainen, R. and Dyer, M. (1989) A modular neural network architecture for sequential paraphrasing of script-based stories. *Proceedings IEEE International Joint Conference on Neural Networks*, pp. II-49–II-56.

Miikkulainen, R. and Dyer, M. (1991) Natural language processing with modular PDP networks and distributed lexicon. *Cognitive Science*, **15**, 343–99.

Miller, L. and Gorin, A. (1992) A structured network architecture for adaptive language acquisition. *Proceedings IEEE International Conference on Acoustics, Speech, and Signal Processing*, **1**, pp. 201–4.

Nowlan, S.J. and Hinton, G.E. (1991) Evaluation of adaptive mixtures of competing experts, in *Advances in Neural Information Processing Systems 3* (eds. R.P. Lippmann, J.E. Moody and D.S. Touretzky), Morgan Kaufmann, San Mateo, CA, pp. 774–80.

Pierce, J. (1961) *Symbols, Signals and Noise*. Harper, New York, NY.

Rumelhart, D. and McClelland, J. (1986) *Parallel Distributed Processing*. MIT Press, Cambridge, MA.

St. John, M. and McClelland, J. (1990) Learning and applying contextual constraints in sentence comprehension. *Artificial Intelligence*, **46**, 217–57.

Tank, D. and Hopfield, J. (1987) Neural computation by concentrating information in time. *Proceedings of the National Academy of Science*, **84**, 1896–1900, April.

Tishby, N. and Gorin, A. (1993) Algebraic learning of statistical associations for language acquisition, in *Neural Networks for Speech and Vision Applications* (ed. R. Mammone), Chapman & Hall, London.

Ullman, J. (1988) *Principles of Database and Knowledge-Base Systems*, **1**. Computer Science Press, Rockville, MD.

Unnikrishnan, K., Hopfield, J. and Tank, D. (1991) Connected-digit speaker-dependent speech recognition using a neural network with time-delayed connections. *IEEE Transactions on Signal Processing*, **39**, 698–713, March.

Winograd, T. (1972) *Understanding Natural Language*. Academic Press, New York, NY.

Winograd, T. (1980) What does it mean to understand language. *Cognitive Science*, **4**, 209–41.

Yarbus, A.L. (1967) *Eye Movements and Vision*. Plenum Press, New York, NY.

Algebraic learning of statistical associations for language acquisition

ALLEN GORIN* and NAFTALI TISHBY†

*AT&T Bell Laboratories, Murray Hill, NJ, USA
†Department of Computer Science and Center for Neural Computation, Hebrew University, Jerusalem, Israel

21.1 Introduction

22.1.1 Statistical language acquisition

Statistical association measures play an important role in many areas of natural language research. An impediment to reliable estimation of such associations is the problem of small-sample statistics, since in any natural corpus there will be many infrequently occurring words. This is a consequence of a general phenomena known as Zipf's law, which states that the frequency of a word is inversely proportional to its rank (Pierce, 1961). According to this law, in a large natural corpus one expects more than half the words to occur only once or twice.

We consider this problem within the context of systems which adaptively acquire language in the sense of Gorin et al. (1991b). A basic principle underlying that work is that the primary function of language is to communicate, with the consequence that language acquisition involves gaining the capability of decoding the intended meaning of an utterance. This principle led to an investigation of language acquisition mechanisms based on connectionist methods, in which the network builds associations between input stimuli and meaningful machine responses to them (Gertner and Gorin, 1993; Gorin et al., 1991a, b; Miller and Gorin, 1991; Miller et al., 1989). In the simplest situation, connection weights were defined to be the **Mutual Information** (MI) (Blachman,

Artificial Neural Networks for Speech and Vision. Edited by Richard J. Mammone. Published in 1993 by Chapman & Hall, London. ISBN 0 412 54850 X

1968; Thomas, 1969) between words and actions. Mutual information is a statistical association measure, calculated there via smoothed relative frequency estimates, and as such it suffers from the problems of small-sample statistics.

One consequence of the small-sample problem can be seen in the lack of **focused learning** of new words in such a language acquisition system. We consider an illustrative example drawn from the Inward Call Management task of Gorin *et al.* (1991a, b), where the range of device actions is to transfer a telephone call to an appropriate department of a large organization. Associations are then learned between words and such actions.

In particular, let us examine the learning scenario when the device encounters a new word. In one case, consider the input message 'I want to buy an etagere', to which the appropriate response is determined to be connection to the **Furniture** department, and where it is the device's first experience with the word **etagere**. In a second case, consider 'I need a mauve sweater', to which the appropriate response is determined to be connection to the **Clothing** department, and where it is the device's first experience with the word **mauve**. It is intuitively clear that, based on context, it would be desirable for the system to greatly strengthen the semantic association (within this task) of **etagere** with **Furniture**, and only slightly adjust the association of **mauve** with **Clothing**. We call this **focused learning**. The smoothed relative frequency estimates of Gorin *et al.* (1991b), however, treat equally all words which occur the same number of times in a particular class, regardless of context. Some of the tradeoffs in selection of smoothing parameters in such situations were investigated previously (Gorin and Levinson, 1989), but were not sensitive to context. A research issue, then, is how to formalize and mechanize our intuitive notions of exploiting context to provide focused learning.

This chapter proposes an alternative method for estimating such associations which both exploits context and circumvents the small-sample issues. The idea is to view sentence/meaning pairs as algebraic equations, rather than as observations of a pattern in some class. Associations are estimated via solving these equations, rather than via relative frequency estimates. Superficially, this is analogous to many classical pattern recognition procedures, which treat the coefficients of a decision rule as abstract parameters to be adjusted to optimize some input/output behavior. In our early experiments with this method, however, we wondered what would happen if one tried to interpret those algebraically-derived parameter values as mutual information, and then solve for the conditional probability distributions. Surprisingly, the probability estimates thus obtained were upon inspection quite good, and in many cases better than those obtained via smoothed relative frequency estimates. The need for a fundamental explanation of this phenomena and an understanding of its generality motivate our theoretical investigations in section 21.2 of the chapter.

21.1.2 Background

Statistical techniques are strongly based on the notion of probability. What is probability and how to estimate it correctly, however, is one of the older and more controversial issues in the history of science. Since its very beginning, probability theory had to face a duality of meaning. On the one hand, there was the practical interpretation of probability as a frequency ratio, attributed to Bernoulli and Borel and exposited, for example in Fine (1973). According to their view, probability is always associated with the relative frequency of the occurrence of some event. Probability should thus be estimated from frequency counts of independent samples. The probability of events that can not be repeated independently, e.g. the destruction of the world in a nuclear war, or having rain tomorrow, is totally meaningless according to this interpretation.

The deficiencies of this narrow interpretation of probability were realized by Laplace (Cox, 1946), who coined the notion of probability as the **reasonable expectation** of an event. Laplace noticed that a naive use of his famous Bayes rule can lead to numbers that are not easily interpretable according to the relative frequency interpretation. Moreover, Laplace wanted to use his theory to calculate probabilities of unrepeatable and never observed events. This was the beginning of a long and bitter dispute between the so-called **Bayesian** and **non-Bayesian** approaches, where the latter dominated the field almost until the middle of the twentieth century. Among other issues, the lack of a simple frequency interpretation of probabilities in statistical and quantum physics, and the successful application of information theoretic inference methods such as the Maximum Entropy principle, eventually legitimized the Bayesian approach. A goal of this paper is to exploit these dual notions of probability to improve our capability of estimating associations in statistical language acquisition.

The notion of information, particularly the mutual information between events, plays an important role in this work. Mutual information occurs in many other areas of natural language research as a statistical association measure. In particular, it has been used for determining associations between words (Church and Hanks, 1974), for determining word units in Chinese text (Sproat and Shih, 1990), for discovering phrase constituent boundaries (Magerman and Marcus, 1990), for clustering words into parts of speech (Jelinek, 1990), and for rule inference (Goodman, *et al.*, 1992). We believe that the methods of this chapter will eventually prove useful in the estimation of MI in these other situations. In the algorithmic and experimental sections of this paper, however, we focus on estimating associations between words and actions, as in Gorin *et al.* (1991b), restricting ourselves to commenting on extensions to these other cases.

21.1.3 Outline and summary

In section 21.2, we develop a theoretical foundation for the dual algebraic/ statistical nature of associations. We begin by focusing on **association measures** as the primary concepts, rather than probabilities as traditionally assumed in statistical modeling. This focus is based on two intuitions. First, that associations are the fundamental quantities to be estimated in the above described language acquisition paradigm. Second, in connectionist models, associations are directly related to the connection weights.

We begin by formulating the general properties of an association measure, in particular investigating the notion of consistent extensibility from elementary to composite and conditional events. Under this mild assumption, we then prove a uniqueness theorem concerning the additivity of associations using a result due to Cox (1946). In particular, let Ω be some set of elementary events, and assume that one is given a real-valued association measure $W:\Omega \times \Omega \to R$, which is extensible to conjunctive and conditional events. We prove that if there exists **any** continuous (and robust) functional relationship amongst $W(ab,c)$, $W(a,c)$ and $W(b|a,c)$ for all a, b and c in Ω, then there exists a monotonic rescaling of W such that $W(ab,c) = W(a,c) + W(b|a,c)$, i.e. any such association measure can be rescaled to be an additive in the above sense.

We then investigate the relationship between connectionism and probability theory, which is an issue of much concern (Bridle, 1989; Rumelhart *et al.*, 1988; Goodman *et al.*, 1992). We prove a uniqueness theorem for additive association measures, using a variant of the Cauchy functional equation. If there exists **any** continuous functional relationship between the association measure and probability, then it must be of the form $P(ab) = P(a)P(b)e^{\beta W(a,b)}$, where β is some parameter. If one solves this formula for W, we see that the association measure must be equal to (up to multiplication by the parameter β) the classical mutual information between a and b (Blachman, 1968; Thomas, 1969). This theorem begins to explain our empirical observations of such a relationship that were mentioned earlier, and to provide some understanding as to the generality of the phenomena.

At the end of section 21.2, we share some intuitions on the relationship between additive association measures and connectionism. In particular, we describe how an association measure can be induced via asymptotic fields in a network, and how this concept extends to conjunctive and conditional events.

In section 21.3, we exploit the above theory to provide an algebraic formulation of the language acquisition problem. In this domain, the elementary events are the occurrences of words in some input utterance, along with the meaningful machine responses to an utterance. A complete utterance is thus a conjunction of elementary events. We assume that there is an additive association measure (to be learned) between words in context and actions, and that semantic supervision is provided via an association score between an utterance and its intended meaning.

The additivity of the measure is used to formulate a linear equation from each utterance/action pair, whose variables are associations between the occurrence of a word in some context and machine actions. For a large amount of training data, the number of variables can grow quite large, although it remains a linear system. In the remainder of the paper, we reduce the size of this system via an independence assumption, equivalent to a bag-of-words language model. The algorithms, however, remain applicable to the general case, since it is always linear.

The result is a linear system of equations of the form $\mathbf{A} = \Lambda \times \mathbf{W}$, where Λ is an indicator matrix for the occurrences of words in the training sentences, $\mathbf{A}$ comprises the semantic supervision information, and $\mathbf{W}$ is the unknown vector of associations. We will see that this formulation provides an interesting split between syntax and semantics, since the matrix Λ depends only on the list of sentences observed in the language, and only the vector $\mathbf{A}$ depends on the semantic supervision. We illustrate this algebraic formulation by computing a small example, with three vocabulary words and three semantic actions.

In general, such a system of equations will be both under and overdetermined. Namely, there will be no exact solution, and infinitely many solutions in the sense of Least Mean Squares (LMS) approximation. It is well known that the set of LMS solutions for such a system can be characterized by a single solution plus an arbitrary vector from the null space of Λ (Golub and Van Loan, 1983). We will explore some of the linguistic and semantic implications of this null space. For example, if a vocabulary word is orthogonal to the null space, then its semantic associations are uniquely determined by this algebraic formulation. On the other hand, if the difference between two utterances is in the null space, then they connote the same action and thus are semantically equivalent for this task. Such semantic equivalences can be used to quantify the notion of synonyms, within the confines of the device's task.

We then describe algorithms which compute solutions to this linear system of equations. In particular, we focus on a batch-mode method using Singular Value Decomposition (SVD), which will be used in the experiments of section 21.4. Some adaptive methods which will serve as the basis for future experiments are reviewed. The adaptive solutions will need to address the fact that not only are the number of equations (input utterances) in Λ increasing, but so are the number of variables (vocabulary words).

In section 21.4, we experimentally evaluate the SVD-based algorithm on 1494 natural language inputs from Miller's 15-class text-based data retrieval experiments (Miller *et al.*, 1989), which comprise a vocabulary of 741 words with a Zipf's Law distribution, and where 53% of the vocabulary words occur only once or twice in the data. We will observe that for infrequently occurring words, the algebraic estimates of associations are much improved over the smoothed relative frequency estimates of mutual information. Furthermore, when these algebraically derived associations are interpreted as mutual information, the resulting probability estimates are quite reasonable even for words which occur only once.

The natural interpretation of this result is via the two classical notions of probability: as **relative frequency**, or as a **reasonable expectation**. Since 67% of the words in this database are orthogonal to the null space of Λ, then their semantic associations are uniquely determined by this algebraic solution. Furthermore, their semantic-conditional probabilities are also uniquely determined, up to the choice of the single parameter β.

The average performance of the algebraically trained network is approximately the same, on this database, as when trained via smoothed estimates of mutual information. In this small system, these improved estimates are manifested in improved dialog stability when learning new words or phrases. In other applications, however, the noisiness of the MI estimates is more severe than in the 15-action text-based task of Miller's data (Miller *et al.*, 1989). Thus, we expect more significant performance gains using this method when applied to a larger data retrieval task, such as the 1000 action text-based Almanac (Miller and Gorin, 1991), and to a system with spoken input (Gorin *et al.*, 1991a).

21.2 Calculus of associations

To establish association measures as the primary concept, we begin by discussing the basic requirements for such a measure. We show that if there is a robust extension of the associations from elementary events to conjunctive and conditional events, then the association measure is additive, up to a monotone rescaling. We prove this by introducing associations between conditional events and following similar arguments to that of Cox (1946) in his formulation of the notion of conditional probability. We then prove that **if there exists** a functional relationship between the **self-association** and the probability of an event, then the association measure is unique and identical to the mutual information, apart from an arbitrary scalar multiplier. Finally, we share some intuitions on deriving associations within a connectionist framework.

21.2.1 Associating events

Consider a set of **elementary events**, $\Omega = \{a, b, c, \ldots\}$. We assume that these events can be either **true** or **false**. (The extension to the case where the events are true with some probability is straightforward, but is not considered here.) Such events might be the occurrence of a particular word in a given location of a sentence, or some specific action to be taken by a device. We also assume that Ω contains a certain event T, i.e. an event that is **constantly true**. We assume that every two elementary events, $a, b \in \Omega$, are **associated** via a measure $W(a,b)$. Our first basic question is what are the fundamental constraints on the possible association functions $W(a,b)$? Based on the definition thus far, associations are allowed to obtain arbitrary real values as long as only elementary events are considered. We call such associations amongst the elementary events **elementary associations**. This picture changes, however, if one tries to extend the measure of association beyond the elementary events. A natural and desirable extension is to associations of composite events, such as $W(a \text{ and } b, c \text{ or } d)$. Associations of events of that kind should be consistent with the familiar logical rules of the **propositional calculus** for composition of events. It is therefore necessary to briefly review this logical structure.

Consider the **algebra** of composite events, $\mathscr{F}(\Omega) \supset \Omega$ as the set closed under the following operations (Fine, 1973). If $a, b \subset \mathscr{F}(\Omega)$ then

1. $ab \equiv a \wedge b$ (read *a joint b*)$\in \mathscr{F}(\Omega)$;
2. $a \vee b$ (read *a or b*)$\in \mathscr{F}(\Omega)$;
3. $\sim a$ (read *not a*)$\in \mathscr{F}(\Omega)$.

With the familiar Boolean rules

$$
\begin{aligned}
aa &= a, \\
ab &= ba, \\
a(bc) &= (ab)c = abc, \\
a(a \vee b) &= a, \\
\sim(ab) &= \sim a \vee \sim b, \\
\sim \sim a &= a,
\end{aligned}
\tag{1}
$$

together with a **certain event**, denoted by $\top$, and an **impossible event**, denoted $\bot \equiv \sim \top$, $\mathscr{F}(\Omega)$ constitute a **Boolean algebra**.

Given some values of elementary associations, $W : \Omega \times \Omega \to R$, one would like to extend it to the full Boolean algebra, $W : \mathscr{F}(\Omega) \times \mathscr{F}(\Omega) \to R$ in a way consistent with the above rules. We will show that if such a functional extension exists for arbitrary values of the elementary associations then certain facts must be true.

For expository purposes, we first explore and reject a relationship involving only conjunctions, i.e. associations of the form $W(ab, c)$, and elementary associations. Assume that $W(ab, c) = G[W(a, c), W(b, c)]$, for some function $G[x, y]$ of two variables. Such a simple extension is unlikely, since it ignores the possible association between a and b, $W(a, b)$, which should clearly influence the joint association $W(ab, c)$. A natural modification is then to assume a relationship $W(ab, c) = F[W(a, c), W(b, c), W(a, b)]$, for some function $F[x, y, z]$. Expressing the alternative forms of $W(abc, d)$ leads to rather unpleasant functional equations for F, namely

$$
F[F(u, z, x), w, F(v, y, x)] = F[F(u, w, v), z, F(x, y, v)],
$$
$$
F(x, y, z) = F(y, x, z),
$$

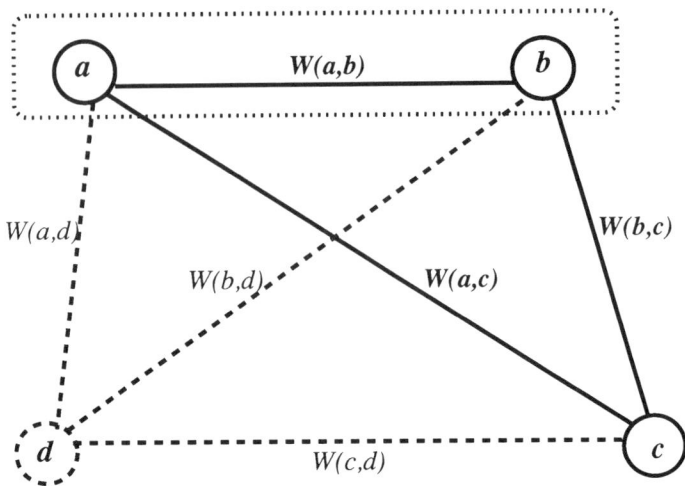

Figure 21.1 *Association of the joint event ab to c depends not only on the associations between a, b and c, but also on their associations to other events in the network.*

for arbitrary real u, v, w, x, y, z, in some interval. The general solution of these equations is unknown to us. Moreover, there is another fundamental reason why this relationship is not satisfactory. The association of joint events can be affected indirectly by any other of associations between other events, thus making the joint association a function of **all** the other elementary associations (see Figure 21.1).

A more tractable and reasonable alternative, similar to the approach taken by Cox (1946) and Fine (1973), is to extend the Boolean algebra to include **conditional events**. The conditional event $a|b$ (read a **conditioned on** b) is the event a given that b is true. The Boolean algebra of events with this binary operation is formally identical to the known structure of a **Heyting algebra** (Johnstone, 1982) if one formally identifies conditioning with the implication operator,[1] denoted $\rightarrow$, namely,

$$b|a \Rightarrow a \rightarrow b. \tag{2}$$

It is convenient to denote the (Heyting) algebra of conditional events of $\mathscr{F}(\Omega)$ by $\tilde{\Omega}$. All the elements of $\tilde{\Omega}$ can be viewed as conditional events, but for simplicity we denote the event $a|\mathsf{T}$ as a so that $\mathscr{F}(\Omega) \subset \tilde{\Omega}$. There are several additional rules for conditional events. For the sake of this chapter, we need only the following additional rules:

$$a|a = \mathsf{T},$$
$$(a|b)|c = a|(bc). \tag{3}$$

---

[1] We are grateful to Fernando Pereira for pointing out this fact and for introducing the Heyting algebra to us.

The main hypothesis of our theorems is that the association of a joint event is functionally related to the conditional association in the following general way

$$W(ab, c) = G\left[W(a, c), W(b|a, c)\right] \tag{4}$$

for some function $G[x, y]$. Furthermore, we assume that this extension is robust, i.e. it is continuous for arbitrary values of the associations, or the arguments x, y, in some interval. This additional requirement guarantees that the same functional relation exists even if the values of the associations slightly change. This requirement expresses the intuitive fact that the association of a joint event must depend only on the association of one of the events and on the conditional association of the other event. It can be thought of as merely a definition of the conditional association, and is similar to the axiom taken by Cox (1946) for conditional probabilities. By dealing with conditional associations we thus avoid and subsume the complication of considering all possible indirect associations.

We now prove a uniqueness theorem for extensible association measures, following a similar theorem due to R.T. Cox (1946) for conditional probabilities.

Theorem 21.1 (Cox) *There exists an association measure $W(a, b)$ on $\tilde{\Omega} \times \tilde{\Omega}$, and a continuous function G, such that $W(ab, c) = G[W(a, c), W(b|a, c)]$ is a robust extension of W for all a, b, c in $\mathscr{F}(\Omega)$, if and only if the function $G(x, y)$ is of the (quasilinear) form*

$$G(x, y) = h^{-1}[h(x) + h(y) + C], \tag{5}$$

for some continuous, strictly monotone, function $h(x)$, and an arbitrary constant C.

Proof: Consider one of the arguments of W as a fixed constant event denoted for simplicity by $\cdot$. The same proof holds for the other argument of W. We examine the alternative evaluations of $W(bcd|a, \cdot)$, using the standard properties (1) and (2):

$$W(dcb|a, \cdot) = W((dc)b|a, \cdot) = G[W(b|a, \cdot), W(dc|ba, \cdot)]. \tag{6}$$

But

$$W(dc|ba, \cdot) = G[W(c|ba, \cdot), W(d|(cb)a, \cdot)] = G[W(c|ba, \cdot), W(d|cba, \cdot)]. \tag{7}$$

Hence

$$W(dcb|a, \cdot) = G[W(b|a, \cdot), G[W(c|ba, \cdot), W(d|cba, \cdot)]]. \tag{8}$$

Similarly,

$$W(bcd|a, \cdot) = W(d(cb)|a, \cdot) = G[W(cb|a, \cdot), W(d|(cb)a, \cdot)] \tag{9}$$

$$= G[G[W(c|ba, \cdot), W(b|a, \cdot)], W(d|cba, \cdot)]. \tag{10}$$

Denoting

$$x = W(b|a, \cdot), \quad y = W(c|(ab), \cdot), \quad z = W(d|(abc), \cdot), \tag{11}$$

and equating the two expressions, equations (7) and (9), we arrive at the following functional equation for G:

$$G(x, G(y, z)) = G(G(x, y), z). \tag{12}$$

This equation is well-known as the associativity equation (Aczél, 1966; Fine, 1973), and it reflects the **group** property of the associations. Its general solution is given by equation (5) as can be easily verified by substitution. It is also known that (4) is the only possible continuous solution, as can be seen by differentiation and solving the obtained differential equation. The parameter C is an arbitrary integration constant (Aczél, 1966; Cox, 1946).

Corollary 21.2 *Under the conditions of Theorem 21.1, the association measure W can always be monotonically rescaled such that*

$$W(ab, c) = W(a, c) + W(b|a, c) + C. \tag{13}$$

Proof: Using equation (5), it is always possible to transform any association measure through the monotone function h

$$\widetilde{W}(a, b) \equiv h(W(a, b)), \tag{14}$$

from which equation (13) immediately follows for $\widetilde{W}$. ∎

We can thus assume, without loss of generality, that W satisfies equation (13). This relation is sufficient to derive most of the results of this chapter. Clearly, a similar relation must hold for the second argument of W.

The value of the constant C is determined by the next corollary:

Corollary 21.3

$$W(\mathsf{T}, a) = W(a, \mathsf{T}) = -C \quad \forall a \in \mathscr{F}(\Omega). \tag{15}$$

Proof: Since

$$W(a, b) = W(a, bb) = W(a, b) + W(a, b|b) + C. \tag{16}$$

∎

Thus the association of **any** event to a **certain** event is a constant, independent of the event. It is natural and desirable that such a null association should be zero, since clearly nothing is learned from the (known) fact that the certain event is true. Thus, without loss of generality, we assume that $C = 0$, which makes equation (13) a simple additivity relation.

Conditioning events are formally extensions of the certain event, T. By applying the preceding corollary, with the convention $C = 0$, to this extended certainty, we obtain that the following associations are all equal to zero.

Corollary 21.4

$$W(a|b, b) = W(a, b|a) = 0 \quad \forall a, b \in \mathscr{F}(\Omega), \tag{17}$$

$$W(a|b, b|a) = 0 \quad \forall a, b \in \mathscr{F}(\Omega). \tag{18}$$

Equation (17) will be crucial to the proof of symmetry in Corollary 21.5.

Using equations (13) and (17) the following relations are obtained:

$$W(ab, a) = W(a, a) + W(b|a, a) = W(a, a). \tag{19}$$

Expanding the **self-association** $W(ab, ab)$, one gets

$$\begin{aligned}
W(ab, ab) &= W(a, ab) + W(b|a, ab), \\
&= W(a, a) + W(b|a, a) + W(a, b|a) + W(b|a, b|a), \\
&= W(a, a) + W(b|a, b|a). \tag{20}
\end{aligned}$$

which is a relation among self-associations only.

Similarly, as an immediate consequence of Corollary 21.4:

$$\begin{aligned}
W(a, a) &= W(a, ab) = W(a, b) + W(a, a|b). \\
&= W(a, b) + W(a|b, a|b), \tag{21}
\end{aligned}$$

so we can express the general association in terms of self-associations

$$W(a, b) = W(a, a) - W(a|b, a|b). \tag{22}$$

So far we haven't been using equation (18), which together with equation (21) yields the following relation:

$$\begin{aligned}
W(ab, ab) &= W(a, ab) + W(b|a, ab) \\
&= W(a, b) + W(a, a|b) + W(b|a, b) + W(b|a, a|b) \\
&= W(a, b) + W(a, a) + W(b, b) - 2W(a, b) \\
&= W(a, a) + W(b, b) - W(a, b). \tag{23}
\end{aligned}$$

The somewhat surprising consequence of equation (23) is the **general symmetry** of the association measure.

Corollary 21.5 *An additive association measure is symmetric.*

$$W(a, b) = W(b, a) \quad \forall a, b \in \mathscr{F}(\Omega). \tag{24}$$

■

From the above relations it is clear that a characterization of the **self-associations** of the events, $W(a, a)$, is sufficient to determine the complete structure. We will relate the self-association to the **likelihood** of the events in the next section.

Finally, we can use the symmetry of the associations equation (24) together with equation (13) to obtain the association to a sequence of joint events.

Corollary 21.6 *For n joint events $S = a_1 a_2 \cdots a_n$ we have*

$$W(c, S) = W(a_1, c) + W(a_2 | a_1, c) + \cdots + W(a_n | (a_1 a_2 \cdots a_{n-1}), c). \quad (25)$$

∎

The last relation can be considered as an equation in the associations between the concept c and the events a_i, given the association of the joint event with the concept. This basic relation will enable us to formulate sets of equations directly in the association measures between words and the corresponding semantic actions, as we now demonstrate.

21.2.2 Associations between words and actions

Let $v_i(t)$ denote the event that **the word v_i occurs at position** t, where v_i are words in a vocabulary of size N, and $1 \leqslant i \leqslant N$. A sentence of length n can be written as the joint event of the form

$$S = (v_{i_1}(t_1) v_{i_2}(t_2) \cdots v_{i_n}(t_n)). \quad (26)$$

If this sentence is known to be associated with a semantic action c_k, as measured by $W(S, c_k)$, then equation (25) is a linear equation in the conditional associations $W(v_{i_l}(t_l) | (v_{i_1}(t_1) \cdots v_{i_{l-1}}(t_{l-1})), c_k)$, $1 \leqslant l \leqslant n$. Given a collection $\mathscr{L}$ of L sentences of this type we can construct a **linear** set of equations in the conditional associations. Observe, however, that the number of unknowns in these equations will tend to grow quite large as the number of sentences increases, since they involve **all orders** of conditioning.

The number of unknowns can be drastically reduced by assuming additional relations between the conditional associations. The simplest such assumption is dropping the dependence on location and order of words altogether, i.e.

$$W(v_i(t) | A(t), c_k) = W(v_i, c_k). \quad (27)$$

Because of this complete lack of order or temporal dependence of the associations, we call this assumption the **bag of words** model. This model will serve to illustrate our methods throughout this paper, though it should be emphasized that our principles are in **no way** restricted to this situation.

In the **bag of words** model, every sentence is represented by an unordered set of words if we omit the time (location) index, t, from the words, writing it (formally) as the joint word event

$$S^l = v_1^l v_2^l \cdots v_n^l, \quad l = 1, \ldots, L. \quad (28)$$

By considering their associations to the K classes

$$W(c^k, S^l) = \sum_{j=1}^{n} W(v_j^l, c^k) \equiv \sum_{j=1}^{n} x_j^k \quad (29)$$

these sentences yield a linear set of L equations for each of the K classes, in the unknowns $x_j^k = W(v_j, c^k)$. Notice that similar linear equations result from any finite order Markovian assumption on the words. For example, for a first order Markov assumption the variables are $x_{j,i}^k = W(v_j(t)|v_i(t-1), c^k)$.

Before we investigate the structure and solutions of these equations we relate our formal measure of association to the more familiar notion of probability in its general sense of reasonable expectation.

21.2.3 Associations and probabilities

We are now ready to investigate the relationship between abstract measures of association and the more familiar notions of probability and mutual information. These relations will allow us to exploit a dual algebraic/statistical interpretation of associations to provide improved probability estimates. Moreover, this will enable us to relate our measure to statistical mechanics and to control the level of associations between the concepts through a **temperature** parameter.

The relationship between self-associations in equation (20) is similar to the familiar relation among conditional probabilities

$$P(ab|\cdot) = P(a|\cdot)P(b|a\cdot), \tag{30}$$

suggesting a possible relation between the two. A natural hypothesis, therefore, is that they are functionally related,

$$W(a, a) = F[P(a)], \tag{31}$$

with some arbitrary continuous function $F(x)$.

The following proposition shows that if such a relationship exists, then it must be of a particular form.

Proposition 21.7 *If there exists a relation between the self-association and the probability of events in the form of equation* (31) *then it must be given by*

$$W(a, a) = -\beta \ln P(a), \tag{32}$$

with some arbitrary real parameter β. If $W(a, a)$ is increasing in $P(a)$ then β is positive.

Proof:
Recalling equation (20)

$$W(ab, ab) = W(a, a) + W(b|a, b|a), \tag{33}$$

in terms of the function $F(x)$, and inserting the conditional probability equation (30), we obtain

$$F(xy) = F(x) + F(y), \tag{34}$$

where $x = P(a)$ and $y = P(b|a)$. This functional equation, which is a variant of the Cauchy functional equation, is well known to have only the (continuous) solution given by equation (32) (Aczél, 1966). ∎

Corollary 21.8 (Mutual Information) *If there exists a functional relation between $W(a,b)$ and probabilities, then it must be given by*

$$P(ab) = P(a)P(b)e^{\beta W(a,b)}, \tag{35}$$

or equivalently

$$W(a,b) = \frac{1}{\beta} \ln \frac{P(ab)}{P(a)P(b)}, \tag{36}$$

corresponding to the mutual information between a and b (Thomas, 1969).

Proof: Follows from equations (32) and (23).   ∎

The probability emerges here as a simple monotonic function of the self-association. The importance of the probability will lie in its empirical relation to the relative frequency, **whenever the latter makes sense.**

So far we have not discussed the role of the normalization of P. Since P is a probability measure, then

$$P(\sim a) = 1 - P(a) \tag{37}$$

for all $a \in \Omega$. We thus obtain the following important relation for any $a \in \mathscr{F}(\Omega)$:

$$P(c^j|a) = \frac{P(c^j)e^{\beta W(a,c^j)}}{\sum\limits_{k=1}^{K} P(c^k)e^{\beta W(a,c^k)}}, \tag{38}$$

where the c^j, $j = 1, \ldots, K$ are the events that correspond to the different possible semantic actions.

Remark. This is analogous to the Gibbs distribution in statistical physics, if the measure W corresponds to the energy. The main difference is that unlike energy, W is not necessarily positive. Via this analogy we understand the meaning of the parameter β as a control parameter, similar to temperature, namely, $\beta = 1/T$, where T is the ensemble temperature. In the high T limit, the concepts **dissociate** and become more independent, whereas at low T the associations are very important. There is therefore a finite intermediate temperature which best corresponds to the correct probabilities of the events. Throughout this work we keep the parameter β fixed to 1 and defer the discussion of different values of the temperature to future work. A variable temperature strategy has been recently proved optimal in other cases of supervised learning (Seung *et al.*, 1991).

The case of $K = 2$ (dichotomies) deserves a special attention. For that case equation (38) can be written as

$$P(c^j|a) = \frac{1}{1 + e^{-\beta \Delta W}} \equiv \psi(\beta \Delta W), \tag{39}$$

where ψ is known as the sigmoid function and ΔW is the difference between the associations of a to the two classes. The parameter β is now clearly also the gain of the sigmoid nonlinearity, as would be expected from a temperature.

Equation (35) gives the direct information theoretic interpretation to the associations and relates it to the mutual information. If we average the association measure with respect to the probability of the joint events $P(ab)$, we obtain

$$\langle W \rangle \sum_{a,b} P(ab)W(a,b) = \frac{1}{\beta} \sum_{a,b} P(ab) \ln \frac{P(ab)}{P(a)P(b)} \equiv \frac{1}{\beta} \mathscr{I}(\mathscr{A},\mathscr{B}), \qquad (40)$$

where $\mathscr{I}(A,\mathscr{B})$ is Shannon's **mutual information** between the events $a \in A \subset \Omega$ and $b \in B \subset \mathscr{F}(\Omega)$ (Thomas, 1969). In particular, if $A = \{a\}$ and $B = \{b\}$, then $\mathscr{I}$ is the mutual information between these single events, as used by Gorin et al. Notice that as defined, $\mathscr{I}$ is also nonnegative if P is normalized over A and B, i.e., $\sum_{a \in A, b \in B} P(ab) = 1$.

21.2.4 Associations and likelihood ratio

For completeness, we review (Duda and Hart, 1973) how equation (25) can be directly computed from the probability interpretation of associations given by equation (35). The posterior probability of the action, c, given the n joint events $S = a_1 a_2 \cdots a_n$ can be written using Bayes' rule

$$
\begin{aligned}
P(c|S) &= P(c) \frac{P(a_1 a_2 \cdots a_{n-1} a_n | c)}{P(a_1 a_2 \cdots a_{n-1} a_n)} \\
&= P(c) \frac{P(a_1|c)P(a_2|a_1 c) \cdots P(a_n|(a_1 a_2 \cdots a_{n-1} c))}{P(a_1 c)P(a_2|a_1) \cdots P(a_n|(a_1 a_2 \cdots a_{n-1}))} \\
&= P(c) \prod_{i=1}^{n} \frac{P(a_i|(a_1 \cdots a_{i-1} c))}{P(a_i|(a_1 \cdots a_{i-1}))},
\end{aligned}
\qquad (41)
$$

or

$$\ln \frac{P(c|S)}{P(c)} = \sum_{i=1}^{n} \ln \frac{P(a_i|(a_1 \cdots a_{i-1} c)}{P(a_i|(a_1 \cdots a_{i-1})}. \qquad (42)$$

This is precisely the basic linear equation in the conditional associations, when taking equation (35) into account. This equation reduces to equation (29) under the bag of words assumptions, i.e. that the probabilities, as the associations, are order independent. The general linear equation, equation (42), is however completely independent of such assumptions.

Another interpretation of the associations W is that of **stochastic complexity**, or **code length** (Rissanen, 1989). The self-association of an event $W(a,a)$ is, up to a constant factor, the number of bits required to encode a with an optimal code, i.e. its description length. The association $W(a,b)$ is, similarly, the additional description length of the joint event ab compared with that of the events a and b independently. This fact allows us also to interpret our method as a Minimum Description Length approach to the problem of weight assignment in a network.

21.2.5 Network connections and associations

One can imagine a realization of these abstract events by threshold units (or 'neurons') in a network. In this realization, the elementary events, Ω, are logical statements of the form **unit i is active** or **unit j is not active**. Later we will allow these threshold units to take real values that correspond to a probability of activity. We also assume that Ω contains a certain event u, or a unit in the network that is constantly active. In the connectionist interpretation one should view the conditional association $W(a|b,c)$, as the additional **local field** on unit c when unit a is turned on **given that unit b is active already**. This local field is meaningful only if we wait long enough such that all the indirect network associations are also taken into account. We do not attempt a rigorous investigation of the relationships between connectionism and associations in this work. Rather, we describe some underlying intuitions which may prove useful to understand our results. Consider a **neural network** comprising M neural units with unrestricted connectivity. At every instance, each unit is under a **local field** as a result of both external and internal interactions. We say that on the unit i there is a local field h_i defined as

$$h_i = \sum_{j=1}^{M} w_{ij}\sigma_j + h_i^{\text{ext}}, \tag{43}$$

where w_{ij} is the value of the connection from unit i to j, σ_j is the output of unit j, and h_i^{ext} is a possible **external field** on unit i. This external field can also be considered as the input to node i. The output value of the unit, σ_i, is traditionally determined from its local field through either a stochastic or deterministic nonlinear transfer function. The difference between the stochastic and deterministic dynamics yields different interpretations of the network's configuration, and both are interesting to consider in our context. In the original formulations of stochastic networks (Hinton and Sejnowski, 1986), the units were random binary variables that can have the value 1 with probability

$$P(\sigma_i = 1) = \psi(\beta h_i) \equiv \frac{1}{1 + e^{-\beta h_i}}, \tag{44}$$

where ψ is the sigmoidal function of equation (39). Otherwise, we assume that $\sigma_i = 0$ (originally it was taken as -1, in analogy with spin systems). In the limit $\beta \to \infty$ (zero temperature), such a network becomes deterministic and the units are 1 if the field is positive, and 0 otherwise. For finite β the units fluctuate, and so do the local fields. It can be shown, however, (using a **mean field approximation** (Hertz *et al.*, 1991)) that the (ensemble) average behavior can still be rather simple

$$\langle \sigma_i \rangle = \psi(\beta \langle h_i \rangle). \tag{45}$$

There is a natural correspondence between such a general dynamical network and associated events:

- The individual units of the network are identified as the elementary events Ω, i.e. to each unit we attach the elementary event: **unit i is active**.
- The output of the unit σ_i is 1 if the event is true and 0 otherwise. In the mean field (deterministic) network, the output naturally corresponds to the probability of the event.
- Associations between events are measured by the local fields on the units. Thus the association of node i with node j is identified as the local field on unit i, h_i, due to unit j being active. Such local fields satisfy the (additive) conditions of Theorem 21.1 thus allowing the corresponding interpretation for associations of joint events. Given a connected network of this type, we can address questions such as the probability of a certain combination of units, given an input (external fields) on other units. The complete algebra, $\mathscr{F}(\Omega)$, corresponds to various activity patterns of the network.
- Conditional association, $W(a|b,c)$ is now naturally defined as the (asymptotic) difference between the two corresponding local fields, such that equation (13) is directly satisfied.
- The network associations evolve with time due to the network's dynamics. Initially only the direct connections between the units generate the fields, however, it is the asymptotic (average) local fields, incorporating to all indirect associations (**network associations**) that should obey our formal relations among associations.
- Self-associations are understood as the reacting local field of the network on a unit, when only this unit is turned on. This field can be measured by creating a duplicate of this unit which is connected in an identical way to the rest of the network. Its self-association is the local field on the 'copy unit' due to the activity of the original one.

An important issue is how to adjust the weights of a network such that the network associations correspond to the **correct** associations of compound events. In what follows we address this question in the context of single-layer feed-forward networks, where there is no distinction between the direct and network associations. The more general question is postponed to future work.

21.3 Semantic supervision as equations in associations

We now proceed to describe an algorithmic solution to equation (29), which is an algebraic formulation of the association-estimation for a bag of words model. We assume semantically supervised sentences, namely, sentences with an *a posteriori* probability of being associated with a semantic action c^k, $1 \leqslant k \leqslant K$. We interpret such supervision as dichotomic, i.e., to each sentence we assign a probability of being associated with the class, for each class independently. This assumption is not totally general, since in many cases the classes are not mutually exclusive, or not independent. It is true for many problems of interest, and we postpone consideration of the general case. Under this simplified assumption, however, the supervision for each class is a simple dichotomy: how much this sentence is associated with **class** k. For each of the training sentences S_l, $1 \leqslant l \leqslant L$, define an association between the sentence and semantic action as

$$A_l^k \equiv \log \frac{P(c^k | S_l)}{P(c^k)}. \tag{46}$$

How these quantities are determined depends on the nature of the supervision. Moreover, the supervision confidence may vary from sentence to sentence. At this point we assume, for simplicity, that these probabilities are a fixed small number ε for the wrong class, and $1 - \varepsilon$ for the right one. In our experiments, we discovered that this method is not very sensitive to the actual value of ε. It may, however, be sensitive to a supervision confidence $\varepsilon(l)$ which varies from sentence to sentence.

Our basic relation, equation (25), can now be written as the system of linear equations

$$A_l^k = \sum_{i_l \in S_l} x_{i_l}^k, \tag{47}$$

the variables x_j^k are defined in equation (29), and S_l are the words in the lth sentence. Introducing the notation: $\Lambda_i^l =$ **the number of occurrences of the word** i **in the sentence** l, we can write these equations in a matrix form

$$\mathbf{A}^k = \Lambda \times \mathbf{x}^k, \tag{48}$$

where Λ is the $N \times L$ matrix (Λ_i^l). In this analysis, it is a matrix of integers, but it can just as well have real values, representing noisy input or the probability of occurrence of a word. This can be important if the data comes from a speech recognizer or from some other noisy channel. We denote the input vector that corresponds to a sentence S by $\lambda(S)$. $\mathbf{A}^k$ denotes the L dimensional (semantic) association for class k, and $\mathbf{x}^k$ is an N dimensional vector of (the unknown) associations between the words and the class. For each class $\mathbf{k}$, these systems of equations are independent. Observe that Λ depends only on the sentences, and that A depends on the semantic supervision.

21.3.1 A very simple example

Consider again a three word/single class problem similar to the one described in the introduction. Despite its simplicity, this example illustrates several of the important features of the algebraic method. The 'sentences':

- 'table'
- 'white table'
- 'chair'

are translated into the following simple set of equations:

$$\begin{pmatrix} A_1 \\ A_2 \\ A_3 \end{pmatrix} = \begin{pmatrix} 1 & 0 & 0 \\ 1 & 1 & 0 \\ 0 & 0 & 1 \end{pmatrix} \times \begin{pmatrix} x_1 \\ x_2 \\ x_3 \end{pmatrix}, \tag{49}$$

where A_i are the supervision associations (equation (46)) of the furniture department for each sentence. The solution of these equations is clearly $x_1 = A_1, x_2 = A_2 - A_1$ and $x_3 = A_3$. When the degree of confidence in the supervision is constant (i.e. $A_1 = A_2$), then $x_2 = 0$. That is, the association of the word **white** with **Furniture** is estimated to be zero, even though it appears once in this class. In contrast, the word **chair** that appears once in the third sentence is directly associated by $x_3 = A_3$, as intuitively expected. Thus, for small numbers of occurrences, this algebraic structure captures the relations between the words and actions better than any relative-frequency statistics. This becomes even more clear when we estimate probabilities using the interpretation of associations as mutual information (equation (35)). Assume that the supervision is correct with probability 99%, and that the prior probabilities are uniform over the three semantic actions. Thus, $A_1 = A_2 = A_3 = \log(0.99/0.33)$. Interpret the x_i as the mutual information between the respective words and the action of connection to the furniture department. Applying equation (25) with $\beta = 1$ then yields

$$p(\textbf{Furniture}|\textbf{table}) = p(\textbf{furniture}|\textbf{chair}) = 0.99$$
$$p(\textbf{Furniture}|\textbf{white}) = 0.33.$$

21.3.2 The null space and its meaning

As observed previously, we obtain linear equations no matter what order of associations are assumed. If we explicitly write these equations for each class k, for the bag of words model, as

$$\begin{pmatrix} A_1^k \\ A_2^k \\ \vdots \\ A_L^k \end{pmatrix} = \begin{pmatrix} 01 \cdots 1 \cdots 10 \\ 10 \cdots 1.1.0 \\ \vdots \\ .10 \cdots 1.01 \end{pmatrix} \times \begin{pmatrix} x_1^k \\ x_2^k \\ \vdots \\ x_N^k \end{pmatrix}, \tag{50}$$

where the rows of the $L \times N$ matrix Λ represent supervised sentences in the training conversations, with 1's in the position of the words. Typically $L > N$ and both are moderately large numbers ($\mathcal{O}(1000)$) in the experiments thus far performed. These equations suffer from the two standard difficulties of linear equations. First, the **sparse** matrix Λ has a rank much lower than $\min(N, L)$, thus no unique solution exists. Second, there are typically no exact solutions at all due to either (very common) supervision errors, or more generically, inadequacy of the model (e.g. lack of word order in the bag of words case). A fascinating property of these equations, however, is that they separate two important aspects of the problem. The **semantic** supervision – with respect to this simplified model – affects only the vector $\mathbf{A}^k$, whereas the structural (or **syntactic**) information is all contained in the matrix Λ, which is class-independent. The rank problem, therefore, is related to the basic structure of the language rather than the semantics. What kind of information can be extracted from the matrix Λ alone?

Let $\mathcal{N} = \ker(\Lambda)$ denote the null space of Λ, namely, a vector $S \in \mathcal{N}$ if $\Lambda \times S = 0$. Let $\mathcal{P}_{\mathcal{N}}$ be the projection operator on the subspace $\mathcal{N}$.

By definition, vectors in $\mathcal{N}$ can not change the l.h.s. of the equations and therefore are **irrelevant** for the discrimination between the classes in the training task. The relevance of a word combination, S, to the task can thus be measured by the relative length, rel(S), of its projection on $\mathcal{N}$, defined as,

$$\mathrm{rel}(S) \equiv 1 - \frac{\| \mathcal{P}_{\mathcal{N}} \mathcal{S} \|}{\| \mathcal{S} \|}, \tag{51}$$

where the norm $\| \ \|$ denotes the Euclidian distance in $\mathbf{R}^N$. The value of rel(S) is 1 when S has no null component at all. Thus the associations (to all the classes) of words that have no component in $\mathcal{N}$ are uniquely determined from the equations, i.e. there is no freedom in choosing their weights. It is important to remember that this uniqueness is a property of the **training set** alone, and invariant to the semantic supervision. The solution, however, does depend on the semantics. However, by adding more sentences (equations) the rank of the system cannot decrease, though the value of the weights might change. It is easy to see that no training sentence can be in the null space.

Semantic equivalence We introduce the notion of **semantic equivalence** with respect to the task. We say that the sentence S_1 is semantically equivalent to S_2 (with respect to the task and the given training sentences) if $\lambda(S_1) - \lambda(S_2) \in \mathcal{N}$, or equivalently,

$$\Lambda \times S_1 = \Lambda \times S_2. \tag{52}$$

Semantically equivalent sentences are indistinguishable, as long as **we use this model** and this training data, for discriminating the given semantic classes. Surprisingly, however, this relationship is **independent** of the semantic supervision. Since the linear algebraic structure remains also when correlations between words to any finite order are taken into account, we can conclude that any **finite memory language** will exhibit a similar peculiar phenomenon, i.e. a notion of semantically equivalent sentences can be defined which depends only on their structure (and not on their meaning). Interestingly enough a similar phenomenon exists also in formal logical models of meaning.

An immediate application of this notion is the identification of **task synonyms**. We call the words v_i and v_j synonyms with respect to our semantic task if replacing v_i by v_j in **any sentence** results in a semantically equivalent sentence. A trivial case of **synonyms** exists when switching these words does not change the matrix Λ at all. This happens, in the bag of words model only if the two words always appear together, or if they appear interchangeably in precisely the same sentences. A more general notion is characterized by the null space.

Proposition 21.8 *A sufficient condition for the words v_i and v_j to be task-synonyms is that* $\mathrm{rel}(\mathbf{s}^{ij}) = 0$, *where the components of* $\mathbf{s}^{ij} \in R^N$ *are defined as* $\mathbf{s}_i^{ij} = -\mathbf{s}_j^{ij} = -1$ *and* $\mathbf{s}_k^{ij} = 0$ *for* $k \notin \{i, j\}$.

Proof: Clearly, switching the word v_i with v_j in a sentence S is equivalent to adding the vector $\mathbf{s}^{ij}$ to $\lambda(S)$. By definition the two sentences are semantically equivalent if their difference is in $\mathcal{N}$. ∎

The generalization of synonyms to larger phrases is simple and natural. In fact the null space of Λ partitions all possible sentences into exactly $L - \dim(\mathcal{N})$ equivalent classes, the dimensionality of the factor space $\mathcal{L}/\mathcal{N}$, through the equivalence relation $\sim$

$$S_1 \sim S_2 \Leftrightarrow \lambda(S_1) - \lambda(S_2) \in \mathcal{N}. \tag{53}$$

These ideas will be experimentally evaluated in section 21.4.4.

21.3.3 Solving the equations

So far we have managed to formulate the learning problem, by exploiting the algebraic structure of the associations, by a simple system of linear equations, equation (48). This linear system is, generally, ill posed, i.e. it is both over and under detemined and a solution can be found only in an approximate sense. Furthermore, there can be infinitely many equally good approximate solutions. The most popular and easy to obtain is the LMS solution which is, in general, not unique,

$$\min_{\mathbf{W}} \| \mathrm{logit}(\mathbf{P}^k) - \Lambda \cdot \mathbf{X} \|^2 = \min_{\{x_i^k\}} \sum_{l=1}^{L} \left(P_l^k - \psi \left(\sum_i \Lambda_{li} x_i^k \right) \right)^2. \tag{54}$$

This system is similar to the one obtained in problems of Information

Retrieval (IR) (Streeter and Lochbaum, 1988). The standard technique for solving such linear optimization problems is by a Singular Value Decomposition (SVD) of the matrix Λ (Golub and Van Loan, 1983). Any matrix can be decomposed into a product of the form

$$\Lambda = \mathbf{UWV}^\mathrm{T}, \tag{55}$$

where $\mathbf{U}$ and V are each orthonormal in the sense that their columns are orthogonal,

$$\sum_{l=1}^{L} U_{lk} U_{ln} = \delta_{kn}, \quad 1 \leqslant k, n \leqslant N, \tag{56}$$

$$\sum_{j=1}^{N} V_{jk} V_{jn} = \delta_{kn}, \quad 1 \leqslant k, n \leqslant N. \tag{57}$$

The matrix $W = \mathrm{diag}(w_j)$ is an $N \times N$ diagonal matrix of the **singular values** which are the natural generalization of the **eigenvalues** of a square matrix. Indeed, when Λ is square and symmetric then $\mathbf{U} = \mathbf{V}$ and the singular values are the eigenvalues.

Since $\mathbf{U}^\mathrm{T}\mathbf{U} = \mathbf{I_L}$ and $\mathbf{V}^\mathrm{T}\mathbf{V} = \mathbf{I_N}$, the matrix

$$\tilde{\Lambda} = \mathbf{VW}^{-1}\mathbf{U}^\mathrm{T}, \tag{58}$$

is a **pseudo inverse** of Λ. An attractive feature of the SVD solution is that it provides both the singular values and the null space of the matrix. In particular, the columns of $\mathbf{V}$ that correspond to the (numerically) zero singular values are a basis of $\mathcal{N}$. Moreover, by eliminating the very small singular values, the numerical sensitivity of the solutions of **ill-conditioned** systems is largely reduced. This is achieved simply by replacing $1/w_j$ by **zero** if the singular value $|w_j|$ is very small (Golub and Van Loan, 1983). The general LMS solution of the system equation (50) is now given by

$$\mathbf{X}^k = \mathbf{V} \cdot [\mathrm{diag}(1/w_j)] \cdot (\mathbf{U}^\mathrm{T} \cdot \mathbf{P}^k) + \mathbf{X}^0, \tag{59}$$

where $\mathbf{X}^0$ is **any** vector in the null space $\mathcal{N}$.

In the space of vectors that minimize equation (54), $\mathbf{X}^0$ is the one with the minimal norm. This particular vector is natural also from an information theoretic point of view in that, to first order, it minimizes the mutual information between the *a posteriori* and *a priori* distributions (Shannon and Weaver, 1949).

Another look at the minimization criteria equation (54) reveals that essentially we use the LMS criterion for the estimation of the parameters (or weights) x_i^k, exactly as in the traditional training of layered neural networks (Rumelhart *et al.*, 1988). Later, however, we apply our interpretation of these weights as measures of associations. This emphasizes the duality of these objects when viewed as algebraic parameters and at the same time as statistical associations.

21.3.4 Other training algorithms

A natural question at this point is when is it possible to apply other training methods to obtain the weights, and then using our general relations, to attempt deriving the distributions from the weights. To test this idea, we used the original perceptron learning rule (Minsky and Papert, 1988) to obtain the weights, and then attempted to interpret them as mutual information. These produced different distributions for the word/class, however still plausible. The advantages in speed and simplicity of such an algorithm over SVD suggest that alternative training methods can be more efficient to estimate probability distribution functions in this context, and the subject is worthy of further research.

21.3.5 Batch and adaptive modes

So far we have discussed learning in a batch mode, where all the information is available at the same time and we can solve all the training equations together. An important aspect of language acquisition and similar learning problems is the need for an adaptive solution. In the case of adaptive language acquisition (Gorin *et al.*, 1991b), the data arrives through a continuous interaction with the environment when updating the associations due to the last conversation. One wouldn't want to solve all the previously obtained equations, nor even to store them in memory. Fortunately, this is a familiar problem in the context of optimization, particularly in solving linear optimization problems. There are several general approaches to the problem. One is known as **Recursive Least Squares** and is used, for example, in adaptive filtering (Honig and Messerschmidtt, 1984). Another general method, which was applied more specifically to the linear case, is successive overrelaxation (SOR) method (Golub and de Pillis, 1990), which we now briefly describe.

Consider the general linear system

$$\mathbf{A}x = f. \tag{60}$$

Imagine that we can split the matrix $\mathbf{A}$ into two terms

$$\mathbf{A} = \mathbf{A}_0 - \mathbf{A}_1, \tag{61}$$

where $\mathbf{A}_0^{-1}$ is known or is easy to compute. For any initial vector x_0 this splitting is used to generate the vector sequence x_k by the following iterative scheme:

$$x_k = \mathbf{B}x_{k-1} + \mathbf{A}_0 f, \quad k = 1, 2, 3, \ldots \tag{62}$$

where we define the iteration matrix as $\mathbf{B} \equiv \mathbf{A}_0^{-1}\mathbf{A}_1$. These iterations converge to a solution of equation (60) if, and only if, the **spectral radius** of $\mathbf{B}$, namely, the largest modulus among its eigenvalues, $\rho(\mathbf{B}) < 1$. We observe empirically that for the experiments of section 21.4, the spectral radius is indeed much less than 1, although we have not addressed the generality of this observation. Moreover, the convergence is asymptotically exponential and the number of iterations scales like

$$\text{step.count} = \frac{-1}{\log \rho(\mathbf{B})}. \tag{63}$$

To apply this method to our case it is necessary to choose the right splitting of the sentences matrix Λ. If Λ_0^{-1} is taken as the previous pseudo inverse, the natural choice for Λ_1 are the added equations from the new sentence(s), which arise from the latest conversation. In addition to the current solution $\mathbf{W}_0$, also the complete SVD decomposition of Λ_0^{-1} from equation (55) matrix has to be stored. It is necessary to separate two cases according to whether there are new words in the last conversation or not. Notice that the last conversation matrix, Λ_1, need not be invertible. If there are no new words, N remains fixed and the additional equations affect only the (orthogonal) $N \times L$ matrix U. This is done by projecting the new conversation on the vectors of U and adding the remaining (orthogonal) component as additional columns of U. This will now produce the new Λ_0^{-1}, by applying the same SVD decomposition. Since for a generic conversation, $\Lambda_0 + \Lambda_1$ is a small perturbation to the original matrix Λ_0, this iterative scheme is likely to converge quickly. For conversations with new words it is necessary to modify the complete SVD representation since both N and L change.

For each iteration the computational requirements for this adaptive algorithm are minimal. The computation of the iteration matrix $\mathbf{B}$ requires a simple multiplication of the given matrix Λ_0^{-1} by the single row matrix Λ_1, i.e. $O(LN^2)$ operations. Only the iteration matrix needs to be stored in addition to the original Λ_0^{-1}. In practice, the equations are very sparse (less than 1% of the entries are non-zero) and a significant saving in both computational and storage requirements can be obtained by using the well known efficient algorithms for the arithmetic of sparse matrices. However, this was not necessary for the database considered in this paper.

21.4 Focused learning for language acquisition

21.4.1 The experimental setup

We have tested our method on the DARPA application which was previously described by Miller *et al.* (1989). This system responds to queries concerning five attributes of three ships. An example query might be **Where is the Ranger?**, to which the machine would respond **The Ranger is in the Atlantic Ocean**.

The data contained $N = 741$ words in $L = 1494$ conversations collected automatically through interaction with ten people. The data contains numer-

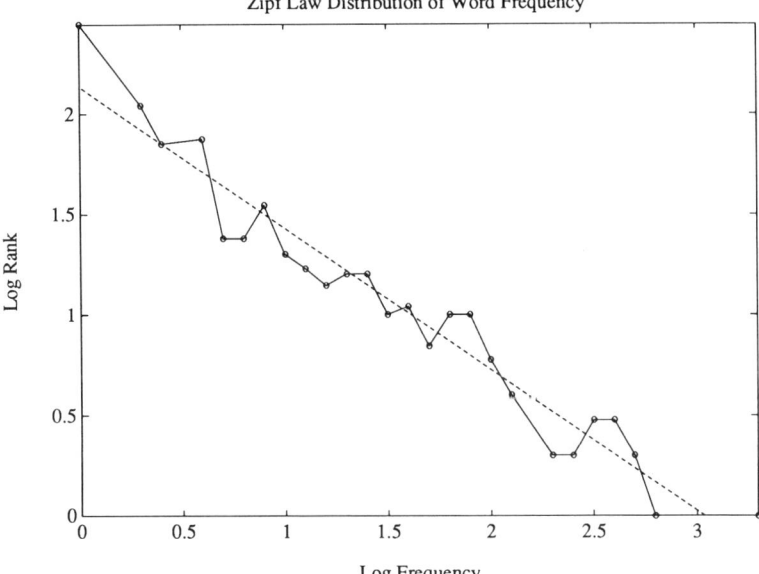

Figure 21.2 *The rank of the words* versus *their frequency for the data used in our experiments (taken from Miller et al. 1989). - - -: a linear regression of the measured data which corresponds to the theoretical Zipf's law*

ous supervision errors and many words that occur only once, as expected from Zipf's law (see Figure 21.2).

Each sentence connotes a two dimensional action, parametrized by the selection of **attribute** and **ship** respectively. The possible **attributes** are as follows:

1. L (FULL LEVEL)
2. C (FUEL CAPACITY)
3. M (MAXIMUM SPEED)
4. E (ECONOMIC SPEED)
5. P (LOCATION)

This experiment focuses on the attribute (5 class) dimension of the task. Similar results were obtained for the ship dimension as well. Notice that this 15 class problem is equivalent to eight linear systems, all with the same matrix Λ but different free terms $\mathbf{P}^k$. The experiment is rudimentary, intended as a first test of our basic ideas.

For this training data we found that the dimension of the null space was $\dim(\mathcal{N}) = 118$ out of a domain dimension of 741. More importantly, we found that 470 (67%) of the words have no component in $\mathcal{N}$ and thus that their associations are uniquely determined by the method. More than 50% of the uniquely determined words (240) appear two times or less in the data, so that their relative frequency estimates are very unreliable. We performed several elementary experiments that specifically address some of the basic problems of the system.

21.4.2 Training and generalization

The first issue is the overall performance of the system. This is normally evaluated by two independent measures, the training and generalization errors (Tishby *et al.*, 1990). By solving the linear equations, using SVD, we obtained 2.7% (16 errors) when testing on the training set of a random selection of 746 sentences. The error on the second half of the data (generalization), using the resulting weights, was 10.4%. There are two issues to be addressed in evaluating such performance. First, why are there any errors on the training data? This can be due to noisy supervision, which is certainly present (Miller *et al.*, 1989), as well as the inadequate bag-of-words model. Second, why such a mismatch between the performance on training and test data? Insufficient training data is certainly an issue, as such a device typically experiences at least one new word per conversation (Gorin *et al.*, 1991b; Miller *et al.*, 1989).

Overfitting of training data may also be an issue, which can be addressed via techniques such as those outlined by Seung *et al.* (1991). The SVD tranining algorithm finds the global minimum of the training error, but due to the supervision noise this minimum is not the one that minimizes the generalization error. There are various ways to address this problem which can be applied here, such as penalizing for over parametrization (e.g. MDI – Rissanen, 1989), or adding thermal noise during the minimization of the training error (Seung *et al.*, 1991; Tishby *et al.*, 1990). The application of such methods to this problem is beyond the scope of the present work. In any case, the obtained final generalization error, even without taking overfitting into account, is not worse than the one obtained in the original system based on relative frequency estimates, which was about 12%.

21.4.3 Probabilities as reasonable expectations

One of the main consequences of our method is the ability to estimate probabilities from very few events. This can be done by translating the weights back into probabilities using the relations discussed in section 21.2. These probability estimates, particularly those that are based on very small samples, should not be considered as an estimate of the relative frequencies of the words, but rather as the measure of their reasonable expecation. In fact, these numbers still depend on the choice of the parameter β, which in this work we take to be 1.0. That is the natural value of β if the probability of supervision error is correctly estimated. Some examples of word-class distributions are given in Table 21.1, together with the corresponding distributions based on word counting. Some comments are in order:

- The semantically null words **too** and **so** have very unreliable statistics because of their small number of observations. This is where the benefit of the algebraic technique is most striking. The word **too**, despite its single occurrence, receives an even distribution among the classes. The word **so** is a neutral word that has a very biased distribution in the data, yet still yields remarkably uniform algebraic associations.
- The word **China** appears in the following sentences in the training:
  (i) **Is the Iowa far from China?**
  (ii) **Can the iowa get to China at full speed without refueling?**
  (iii) **Is the iowa near china?**
  Despite this poor statistic, **China** is associated (algebraically) primarily with **position** and receives about even associations to the other attributes.
- The word **what** appears 305 times, and we expect it to be about evenly distributed between the classes. Both methods give a rather flat, though different, distribution.
- The word **position** receives high association to the **position** class in both methods.

Many words that appear in long sentences can get very distorted associations by the new method due to the fact that the probability of correct supervision and model is taken to be constant, independent of the sentence. This can be improved in the adaptive mode of the algorithm, as previously discussed.

21.4.4 Null space projections

We examined the null space projections for this training data. Somewhat surprisingly we found that about 65% of the words have no component in

Table 21.1 *For each word, the first line is an algebraic estimate of the conditional probability of the semantic action given a word, and the second is the measured relative frequency distribution. The mass is the number of times the word occurs in the database.*

No.	Word	Mass	L	C	Classes M	E	P
1	too		0.15	0.12	0.47	0.12	0.13
		1		1.00			
2	so		0.16	0.26	0.20	0.19	0.17
		15			0.40	0.47	0.13
3	China		0.08	0.13	0.11	0.10	0.58
		3	0.33				0.67
4	what		0.15	0.30	0.20	0.20	0.15
		305	0.12	0.13	0.22	0.28	0.25
5	position		0.01	0.02	0.02	0.03	0.92
		25	0.04		0.04		0.92

$\mathcal{N}$, so that their associations are uniquely determined from the training data. Some words that were not uniquely determined are: **call** (**rel** $= 0.75$); **these** (0.71); **course** (0.54); **also** (0.53); **fairly** (0.54). On the other hand words like **ships**; **type**; **world**; **reveals**;... all had **rel** $= 1$. This by itself is certainly data specific, and its general significance is not clear.

Of more interest are some task–synonyms (e.g. **speeding/towards**; **answer/question**; **chased/outrun**; **once/maybe**; **latitude/longitude**; **relevant/info**; **likely/eaten**; **grows/corn**; **donde/esta**;...). All of these synonyms, however, are mostly coincidental. These words appear always together in this small data set. We couldn't identify more interesting cases in this limited data.

The null projection can serve, however, as a tool to investigate structural relations in linguistic data, as even this limited test demonstrates.

21.4.5 Dialog stability

A side-effect of noisy learning is the phenomenon of dialog instability, as described by Miller *et al.* (1989). We have tested our scheme on six examples of such instability in the original system, and in five of them the problem disappeared after training using the algebraic method.

21.5 Conclusions

By considering the associations between events as the primary concept in learning, we have proposed a novel approach for estimating statistical quantities in linguistic data. Rather than estimating probabilities from empirical frequency ratios of generically rare events, sentences are viewed as algebraic equations in the associations between words and semantic actions. We showed that if there exists any functional relationship between an additive association measure and probability, then the association can be monotonically rescaled so that it is the familiar measure of mutual information. This, in turn, enables us to derive complete probability distributions from the association measures interpretable as reasonable expectations of events rather than relative frequency estimates. We find that these distributions can be very different from, but often much more reliable than, those which result directly from relative frequency estimates. Even for rare events that appear only once or twice in the data, the algebraic estimate often yields quite reasonable distributions.

The reason for this somewhat surprising behavior is that the equations exploit the context via the associations of the other words in the sentence. Information is indirectly shared, through the equations, between different words in the training data, increasing the effective available data dramatically. Our method is general, and applies to the ordered-word situation as well.

Another intriguing feature of this approach is the separation of syntactic and semantic linguistic properties in any finite memory model, as expressed by equations (48). It turns out that all the syntactic information is contained in the structure of the matrix Λ, whereas the semantic supervision is all in the free term $\mathbf{P}^k$ of these equations. The emerging algebraic structure of the sentences can also provide structural linguistic information such as synonyms and semantically-equivalent phrases, arising from projection operators on the corresponding null space of the equations.

We have tested our approach in a set of rudimentary experiments on a simple database query task. The results indicate that these algebraic methods can overcome several difficulties of the relative frequency training procedures, such as unfocused learning and dialog instabilities. We demonstrate the ability to estimate a probability distribution even from a single occurrence of the word, and find that more than 65% of the associations are completely determined from the available training data. Many of the remaining difficulties of the method can be addressed more properly in an adaptive learning mode. In particular, we can avoid the unnecessary assumption of a fixed level of supervision by adjusting the free term of the equation by the current prediction of the system.

The intriguing algebraic structure of associations suggests a natural connectionist interpretation in a fully connected network of nodes that corresponds to the elementary events. The field of compound events is then mapped directly to a general activation pattern of the network. The short time dynamics of such a network generates associations between different configurations thus allowing much more complex and time dependent semantic tasks. We consider this direction as the most promising extension of our ideas, with a variety of possible applications.

We believe that our results indicate that algebraic methods can be very powerful when added to purely statistical techniques. Moreover, the duality of associations, which have both statistical and algebraic characteristics, is proved useful for combining the connectionist and statistical frameworks for language and speech understanding.

Acknowledgements

We are most grateful to Laura Miller for providing the data and for her help in carrying out the experiments, and to Fernando Pereira, Steve Levinson and Jan van Santen for very insightful comments and useful discussions.

References

Aczél, J. (1966) *Functional Equations and Their Applications.* Academic Press, New York, NY.

Blachman, N.M. (1968) The amount of information that y gives about x. *IEEE Transactions on Information Theory,* **14**(1), January.

Bridle, J.S. (1989) Probabilistic interpretation of feedforward classification network outputs, with relationship to statistical pattern recognition, in *Neuro-Computing:*

Algorithms, Architectures, and Applications (eds. F. Fougelman-Soulie and J. Herault), Springer-Verlag, Berlin.

Chomsky, N. (1957) *Syntactic Structures*, Mouton Publishers, Paris.

Church, K.W. and Hanks, P. (1974) *Word Association Norms, Mutual Information and Lexicography*. Proc. 27th meeting of the association for computational linguistics, pp. 76–83.

Cox, R.T. (1946) Probability, frequency and reasonable expectation. *American Journal of Physics*, **14**(1), 1–13.

Duda, R.O. and Hart, P.E. (1973) *Pattern Classification and Scene Analysis*. Wiley, New York.

Fine, T.L. (1973) *Theories of Probability*. Academic Press, New York.

Gertner, A.N. and Gorin, A.L. (1993) Adaptive language acquisition for an airline information subsystem. AT&T Bell Laboratories, *Technical Memorandum* (in preparation).

Golub, G.H. and de Pillis, J.E. (1990) *Iterative Methods for Large Linear Systems*. Academic Press, New York.

Golub, G.H. and Van Loan, C.F. (1983) *Matrix Computation*. John Hopkins University Press, Baltimore.

Goodman, R.M., Higgins, C.M., Miller, J.W. and Smythe, P. (1992) Rule-Based Neural Networks for Classification and Probability Estimation, *Neural Computation* **4**(6), 781–804.

Gorin, A.L. and Levinson, S.E. (1989) On adaptive acquisition of language. AT&T Bell Laboratories *Technical Memorandum* (unpublished).

Gorin, A.L., Levinson, S.E. and Gertner, A.N. (1991a) *Adaptive Acquisition of Spoken Language*. Proceedings ICASSP91, May, pp. 805–8.

Gorin, A.L., Levinson, S.E., Gertner, A.N. and Goldman, E.R. (1991b) On adaptive acquisition of language. *Computer Speech and Language*, April, 101–32.

Hertz, J., Krogh, A. and Palmer, R.G. (1991) *Introduction to the Theory of Neural Computation*. Addison Wesley, Reading, MA.

Hinton, G.E. and Sejnowski, T.J. (1986) *Parallel Distributed Processing vol. 1*. MIT Press, Cambridge.

Honig, M.L. and Messerschmidtt, D.G. (1984) *Adaptive Filters*. Kluwer, Dordrecht.

Jelinek, F. (1990) Self-organizing language modeling for speech recognition, in *Readings on Speech Recognition* (eds. Waibel and Lee), Morgan Kaufmann, San Mateo, CA, pp. 450–506.

Jelinek, F. and Mercer, R. (1980) Interpolated estimation of Markov source parameters from sparse data. *Proceedings Workshop on Pattern Recognition in Practice*, North-Holland, Amsterdam.

Johnstone, P.T. (1982) *Stone Spaces*. Cambridge University Press, Cambridge, pp. 7–11.

Magerman, D.M. and Marcus, M.P. (1990) *Parsing a Natural Language using Mutual Information*. Proc. of the AAAI, Boston.

Miller, L.G. and Gorin, A.L. (1991) Adaptive language acquisition for a data retrieval task. AT&T Bell Laboratories, *Technical Memorandum* (unpublished), May.

Miller, L.G., Gorin, A.L. and Levinson, S.E. (1989) Adaptive language acquisition for a database query task. AT&T Bell Laboratories, *Technical Memorandum* (unpublished), December.

Minsky, M.L. and Papert, S.A. (1988) *Perceptrons*. MIT Press, Cambridge, MA, pp. 161–227.

Pierce, J.R. (1961) *Symbols, Signals and Noise*, Harper, New York, NY.

Rissanen, J. (1989) *Stochastic Complexity in Statistical Inquiry*. World Scientific, NJ.

Rumelhart, D.E., McClelland, J.L. *et al.* (1988) *Parallel Distributed Processing*, MIT Press, Cambridge, MA.

Seung, H.S., Sompolinsky, H. and Tishby, N. (1991) Statistical mechanics of learning from examples. *Physical Review A* (submitted).

Shannon, C. and Weaver, W. (1949) *Mathematical Theory of Communication*. University of Illinois Press, IL, pp. 9–18.

Sproat, R. and Shih, C. (1990) A statistical method for finding word boundaries in Chinese text. *Computer Processing of Chinese and Oriental Languages*, **4**(4), 336–51.

Streeter, L.A. and Lochbaum, K.E. (1988) *Who Knows: A System Based on Automatic Representation of Semantic Structure*. Proc. Conference on User-Oriented Content-Based Text & Image Handling, MIT Press, Cambridge, MA, pp. 380–8.

Thomas, J.B. (1969) *Statistical Communication Theory*. Wiley, New York, NY.

Tishby, N., Levin, E. and Solla, S. (1990) A statistical approach to learning and generalization. *Proceedings of the IEEE*, **78**(10), 1568–74.

Incremental algebraic learning for adaptive language acquisition

K.R. FARRELL*, RICHARD J. MAMMONE* and ALLEN L. GORIN†
*CAIP Center, Rutgers University, Piscataway, NJ 08855, USA
† AT&T Bell Laboratories, Murray Hill, NJ 07974, USA

22.1 Introduction

Language acquisition consists of gaining the ability to extract information from a natural language message. This is a consequence of the principle that the function of language is to communicate meaning (Gorin et al., 1991a). This principle forms the basis for language acquisition models based on **connectionist** methods that build associations between input stimuli and meaningful responses to them.

This chapter explores the application of new algorithms to the adaptive language acquisition model formulated by Gorin et al. (1991a). The new methods consist of incremental approaches for the algebraic learning of statistical associations proposed by Tishby and Gorin (1993). The incremental methods are evaluated on a natural language experiment, namely the Inward Call Manager (Gorin et al., 1991a) database. Performance is evaluated with respect to the alternative methods: the smoothed mutual information method (Gorin et al., 1991a) and the pseudo-inverse solution (Tishby and Gorin, 1993).

The following section reviews the formulation for adaptive language acquisition proposed in Gorin et al. (1991a), and describes the natural language experiment considered in this chapter. This section is followed by the motivation for the current work. The algebraic formulation for language

Artificial Neural Networks for Speech and Vision. Edited by Richard J. Mammone.
Published in 1993 by Chapman & Hall, London. ISBN 0 412 54850 X

acquisition is then presented followed by the description of the new incremental methods that are based on this model. Preliminary results show the incremental methods to offer performance advantages over the direct pseudo-inverse methods with respect to cross-validation, in addition to computational and memory requirements. Experimental results that demonstrate the performance of the new algorithms are provided in section 22.6 and are followed by the conclusions and future work.

22.2 Adaptive language acquisition

As described above, language acquisition refers to gaining the ability to decode the intended meaning of a message. This is based on the principle that the function of language is to communicate meaning. A second principle is that language is acquired by interacting with a complex environment. Such interaction provides feedback as to the appropriateness of a machine's response to a particular input. This technique of monitoring learning via feedback is known as **reinforcement learning** (Barto and Anadan, 1985). The use of reinforcement feedback for governing the learning of a machine has been termed **learning by doing** in Gorin *et al.* (1991a). This approach is contrasted to that of **learning by example** in which both the input and desired output are provided during the training phase. For language acquisition, the **learning by doing** method acquires language throughout the course of performing its task and, hence, has been termed **adaptive** language acquisition (Gorin *et al.*, 1991a). The model for adaptive language acquisition is shown in Figure 22.1.

In Figure 22.1, an input (i.e. a sentence) is applied to the network, which determines the appropriate action. The user then decides if this action is appropriate and correspondingly rewards or punishes the network via a **semantic-level error signal**. The system modifies its parameters accordingly, based on this feedback. Initially, the system will be capable of only 'guessing'

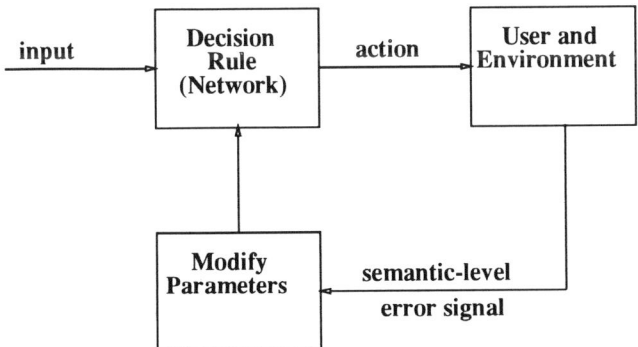

Figure 22.1 *Learning by doing model.*

the correct action, but as more sentences are encountered, it will 'converge' to a correct understanding.

The database used in this chapter for evaluation of the new algorithms is the Inward Call Manager database (Gorin *et al.*, 1991a). The Inward Call Manager database consists of requests to an operator in a department store that may be routed to the **furniture**, **clothing** or **hardware** departments. An example of a natural language dialog between human and machine for the Inward Call Manager is shown as follows:

Machine:	HELLO.
	THIS IS THE J.C. BELL DEPARTMENT STORE.
	WE SELL FURNITURE, CLOTHING, AND HARDWARE.
	HOW MAY I HELP YOU?
User:	*I'm looking for a sofa.*
Machine:	MAYBE I SHOULD CONNECT YOU TO THE
	CLOTHING DEPARTMENT?
User:	*No, a sofa would be in the department with chairs and couches.*
Machine:	I WILL CONNECT YOU TO THE FURNITURE
	DEPARTMENT.
User:	*Yes, that will be fine.*

In this dialog, the machine incorrectly responded to the first user request, but corrected itself after the second user entry, i.e. the semantic-level error signal plus a clarifying message obtained from the convergent dialog. The portion of this dialog that is used for the experiments considered in this chapter is the first sentence from the human, in addition to the action label. This particular experiment is for **supervised training** and not **learning by doing**. However, it provides an initial criterion for evaluating the new incremental methods, after which the adaptive scheme will be a straightforward modification.

The parameters that allow the network to determine an action given a sentence are the word/action associations. The word/action association as determined by the smoothed mutual information technique (Gorin *et al.*, 1991a) provides an estimate of the posterior probability that an action will occur given a word. It was shown in Tishby and Gorin (1993) that algebraic methods can be used as an alternative to obtain word/action associations that are **related** to the associations provided by the smoothed mutual information estimates. This chapter extends upon the algebraic methods for estimating word/action associations.

22.3 Motivation

The methods for determining word/action associations in Gorin *et al.* (1991a,b), Miller and Gorin (1993) and Sankar and Gorin (1993) rely on mutual information estimates. The mutual information for word/action associations can be computed using smoothed relative frequency estimates, i.e. using the number of occurrences of a given word and the number of times an action occurred for sentences containing that word. That method for determining word/action associations is **context independent**, meaning that the update of a word/action association for a given word is independent of the other words that occur along with it in the sentence. This trait is undesirable, and leads one to formulate the problem of **focused learning** (Tishby and Gorin, 1993), referring to the ability to concentrate on words that convey most of the meaning of a sentence.

As an example of focused learning, consider two sentences from the Inward Call Manager database. The two example sentences are: 'I'm looking for a *mauve* sweater', and 'I need a new *etarge*', where italic type denotes a new vocabulary word. The smoothed mutual information method will estimate an equal level of association of the words **mauve** and **etarge** with their corresponding classes, namely **clothing** and **furniture**. This is due to the algorithm only using the information that it has seen **mauve** occur once for the **clothing** category, and **etarge** occur once for the **furniture** category.

The desired response of an algorithm would be to create a relatively small association of **mauve** with clothing and a relatively large association of **etarge** with furniture. For example, the appropriate action can be determined when given the word **etarge**, but cannot be identified when only given the word **mauve**. Intuitively, this motivates the use of an algorithm whose update for the word/action association is proportional to the error signal. In the above example, the first sentence would probably be classified correctly, thus having a small error, whereas the second sentence would probably be misclassified, hence having a large error. Formulating the language acquisition problem as a system of linear equations (Tishby and Gorin, 1993), i.e. algebraic learning, is our proposed means of incorporating the error signal in the update for the word/action association.

Algebraic learning consists of modeling the language acquisition problem as a system of linear equations, where each equation represents a sentence/action pair and each variable denotes a word/action association. The pseudo-inverse solution for this system of linear equations has been found to provide connection weights that are less sensitive to small numbers of samples than are the smoothed relative frequency estimates. The pseudo-inverse solution in Tishby and Gorin (1993) was computed using a Singular Value Decomposition (SVD). However, the direct computation of the pseudo-inverse has some limitations. It is costly to use for updating weights, and is found to provide suboptimal performance for cross-validation. In this chapter, we present two methods of incremental learning to overcome the drawbacks of the pseudo-inverse solution. The next section reviews how the language acquisition problem can be formulated as a system of linear equations, and is followed by the description of the new incremental methods.

22.4 Problem formulation

Our most basic language acquisition model can be interpreted as a single layer neural network, as illustrated in Figure 22.2. The input nodes V_i are word detectors whose outputs O_i represent the probability that a word is in sentence s. In this text-based experiment, the output of the word detectors is either 0 or 1. Note that the number of input nodes M increases in time as the vocabulary grows. The connection weights w_{ij} represent the word/action association and were defined in Gorin *et al.* (1991a) as the **mutual information** between words and actions. The output nodes C_j correspond to the set of N possible actions and are evaluated as the inner product of O and W_j. The action A_j is chosen according to which output node C_j has the largest value.

It was shown in Tishby and Gorin (1993) that the language acquisition model described above can be characterized as a set of linear equations. In particular, given a sentence/action pair for the jth sentence, define a vector λ_j as

$$\lambda_j = \langle 00 \cdots 0100 \cdots 10 \rangle \tag{1}$$

where a 1 or 0 in position i indicates the presence or absence of word i. A straightforward generalization uses word probabilities in place of the 0s and 1s (Gorin *et al.*, 1993). Note that the dimension of λ is equal to the number of words in the vocabulary, namely M, which grows over time. An equation derived for a sentence/action pair is thus

$$\langle \lambda_j, W^k \rangle = A_j^k = \begin{cases} 1 & \text{if } \lambda_j \in \text{action } k \\ 0 & \text{if } \lambda_j \notin \text{action } k \end{cases}. \tag{2}$$

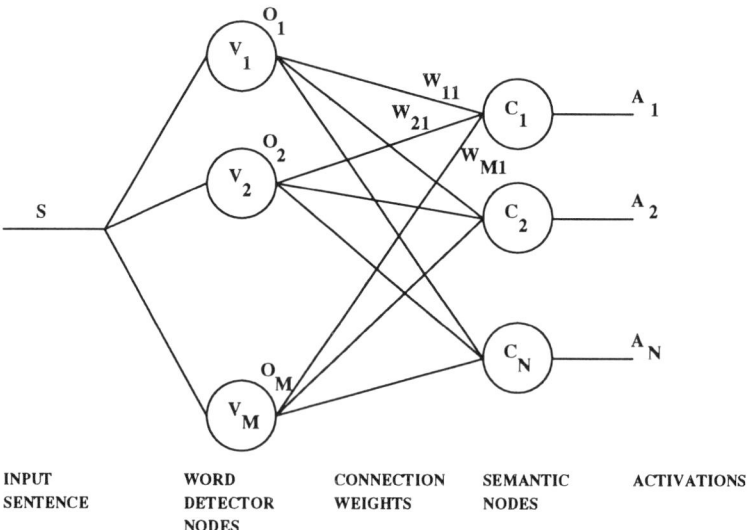

Figure 22.2 *Single-layer neural network for sentence/action mapping.*

This equation is independent of word order in a sentence, and can thus be characterized as a **bag of words** model. Tishby and Gorin (1993) showed how to extend this model to depend on word order, which we do not consider in this work. By using the formulation in equation (2) for each sentence in the system, one obtains a system of linear equations

$$\Lambda W^k = A^k, \quad 1 \leqslant k \leqslant N. \tag{3}$$

In equation (3), Λ is an M by P matrix, whose row vectors are that as given in equation (1). The variable P represents the number of sentences, which also grows over time, W^k is an M dimensional vector containing the connection weights for the kth action, and A^k is a P dimensional vector representing the labels for the kth action. In this experiment, we consider the case where the labels $A^k \in \{1, 0\}$ denote whether or not the sentence corresponds to the kth action.

The pseudo-inverse solution to equation (3) is denoted as

$$W^{k\dagger} = \Lambda^\dagger A^k, \tag{4}$$

where the pseudo-inverse matrix $\Lambda^\dagger$ for equation (4) can be computed using the SVD of Λ (Noble and Daniel, 1988). For example, the SVD decomposes the Λ matrix as a product of the unitary matrices U, V and a diagonal matrix Σ containing the singular values of Λ

$$\Lambda = U\Sigma V^T. \tag{5}$$

The pseudo-inverse matrix $\Lambda^\dagger$ is computed by inverting the nonzero singular values and letting the zero singular values stay zero:

$$\Lambda^\dagger = V\Sigma^{-\dagger}U^T. \tag{6}$$

In practice, singular values below some threshold are set to zero and are not inverted.

22.5 Incremental methods

Two incremental methods are evaluated for solving the system of equations (3) for W^k. The first method minimizes the quantity

$$E_k^2 = \sum_{j=1}^{P} [A_j^k - \langle \lambda_j, W^k \rangle]^2, \tag{7}$$

where j is the sentence index. For each k, W^k is selected to minimize E_k^2. The superscript k is omitted in the remaining discussion for simplicity of notation. The method used to minimize the error quantity in equation (7) is known as the Row-Action Projection (RAP) algorithm (Mammone, 1992), and can be used to incrementally calculate the pseudo-inverse solution of equation (3). The RAP algorithm for the system in equation (3) is implemented by using the update equation

$$W^{(i+1)} = W^{(i)} + \mu \frac{\varepsilon_j}{\|\lambda_j\|} \frac{\lambda_j^T}{\|\lambda_j\|}, \tag{8}$$

where

$$\varepsilon_j = A_j - \langle \lambda_j, W^{(i)} \rangle. \tag{9}$$

In expressions (8) and (9), the superscript i denotes the iteration, the vector λ_j refers to the jth row vector of the matrix Λ, ε_j is called the error, and μ is a gain parameter, which is usually chosen between zero and two. Intuitively, the weight vector W in equation (8) is updated by projecting in the direction of the unit vector $\lambda_j^T/\|\lambda_j\|$, by an amount given by the scaled error $\varepsilon_j/\|\lambda_j\|$. The choice of μ contributes to the trade-off between rate of the convergence and the accuracy of the solution. The RAP method minimizes the error quantity E in equation (7) by cycling over the P equations until the error is below some threshold. Each cycle over the P equations will henceforth be referred to as an epoch.

Asymptotically, the RAP algorithm will converge to the pseudo-inverse solution of equation (4). However, in the short term, the RAP algorithm de-emphasizes the inversion of small singular values and provides a **regularized** inverse solution as described in Mammone (1992). The resulting singular value taper is given by

$$\sigma_i = \frac{1}{\sigma_\Lambda} \left[1 - \left(1 - \frac{\lambda}{N} \sigma_\Lambda^2 \right)^{l+1} \right], \tag{10}$$

where σ_Λ and σ_i are the singular values of the data matrix and its inverse, N is the dimension of the solution, and l is the iteration index for the block of P equations.

Regularization is typically implemented by appending a penalty function to the cost function. The cost function in this case is the minimization of L_2 norm of the error quantity in equation (7). The regularized cost function is of the form:

$$\text{minimize} \quad E_k^2 + \alpha P_k, \tag{11}$$

where α is a scaling parameter and P_k is a penalty function. The addition of the penalty function prevents the quantity E_k^2 from being minimized to the point that the data is overfit. Thus, regularization should improve generalization. This can also be viewed as reducing the sensitivity to ill-conditioned data by tapering the spectral components during a matrix inversion (Doherty, 1990). Regularization is particularly useful for ill-conditioned problems (Tikhonov and Arsenin, 1977).

Equations (8) and (9) represent a regularized solution that is more robust to noise than the pseudo-inverse solution (Mammone, 1992). This regularization tends to improve the classification of test data since the inversion of small eigenvalues, as performed in the SVD computation of the pseudo-inverse solution, tends to overfit the training data.

A second approach is a nonlinear incremental method, which minimizes the error quantity

$$E_k^2 = \sum_{j=0}^{P} [A_j^k - f(\langle \lambda_j, W^k \rangle)]^2.$$ (12)

The function $f(\ )$ used in equation (12) is the sigmoid activation function (Rumelhart and McClelland, 1986):

$$f(\langle \lambda_j, W \rangle) = \frac{1}{1 + e^{-\langle \lambda_j, W \rangle}} = y_j.$$ (13)

The effect of the nonlinear activation is to replace the error term ε_j in equation (9) with $\tilde{\varepsilon}_j$, which is given as

$$\tilde{\varepsilon}_j = y_j(1 - y_j)(A_j - y_j).$$ (14)

In equation (12), since $A_j^k \in \{0, 1\}$ and $0 < f(\ ) < 1$, the error for the jth sentence is bounded by $0 < |E_j| < 1$. Thus, large errors of the same sign are de-emphasized. The use of the sigmoid activation function introduces a different error norm that is more robust to this type of error (Huber, 1981).

22.6 Experimental results

The two incremental methods were applied to the text-based Inward Call Manager database. This system consists of 1105 sentences comprised of the first sentence in each dialogue of a natural language experiment. The vocabulary size of the 1105 sentences is 1356. All experiments reported in this chapter use the first 800 sentences for training, which contains 1122 vocabulary words.

Figures 22.3 and 22.4 show the learning curves for the two algorithms. These plots illustrate the performance when the system is trained on 800 sentences and tested with (1) the training set, (2) the test set (305 sentences), and (3) the subset of the test set (202 sentences) containing known **salient** words. For example, in the test sentence 'I'm looking for a table', if **table** was encountered in the training set, then this sentence would be labeled as containing a known **salient** word. Similarly, for the test sentence, 'I need a new etarge', if **etarge** was not encountered in the training set, then this sentence would not be labeled as salient.

The peak classification performance for both methods and test sets occurs at roughly 15 epochs. At the peak operating point, the linear method correctly classified 99% of the training set, 85% of the 202 test set, and 72% of the 305 test set. The nonlinear method correctly classifies 98% of the training set, 84% of the 202 test set, and 72% of the 305 test set. The pseudo-inverse as

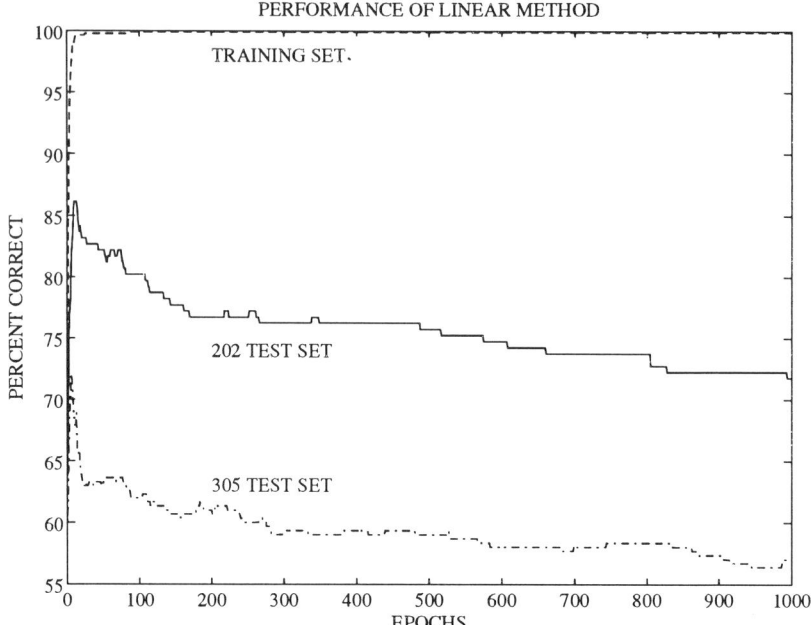

Figure 22.3 *Linear method.*

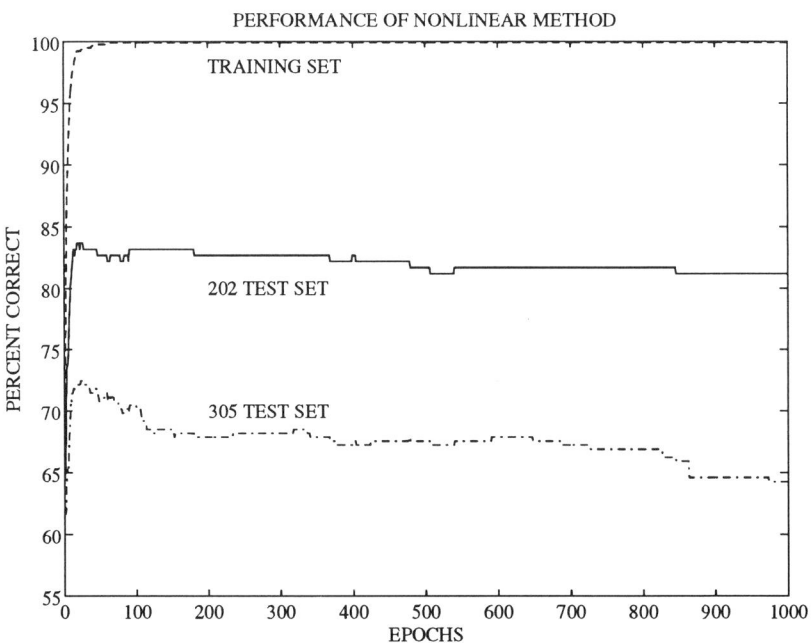

Figure 22.4 *Nonlinear method.*

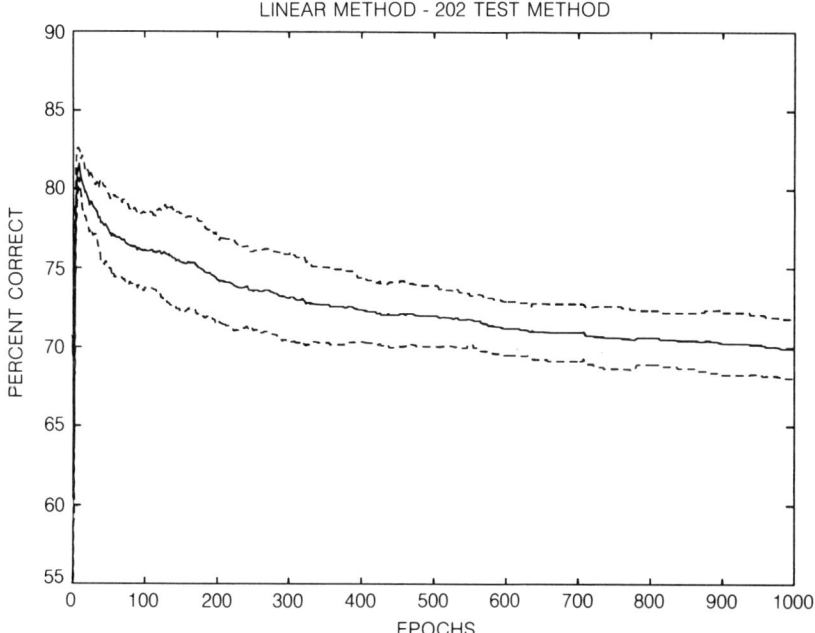

Figure 22.5 *Linear method random training.   : mean;   : standard deviation.*

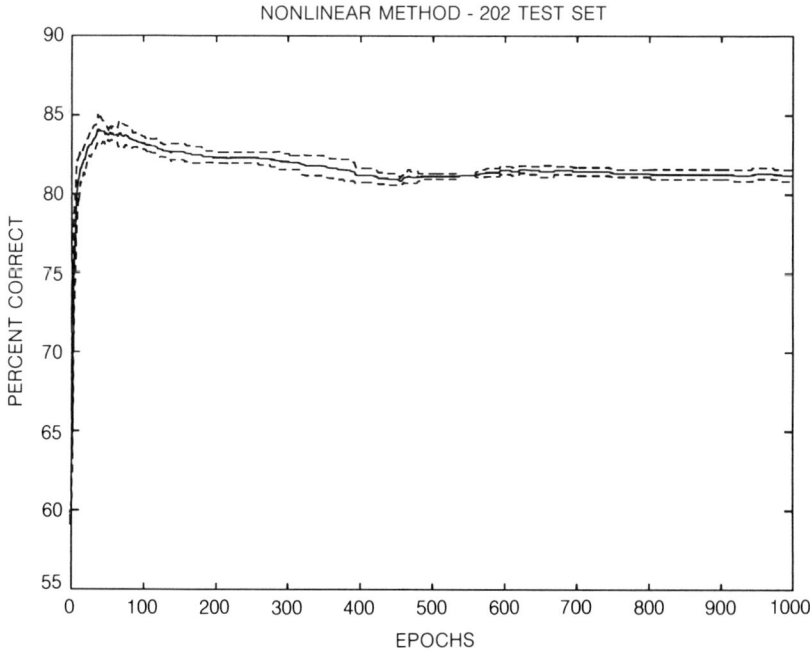

Figure 22.6 *Nonlinear method – random training. ——: mean; - - -: standard deviation.*

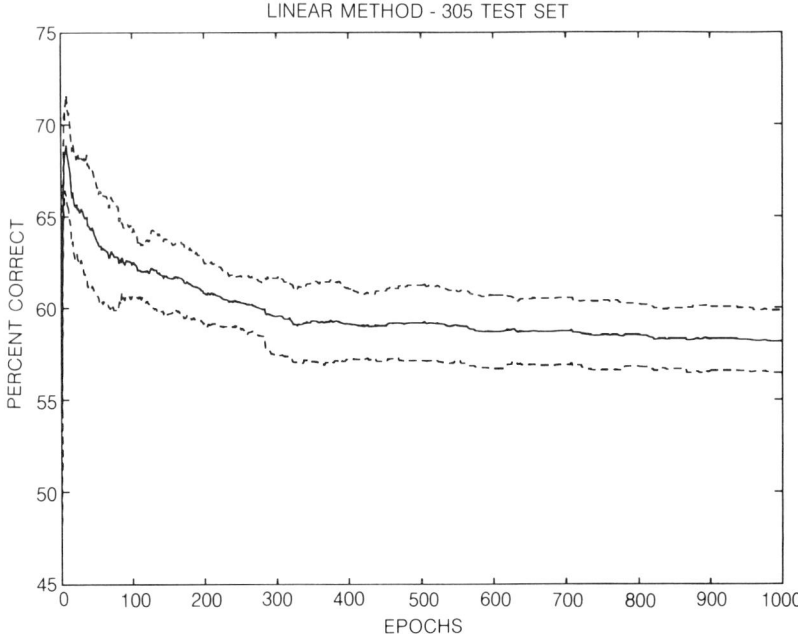

Figure 22.7 *Linear method – random training.* ———: *mean;* - - -: *standard deviation.*

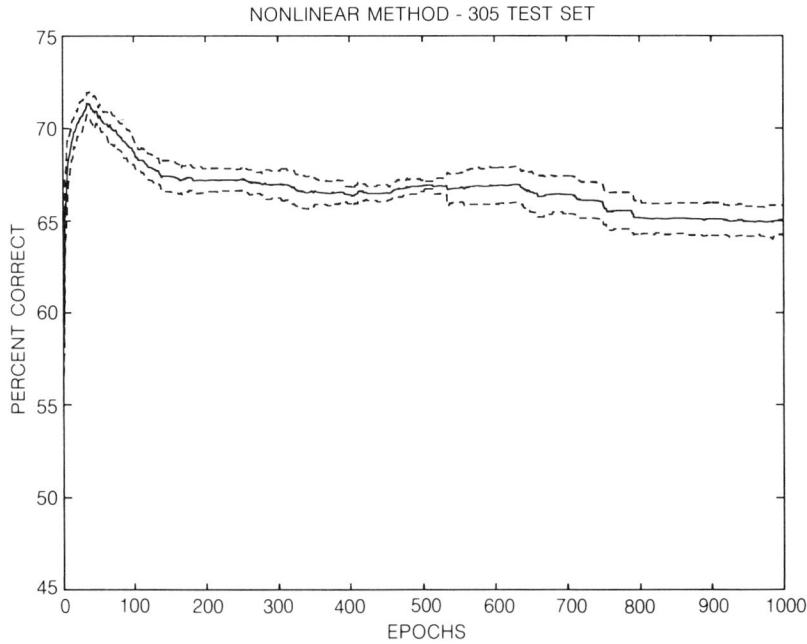

Figure 22.8 *Nonlinear method – random training.* ———: *mean;* - - -: *standard deviation.*

Table 22.1 *Classification performance*

Method	Training (%)	Test (305) (%)	Test (202) (%)
SMI	93	73	83
SVD	99	57	69
Linear-peak	99	72	85
Nonlinear-peak	98	72	84
Linear-1000	99	57	72
Nonlinear-1000	99	64	81

computed with an SVD (thresholding singular values less than 0.1) correctly classifies 99% of the training set, 69% of the 202 test set, and 57% of the 305 test set. These results are summarized in Table 22.1, along with the Smoothed Mutual Information (SMI) estimates.

Though the peak performance of both incremental algorithms is roughly equal, the nonlinear method maintains its classification performance as opposed to the linear method, whose performance degrades after numerous iterations. An additional experiment was performed, where the 800 training sentences are randomly ordered prior to estimating the performance. Note that this does not change the final solution to the system of equations. However, the path that the weights take towards their optimum will be different and hence affect performance. Eight random orderings were tested, whose mean and one standard deviation for classification performance on the 202 and 305 test sets are shown in Figures 22.5–22.8. For the 202 test set, the standard deviation at the 1000th epoch is 0.375 for the nonlinear method and 1.866 for the linear method. The standard deviation at the 1000th epoch for the 305 test set is 0.802 for the nonlinear method and 1.606 for the linear method. Hence, the nonlinear method is more robust than the linear method with respect to order sensitivity.

22.7 Conclusions and future work

Two incremental methods have been evaluated on the adaptive language acquisition problem. For the 305 test set, the incremental methods correctly classify 72% of the test sentences at their peak operating point. When evaluated on a subset of the test set containing known salient words, the incremental methods correctly classify 84% of the test sentences. The non-linear incremental method is found to maintain its level of generalization while the linear method is more vulnerable to overtraining. The nonlinear method is also less sensitive to equation ordering. Both methods perform significantly better than the pseudo-inverse, which correctly classifies about 57% and 69% of the sentences in the 305 and 202 test sets, respectively. The performance of the incremental methods is similar to that of the smoothed mutual information method for the test set, but yields better performance for the training set.

The incremental methods presented in this chapter for the algebraic learning of statistical associations are encouraging alternatives to the smoothed mutual information method. Research is currently in progress to extend the incremental methods to the adaptive mode of language acquisition. Issues that will come into consideration for the adaptive mode include step size and optimal cycling strategies. For example, if the system has been trained on 1000 sentences, how will the weights be updated upon encountering the 1001st sentence? One possible method is to store only the sentences that lie near the discriminant boundary and just perturb the discriminant upon receiving a new sentence (Agrawal and Mammone, 1992). Other methods may involve optimal choice of step size (Gorin, private communication). Another issue to be considered is that of a stopping criteria for training. These topics are among the numerous areas that will be further investigated during this research.

References

Agrawal, A. and Mammone, R.J. (1992) An on-line training algorithm to overcome catastrophic forgetting. *Proceedings ANNIE '92*, St. Louis, MO.

Barto, A.G. and Anadan, P. (1985) Pattern recognizing stochastic learning automata. *IEEE Trans. on Systems, Man, and Cybernetics*, **15**, 360–75.

Doherty, J.F. (1990) Regularized adaptive processing of ill-conditioned data. *PhD thesis*, Rutgers University.

Gorin, A.L., Levinson, S.E., Gertner, A.N. and Goldman, E.R. (1991a) On adaptive acquisition of language. *Computer, Speech, and Language*, April, 101–32.

Gorin, A.L., Levinson, S.E. and Gertner, A.N. (1991b) Adaptive acquisition of spoken language. *Proceedings IEEE ICASSP 91*, Toronto, Canada, May.

Gorin, A.L., Miller, L.G. and Levinson, S.E. (1993) Some experiments in spoken language acquisition. *Proceedings IEEE ICASSP '93*, Minneapolis, MN, April.

Huber, P.J. (1981) *Robust Statistics*. Wiley, New York, NY.

Mammone, R.J. (1992) *Computational Methods of Signal Recovery and Recognition*. Wiley, New York, NY.

Miller, L.G. and Gorin, A.L. (1993) Structured networks for adaptive language acquisition. *International Journal of Pattern Recognition and Artificial Intelligence* (to appear).

Noble, B. and Daniel, J.W. (1988) *Applied Linear Algebra*. Prentice Hall, Englewood Cliffs, NJ.

Rumelhart, D.E. and McClelland, J.L. (1986) *Parallel Distributed Processing*. MIT Press, Cambridge, MA.

Sankar, A. and Gorin, A.L. (1993) Visual focus of attention in adaptive language acquisition, in *Neural Networks for Speech and Vision Processing* (ed. R.J. Mammone), Chapman & Hall, London.

Tikhonov, A.N. and Arsenin, V.Y. (1977) *Solutions to Ill-Posed Problems*. V.H. Winston and Sons, Washington, DC.

Tishby, N. and Gorin, A. (1993) Algebraic learning of statistical associations for language acquisition, in *Neural Networks for Speech and Vision* (ed. R.J. Mammone), Chapman & Hall, London.

23

Adaptive language acquisition for an airline information subsystem

A.N. GERTNER and ALLEN L. GORIN

AT&T Bell Laboratories, 600 Mountain Avenue, Murray Hill, NJ 07974, USA

23.1 Introduction

The goal of this chapter is to extend our principles and mechanisms for adaptive language acquisition to moderate complexity tasks. In our previous work (Gorin *et al.*, 1991a), a basic principle was that the primary function of language is to convey meaning, with the consequence that language acquisition involves gaining the capability of decoding that meaning. This led us to investigate a language acquisition mechanism based on connectionist methods, in which the network builds associations between messages and meaningful responses to them.

In that previous work, we experimentally evaluated our principles and mechanisms on some elementary tasks. As a task increases in complexity, however, so does the mapping from message to meaning.

In order to provide improved generalization capability in language acquisition, we investigate how one might reflect our knowledge of the device periphery and language structure in a network architecture, to provide improved generalization capability in language acquisition. This chapter, in particular, proposes to incorporate intermediate layers into the network which reflect such structure, and to factor the phrase/action associations through those intermediate nodes. We then experimentally evaluate this network on a subset of an Airline Information task.

Artificial Neural Networks for Speech and Vision. Edited by Richard J. Mammone.
Published in 1993 by Chapman & Hall, London. ISBN 0 412 54850 X

The remainder of this introduction proceeds as follows. First, for completeness, we briefly review the basic principles and mechanisms underlying this research program, as detailed in Gorin *et al.* (1991a). We then propose two corollaries to these basic principles, thereby motivating extensions of our earlier experimental mechanisms to more complex devices. Finally, we define a subset of an Airline Information task on which to experimentally evaluate these ideas.

23.1.1 *Background*

This chapter continues our investigation into devices which adaptively acquire the language for their task. There have been two basic principles underlying this work, as exposited in Gorin *et al.* (1991a). A **first principle** is that the primary function of language is to communicate. A consequence of this principle is that language acquisition involves gaining the capability of decoding the message, i.e. of extracting the intended meaning. This is in contrast to much of the research on automated language acquisition, which focuses on discovering syntactic structure, often specifically to the exclusion of meaning. This first principle led us to investigate a language acquisition mechanism based on connectionist methods, in which the network builds associations between input stimuli and meaningful machine responses to them.

A **second principle** is that language is acquired by interacting with a complex environment. A consequence of this principle is that the interaction involves feedback as to the appropriateness of a machine response to a particular input stimulus. Govering learning via such feedback is called **reinforcement learning** (Barto and Anadan, 1985; Kaebling, 1990) and can be contrasted with **learning by example**. When reinforcement feedback is provided judging the appropriateness of a machine action, we've called this **learning by doing**, and the reinforcement a **semantic-level error signal**. This second principle led us to investigate a mechanism for human–machine interaction based on control-theory methods, where the system's input is a message and the error signal is a measure of the appropriateness of the machine's response.

The generic mechanism inspired by these two principles is illustrated in Figure 23.1, namely an information-theoretic connectionist network embedded in a feedback control system, where connections are strengthened or weakened depending upon feedback as to the appropriateness of the machine's response to input stimuli. In our earliest text-based experiments (Gorin *et al.*, 1991a), we employed a multilayer network, as illustrated in Figure 23.2, where the input nodes correspond to a growing list of vocabulary words, the intermediate layer corresponds to an (also growing) list of observed word-pairs, the output nodes correspond to a fixed discrete set of possible machine actions, and the connection weights are defined to be the **mutual information** (Thomas, 1969) between words (or phrases) and actions. The mutual information is calculated

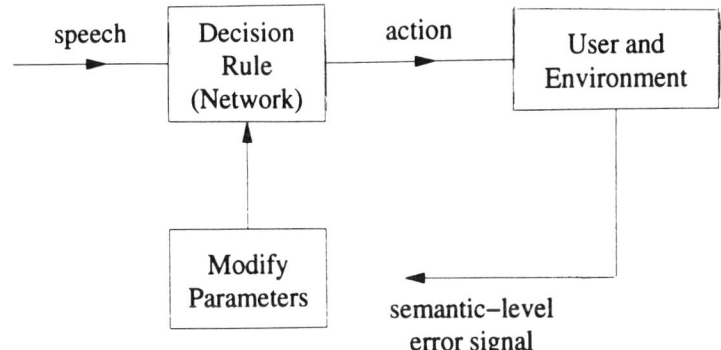

Figure 23.1 *Adaptive language acquisition.*

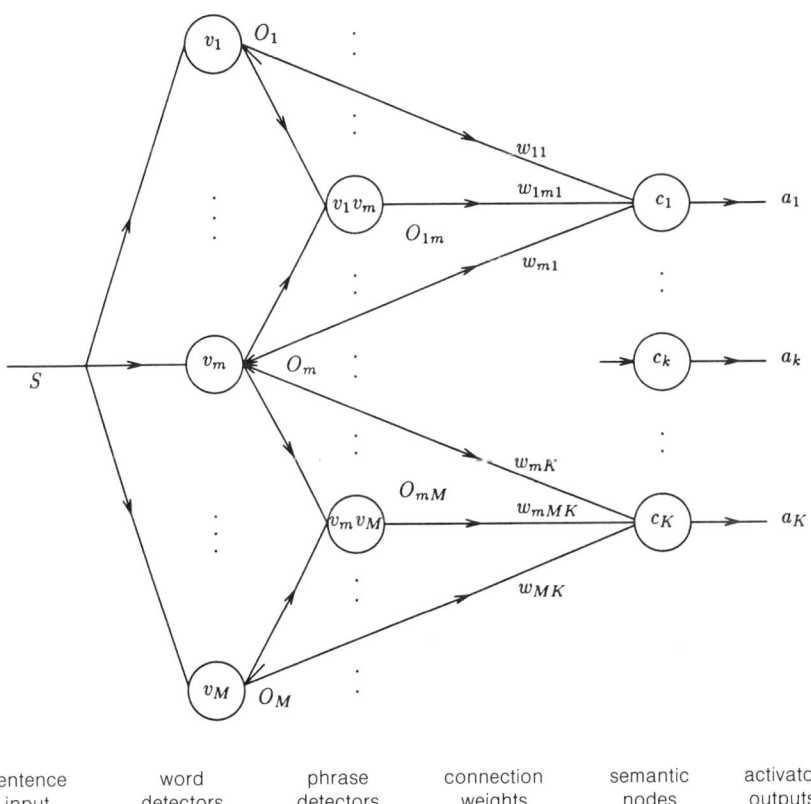

Figure 23.2 *Multi-layer network.*

via smoothed relative frequency estimates, which is a naturally sequential computation. It can be shown that the information-theoretic adaptation step is guaranteed to decrease the single-step error function (Gorin and Levinson, 1989), although **no** gradient is computed.

In the text-based experiment of Gorin *et al.* (1991a), the application scenario was an Inward Call Manager, where the possible machine actions were to transfer a telephone call to an appropriate department. The device was initialized with only the words **no** and **ok**, comprising a prefabricated one bit encoding of the semantic-level error signal. During the course of performing its task, in over 1000 dialogs with 10 users, the device acquired a vocabulary of over 1500 words. Learning was stable in that it retained 99% of what it was taught. (More details on that experiment can be found in Gorin *et al.*, 1991a.) An extension of that experiment to a spoken language acquisition system is described in Gorin *et al.* (1991b).

23.1.2 Extension to large and complex tasks

As a task and language increase in complexity, so does the mapping from message to meaning. It is then reasonable to question the capability of the proposed networks and training procedures to learn such complex mappings. There does, indeed, exist a body of theory addressing such issues (Cybenko, 1989; Judd, 1988; Baum and Haussler, 1988). Those results, however, tend to be asymptotic in nature, requiring large numbers of examples for learning to occur. In contrast, a striking feature of human language acquisition is our ability to make sweeping generalizations from small numbers of observations. For example, a single occurrence of a new word, in the appropriate context, can be sufficient to acquire its pronunciation, its syntactic role and its semantic associations.

Thus, although a homogeneous network architecture might, given sufficient data, be capable of learning the associations between messages and meaningful responses for complex tasks, we are not satisfied with such asymptotic results. An alternative is to investigate how one might reflect our knowledge of task and language structure in a network architecture, in order to provide improved generalization capability in language acquisition.

We thus propose a **third principle**, that a language acquisition device should be well-matched to its environment and I/O periphery, as measured by its ability to rapidly adapt and generalize. One can anthropomorphize this principle by considering the input and error channels in Figure 23.1 to comprise the device's sensory periphery, the output channel to comprise its motor periphery, and the network architecture and learning procedure to comprise its innate knowledge. The adaptive training of the network parameters then corresponds to learning during the lifetime of an individual organism. It is intuitively clear that the better matched the innate knowledge of an organism is to its sensory-motor periphery and environment, the better it will be able to generalize from what it experiences. Indeed, one can take this as a definition of **well-matched**, since the ability to generalize implies faster learning and adaptation, which is clearly a critical aspect of intelligence. This anthropomorphic viewpoint is pursued by Sankar and Gorin (1992), who show how to exploit sensory input structure in a network architecture, which they evaluate in a Blocks World task.

Given a device whose range of actions can be formally described, this third principle led us to investigate methods by which to reflect the structure of that action space in the network architecture. A simple, yet still interesting situation, occurs when the set of programs which the device can execute are specified by n parameters. We view the selection of each parameter as a hidden subaction, denoted a **semantic primitive**. These primitives are then combined to form an observable meaningful action. In this case, the action space can be characterized by a Cartesian product of these semantic primitives.

In order to reflect this action space structure in a network architecture, Miller and Gorin (1992) proposed the concept of a **product network**, comprising n independent networks, one for each semantic primitive. Each is of the form of Figure 23.2, where the outputs of the individual networks are combined to form activations for action nodes which correspond to ordered n-tuples of semantic primitive values.

In particular, a twofold product network has been experimentally evaluated on a 1000-action Almanac data retrieval task (Miller and Gorin, 1992) with text input, responding to queries for some attribute of one of the 50 states in the USA. Denote by N the subnetwork corresponding to the semantic primitive which selects the state parameter, and denote by A the subnetwork which selects the attribute parameter. Abusing notation, we also denote the set of values for the state parameter as N (where the network N has one output node for each possible value), and similarly for A. Thus, one can describe the action space for this task as isomorphic to $N \times A$.

23.1.3 Emergent nonterminals

Given a task such as the Almanac, let us consider the collection of words and phrases which cause the subnetwork N to fire. Upon inspection, one observes that these mostly comprise place names. Let us hypothesize that this set of words is a **part of speech**. So as to avoid raising a linguistic storm, we will characterize this nonterminal abstractly as N, rather than as a **noun**.

Another perspective on this hypothesis is provided via Goodman *et al.*'s (1989) approach to rule inference. If one conjectures a production rule $N \rightarrow v$, where v is a vocabulary word or phrase, they have proposed a priority measure based on the mutual information between the clauses, i.e. $I(v, N)$. This is precisely the output of the information-theoretic subnetwork N, raising the specter of exploiting meaning to govern the acquisition of nonterminals in a language. This is in contrast to much of the literature on grammatical inference, where meaning plays little or no role.

23.1.4 Developmental learning

People use concepts acquired in simple tasks as building blocks to learn more complex ones. We propose a **fourth principle**, which is that language acquisition should proceed in developmental stages, beginning with mastery of simple tasks, and only then continuing to complex ones. This leads us to consider a mechanism whereby subnetworks are initially trained within a simple task, where their outputs are directly tied to a semantic primitive for that task. These stable subnetworks can then be exploited as nonterminals in higher complexity tasks.

In this work, we investigate a device whose action space is characterized via an ordered pair of places. The application scenario is a subset of an Airline Information Task, in particular the display of a flight table between some pair of cities. This is a time-honored domain for research in natural language interpretation (Watt, 1968; Woods, 1968; Levinson and Shipley, 1980; Price, 1991). If C denotes the set of possible cities, then the action space is isomorphic to $C \times C$. While again a product space, a little thought shows that the product network mechanism will not suffice to provide rapid adaptation and generalization. This will be illustrated in the sample dialogs below. We instead proceed developmentally, according to our fourth principle, assuming that a stable subnetwork corresponding to the nonterminal for place names was acquired in an earlier task (e.g. the subnetwork N from the Almanac task.)

A network, analogous to that of Figure 23.2, is constructed, but where the nodes correspond to nonterminals. The structure is hierarchically self-similar, in that each nonterminal is itself a copy of Figure 23.2, but with nodes corresponding to vocabulary words (terminals). Thus, the construction of associations between words and actions is factored through these intermediate nonterminals. This network will be described in detail in section 23.4.

As demonstrated in the sample dialogs below, this leads to rapid adaptation and generalization. For the sake of an interesting example, we have chosen the input messages to involve the Nepali language, which uses postpositional rather than prepositional modifiers (Yarowsky, private communication, 1990). After session one, any reasonable network architecture would have memorized the association between that particular sentence and the appropriate action. A product network would even be able to generalize that the phrase **chicago bata** is associated with Chicago being the departure city (a semantic primitive). One would hope, however, that the system would furthermore learn that these two new words modify the semantics of **any** city name, not just the ones with which they were observed. One, indeed, observes this generalization in session two, illustrating the efficacy of factoring the word/ action associations through intermediate nonterminals. Detailed experimental results are described in section 5.

Session one

I CAN SHOW YOU THE FLIGHT TABLE BETWEEN ANY PAIR OF CITIES.

chicago bata detroit sama

DO YOU WANT TO SEE THE FLIGHTS FROM DETROIT TO CHICAGO?

no, the other way around.

I WILL SHOW YOU THE FLIGHTS FROM CHICAGO TO DETROIT.

Session two

ARE YOU INTERESTED IN OTHER FLIGHTS?

washington sama boston bata

I WILL SHOW YOU THE FLIGHTS FROM BOSTON TO WASHINGTON.

23.2 Task structure

We consider now, in detail, the subset of the Airline Information Task proposed in the introduction, namely the display of flight tables between any pair of cities. We call the collection of all such possible displays the **semantic actions** for this device. The action space is thus specified by an ordered pair of parameters, the first denoting the origin city and the second denoting the destination city. We view the individual selection of these parameters as **hidden semantic actions**, which we denote by **semantic primitives**. These are then combined to form the observable semantic actions, namely display of a flight table.

We can define the action space for this device by a formal grammar. We remark that this grammar defines the **action space**, not the language for the task. A semantic action is determined by two semantic primitives, namely selection of the origin and destination cities:

$$\langle \text{Semantic Action} \rangle \rightarrow \langle \text{Origin} \rangle \langle \text{Destination} \rangle$$

The origin and destination primitives are in turn determined by a selection of a city,

$$\langle \text{Origin} \rangle \rightarrow \langle \text{City} \rangle$$
$$\langle \text{Destination} \rangle \rightarrow \langle \text{City} \rangle$$

where $\langle \text{City} \rangle$ is a nonterminal in the grammar which can in turn take on one of five values,

$$\langle \text{City} \rangle \rightarrow \langle \text{Boston} \rangle$$
$$\langle \text{City} \rangle \rightarrow \langle \text{Chicago} \rangle$$
$$\langle \text{City} \rangle \rightarrow \langle \text{Detroit} \rangle$$
$$\langle \text{City} \rangle \rightarrow \langle \text{NYC} \rangle$$
$$\langle \text{City} \rangle \rightarrow \langle \text{Washington} \rangle.$$

We remark that one needs to distinguish the semantic event $\langle \text{NYC} \rangle$ from the linguistic event of 'NYC' occurring in an input message. We thus introduce notation for the event that a semantic primitive takes on some particular value,

$$C_{iF} = \{\text{Origin is City number } i\}$$
$$C_{jT} = \{\text{Destination is City number } j\}.$$

The grammar for the action space is reminiscent of the one proposed by Miller and Gorin (1992) for the Almanac Data Retrieval Task, excepting that the two semantic primitives are decidedly **not** independent. In section 23.4, we will describe how these semantic primitives correspond to intermediate nodes in an information-theoretic network which maps input messages to semantic actions. We remark that one could also refer to semantic primitives as nonterminals in the formal grammar for the action space. This would be confusing, however, so we reserve the name nonterminals for use in describing the language.

23.3 Language structure

Embedded in the network architecture of section 23.4 are some mild hypotheses on grammatical structure and its relation to the task semantics, which we make explicit in this section. We will observe in section 23.5, however, that input is **not** restricted to sentences with this structure, and that the system will make reasonable inferences even for sentences which do not conform to these hypotheses.

First, we hypothesize a linguistic nonterminal which produces terminal strings referring to the various cities. In the introduction, we described how such a nonterminal can emerge as an abstraction of a semantic primitive. We denote this nonterminal by N, and in this work assume that it can take on one of K possible values,

$$N \rightarrow N_1 | N_2 | N_3 | \cdots | N_K,$$

where the N_k can in turn produce terminal strings in the language, referring to the kth city. Examples of such strings would be **New York City** or **The Big Apple.**

Given an input message, denoted S, we hypothesize a segmentation into phrases, some derived from N, with the remainder denoted by the nonterminal X (including the null string), i.e.

$$S \to (XN)^*X.$$

We now hypothesize that X can produce four classes of terminal strings. These are semantically motivated as containing prefix and suffix phrases which indicate whether the phrase produced by an N should be associated with the Origin or Destination semantic primitives. More generally, given a task where a place-name could be associated with one of M semantic primitives, one could hypothesize $2M$ classes of strings produced by X. One could further generalize by considering non-adjacent modifiers, triples, etc.

We denote, for this device, a coarse subdivision of X via the nonterminals A and B, denoting suffix (A denoting after), and prefix (B denoting before) phrases respectively, i.e.

$$XN \to BN$$
$$NX \to NA.$$

Finally, denote the semantically-motivated subdivision of A and B via

$$A \to F_A | T_A | \varepsilon$$
$$B \to F_B | T_B | \varepsilon,$$

where ε is the null string, where F_B is a nonterminal which produces prefixes indicating that the associated place-name phrase is the origin city (F denoting from), and with analogous definitions for F_A, T_A and T_B.

In the network of section 23.4, we will introduce intermediate nodes corresponding to these nonterminals and pairs thereof, constructing associations, for example, between the linguistic event $F_B N_3$ with the semantic primitive C_{3F} (which denotes the semantic event that the desired origin is city number 3).

23.4 A network with an intermediate layer of nonterminals

A multilayer network of nonterminals is illustrated in Figure 23.3. The input layer comprises a collection of nonterminal detectors, whose outputs are indicative of the presence of an input string produced by that nonterminal. The intermediate layer comprises nonterminal pair detectors, whose outputs are indicative of an adjacent pair of nonterminals. The output layer contains nodes corresponding to semantic primitives for the device. This network is analogous to the multilayer network of Gorin *et al.* (1991a), that was illustrated in Figure 23.2, except in that work the nodes correspond to word-detectors, phrase detectors and semantic actions. As was observed in Gorin *et al.* (1991a), the network architecture is straightforwardly extensible

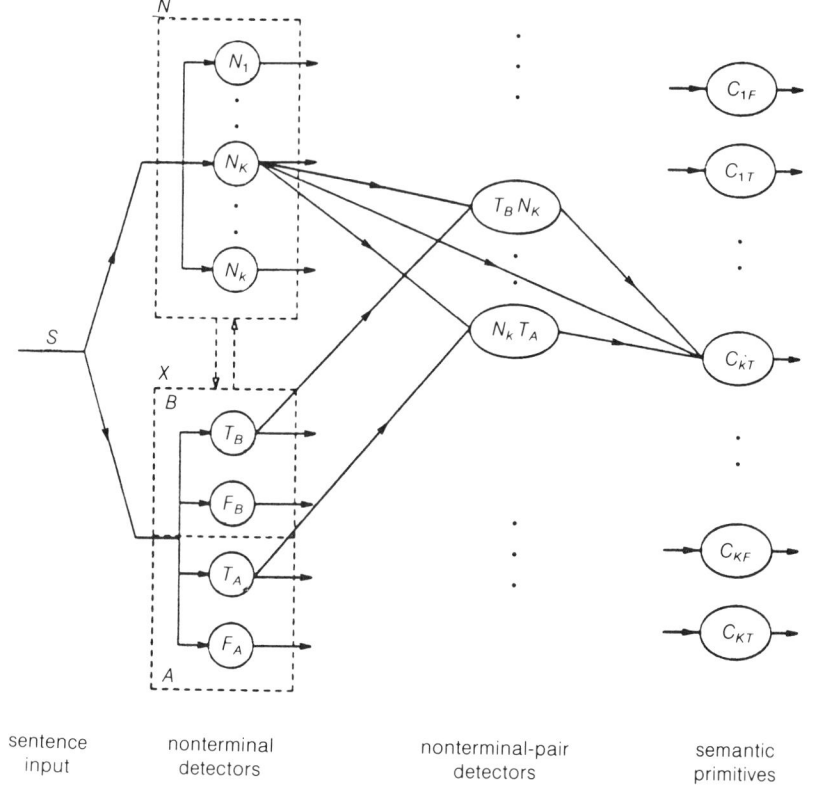

sentence   nonterminal   nonterminal-pair   semantic
input   detectors   detectors   primitives

Figure 23.3 *Multi-layer network of nonterminals.*

to include phrases of nonadjacent input symbols which can be of arbitrary
length. Each of the nonterminal detectors in Figure 23.3 are themselves a
word-level multilayer network (cf. Figure 23.2).

The outputs of the semantic primitive nodes are then combined in a Cartesian
product, as described by Miller and Gorin (1992), to obtain activations for
each of the possible semantic actions in the task. In Miller's work, the input
to the semantic action nodes was provided by two independent networks.
In this work, the input is provided by pairs of nodes from the same network.

The overall operation of the network is as follows. Rather than constructing
associations directly between words and device actions, one factors these
associations through intermediate nodes corresponding to nonterminals in
the language and semantic primitives for the device. We observed in section
23.2 that one can view semantic primitives as nonterminals in the formal
grammar describing the device's action space. This terminology is confusing,
however, so will be avoided. In the remainder of this section we will detail
the definition of each of these nodes and connections. For the purposes of

experimental expediency, some of these connections are prespecified, which values are intepretable as mutual information between events. The other connections are trainable, using the methods of Gorin *et al.* (1991a) for estimating mutual information.

In subsection 23.4.1, we describe a dynamic programming procedure for segmenting sentences into substrings associated with the hypothesized non-terminals. In subsections 23.4.2 and 23.4.3 we describe the input layer of Figure 23.2, in particular the nonterminal-detector networks N, A and B. In subsection 23.4.4, we describe the nonterminal-pair nodes, and, in subsection 23.4.5, the final layers comprising semantic primitive and semantic action nodes.

23.4.1 Segmentation

The first stage segments the input sentence into a sequence of phrases $P_0, P_1,$ $P_2, \ldots, P_N$ which are alternately city names (N) or not (X). Since X can produce a null string, we can without loss of generality require that the odd segments, $P_1, P_3, P_5, \ldots$, are city names and the even segments $P_0, P_2, P_4 \ldots$ are not. We observe that this notion of phrase may not exactly correspond to the classical linguistic definition.

Given networks which, for each substring, produce a score for each of the nonterminals, an algorithmic solution to the segmentation problem is provided by dynamic programming. We do not describe this algorithm in any detail, since it is standard. In particular, one solves the optimization problem of finding that segmentation of the input sentence for which the sum of the network activations is maximum. This method was used, for example, in Pieraccini *et al.* (1991), although in the context of HMMs rather than networks.

As will be described in the subsections 23.4.2 and 23.4.3, each nonterminal detector is a second-order multi-layer network as described in Gorin *et al.* (1991a). These networks capture associations between rudimentary syntactic structure and semantics. As in that work, we adjoin special symbols to each string to denote Beginning Of Phrase (BOP), End Of Phrase (EOP), Beginning Of Sentence (BOS) and End Of Sentence (EOS).

To illustrate such segmentation, consider the input sentence 'Chicago is the city where I am now. Next week, I am going to leave Chicago. Detroit is my destination, since my brother lives in Detroit', which when segmented yields:

$P_0 = \{BOS\ EOP\}$
$P_1 = \{BOP\ Chicago\ EOP\}$
$P_2 = \{BOP\ is\ the\ city\ where\ I\ am\ now.\ Next\ week,\ I\ am\ going\ to\ leave\ EOP\}$
$P_3 = \{BOP\ Chicago\ EOP\}$
$P_4 = \{BOP\ EOP\}$

$P_5 = \{BOP\ Detroit\ EOP\}$
$P_6 = \{BOP\ is\ my\ destination,\ since\ my\ brother\ lives\ in\ EOP\}$
$P_7 = \{BOP\ Detroit\ EOP\}$
$P_8 = \{BOP\ EOS\}.$

In this analysis, there are two distinct time scales, one for word intervals, the second for phrase intervals. We clarify and illustrate this issue as follows:

- Let $S = v_{m_1}v_{m_2}\ldots v_{M_L}$ be the sequence of the L words in a sentence, indexed by the discrete variable t.
- Let $S_p = P_0P_1\ldots P_N$ be the sequence of phrases in that same sentence, indexed by the discrete variable τ.
- Let $(M + 1)$ denote the number of city names that occurred in the input sentence, and $(M + 2)$ the number of other phrases.

The total number of phrases in the segmented sentence S_p is then $N = (2M + 3)$. The two time scales are illustrated in Figure 23.4, where t is word-time and τ is phrase-time.

Observe that $(t_{i+1} - t_i)$ is the duration of the phrase P_i (number of words in P_i). For odd τ, P_τ is the city name that occurred at time τ in S_p, $S_{\tau-1}$ is the phrase that occurred before the city name P_τ, and $P_{\tau+1}$ is the phrase that occurred after the city name P_τ.

The phrases are presented to the network as a sequence of overlapping triplets. A sliding window of width 3 is centered at successive city-name non-terminals. The resulting triplet is then input to the network as illustrated in Figure 23.5.

Recall that the first layer in Figure 23.3 comprised three subnetworks, one each for prefixes (B), city names (N) and suffixes (A). The N subnetwork computes associations between the phrases $P_\tau, \tau = 1, 3, \ldots 2M + 1$ in the input

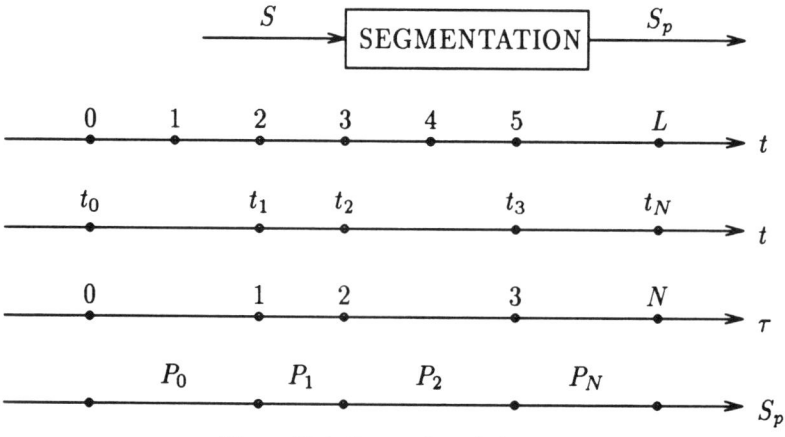

Figure 23.4 *Sequencing of phrases.*

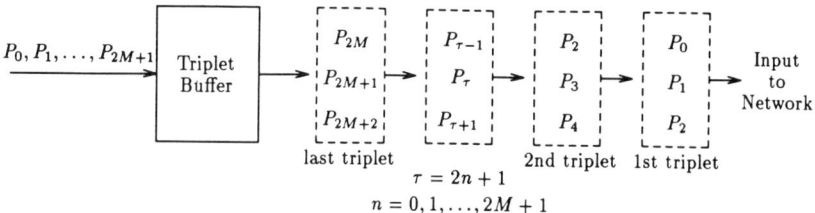

Figure 23.5 *Phrase triplet.*

sentence S_p and the specific city-name values N_k, where $1 \leqslant k \leqslant K$ and K is the number of the city names in the system. The initial phrase in a triplet, $P_{\tau-1}$, is processed by the subnetwork B, and the final phrase in a triplet, $P_{\tau+1}$, is processed by the network A. Subnetwork B computes associations between words (and word-pairs) and the prefix values F_B and T_B. The network A computes associations between words (and word-pairs) and the suffix values F_A and T_A. Figure 23.6 illustrates how the segmented triplets are input to the first layer of network of Figure 23.3.

23.4.2 The city-name subnetwork

The input to the city-name subnetwork (N) is the center phrase of the triplet P_τ, comprising a subsequence of words from the input message, as was illustrated in Figure 23.6. There are k outputs, one for each city in the task, $N_1, N_2, \ldots N_K$. The kth output at time τ is denoted $O(\tau, N_k)$ which in general will be some value between 0 and 1. In the sense of Sankar and Gorin (1993), this output is indicative of the probability that phrase P_τ is an exemplar of the nonterminal N_k.

To illustrate this definition, Figure 23.7 shows three outputs of the network N for the following example. Consider an input message S_p containing three city names: N_1 occurred at $\tau = 3$; N_3 occurred twice – at $\tau = 1$ and $\tau = 2M + 1$;

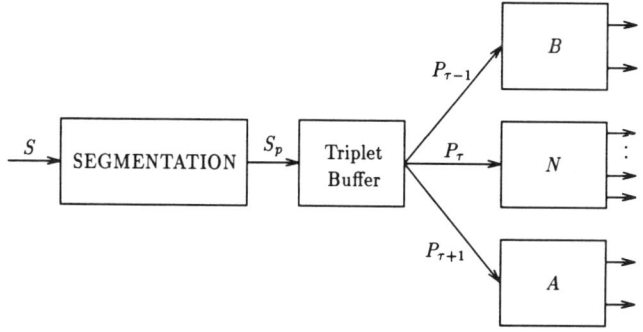

Figure 23.6 *Segmented input to the first layer of the network.*

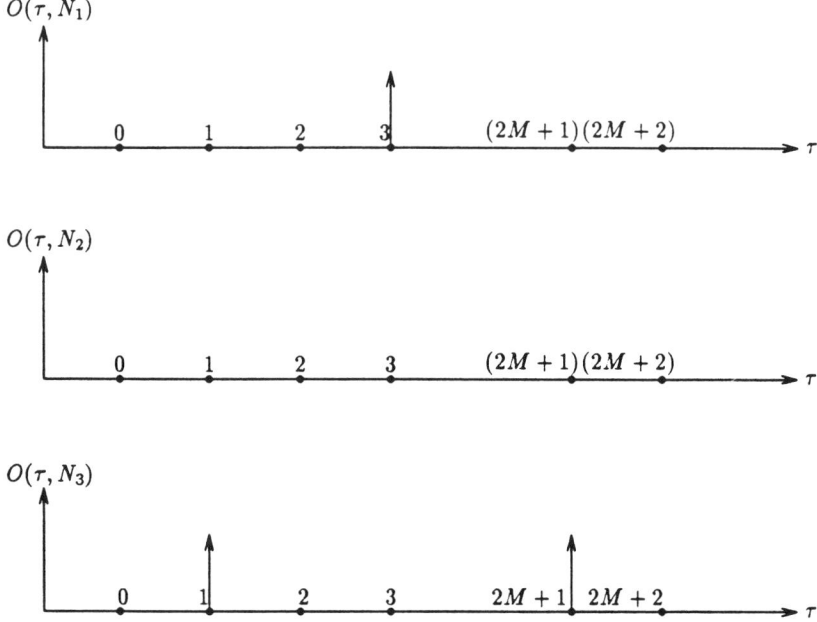

Figure 23.7 *Occurrence of the city names in the sentence is indicated by outputs* $O(\tau, N_k)$.

N_2. Thus, the output of the network is a vector-valued discrete time series, where the vector is of dimension K and time is indexed by τ: $O(\tau, N_k), \tau = 1, 3, \ldots,$ $2M + 1, k = 1, 2, \ldots, K$. The output indicates both the presence of city names and the time of their occurrence in the sentence. These outputs, as was illustrated in Figure 23.3, are provided as inputs to the nonterminal-pair detectors.

In the network of Figure 23.3, the output of the first layer of nonterminal detectors is connected to both nonterminal-pair nodes and the semantic primitive nodes. The latter connections utilize a time-integrated output of the network N, which we denote $\mathbf{O}(N_k)$, defined as the Boolean OR of the $O(\tau, N_k)$ via

$$\mathbf{O}(N_k) = \bigcup_{\tau} \{O(\tau, N_k)\} = \bigoplus_{\tau} \{O(\tau, N_k)\}$$

$$= \begin{cases} 1 & \text{if } \exists \tau S T O(\tau, N_k) = 1 \\ 0 & \text{for } \forall \tau O(\tau, N_k) = 0. \end{cases} \tag{1}$$

This definition suffices for experiments of section 23.5 where the $O(\tau, N_k)$ are 0 or 1. In general, one would utilize a **soft** OR function valid for $O(\tau, N_k)$ between 0 and 1. The values of $O(\tau, N_k)$ corresponding to the example of

Figure 23.6 are

$$\mathbf{O}(N_1) = 1$$
$$\mathbf{O}(N_2) = 0 \qquad\qquad (1a)$$
$$\mathbf{O}(N_3) = 1.$$

The connection weights between the nonterminal-network node for N_k and the semantic primitive C_{jT} are given by the mutual information between the two. While this is in general trainable via the methods of Gorin *et al.* (1991a), in this experiment we preset them as

$$I(N_k, C_{jT}) = \begin{cases} 0 & \text{if } k \neq j \\ \log \dfrac{P(C_{kT}|N_k)}{P(C_{kT})} & \text{if } k = j. \end{cases} \qquad (2)$$

Assuming $P(C_{kT}|N_k) = 0.5 - \varepsilon$, for some small ε, we then define the connection weight

$$w_k^+ = \log \frac{0.5 - \varepsilon}{P(C_{kT})}. \qquad (3)$$

Although not shown in Figure 23.3, we also compute an association between the non-occurrence of nonterminal N_k and C_{kT} as

$$\omega_k^- = \log \frac{\varepsilon}{P(C_{kT})}. \qquad (3a)$$

23.4.3 Prefix and suffix networks

The initial and final phrases of a phrase triplet $P_{\tau-1}$ and $P_{\tau+1}$ are, respectively, input to the prefix and suffix subnetworks, B and A, as was shown in Figure 23.3. Observe that since the triplet windows overlap, any particular modifier phrase will be input to A on one cycle, and B on the subsequent cycle. Each network, B and A, is a copy of the second-order multi-layer network as was illustrated in Figure 23.2 (Gorin *et al.*, 1991a). The B network has two outputs, corresponding to the two occurrences of the prefix modifiers, F_B and T_B, connoting **from** and **to** respectively.

For a particular triplet, $P_{\tau-1}P_{\tau}P_{\tau+1}, \tau$ odd, the networks B and A produce 4 activations: $a_{F_B}(P_{\tau-1})$, $a_{T_B}(P_{\tau-1})$, $a_{F_A}(P_{\tau+1})$, $a_{T_B}(P_{\tau+1})$, according to the algorithm of Gorin *et al.* (1991a). We transform these activations to outputs (between 0 and 1) as follows. First, we compute activation differences

$$d_{F_B} = a_{F_B} - a_{T_B} \quad d_{T_B} = a_{T_B} - a_{F_B} = -d_{F_B}$$
$$d_{F_A} = a_{F_A} - a_{T_A} \quad d_{T_A} = a_{T_A} - a_{F_A} = -d_{F_A} \qquad (4)$$

and then apply the nonlinear threshold $s(x) = 1/(1 + e^{-x})$ to each difference,

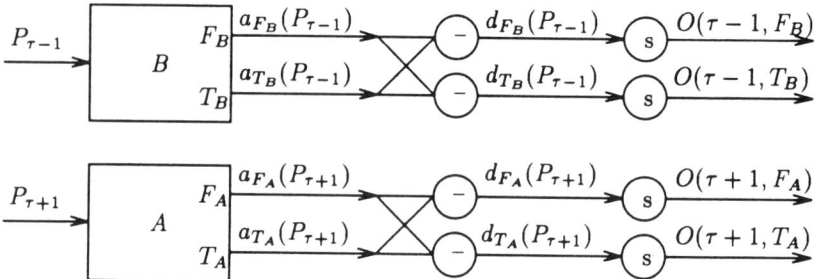

Figure 23.8 *Prefix and suffix networks.*

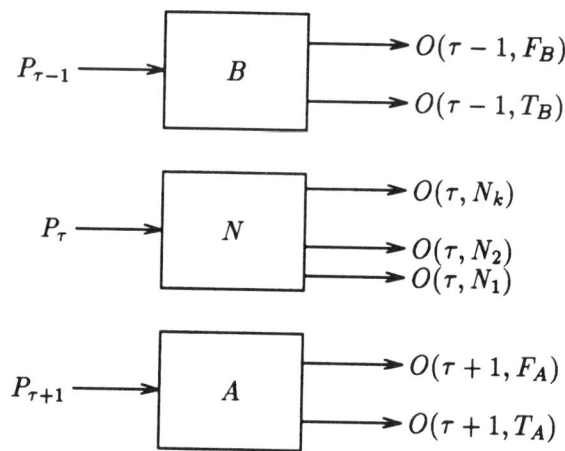

Figure 23.9 *The first layer's output at time* τ.

obtaining

$$O(\tau - 1, F_B) = s[d_{F_B}(P_{\tau - 1})]$$
$$O(\tau - 1, T_B) = s[d_{T_B}(P_{\tau - 1})]$$
$$O(\tau + 1, F_A) = s[d_{F_A}(P_{\tau + 1})]$$
$$O(\tau + 1, T_A) = s[d_{T_A}(P_{\tau + 1})].$$

We will show experimentally in subsection 23.5.3 that the nonlinearity $1/(1 + e^{-x})$ is a good approximation to convert activation-differences to probabilities. Figure 23.8 demonstrates how the B and A networks are constructed from the second-order network of Figure 23.2.

To summarize: for each triplet buffer of phrases $P_{\tau - 1}P_{\tau}P_{\tau + 1}$, the following output is generated by the first layer of Figure 3 (as illustrated in Figure 23.9):

$O(\tau - 1, F_B)$ is indicative of the probability of the event that phrase $P_{\tau - 1}$ is a prepositional modifier connoting **from**.

$O(\tau - 1, T_B)$ is indicative of the probability of the event that phrase $P_{\tau-1}$ is a prepositional modifier connoting **to**.

$O(\tau, N_k)$ is indicative of the probability of the event that the phrase P_τ is a city name connoting the kth city.

$O(\tau + 1, F_A)$ is indicative of the probability of the event that phrase $P_{\tau+1}$ is a postpositional modifier connoting **from**.

$O(\tau + 1, T_A)$ is indicative of the probability of the event that phrase $P_{\tau+1}$ is a postpositional modifier connoting **to**.

23.4.4 Nonterminal-pair nodes

We define by $F_B N_k$ the adjacent occurrence of the nonterminals N_k and F_B. The output of the nonterminal-pair nodes is denoted $O(\tau, F_B N_k)$, which is indicative of the probability that the terminal string comprising $P_{\tau-1} P_\tau$ is an exemplar of $F_B N_k$. The inputs to this node are the outputs of the nonterminal detectors. We compute $O(\tau, F_B N_k)$ via a soft *AND* operation (i.e. multiplication) with a unit time delay,

$$O(\tau, F_B N_k) = O(\tau - 1, F_B) * O(\tau, N_k). \tag{5}$$

Similarly, $O(\tau, N_k F_A)$ is computed via

$$O(\tau, N_k F_A) = O(\tau, N_k) * O(\tau + 1, F_A). \tag{6}$$

23.4.5 Semantic primitive nodes

Recall that C_{kF} is the semantic primitive connoting that the kth city is the origin city, and that C_{jT} analogously connotes that the jth city is the destination city. The activations of these nodes are computed as the second-order network of Gorin *et al.* (1991a):

$$a_{c_{kF}} = \sum_{\tau \text{ odd}} [O(\tau, F_B N_k) + O(\tau, N_k F_A)] + w_k^+ \mathbf{O}(N_k) + w_k^- [1 - \mathbf{O}(N_k)] + w_{c_{kF}}, \tag{7}$$

where the second-order terms $O(\tau, F_B N_k)$ and $O(\tau, N_k F_A)$ were defined in formulas (5) and (6); the connection weights from the second-order terms are 1 for nodes involving the same city and 0 otherwise; the first-order connection weight w_k was defined in formulas (3) and (3a); and the biases $w_{c_{kF}}$ are $\log P(C_{kF})$.

We similarly compute

$$a_{c_{jT}} = \sum_{\tau \text{ odd}} [O(\tau, T_B N_j) + O(\tau, N_j T_A)] + w_j^+ \mathbf{O}(N_j) + w_k^- [1 - \mathbf{O}(N_j)] + w_{c_{jT}}. \tag{8}$$

Finally, the semantic primitive activations are summed to form activations for the semantic actions, following the method of Miller and Gorin (1992), but in this application restricted to $k \neq j$

$$a_{c_{kF}c_{jT}} = a_{c_{kF}} + a_{c_{jT}}, \tag{9}$$

with the output action selected via computing the maximum of $a_{c_{kF}c_{jT}}$ over all $j \neq k$. In that work, the semantic primitive activations were derived from two independent networks. In this work, the semantic primitive activations arise from different output nodes of a single network.

23.5 Experimental evaluation

23.5.1 Anecdotal evaluation on natural language input

We briefly describe some anecdotal natural language interactions with a conversational-mode system initialized on the artificially generated database of subsection 23.5.2, utilizing the network of section 23.4 and the dialog control model of Gorin *et al.* (1991a).

Session one illustrates the dialog control system, where the proposed action is determined by averaging the activation array for each input sentence, and subtracting the error signal, as was described in Gorin *et al.* (1991a). The next two dialogs illustrate the generalization capability of the network. (These also appeared in the introduction.) For those interested, **bata** and **sama** are postpositional modifiers in the Nepali language, connoting point of departure and destination respectively (this example is compliments of David Yarowsky, who spent some time teaching in Nepal). The network is adapted at the end of this convergent dialog. Session two illustrates the dialog control and error recovery, as above. Session three illustrates the generalization capability provided by the innate knowledge of language reflected in the network architecture. Finally, session four demonstrates the robustness of the system to violations of its syntactic hypotheses (cf. section 23.3), where it sorts through all sorts of irrelevancies to arrive at a reasonable conclusion.

Session one

Machine: HELLO.
           I CAN SHOW YOU THE FLIGHT TABLE BETWEEN ANY
           PAIR OF THE FOLLOWING CITIES: NEW YORK,
           BOSTON, CHICAGO, DETROIT AND
           WASHINGTON.
           HOW MAY I HELP YOU?
User: *I'd like to go to Detroit.*
Machine: WOULD YOU LIKE TO SEE THE FLIGHT TABLE
           FROM BOSTON TO DETROIT?
User: *no, from nyc*

Machine: WOULD YOU LIKE TO SEE THE FLIGHT TABLE
FROM NYC TO DETROIT?

User: *yes*

Machine: HERE IS THE LIST OF THE FLIGHTS FROM NYC
TO DETROIT.

* *
* *

Session two

Machine: ARE YOU INTERESTED IN OTHER FLIGHTS?

User: *chicago bata detroit sama*

Machine: WOULD YOU LIKE TO SEE THE FLIGHT TABLE
FROM DETROIT TO CHICAGO?

User: *no, the other way around.*

Machine: I WILL SHOW YOU THE FLIGHT TABLE FROM
CHICAGO TO DETROIT.

User: *yes*

Machine: HERE IS THE LIST OF THE FLIGHTS FROM
CHICAGO TO DETROIT.

* *
* *

Session three

Machine: ARE YOU INTERESTED IN OTHER FLIGHTS?

User: *washington sama boston bata*

Machine: I WILL SHOW YOU THE FLIGHT TABLE FROM
BOSTON TO WASHINGTON.

User: *ok*

Machine: HERE IS THE LIST OF THE FLIGHTS FROM
BOSTON TO WASHINGTON.

* *
* *

Session four

Machine: ARE YOU INTERESTED IN OTHER FLIGHTS?

User: *I was thinking about going to Washington to see the cherry
blossoms because they're so pretty, but I can't. Instead,
I have to go to Detroit on business, departing from
NYC, as usual.*

Machine: WOULD YOU LIKE TO SEE THE FLIGHT TABLE
FROM NYC TO WASHINGTON?

User: *No, to Detroit.*

Machine: I WILL SHOW YOU THE FLIGHT TABLE FROM
NYC TO DETROIT.

User: *Yes, that's what I need.*
Machine: HERE IS THE LIST OF THE FLIGHTS FROM
             NYC TO DETROIT.

             *
             *

23.5.2 Database

We report on a preliminary experimental evaluation of the proposed network using an artificially generated data set. This is a precursor to evaluation using natural language interactions, as in our previous efforts. The sentence/ action pairs were generated automatically from an augmented phrase structure grammar (Pereira and Wright, 1991). The goal of the specification was to generate a few representative sentences of several types. The grammar is far from complete, as there are many reasonably natural language constructions that are not included in the specification. In this case, the specification of the phrase structure grammar was quite simple: a vocabulary of 43 words (terminal symbols), embedded in a non-recursive grammar with maximum parse tree depth of 8. The number of valid sentences in the grammar is 70550, and the perplexity is 3.4. The maximum length of the sentence is about 20 words, the average length is about 11 words. Since this grammar is non-recursive, there is a simple mapping to a finite state machine (Pereira and Wright, 1991), and this finite state machine was used to generate the sentences. We remark that this same database was utilized to evaluate a segmentation method in Price (1991).

This experiment considers traveling between five cities: Boston, Chicago, Detroit, NYC and Washington. In line with the principle of developmental learning proposed in the introduction, the N network was pretrained on the occurring city names, so that segmentation into N and X phrases was straightforward and error-free. The database consists of 825 sentence/meaning pairs. Most sentences contain two city name occurrences, but 82 of these sentences have three city names (where one city name is repeated twice).

A few examples of the training sentences from this database are shown below. The two letters before the colon are codes for the origin and destination city respectively. (For example, '*b c:*' stands for origin = **boston**, destination = **chicago**.) These codes are used in the experiments for training and evaluation.

Examples of Sentences/Action Pairs

1) *w n: flying to nyc, i want to fly going from washington.*
2) *b c: i am arriving in chicago and i am in boston now.*
3) *w b: i want to travel into boston and i am interested in flights between boston and washington.*
4) *b c: i am interested in flights between boston and chicago and i want to arrive at chicago.*

23.5.3 Experiments

In the first experiment, we describe the vocabulary and connection weights which result from training on the 825 sentence/meaning pairs of subsection 23.5.2. Table 23.1 shows the vocabulary list of the modifier network B, the

Table 23.1 *The vocabulary list of words with prefix associations modifier (Network B)*

	Number of occurrences			Relative frequency		Connected weights	
	Total	F	T	F	T	F	T
from	474	474		1.00		0.69	−6.16
leaving	104	104		1.00		0.69	−4.95
of	134	134		1.00		0.69	4.91
departing	111	111		1.00		0.69	−4.72
depart	76	76		1.00		0.69	−4.34
leave	74	74		1.00		0.69	−4.32
tonight	12	11	1	0.92	0.08	0.57	−1.47
into	212		212		1.00	−5.36	0.69
arriving	160		160		1.00	−5.08	0.69
at	71		71		1.00	−4.28	0.69
arrive	67		67		1.00	−4.22	0.69
be	53		53		1.00	−3.99	0.68
now	22		22		1.00	−3.14	0.67
destination	21		21		1.00	−3.09	0.67
is	21		21		1.00	−3.09	0.67
my	21		21		1.00	−3.09	0.67
start	73	19	54	0.26	0.74	−0.64	0.39
to	1019	287	732	0.28	0.72	−0.57	0.36
and	535	271	264	0.51	0.49	0.00	0.00
am	568	321	247	0.57	0.43	0.00	0.00
between	82	32	50	0.39	0.61	0.00	0.00
flights	82	32	50	0.39	0.61	0.00	0.00
flying	63	35	28	0.56	0.44	0.00	0.00
fly	148	50	98	0.34	0.66	0.00	0.00
i	1257	608	649	0.48	0.52	0.00	0.00
head	82	30	52	0.37	0.63	0.00	0.00
go	59	21	38	0.36	0.64	0.00	0.00
going	144	53	91	0.37	0.63	0.00	0.00
heading	68	39	29	0.57	0.43	0.00	0.00
want	689	287	402	0.42	0.58	0.00	0.00
interested	82	32	50	0.39	0.61	0.00	0.00
in	246	86	160	0.35	0.65	0.00	0.00
out	295	200	95	0.68	0.32	0.00	0.00
starting	88	47	41	0.53	0.47	0.00	0.00
travel	57	17	40	0.30	0.70	0.00	0.00
traveling	88	42	46	0.48	0.52	0.00	0.00
BOS	825	409	416	0.50	0.50	0.00	0.00
BOP	907	457	450	0.50	0.50	0.00	0.00
EOP	1732	866	866	0.50	0.50	0.00	0.00

number of occurrences of each word, its relative frequency in the two output classes (F_B or T_B), and the first-order connection weights. The small vocabulary arises from the artificially generated data, and reminds us of the preliminary nature of this experimental evaluation.

The second experiment evaluates the performance of the total network and illustrates its adaptive behavior. 100 sentence/meaning pairs were randomly selected for training data, and the remaining 725 reserved for testing. In Figure 23.10, we plot the error rate (of correct semantic interpreta-

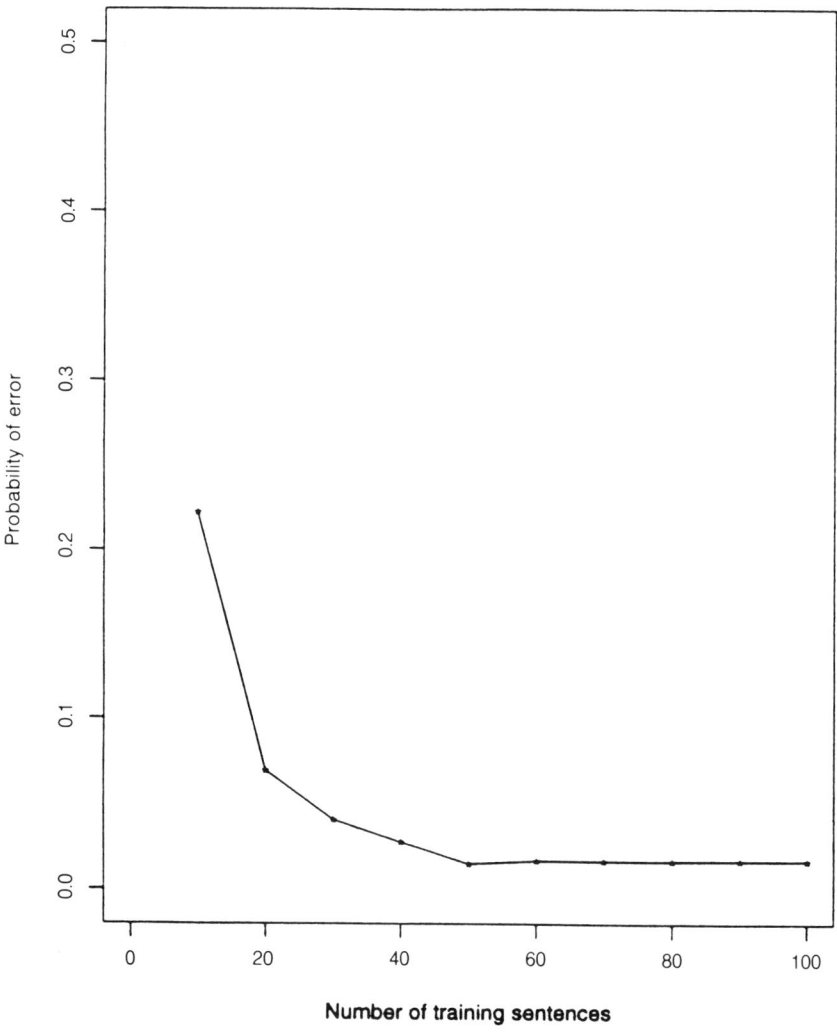

Figure 23.10 *Dependence of error rates on training data (training on 100 first sentences; tests conducted on remaining 725 sentences).*

tion on the 725 testing sentences) after training on sequentially increasing subsets of the 100 training sentences. The error rate asymptotes at 1.7% after 50 training pairs. Essentially the same behavior occurs for other random selections of 100 training sentences. Upon inspection, one observes that these errors occur mostly on sentences with three city name occurrences. The second best choice, however, is always correct illustrating the robustness of the full system to violations of the hypotheses of section 23.3.

The purpose of the third experiment is to investigate the dependence of the probability of error for modifier classification. This experiment was motivated in the discussion of the nonterminal-detector nodes in subsection 23.4.3, where we proposed transforming activation-differences into outputs via the nonlinear threshold function $1/(1 + e^{-x})$. The database for this experiment is again the 825 artificial sentences of the database discussed in subsection 23.5.2. During training, each modifier phrase in each sentence was

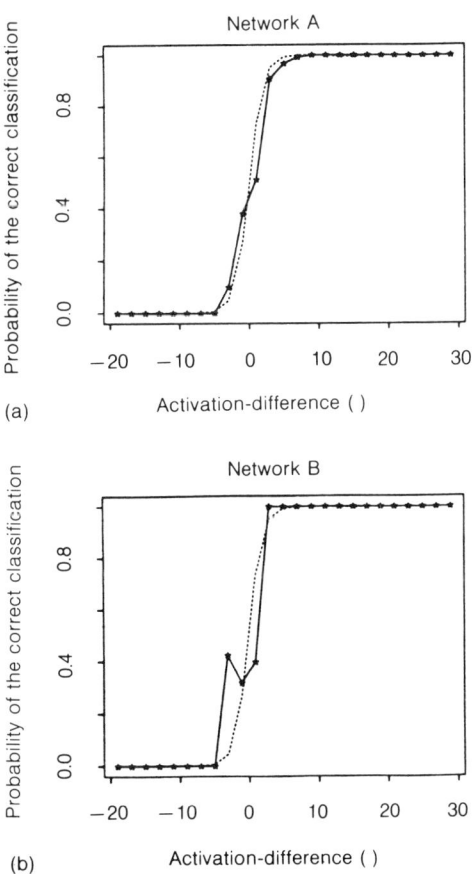

Figure 23.11 *Dependence of correct activations on differences between activations.*

automatically labeled as one of the nonterminals F_B, T_B, F_A, T_A, according to the adjacent city-name phrase and the sentence's semantic label. The sentences were input to the network, and the outputs d_{F_B} and d_{F_A} were computed for each phrase (as in formula (4)). Figure 23.11a shows a plot of the measured probability that a modifier phrase is an exemplar of F_A, conditioned on the activation-difference d_{F_A}. Figure 23.11b shows the analogous result for d_{F_B}. The curves for d_{T_A} and d_{T_B} are identical to Figures 23.11a, b, respectively, due to formula (4). In both cases, the curve $1/(1 + e^{-x})$ is overlaid, showing a reasonable approximation in each case.

In the fourth experiment, we evaluate the effect of using the multi-layer versus the single-layer network for the nonterminal detectors, i.e. the input

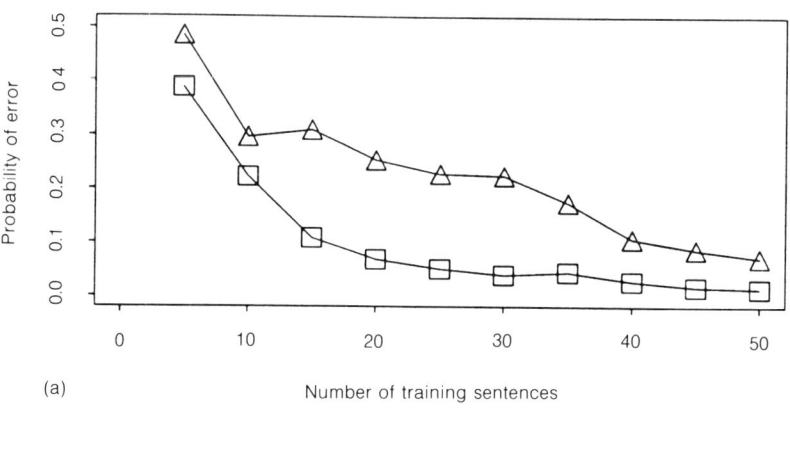

(a)

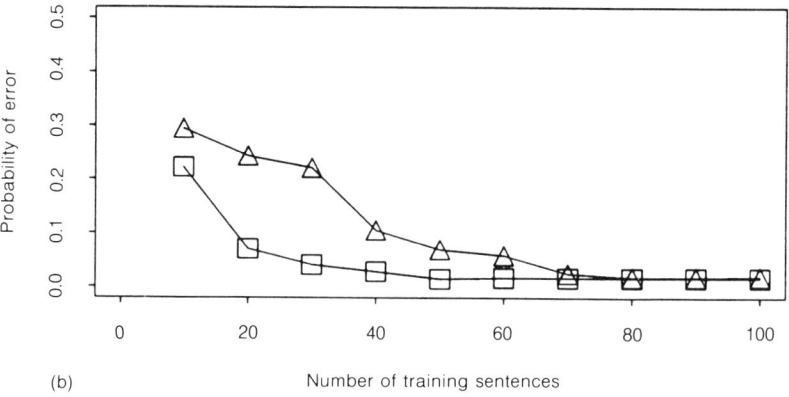

(b)

Figure 23.12 *Performance of the single- and multi-layer network.* □: *multi-layer;* △: *single-layer. (a) Training on 50 sentences, tests conducted on remaining 775 sentences, (b) training on 100 sentences, tests conducted on remaining 725 sentences.*

of the intermediate layer word-pair nodes. Repeating the second experiment with this variation, after 50 training sentences, the error rate of the multi-layer network is 1.7% *versus* 7.1% for the single-layer, an improvement of 5.4%. These results are depicted over a range of 5 to 50 training sentences in Figure 23.12a. For a training set of 100 sentences, the results are shown in Figure 23.12b. The multi-layer network achieves its best performance on this specific database after 50 training sentences. The single-layer performs best after 80 sentences. Thus, the multi-layer network learns faster than the single-layer.

23.6 Conclusions

We have proposed methods for extending our principles and mechanisms for adaptive language acquisition to moderate complexity tasks. In particular, we have introduced intermediate layers into an information-theoretic network corresponding to nonterminals in the language and semantic primitives for the device.

We've reported on a preliminary experimental evaluation of this network using a small text-based subset of the Airline Reservation Task. It is preliminary in the sense that training and testing data were artificially generated, rather than via exposure to natural language interactions. A short-term issue is to perform an online data collection and evaluation of the system.

A medium-term issue arising from this work is how to apply these methods to a larger system such as the DARPA Airline Travel Information System (ATIS). Based on preliminary discussion (Tzoukermann, private communication, 1991) the ATIS task (Price, 1991) involves approximately 45 semantic primitives. It would be worthwhile to describe those via a formal grammar, to apply the methods of this chapter to reflect that device structure in a network architecture, and explore how these ideas scale.

A long-term issue arising from this work is to automatically acquire network architecture which reflects language and task structure. There are a variety of methods which have been proposed in the literature for automated inference of nonterminals. Those methods have, for the most part, exploited only a text corpus without regard for meaning. It would be worthwhile to expand on the concept of emergent nonterminals introduced here to exploit meaning to acquire nonterminals in a language.

Acknowledgements

We thank David Roe for providing the database of sentence/action pairs used in our experiments, and thank Steve Levinson for many insightful conversations. We also thank Julia Hirschberg, Mark Jones, Fernando Pereira, Roberto Pieraccini and Ananth Sankar for their review of the manuscript. Finally, we thank Larry Rabiner for suggesting the Airline Information Task as a vehicle for this work.

References

Barto, A.G. and Anadan, P. (1985) Pattern recognizing stochastic learning automata. *IEEE Trans. on System, Man and Cybernetics*, **15**(3), 360–75.

Baum, E. and Haussler, D. (1989) What size of net gives valid generalization. *Neural Computation*, **1**, 151–60.

Cybenko, G. (1989) Approximation by superpositions of sigmoidal function. *Mathematics of Control, Signals, and Systems*, **2**, 303–14.

Goodman, R.M., Miller, J.W. and Smyth, P. (1989) An information-theoretic approach to rule-based connectionist expert systems. *Advances in Neural Information Processing Systems*, Morgan-Kaufmann, San Mateo, CA.

Gorin, A.L. and Levinson, S.E. (1989) A perceptron with information-theoretic connection weights. *AT&T Bell Laboratories, Technical Memorandum*, December (unpublished).

Gorin, A.L., Levinson, S.E., Gertner, A.N. and Goldman, E. (1991a) Adaptive acquisition of language. *Computers, Speech and Language*, **5**(2), 101–32.

Gorin, A.L., Levinson, S.E. and Gertner, A.N. (1991b) Adaptive acquisition of spoken language. *Proc. International Conference on Acoustics, Speech and Signal Processing (ICASSP)*, May, pp. 805–8.

Judd, S. (1988) On the complexity of loading shallow neural networks. *Journal of Complexity*, **4**, 177–92.

Kaebling, L. (1990) Learning in embedded systems. *PhD Thesis*, Computer Science Department, Stanford University.

Levinson, S.E. and Shipley, K.L. (1980) A conversational mode airline information and reservation systems using speech input and output. *Proc. Int. Conf. on Acous., Speech, and Sig. Processing*, Denver, CO, April, pp. 203–8.

Miller, L.G. and Gorin, A.L. (1992) A structured network for adaptive language acquisition (submitted for publication).

Pereira, F. and Wright, R. (1991) Finite-state approximation of phrase structure grammar. *Proc. 29th ACL Meeting*, pp. 246–55.

Pierarccini, R., Levin, E. and Lee, C.H. (1991) Stochastic representation of conceptual structure in the ATIS task. *Proc. DARPA workshop on speech and natural language*. Asilomar, CA. February.

Price, P. (ed.) (1991) *Proc. DARPA workshop on speech and natural language*. Asilomar, CA. February.

Sankar, A. and Gorin, A.L. (1993) Visual focus of attention in language acquisition, in *Neural Networks for Speech and Vision* (ed. R. Mammone), Chapman & Hall, London.

Thomas, J.B. *Statistical Communication Theory*, Wiley, New York, NY.

Watt, W.C. (1968) Habitability. *American Documentation*, July, 338–51.

Woods, W.A. (1968) Procedural semantics for a question answering machine. *Proc. of AFIPS*.

Part Three
ANN applications in vision

24

A miniaturized space-variant active vision system: Cortex-I

BENJAMIN B. BEDERSON,* RICHARD S. WALLACE[†] and
ERIC L. SCHWARTZ[‡]

*Bellcore MRE 2D-336, 445 South Street, Morristown, NJ 07962, USA

[†] Courant Institute of Mathematical Sciences, New York University, 251 Mercer Street, New York, NY 10012, USA

[‡] Department of Cognitive and Neural Systems, Boston University, 111 Cummington Street, Boston, MA 02146, USA

24.1 Introduction

Computer vision is a field that typically requires fast and expensive machines. One reason for this is the need to process images of size $O(N^2)$, for $N = 250 \rightarrow 1000$ at frame rates of 30–60 Hz. By using a novel image architecture, image processing and actuation technologies, we have been able to construct a system that is competitive in performance to existing systems which are orders of magnitude larger and more costly to build. In other work, a detailed examination of the design considerations and advantages of space-variant sensing is provided (Rojer and Schwartz, 1990), and it is shown that the human visual system, which uses a similar space-variant sensor design, achieves up to four orders of magnitude of image compression from this strategy.

Any system that uses a space-variant sensor must aim the sensor properly. Since space-variant sensors only have high resolution in the fovea, the current region of interest must be continuously tracked or foveated. Such a sensor must be mounted in a device that can aim the sensor with precision. A system with this capability is an example of an active or attentive vision system (Bajcsy, 1988; Ballard, 1989). In other words, the advantages of space-variant sensing are provided at the cost of increased algorithmic and robotic complexity: high speed and accurate actuators and control strategies, attentional

Artificial Neural Networks for Speech and Vision. Edited by Richard J. Mammone. Published in 1993 by Chapman & Hall, London. ISBN 0 412 54850 X

algorithms, and novel image processing and pattern recognition approaches must be developed.

In this chapter, we describe Cortex-I, a prototype miniaturized active vision system with a space-variant image architecuture. This system integrates a CCD sensor, miniature pan-tilt actuator, controller, general purpose processor and display (Figure 24.1). The system may be connected to a host processor for applications development, integrated as the visual module of a larger robotic system, or operated in a stand-alone configuration.

As an architecture for image processing and computer vision, our prototype represents a significant departure from the types of large-scale parallel vision systems we and others have previously investigated (Rizzi *et al.*, 1991; Schwartz, 1977; Schwartz *et al.*, 1988; Weiman and Chaikin, 1979). Our design is a small, loosely coupled network of embedded microcomputer modules, integrated directly with a sensor and robotic pan-tilt actuator. Moreover, our architecture has benefited from research into the space-variant nature of the human visual system (Schwartz, 1977; Schwartz *et al.*, 1988; van der Spiegel *et al.*, 1989; Weiman and Chaikin, 1979). We use a logmap sensor which is a useful type of space-variant sensor that is modeled on the human visual system. The space complexity aspect of logmap sensors is particularly attractive and has been analysed in detail (Rojer and Schwartz, 1990).

Other researchers have developed a variety of active vision systems that mimic some biological functions such as pan, tilt, vergence and focus control,

Figure 24.1 *Cortex-I prototype miniaturized active vision system.*

attentional algorithms and real-time tracking (Abbott and Ahuja, 1990, 1991; Allen *et al.*, 1991; Baloch and Waxman, 1991; Brown, 1988; Clark and Ferrier, 1988; Dickmanns and Graefe, 1988; Kawarabayashi *et al.*, 1991; Krotkov *et al.*, 1988). Through implementing image processing at the low data rate of logmap sensor, and exploiting our novel pan-tilt mechanism, our prototype demonstrates a significant subset of these capabilities with only modest processing power and inexpensive components. The two principles taken together of embedded system design and space-variant active sensing, enable us to flexibly develop new applications at a very low cost.

24.2 Space-variant images

A space-variant image sensor is characterized by an irregular pixel geometry. We have experimented with several sensor designs, including custom VLSI (in collaboration with Synaptics, Inc.). Their common features are large scale changes between the smallest and largest pixels, wide field of view, and a pixel population far smaller than that of a conventional uniform image sensor. One such space-variant sensor is the logmap (Rojer and Schwartz, 1990; Rojer, 1989), in which the pixel pattern approximates the sensor geometry of the human eye.

The logmap is illustrated in Figure 24.2. It is convenient to represent the point in the domain P_1 as $re^{i\theta}$, and the point in the range P_2 as the complex number $x + iy$. If we take the log of P_1, we get

$$\log(re^{i\theta}) = \log r + i\theta.$$

Substituting

$$x = \log r \quad \text{and} \quad y = \theta,$$

we get

$$\log(re^{i\theta}) = x + iy$$

or

$$\log(P_1) = P_2,$$

so the (complex) logarithm of a point in polar coordinates is transformed to a point in rectangular coordinates.

This mapping has some interesting geometric properties. Specifically, fovea-centered circles get mapped to vertical lines and radial lines get mapped to horizontal lines. This has the effect of transforming scale and rotation in fovea-centered retinal images to translation in cortical images. Computationally, translation is easier to handle than scaling or rotation, so this provides another justification for a complex log sensor geometry, which has attracted considerable interest during the past fifteen years. In the present work, we do not attempt to make use of this feature of the complex log mapping, and merely use it as a convenient representation for space-variant sensing, and one which is motivated by the similar structure of the human visual system.

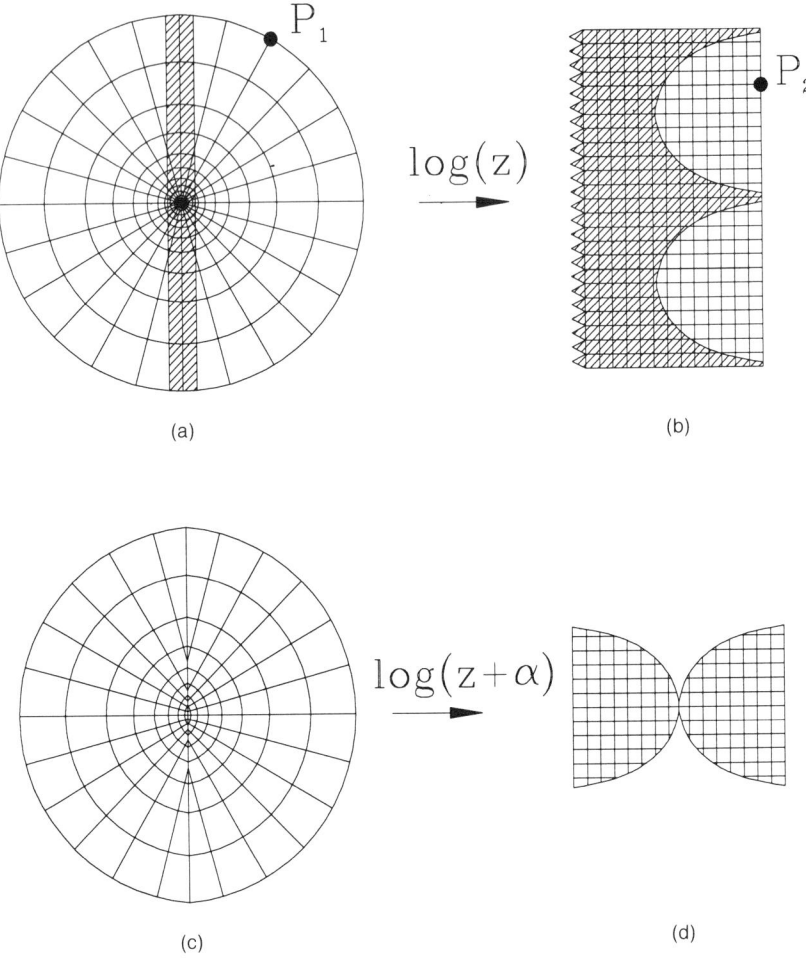

Figure 24.2 *Complex* log *map* log(z) *in (a) and (b) and its relative, the mapping,* log(z + α) *in (c) and (d). It can be seen that the* log(z + α) *map results from cutting the hatched region out of the* log(z) *map. Note that rings centered around the fovea in the domain get mapped to vertical lines in the range, and radial lines get mapped to horizontal lines. Here, P_1 gets mapped to P_2. The* log(z) *map has a singularity in the center, while the* log(z + α) *map has a branch-cut along the vertical meridian.*

One problem in using an analytic space variant mapping, such as the logarithm, is the existence of a singularity at the origin of the coordinate system. Figure 24.2b shows this singularity. The left points of each triangle in the range all represent the same single point in the domain. Our solution to this problem is to introduce a small real constant α into the mapping and using a map function of the form log(z + α). The constant α is used in an analogous fashion in models of the human visual system: it is a measure of the size of the central linear representation of the human fovea (Schwartz, 1977).

As can be seen in Figure 24.2d, the pixels on the edge are cut off in different places yielding 3, 4 and sometimes 5-sided pixels. This greatly complicates image processing. Even simple operators, such as convolution, are difficult to implement. We have found a general solution to this problem, which in effect generalizes image processing to sensors of arbitrary neighborhood relations, or topology. This work is described in detail in section 24.4.2.

We have followed two approaches to acquiring logmap images in real time. The first involves the design and fabrication of a custom VLSI sensor, in collaboration with Synaptics, Inc. This work is in an early stage, and we do not describe it further here. The second approach is to use an embedded processor, together with a conventional CCD imaging chip, to produce the logmap transformation by a real-time lookup table technique. Thus we can formally define the logmap as a mapping from a TV image, $I(i, j)$, where $i \in \{0, \ldots, \text{NROWS} - 1\}$ and $j \in \{0, \ldots, \text{NCOLS} - 1\}$. Let $L(u, v)$ be the logmap, with $u \in \{0, \ldots, \text{NSPOKES} - 1\}$ and $v \in \{0, \ldots, \text{NRINGS} - 1\}$.

The forward mapping from TV image space to logmap space is specified by the spoke and ring lookup tables, $S(i, j)$ and $R(i, j)$ (Figure 24.3), where again $i \in \{0, \ldots, \text{NROWS} - 1\}$ and $j \in \{0, \ldots, \text{NCOLS} - 1\}$. Let $a(u, v)$ be the area (in TV pixels) of a logmap pixel (u, v)

$$a(u, v) = \sum_{i,j} 1 \,|\, S(i, j) = u \quad \text{and} \quad R(i, j) = v. \tag{1}$$

The logmap (or forward map) image (Figure 24.4c) is defined by

$$L(u, v) = \frac{1}{a(u, v)} \sum_{i,j} I(i, j) \,|\, S(i, j) = u \quad \text{and} \quad R(i, j) = v. \tag{2}$$

The inverse map, illustrated in Figure 24.4b, is

$$L^{-1}(i, j) = L(S(i, j), R(i, j)). \tag{3}$$

The relationship between a space-variant image and the lookup tables $S(i, j)$ and $R(i, j)$ is illustrated by comparing Figure 24.3 with Figure 24.4. The values in the lookup tables depict the row and column addresses of pixels in the space-variant image array. We observe that if n is the number of pixels for which $a(u, v) > 0$, then $n \leqslant \text{NSPOKES} \times \text{NRINGS}$, and we define $\text{NPIXELS} = n$.

24.2.1 Fast logmap computation

We have developed a fast algorithm to compute the logmap based on a run-length mapping.[1] This algorithm avoids accessing the lookup tables for each pixel and it executes with an average of just over one instruction per

---

[1] Patent pending.

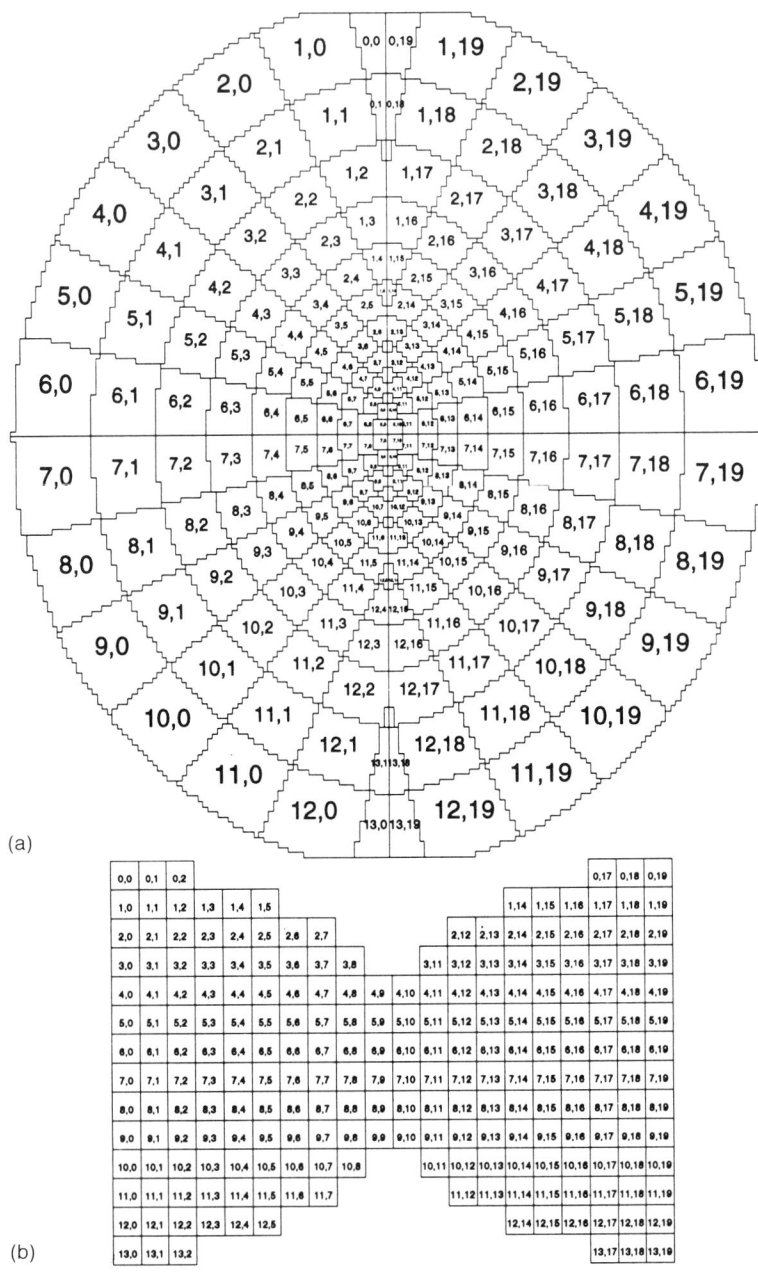

Figure 24.3 *(a) The lookup tables* $S(i,j)$ *and* $R(i,j)$ *combined into one figure,* *(b) the forward map space. The correspondence between inverse and forward map pixels is shown.*

(a)

(b)

(c)

Figure 24.4 *Sample of (a) a TV image $I(i,j)$, (b) the inverse logmap image $L^{-1}(i,j)$, and (c) the forward logmap image $L(u,v)$.*

TV pixel. The $S(i,j)$ and $R(i,j)$ lookup tables of the previous section are run-length encoded off-line with the algorithm **run_length_encode**. The CCD image is then mapped, line by line, as it is read out into the logmap image with the algorithm **fastmap**.

The algorithm **run_length_encode** analyses $S(i,j)$ and $R(i,j)$ in raster order to find the **runs**, or sequences of length ℓ in which

$$S(i,j) = \cdots = S(i,j+\ell-1) \quad \text{and} \quad R(i,j) = \cdots = R(i,j+\ell-1)$$

We partition the raster scan of the TV image into a sequence of NRUNS runs where run_len[k] is the length of the kth run and run_addr[k] is the address of the logmap pixel of the kth run.

The **fastmap** algorithm first zeros the logmap. It then goes through the TV image in raster order and through the runs in linear order. For each run, k, it adds run_len[k] TV pixels to the logmap pixel indexed by run_addr[k]. After the entire image has been mapped, the resulting logmap image must be normalized. For each logmap pixel $L(u,v)$, we set $L(u,v) = L(u,v)/a(u,v)$. **fastmap** shows the pixels in each run being summed in a loop. However, in practice we avoid the overhead associated with each loop iteration by unrolling the loops. We call a routine, **map**$_n$ which consists of n inline summing statements of the form *lm_addr + = I (tv_index + +).

The number of runs NRUNS depends on the mapping function given by the lookup tables $S(i, j)$ and $R(i, j)$. For a wide variety of interesting mappings, such as the logmap, NRUNS $\ll$ NROWS $\times$ NCOLS and NSPOKES $\times$ NRINGS $\ll$ NROWS $\times$ NCOLS. Let us assume that the statements in **fastmap** that add the TV pixel to the logmap pixel and increment the TV pixel address take one assembly language instruction. Let us also assume that we either unroll the loop computing each run (or use a DSP processor with zero-overhead loops) so that there is no overhead during each run. If the overhead between each run takes b instructions, then the mapping will take NROWS $\times$ NCOLS $+ b \times$ NRUNS $+ 2 \times$ NSPOKES $\times$ NRINGS instructions, or $1 + (b \times$ NRUNS$)/($NROWS $\times$ NCOLS$) + (2 \times$ NSPOKES $\times$ NRINGS$)/$ (NROWS $\times$ NCOLS) instructions per TV pixel.

Our system uses a TV image of $165 \times 192 = 34\,650$ pixels and there are 6074 runs. The logmap image is $34 \times 56 = 1904$ pixels, and the number of 'overhead' instructions between each run, b, is 4. Then the mapping takes 1.81 instructions per TV pixel.

Algorithm: run_length_encode

Function: This creates the run length and address tables for a mapping based on the spoke and ring look-up-tables.

Input: $S(i, j)$ and $R(i, j)$ look-up-tables

Output: Run length table, run_len and run address table, run_addr.

```
length ← 0
run_index ← 0
old_address ← − 1
For each TV pixel, (i, j), in raster order
    If ((j = NCOLS − 1) OR (R(i, j) = invalid)) Then
        address ← − 1
        spoke ← 0            {a(spoke, ring) must equal 0}
        ring ← NSPOKES/2
    Else
        address ← S(i, j) × NRINGS + R(i, j)
        spoke ← S(i, j)
        ring ← R(i, j)
    End If
    If (((j > 0) AND (address ≠ old_address)) OR (j = NCOLS − 1)) Then
        run_len[run_index] ← length
        run_addr[run_index] ← old_spoke × NRINGS + old_ring
        run_index ← run_index + 1
        length ← 1
    Else
        length ← length + 1
```

End if
old_address ← address
old_spoke ← spoke
old_ring ← ring
End For
NRUNS ← run_index

Algorithm: fastmap
Function: This maps the uniform TV image, $I(i, j)$, to the logmap image,
             $L(u, v)$. It uses the run length and address tables computed by
             run_length_encode.
Input: run_len and run_addr run tables
             TV image, $I(i, j)$
Output: Logmap image, $L(u, v)$

tv_index ← 0   {The TV image I is accessed in raster order with
                         the index, tv_index.}
For each pixel $p \in L$ {Zero logmap}
   $L(p) ← 0$
End For
For each run, k
   Im_addr ← address_of(L) + run_addr[k]
   For $l = 0$ to (run_len[k] − 1)
              {The next two lines can be written with one C
              instruction, *Im_addr + = I (tv_index + +). Note
              that the '*Im_addr' notation denotes the memory
              location referenced by Im_addr}
      *Im_addr ← *Im_addr + I(tv_index)
      tv_index ← tv_index + 1
   End For
End For
For each pixel $p \in L$ {Normalize logmap}
   $L(p) ← L(p)/a(p)$
End For

24.3 System description

Cortex-I consists of the emulated logmap sensor, a miniature pan-tilt
actuator, controller, general purpose processor, display and optional video
telephone interface. The controller consists of a camera driver, a 2 MIPS
programmable microcontroller (Motorola MC68332), a video display driver
and three 12 MIPS digital signal processors (Analog Devices AD2101). The
actuator and camera are mounted to the electronics chassis ($14 \times 22 \times 22$ cm)

and connected by twisted-pair cables. The system is powered from a standard 110 volt AC line, but uses less than 25 watts and could be battery powered.

The camera consists of a miniature, commercially available CCD image sensor and a custom lens assembly (fabricated in collaboration with Barry Levin) mounted in the actuator. The camera image is mapped to a logmap image with a fast lookup-table algorithm (section 24.2.1). For a choice of mapfunction that we have used extensively, the maximum resolution is 0.175 degrees per pixel and the horizontal field of view measures 33°. The sensor has a fixed focus 4 mm lens with a set of fixed, manual apertures (3 sizes). Since objects that are more than 10 focal lengths from the camera have essentially infinite depth of field, we avoid the need of focus for working distances which are larger than about 40 mm. The system outputs up to 30 frames per second and measures 256 gray levels per pixel. The camera head (CCD and lens assembly) measures only $8 \times 8 \times 10$ mm, and is controlled by a lab-built driver board that provides timing signals to the sensor and converts analog sensor data to 8-bit digital data for the processors.

The Spherical Pointing Motor (SPM) is a novel pan-tilt actuator using three orthogonal motor windings to achieve open-loop pan-tilt actuation of the camera sensor in a small, low-power package. The SPM can orient the sensor through approximately 60° pan and tilt, at speeds of several hundred degrees per second. It measures $4 \times 5 \times 6$ cm and weighs 170 grams. It is actuated by currents of roughly 50 mA in each of the three coils.

The MC68332 controls the SPM and runs the application softwave. The MC68332 may be connected to a host processor for applications development, to upload sensor data, or to receive pan-tilt commands. The MC68332 is a 32-bit 16 MHz microcontroller integrating peripheral controls, such as programmable digital control lines and timing signals, directly on chip. We connected 192 kbytes RAM and 128 kbytes EPROM to the microcontroller. The logmap data is output via a high speed serial interace, either to an external device such as a host computer, to the internal display driver, or to the video telephone transmitter.

Several image processing demonstrations have been implemented in the microcontroller ROM. These include a simple motion tracking program, that turns the camer to center the observed motion field, at 16 frames per second (fps). The ROM also contains a test pattern, image binarization (22 fps) and a motor motion demo. Other demonstrations illustrate the connectivity graph (section 4.2) to implement image smoothings (3 fps), edge detection (2 fps) and connected components (1 fps), illustrating both the generality of the programming model and the limitations of the relatively low power microcontroller used in the current implementation of Cortex-1.

The Analog Devices 2101 Digital Signal Processor (DSP) provides additional real-time image processing capabilities. The DSP controls the CCD readout, computes the log map and sends the logmap image to the MC68332 via a high-speed serial connection. The DSP board combines an AD2101 12 MHz

DSP having two 2 MHz serial ports, 8 kbytes internal RAM, 80 kbytes external RAM, and 64 kbytes boot EPROM. A second identical DSP board functions as a video display driver, generating an RS-170 video output suitable for display on a standard TV monitor. An optional third DSP board is used as a video transmitter that can send four (uncompressed) frames per second of logmap images over a standard voice-grade telephone line. To achieve this, the DSP implements a custom analog modem protocol which encodes the logmap frames.

24.3.1 Camera sensor

We have pursued two routes to real-time acquisition of logmap images. The first is to develop a custom VLSI sensor chip with a logmap geometry that will consist of varying size pixels arranged in a logmap geometry. The second is to use a commercially available sensor chip that returns conventional rectangular images and map them into logmap images.

The main advantages of a custom logmap sensor chip are the high frame rate and small resultant system size. This is because the geometry of the chip performs the mapping intrinsically. We expect that a frame rate of several thousand frames per second could be supported, contingent on the ambient light intensity. However, at the present time, we do not have a fully working space-variant chip.

The main advantages of an off-the-shelf conventional (uniform) sensor chip are low price, high image quality, and immediate availability. Because uniform sensors have been refined for many years they have extremely high quality which is difficult to match with custom sensor chips. The image from a uniform sensor, however, must be mapped to a logmap image (Section sec-fastmap).

24.3.2 Spherical pointing motor

A pan-tilt mechanism is a computer-controlled actuator designed to point an object such as a camera sensor. For applications in active vision, we prefer a pan-tilt mechanism to be accurate, fast, small, low-power and inexpensive. We have constructed two actuators meeting these requirements: one based on a parallel linkage actuated by two identical small stepper motors (Bederson, 1992; Bederson *et al.*, 1992b); the other incorporates both pan and tilt into a single 2-axis actuator (Figure 24.5). The SPM[2] is described in detail in Bederson *et al.* (1992a), but is summarized here. The SPM consists of three orthogonal motor windings in a permanent magnetic field, configured to move a small camera attached to a gimbal.

---

[2] Patent application #07/731,639, entitled 'Spherical Pointing Motor' was submitted to the US Patent Office in 1991.

Figure 24.5 *Spherical Pointing Motor (SPM). At the center is a miniature camera consisting of a single CCD sensor chip and a lens assembly that fits on the rotor of this motor.*

The simplest and most obvious direct drive pan-tilt mechanism is the two-stage Motor-On-Motor (MOM) design. The first motor turns the mechanism through one degree of freedom, usually pan, and the second through the other d.o.f., usually tilt. The second motor must be powerful enough to move the camera sensor. The first must move both the camera and the second motor. The MOM design therefore usually consists of one larger motor and one smaller one. Because of the large accelerations involved in starting and stopping a high-speed device accurately, the extra inertial load presented by the MOM design requires very large torques in the main motor.

An alternative to the direct drive MOM design requires some form of linkage to couple the camera to the motor. We have built a stepper motor actuated modified Stewart platform device, but it is our impression that direct drive DC motors are advantageous, except for the above noted limitations of the MOM design. It is clear that some form of direct drive design, in which the MOM design was avoided, but in which no linkages were required, would be ideal. We have designed such an actuator, which provides a spherically symmetric direct drive DC motor actuator, which we call the Spherical Pointing Motor (SPM).

Background Pan-tilt mechanisms have been a source of inspiration and frustration to computer vision researchers. One source of inspiration is nature, since humans and animals rely on their pan-tilt apparatus to achieve wide field-of-view visual sensing.

The argument from nature is not by itself a compelling reason to build robot eyes that pan and tilt. The alternative to mechanical pan-tilt action is electronic scanning, i.e. computer control of a fixed set of cameras having a combined wide field-of-view. Selective attention can be implemented by a variety of addressing methods, for example the inverted pyramid of Burt (1988). Such 'software pantilt' mechanisms are considerably more convenient and reliable than their motorized counterparts, but we argue that they will be ultimately more expensive. In effect, software pan-tilt trades memory and processor bandwidth for motors. A large sensor, which is required to efficiently use software pan-tilt, has a quadratically increasing pixel load. The alternative to providing the extra processor bandwidth and memory needed for such an approach is to physically move the sensor, as is the usual choice in 'active-vision' approaches. It is our opinion that at the current state of technology, this is a considerably more economical approach.

One source of frustration with pan-tilt devices is acquiring or building, then calibrating and controlling the mechanism itself. Until recently, no manufacturers have provided devices specifically designed for computer control of robot cameras. It is now possible to purchase pan-tilt mechanisms from a variety of sources. The security, motion picture and optics industries all produce pan-tilt actuators, but they tend not to satisfy our requirements, usually combining several of the problems of being too bulky, slow, inaccurate, or expensive.

Perhaps because of their familiarity and availability, if not their generality and programmability, robot arms have often been the method of choice for vision researchers trying to actuate their cameras (Baloch and Waxman, 1991; Allen et al., 1991; Raviv and Shapira, 1991). Finally, a number of researchers, including ourselves, have embarked on building their own pan-tilt devices from scratch (Krotkov, 1989; Abbott and Ahuja, 1990; Kawarabayashi et al., 1991; Dickmanns and Graefe, 1988; Clark and Ferrier, 1988; Brown, 1988). Although many vision researchers are also interested in controlling parameters other than pan and tilt such as focus, zoom, aperture and vergence, these interesting subjects will remain outside the scope of the present discussion.

Spherical Pointing Motor theory   The Spherical Pointing Motor (SPM) is an absolute positioning device designed to orient a small camera sensor in two degrees of rotational freedom. The basic principle is to orient a permanent magnet in three orthogonal motor windings[3] by applying the appropriate ratio of currents to the three coils. The SPM can either have the coils on

---

[3] Strictly speaking, the coils must only be linearly independent, but then the transfer function becomes more complicated.

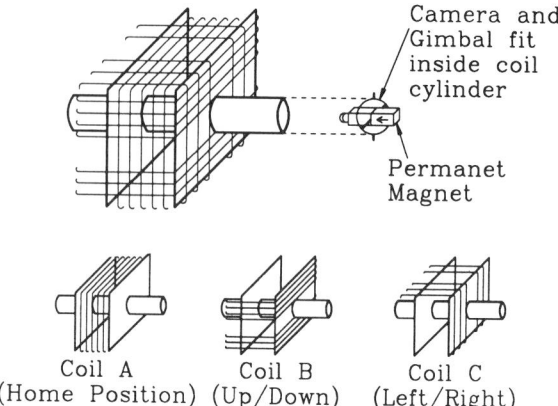

Figure 24.6 *External SPM shown in its home position with labels for the three coils.*

the outside with the permanent magnet rotating on the inside, or *vice versa.* Figure 24.6 depicts an example of the former.

In this section, we look at the transfer function taking input current to pan and tilt angles. We point out some design constraints on the configuration of the coils and the permanent magnets, and discuss briefly calibration and accuracy of the motor. In the derivation, we use the external coil motor, but the derivation for the internal coil motor is almost identical.

Both designs are constrained by two principles that affect the range of motion of the motor. The SPM is meant to be used as a pointing device. As such, it has a 'home position', defined as the initial resting position from which the motor can make pan or tilt excursions of limited extent. Assuming that we want the home position to be centered within the possible excursions, we are led to the following constraints:

1. The permanent magnets must be positioned so that the field they define is orthogonal to both axes of rotation of the gimbal when it is in home position.
2. The camera must be positioned on the rotor so that its optical axis is orthogonal to both axes of rotation of the gimbal when it is in home position. Note that this is equivalent to being aligned with the magnetic field if the first design constraint is satisfied.

These design principles arise because the motor is limited to two mechanical degrees of freedom and because the motor rotation cannot be controlled about an axis aligned with the permanent magnetic field.

We assume that the two rotational axes of the gimbal are orthogonal and intersect at a point, so that the kinematics of the SPM are trivial. That is, Θ and Φ are both the input and output variables. Our problem is to determine the variables Θ and Φ as a function of currents i_A, i_B and i_C in the three coils A, B and C.

Given a coil of wire in a magnetic field $\mathbf{B}$, the torque τ exerted on the coil is the cross product

$$\tau = \bar{\mu} \times \mathbf{B} \tag{4}$$

where $\bar{\mu}$ is the magnetic dipole moment having direction perpendicular to the coil and magnitude

$$|\bar{\mu}| = NiA \tag{5}$$

where i is the current in the wire, N is the number of windings in the coil, and A is the area inside each winding (Halliday and Resnick, 1981). The orientation of $\bar{\mu}$ is determined by the direction of current in the wire loop. When a nonzero current i flows through the loop, there will be a torque on the loop so that it will rotate to its minimum energy configuration where $\tau = 0$, i.e. $\bar{\mu}$ is aligned with $\mathbf{B}$.

In the SPM, the three orthogonal coils, A, B and C are modeled in terms of magnetic dipole moments $\bar{\mu}_A$, $\bar{\mu}_B$ and $\bar{\mu}_C$, respectively. Writing $K = NA$ as a constant for each of these dipole moments, the SPM rotated to Θ and Φ creates three torques, τ_A, τ_B and τ_C, one for each winding. When currents i_A, i_B and i_C flow in the three coils, we obtain three magnetic dipole moments:

$$\bar{\mu}_A = K_A i_A (\cos \Theta \cos \Phi, \sin \Theta, -\cos \Theta \sin \Phi)$$
$$\bar{\mu}_B = K_B i_B (-\sin \Theta \cos \Phi, \cos \Theta, \sin \Theta \sin \Phi)$$
$$\bar{\mu}_C = K_C i_C (\sin \Phi, 0, \cos \Phi).$$

The SPM rotates so that the sum of the three torques is zero, i.e.

$$\tau_A + \tau_B + \tau_C = 0. \tag{6}$$

We can write equation (6) as

$$(\bar{\mu}_A + \bar{\mu}_B + \bar{\mu}_C) \times \mathbf{B} = 0 \tag{7}$$

and solve for Θ and Φ

$$\Theta = \tan^{-1} \left(\frac{-K_B i_B}{K_A i_A} \right) \tag{8}$$

$$\Phi = \tan^{-1} \left(\frac{K_C i_C}{K_B i_B \sin \Theta - K_A i_A \cos \Theta} \right). \tag{9}$$

Thus we can write the pan and tilt angles of the gimbal as a function of the currents applied to the three coils. We can now illustrate the first design constraint. When the gimbal is panned so that $\Phi = 90°$, assuming $i_C \neq 0$, equation (9) shows that

$$K_B i_B \sin \Theta - K_A i_A \cos \Theta = 0$$

or

$$\tan \Theta = \frac{K_A i_A}{K_B i_B},$$

which can be true along with equation (8) only when $i_A = i_B = 0$. But by equation (8), Θ is undefined when $i_A = i_B = 0$. Therefore, when the SPM is panned 90°, there is no control of tilt.

SPM calibration and control   The calculation of motor position for specified currents would be feasible in the ideal case that all three coils were perfectly symmetrical, had the same number of turns, and were the same size. In general, none of these things are true, and it is a complex problem to realistically model the electromagnetic forces that are present. The calculated currents under the simplifying approximations that we have used give only an approximation to the resultant position of the motor. Therefore, the motor must be calibrated to associate motor positions with the related set of currents that moves the motor to these positions.

We developed a procedure for automatic calibration of the SPM (Bederson, 1992; Bederson *et al.*, 1992c). It is based on image feedback from a camera mounted on the rotor of the motor. It assumes that a calibrated image sensor and lens are used, i.e. that it is known how many degrees each pixel subtends, and that this is constant throughout the field-of-view. The calibration algorithm uses a scene of black dots on a white background. For each motor position that is to be calibrated, the algorithm moves the motor approximately to that position using the calculated currents. The algorithm analyses the image and uses the position of the relevant dot to calculate the actual position of the motor. It then associates this position with the coil currents and stores it in a look-up-table.

The dynamics of the SPM are that of a simple second order system. When a new set of currents are applied to the coils, a torque is created that moves the rotor to the new position. This torque is dependent on the angle between the initial motor position and the destination position. Let us call this angle Ψ.

The motor will accelerate towards the destination position with the torque decreasing as it is reached. However, it will overshoot and ring around the final position. The ringing is described as follows. The torque $\tau = \kappa \sin \Psi$ for some κ. For small angles, $\sin \Psi \approx \Psi$. Then the position of the motor will follow equation (10) (Halliday and Resnick, 1981, p. 228):

$$-\kappa\Psi - b\frac{\mathrm{d}\Psi}{\mathrm{d}t} = I\frac{\mathrm{d}^2\Psi}{\mathrm{d}t^2} \tag{10}$$

where b is the damping constant and I is the rotational inertia of the rotor. The approximate (small-angle) solution to this is

$$\Psi = A\mathrm{e}^{-bt/2I}\cos(\omega t + \alpha) \tag{11}$$

where A and α are constants, and the exponential function describes the magnitude envelope of the ringing. The frequency of the ringing is $\omega \approx \sqrt{\kappa/I}$.

In practice, this ringing can be greatly reduced by moving the motor in small decreasing increments. This way, the motor velocity is traded off for control. The simplest method is to move a fixed percentage of the distance between the initial position and final position. This will decrease the motor movement with each step.

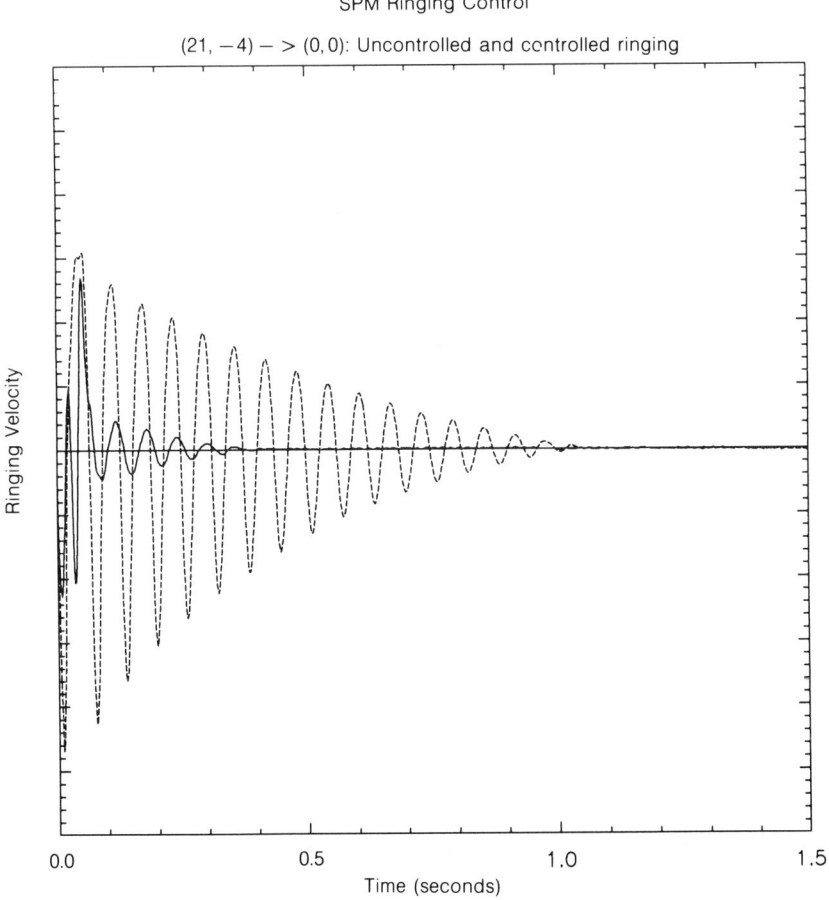

Figure 24.7 *Measurement of two-step open-loop control strategy to reduce SPM ringing. Results are shown for the same movement of 21.4° with and without control. The motor currents are changed to hold the motor at the final position when the motor is expected to have zero velocity. Because the midpoint and timing are not exactly correct, the ringing is not completely eliminated. ---: uncontrolled ringing; ——: controlled ringing.*

A second slightly more complicated open-loop control strategy based on traditional stepper motor control theory yields better results than the fixed percentage method. This strategy is based on the fact that the SPM rotor oscillates with an approximately constant period. We first step the motor to a point midway between the initial and destination positions. This midpoint is determined from the motor's calibration. We then wait for the ringing velocity to be zero at which point we apply a second step to hold the rotor at this position of zero velocity. The energy of the ringing will be largly dissipated, and the rotor will be at the destination position. Although we don't know exactly when to apply the second step, we can estimate it by waiting half the period of oscillation. This assumes that the period of oscillation is constant, which is not true, but is a close approximation. In practice, because neither the midpoint nor the time at which the currents are changed are exactly correct, not all of the ringing energy is dissipated, and a little ringing of the same period remains, but with vastly reduced amplitude. This approach is unusual in that it takes a constant time to move any distance, where the time is half the period of oscillation. A sample result of this approach is shown in Figure 24.7.

The accuracy (or repeatability) of the motor is determined largely by the friction of the bearings. There is no iron core, and thus no hysteresis. Driving the coils with a constant current source, the final position of the rotor is in principle exactly reproducible. We measured the accuracy of the SPM by reflecting a laser beam off a reflective surface attached to the rotor, and found the motor to be accurate to $0.15°$ which corresponds to about one pixel for our camera.

24.3.3 Microcontroller board

A Motorola MC68332 microcontroller controls the SPM and runs some applications software. The MC68332 may be connected to a host processor for applications development, or to upload sensor data and to receive pan-tilt commands. The MC68332 is a 32 bit 16 Mhz microcontroller integrating peripheral controls, such as programmable digital control lines and timing signals, directly on chip. The logmap data is output via a high speed serial interface, either to an external device such as a host computer or to the internal display driver.

We have implemented image processing demonstrations in the micro-controller ROM. A simple motion tracking program, which turns the camera to center the observed motion field, runs at 16 frames per second (16 fps). The ROM also contains a test pattern, image binarization (22 fps) and a motor scan sequence demo. We also use the connectivity graph (section 24.4.2) to implement image smoothing (3 fps), edge detection (2 fps) and connected components (1 fps), illustrating both the generality of the programming model and the limitations of the microcontroller in the current prototype.

24.3.4 Digital Signal Processors

The Analog Devices AD-2101 Digital Signal Processor (DSP) provides additional real-time image processing capabilities on logmap images. The DSP board might be programmed to control a robot hand, to perform real-time pattern recognition tasks, or even for voice output. The DSP reads the camera board, computes the log mapping and sends the logmap image to the MC68332 via a high-speed serial connection. The DSP board combines an AD-2101 12 MHz DSP having two 2 MHz serial ports, 8 K bytes internal RAM, 80 K bytes external RAM, and 64 K bytes boot EPROM.

An second identical DSP board functions as a video display driver, generating an RS-170 video output suitable for display on a standard TV monitor.

An optional third DSP board is used as a video transmitter that can send four frames per second of logmap images over a standard voice-grade telephone line.

24.4 Programming and development model

24.4.1 Embedded system model

Each of the three microprocessors in out prototype is a general purpose computer, so the programming model bears great resemblance to that for embedded control systems on general purpose processors. One of the key elements in this model is a distinction between a development system and a target system. We initially developed our applications on a Sun workstation based system. This development system simulates the target system to a high degree: it combines a robotic pan-tilt actuator made by Klinger Scientific, a Sony XC-77RR camera and Analogic video digitizer, with software tools to simulate a variety of sensor geometries.

There are four stages to developing an application.

1. We design a prototype program on the development host. At this stage, there are few memory, timing or numeric precision restrictions. The commercial camera and actuator provide a high degree of reliability.
2. Development continues on the host, but we use the camera and actuator of Cortex-I. The host controls the SPM by sending commands over an RS-232 serial line, and receives the logmap image from the miniature camera, digitizing the video signal output. This allows the same software to be tested using the new hardware.
3. The application is debugged on the target hardware using the host as a terminal. Since *C* language cross-development environments are available for both the DSPs and the microcontroller used in this system, we develop *C* code on the Sun host, then download it to the target system. The code must account for the more stringent hardware restrictions such as integer arithmetic, less memory and less processing power. Such restrictions are

a result of the inherent tradeoff between a highly flexible, programmable development system and an inexpensive target system.

4. We burn the application into the ROM of the target system at which point we can take the target system 'into the field'. Some applications, like an attentional OCR program for reading license plates (Ong, 1992; Ong *et al.*, 1992), are at stage two, while many simpler image processing algorithms, such as motion tracking, are at stage four.

24.4.2 Space-variant image processing

As mentioned earlier, the complex log mapping has a singular point at the origin, and a branch cut associated with the 'phase-wrapping' of the angles 0 and 2π. In addition, the local pixel connectivity does not generally possess the simple 4-connectivity or 8-connectivity familiar in conventional computer graphics and image processing. The local topology of the complex log sensor is variable and complicated, and this is a feature that might be shared by other novel sensor architectures. To deal with image processing on an arbitrary sensor topology, we developed an approach to image processing based on the use of a connectivity graph. We define the connectivity graph $G = (V, E)$ to be the graph whose vertices V stand for sensor pixels, and the edges E represent the adjacency relations between pixels. Associated with a vertex p is a pixel address (u, v). Thus we write $(u(p), v(p))$ for a pixel coordinate identified by its graph vertex, or $p = \phi(u, v)$ for a vertex identified by its pixel coordinate. Then, $V = \{p_0, \ldots, p_{\text{NPIXELS}-1}\}$.

The definitions of $S(i, j)$ and $R(i, j)$ do not constrain the mapping. Some sensor mappings, such as the $\log(z)$ mapping (Figure 24.2a), are defined such that adjacent pixels in the TV image map to pixels that are also adjacent in the forward map image. In this case, the connectivity relations are straightforward. Let E_F be the set of edges representing connections between pixels in the forward map. The edge $(p, q) \in E_F$ provided $(u(p), v(p))$ is a neighbor of $(u(q), v(q))$. For the $\log(z + \alpha)$ mapping (Figure 24.2c) E_F does not contain the connections across the vertical meridian. To obtain all the connections in the sensor, we place the inverse image adjacency relations in the edge set E_I

$$
\begin{aligned}
(p, q) \in E_I \quad &\text{provided } \exists i, j, k, l \text{ such that} \\
&S(i, j) = u(p), R(i, j) = v(p) \text{ and} \\
&S(k, l) = u(q), R(k, l) = v(q) \text{ and} \\
&(i, j) \text{ is a neighbor of } (k, l)
\end{aligned}
\tag{12}
$$

The connectivity graph edge set E may be $E = E_I$ or $E = E_I \cup E_F$, depending on the map. Resulting from the discretization of the complex log function $\mathbf{w} = \log(\mathbf{z} + \alpha)$ in the tables $S(i, j)$ and $R(i, j)$, some of the 8-adjacent neighbors in the forward map correspond to nonadjacent pixels in the inverse map. In this case, we chose $E = E_I \cup E_F$.

The algorithm to compute the connectivity graph is simple. One vertex $p \in V$ is allocated for each pixel (u, v). The graph edges in E_F are just the 8- or 4-edges from the forward map image. The graph edges in E_I are computed by scanning the look-up-tables $S(i, j)$ and $R(i, j)$ with a 3×3 operator. The following algorithm, **compute_inverse_map_edges**, finds the edges E_I for the 4-neighbors:

Algorithm: compute_inverse_map_edges
Function: Computes the edges from the inverse map for the connectivity
graph.
Input: Spoke and ring look-up-tables, $S(i, j)$ and $R(i, j)$
Output: Inverse map edges, E_I

$E_I = \{ \ \}$
For each TV pixel (i, j)
   $u = S(i, j)$
   $v = R(i, j)$
   For each $(k, l) \in \{(i + 1, j), (i, j + 1), (i - 1, j), (i, j - 1)\}$
     $w = S(k, l)$
     $z = R(k, l)$
     If $(u \neq w$ **or** $v \neq z)$ **and** $e = (\phi(u, v), \phi(w, z)) \notin E_I$
     Then $E_I = E_I \cup \{e\}$.
   End For
End For

The **compute_inverse_map_edges** algorithm can be changed in a trivial way to pick up 8-neighbors. Another detail is that some points (i, j) may be outside the domain of the map, and $S(i, j)$ and $R(i, j)$ are undefined at those points. Also, this simplified algorithm does not take into account the fact that not all points (k, l) lie inside the bounds of the TV image.

Each graph node p in the connectivity graph is represented by a constant size data structure in memory. The graph edges $\{(p, q)\}$ are represented by one field containing a list of pointers. The structure for p may also contain fields such as the pixel array coordinates $(u(p), v(p))$, the pixel centroid $\mu(p)$, the pixel area $a(p) = a(u(p), v(p))$, and the number of neighbors $|\mathcal{N}(p)|$. The pixel centroid $\mu(p)$ represents the centroid of the TV pixels that map to p and is given by

$$\mu(p) = \frac{1}{a(p)} \sum_{i,j} (i, j)^T \mid S(i, j) = u(p) \quad \text{and} \quad R(i, j) = v(p). \tag{13}$$

We define the set of neighbors of p to be denoted by

$$\mathcal{N}(p) = \{q \mid (p, q) \in E\}. \tag{14}$$

We can define a space-variant sensor geometry that is not a complex

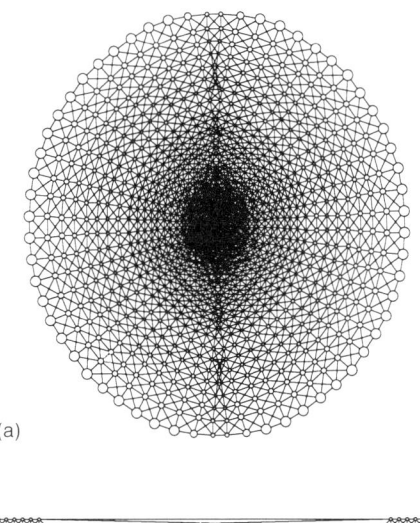

(a)

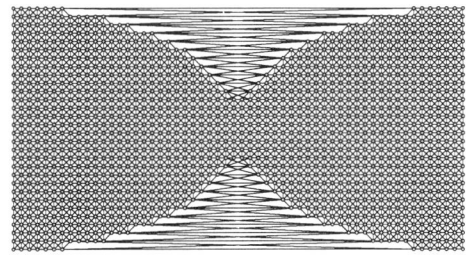

(b)

Figure 24.8 *Connectivity graph for a* $\log(z + \alpha)$ *sensor geometry. Circles stand for graph vertices and lines stand for graph edges. The diameter of the circles in the inverse map is proportional to the area of the pixel. The graph explicitly represents the neighbor relations across the vertical meridian. (a) Inverse map, (b) forward map.*

logarithm, but is the result of a stochastic process. We define this map by placing seed points randomly within the image space with a density function defined so that more points will be in the center of the image. The map is then created by growing each seed point until its neighbor is met using a simple relaxation procedure. The map is called the random map and is illustrated in Figure 24.9. To obtain the connectivity graph for this mapping, we use only $E = E_I$.

One application for the random map would be to use it with large area CCD image sensors with defective pixels. Large CCD sensors (1K × 1K or 2K × 2K pixels) are extremely expensive because of their low production yield. These sensors are much cheaper when they have defective pixels. A random map with the associated connectivity graph could be created for each of these sensors, skipping the bad pixels. This would allow for a very high resolution camera that would not be prohibitively expensive.

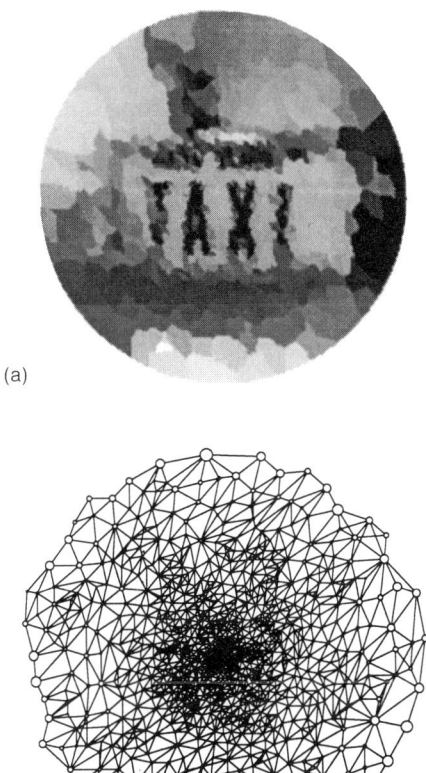

(a)

(b)

Figure 24.9 *(a) The image from a sensor having a random pixel geometry, (b) the connectivity graph for this sensor.*

A variety of space-variant sensors have been designed and fabricated (Chaikin and Weiman, 1981; Rojer and Schwartz, 1990, Rojer, 1989; Sandini *et al.*, 1989a, b; van der Spiegel *et al.*, 1989). The connectivity graph can be defined for any of these mappings, and then used to develop a library of image processing routines that can run on data from any of these sensors, and therefore we provide a generic approach to image processing on an unconstrained sensor geometry (Wallace *et al.*, 1991).

Using the connectivity graph, we define a variety of image processing operations. For example, if p represents a pixel, $L(p)$ its gray value and $\mathcal{N}(p)$ its neighbors, then we can define a simple edge operator $e(p)$ as

$$e(p) = \frac{1}{|\mathcal{N}(p)|} \sum_{q \in \mathcal{N}(p)} (L(p) - L(q))^2. \tag{15}$$

Note that the definition of $e(p)$ contains no special cases for pixels having different numbers of neighbors, and thus applies equally to pixels at the boundary of the image and to those in the interior.

Another simple example is the Laplacian, in sensor coordinates, $\ell(p)$, given by

$$\ell(p) = |\mathcal{N}(p)|L(p) - \sum_{q \in \mathcal{N}(p)} L(q). \tag{16}$$

Using such definitions we can build a library of image processing routines that is independent of the sensor geometry. We report the details of the connectivity graph elsewhere (Wallace *et al.*, 1991), where we show how to develop programs for template matching, connected components analysis, pan-tilt calibration, and pyramid operations.

24.5 Applications

24.5.1 Motion tracking

We have implemented a motion-tracking application on Cortex-I in ROM that integrates all the capabilities of the system. It is based on a simple frame-differencing algorithm and is able to track moving objects at approximately five frames per second.

The algorithm subtracts successive pairs of frames, computes the centroid of motion, and moves the motor to point the camera at the computed centroid. Because this algorithm needs two frames to compute the centroid of motion, and then misses a frame while the motor is moving, it can only make one motor movement every three frames. Therefore, although it can compute the frame difference and centroid at 16 Hz, the motor is only moved about five times per second.

24.5.2 License plate tracking and reading

We solved a difficult tracking and pattern recognition problem using a combination of Cortex-I and a Sun Sparcstation, bringing it to the second stage of development. This application is described in detail elsewhere (Ong, 1992; Ong *et al.*, 1992), but is summarized here. The task is to find the license plate on a moving car, track it as the car moves towards the camera, and finally read the characters on the license plate when it gets close enough to the camera.

The experimental setup consists of a real license plate attached to a toy truck that is pulled by a string wound around a motor-driven pulley. The truck moves at approximately two inches/second. It is tracked for about six feet before the license plate is read.

Cortex-I is set up to allow commands sent via an RS-232 serial port to control the SPM position. The commands specify the pan and tilt angles of the motor in tenths of a degree. Cortex-I outputs a standard RS-170 video signal that contains the inverse logmap image. This signal is then digitized on a Sun SPARC-2, and the forward logmap is computed from the invese image just as if it were a TV image. This method is very inefficient as it wastes communication bandwidth in transmitting an inverse image, and computational resources in computing the forward map from the inverse map. We chose this approach because it allows the existing application running on the host to use the Cortex-I hardware.

We track the license plate using a combination of three techniques which are a modified Hough transform (Rojer, 1989), a foreground-background segmentation and a corner detector. We assume that the car moves at a constant velocity, and the license plate's position is estimated each frame using a Kalman filter. When the car is close enough, and thus the characters on the license plate are big enough, the camera scans the license plate from left to right with five frames. The program analyses each frame to segment the characters and perform OCR. It then merges the results from the five frames to yield the string of characters on the license plate.

24.5.3 Cortex-I limitations

The development of the application described in the previous section provides a better understanding of some of the limitations of using Cortex-I in a real situation. We found that although Cortex-I works well, it is limited in several ways:

- *Not enough processing power* The Motorola MC68332, which is capable of about 2 MIPS, performs all of the image processing in the system as well as controlling the motor. This is not enough to track the license plate even at these low speeds.
- *Not enough memory* The MC68332 board has only 192 Kbytes of RAM. This is not enough to hold the OCR tables, and thus the application could not be advanced further than stage two at this point.
- *Not enough sensor resolution* By the time the license plate is near enough to the camera so that the characters are reliably recognizable, the truck is so close to Cortex-I that there is not enough time to scan the license plate and read the characters. Because of this, the characters on the license plate must be read while the license plate is still too far away, resulting in the imperfect recognition results.
- *Camera doesn't rotate about its focal point* The application software assumes the camera rotates about its focal point when it scans the license plate to read the characters. Because the camera doesn't in fact rotate about its focal point, the rotation results in an effective translation which throws off the expected position of the camera. Because of this, the OCR

results from the different frames are not merged accurately, yielding an incorrect resultant string.

24.6 Conclusion

To build a miniature system, it is necessary that **every** component be miniature. We have successfully built a working miniature system which consists of a miniature camera, actuator, DSP board to read out and map the camera image to a logmap image, microcontroller board to control the motor and process the images, DSP board to display the image, and a DSP board to transmit the images over a voice-grade telephone line at four frames per second.

We have shown that relatively little processing power is required to perform significant real-time vision using a logarithmically structured sensor architecture. Our current system has roughly 2 MIPS of processing power. For a future version, we estimate that 50 MIPS would provide enough power for extensive real-time applications of computer vision.

Although we are currently participating in the fabrication of a custom VLSI sensor, we have been able to emulate a logmap sensor with commercially available hardware. This sensor architecture, coupled with currently available general purpose microcontrollers and DSPs, enables the building of a high performance machine vision system without extensive investment in custom VLSI.

The Spherical Pointing Motor is comparable in capabilities, yet at least an order of magnitude less in size and cost than other similar pan-tilt actuators. The current prototype (camera and motors) is about 5 cm on a side, draws about 10 watts, and is able to actuate our 6 gram camera at speeds of several hundred degrees per second. It is also easy to use as it is an absolute positioning device and is run open-loop. A set of currents applied to the coils moves the motor and holds it at a fixed position, which can be specied to a fraction of a pixel.

The long-range goal of this project is to demonstrate that major new applications of robotics will become feasible when small low-cost machine vision systems can be mass-produced. This notion of 'commodity robotics' is expected to parallel the impact of the personal computer, in the sense of opening up new application niches for what has until now been expensive and therefore limited technology.

Acknowledgements

This work supported in part by DARPA/ONR Contract #N00014-90-C-0049 and AFOSR Contract #88-0275, and performed at Vision Applications, Inc., currently in Boston, MA.

References

Abbott, A.L. and Ahuja, N. (1990) Active surface reconstruction by integrating focus, vergence, stereo, and camera calibration. *International Conference on Computer Vision. IEEE Computer Society Press*, Osaka, Japan.

Abbott, A.L. and Ahuja, N. (1991) The University of Illinois active vision system. *Technical Report CV-91-8-2*, University of Illinois, Beckman Institute.

Allen, P.K., Yoshimi, B. and Timcenko, A. (1991) Real-time visual servoing. *Proceedings IEEE International Conference on Robotics and Automation*, 851–6, April. IEEE Computer Society Press, Sacramento, CA.

Bajcsy, R. (1988) Active perception. *IEEE Proceedings*, **76**(8), 996–1005.

Ballard, D.H. (1989) Animate vision. *Technical Report, Computer Science Department University of Rochester.*

Baloch, A.A. and Waxman, A.M. (1991) Behavioral control of the mobile robot mavin, in *Neural Networks: Concepts, Applications, and Implementations, Volume IV* (eds. Antognetti and Milutinov) Prentice Hall, Englewood Cliffs, NJ.

Bederson, B.B. (1992) A miniature space-variant active vision system: Cortex-I. PhD thesis, *Computer Science Department*, GSAS, New York University.

Bederson, B.B., Wallace, R.S. and Schwartz, E.L. (1992a) A miniature pan-tilt actuator: The spherical pointing motor. *Technical Report 264*, New York University, Computer Science, Robotics Research.

Bederson, B.B., Wallace, R.S. and Schwartz, E.L. (1992b) Two miniature pantilt devices. *IEEE International Conference on Robotics and Automation*, May. IEEE Computer Society Press, Nice, France.

Bederson, B.B., Wallace, R.S. and Schwartz, E.L. (1992c) Calibration of the spherical pointing motor. *SPIE Conference on Intelligent Robots and Computer Vision*, November. International Society for Optical Engineering, Boston, MA.

Brown, C. (ed.) (1988) The rochester robot. *Technical Report 257*, University of Rochester.

Burt, P.J. (1988) Smart sensing within a pyramid machine, *IEEE Proceedings*, **76**(8), 1006–15.

Chaikin, G.M. and Weiman, C.F.R. (1981) Image processing system. *U.S. Patent No. 4,267,573*, May.

Clark, J.J. and Ferrier, N.J. (1988) Modal control of an attentive vision system. *Second Int. Conf. Computer Vision*, 514. *IEEE Computer Society Press*, Tampa, FL.

Dickmanns, E.D. and Graefe, V. (1988) Applications of dynamic monocular machine vision. *Machine Vision and Applications*, **1**, 241–61.

Halliday, D. and Resnick, R. (1981) *Fundamentals of Physics, Second Edition, Extended Version.* Wiley, New York.

Kawarabayashi, H., Watanabe, M., Shirai, Y., Asade, M. and Miura, J. (1991) Tracking of a moving object using an active vision system. *Japan Mechanical Society, Robotics Mechatronics Conference Proceedings*, 207–12, June.

Krotkov, E.P. (1989) *Active Computer Vision by Cooperative Focussing and Stereo.* Springer-Verlag, NY.

Krotkov, E., Fuma, F. and Summers, J. (1988) An agile stereo camera system for flexible image acquisition. *IEEE J. Robotics and Automation*, **4**, 108–13.

Ong, P.-W. (1992) Image processing, pattern recognition and attentional algorithms in a space-variant active vision system. *PhD thesis, Computer Science Department*, GSAS, New York University.

Ong, P.-W., Wallace, R.S. and Schwartz, E.L. (1992) Space-variant optical character recognition. *11th International Conference on Pattern Recognition. IEEE Computer Society Press*, The Hague, Netherlands.

Raviv, D. and Shapira, A. (1991) Miniature vision-based flight simulator. *4th Annual Conference on Recent Advances in Robotics*, 81–6. *Tech. report*, Florida Atlantic University, Florida.

Rizzi, A.A., Whitcomb, L.L. and Koditschek, D.E. (1991) Distributed real-time control of a spatial robot juggler. *IEEE Computer Magazine* (submitted).

Rojer, A.S. (1989) Space-variant computer vision with a complex-logarithmic sensor geometry. *PhD thesis, Computer Science Department*, GSAS, New York University.

Rojer, A.S. and Schwartz, E.L. (1990) Design considerations for a space-variant visual sensor with complex-logarithmic geometry. *10th ICPR*, **2**, 278–85. *IEEE Computer Society Press*, Atlantic City, NJ.

Sandini, G., Bosero, F., Bottino, F. and Ceccherini, A. (1989a) The use of an anthropomorphic visual sensor for motion estimation and object tracking. *Image Understanding and Machine Vision Workshop*, 1–5. Optical Society of America, North Falmouth, MA.

Sandini, G., Dario, P. and Debusschere, I. (1989b) Active vision based on space-variant sensing. *5th International Symposium on Robotics Research*, August. MIT Press, Tokyo, Japan.

Schwartz, E.L. (1977) Spatial mapping in primate sensory projection: analytic structure and relevance to perception. *Biological Cybernetics*, **25**, 181–94.

Schwartz, E.L., Merker, B., Wolfson, E. and Shaw, A. (1988) Computational neuro-science: Applications of computer graphics and image processing to two and three dimensional modeling of the functional architecture of visual cortex. *IEEE Computer Graphics and Applications*, **8**(4), 13–28.

van der Spiegel, J., Kreider, F., Claeys, C. *et al.* (1989) A foveated retina-like sensor using ccd technology, in *Analog VLSI Implementations of Neural Networks* (eds. C. Mead and M. Ismail), Kluwer, Boston.

Wallace, R.S. and Howard, M.D. (1989) Hba vision architecture: built and benchmarked. *IEEE Transactions on Pattern Analysis and Machine Intelligence*, **11**(3).

Wallace, R.S., Ong, P.-W., Bederson, B.B. and Schwartz, E.L. (1991) Space-variant image processing. *Technical Report 256*, New York University, Computer Science, Robotics Research.

Wallace, R.S., Webb, J.A. and Wu, I.-C. (1989) Architecture independent image processing: performance of apply on diverse architectures. *Computer Vision, Graphics and Information Processing*, **48**, 265–76.

Weiman, C.F. and Chaikin, G. (1979) Logarithmic spiral grids for image-processing and display. *Computer Graphics and Image Processing*, **11**, 197–226.

25

A biologically based synthetic nervous system for a real-world device

GEORGE N. REEKE, JR., OLAF SPORNS, W. EINAR GALL,
GIULIO TONONI, and GERALD M. EDELMAN
Neuroscience Institute, New York, NY, USA

25.1 Introduction

To understand better the complex interactions that occur at multiple levels in the nervous system during behavior, we have developed an approach called Synthetic Neural Modelling (SNM) (Reeke *et al.*, 1990a).[1] Because a mathematical analysis of behavior is frustrated by the nonlinearity of neuronal responses and the extreme variability of individual brain anatomy, SNM depends heavily on computer simulation of the working nervous system. To avoid the pitfalls inherent in the interpretation by an observer of neuronal firings as encoding or representing information (Reeke and Edelman, 1988), we have chosen to embed our neural models in simple automata with designed phenotypes that behave in a specified environment. In this way, we can be assured that no part of a theory of behavior is inadvertently hidden in an observer's interpretation of neural responses. Our models can be assessed independent of any theory of 'neural information' and the results compared with a wide range of animal psychology experiments.

25.1.1 The Theory of Neuronal Group Selection

While the comparison of results from models with experiment should be direct and theory-free, modeling itself can only be meaningful as a scientific

[1] The discussion in this chapter is based in part on Edelman and Reeke (1990) and on Edelman *et al.* (1992)

Artificial Neural Networks for Speech and Vision. Edited by Richard J. Mammone.
Published in 1993 by Chapman & Hall, London. ISBN 0 412 54850 X

paradigm if it is based on a theoretical framework. Models so constructed function to predict experimental consequences of a given theory, thereby providing a means to test that theory. In the work reported here, we have based the operation of the simulated nervous system of NOMAD on the Theory of Neuronal Group Selection (TNGS) or neural Darwinism (Edelman 1978, 1987, 1989).

The central idea of the TNGS is that selective processes operate in the nervous systems of individual animals to generate working circuitry that is adapted to the needs of the particular individual in a particular econiche. These processes are related to those that operate in biological evolution, but their substrate (developmentally established repertoires of interconnected neuronal groups) and mechanisms (modification of synaptic strengths modulated by the action of systems capable of sensing the adaptive value of behavior) are totally different. In particular, the TNGS proposes that brain function is based on: (1) selectional events occurring among interacting cells in the developing embryo to form neuroanatomy; (2) further selectional events occurring among populations of synapses to enhance neuronal responses having adaptive value for the organism; and (3) reentrant signals exchanged via massively parallel connections to integrate response patterns among functionally segregated brain areas (see Figure 25.1). The TNGS claims that these means are sufficient to account for a variety of brain functions ranging from perception to motor responses. The TNGS is supported by recent experimental findings and is consistent with current knowledge of neuro-anatomy and physiology (Edelman, 1993).

Embryological development must provide sufficient neuronal components if this scheme is to work. This aspect of development is clearly under overall genetic (and epigenetic) control – the general arrangement of brain areas, the kinds and numbers of cells within each, and their overall patterns of connectivity are characteristic of each species. In the course of development, neural units must be generated that are potentially capable of responding to all relevant stimulus features. These responses must exist *a priori* for selection to occur, but may be enhanced after experience. To satisfy this requirement, the TNGS postulates that mechanisms exist actively to generate variance at the finest ramifications of the nervous system (i.e. such variance is not just 'noise' in the system). These mechanisms operate to produce neural elements with sufficient variation to assure that the space of possible input features is covered by several *repertoires* of variant recognizing units. Recent studies on the mechanism of action of cell adhesion molecules, which serve to 'glue' neurons together, indicate that they contribute dynamically to the origin of diversity of such repertoires in the neuroanatomy of the developing nervous system (Edelman, 1986, 1988).

Selection upon this diversity to yield adaptive behavior begins before completion of the repertoires (indeed, selection is a key mechanism of development) and continues throughout life. In this process, sensory signals arriving

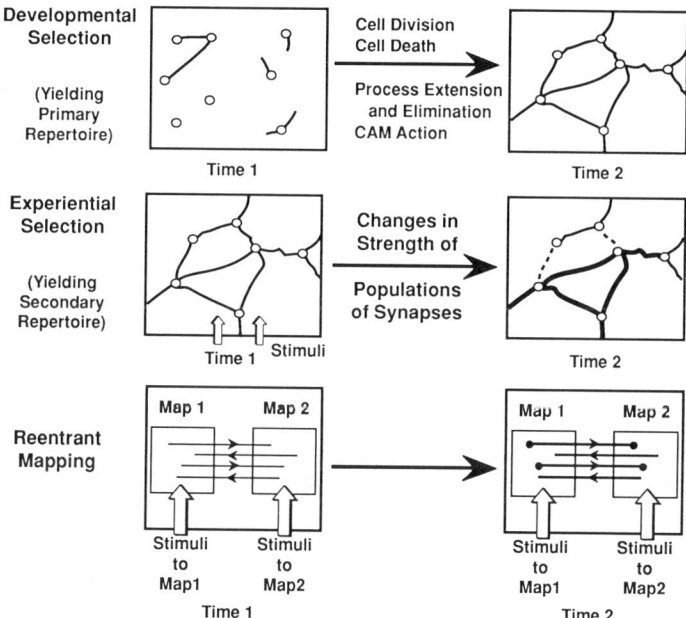

Figure 25.1 *Three fundamental mechanisms in neuronal group selection. (1) Developmental selection occurs through interaction of the primary processes of cell division, cell migration and cell death with regulatory events involving cell and surface adhesion molecules, growth factors and other regulatory molecules to yield networks with variant anatomy in each individual. Such networks constitute* primary repertoires. *Small circles schematically indicate neurons, lines indicate neuronal processes forming synaptic pathways connecting neurons. (2) Selective strengthening or weakening of particular populations of synapses as a result of behavior leads to the modulation of circuits in the primary repertoire to form a* secondary repertoire *of neuronal groups. Heavy lines indicate strengthened pathways, dotted lines indicate weakened pathways. (3) Reentry, a process by which linkage of maps occurs through parallel selection and correlation of neuronal groups in different areas receiving disjunct but possibly correlated inputs. This process provides a basis for perceptual categorization. Lines with arrows indicate connections between neuronal maps indicated by inner rectangles. Dots at the ends of active reciprocal connections indicate strengthened synapses in reentrant paths. Strengthening or weakening can also occur in extrinsic connections. The designations 'Time 1' and 'Time 2' refer to earlier and later times within each pair of panels but do not refer to the same times in stages (1), (2) and (3), although these stages may to some extent overlap in time. (Figure from* The Remembered Present *by Gerald Edelman. Copyright © 1990 by Basic Books, Inc. Reprinted by permission of Basic Books, a division of HarperCollins Publishers.)*

at the brain excite varying subsets of the preformed neural repertoires. The exact pattern of responses at any time depends on the environment as well as on the context and on the history and affective state of the subject. The groups that respond directly to sensory input in turn excite (or inhibit) other groups, until eventually motor units are activated, resulting in behavior. Such behavior may or may not contribute to the well-being of the organism; it is the function of selection to amplify neural responses contributing to behavior having adaptive value and to suppress those which do not. The mechanism of selection is proposed to be the modification of synaptic strengths between neurons, both within and among neuronal groups. Such differential changes affect the composition of individual groups as well as their relative contributions to future responses, correlating responses from one period of time to those of another. Synaptic modification in the TNGS is thus analogous to the role of differential reproduction in the theory of natural selection.

No global learning algorithm (Rumelhart et al., 1986) is required to calculate precisely the amount of change at each synapse. According to the TNGS, an animal possesses innate mechanisms to assess its behaviors and to transmit the results of these assessments to collections of synapses, where mechanisms based on purely local activity in the recent past act to determine the direction of change. These assessment mechanisms are referred to as 'value schemes' (Edelman, 1987; Reeke and Edelman, 1987; Reeke et al., 1990a). Generally, value schemes respond to easily evaluated consequences of behavior in homeostatic systems. For example, the elevation of blood glucose levels following ingestion of appropriate foods might form a suitable basis for a value scheme. Value schemes instantiate the ability to evaluate the consequences of behaviors, but they embody no immediate categorical or procedural knowledge (although they may themselves be modified and extended through selection during the lifetime of the individual). With the use of value schemes, selection acts to enhance appropriate behavioral responses in particular contexts without the intervention of external agents, such as those employed in 'supervised' learning (Rosenblatt, 1958).

Reentry is the third major mechanism of the theory. It is a form of ongoing, reciprocal exchange of signals between neuronal repertoires along parallel anatomical connections. It functions to ensure that responses of neuronal groups are correlated across different brain areas at any one time and across similar sensory signaling patterns occurring at different times. This correlation is facilitated in many brain areas by the arrangement of neuronal groups in mappings which place groups with similar response patterns in neighboring positions. Anatomically regular reentrant pathways can thus link groups with similar responses in different areas. Models have been constructed to show how reentry enables integration of visual responses in multiple cortical areas (Finkel and Edelman, 1989; Tononi et al., 1992), providing solutions to the problems of figure/ground discrimination and perceptual grouping (Sporns et al., 1991).

25.1.2 Darwin III

The first of our automata to fully embody the principles of SNM was Darwin III (Reeke et al., 1990a, 1990b), a simulated sessile organism with a moveable eye and a four-jointed arm. Darwin III possessed neural repertoires subserving senses of contrast vision, light touch, and kinesthesia. A detailed set of neuroanatomical and neurochemical constraints embedded within its structure provided the basis for selection, giving rise to simple behavioral patterns. These constraints were designed to embody the results of prior evolutionary and developmental steps leading to the Darwin III phenotype. These steps were not explicitly modelled.

The environment of Darwin III consisted of objects of different shapes that appeared and moved across its visual field. These objects were chosen and driven by a random number generator. A naive individual with its neural connections and initial activity also driven by random number generators was exposed to these stimuli. After sufficient experience, selection among its neuronal repertoires constrained by criteria of value resulted in consistent patterns of visual tracking, reaching with the arm, and discrimination among different objects.

The simplified, completely predesigned structure and interaction dynamics of the objects in Darwin III's environment, however, could have led to inadvertent bias in the simulations, and the resulting limited behavior could not readily be compared with that of animals. For example, in most simulations the visual input was presented at rather low resolution with carefully controlled noise content and a featureless background. The environment was two dimensional, and the arm and the objects it manipulated were not subject to inertia or friction.

25.1.3 Darwin IV

To avoid these limitations of Darwin III, we extended SNM techniques to incorporate a real-world artifact (NOMAD) in a new automaton, Darwin IV. In Darwin IV, the automaton and its environment are real; only the nervous system is simulated. NOMAD moves about in the environment and provides visual and other sensory inputs to the simulated nervous system; in turn, it receives computed neural signals that activate its motor effectors. Darwin IV can execute built-in reflexes and, in addition, possesses modes of behavior that are subject to selection under principles of the TNGS. These behavioral modes and reflexes become linked during experience to perform a number of exemplary tasks.

25.2 Materials and methods

25.2.1 The mobile device

NOMAD (Neurally Organized, Multiply Adaptive Device) was built to meet several design criteria. It is small enough to move about effectively in a small experimental room, but large enough for easy construction and adjustment.

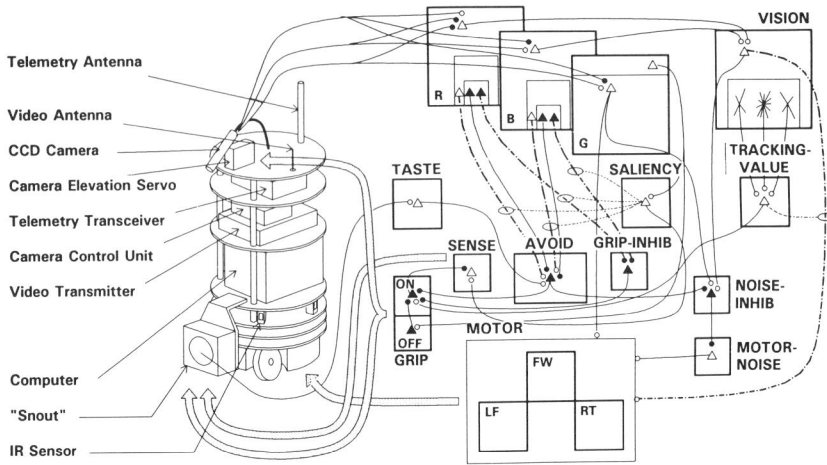

Figure 25.2 *Schematic diagram of Darwin IV showing the major components of the mobile artifact (left) and the simulated nervous system used for the block sorting task (right). Boxes represent neuronal repertoires. Open and filled triangles denote excitatory and inhibitory cells, respectively. Lines connecting cells or repertoires indicate neuronal pathways (only a few representative cells and connections are shown); heavy arrows indicate efferent motor pathways. Open and filled circles indicate excitatory and inhibitory synapses, respectively. Synaptic pathways subject to value-dependent selective amplification are indicated by dot-dash lines. Dashed lines originating at the value systems involved end in loops around the affected pathways. Beginning at the upper left, the red, blue and green channels from the CCD video camera provide input to color-opposition cells in areas R, B and G, respectively. Areas R and B jointly provide input to a VISION repertoire (top right), which directly excites MOTOR areas FW (for forward motion), LF (for left motion), and RT (for right motion), bottom center (see also Figure 25.4). These areas in turn activate NOMAD's wheels to produce locomotion. MOTOR neurons also receive noise input from MOTOR-NOISE area, which generates spontaneous (exploratory) motions of NOMAD. MOTOR-NOISE is inhibited by activity in NOISE-INHIB, which is excited by VISION, thereby reducing spontaneous locomotion when a potential tracking target is in sight. Connections from VISION to MOTOR are amplified under the selective influence of the TRACKING-VALUE repertoire. TRACKING-VALUE responds most strongly to light falling directly in front of NOMAD, which excites the rectangular area near bottom of VISION repertoire, corresponding to the proximal region of the field of view (trapezoidal area in Figure 25.3). Cells in the foveal and perifoveal regions of R and B (smaller rectangles at bottoms of R and B repertoires) are also connected via selectively modified synapses (see below) to excite area AVOID and to inhibit area GRIP-INHIB when an object is sighted at a moderate distance. After training, these areas are responsible, respectively, for initiating the avoidance and preventing the gripping reflexes discussed in the text. GRIP-INHIB is normally active, leading to inhibition of GRIP. When GRIP-INHIB is itself inhibited, GRIP is released from inhibition and can activate the snout magnet and camera elevation effectors, but only when excitatory input is received at the same time from TRACKING-VALUE, causing NOMAD to pick up objects that have been foveated. AVOID acts by inhibiting both NOISE-INHIB and GRIP, causing NOMAD to move randomly without activating its gripping magnet. The green (G) visual repertoire is responsible for recognition of the green home area. When the camera has been elevated*

(continued)

It is modular, permitting sensor and effector elements to be changed without major redesign. It is autonomous, capable of operating under battery power and of communicating by radio and video telemetry with the computer in which its nervous system is simulated. Wherever possible, it uses commercially available components.

NOMAD's base is a mobile platform (RWI Inc., Dublin, NH) with three steerable wheels that permit independent translational and rotational motion (Figure 25.2, left). Modules stacked on the platform provide effectors, sensors, and a telemetry interface to the nervous system, which is simulated on an nCUBE/10 parallel computer (Beaverton, OR). A rigid 'snout' fitted with an electromagnet permits NOMAD to grip small metal objects. Visual input is provided by a miniature color CCD video camera (Toshiba IK-M30A) mounted near the top of the device. Camera azimuth can be varied by rotation of the platform as a whole; elevation is controlled by a model airplane servo that is directly linked to NOMAD's nervous system. Additional 'senses' are provided by electrical contacts in the snout (Figure 25.2, left), which can detect the conductivity of objects gripped by the electromagnet ('taste'), as well as by infrared (IR) proximity sensors (Banner SM312D) mounted around the periphery of the base. In current versions of NOMAD, the primary function of the IR sensors is to redirect the motion of the base when a collision with a large fixed object, such as a wall, is imminent.

A VME-bus computer (Oettle & Reichler Industrial Computers, Augsburg, Germany) with a 68020 processor running under OS-9 (Microware Systems Corp., Des Moines, IA) provides interfaces linking the various sensors and effectors in a standardized way to the simulated nervous system. All signals exchanged between the nCUBE and this on-board computer are in the form of encoded neuronal responses. The on-board computer initiates no behavior by itself other than manual override and collision avoidance.

25.2.2 NOMAD's environment

Experiments with NOMAD are carried out in a specially constructed frame (Figure 25.3a) containing an 8' × 10' raised floor that may be covered with either opaque or translucent plexiglass. This floor is surrounded by 'walls'

---

and the green target is seen from a distance (when cells at bottom of G are active), MOTOR and NOISE-INHIB are excited, causing NOMAD to move towards the green target. When the target is reached, other cells (top of G) become active, exciting GRIP-OFF cells and providing the SALIENCY signal. SALIENCY immediately excites SENSE neurons, activating the conductivity sense in the snout. 'Bad taste' activates TASTE cells, which excite reflex avoidance via a direct pathway to AVOID. Activation of AVOID by this mechanism while SALIENCY is still active leads to strengthening of connections from R or B (whichever was active when the object was recently viewed) to AVOID; as a consequence, after training, avoidance can be activated directly by visual signals without need for the object to be tasted.

(a)

Environment

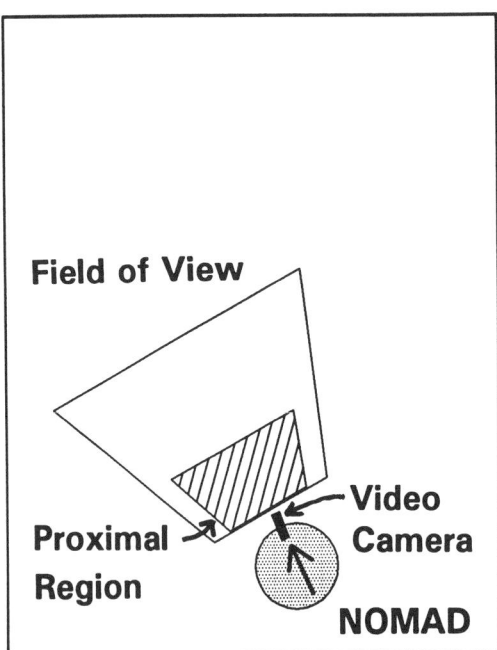

(b)

Figure 25.3 *(a) NOMAD in its environment as arranged for the block sorting experiments (showing NOMAD, randomly distributed blocks, and the landmark for 'home position'). Blue blocks are labeled with an asterisk; (b) schematic view of NOMAD (stippled), its environment and its field of view. The hatched region indicates the proximal part of the visual field.*

consisting of projection screens. Depending on the studies to be carried out, the experimental area may be configured to include a collection of objects and can contain real or projected landmarks upon the floor or walls. The area under the raised floor contains a second mobile platform controlled by a conventional robotics program. This platform carries a flashlight which projects a stimulus upward through the translucent floor for tracking by NOMAD. A television camera mounted on the ceiling is used to record the behavior of NOMAD for later evaluation.

25.2.3 The nervous system

A computer program developed at The Neurosciences Institute for simulating biologically realistic neuronal networks (CNS, Reeke *et al.*, 1990b) was used to construct the nervous system of Darwin IV (Figure 25.2, right) and to collect performance data. The previous network specifications for Darwin III (Reeke *et al.*, 1990a, 1990b) served as a prototype for the development of the new networks that were required to extend the simulation to real-world sensors and effectors. A topographically mapped visual network receives input from the three color chanels of the video camera and projects to three groups of motoneurons, one each for translation, for rotation to the left, and for rotation to the right (Figure 25.2). Other networks handle sensory and motor pathways pertaining to the snout.

Neuronal responses are updated in discrete time steps using rules for cellular activity and synaptic modification similar to those employed in Darwin III (for detailed descriptions see Reeke *et al.*, 1990a, 1990b). Visual units are subject to simulated cellular depression which causes them to respond less efficiently to visual images that remain stationary for a time than to new stimuli. Synaptic modification depends not only on pre- and post-synaptic activity, but also on the activity of value systems that respond to easily sensed indications of the adaptive value of behavior. As described in Reeke *et al.* (1990a, 1990b), value systems provide broad constraints for possible adaptive behaviors but do not specify those behaviors in detail. To be biologically plausible, value systems must be based on consequences of behavior that can be sensed independent of a teacher by parts of the nervous systems that might have arisen as a result of evolutionary selection. Darwin IV contains two distinct value systems. The first is implemented by visual units that respond more strongly when an illuminated target appears in the region of the visual field adjacent to NOMAD's snout. Its activity influences the probability of changes in synaptic strength between visual and motor networks and leads to tracking (Figure 25.2, right). The second value system, referred to as 'saliency', is triggered whenever Darwin IV activates its snout sensor to assess surface conductivity. 'Saliency' modulates changes in the strength of the connections linking visual repertoires with reflex centers (Figure 25.2, right) and permits a form of classical conditioning to occur in these pathways. Conditioning leads to control of snout gripping activity by stimulus color, as described in the following section.

25.3 Results

25.3.1 Tracking

The first task for which we trained Darwin IV was to approach and track a light that was projected upward from a platform moving randomly in the space below the translucent floor of the environment. For these experiments, NOMAD's video camera pointed at an angle roughly 45° below the horizontal from a position at the top front of the device. Figure 25.3b illustrates the relative sizes of NOMAD, the environment, and the field of view of the camera, which covered 14% of the entire environment under unobstructed conditions. Note that there is keystone distortion due to the oblique angle of the camera and that distant stimuli appear to grow larger when approached.

Darwin IV's motor system includes spontaneously active units that feed input to the neuronal repertoires that control locomotion. In the absence of a visual stimulus, NOMAD rotates and translates at random, driven by this spontaneous activity (search mode). When a stimulus appears and motoneurons are directly activated by the visual network (tracking mode), spontaneous activity is inhibited by separate connections from the visual area. After a movement has occurred, the synaptic populations giving rise to this movement are probabilistically strengthened or weakened by selection (see Figure 25.4), depending on whether or not the movement resulted in an increase in value. After some time, those movements that facilitate close approaches and tracking occur more frequently than others. During training, the visuomotor connections automatically adapt to any nonlinearities resulting from the distorted visual image and from the mechanics of NOMAD's motor apparatus.

During early trials, NOMAD rarely approaches the light (Figure 25.5). Even if it does so by chance, it cannot track the target's movements because it has no innate adaptation to carry out this task. After experience and the concomitant selectional events in the visuomotor projections, NOMAD consistently tracks the light along complicated trajectories (Figure 25.5) and loses contact only occasionally. When contact is lost, NOMAD briefly reverts to search mode, but it resumes tracking after encountering the light again.

25.3.2 Sorting

Following successful training on the tracking task, we used the networks developed by Darwin IV for tracking as a partial basis for training on the different but related task of locating and approaching stationary objects. An opaque floor was installed on the environmental platform and NOMAD was placed on this floor under roomlight illumination. Colored blocks (hollow

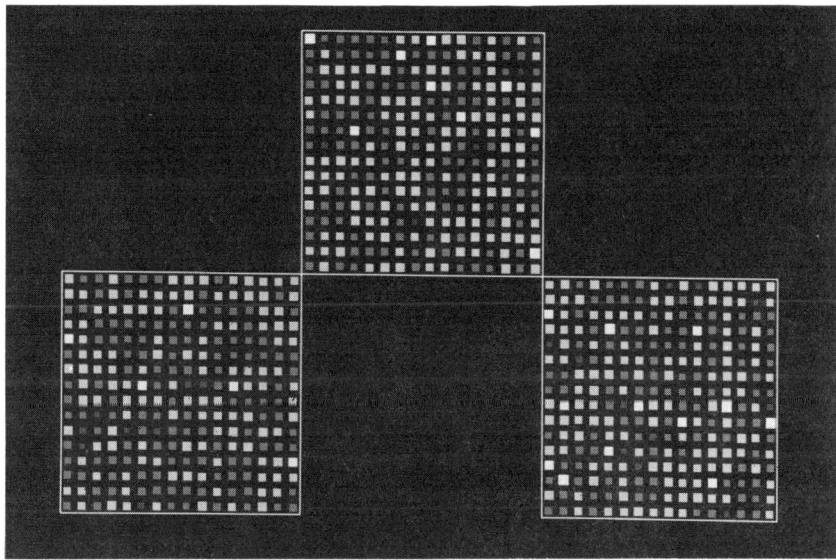

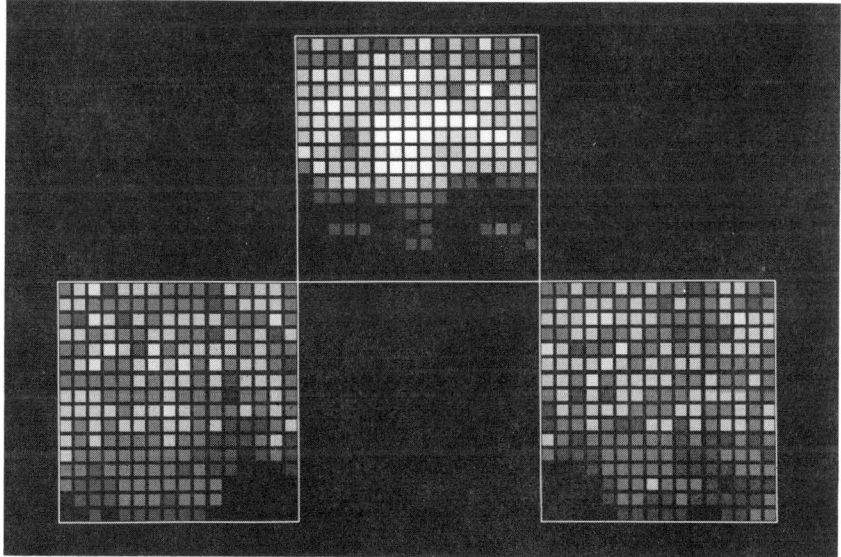

Figure 25.4 *Strengths of connections between VISION and MOTOR repertoires before (a) and after (b) training. Stronger connections are indicated by larger and lighter squares.*

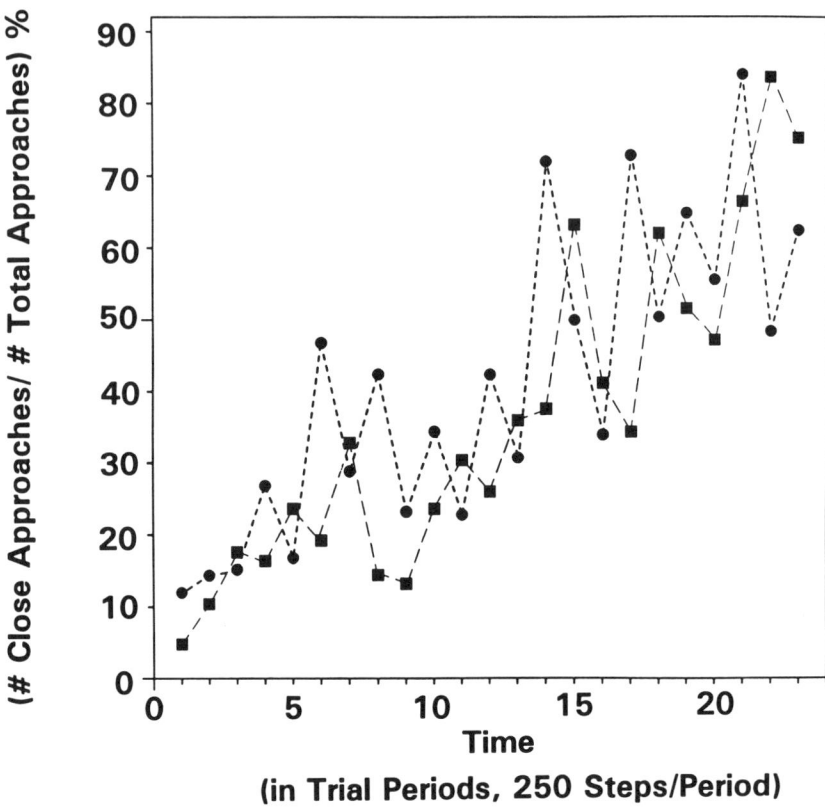

Figure 25.5 *Training curve for two individual runs of Darwin IV's tracking system. Time is given in trial periods, with each trial period lasting for 250 time steps. The success rate is given as the percent of total time that the target was in the proximal part of NOMAD's visual field (Figure 25.3).*

4″ cubes) made of thin sheet steel (Figure 25.3a) were placed at random positions on the floor. Translucent plastic sheets, either electrically conductive (Southwall Technologies, Palo Alto, CA) or not, were used to coat the surface of each block. The conductivity of each block was associated arbitrarily with its color – conductive blocks were blue and nonconductive blocks were red. No information was provided to Darwin IV about the positioning of the blocks or the nature of the correlation of conductivity with color. In one part of the environment (see Figure 25.3a), a raised green landmark signaled the 'home position', a potential collection point for colored blocks.

Each color channel (red, green or blue) from the video camera was transmitted to a separate primary neuronal visual map, and these in turn were topographically mapped to the tracking vision network (Figure 25.2). This arrangement gave the device the potential to distinguish blocks of different colors.

Four motor reflex networks provided behavioral patterns suitable for selection. One, the 'gripping reflex', turns the snout magnet on whenever an object appears in its immediate vicinity. Prior to training, the probability of activation of this network is about 50% when suitable visual input is received, and, as a result, NOMAD picks up blocks at random with about this frequency. Value-dependent modification of connections from the red and blue color networks can modify this probability. A second reflex network controls the elevation of the camera. In the sorting experiment, the camera is positioned either (1) 45° down from the horizon while searching for blocks, or (2) horizontally while searching for the 'home position'. Normally the camera is in position (1), but the elevation reflex automatically moves it to position (2) when the snout magnet is turned on and releases it back to (1) when the magnet is turned off. A third reflex is triggered whenever the green landmark activates the upper portion of the visual field (signaling proximity to home): NOMAD stops, the camera moves to the downward position, and conductivity receptors in the snout are activated. The fourth reflex network strongly activates the repertoire generating spontaneous locomotion if a conductive block ('bad taste') is sensed via the snout, resulting in an avoidance response. This network also receives modifiable connections from the red and blue color networks.

To test the behavior of Darwin IV in locating, approaching, and retrieving objects, we used the conductive blue blocks and nonconductive red blocks to set up a simple block sorting task. The aim was to see whether Darwin IV, through experience with 'good' and 'bad' tasting blocks, could be trained to avoid the blocks whose color was associated with 'bad taste' without the need to approach and grip them. Before training, NOMAD approached all blocks in its vicinity under the guidance of its tracking system and picked up approximately 50% of these with the magnetic snout by virtue of the gripping reflex described above. In these cases, the camera was raised by the elevation reflex into the horizontal position and NOMAD searched for the home position while pushing the block with its snout across the floor. When the home position was reached, the camera turned downward again towards the block and the conductive properties of the block were sensed with the snout, leading to a strong signal in the 'saliency' value system (Figure 25.2). This signal is so named because it increases the probability of synaptic changes within the nervous system regardless of whether the block is in fact conductive or nonconductive. One result is a strengthening of the association between active vision repertoires and the gripping reflex, increasing the probability of gripping objects that later come into the visual field. A second result is that an association is formed between neurons signalling the color of the object in the foveal region and the avoidance response that occurs by reflex if high conductivity ('bad taste') is sensed. After selection of connections

Table 25.1 *Response frequencies in the block sorting task. Data was collected from five test sessions while value was disabled and five test sessions while value was enabled; each test session lasted 150 time steps. At the beginning of a session, 14 colored blocks (7 red and 7 blue) were distributed at random over the environmental platform and NOMAD began its search from the edge of one side of the platform. COLOR, color of blocks to which data refer. CONTACT, number of times NOMAD established physical contact with a block, GRIP, number of times NOMAD gripped the encountered block with its magnet. HOME, number of times NOMAD reached the home position with a block attached to its snout. AVOID, number of times NOMAD actively avoided a blue block that came into view. The difference between GRIP and HOME results from accidental losses of blocks due to collisions with other blocks in the environment.*

	COLOR	CONTACT	GRIP	HOME	AVOID
'Block Collection'	Red	24	15	11	0
(Value Disabled)	Blue	34	16	13	0
'Block Sorting'	Red	30	30	21	0
(Value Enabled)	Blue	0	0	0	32

supporting this association, the appearance in the perifoveal region of an object of the color (conditioned stimulus) previously sensed as having bad taste (unconditioned stimulus) is sufficient to trigger an avoidance response and such objects are no longer gathered to the home position. This result represents a simple form of Pavlovian conditioning.

Results are shown in Table 25.1. If conductivity sensing in the snout and the corresponding value network are disabled, NOMAD collects red and blue blocks but does not discriminate them according to color. When the value network is enabled, NOMAD sorts the blocks according to color after just a few encounters with 'bad-tasting' blocks: only red blocks are taken to the home position, while blue blocks are actively avoided.

25.4 Discussion

The experiments described here and in Edelman *et al.* (1992) were deliberately limited to very simple tasks. Our initial objective was to demonstrate the feasibility of extending SNM to an artifact capable of performance in the real world. With Darwin IV, we were able to conduct long-lasting runs and to record neural and behavioral data continuously. These data could be used for the analysis of cross-level interactions among synaptic changes, environmental stimuli, phenotypic variations and behavior.

Darwin IV's behavioral repertoire includes several reflex responses (gripping, camera elevation, snout sensing, and avoidance) as well as adaptive behaviors resulting from sensorimotor interactions (such as random search, tracking, approaching and homing). In general, adaptive behaviors depend upon experience and are not predictable in detail, although they follow constraints posed by value schemes. Tasks like Darwin IV's block sorting task require the successful combination, based on experience, of sequences of reflex and adaptive behaviors. Within bounds, Darwin IV even shows a degree of opportunism, being able to transfer 'learned' behaviors (such as approaching and tracking) to different environmental situations. For example, after training it was possible to use the same networks for tracking a moving light and for approaching stationary colored blocks or a colored home position on the basis of the differential reflectance of these various stimuli relative to the background.

Workers in robotics have also attempted to design mobile devices operating in a real-world environment (for a review see Iyengar and Elfes, 1991). Despite much effort, however, 'classical' AI programs have generally been unable to deal effectively with autonomous behavior within a rich environment (Reeke and Edelman, 1988). More recent work (Maes, 1990; Meyer and Wilson, 1991; Brooks, 1991; Beer, 1990; Connell, 1990) on real or simulated behaving robots has emphasized how systems composed of independent modules can, in fact, give rise to composite behaviors in the absence of centralized control. The design used for many of these systems is based on invertebrates (particularly insects) and, unlike Darwin IV, is usually hard-wired and non-plastic. Direct interactons between the constituent modules are minimized.

While the simple behaviors we have modeled so far using Darwin IV bear certain resemblances to work using these systems, our approach differs in several fundamental respects. Darwin IV's behavioral repertoire consists of a combination of built-in reflexes with various modes of ongoing adaptive behaviors emerging from the encounters of a selectionally-based nervous system with an environment. Most of the elementary behaviors are subject to value-dependent modification of synapses. Sensor-driven modes depend directly on selective synaptic processes to mold the resulting behavioral patterns. As a consequence of selective synaptic change, the elementary bchaviors combinc with cach othcr and with rcflcxcs during cxpcricncc to yield associative sequences that allow sorting of objects in the absence of a fixed sequence of programmed instructions. Each behavior is controlled by multiple repertoires in the nervous system; a strict one-to-one mapping does not exist between neural centers and the behaviors elicited by their activation.

NOMAD, as embedded within the Darwin IV simulation, provides a valuable testing ground for biologically based neural models in a real-world environment, making it possible to explore the interactions of many combinations of phenotypic structure and neuronal architecture. Our present studies provide a basis for incorporating increasingly complex neuronal structures into the simulation, for evaluating their impact on behavior, and for understanding how adaptive action in a rich environment is initiated and controlled by the nervous system. New insight into this key scientific problem will have broad implications not only for biology and medicine, but also for computer science and robotics.

Acknowledgements

We thank Ariel Ben-Porath for his invaluable assistance with mechanics, electronics and programming. This work was carried out as part of the Institute Fellows in Theoretical Neurobiology program at The Neurosciences Institute, which is supported by the Neurosciences Research Foundation. The Foundation received major support for this research from the J.D. & C.T. MacArthur Foundation, the Lucille P. Markey Charitable Trust and the van Ameringen Foundation. O.S. is a W.M. Keck Foundation Fellow.

References

Beer, R.D. (1990) *Intelligence as Adaptive Behavior. An Experiment in Computational Neuroethology.* Academic Press, Boston, MA.

Brooks, R.A. (1991) New approaches to robotics. *Science* **253**, 1227–32.

Connell, J.H. (1990) *Minimalist Mobile Robotics. A Colony-Style Architecture for an Artificial Creature.* Academic Press, Boston, MA.

Edelman, G.M. (1978) Group selection and phasic reentrant signaling: A theory of higher brain function, in *The Mindful Brain: Cortical Organization and the Group-Selective Theory of Higher Brain Function* (eds. G.M. Edelman and V.B. Mountcastle), MIT Press, Cambridge, MA, pp. 51–100.

Edelman, G.M. (1986) Cell adhesion molecules in the regulation of animal form and tissue pattern. *Annu. Rev. Cell Biol.*, **2**, 81–116.

Edelman, G.M. (1987) *Neural Darwinism: The Theory of Neuronal Group Selection.* Basic Books, New York, NY.

Edelman, G.M. (1988) *Topobiology: An Introduction to Molecular Embryology.* Basic Books, New York, NY.

Edelman, G.M. (1989) *The Remembered Present: A Biological Theory of Consciousness.* Basic Books, New York, NY.

Edelman, G.M. (1993) Neural Darwinism: Selection and reentrant signalling in higher brain function. *Neuron* (in press).

Edelman, G.M. and Reeke, G.N., Jr. (1990) Is it possible to construct a perception machine? *Proc. Am. Philos. Soc.*, **134**, 36–73.

Edelman, G.M., Reeke, G.N., Jr., Gall, W.E. *et al.* (1992) Synthetic neural modeling applied to a real-world artifact. *Proc. Natl. Acad. Sci. USA*, **89**, 7267–71.

Finkel, L.H. and Edelman, G.M. (1989) The integration of distributed cortical systems by reentry: A computer simulation of interactive functionally segregated visual areas. *J Neurosci.*, **9**, 3188–208.

Iyengar, S.S and Elfes, A. (1991) *Autonomous Mobile Robots: Control, Planning, and Architecture.* IEEE Press, Los Alamitos, CA.

Maes, P. (ed.) (1990) *Designing Autonomous Agents: Theory and Practice From Biology to Engineering and Back.* MIT Press, Cambridge, MA.

Meyer, J.-A. and Wilson, S.W. (eds) (1991) From animals to animats. *Proc. First Int. Conf. on Simulation of Adaptive Behavior,* MIT Press, Cambridge, MA.

Reeke, G.N., Jr. and Edelman, G.M. (1987) Selective neural networks and their implications for recognition automata. *Int. J. Supercomput. Appl.*, **1**, 44–69.

Reeke, G.N., Jr. and Edelman, G.M. (1988) Real brains and artificial intelligence. *Daedalus, Proc. Am. Acad. Arts Sci.*, **117**, 143–73.

Reeke, G.N., Jr., Finkel, L.H., Sporns, O. and Edelman, G.M. (1990a) Synthetic neural modeling: A multilevel approach to the analysis of brain complexity, in *Signal and Sense: Local and Global Order in Perceptual Maps* (eds. G.M. Edelman, W.E. Gall and W.M. Cowan), Wiley, New York, pp. 607–706.

Reeke, G.N., Jr., Sporns, O. and Edelman, G.M. (1990b) Synthetic neural modeling: The 'Darwin' series of automata. *Proc. IEEE*, **78**, 1498–1530.

Rosenblatt, F. (1958) The perceptron: A probabilistic model for information storage and organization in the brain. *Psychol. Rev.*, **65**, 386–408.

Rumelhart, D.E., Hinton, G.E. and Williams, R.J. (1986) Learning representations by back-propagating errors. *Nature*, **323**, 533–6.

Sporns, O., Tononi, G. and Edelman, G.M. (1991) Modeling perceptual grouping and figure-ground segregation by means of active reentrant conditioning. *Proc. Natl. Acad. Sci. USA*, **88**, 129–33.

Tononi, G., Sporns, O. and Edelman, G.M. (1992) Reentry and the problem of integrating multiple cortical areas: Simulation of dynamic integration in the visual system. *Cerebral Cortex*, **2**, 310–35.

Dynamic formation and reset of coherent visual segmentations by neural networks

GREGORY FRANCIS[1], STEPHEN GROSSBERG[2] and
ENNIO MINGOLLA[3]
Center for Adaptive Systems and Department of Cognitive and Neural Systems, Boston University, 111 Cummington St., Boston, MA 02115, USA

26.1 Introduction

Humans and other animals are capable of forming useful visual representations of rapidly changing scenes. A segmentation or feature binding process helps to generate these representations. The segmentations corresponding to stationary parts of the scene may remain stable and coherent even as the segmentations corresponding to changing parts of the scene are rapidly reset and updated to prevent image smearing. Thus the formation and reset of visual segmentations is context-dependent, and can track the statistics of different scenic parts.

Since the turn of the century, psychophysicists have investigated the response time of the human visual system to changes in visual imagery, notably to onsets and offsets of visual stimuli – see Breitmeyer (1984) for a

[1] This material is based upon work supported under a National Science Foundation Graduate Fellowship.
[2] Partially supported by the Air Force Office of Scientific Research (AFOSR 90-0175), the Defense Research Projects Agency (AFOSR 90-0083 and ONR N00014-92-J-4015), and the Office of Naval Research (ONR N00014-91-J4100).
[3] Partially supported by the Air Force Office of Scientific Research (AFOSR 90-0175).

Artificial Neural Networks for Speech and Vision. Edited by Richard J. Mammone.
Published in 1993 by Chapman & Hall, London. ISBN 0 412 54850 X

historical review. This chapter explains how a neural network theory of visual perception proposed by Grossberg and Mingolla (1985a, 1985b, 1987) accounts for many percepts of stimulus offset, notably visual persistence after the inducing stimulus shuts off. The theory suggests that a key process governing these percepts is the time taken to reset a segmentation. These results have implications for biological as well as machine vision systems. In this chapter we describe the model architecture, demonstrate the system's ability to process synthetic aperture radar images, explain how hysteresis in the segmentation network corresponds to visual persistence, and finally show that properties of the hysteresis quantitatively match key psychophysical data on visual persistence.

26.2 Feature binding by the boundary contour system

Luminance contrast has long been recognized as an important stimulus to the visual system. Although luminance edges are of great significance for perception, what we typically see are surface regions of color and brightness (Cohen and Grossberg, 1984; Grossberg, Mingolla and Todorović, 1989; Grossberg and Todorović, 1988; Todorović, 1987). Other authors suggested that color and brightness fill-in from edges or other segmented contrasts to the interiors of stimuli (Gerritts and Vendrik, 1970). The same mechanisms clarify early visual processing of textures and shading (Beck, Graham and Sutter, 1991; Grossberg and Mingolla, 1985b, 1987; Sutter, Beck and Graham, 1989; Todd and Akerstrom, 1987).

One of the primary insights of the vision theory proposed by Cohen and Grossberg (1984) and Grossberg and Mingolla (1985a, 1985b) is the role of edges, or other regions of relatively high spatial contrast change, in the filling-in process. The theory proposes that edges have two functions. First, the computations of color and brightness take place at edges; color and brightness then flow from the edges to fill-in the enclosed surfaces of an image. If the boundaries of the surface are not defined, however, then the color and brightness could fill-in the entire visual field. A second property of edges is thus to define the boundaries of objects and to stop the filling-in process from extending outside the surfaces of the proper stimuli.

Thus there are two parallel contour-sensitive systems, a Feature Contour System (FCS) and a Boundary Contour System (BCS). The FCS represents surface color and brightness and performs the filling-in process. The BCS represents surface boundaries and blocks the filling-in process. Although we 'see' filled-in color and brightness, boundary signals are necessary for the preception of visible color and brightness, and the spatial organization of boundary signals can be recognized as groupings or bindings of visual features (Grossberg, 1987a, 1987b; Grossberg and Mingolla, 1985a, 1985b).

Algorithms based on BCS/FCS dynamics have been developed for image processing applications. Figure 26.1 displays the results of such processing

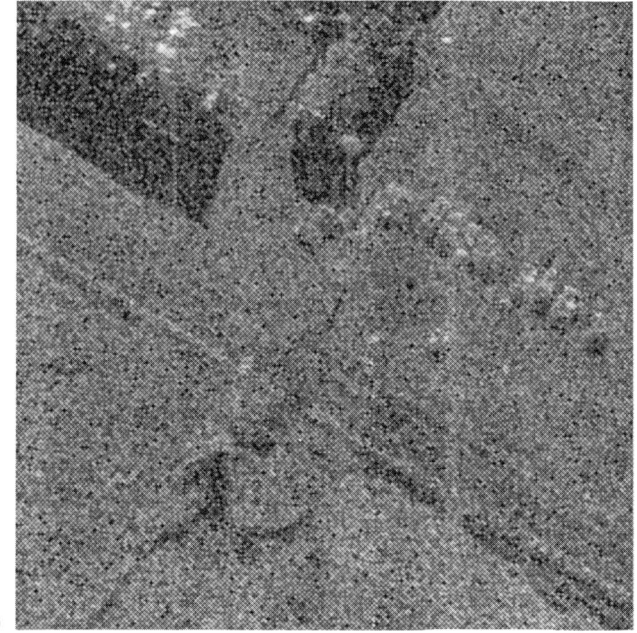

(a)

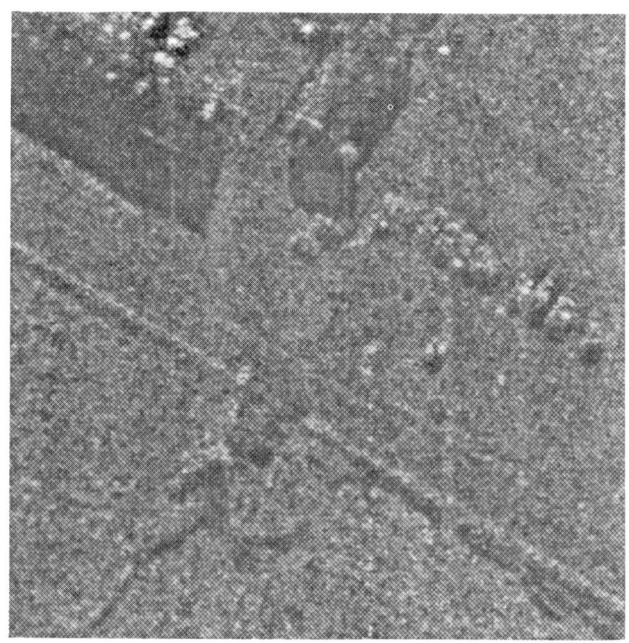

(b)

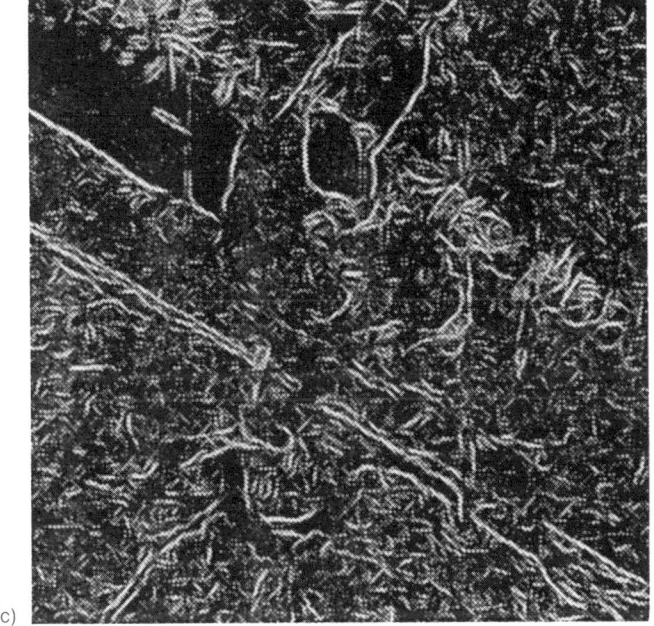

(c)

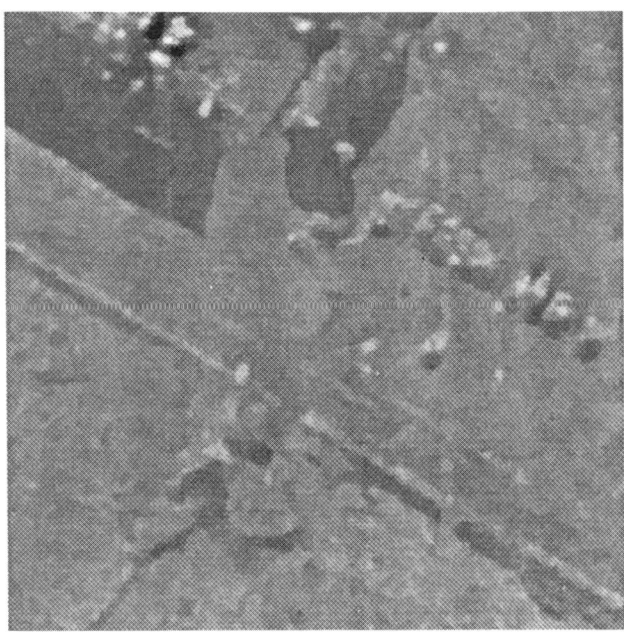

(d)

Figure 26.1 *Four transformations of a 400 × 400 pixel synthetic aperture radar image showing two buildings (upper left) and a row of parked cars near a roadway.*

applied to a synthetic aperture radar image. The original image data represents the intensity of the reflection of a radar beam, and typically covers more than five orders of magnitude of intensity variation. Thus, simply displaying the image data in, for example, 256 gray levels requires some sort of compressive transformation. The results of such a conventional transformation are shown in the upper left quadrant of Figure 26.1. The FCS includes a feed-forward stage of 'center-surround' shunting inhibition, which is itself capable of localized gain control; the results of initial FCS processing are shown in the upper right quadrant of Figure 26.1. Another difficulty presented to the human observer of synthetic aperture radar images is that they typically include a large component of 'speckle' (multiplicative noise). BCS/FCS processing can remove a great deal of this high spatial frequency noise while preserving sharp edges at coherent transitions between regions. The lower left quadrant shows the boundary signals computed by the BCS. Finally, the lower right quadrant shows the results of letting the FCS signals diffuse (filling-in) within the BCS signals. Expert photointerpreters with years of experience with synthetic aperture radar images report that those processed by the BCS/FCS algorithm afford quicker scanning for significant features and greater ease of interpretation of image structures than do conventionally transformed images. A complete description of these images and the network processing can be found in Cruthirds et al. (1992).

Cohen and Grossberg (1984) suggested that the filling-in process takes place at a syncytium of closely connected cells such that contiguous cells can easily pass signals between each other's compartment membranes. The diffusion of signals between cells spreads out until it is blocked by the presence of boundary signals. To fill-in large regions of the visual field, the passive decay parameter of each cell in the syncytium must be small relative to the diffusion coefficients (Grossberg and Todorović, 1988, equation A22). Since the passive decay term is small relative to the sizes of input activations, the activities in the syncytium will persist beyond stimulus offset as long as the corresponding boundary signals remain active to support the segmentation of surface properties. Therefore, the dynamical behavior of the BCS primarily determines the properties of visual persistence. This chapter makes the assumption that the persistence of boundary signals directly relates to the persistence of the perceived brightness and color of the visual stimulus.

To effectively build up boundary signals, an early level of the BCS must determine the orientation of a boundary at every position. To accomplish this, the cells at the first stage of an oriented filter possess orientationally tuned simple cell receptive fields. Such simple cells, or cell populations, respond selectively to orientations that activate a prescribed small region of the retina, and their orientations lie within a prescribed band of orientations with respect to the retina. A collection of such orientationally tuned cells exists at every network position, such that each cell type is sensitive to a different band of oriented contrast within its prescribed small region of the scene, as in the hypercolumn model, which was developed to explain the responses of simple cells in the area V1 of the striate cortex (Hubel and Wiesel, 1977).

These oriented receptive fields are oriented **local contrast** detectors, rather than edge detectors. This property enables them to fire in response to a wide variety of spatially nonuniform image contrasts, including edges, spatially nonuniform densities of unoriented textural elements, and spatially nonuniform densities of surface gradients. Thus, by sacrificing a certain amount of spatial resolution in order to detect oriented local contrasts, these masks achieve general detection characteristics that can respond to edges, textures and surfaces.

The fact that the receptive fields of the oriented filters are **oriented** greatly reduces the number of possible groupings into which their target cells can enter. On the other hand, in order to detect oriented local contrasts, the receptive fields must be elongated along their preferred axis of symmetry. Then the cells can preferentially detect differences of average contrast across this axis of symmetry, yet remain silent in response to differences of average contrast that are perpendicular to the axis of symmetry. Such receptive field elongation creates greater positional uncertainty about the exact locations within the receptive field of the image contrasts that fire the cell. This positional uncertainty becomes acute during the processing of image line ends and corners.

Oriented receptive fields cannot easily detect the ends of thin scenic lines or corners (Grossberg and Mingolla, 1985b). This property illustrates a basic uncertainty principle that says: Orientational 'certainty' implies positional 'uncertainty' at the ends of scenic lines whose widths are neither too small nor too large with respect to the dimensions of the oriented receptive field. If no BC signals are elicited at the ends of lines, however, then in the absence of further processing within the BCS, boundary contours will not be activated to prevent color and brightness signals from flowing out of the line ends within the FCS during filling-in. Many percepts would hereby become badly degraded by featural flow.

The BCS needs later processing stages to recover both the positional and the orientational information that are lost in this way, so that boundaries at line ends and corners can be completed before they are mapped into the FCS to control filling-in of surface brightness and color. Grossberg and Mingolla (1985b) have called the process that completes the boundary at a line end an **end cut**. End cuts actively reconstruct the line end at a processing stage higher than that of the oriented receptive field. Interactions between simple cells, complex cells, and hypercomplex cells were predicted to generate these perpendicular end cuts.

The processing stages that are hypothesized to generate end cuts are diagrammed in Figure 26.2. First, oriented simple-cell receptive fields of like position and orientation but opposite direction of contrast generate rectified

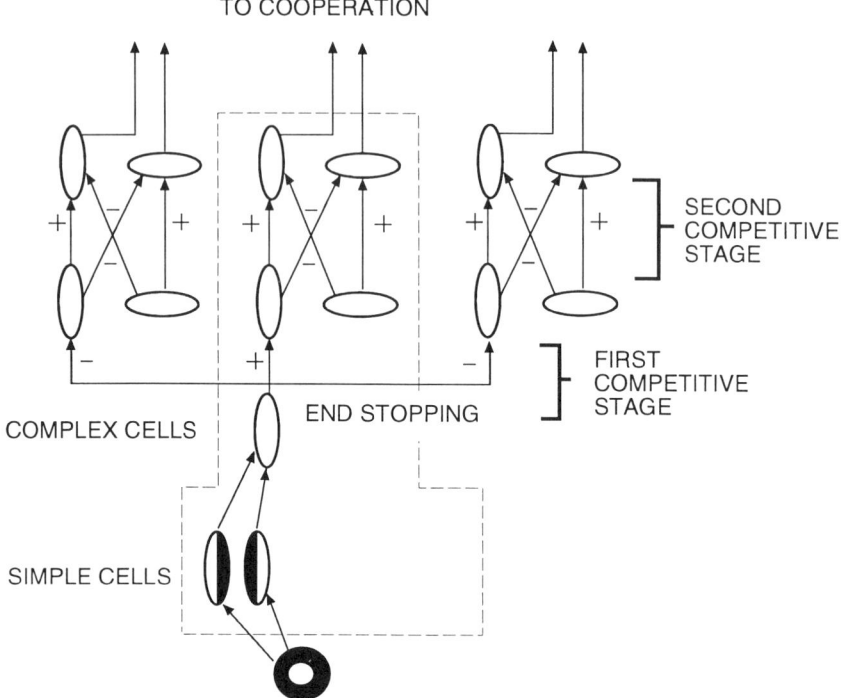

Figure 26.2 *Early stages of oriented filtering.*

output signals that summate at the next processing stage to activate complex cells whose receptive fields are sensitive to the same position and orientation as their own, but are insensitive to direction of contrast. To generate boundary detectors that can detect the broadest possible range of luminance or chromatic contrast reversals, these complex cells maintain their sensitivity to **amount** of oriented contrast, but not to the **direction** of this oriented contrast.

The rectified output from the complex cells activates a second filter, which is composed of two successive stages of spatially short-range competitive interactions whose net effect is to generate end cuts. First, a cell of prescribed orientation excites like-oriented cells corresponding to its location and inhibits like-oriented cells corresponding to nearby locations at the next processing stage. In other words, an on-center off-surround organization of like-oriented cell interactions exists at each perceptual location, analogous to the neurophysiological operation of end stopping that converts complex cells into hypercomplex cells (Hubel and Wiesel, 1965; Orban, Kato and Bishop, 1979). A version of this double filter model has been used by Beck, Graham and Sutter (1991) and Sutter, Beck and Graham (1989) to fit their data on texture segregation. It is often called the **Static Oriented Contrast Filter** (SOC Filter).

The outputs from this competitive mechanism interact with the second competitive mechanism. Here, hypercomplex cells that represent different orientations, notably perpendicular orientations, compete at the same perceptual location. This competition defines a push-pull opponent process. Excitation of a given orientation inhibits its perpendicular orientation. Inhibition of a given orientation excites its perpendicular orientation via disinhibition.

The combined effect of these two competitive interactions generates end cuts as follows. The strong vertical activations along the edges of a scenic line inhibit the weak vertical activations near the line end. In turn, these inhibited vertical activations disinhibit horizontal activations near the line end, thereby generating a horizontal end cut that is perpendicular to the inducing vertical line end. Thus, the positional uncertainty generated by orientation certainty is eliminated at a subsequent processing level by the competitive interactions.

The first and second competitive stages ensure the formation of boundary signals at all luminance edges. However, the retinal image is rarely uncontaminated; for example, retinal veins and the blind spot frequently occlude parts of the image. Since the oriented filters and the two competitive stages respond to spatial changes in luminance, the model as stated so far would create boundaries along the outline of the shadows of the retinal veins. We do not typically perceive boundaries of retinal veins and the blind spot if only because they are stabilized images and such images perceptually fade away. However, after these spurious boundaries fade away, the remaining boundary signals along the stimulus contours would have gaps wherever they were crossed by these occluding retinal structures. As a result, during the filling-in process, color and brightness would flow out of the region defining the stimulus surface through the gaps produced by the retinal veins.

Grossberg and Mingolla (1985a, 1985b) showed how a cooperative feedback process completes boundary signals across the gaps and thereby restores the occluded visual boundaries. Such a process needs to be able to rapidly complete boundaries over variable distances without a loss of acuity. Through an analysis of a large psychophysical data base, Cohen and Grossberg (1984), Grossberg (1984), and Grossberg and Mingolla (1985a, 1985b) were led to hypothesize the existence, at each orientation and position, of a cooperative bipole cell with two independent receptive fields. Each of the bipole cell's oriented receptive fields receives similarly oriented boundary signals over a large region of space. The bipole cell fires only if both sides of its receptive field are excited (Figure 26.3). Thus a horizontal bipole cell will respond to horizontal boundary signals located to the left and right of the center of the bipole receptive field, but will not respond to boundary signals, even of the same total strength, located on only the left or the right. Neurophysiological support for the prediction that bipole cells exist was soon provided by the work of von der Heydt, Peterhans and Baumgartner (1984).

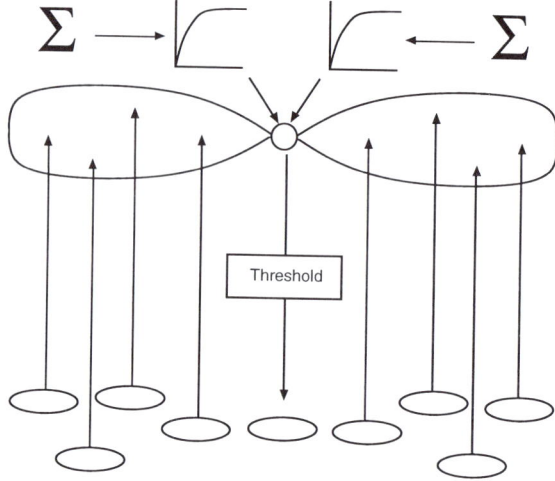

Figure 26.3 *Oriented bipole cells receive excitatory inputs from similarly oriented boundary signals. The weighted sum of signals on each half of a bipole cell receptive field is independently squashed by a saturating function. The threshold to generate a bipole cell output is set above the saturation level so that both sides of the receptive field must be stimulated to produce an output signal.*

Such a boundary completion process realizes a type of real-time statistical decision theory that chooses the globally most salient boundary segmentations and suppresses less favored groupings. Each bipole cell is sensitive to the position, orientation, density, and size of the inputs that it receives from the second competitive stage. Each bipole cell performs like a type of statistical 'and' gate, since it can only feed back signals to the first competitive stage if both of its receptive field branches are sufficiently activated. In response to a continuous image edge, the boundary completion process generates boundary activations simultaneously along the full length of the edge. In response to a widely separated pair of inducers, such as in a Kanizsa square, only a subset of bipole cells may be able to bridge the gap on the first feedback cycle and thereby activate hypercomplex cells near the midpoint of the gap. Then rapid parallel completion by simultaneously acting arrays of bipole cells can occur on the second and subsequent cycles (Grossberg and Mingolla, 1985a). This inward action of the bipole cells enables boundary segmentations to form, as desired, over variable distances in a self-scaling fashion that maintains boundary sharpness, speed of formation, and insensitivity to image noise. Computer simulations showing boundary completion of a circle, a reverse contrast Kanizsa square, and an Ehrenstein figure were first reported in van Allen and Kolodzy (1987). Such a boundary completion process can also complete boundaries across the gaps produced by retinal veins, the blind spot, or other types of retinal noise.

If all the signals to the bipole cells were excitatory, boundary signals could form at inappropriate locations on the image. For example, in a 2D cartoon drawing of a person standing in a grassy field, the horizontal contours where the ground touches the sky do not generate horizontal emergent boundaries that cut the person's vertical body in half. The same is true of many images in which collinear orientations on both sides of a noncollinear region of contours cannot generate emergent boundaries that span, or penetrate, the noncollinear contours. Grossberg and Mingolla (1985b) called this property **spatial impenetrability** and they realized it computationally as follows. Whereas, say, collinear horizontal boundary signals can excite the horizontal bipole cells, vertical boundary signals inhibit horizontal bipole cells. Likewise, horizontal boundary signals inhibit vertical bipole cells. Grossberg and Mingolla (1985b) described a more complex interaction during which, say, vertical on-cells at each location inhibit horizontal on-cells at that location, which disinhibit horizontal off-cells, which inhibit horizontal bipoles that pass through their location. In this scheme horizontal on-cells excite and horizontal off-cells inhibit horizontal bipole cells. This sort of orientation-sensitive inhibition prevents bipole cells from completing boundary signals across contours of different orientation. The net feedback from the bipole cells is then the result of a cooperative-competitive weighting of the relative strength and spatial layout of the variously oriented boundary signals across the scene. Figure 26.4 describes the full BCS consisting of the oriented filters, the first and second competitive stages, and bipole feedback with spatial impenetrability. The two competitive stages and the cooperative feedback loop are referred to as the Cooperative-Competitive Loop (CC Loop).

As noted above, if a stimulus provides inputs to both sides of a bipole receptive field, the feedback from the bipole cell can produce an illusory contour. Consider a horizontal bipole cell centered between two horizontally oriented inducers. The bipole cell receives strong horizontal signals from the inducers on both sides of its receptive field and feeds back a boundary signal midway between the inducers. This new boundary signal can then excite spatial arrays of other bipole cells that complete the entire horizontal illusory line between the inducers.

With some modifications of signal strength and timing, the same process occurs for real contours. The feedback signals will first be strongest in the middle of the contour. The boundary signals in the middle then help to recruit the bipole cells closer to the ends of the contour. The feedback process for both real and illusory contours develops first in the middle of the contour and then grows outward toward the ends. We will show that exactly the opposite happens at stimulus offset. The boundary signals then erode away from the contour ends toward the middle. While Figure 26.1 shows results of theoretical insights of static visual segmentation, the remainder of this chapter is concerned with the problems associated with the need for dynamic reset of such visual segmentations in real time.

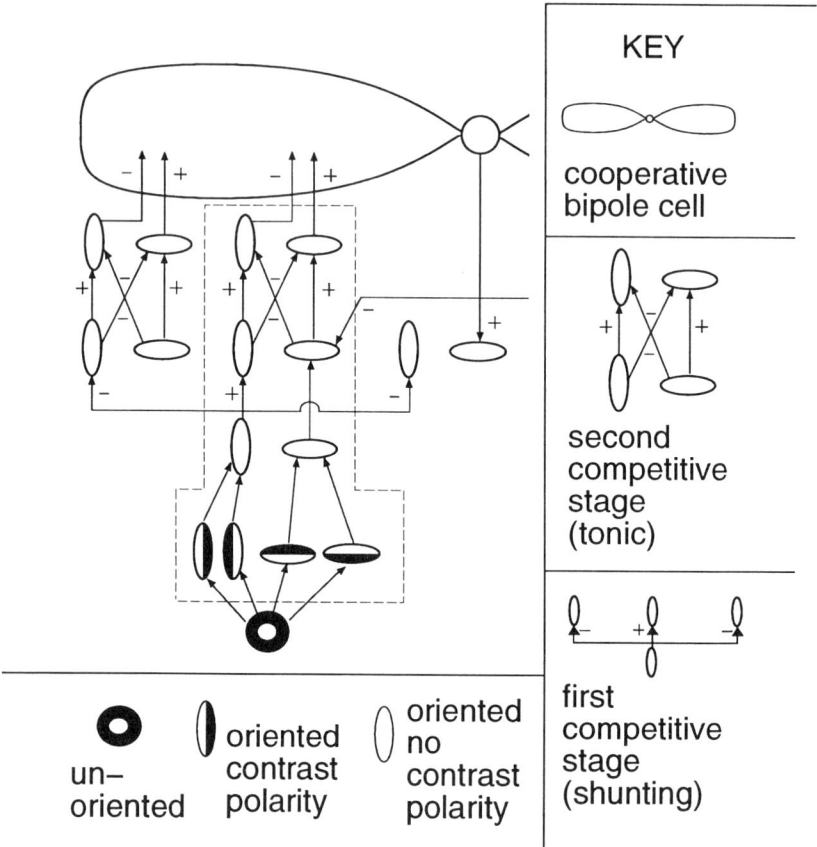

Figure 26.4 *Boundary contour system.*

26.3 Feature binding as a source of visual persistence

In both biological and machine vision systems there are many sources of persistence. In the human visual system, for example, the chemical interactions at the retina and subsequent neural cells throughout the cortex must have persisting activities beyond stimulus offset (Coltheart, 1980; Long and Sakitt, 1980). Similarly, the sensors and electrical circuits of a machine vision system must also have some persistence, although of a much shorter duration than the chemical sources in biological vision. In the context of the BCS, however, the feedback from the cooperative bipole cells to the lower competitive levels is the rate-limiting source of visual persistence within the model. The positive feedback completes an emergent boundary segmentation that coherently binds together appropriate feature combinations in the image. Such a positive feedback process also creates hysteresis which, in the absence of some compensatory reset mechanism, could lead to undesirably long persistence times after stimulus offset. Thus, both biological and machine vision systems can have substantial visual persistence.

Figure 26.5 summarizes these hysteretic properties of the CC Loop. At stimulus offset, the signals from the oriented simple and complex cell filters passively decay away while the signals from the feedback loop persist. Since the bipole cell fires whenever it has sufficient input on both sides of its receptive field, before stimulus offset all boundary signals along the stimulus contour, except those at the ends, receive strong feedback. Unpon stimulus offset, the boundary signals at the ends of the contour receive neither feedback support nor signals from the oriented filter. As a result they quickly fade away. On the other hand, toward the middle of the contour, boundary signals continue to receive bipole feedback even after the signals from the oriented

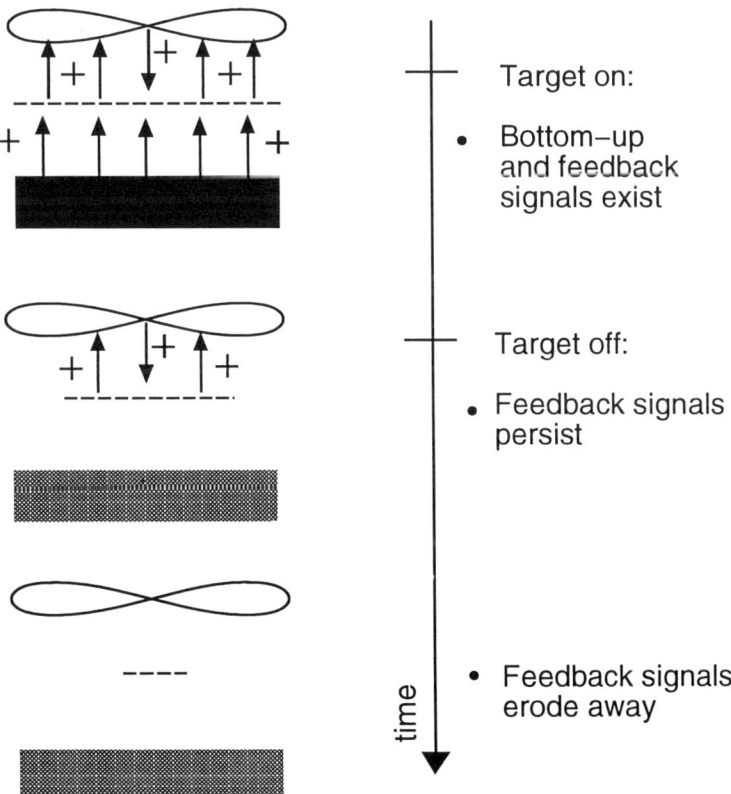

Figure 26.5 *The hysteretic properties of the CC Loop can keep the representation of a stimulus contour active for a significant length of time after a stimulus offset.*

filter have disappeared, because the bipole cells in the middle of the contour continue to receive inputs on both sides. Thus, the CC Loop contour representation erodes away from the ends because as boundary signals fade away, new 'ends' are exposed which do not receive feedback support.

The left side of Figure 26.6 shows a simulation of the hysteretic property of the CC Loop. Each frame shows the strength of the boundary signals at a successive time. The first frame shows the boundary signals with the stimulus

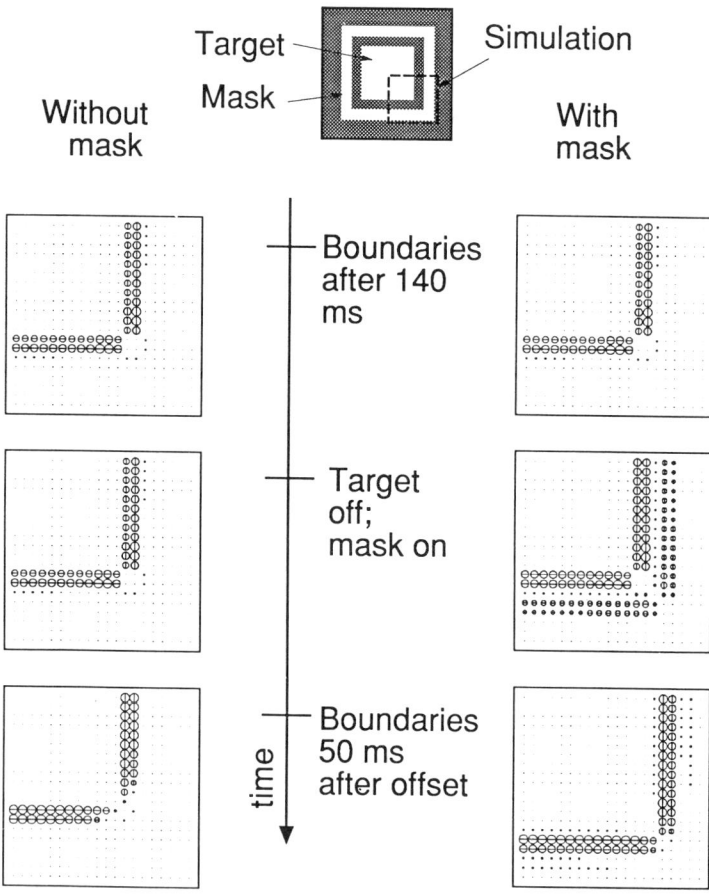

Figure 26.6 *Persistence of boundary signals without (left) and with (right) a subsequent masking stimulus. Boundary strength at each pixel is coded by the size of the circle. Boundary orientation is coded by the orientation of the line inside the circle. Although the entire image plane (shown at top) was simulated, only the lower right corner of the image plane is shown. The presence of the mask's boundary signals inhibits the persisting boundary signals of the target via the first competitive stage. Without such inhibition (left) the target boundaries remain quite strong at the same point in time.*

(a bright square on a dark background) present on the image plane. The next frame shows the boundary signals a few (simulated) milliseconds after removal of the bright square from the image plane. In the second frame the signals at the oriented filters have not yet decayed away, so the boundary signals are essentially unchanged. The final frame shows the boundary signals 50 milliseconds after stimulus offset; the ends of the contour representation, at the corner, have started to disappear, while the middle of the contour representation persists due to the feedback support. Additional frames would show that eventually all boundary signals disappear as the contour representation erodes from the ends. The existence of the boundary signals beyond stimulus offset is assumed to directly relate to subjects' persisting percepts of the stimulus because the filling-in of brightness and color requires the boundary signals to produce a percept. Note that the model predicts the erosion of boundary signals **inward** from the ends of a contour.

Independent of these details, the very existence of an emergent segmentation process that cooperatively binds features together creates a potentially serious problem for the sensory processing of changing imagery. If left unchecked, persistence of the boundaries engendered by a moving stimulus would produce a smear of boundary signals which could seriously hinder object recognition. Thus from a purely computational standpoint, any model of feature binding requires sources of inhibition to control the duration of boundary signals, after the offset of their visual inducers. Grossberg (1991) suggested that the same circuit of on-cells and off-cells that controls spatial impenetrability also controls the rapid reset of resonating segmentations. Properties of binocular rivalry and negative afterimages have also been accounted for by this circuit (Grossberg, 1987b). Our present work computationally develops these qualitative observations into a quantitative model capable of explaining parametric details of the psychophysical data on visual persistence.

26.4 Control of smearing due to moving images

The persistence of boundary signals described in the previous section has the potential to cause massive smearing as an image moves across the retina. Although images moving very quickly can be perceived as a smear, estimates of visual persistence duration suggest that, without some mechanism to inhibit persistence, we should perceive smear at much slower velocities (Burr, 1980). Psychophysical studies of this mechanism have revealed that the duration of persistence for a target stimulus depends on the spatial separation between the target and a subsequently presented masking stimulus. Placing the mask stimulus spatially further away from the target increases the duration of the target's persistence. Thus, inhibition from spatiotemporally nearby stimuli might remove the persistence of trailing representations of a moving stimulus and reduce smearing (Farrell, 1984; DiLollo and Hogben, 1987; Farrell, Pavel

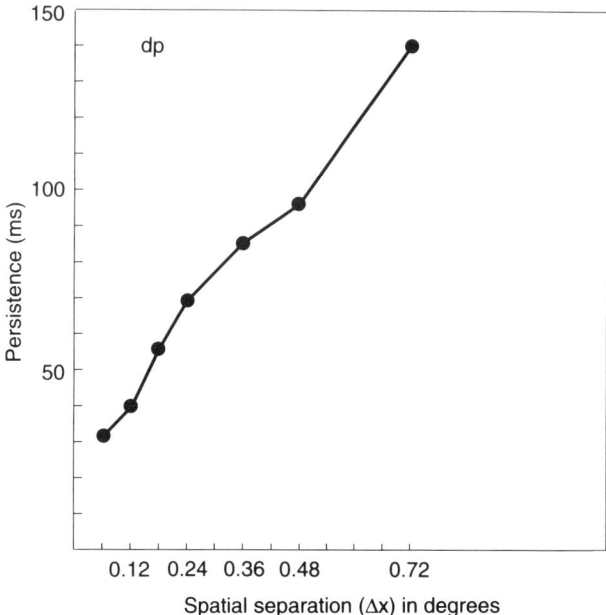

Figure 26.7 *The persistence of thin lines moving in stroboscopic motion depends upon the spatial separation between successive images. (Reprinted with permission from Farrell et al., 1990).*

and Sperling, 1990). Figure 26.7 (from Farrell *et al.*, 1990) illustrates how visual persistence decreases with the spatial separation of the target and masking stimuli.

The presence of a mask apparently inhibits the persistence of the target; and the strength of the inhibition decreases with spatial distance. The BCS contains precisely this type of inhibition (Figure 7.2) in the first competitive stage (Grossberg and Mingolla, 1985b, equation A4). The right side of Figure 26.6 shows how inhibition from the first competitive stage can remove persisting boundaries of the target. In the first frame the image plane contains the target and the system has responded to the boundaries of the image. In the second frame the target has been removed and the masking annulus has been turned on; the BCS then briefly represents the boundaries from both the target and the mask. The final frame shows that 50 milliseconds after target offset, the boundary signals from the mask have completely inhibited the boundary signals of the target. In contrast, without the mask, as on the left side of Figure 26.6, the boundary signals continue to be quite strong 50 milliseconds after target offset.

Figure 26.8 shows a number of such simulations with various spatial separations between the contours of the target and the mask. Within the

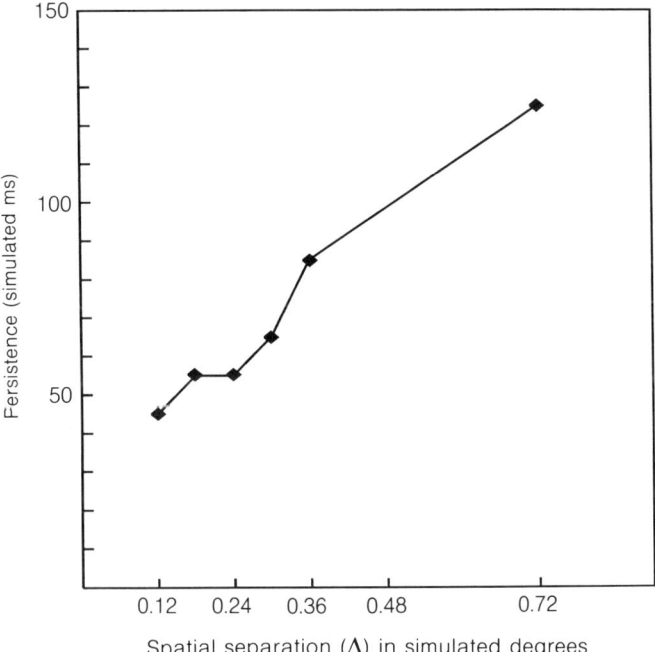

Figure 26.8 *Computer simulation of boundary signal persistence as a function of the spatial separation between contours of the target and the mask. Compare with the data of Farrell* et al. *(1990).*

BCS, persistence of boundary signals increases with spatial separation between the target and mask stimuli. This result should be compared to the data of Farrell *et al.* (1990), shown in Figure 26.7. The close correlation between the modeling and experimental results leads us to propose that the interactions of the first competitive stage provide the spatial inhibition needed to account for the data of Farrell *et al.* (1990).

26.5 Gated dipole: production of a reset signal

Although inhibition from the first competitive stage might prevent smearing of moving stimuli, it does not help to explain the remaining key data on visual persistence. Reviews by Coltheart (1980) and Breitmeyer (1984) conclude that across many experimental methods, visual persistence is inversely related to stimulus duration and stimulus luminance. Figure 26.9 (taken from Bowen, Pola and Matin, 1974) is an excellent example of these properties for one subject. The figure clearly shows that, except for very brief stimuli, persistence is inversely related to luminance; and for each luminance curve, persistence is inversely related to duration.

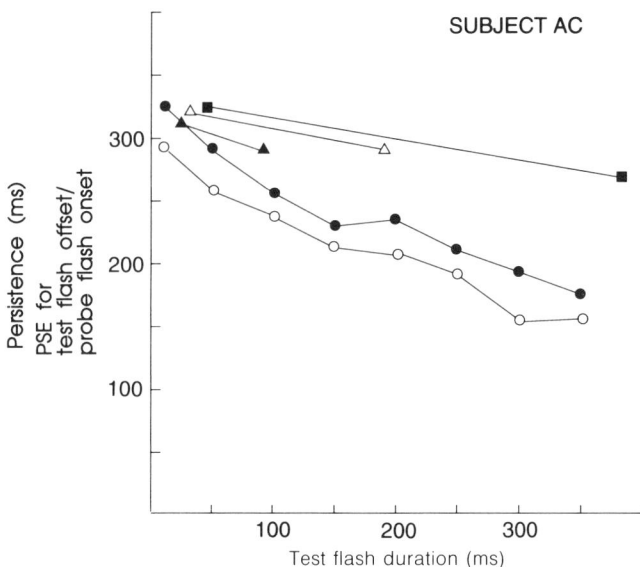

Figure 26.9 *Persistence is inversely related to flash luminance and flash duration. (Reprinted with permission from Bowen* et al., *1974.) Test flash luminance* $+ O$: 0.45 log *FT LAM;* ●: -0.49 log *FT LAM;* ▲: -0.82 log *FT LAM;* △: -1.11 log *FT LAM;* ■: -1.42 log *FT LAM.*

   The inverse relationship between persistence and flash luminance and duration seems paradoxical. Most visual tasks become easier as luminance and duration increase, implying that the visual system creates a strong representation of such images. If the representation of brighter and longer flashes is stronger, then why do they disappear more quickly than dim, brief flashes which presumably are not well represented? We suggest that some source of inhibition at stimulus offset modulates visual persistence. We call this source of inhibition a **reset signal**. The primary issue of this section is to discover how the strength of the reset signal can be made to increase with stimulus duration and luminance. If such a reset signal can be understood, then the data of Bowen *et al.* (1974) can, in principle, be explained because a stronger reset signal will more quickly remove persistence. In this scheme, even though a bright and long flash may create the strongest representation in the visual system, it also produces the strongest reset signal which more quickly removes that representation.

   If a system creates a reset signal, it must respond to the offset of the stimulus. Grossberg (1972) described an opponent processing module called the **gated dipole** which produces a transient off-cell output signal in response to the offset of a stimulus. We use the offset response of a gated dipole as our reset signal. In an early description of the BCS, Grossberg and Mingolla

(1985b) referred to a field of gated dipoles in the discussion of spatial impenetrability. Whereas they modeled the dipoles by a simple subtraction and ignored the slower temporal variables at the gates, we show that full use of the gated dipole provides a reset signal which actively inhibits the persisting stimulus representation in accordance with the data of Bowen *et al.* (1974).

The gated dipole module, shown in Figure 26.10, consists of two competing parallel channels of on-cells and off-cells. The rectangle in each pathway represents a habituating chemical transmitter that gates, or multiplies, the signal in its pathway. The habituation operates on a slower time scale than the action potentials of the neurons. Both channels of the network receive a common tonic input which, without previous or present external inputs, produces no net signal in either channel after competition. Should one channel receive a phasic external input, that channel will produce an output signal and inhibit the opposite channel. As the time plots next to each cell and gate indicate, the transmitter gate in the stimulated channel habituates (because inputs above the tonic level require additional transmitter to send the signal between cells) and the net strength after competition of the on-cell signal drops. Upon stimulus offset, the action potentials of the neurons quickly

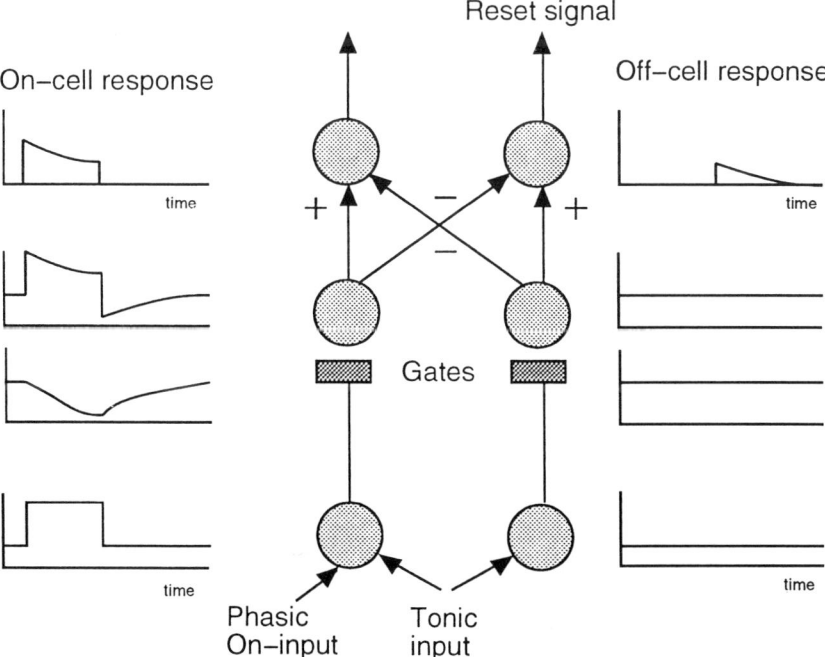

Figure 26.10 *A gated dipole circuit produces a brief off-cell rebound of activity upon offset of a phasic input to the on-cell channel.*

adjust to the tonic input level, but because it has habituated and takes some time to recover, the stimulated on-cell channel now has a net signal below the baseline activity. As a result, the off-cell channel has a net signal larger than that of the stimulated channel. This bias produces a rebound of activity in the non-stimulated off-cell channel. As the stimulated channel recovers from the habituation, the strength of the rebound signal decreases toward zero. Thus offset of the input triggers a neural response which we use as a reset signal to break the feedback hysteresis in the CC Loop and thereby control persistence.

Using a gated dipole to create the reset signal explains why persistence is inversely related to luminance and duration. The greater the strength or duration of a phasic input to a channel in a gated dipole, the more habituated becomes the transmitter gate of that channel, and hence, the stronger is the rebound signal in the non-stimulated channel. A stronger rebound generates

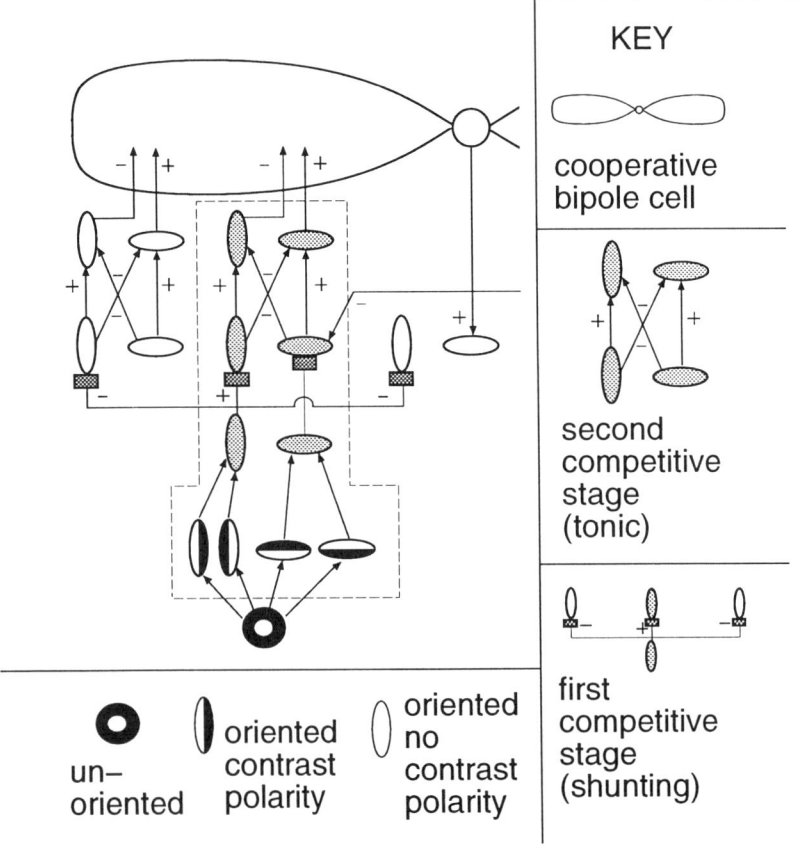

Figure 26.11 *Boundary contour system with embedded gated dipoles.*

a larger reset signal which more quickly inhibits the feedback process and removes persistence.

Figure 26.11 shows a natural way to embed a gated dipole in the BCS. With habituating transmitter gates feeding the competition between orthogonal orientations and a tonic signal to establish a baseline of activity that energizes rebounds, the BCS creates a reset signal at stimulus offset. For example, when stimulated the horizontal pathway habituates, and at offset of the horizontal stimulation the vertical pathway will show a rebound of activity. Through the process of spatial impenetrability, the vertical signal

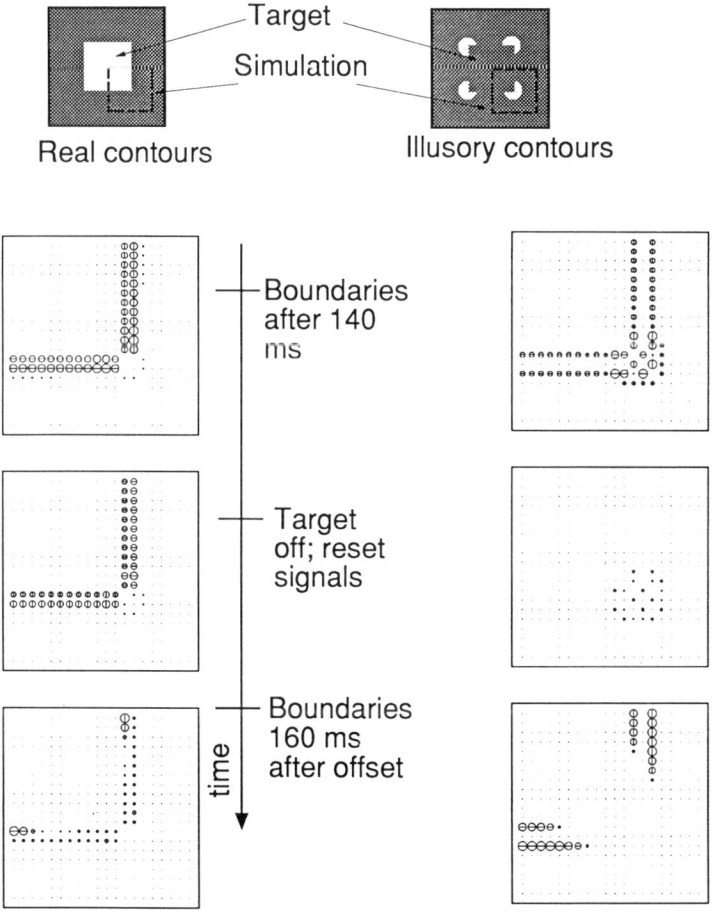

Figure 26.12 *Simulated behavior of the BCS in response to real contour (left) and an illusory contour (right). The illusory contour is more complete at times when the real contour is almost entirely removed due to the fewer reset signals produced by the illusory stimulus.*

inhibits the horizontal bipole cells, weakens the horizontal feedback signals, and thus reduces persistence.

The left side of Figure 26.12 shows a simulation of the BCS with reset signals created by a gated dipole. In the first frame the system accurately represents the horizontal and vertical boundaries of the square stimulus. The next frame shows the reset signals produced shortly after offset of the square. Careful examination of the icons reveals that wherever there is a vertical (horizontal) boundary signal in the first frame there is a corresponding horizontal (vertical) reset signal in the second frame. The final frame shows the boundary signals 160 milliseconds after the square offset. Nearly all of the boundary signals have been removed.

The results of a number of simulations of the BCS with gated dipoles are shown in Figure 26.13 which shows how stimulus luminance and duration modulates the persistence of the boundary signals. The results are quite similar to the data of Bowen *et al.* (1974), shown in Figure 26.9. In particular,

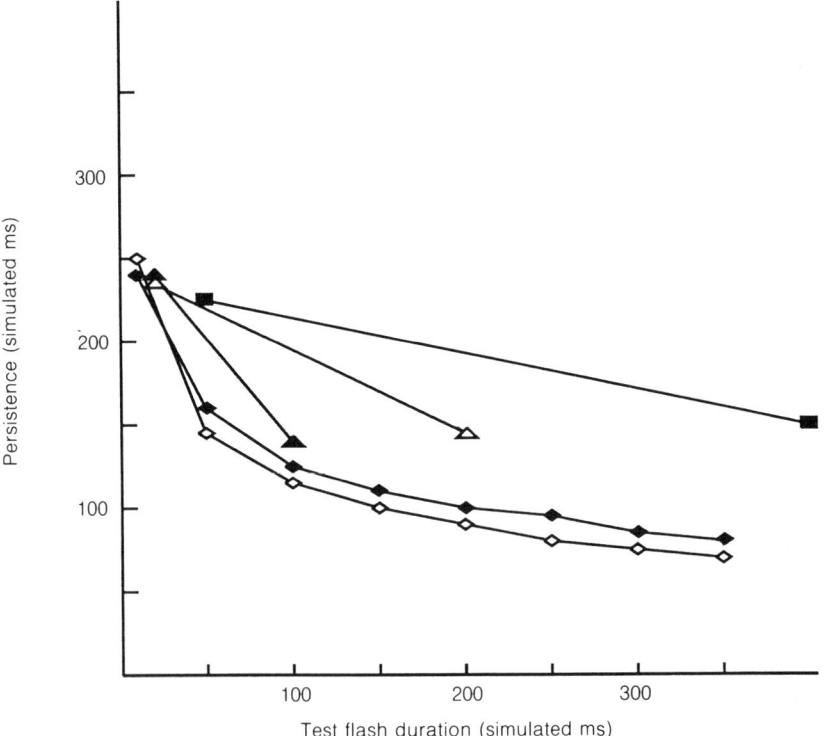

Figure 26.13 *Computer simulation of boundary signal persistence as a function of flash duration and luminance. Compare with the data of Bowen* et al. *(1974). Simulated test flash luminance* $-\diamondsuit$: *+0.45 log FT LAM;* $\blacklozenge$: *−0.49 log FT LAM;* $\blacktriangle$: *−0.82 log FT LAM;* $\triangle$: *−1.11 log FT LAM;* $\blacksquare$: *−1.42 log FT LAM.*

persistence of boundary signals is inversely related to both stimulus luminance and duration.

While **global** properties of the system produce persistence, **local** mechanisms produce reset signals. This distinction becomes particularly relevant for the reset of illusory contours.

26.6 Persistence of illusory contours

The above description of the BCS suggested how illusory contours are formed. In this section we suggest how illusory contours are reset. Meyer and Ming (1988) compared the persistence of real and illusory contours. Figure 26.14 shows that illusory contours persist substantially longer than real contours. Perceptually, subjects reported that after the inducers disappeared the illusory contour appeared to persist by itself. Figure 26.14 also indicates that the duration of persistence for illusory contours is not inversely related to stimulus duration but peaks at some intermediate duration.

Neurophysiological support for the extended persistence of illusory contours comes from a study by von der Heydt and Peterhans (1989). Figure 26.15 shows the responses of a cell in V2 to a real contour and an illusory contour.

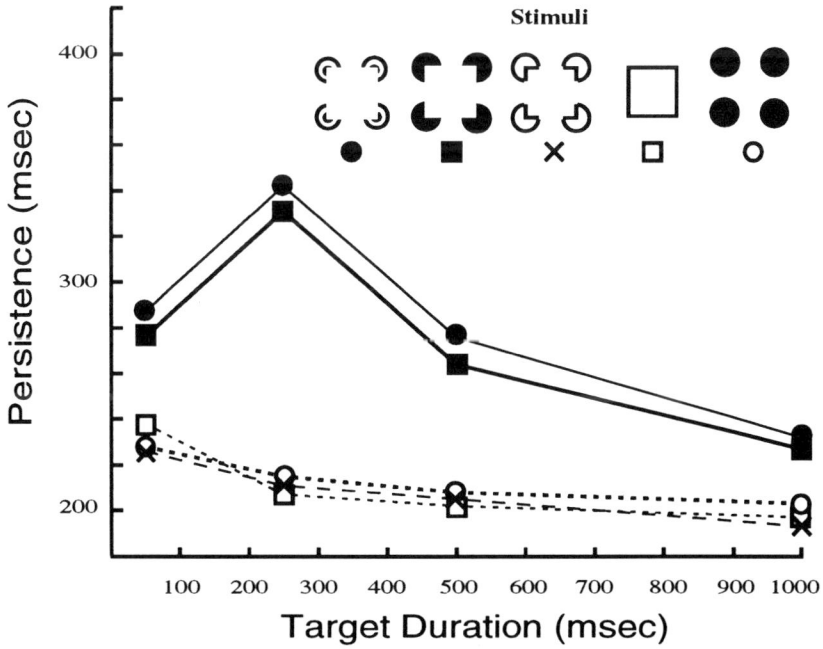

Figure 26.14 *Persistence of illusory contours is greater than persistence of real contours. Persistence of illusory contours is maximal at an intermediate duration of the stimulus. (Reprinted with permission from Meyer and Ming, 1988.)*

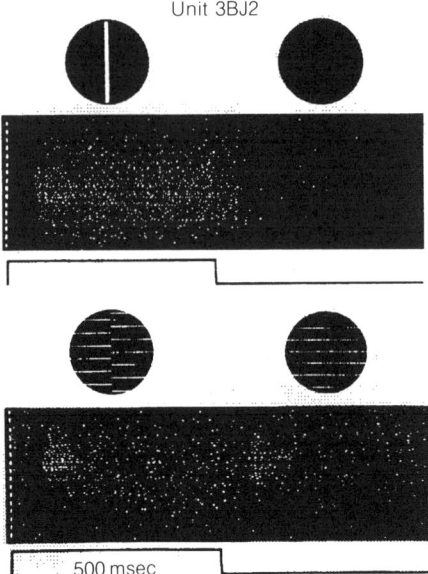

Figure 26.15 *Behavior of one cortical cell in response to onset and offset of a real (top) and illusory (bottom) contour. Each row, indicated by the white bars to the left, marks a different orientation of the stimulus. Each white dot in the row marks an action potential of the cell at a specific point in time. The response of the cell to the illusory contour persists longer than the response to the real contour. (Reprinted with permission from von der Heydt and Peterhans, 1989.)*

Although the cell responds well to both contours, after stimulus offset its firing rate remains high longer for an illusory contour than for a real contour. It should be noted that the model of illusory contour formation proposed by Peterhans and von der Heydt (1989) contains only feedforward interactions that cannot explain the different offset behaviors of this cell.

In contrast, the BCS with the gated dipole can explain the extended persistence of illusory contours. Figure 26.16 shows in cartoon format the reason that illusory contours persist longer than real contours. As is schematized on the left side of the figure, both real contours and illusory inducing contours can produce similar boundary signals, in this case in the shape of a square. At stimulus offset, however, real contours produce reset signals (gray oriented lines) everywhere along the contour, while a stimulus with an illusory contour produces reset signals only at the inducers. With fewer reset signals to inhibit the feedback process, illusory contours persist longer than real contours.

Figure 26.12 shows a computer simulation of the differences in boundary signal persistence for a real contour and an illusory contour. In the first frame of each simulation, the bright square or the illusory contour inducers

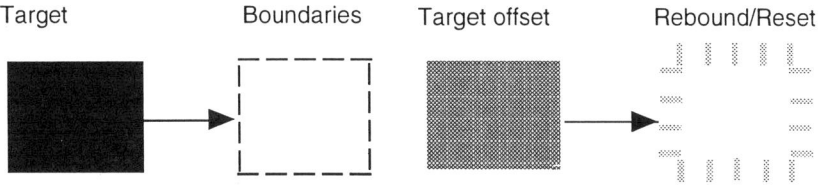

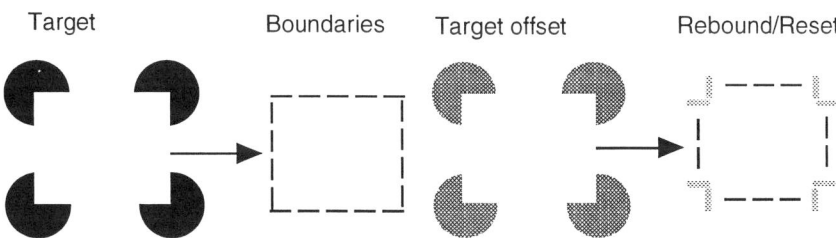

Figure 26.16 *During presentation of a real contour or an illusory contour the boundary signals are similar. At stimulus offset, however, the real contour produces reset signals all along the contour, whereas the illusory contour produces reset signals only at the location of the inducers. The fewer signals allow the illusory contour to persist for longer.*

at the image plane produce strong boundary signals along both real and illusory contours. Shortly after stimulus offset the reset signals, as shown in the second set of frames, inhibit the feedback. Although the real contour produces reset signals wherever there is a boundary signal in the first frame, the image with an illusory contour produces reset signals only at the location of the illusory contour inducers. The final frame shows the significance of the different reset signals. At 160 milliseconds after offset of each stimulus the boundary signals of the real contour are almost entirely removed, but the signals for the illusory contour remain quite evident.

Figure 26.17 presents the results of parametric simulations of this type, with appropriate variations in stimulus duration but identical parameters. Figure 26.17 shows that the boundary signals in the BCS persist in a manner quite similar to the results of Meyer and Ming (1988) summarized in Figure 26.14. As in the data, an intermediate stimulus duration produces the longest persistence of an illusory contour in the model, because it takes a significant length of time for the illusory contour to reach its full strength via cooperative feedback in the CC Loop. As a result, very brief stimuli are not strongly represented and more easily fade away, while stimuli of much longer durations create very strong reset signals which more quickly remove the persisting

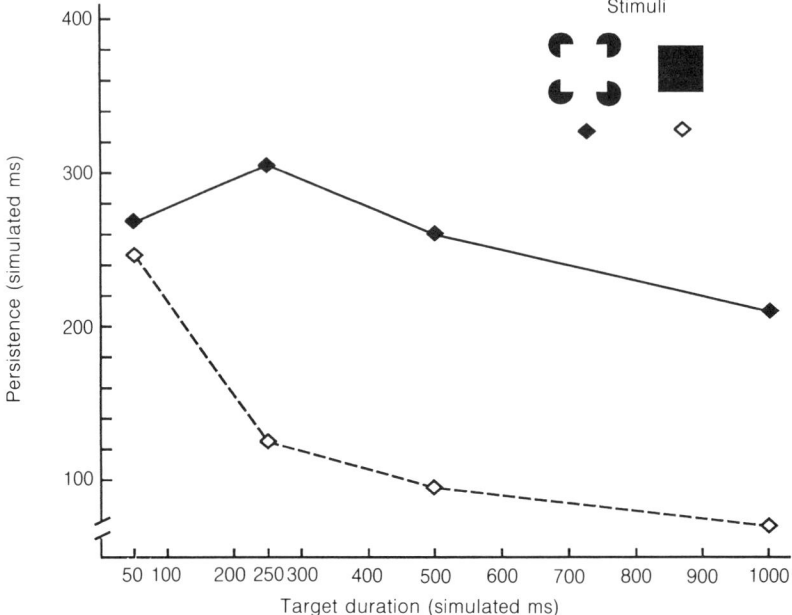

Figure 26.17 *Computer simulation of real and illusory boundary persistence as a function of flash duration. The boundaries produced in response to the illusory contours persist longer than the boundaries produced in response to the real contours. Persistence of illusory contours peaks at an intermediate stimulus duration, as in Figure 26.13.*

representation. Stimuli of intermediate durations establish a strong feedback hysteresis, but do not create particularly strong reset signals at stimulus offset. Real contours can more quickly instigate the feedback process and so do not generally violate the inverse relationship between persistence and stimulus duration (but see data in Haber and Standing, 1970, which shows that under some conditions very brief veridical stimuli have little persistence).

26.7 Conclusions

This chapter has described a model architecture for visual processing, demonstrated the abilities of the system to handle real-world images, and shown that its behavior matches key psychophysical data on visual persistence. A key point in this discussion is that the visual system requires a cooperative-competitive feedback process to rapidly choose from the infinitude of possible completions within a spatial distribution of boundary signals. The necessity of feedback means that both machine and biological vision systems must control persistence to prevent smearing and temporal interference.

   In addition to the data described in this chapter, our analysis explains how orientation-specific adaptation modulates visual persistence (Meyer, Lawson and Cohen, 1975), and why high spatial frequency gratings persist longer than low spatial frequency gratings (Meyer and Maguire, 1981). A discussion of these topics and a further description of the computer simulations can be found in Francis, Grossberg and Mingolla (1992).

We have shown how a quantitative development and analysis of the BCS/FCS architecture can offer new mechanistic and functional explanations of data on such phenomena as visual persistence. These explanations preserve the theory's previous explanations of boundary completion, texture segmentation, shape-from-shading, and 3D vision, while extending its explanatory range still further into the difficult temporal phenomena of visual persistence. The functional role of the feature binding and reset mechanisms responsible for persistence suggests links between persistence and fundamental issues in the formation and breakup of groupings in a dynamically fluctuating environment. Thus, data on persistence provides important clues about some of the most fundamental processes of preattentive vision, and neural models that are being devised to explain and simulate them.

References

Beck, J., Graham, N. and Sutter, A. (1991) Lightness differences and the perceived segregation of regions and populations. *Perception & Psychophysics*, **49**, 257–69.

Bowen, R., Pola, J. and Matin, L. (1974) Visual persistence: Effects of flash luminance, duration and energy. *Vision Research*, **14**, 295–303.

Breitmeyer, B. (1984) *Visual Masking: An Integrative Approach*. Oxford University Press, New York, NY.

Burr, D. (1980) Motion smear. *Nature*, **284**, 164–5.

Cohen, M. and Grossberg, S. (1984) Neural dynamics of brightness perception: Features, boundaries, diffusion, and resonance. *Perception & Psychophysics*, **36**, 428–56.

Coltheart, M. (1980) Iconic memory and visible persistence. *Perception & Psychophysics*, **27**, 183–228.

Cruthirds, D., Gove, A., Grossberg, S., Mingolla, E., Nowak, N. and Williamson, J. (1992) Processing of synthetic aperture radar images by the boundary contour system and feature contour system. *Technical Report CAS/CNS-92-010*, Boston University, Boston, MA.

DeYoe, E. and van Essen, D. (1988) Concurrent processing streams in monkey visual cortex. *Vision Research*, **22**, 545–59.

DiLollo, V. and Hogben, J. (1987) Suppression of visible persistence as a function of spatial separation between inducing stimuli. *Perception & Psychophysics*, **41**, 345–54.

Farrell, J. (1984) Visible persistence of moving objects. *Journal of Experimental Psychology: Human Perception and Performance*, **10**, 502–11.

Farrell, J., Pavel, M. and Sperling, G. (1990) The visible persistence of stimuli in stroboscopic motion. *Vision Research*, **30**, 921–36.

Francis, G., Grossberg, S. and Mingolla, E. (1992) Cortical dynamics of feature binding and reset: Control of visual persistence. *Technical Report CAS/CNS-92-026*, Boston University, Boston, MA.

Gerrits, H. and Vendrik, A. (1970) Simultaneous contrast, filling-in process and information processing in man's visual system. *Experimental Brain Research*, **11**, 411–30.

Grossberg, S. (1972) A neural theory of punishment and avoidance: II. Quantitative theory. *Mathematical Biosciences*, **15**, 253–85.

Grossberg, S. (1976) Adaptive pattern classification and universal recoding, II: Feedback, expectation, olfaction, and illusions. *Biological Cybernetics*, **23**, 187–202.

Grossberg, S. (1980) How does the brain build a cognitive code? *Psychological Review*, **87**, 1–57.

Grossberg, S. (1983) The quantized geometry of visual space: The coherent computation of depth, form, and lightness. *Behavioral and Brain Sciences*, **6**, 625–92.

Grossberg, S. (1984) Outline of a theory of brightness, color, and form perception, in *Trends in Mathematical Psychology* (eds. E. Degreef and J. van Buggenhaut), Elsevier/North-Holland, Amsterdam, pp. 59–86.

Grossberg, S. (1987a) Cortical dynamics of three-dimensional form, color, and brightness perception I: Monocular theory. *Perception & Psychophysics*, **41**, 97–116.

Grossberg, S. (1987b) Cortical dynamics of three-dimensional form, color, and brightness perception II: Binocular theory. *Perception & Psychophysics*, **41**, 117–58.

Grossberg, S. (1991) Why do parallel cortical systems exist for the perception of static form and moving form? *Perception & Psychophysics*, **49**, 117–41.

Grossberg, S. (1992) 3-D vision and figure-ground separation by visual cortex. *Technical Report CAS/CNS-Tr-92-019*, Boston University, Boston, MA.

Grossberg, S. and Mingolla, E. (1985a) Neural dynamics of form perception: Boundary completion, illusory figures, and neon color spreading. *Psychological Review*, **92**, 173–211.

Grossberg, S. and Mingolla, E. (1985b) Neural dynamics of perceptual grouping: Textures, boundaries, and emergent segmentations. *Perception & Psychophysics*, **38**, 141–71.

Grossberg, S. and Mingolla, E. (1987) Neural dynamics of surface perception: Boundary webs, illuminants, and shape-from-shading. *Computer Vision, Graphics, & Image Processing*, **37**, 116–65.

Grossberg, S. and Mingolla, E. (1992) Neural dynamics of visual motion perception: Local detection and global grouping, in *Neural Networks for Vision and Image Processing*, (eds. G. Carpenter and S. Grossberg), MIT Press, Cambridge, MA, 293–342.

Grossberg, S., Mingolla, E. and Todorović, D. (1989) A neural network architecture for preattentive vision. *IEEE Transactions on Biomedical Engineering*, **36**, 65–84.

Grossberg, S. and Todorović, D. (1988) Neural dynamics of 1-D and 2-D brightness perception: A unified model of classical and recent phenomena. *Perception & Psychophysics*, **43**, 241–77.

Haber, R. and Standing, L. (1970) Direct estimates of the apparent duration of a flash. *Canadian Journal of Psychology*, **24**, 216–29.

Hubel, D. and Wiesel, T. (1965) Receptive fields and functional architecture in two nonstriate visual areas (18 and 19) of the cat. *Journal of Neurophysiology*, **28**, 229–89.

Hubel, D. and Wiesel, T. (1977) Functional architecture of macaque monkey visual cortex. *Proceedings of the Royal Society of London (B)*, **198**, 1–59.

Long, G. and Sakitt, B. (1980) The retinal basis of iconic memory: Eriksen and Collins revisited. *American Journal of Psychology*, **93**, 195–207.

Meyer, G., Lawson, R. and Cohen, W. (1975) The effects of orientation-specific adaptation on the duration of short-term visual storage. *Vision Research*, **15**, 569–72.

Meyer, G. and Maguire, C. (1981) Effects of spatial-frequency specific adaptation and target duration on visual persistence. *Journal of Experimental Psychology: Human Perception and Performance*, 7, 151–6.

Meyer, G. and Ming, C. (1988) The visible persistence of illusory contours. *Canadian Journal of Psychology*, **42**, 479–88.

Orban, G., Kato, H. and Bishop, P. (1979) Dimensions and properties of end-zone inhibitory areas in receptive fields of hypercomplex cells in cat striate cortex. *The Journal of Neurophysiology*, **42**, 833–49.

Peterhans, E. and von der Heydt, R. (1989) Mechanisms of contour perception in monkey visual cortex II. Contours bridging gaps. *The Journal of Neuroscience*, **9**, 1749–63.

Sutter, A., Beck, J. and Graham, N. (1989) Contrast and spatial variables in texture segregation: Testing a simple spatial-frequency channels model. *Perception & Psychophysics*, **46**, 312–32.

Todd, J. and Akerstrom, R. (1987) Perception of three-dimensional form from patterns of optical texture. *Journal of Experimental Psychology: Human Perception and Performance*, **13**, 242–55.

Todorović, D. (1987) The Craik–O'Brien-Cornsweet effect: New varieties and their theoretical implications. *Perception & Psychophysics*, **42**, 545–60.

van Allen, E. and Kolodzy, P. (1987) Application of a boundary contour neural network to illusions and infrared sensor imagery, in *Proceedings of the IEEE First International Conference on Neural Networks, IV*, (eds. M. Caudill and C. Butler), IEEE Press, Piscataway, NJ, pp 193–7.

von der Heydt, R. and Peterhans, E. (1989) Mechanisms of contour perception in monkey visual cortex. I. Lines of pattern discontinuity. *The Journal of Neuroscience*, **9**, 1731–48.

von der Heydt, R., Peterhans, E. and Baumgartner, G. (1984) Illusory contours and cortical neuron responses. *Science*, **224**, 1260–2.

Recognition of space-time gestures using a distributed representation

TREVOR J. DARRELL and ALEX P. PENTLAND

Vision and Modeling Group, The Media Laboratory, Massachusetts Institute of Technology, 20 Ames St., Cambridge, MA 02139, USA

27.1 Introduction

The location and orientation of head, hand and eyes is a critical element of all human dialog. The ability to follow objects moving through space and recognize particular motions as meaningful gestures is therefore essential if computer systems are to interact naturally with human users (Bolt, 1984; Negroponte, 1980). Currently, however, this information is largely unavailable to computing machines. An important new application of machine vision, therefore, is to extend the interface between man and machine, allowing the machine to directly perceive what its user is doing (Mase, 1991; Torige and Kono, 1992; Yamato *et al.*, 1992; Ishibuchi *et al.*, 1992). This chapter reports a system that can recover such information in real time, so that it can help mediate human–machine interaction.

To accomplish this goal, we have adopted a view-based representation of objects and actions, since such an approach places few restrictions on the range of shapes and behaviors that can be described. This allows us to model complex, articulated objects for which no simple 3D model or recovery method is available. Moreover, the use of a view-based approach allows us to learn our models by observation, rather than needing precise CAD models.

The drawback of such an approach is that complex, articulated objects (such as hands) have a very large range of appearances, making traditional approaches to view-based matching difficult. We have therefore adopted a

Artificial Neural Networks for Speech and Vision. Edited by Richard J. Mammone. Published in 1993 by Chapman & Hall, London. ISBN 0 412 54850 X

representation based on **interpolation** of appearance from a relatively small number of views. This is similar to the ideas of Ullman and Basri (1991) and Poggio and Edelman (1990) for representing 3D objects by interpolating between a small set of 2D views. We are extending this idea in two ways: first, by building the representation using an ensemble of matched filters rather than feature sets; and second, by addressing the problem of recognizing the behavior of articulated objects in space-time.

In our system the match statistic is the normalized correlation between the image and a set of learned **view models**. Each model is based on one or more example images of a view of an object, from which mean and variance statistics about each pixel in the view are computed. The view models capture the reliable portions of the appearance of a particular view of an object, and exclude pattern details that vary across learning trials. Areas with highlights and high-frequency geometric details are typically excluded from a view model.

A particular view model will have a range of parameter values of a given transformation (e.g. rotation, scale, articulation) for which the match statistic shows a roughly convex 'tuning curve'. If we have a set of views models which sample the transformation parameter finely enough, we can infer the actual transform parameters for new views by examining the **set** of model correlation scores. For example, Figure 27.1a shows three images of an eyeball that were used to create view models for gaze tracking; one looking 30 degrees left, one looking center-on, and one looking 30° to the right. The three views span a $\pm 30°$ subspace of the gaze direction parameter. Figure 27.1b,c,d shows the normalized correlation score for each view model when tracking a rotating eyeball. Since the tuning curves produced by these models are fairly broad with respect to gaze angle, one could interpolate from their responses to obtain a good estimate of the true angle.

For a correctly-chosen set of view models, the set of correlation scores is theoretically adequate to permit recovery of the object's parameter values. However this requires knowing the parameter values associated with each model, information that is often difficult to obtain. Fortunately, this information is not required to recognize stereotyped behaviors, such as the hand gestures shown in Figure 29.2. Because the parameter values underlying the object pose are associated with the set of correlation scores, we can characterize a behavior by the pattern of view model scores directly.

To recognize a gesture in this way we first measure the scores of a set of view models for each frame of an image sequence. Then instead of deriving parameter values from this data, we ask which known behavior (gesture) most closely matches the observed **space-time** pattern of model scores. That is, rather than transforming sets of view model scores to parameters and then matching in parameter space, we match in the model-score space directly. This allows us to recognize gestures without explicit knowledge of the transformation parameters.

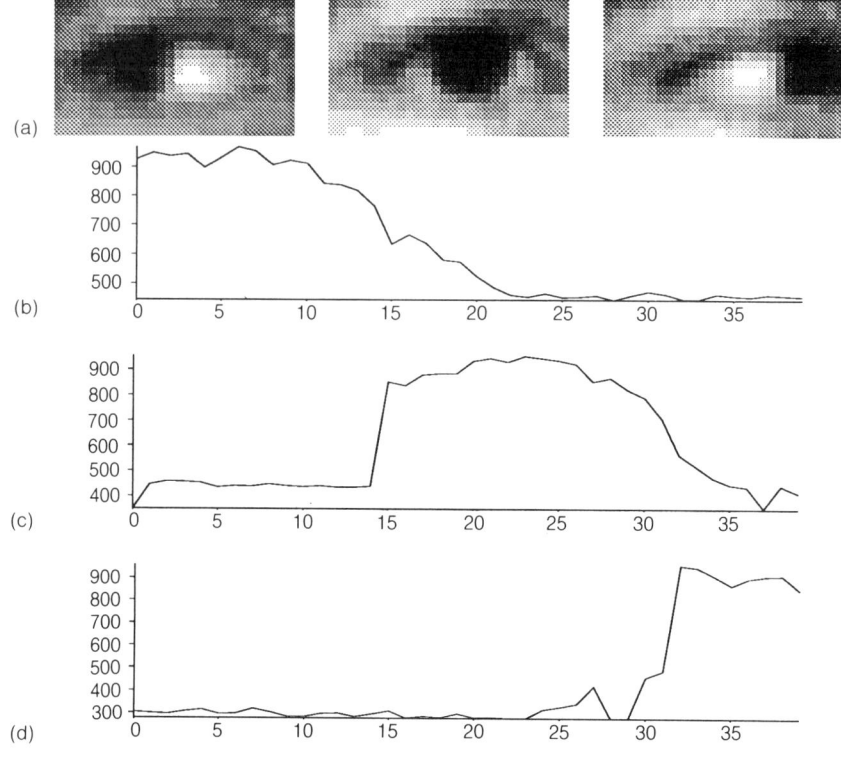

Figure 27.1 *(a) Three views of an eyeball: + 30°, 0° and − 30° of gaze angle; (b) normalized correlation scores of the + 30° view model when tracking a eyeball rotating from approximately − 30° to + 30° of gaze angle; (c) score for 0° view model; (d) score for − 30° model.*

The domain of human gesture recognition seems particularly promising for this approach. It is known, for instance, that the human ability to interpret American Sign Language remains accurate even for 32 × 32 pixel high-contrast images with a frame rate of 16 images per second (Sperling *et al.*, 1985). The ability to 'read' sign language from very low-resolution, poor quality imagery indicates that humans do not require precise contours, shading, texture, or 3D properties. What they require is a coarse 2D description of hand appearance and an accurate representation of the hand's 2D trajectory. This mix of coarse 2D shape information and precise trajectory information is exactly what a fast, view-based interpolation approach can hope to provide.

We have implemented a system which automatically builds a view-based object model and its contextual dependencies while tracking the object through space and time. Special hardware for real-time normalized correla-

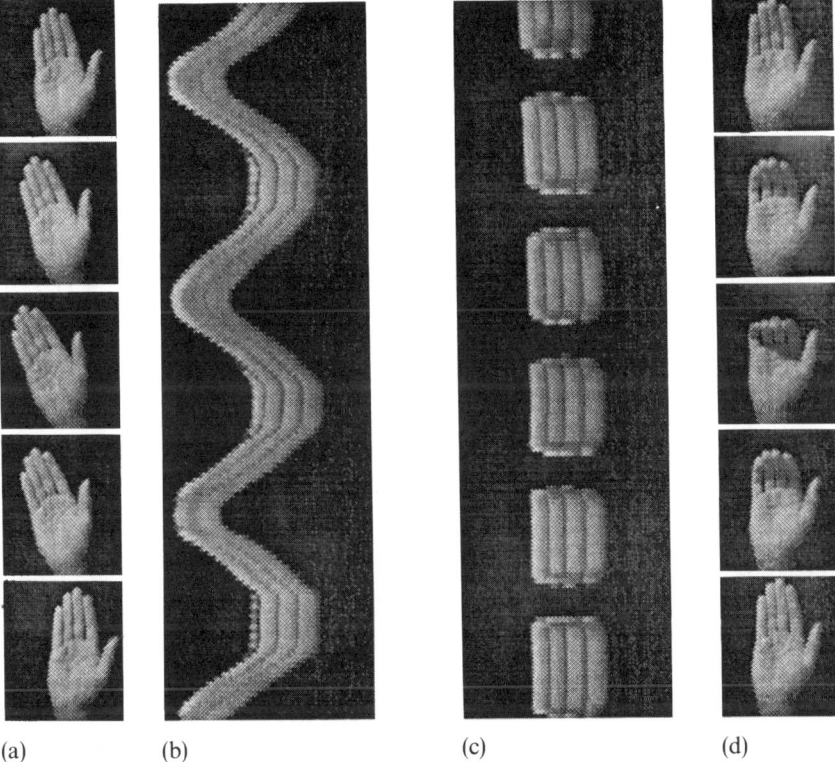

(a)   (b)   (c)   (d)

Figure 27.2 *Space-time pattern of two hand waving gestures. (a,b) 'hello', (c,d)*
'goodbye'. (a) and (d) show frame numbers 0, 5, 10, 15, 20 sampled from a sequence of
70 frames; (b) and (c) show a horizontal spatio-temporal slice through the sequence,
taken just above the position of the thumb in the image.

tion is used to match views in 2D images, the results of which are integrated
over time to match gestures in 3D (e.g. to match a space time sequence of
views). The following sections discuss in detail the view-based model acquisition and context sensitive searching, and then the extension to model and
recognize gestures. We will show results of a real-time implementation
tracking simple and complex objects, and on recognizing the hand gestures
shown in Figure 27.2.

27.2 Learning view models

A key problem for this approach is how to learn an appropriate set of view
models, given the requirement that they adequately sample the parameters
of the transformations an object may undergo. For simple transforms such
as rotation or scale, analytic methods can often provide an optimal set of

sample points. For more complex situations, such as articulated or unfamiliar objects, we have no adequate analytic model. Therefore, we have developed a data-driven method of automatically constructing a set of view models whose normalized correlation scores can be meaningfully interpolated.

27.2.1 Correlation-based search

Our tracking system performs a normalized correlation search using a set of view models. Given a set of models indexed by the variable m, $1 \leqslant m \leqslant M$, the search function is

$$R_m(i, j)$$
$$= \frac{n_m \sum_{V_m(u,v) < \gamma} T_m(u, v) I(i + u, j + v) - \sum_{V_m(u,v) < \gamma} T_m(u, v) \sum_{V_m(u,v) < \gamma} I(i + u, j + v)}{n_m^2 \sigma_I \sigma_{T_m}}.$$

(1)

where $T_m()$, $V_m()$ are the mean and variance of pixels in the set of example images for model m, $I()$ is the new image being searched, n_m is the number of valid pixel locations in the view model, γ is the 'don't-care' threshold on model variance, and σ_I, σ_{T_m} are the standard deviation of the offset and model images, respectively:

$$\sigma_I = \sqrt{\frac{1}{n_m} \sum_{V_m(u,v) < \gamma} I^2(i + u, j + v) - \left(\frac{1}{n_m} \sum_{V_m(u,v) < \gamma} I(i + u, j + v)\right)^2}$$

$$\sigma_{T_m} = \sqrt{\frac{1}{n_m} \sum_{V_m(u,v) < \gamma} T_m^2(u, v) - \left(\frac{1}{n_m} \sum_{V_m(u,v) < \gamma} T_m(u, v)\right)^2}.$$

We find the spatial maxima and the corresponding image offsets for each view model:

$$r_m - \max_{i,j} r_m(i, j); \quad (x_m, y_m) = \arg \max_{i,j} r_m(i, j).$$

27.2.2 Adaptive model acquisition

The system begins with one initial model ($M = 1$), specified by the user using a cursor. The target object is then tracked by using the search function given above. When the search function score falls below a certain threshold a new model is added to the search set, using the image at the offset associated with the current best score. Over time, this results in a family of view models that sample the aspect space. Once a fixed set of models has been acquired, the system can update the pixel statistics for each model using a nearest-neighbor refinement rule.

Adding view models   A new view model is added when the current maximum correlation score is degraded, but the system has not completely lost track of the model (i.e. if the object is completely removed from the field of view). A threshold θ_0 establishes the 'base' tracking level, below which we assume we have lost track of the object. A second threshold, $\theta_1, \theta_1 < \theta_0$ sets the level at which a new model should be added. The full rule is given by

Let $m^* = \arg \max_{1 \leqslant m \leqslant M} r_m$

If $\theta_0 < r_{m^*} < \theta_1$ $\qquad\qquad\qquad\qquad\qquad\qquad (2)$

Then $T_M(i,j) = I(x_{m^*} + i, y_{m^*} + j), \quad 1 \leqslant i, j \leqslant \sqrt{n_M} \quad M = M + 1,$

where n_M is the number of pixels in the initial view model. In the current system the size of the view model is set by the user when specifying the initial model. However, during the refinement phase described below pixel variances are computed and unreliable pixels effectively removed from the model, thus allowing it to have variable size. (During model acquisition the model variance is undefined, and is ignored by the search function.)

The relationship of these thresholds is shown diagrammatically in Figure 27.3. Currently they are set by the user after an initial training phase which establishes the sensitivity of the view model matches. For all of the examples in this chapter we used $\theta_0 = 0.6$ and $\theta_1 = 0.7$. We are currently exploring additional techniques to automatically set these thresholds by specifying a desired number of view models.

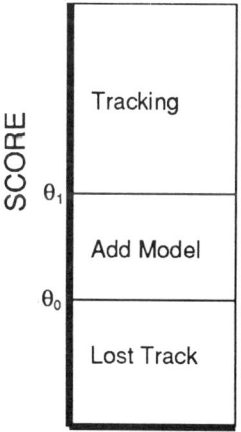

Figure 27.3 *States in adaptive model training as a function of the current maximum model score. When the current score is degraded but still above a minimum 'lost-track' threshold, a new model is added using an image centered at the current track position.*

Refining view models   Once a fixed number of view models has been found to coarsely interpolate the set of observed images, one can refine the view models by collecting statistics about multiple images of each view. Using a nearest-neighbor update rule, the models can be modified so that they optimally cover the view space in terms of RMS error (Makhoul *et al.*, 1985). The refinement stage functions by first classifying new images as nearest to one of the existing models, and then modifying the pixel statistics for that model. In this way we compute the pixel variance $V_m(u, v)$ used by the search function.

Example of data-driven model acquisition   For simple objects and transformations, this adaptive scheme can build a model which adequately covers the entire space of possible views. For example, for a convex rigid body undergoing a 1D rotation with fixed relative illumination, a relatively small number of view models can suffice to track and interpolate the position of the object at any rotation. Figure 27.4 illustrates this with a simple example of a rotating box. The adaptive tracking scheme was run with a camera viewing a box suspended by wire. (The axis of rotation was not parallel to any of the three principle axes of the box.) Figure 27.4a shows the view models in use when the algorithm converged, and all possible rotations were matched with $r_{m^*} > \theta_0$. To demonstrate the tuning properties of each model under rotation, Figure 27.4b shows the correlation scores for each model plotted as a function of input frame number of a demonstration sequence. In this sequence the box was held fixed at its initial position for the first five frames, and then rotated continuously from 0–340 degrees. The responses of each model are broadly tuned as a function of object angle, with a small number of models sufficing to represent/interpolate the object at all rotations.

27.3 Using temporal context to guide search

For a static search task, the search rule specified above evaluates the correlation score for each model and picks the maximum. If, however, we are processing a stream of video images, we can exploit temporal correlation between frames of an image sequence to make the search task more efficient.

If the rate of temporal sampling is fast enough, an object can only move a limited amount from frame to frame. Thus we can spatially restrict our search to be within a window around x_{m^*}, y_{m^*}, if our current match score is above the base threshold ($r_{m^*} > \theta_0$). (If we have more prior knowledge about the object being tracked, we can also use a more powerful predictive model incorporating the object dynamics.) If the object is not found within the reduced window, then the current position information is considered invalid and an exhaustive search is conducted over the entire image.

Similarly, by modeling the expected view model score conditional on the current scores, we can predict which views will most likely be seen at the next instant. When a particular view of an object is seen at one instant, not

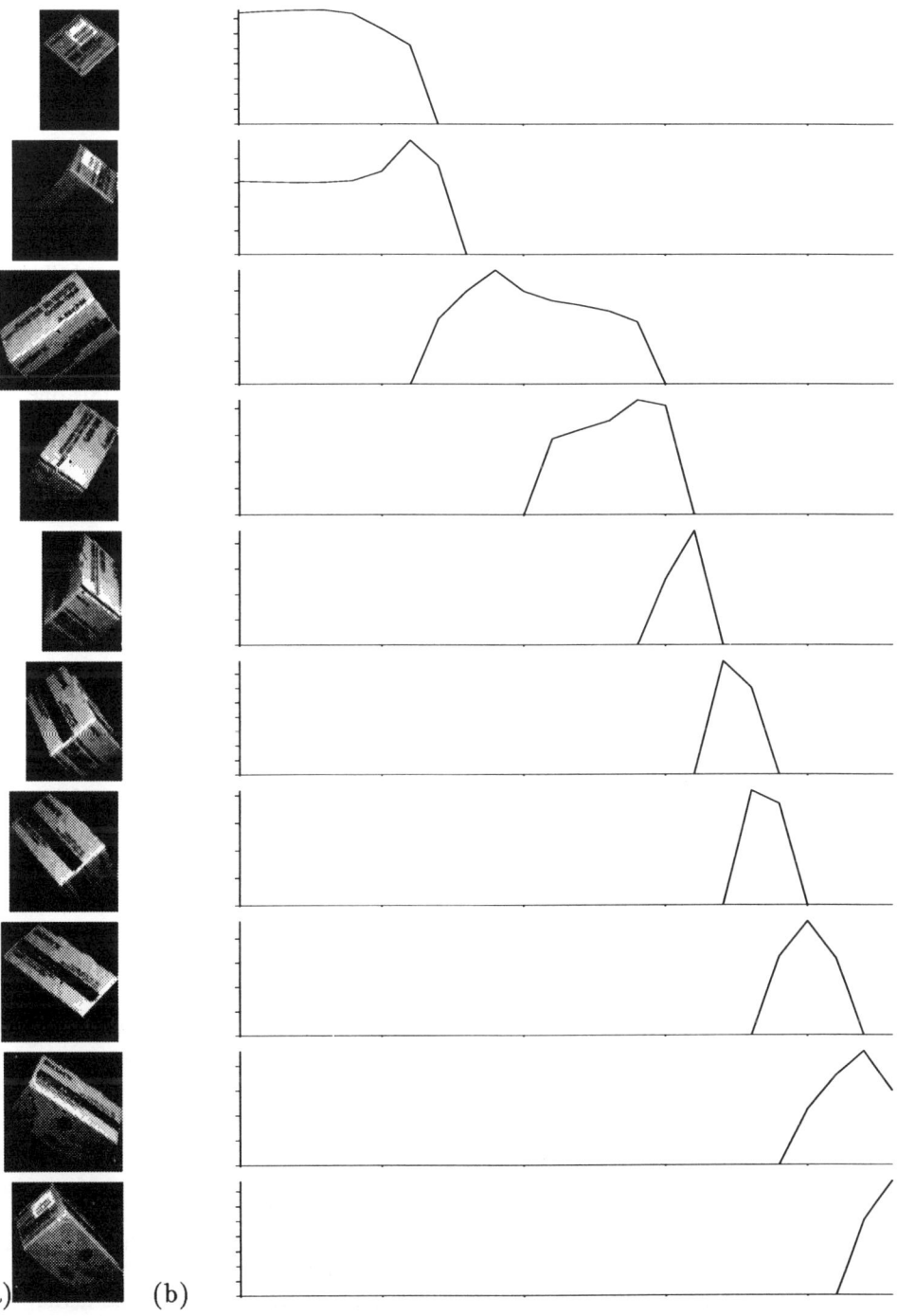

(a)   (b)

Figure 27.4 *(a) Models automatically acquired from a sequence of images of a rotating box; (b) normalized correlation scores for each model as a function of image sequence frame number.*

all other views are equally likely to be seen at the next instant (except for certain pathologic objects like a sphere!). We can use this information to order the computation of match scores and/or only compute scores for a subset of the view models.

In essence, we wish to compute the conditional expected score and position of **all** of the view models at time $t + 1$, given the current vector of *all* the view model responses at time t: $E(\mathbf{r}[t + 1]|\mathbf{r}[t])$, where $\mathbf{r} = \{r_1, \ldots, r_M\}$. To estimate this numerically we represent the vector of responses $\mathbf{r}$ as a discrete set of states. The simplest discretization is to define the match state to be the view model with the current maximum score, $m^*[t] = \arg\max_m r_m[t]$. More complex discretizations are also possible, but we have found this one to be intuitive and give good results.

When the system is in context training mode, it collects the following simple statistical observations:

$$A(m, m^*[t - 1]) = A(m, m^*[t - 1]) + r_m[t] \quad \forall m \text{ s.t. } r_m[t] > \theta_0$$
$$B(m^*[t - 1]) = B(m^*[t - 1]) + 1.$$

The expected score of the mth model in the next time step is therefore:

$$E(r_m[t + 1]|m^*[t]) = \frac{A(m, m^*[t])}{B(m^*[t])}.$$

When being run in matching mode (non-training), this information guides the search computation. We search a reduced set of view models expected to exceed a certain score first, and if we find above-threshold scores within this set we return only the subset of their scores and positions. If no match is found in this subset, we evaluate the search scores of the remaining view models, and return the scores for the full set.

27.4 Non-rigid objects and sparse view spaces

When objects are non-rigid, either constructed out of flexible materials or an articulate collection of rigid parts (like a hand), then the dimensionality of the space of possible views becomes much larger. Full coverage of the view space in these cases is usually not possible since enumerating it even with very coarse sampling would be prohibitively expensive in terms of storage and search computation required.

However, many parts of a high dimensional view space may never be encountered when processing real sequences, due to unforeseen additional constraints. These may be physical (some joints may not be completely independent), or behavioral (some views may never be used in the actual communication between user and machine). A major advantage of our adaptive scheme is that it has no difficulty with sparse view spaces, and derives from the data which regions of the space are full.

In the context of developing a user interface, the ability to only model the relevant information can be of critical importance. If there are only a small number of gestures that need to be recognized, then it would be wasteful to model views not actually used by these gestures. To cover completely the possible view-space of a human hand would require a prohibitively large number of view models. However if there are only N gestures to be recognized, each with M frames then at worst we will need to cover a space of $N*M$ views. In general this will require far fewer than $N*M$ view models, since there is almost always some correlation between frames in a sequence which can be exploited.

27.5 Training gestures

A gesture can be thought of as a set of views observed over time. Since each view is characterized by the outputs of the view models used in tracking, a gesture can be modeled as the set of model outputs (both score and position) over time. We thus recognize previously trained gestures by collecting the model outputs produced when viewing a novel sequence and comparing them to a library of stored patterns.

To compare a novel sequence of view model outputs to a stored gesture model we must take into account expected variations in those outputs. Our gesture representation incorporates a statistical model of correlation scores, so view models which are less highly correlated with the actual gesture are given less weight in the matching. To account for variation in the overall length of the gesture, we allow the observed sequence to be arbitrarily time-warped to the stored gesture models.

We train a gesture model by providing several temporally segmented examples of the gesture, and computing the mean and variance of the view model correlation scores as a function of time. Each example is time-warped to be the same length as the longest example before computing statistics on the correlation scores.

27.5.1 Dynamic Time Warping

The Dynamic Time Warping (DTW) method involves the use of dynamic programming techniques (Bellman, 1957) to solve an elastic pattern matching task. This method was developed to solve the time alignment problem in the speech and signal processing literature (Sakoe and Chiba, 1980), and is easily applied to our task. To temporally align two sequences, $\mathbf{r}[t]$, $0 < t < T$, and $\mathbf{r}'[t]$, $0 < t < T'$, using the DTW method, we consider the grid whose horizontal axis is associated with $\mathbf{r}$ and whose vertical axis is associated with $\mathbf{r}'$. Each element of a grid contains a distance measure $D_{i,j}$ measuring the distance between $\mathbf{r}[i]$ and $\mathbf{r}'[j]$. During the gesture training phase we have used Euclidean distance for $D_{i,j}$, however other metrics are possible.

The best time warp will minimize the accumulated distance along a monotonic path through the grid from $(0,0)$ to (T, T'). The DTW algorithm uses a partial sum variable $C_{i,j}$, to recursively compute a minimal solution; $C_{i,j}$ is defined to be the minimum cost to align $\mathbf{r}[0\ldots i]$ with $\mathbf{r}'[0\ldots j]$. Using a simple form of the DTW method, we have

$$C_{i,j} = D_{i,j} + \min(C_{i-1,j-1}, C_{i-1,j}, C_{i,j-1}), \tag{3}$$

where

$$C_{1,1} = D_{1,1}$$
$$C_{i,1} = D_{i,1} + C_{i-1,1}$$
$$C_{1,j} = D_{1,j} + C_{1,j-1}.$$

When the recursion is complete, the minimum distance between the two patterns is simply $C_{T,T'}$. To find the optimal path and thus the actual alignment we simply backtrack through $C_{i,j}$ along the directions of partial sum minima.

27.5.2 Classifying time-aligned patterns

Once the view model outputs for each example sequence have been time-aligned, we can build a new gesture model $\mathbf{g}$, by computing the mean values and variance of the model outputs at each time step. Denoting the mean value of view model m at time t for gesture $\mathbf{g}$ as $\tilde{g}_m[t]$, we also find its corresponding variance, $\sigma^2(g_m[t])$.

Given a set of gesture models we detect their presence in a novel sequence by matching each gesture against the most recently observed view model outputs ($\mathbf{r}[t]$). We apply the DTW method to compute the gesture model scores, using a distance function that takes into account the statistics of the gesture examples:

$$D_{i,j} = \sum_{m<M} \frac{1}{\sigma^2(g_m[i])} (\tilde{g}_m[i] - r_m[j])^2. \tag{4}$$

When time-warping gesture models to new observations, we perform the matching backwards in time, so that the current time step is zero for the time-warping algorithm. Thus, both the observed sequence and the gesture pattern must be aligned at the current time step. We relax the requirement that a fixed amount of the observations be used in the time-warped match; the score of a gesture model is defined to be the minimum of any of the partial sums which account for all of the time samples in the gesture:

$$\mathscr{D}(\mathbf{g}, \mathbf{r}') = \min_{0 \geqslant t \geqslant T'} C_{T,t'},$$

where T is the number of time samples in $\mathbf{g}$ and T' is the number of time steps in the input buffer $\mathbf{r}'$. Finally, the score function for a given gesture is defined as the inverse distance to the current sequence of observations.

27.6 A gesture recognition example

As an example, we trained our system to recognize the gestures shown in Figure 27.2. The first gesture was of a person waving 'hello' to a camera; in the second gesture a person waved 'goodbye'. The adaptive training procedure described in section 27.2 was used to acquire a set of view models that covered (i.e. was able to interpolate) all of the views generated by the two gestures; these are shown in Figures 27.5.

Figure 27.6 shows the correlation scores for these models for an example of the 'hello' gesture. In this gesture, one can see the high scores oscillating between the view models which contain the rotated versions of the hand. Figure 27.7 shows the correlation scores for an example of the 'bye' gesture; one can see the output oscillating between the view for the extended hand and the view of the compressed hand. Figure 27.8 shows the gesture data displayed as a surface plot depicting 'view-space-time', the pattern of view scores over time.

Figure 27.9 shows the pattern of view scores for novel sequence which contained three instances of each gesture. At each time step of the observed sequence, the time-warped distance metric was evaluated (in real-time) for each stored gesture pattern. The inverse distance is plotted as a function of frame number next to each of the gesture models. Each gesture in the observed sequence yields a distinct peak in the score of the appropriate gesture model.

27.7 Implementation issues and real-time performance

We have implemented the method described above in a hybrid general/special purpose computing environment. Our system has been designed for real-time performance, and all of the examples demonstrated above ran at 10 Hz or better (except during the training phase, which has latencies on the order of a second when a new view model is added.)

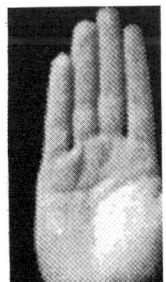 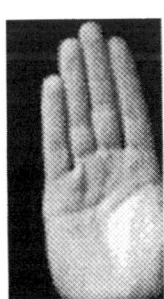 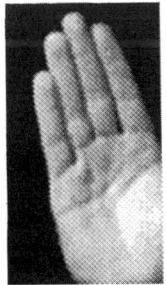 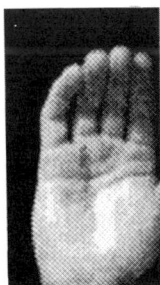

Figure 27.5 *Four view models used in recognizing the gestures shown in Figure 27.2. The first model was specified with a window provided by the user, and the remaining models were adaptively acquired from a training sequence containing both gestures.*

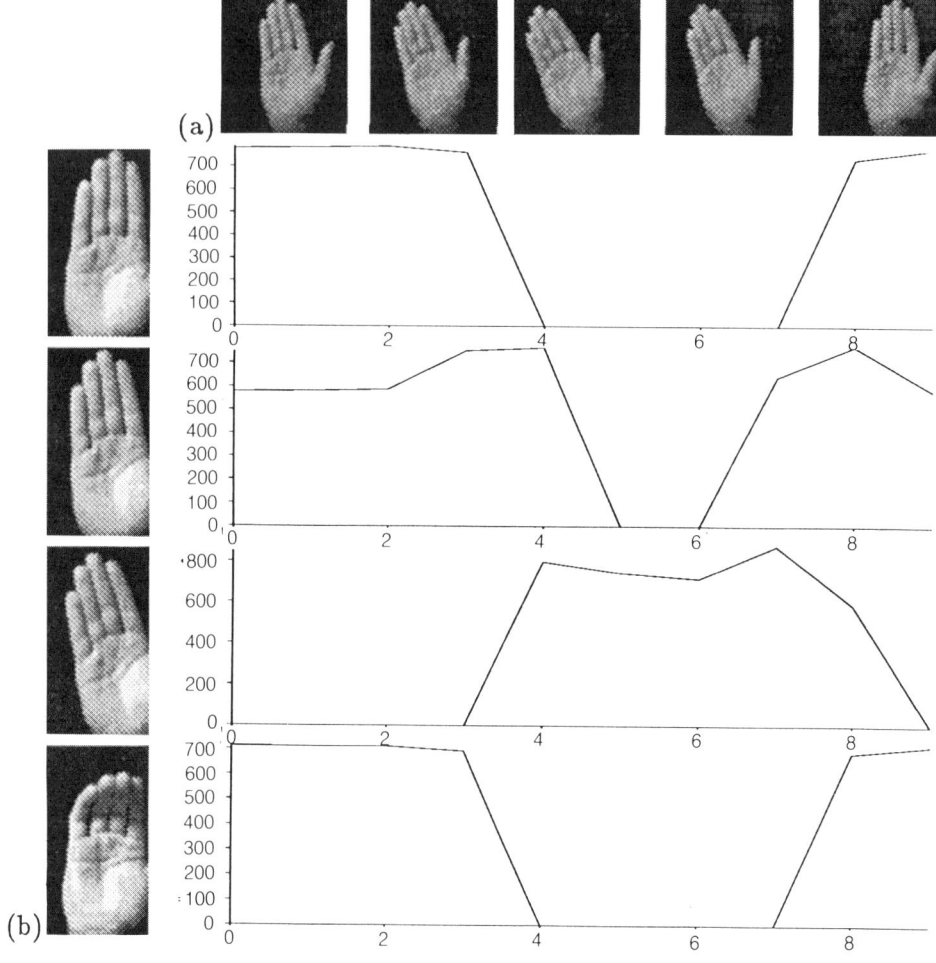

Figure 27.6 *Training the 'hello' gesture. (a) Samples from sequence of frames used to train the gesture; (b) scores for each of the model views as a function of frame number.*

The majority of the computational burden in this method involves finding the peak view model correlation scores. To compute correlation scores, we rely on a special-purpose image processing computer which is designed for quick correlation searching. The view model acquisition, evaluation, and maxima finding are implemented on a Cognex 4400 vision processor developed by the Cognex Corporation. We have found that for the domain of recognizing hand gestures where the hand fills 1/8 to 1/4 of the frame, it is possible to subsample input images by 4 in both directions (for a final resolution of 128×120) and achieve good recognition performance. We have tested our

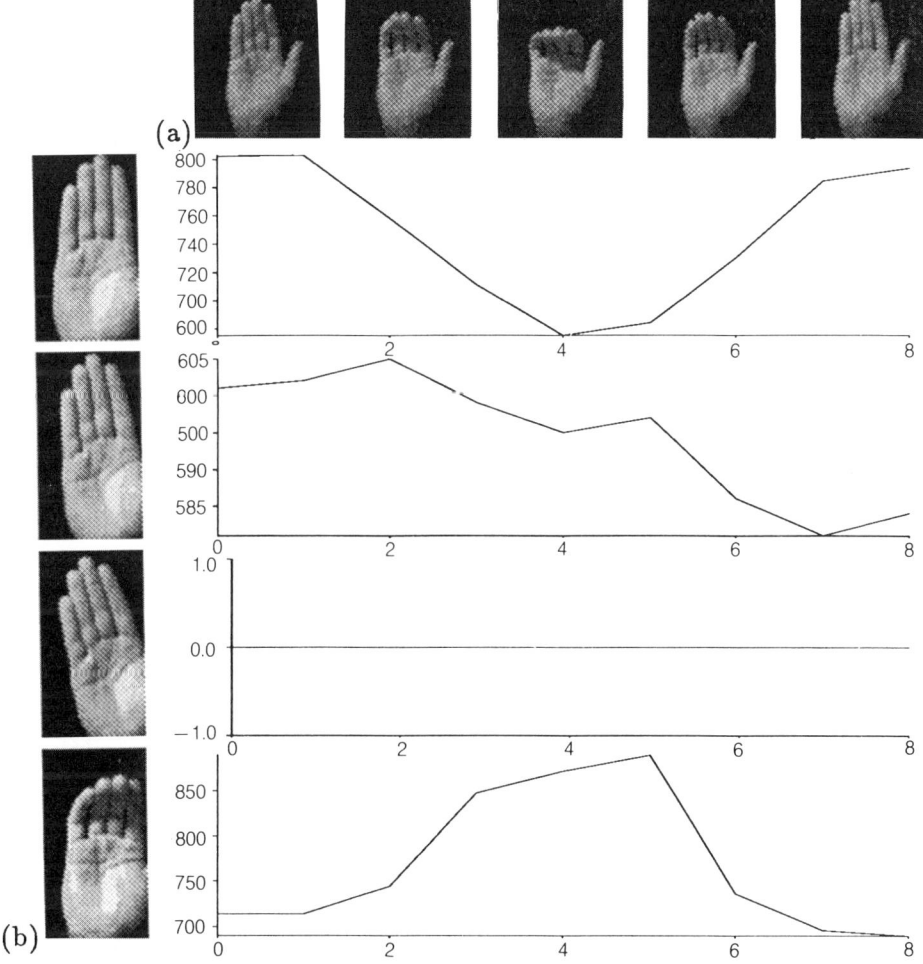

Figure 27.7 *Training the 'bye' gesture. (a) Samples from sequence of frames used to train the gesture; (b) scores for each of the model views as a function of frame number.*

system at this resolution on examples which used up to 40 models (on a modified version of the box example); the time required to exhaustively search all models in this case was in the order of 200–300 ms. (At this resolution our system can store up to 100 view models in memory accessible by the searching hardware.) Using the predictive searching mechanism described in section 27.3 we were able to reduce the processing time for this example to under 100 ms.

The Cognex 4400 is connected via serial line and shared memory to a host Sun 4/330. The correlation scores are transmitted to the Sun workstation,

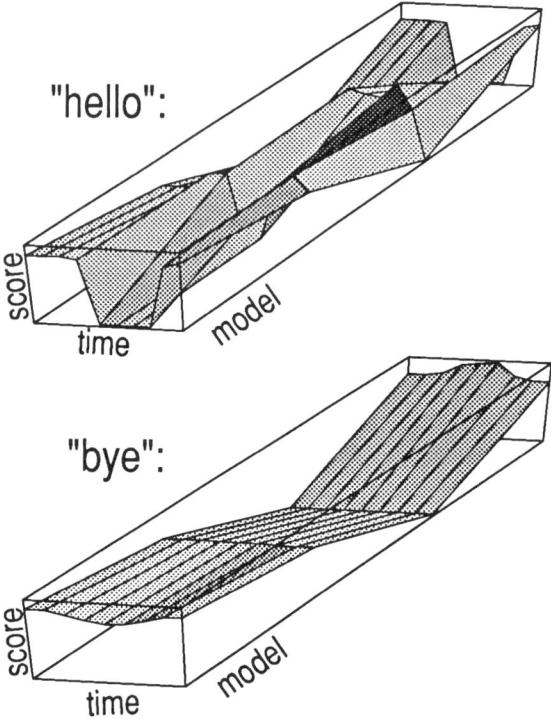

Figure 27.8 *Surface plots of gesture models using data from Figures 27.6 and 27.7.*

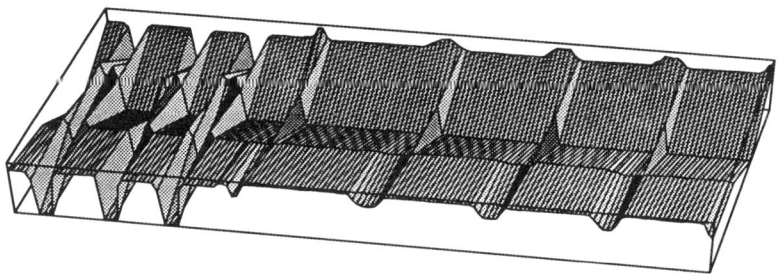

(a)

Figure 27.9 *Matching the 'hello' and 'bye' gestures against observed data. (a) Output of the view models for a sequence in which the user waves 'hello' three times and then 'bye' three times; (b) 'hello' gesture model; (c) gesture score as a function of time; (d) 'hello' gesture model; (e) gesture score as a function of time. Three peaks are evident in each score plot, indicating a match for each of the gestures.*

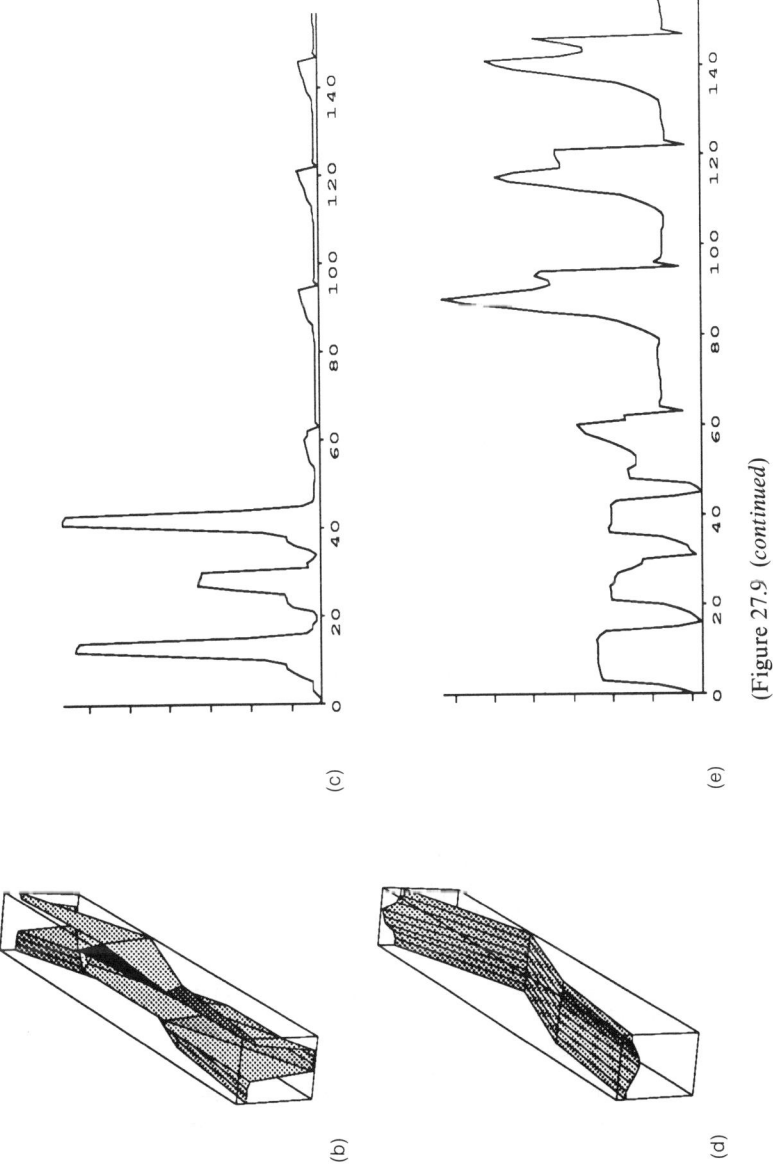

(c)

(e)

(b)

(d)

(Figure 27.9 (continued)

which stores the gesture models and performs the dynamic time warping procedure. The $(2T^*)$ most recent score vectors are buffered, where T^* is the length of the longest sequence in the gesture library. After each frame the DTW scores for each gesture are evaluated, matching backwards in time. Our implementation of DTW on the Sun takes considerably less than 100 ms to warp two 20 element sequences, where each element is a vector of 10 model scores. The entire tracking and recognition system can thus perform in real time or near real time for non-trivial tasks.

27.8 Conclusions

We have developed and implemented a real-time system for learning, tracking and recognizing complex objects and gestures. The use of a view-based representation allows us to model (and search) only the portion of an object's view-space which is actually used by a user in the gestures to be recognized. Capturing the temporal correlation of view model scores is an important portion of this work, since it can reduce the amount of computation that needs to be performed by an order of magnitude. Together with the Cognex hardware described above, this allows us to achieve real-time performance when tracking objects with many views.

Modeling gestures as a set of view scores over time allows us to reduce the dimensionality of the space-time pattern without having to recover exactly the underlying object pose parameters. Using dynamic time warping and a statistical recognition approach, real-time recognition of human gestures is possible using computational equipment of modest power.

References

Bellman, R.E. (1957) *Dynamic Programming*. Princeton University Press, Princeton, NJ.

Bolt, R. (1984) The Human Interface, where people and computers meet. *Lifetime Learning Publications*, Belmont, CA.

Ishibuchi, K., Takemura, H. and Kishino, F. (1992) *Real Time Hand Shape Recognition using Pipe-line Image Processor*. IEEE Workshop on Robot and Human Communication, pp. 111–16.

Makhoul, J., Roucos, S. and Gish, H. (1985) Vector quantization in speech coding. *Proc. IEEE*, **73**(11), 1551–87.

Mase, K. (1991) Recognition of facial expression from optical flow. *ICICE Transactions*, **74**(10), 3474–83.

Negroponte, N. (1980) *The Architecture Machine*. MIT Press, Cambridge, MA.

Poggio, T. and Edelman, S. (1990) A network that learns to recognize three dimensional objects. *Nature*, **343**(6255), 263–6.

Sakoe, H. and Chiba, S. (1980) Dynamic programming optimization for spoken word recognition. *IEEE Trans. Acoust., Speech, Signal Processing*, **26**, 623–5.

Sperling, G., Landy, M.S., Cohen, Y. and Pavel, M. (1985) Intelligible encoding of ASL image sequences at extremely low information rates. *Computer Vision, Graphics, and Image Processing*, **31**, 335–91.

Torige, A. and Kono, T. (1992) *Human-Interface by Recognition of Human Gesture with Image Processing Recognition of Gesture to Specify Moving Direction.* IEEE Workshop on Robot and Human Communication, pp. 105–10.

Ullman, S. and Basri, R. (1991) Recognition by linear combinations of models. *IEEE Trans. PAMI,* **13**(10), 992–1007.

Yamato, J., Ohya, J. and Ishii, K. (1992) *Recognizing Human Action in Time-Sequential Images using Hidden Markov Model.* IEEE Proc. CVPR-92, pp. 379–85.

Face recognition using transform coding of gray scale projections and the neural tree network

JOSEPH WILDER

Rutgers University Center for Computer Aids for Industrial Productivity (CAIP), Piscataway, NJ, USA

28.1 Introduction

There is an urgent need, in today's political and technological environment, for systems that can identify people reliably. In many instances, access to privileged information or premises is restricted to authorized individuals. A need to identify suspected terrorists or others involved in criminal activities also exists. Current identification media are manifold – including badges, cards and personal identification numbers – some of which can be subverted by theft. An alternative approach, that has received considerable attention in recent years, identifies people by recognizing facial features. Humans have a remarkable ability to recognize thousands of faces. We can perform reliably under difficult viewing conditions, e.g. poor illumination, extreme viewing angles and partial obscuration by hats, glasses and facial hair. We can also account for aging and change in expression. An automatic recognition system that can approach the human capability to recognize faces would represent a significant step forward in personnel identification.

Face recognition systems would also prove useful in other areas. Film processing could be improved with automatic equipment that detects the presence of faces in photographs to adjust tints for accurate reproduction of flesh tones (as suggested in Turk and Pentland, 1991). Furthermore, identify-

Artificial Neural Networks for Speech and Vision. Edited by Richard J. Mammone. Published in 1993 by Chapman & Hall, London. ISBN 0 412 54850 X

ing the orientation of portrait photos would also be useful in film development laboratories.

Applications for face recognition techniques can also be found in medicine. For example, changes in facial features due to post-operative swelling could be monitored (Dunn, Keizer and Yu, 1989). Changes in expression could also be detected and related to changes in mood experienced by emotionally disturbed individuals.

This chapter reviews previous efforts to develop face recognition systems and presents a new approach to building robust, cost-effective systems. It also discusses issues that must be addressed in developing such a system.

28.2 Approaches to face recognition

Face recognition has been a subject of interest for many years in the pattern recognition community (Samal and Iyengar, 1992, give a current survey). As mentioned above, this interest can be linked to the amazing human ability to recognize thousands of faces learned over time under a variety of viewing conditions. However, achieving highly reliable recognition of a significant number of individuals under realistic viewing conditions has proved difficult, since faces are complex objects that vary in appearance with time.

The most widely pursued approach to face recognition involves the detection and characterization of individual facial features such as eyes, nose and mouth and their geometric relations with each other. Goldstein, Harmon and Lesk (1971) developed such a system based on subjective human judgements. Takao Kanade (1973) was among the first to apply computer vision techniques to extract and use geometric features for face recognition. Kanade extracted edges from full-face images and extracted chin and cheek contours and location points obtained from the eyes, nose and mouth. His algorithm worked reasonably well under ideal conditions (91% correct), but could not work with glasses (2%) or beards (0%). Performance also dropped off sharply with small turns and tilts of otherwise well positioned faces (80%). More recently, Brunelli and Poggio (1992) carried out a similar experiment. Shackleton and Welsh (1991) and Yuille (1991) matched facial features to deformable templates. Nakamura, Mathur and Minami (1991) used isodensity maps as a source of features.

While some success has been reported on small data sets under controlled conditions, the geometric feature approach is not likely to prove robust in practical applications for the following reasons. First, finding individual facial features requires powerful adaptive segmentation algorithms that can separate these features from their surrounding background. Such algorithms must deal with the large dynamic range of reflectivity and the variation in surface properties occurring on faces of widely varying skin color and texture. Variations in intensity and uniformity of illumination will also make segmentation more difficult. Second, geometric distortion due to varying perspectives in viewing faces that are not head-on will prove difficult. Third, obscurants like glasses will severely limit performance. Finally, such systems will not be robust under changes in facial expressions.

Another approach is based on a global or holistic analysis. Recent research into the cognitive processes involved in face recognition suggests that certain higher level aspects of faces contribute to their 'familiarity' (Young and Yamane, 1992). This approach involves the encoding of the entire face image and treating it as a point in a high-dimensional feature space (e.g. Kohonen and Lahtio, 1981; Sirovich and Kirby, 1987; Kirby and Sirovich, 1990; Turk and Pentland, 1991). The latter two used principle component analysis (or Karhunen–Loeve expansion) to find the vectors that best account for the distribution of face images within the entire image space. They label these vectors 'eigenfaces'. Kirby and Sirovich (1990) demonstrated the usefulness of this approach under controlled conditions, and Turk and Pentland (1991) under more varied conditions. Also included in the holistic approach are experiments using a neural network to train on complete face images (e.g. Kohonen and Lahtio, 1981; and Cottrell and Fleming, 1990). For example, Cottrell and Fleming used 64×64 pixel images of faces as 4096 dimensional input feature sets to train a neural network. 64 images of 11 subjects were used for training. The complete training operation took more than two days of real-time processing on a Sun4 workstation. However, the system performed well on recognition, even when faces were partially obscured. Although these initial experiments on holistic face recognition were carried out on small training and test sets, this approach shows promise of being more robust than the more detailed geometric approach under realistic viewing conditions.

28.3 Face recognition using gray scale projections

Recently, a holistic face recognition system was demonstrated at the Rutgers University Center for Computer Aids for Industrial Productivity (CAIP) (Wilder, 1992). As with Sirovich and Kirby (1987) and Turk and Pentland (1991) it involves transform coding of gray scale face images. It differs from their approach in that it involves a preliminary data reduction step, gray scale projections, and a fast transform technique that greatly reduces the computational complexity of the problem and, consequently, the cost of high speed implementation. This system also uses a new, extremely cost-effective neural network, the Mammone/Sankar Neural Tree Network (NTN) for its decision function (Sankar and Mammone, 1991). The CAIP system was developed during a short-term demonstration project, and was designed to recognize full-face, consistently positioned and illuminated faces. Subsequently, it was shown to be robust when these conditions were relaxed. The following paragraphs describe the details of that system.

28.3.1 Feature extraction

Gray scale projections have proven to be effective in industrial pattern recognition and pattern verification applications (Wilder, 1983). The gray values of pixel data are added along specific directions within a region of interest to create a series of one-dimensional signatures to represent two-dimensional data. Unlike tomographic applications, where image reconstruction is the goal, a small number of projections can provide sufficient information for classification. Horizontal and vertical projections are adequate in some applications, and horizontal, vertical and $+/- 45°$ in others. It is interesting to note that Kanade (1973) and Brunelli and Poggio (1992) used horizontal and vertical projections to locate facial features, but did not use those projections as a source of feature data for classification.

The Rutgers system uses horizontal and vertical projections within a window that extends vertically from just above the chin to the upper portion of the forehead and horizontally to include a small portion of both ears. The images are captured by a moderate resolution, RS170, monochrome CCD camera (Sony XC-38). There are 416 rows and 320 columns in the window. An example of a face image and its projections is shown in Figure 28.1. Note that in the horizontal projection (rotate it 90° clockwise) the mouth, nose, eyes and eyebrows are clearly delineated. The eyes, nose and edges of the cheeks can be located in the vertical projection.

Raw input features are extracted from the gray scale projections by integrating them over bands whose width is narrow enough to resolve the main features and, at the same time, wide enough to ignore fine features, such as facial texture, that could vary over time. Furthermore, the wider the bands, the less sensitive the system is to small variations in horizontal and vertical position. The widths chosen for the initial design divided each projection into 16 bands. The integrals corresponding to the projections in Figure 28.1 are shown in Figure 28.2. Thus, the original two-dimensional image within the window, which contains 133120 pixels, is reduced to two one-dimensional profiles described by 16 numbers each.

The raw projection features are then subjected to a transform into the spatial frequency domain, using a unitary, orthogonal transform. There are several reasons why this step can be advantageous. Unitary transforms are energy and entropy preserving, decorrelate highly correlated input vectors, and tend to pack a large fraction of the average energy (and information) of the image into the low spatial frequencies (Jain, 1989). For classification purposes, the low spatial frequency and selected high frequency components are retained to differentiate those patterns that are similar except for some small details. The remaining components, generally the highest frequency terms, contain very little energy (Figure 28.4), and can be discarded without sacrificing information that is significant for classification.

There is also a practical implication of the decorrelation property of these transforms in the face recognition application. Since every transform compo-

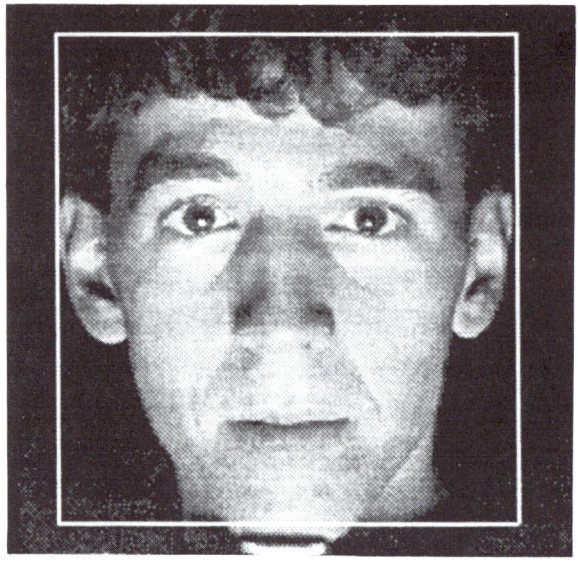

(a)

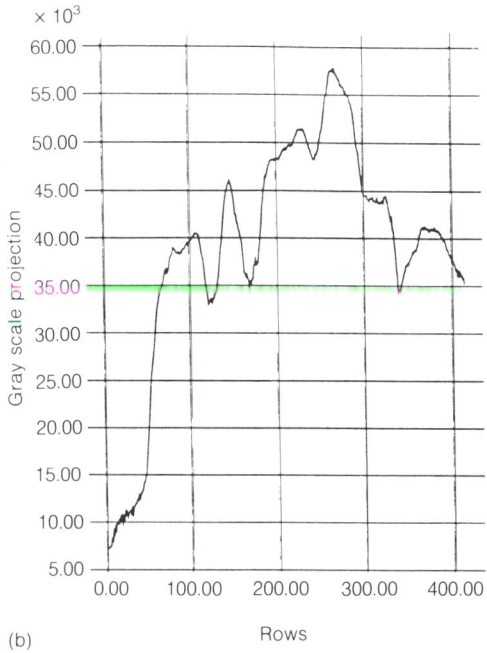

(b)

Figure 28.1 *(a) Sample face image and its (b) horizontal and (c) vertical gray scale projections within the bounding box.*

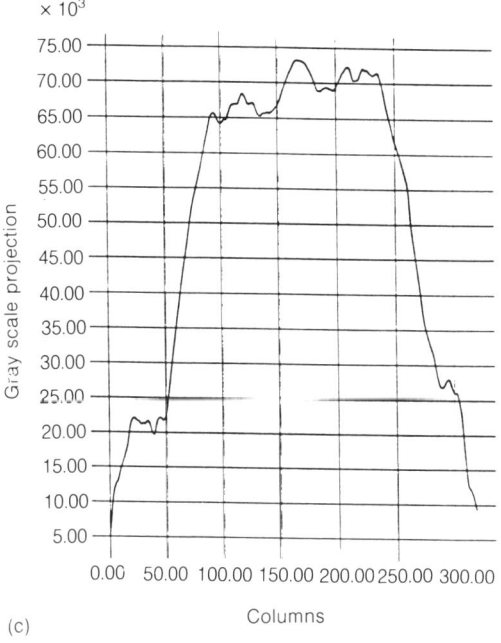

(c)

Figure 28.1 (*continued*)

nent is a linear combination of all the input features, pattern distortion due
to alteration of a group of neighboring input features is distributed over all
the output features. Hence, addition of glasses or changing from a smile to
a frown will not have a catastrophic effect on the transformed pattern vector.

Three orthonormal transforms; Hadamard, Discrete Cosine (DCT) and
Karhunen–Loeve (KLT) were applied to the raw input feature data. All
produced similar results, in terms of class separability and recognition rate,
with the DCT and KLT performing slightly better than the Hadamard. The
similarity in performance is not surprising since all have similar basis
functions, as shown in Figure 28.3 (from Jain, 1989). Unlike the KLT, the
DCT has a fast algorithm and can be efficiently computed using software or
dedicated hardware. The DCT was the transform of choice. The DCT's of
the input features in Figure 28.2 are shown in Figure 28.4. In the initial tests
of the CAIP system, DCT components 1 (the DC term) through 12 of the
horizontal projections and 2–13 of the vertical projections were retained.
Note that the DC term, which represents overall skin tone, contains important
information for classification of faces when illumination conditions are well
controlled.

It is instructive to examine the relationship between the one-dimensional
transforms of the horizontal and vertical gray scale projections and the

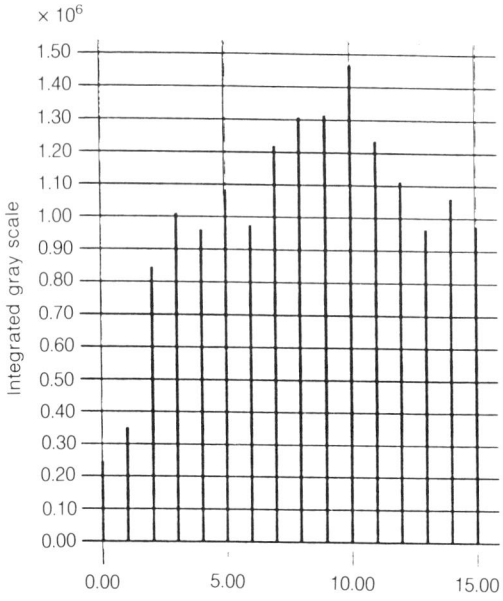

(a)

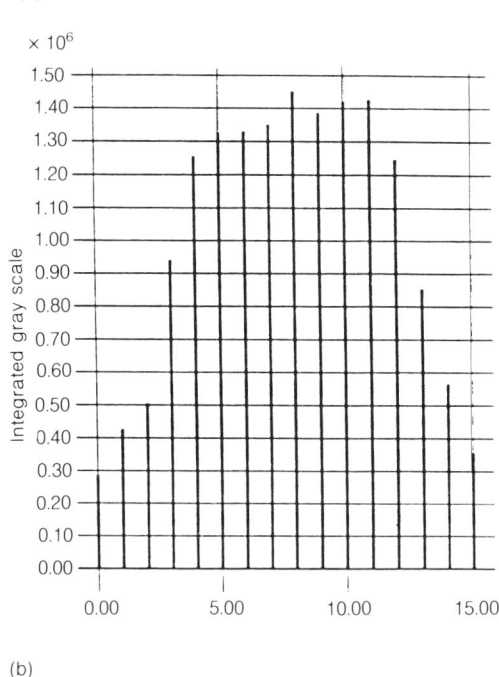

(b)

Figure 28.2 *Integrals over 16 bands of the horizontal (a) and vertical (b) gray scale projections shown in Figure 28.1.*

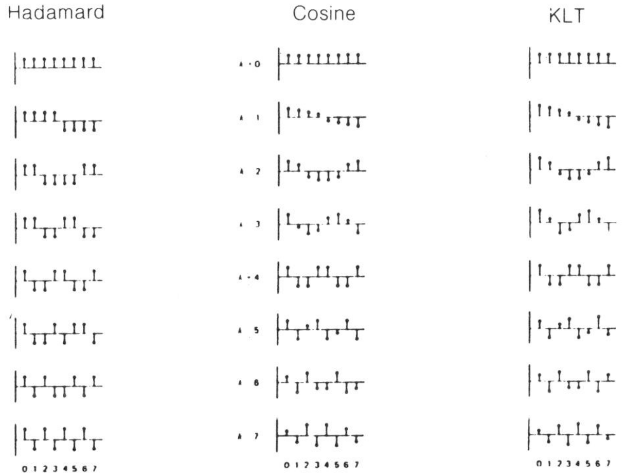

Hadamard	Cosine	KLT

Figure 28.3 *Basis functions of the Hadamard, Discrete Cosine and Karhunen–Loeve transforms (from Jain, 1989).*

two-dimensional transforms of the original images. Observe the basis functions of the two-dimensional transforms shown in Figure 28.5 (from Jain, 1989). Note that the first row and first column of the two-dimensional transforms are computed from vertical and horizontal projections, respectively. If, as mentioned above, the highest frequency projection transform components are discarded, the selected components represent a low-pass filtered version of the two-dimensional transformed image. Such high frequency components as are retained from the projections are relatively insensitive to positional errors, i.e. the horizontal projections are insensitive to small horizontal translations (neglecting effects at the edge of the window), and the vertical projections are insensitive to small vertical translations.

In summary, gray scale face images can be represented by a small number of relatively uncorrelated spatial frequency components that emphasize the low spatial frequency content of the images but, as the same time, include sufficient high frequency information to describe significant differences between subjects. The high frequency components are relatively insensitive to small, within-class positional variations between images.

28.3.2 Classification

A hierarchical pattern classifier, the Neural Tree Network (NTN), carries out the decision function in the CAIP face recognition system. The NTN effectively combines neural networks and decision trees. It has demonstrated performance superior to that of MLP's and decision trees (Sankar and Mammone, 1991). Unlike the MLP, the number of neurons does not have

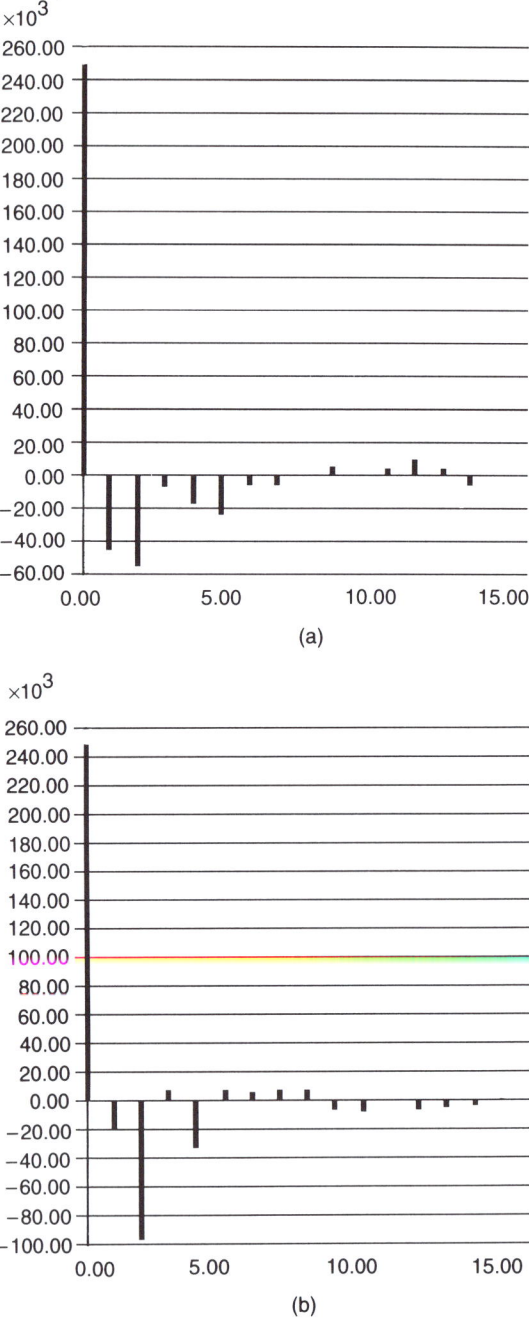

Figure 28.4 *Discrete Cosine Transform of the (a) horizontal and (b) vertical gray scale features shown in Figure 28.2.*

HADAMARD   COSINE   KLT

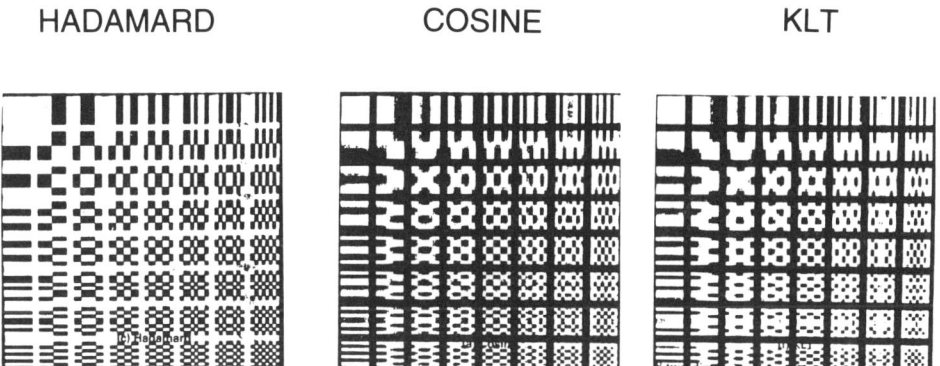

Figure 28.5 *Two-dimensional basis images.*

to be specified in advance. The NTN grows as it learns, and has only as many neurons as required to solve the classification problem at hand. Furthermore, the NTN does not have problems with local minima – it always converges to a solution. Standard decision trees also grow their tree during the learning process. However, the standard decision tree training algorithms are extremely complex, in comparison with the NTN. The NTN can be implemented with simple hardware. In fact, a single neuron can be programmed with a sequence of sets of weights. An example of the tree structure and a hardware implementation is shown in Figure 28.6. The details of the NTN are discussed in the above cited reference and also elsewhere in this volume.

28.3.3 System hardware

The initial experiments with the CAIP face recognition system were carried out on well positioned, near-full-face images with consistent illumination.

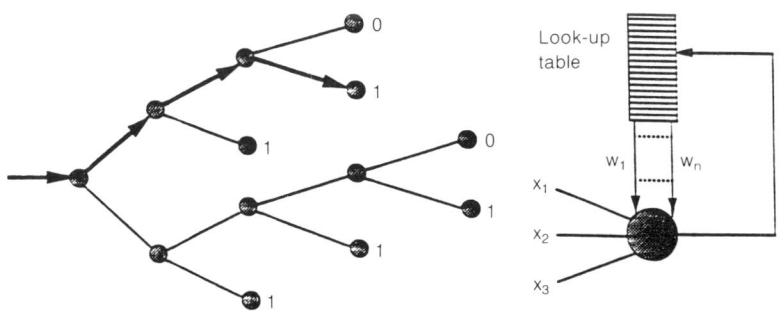

Figure 28.6 *Neural tree network.*

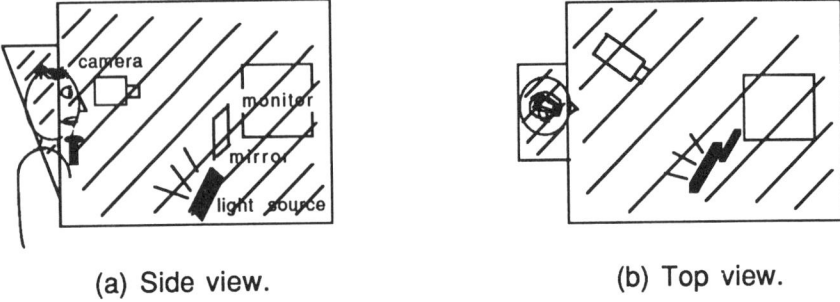

(a) Side view.   (b) Top view.

Fig. 6. Face recognition image capture module.

Figure 28.7 *Face recognition image capture model.*

Positioned by a small chin rest, subjects looked into a window in a booth containing a camera, light source, mirror and monitor. During training, the subjects observed their image in the monitor and aligned their faces roughly within a box appearing on the monitor (see Figure 28.7). The camera and mirror provided a nearly-full-face image of the subject. The light source was deliberately placed off-axis to create shadows which helped to delineate facial features. Another reason for placing the light source off-axis is to create as much asymmetry as possible about the vertical axis. Since the odd components of the DCT are zero for symmetrical signals, as can be inferred from Figure 28.3, odd component features from asymmetric images will yield more information.

The image capture and pre-processing is carried out on a Data Cube MV20 image processing system. The MV20 processes images at 20 Mpixels/s and has special hardware that extracts gray scale projections at that pixel rate. A Sun Sparc1 workstation served as the host computer. With this hardware, all pre-processing and feature extraction can be carried out in under 10 ms. In the experiments performed at CAIP, the neural network was implemented on the Sun workstation. At a demonstration of the system at *Supercomputing '91*, the neural network was implemented on the Motorola/ MIT Monsoon multiprocessor computer.

28.4 Experimental results

The first experiment was carried out with 32 subjects, six images/subjects (to be called the Rutgers data base). Recognition was tested on 20 combinations of three images for training and three for testing, i.e. 96 training and 96 test samples per combination. The average error rate over all 20 combinations was 97%. The number of errors (out of 96 test samples) ranged from 0–5.

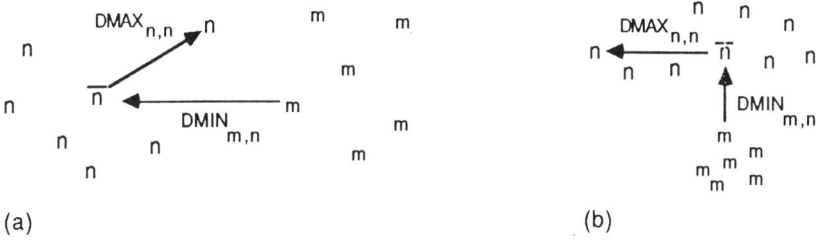

(a)   (b)

Figure 28.8 *(a) Example of linearly separable classes for which $S_{m,n} > 1$; (b) example of linearly separable classes for which $S_{m,n} < 1$.*

It is interesting to examine the feature data and relate it to these recognition results. Pairwise class separability was calculated for the six samples available from each class. The separability of classes m and n, $S_{m,n}$, is defined below and illustrated in Figure 28.8:

$$S_{m,n} = \frac{DMIN_{m,n}}{DMAX_{n,n}} \tag{1}$$

$$S_{m,n} = \frac{MIN \text{ distance of class } m \text{ samples to mean of class } n}{MAX \text{ distance of class } n \text{ samples to its mean}} \tag{2}$$

if $S_{m,n} > 1$, classes m and n are linearly separable (Figure 28.8a) (3)

if $S_{m,n} \leqslant 1$, classes m and n are not necessarily overlapping (Figure 28.8b)

(4)

$$S_{m,n} = S_{n,m} \tag{5}$$

Of the $32 \times 31 = 992$ pairwise computations of $S_{m,n}$ carried out on the Rutgers data base, 20 were < 1. All of the 20 instances occurred within only five of the 32 classes, suggesting that for this data set, 27 of the 32 classes were linearly separable. The NTN tree for a combination that resulted in five errors is shown in Figure 28.9, and also supports the contention that 27 of the 32 classes were linearly separable. This analysis supports the contention that the features extracted in the CAIP system produced well separated classes under the imaging conditions imposed.

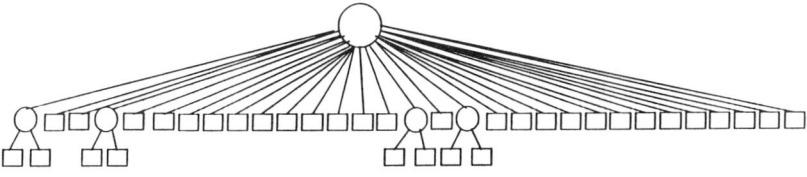

Figure 28.9 *The NTN for an example from the Rutgers data base for which five errors occurred. ○: node; □: leaf: no. of levels = 2; no. of nodes = 5; no. of leaves = 35.*

The second experiment was conducted at *Supercomputing '91*, when the imaging booth was set up on the convention floor. There were 269 subjects, three images per subject. Recognition was tested on six combinations of two images for training and one for testing. The average error rate was 90%. Additionally, a number of subjects tried to fool the system by putting on or taking off their glasses, or changing their expression from a smile to a frown. The subjects were always recognized.

A number of additional experiments were carried out on groups of 10–20 subjects with three training samples per subject. During the testing phase in these experiments, the subjects tilted, translated and rotated their faces, put on and removed glasses and changed their expressions. The system was highly reliable for sizeable variations in these conditions within the constraints of approximately full-face imaging within the test window.

28.5 Development of a practical face recognition system

The requirements to be met by a useful face recognition system are application specific. However, it is possible to discuss general considerations of reliability, flexibility and cost effectiveness inherent to most applications. What follows is a compendium of technical issues, some of which are essential to the development of basic systems, and some exploratory issues for potentially more advanced systems.

28.5.1 Removing positional restraints

The positional restraints permitted vary from application to application. They range from full-face, close-up images that would be reasonable in secure access systems, e.g. logging on to a secure workstation or gaining access to a secure building, on the one hand, to finding, tracking and identifying moving subjects passing through a corridor on the other. Even in the most restricted environments, however, a recognition system should be robust in the presence of some variations in translation and scale. For example, in an access system where a subject is required to stand in front of a window in full-face, the position within that viewing window must still be determined (translation) and variations in magnification due to varying distances from the window (scale) must be compensated. The gray scale projection technique employed in the CAIP system is particularly amenable to compensation for translation and scale. In fact, because fine details of the face have been found to be less important than global appearance, considerable variations in scale, i.e. viewing from a large distance, can be accommodated without degradation in performance.

The CAIP system, in its present form (i.e. single camera, near head-on), can also accommodate small rotations and tilts in virtually any combination. However, in many less restricted applications, more than one view will be required to accommodate the full range of positions and perspectives encountered. Multiple views can be acquired with multiple cameras, or a single camera operating over multiple paths. Since the cost of video cameras has dropped dramatically in recent years, the relative costs of the two approaches would have to be analysed in detail for any application. A multiple view system also places computational demands on the image processing and decision-making hardware. As mentioned above, the CAIP system performs all major image processing and feature extraction functions, using commercially available image processing hardware, in under 10 ms, so dealing with multiple views would not be a problem.

28.5.2 *Accommodating variations in background illumination*

Intensity, uniformity and spectral nature of the illumination and variations of these quantities over time are important factors in the design of any imaging system that must perform consistently. The illumination source, the objects viewed and the sensor must all be matched in dynamic range and spectral response. A successful face recognition system will most likely need to provide its own controlled source of illumination and include a method for filtering out and masking out the normal surrounding background illumination. This operation can be carried out in a variety of ways. In some access applications, of course, a hood would be very effective in controlling the environment. In less restricted environments, narrow band light sources in combination with narrow band filters could exclude background illumination (if face color is used as a source of information, this will affect the design of a narrow band system). Infrared sources and cameras, and systems with flash lamps can also be used in non-intrusive ways to provide controlled illumination. One requirement of any illumination design is that it emphasize facial features (e.g. creases, shape of the nose) by creating shadows or other image artifacts that relate directly to the shape of the face.

Robustness in the presence of variations in illumination can also be achieved algorithmically. A number of algorithms exist that reduce the effects of such variations. The use of these algorithms must be tempered, however, by the need to retain variations in facial skin tones which contribute important information in discriminating one face from another. It should be noted that once a face is located, it is possible to use high-speed image processing hardware to fit an oval mask around a face image that will effectively eliminate those portions of the image that do not pertain to the face itself.

An effective face recognition system must include elements of both illumination and algorithmic design to be successful.

28.5.3 *Enriching the input data*

Most face recognition systems tested to date acquire reflectance data from a conventional monochrome TV camera. Facial features are extracted from the patterns of light and dark in the image. There are other sensing systems that, potentially, are a much richer source of facial feature data. In shape-from-shading, for example, a series of images (usually three) is acquired from a camera when the illumination comes from different directions. The images, acquired with different shadings can be combined to produce a map of surface normals, i.e. a map of the direction each surface patch is facing. While not providing true 3D imagery, it does produce considerably more information about shape than a conventional camera image. It is also possible to compute true 3D images either by using multiple views, e.g. stereo image pairs, triangulation using structured light, or depth-from-defocus techniques, which can be fast, effective and inexpensive (Wilder *et al.*, 1992). Color, of course, is another potential source of enriched face data. All of the above data collection techniques can be used in conjunction with the CAIP face recognition system.

28.5.4 Using 3D modeling

It is possible, using 3D modeling techniques, to construct a close approximation of the face from multiple views, surface normals or range data. Such a model could be translated, rotated and scaled to match virtually any view of a subject acquired on-the-fly. This type of image manipulation is currently within the computing power of present-day workstations. Matching to a 3D model would be extremely useful in unconstrained environments where the viewing perspective cannot be controlled.

28.5.5 Developing the recognition functions

In addition to determining which of a pre-trained collection of faces is being viewed, most systems will need to detect the presence of a face(s) in the field of view, and distinguish between faces for which the system was trained and all others. These functions can be implemented easily in the CAIP system, with appropriate modifications to the training routines in its Neural Tree Network. In secure access applications, the system will frequently be used in a verification mode to corroborate other means of identification. This, too, will be easy to implement.

Another important issue in developing the recognition function is ease of training. In addition to a rapid initial training routine, a useful system should include the capability of deleting and adding subjects to the training data base without a lengthy re-training procedure. The Mammone/Sankar NTN mentioned above fulfills these requirements.

28.6 Summary

This chapter has addressed some of the key issues in the development of face recognition systems. A review of the literature and tests of the CAIP face recognition system suggest that a global or holistic approach to face recognition shows great promise. The CAIP system was tested on several face image data sets and performed reliably under significant variations in facial appearance. These results suggest that transform coding of gray scale projections and the NTN, the main elements of the CAIP approach, can contribute to the development of robust, cost-effective face recognition systems.

Acknowledgements

This work represents the efforts of a team of people who carried out the project over a three month period. The image processing and feature extraction work was carried out, primarily, by Stephen Juth, Augustine Tsai and Joseph Wilder of CAIP. The neural network decision processes were developed, primarily, by Richard Mammone and Xiaou Zhang of CAIP. The programming of the NTN on the Motorola/MIT Monsoon computer and the data collection at *Supercomputing 91* was carried out, primarily, by Venkat Natarajan of Motorola.

References

Brunelli, R. and Poggio, T. (1992) Face recognition through geometrical features. *Proc. of ECCV '92*, Genova, Italy, May, pp. 792–800.

Cottrell, G.W. and Fleming, M.K. (1990) Faces recognition using unsupervised feature extraction. *Proc. International Neural Network Conference*, Paris, France.

Dunn, S.M., Keizer, R.L. and Yu, J. (1989) Measuring the area and volume of the human body with structured light. *IEEE Trans. on Systems, Man, and Cybernetics*, **19**(6), 1350–64.

Goldstein, A.J., Harmon, L.D. and Lesk, A.B. (1971) Identification of human faces. *Proc. IEEE*, **59**, 748, May.

Jain, A.K. (1989) *Fundamentals of Digital Image Processing*. Prentice-Hall, Englewood Cliffs, NJ.

Kanade, T. (1973) *Picture Processing System by Computer Complex and Recognition of Human Faces*, doctoral thesis submitted to Department of Information Sciences, Kyoto University, Japan.

Kirby, M. and Sirovich, L. (1990) Application of the Karhunen–Loeve procedure for the characterization of human faces. *IEEE Trans. on Pattern Analysis and Machine Intelligence*, **12**(1), 103–8.

Kohonen, T. and Lahtio, P. (1981) Storage and processing of information in distributed associative memory systems, in *Parallel Models of Associative Memory* (eds. G.E. Hinton and J.A. Anderson), Erlbaum, Hillsdale, NJ pp. 105–43.

Nakamura, O., Mathur, S. and Minami, T. (1991) Identification of human faces based on isodensity maps. *Pattern Recognition* **24**(3), 263–71.

Samal, A. and Iyengar, P.A. (1992) Automatic recognition and analysis of human faces and facial expressions: a survey. *Pattern Recognition*, **25**(1), 65–77.

Sankar, A. and Mammone, R. (1991) Neural tree networks, in *Neural Networks: Theory and Applications* (eds. R. Mammone and Y. Zeevi), Academic Press, New York, NY, pp. 281–302.

Shackleton, M.A. and Welsh, W.J (1991) Classification of facial features for recognition.

Proceedings Computer Vision and Pattern Recognition, Conference, Maui, June 3–6, IEEE, pp. 573–9.

Sirovich, L. and Kirby, M. (1987) Low-dimensional procedure for the characterization of human faces. *Journal of the Optical Society of Amer.*, **4**(3), 519–24.

Turk, M. and Pentland, A. (1991) Eigenfaces for recognition. *Journal of Cognitive Neuroscience*, **3**(1).

Wilder, J. (1983) A machine vision system for inspection of keyboards. *Signal Processing*, **5**(5), 413–21.

Wilder, J. (1992) *Face Recognition Using Transform Coding of Grey Scale Projections and the Neural Tree Network*. FAA/CAIP Neural Network Workshop, October.

Wilder, J., Brajovic, V., Prasad, K.V. *et al.* (1992) Capture of 3D image data with an on-axis, real-time range mapper. Report to the New Jersey Commission on Science and Technology under Innovation Partnership, *Grant No. 90-240510*, March.

Young, M.P. and Yamane, S. (1992) Sparse population coding of faces in the inferotemporal cortex. *Science*, **256**, 1327–31, May.

Yuille, A.L. (1991) Deformable templates for face recognition. *Journal of Cognitive Neuroscience*, **3**(1).

A discrete Radon transform method for invariant image analysis using artificial neural networks

JOHN F. DOHERTY and OSAMA K. AL-SHAYKH

Department of Electrical Engineering and Computer Engineering, Iowa State University, Ames, IA 50011, USA

29.1 Introduction

Many of the real life applications of image processing aim to describe and classify objects in images. Mail sorting, text reading, chromosome analysis, tumor detection, parts identification on assembly lines, non-destructive evaluation, motion control for robots, fingerprint matching and target detection and identification are examples of such applications.

While extracting features from objects, we make little use of the position, size or orientation of the object in the image. Rather, the information is contained in the shape of the object, which might be defined as those properties of an object which are invariant under rigid-body motion (Wong and Steppe, 1969). It is rare that we want to recognize an object from a transformed version of it. An example of this is recognizing '6' from '9'.

Invariant recognition (**recognition of visual patterns irrespective to their position, orientation, scale and deformation**) has long been one of the main concerns of researchers in the fields of pattern recognition and neural networks. Pitts and McCulloch (1947) described a neural mechanism which exhibits invariant recognition of forms. Since then several methods have been proposed.

Many researchers have found the application of Artificial Neural Networks (ANN) to invariant pattern recognition particularly attractive because of the

Artificial Neural Networks for Speech and Vision. Edited by Richard J. Mammone. Published in 1993 by Chapman & Hall, London. ISBN 0 412 54850 X

possible relationship between ANN and biological neural nets (Barnard and Casasent, 1991). There are three techniques to render neural networks invariant to transformations (Barnard and Casasent, 1991):

1. Invariant feature space.
2. Invariance by training.
3. Invariance by structure.

Invariant feature space includes using Fourier descriptors, method of moments or any other invariant features of the object. These features are used as the input to the neural network.

Invariance by training is achieved by presenting transformed versions of the input to the neural network in the training phase. A major drawback of this approach is the need for large networks and memory matrices to store these patterns.

Imposing invariance into the structure of the neural network is done by creating connections between the neurons which force transformed versions of the same input to have the same output (Barnard and Casasent, 1991). The neucognitron (Fukushima and Wake, 1991), Widrow's network (Widrow et al., 1988; Fukumi et al., 1992), and higher neural networks (Maxwell and Giles, 1986; Kollias et al., 1991) are examples of these networks.

In this chapter, an approach that falls under the invariant feature space category is presented. This approach is based on utilizing the projections (Radon transform) of the image to achieve invariant features. The singular values of the projection matrix, constructed by row-stacking each projection, are used as the invariant features.

29.2 The Radon transform

The Radon transform, ray sum, shadowgram or projections of a function, denoted as $g(s, \theta)$, is defined as its line integral along a line inclined at an angle θ from the y axis at a distance s from the origin (Jain, 1989), i.e.

$$g(s, \theta) = \mathbf{R}(f) = \iint f(x, y)\delta(x\cos\theta + y\sin\theta - s)\, dx\, dy \quad -\infty < s < \infty, 0 \leqslant \theta < \pi.$$

$$(1)$$

The Radon transform has several useful properties which can be utilized to achieve invariant features of the image in the Radon transform. These properties were used to process images using one dimensional systems (Sanz et al., 1988).

Let $g(s, \theta)$ be the projections, Radon transform, of an image, two dimensional function, $f(x, y)$ or $f_p(r, \phi)$ in the polar coordinates; then the following properties hold (Jain, 1989):

• Linearity

$$\mathbf{R}\{a_1 f_1(x, y) + a_2 f_2(x, y)\} = a_1 g_1(s, \theta) + a_2 g_2(s, \theta) \qquad (2)$$

- Symmetry

$$g(s, \theta) = g(-s, \theta \pm \pi) \tag{3}$$

- Translation

$$\mathbf{R}\{f(x - x_0, y - y_0)\} = g(s - x_0 \cos \theta - y_0 \sin \theta) \tag{4}$$

- Rotation

$$\mathbf{R}\{f_p(r, \phi + \phi_0)\} = g(s, \theta + \phi_0) \tag{5}$$

- Scaling

$$\mathbf{R}\{f(\alpha x, \alpha y)\} = \frac{1}{|\alpha|} g(\alpha s, \theta) \tag{6}$$

- The moments of the image are related to the moments of its projections by

$$m^i(\theta) = \sum_{j=0}^{i} \binom{i}{j} M^{i,j} \cos^j \theta \sin^{i-j} \theta \tag{7}$$

- Convolution

The Radon transform of the convolution is the convolution of the Radon transforms (Deans, 1983)

$$\mathbf{R}\{f_1 * f_2\} = g_1 * g_2. \tag{8}$$

29.3 Singular Value Decomposition (SVD)

Let $\mathbf{A}$ be a linear operator between separable Hilbert spaces $\mathbf{X}, \mathbf{Y}$

$$\mathbf{A}:\mathbf{X} \to \mathbf{Y}. \tag{9}$$

The triple $\{\mathbf{u}_n, \mathbf{v}_n, \sigma_n\}_{n \geqslant 0}$ is called a Singular Value Decomposition (SVD) of the operator A if

$\{\mathbf{u}_n\}_{n \geqslant 1}$ is a complete orthonormal system in X.
$\{\mathbf{v}_n\}_{n \geqslant 1}$ is an orthonormal system in Y.
$\{\sigma_n\}$ is a set of non-negative and real numbers.

$$\mathbf{A}\mathbf{u}_n = \sigma_n \mathbf{v}_n \quad \text{and} \quad \mathbf{A}^*\mathbf{v}_n = \sigma_n \mathbf{u}_n$$
$$\mathbf{A}^* \text{ is the adjoint of } \mathbf{A}.$$

The singular values σ_n are usually ordered such that $\sigma_1 \geqslant \sigma_2 \geqslant \cdots \geqslant \sigma_n > 0$ (Maass, 1991).

The singular functions $\{\mathbf{u}_n\}$ are sometimes called the generalized eigenfunctions, since

$$(\mathbf{A}^*\mathbf{A})\mathbf{u}_n = \sigma_n^2 \mathbf{u}_n. \tag{10}$$

A can be constructed from the triple by

$$\mathbf{A} = \sum \sigma_n \mathbf{v}_n \mathbf{u}_n^*. \tag{11}$$

29.4 Projection-based invariant features

Any image can be approximately reconstructed from a finite subset of its projections. The angular resolution at which projections are taken depends on the maximum reconstruction error acceptable. The linearity, shift, rotation and scaling properties of the Radon transform can be utilized to achieve an invariant feature vector. Here, an algorithm that utilizes these properties to achieve invariance to translation, rotation and scaling is presented. The singular value of a matrix, constructed by row-stacking projections, is used to construct the invariant feature vector. This feature vector will be used as input to a classifier, which is the back-propagation neural network followed by a maximum-output-selector. A performance function is introduced to evaluate the performance of the recognition system. This performance function can also be used to indicate how closely the pattern matches the decision template.

The invariance with respect to translation, rotation and scaling will be discussed separately. Afterwards, all procedures will be incorporated in a complete system that can achieve invariance to translation, rotation and scaling.

29.4.1 Invariance to translation

If an object is translated then, according to the shift property of the Radon transform, each projection will be translated by a distance which is a function of the translation distance and the projection angle, i.e.

$$s_\theta = x_0 \cos \theta + y_0 \sin \theta, \tag{12}$$

where s_θ is the projection translation caused by a translation of (x_0, y_0) at a projection angle θ.

Centering each projection around its center of mass will eliminate the translation effect. This can be justified by the fact that centering each projection around its center of mass will result in centering the object around its center of mass. This is because

$$\hat{s} = \frac{m^1}{m^0} \tag{13}$$

where

$$m^0(\theta) = \iint f(x, y) \, dx \, dy = M \tag{14}$$

$$m^1(\theta) = M_x \cos \theta + M_y \sin \theta \tag{15}$$

where $\hat{s}$ is the center of mass of the projection taken at angle θ. The quantities m^0 and m^1 are the average and first order moment of the projection. M, M_x

and M_y are the average and the moments in the x and y directions of the object, respectively.

29.4.2 Invariance to rotation

Invariance to rotation of an object by an arbitrary angle is achieved by extracting features that are independent on the ordering of the projections, i.e. if each projection is placed in a row of a matrix (Figure 29.1), the features must be independent of the way the rows of the matrix are organized. There are few algebraic parameters which are invariant to the order of the rows of a matrix, but not all are distinct for each matrix, e.g. the trace. However, the singular values of the projection-matrix are invariant to the order of the rows. This means that singular values are invariant to rotation of integer multiple of angular resolution of projections.

It can be shown that the image can be represented as a sum of multiplications of the singular values with functions of the radial distance from the origin and of the angle taken from the abscissa, i.e. the image in polar coordinates can be described by

$$f(r, \phi) = \sum_k \frac{\sigma_k}{2\pi^2} \int_0^\pi u_k(\theta) \, d\theta \left\{ \int_s \frac{[\partial w_k(s)/\partial s]}{r \cos(\theta - \phi) - s} \, ds \right\} \qquad (16)$$

where

σ_k = singular values of the Radon transform
$w_k(s)$ = right singular vector spanning the domain of the projections
$u_k(\theta)$ = left singular vector spanning the angle θ of the projections
k = runs over the rank of the projection-matrix.

The Radon transform is taken over $[0°, 180°]$. The symmetry property of the Radon transform equates the projection at angle θ with the abscissa

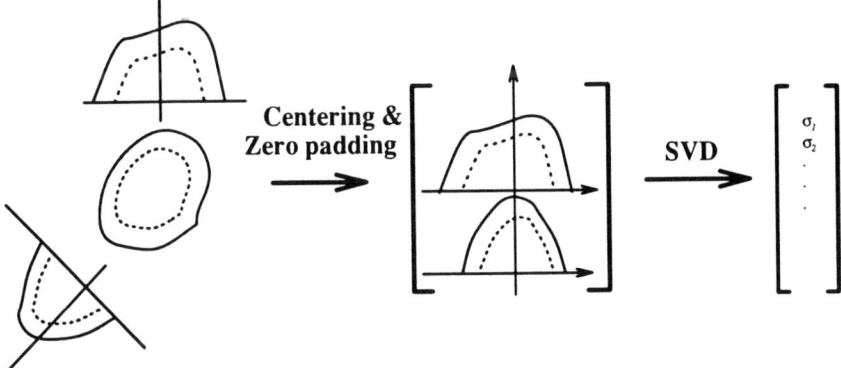

Figure 29.1 *Steps to achieve invariant feature vector.*

reversed projection at angle $\theta + 180$. As a result, if the image is rotated then at least one row of the matrix will be reversed. Hence, the singular values won't be the same. However, taking projections over the whole $360°$ range would give invariance at increments of $180/N°$, where N is the number of projections taken over the image. This can also be done by utilizing the symmetry property, i.e. by reversing the projections alternately. This will result in a $360°$ coverage.

The rotation angle can be estimated by calculating the translation in the left singular vectors spanning the angle. This is because

$$\mathbf{R}f(r, \phi + \phi_0) = g(s, \theta + \phi_0)$$

$$= \sum_k \sigma_k u_k(\theta + \phi_0) w_k(s) \tag{17}$$

where ϕ_0 is the angle of rotation.

29.4.3 Invariance to scaling

If an object, $f(x, y)$, is scaled by a scaling factor α, the scaled object, $f_\alpha(x, y)$, will be

$$f_\alpha(x, y) = f(\alpha x, \alpha y). \tag{18}$$

When the object is scaled, the left singular vector spanning the angle of the projection won't be affected. However, the right singular vector spanning the domain of the projections as in equation (2) will change, i.e.

$$\mathbf{R}\{f_\alpha(x, y)\} = g_\alpha(s, \theta)$$

$$= \frac{g(\alpha s, \theta)}{|\alpha|}$$

$$= \sum_k \frac{\sigma_k}{\alpha^{3/2}} u_k(\theta)[\sqrt{\alpha} w_k(\alpha s)]. \tag{19}$$

The right singular vector would be $\sqrt{a} w_k(\alpha s)$ and the singular values are $\sigma_k/\alpha^{3/2}$. Consequently, when the object is scaled by a scaling factor of α, the l_2 norm of the singular-value vector (i.e. the Frobenius norm of the projection matrix) would be scaled by $\alpha^{-3/2}$.

29.4.4 Constructing invariant feature vector

The following summarizes the projection-based algorithm (Figure 29.1) to achieve invariance to translation, rotation and scaling:

1. Projections are taken over $360°$. In most practical systems, only $180°$ coverage is available. However, the coverage can be extended to $360°$ by alternately reversing the projections.

2. Each projection is centered around its center of mass. This will center the image and introduce translation invariance in the extracted features.
3. A projection image matrix is constructed, where the row vectors are the centered projections, as illustrated in Figure 29.1.
4. SVD is applied to the projection matrix. The order of the singular values is invariant to rotation with the angular resolution.
5. The singular value vector is normalized to achieve invariance to scaling.

29.5 Recognition system

After the feature vector is constructed, it is applied to the input of the recognition block or the classifier. The classifier used here is a back-propagation neural network followed by a maximum-output-selector.

The adaptive nature of neural networks as well as their ability to generalize from training data justifies their use for classification in our system. They are expected to overcome the rotation resolution invariance problem. This will be illustrated by the results obtained for worst case resolution, i.e. when the angle of rotation taken is in the middle of the angular sampling period.

The performance of the recognition system involves studying the recognition rate, the similarity of features extracted from patterns of the same class, and the differences in features extracted from patterns of different classes. To incorporate these parameters, we consider as a performance measure a function that sums all the normalized differences between the output nodes and the output of the node corresponding to the correct class, i.e.

$$P(n) = \frac{\sum_{\substack{k=1 \\ k \neq n}}^{N} Y(n) - Y(k)}{N-1} \tag{20}$$

where $0 \leqslant Y(i) \leqslant 1$ is the output of node i of the neural network, n is the node corresponding to correct output class, and N is the number of output nodes of the neural network.

This performance measure takes values between -1 and 1. It gives its best output (1.0) when the output of the node corresponding to the correct class equals 1.0 and the output of the rest of the nodes equal 0. It gives its worst output when all the output nodes have values of 1.0 and the output of the node corresonding to the correct class equals 0.

This function is used to give an indication of how closely a pattern matches the template the system classified. This function is analogous to the membership function defined in fuzzy set theory (Zadeh, 1965). Along with some defined rules, it can be used to give a syntactic description of the output of the neural network. When this function is used as a membership function, its range will be $[0, 1]$. This is because $Y(n) \geqslant Y(k)$ for all $k \neq n$. Table 29.4

Table 29.1 *Feature vector length experiment*

Parameter	Value
No. of projections	Variable
No. of training patterns	5 (Original)
No. of testing patterns	$5 \times 10 = 50$ each
S/N	∞

Table 29.2 *Feature vector robustness*

Parameter	Value
No. of projections	18
No. of training patterns	N/A
No. of testing patterns	$5 \times 10 = 50$
S/N	∞

Table 29.3 *Effect of white noise experiment*

Parameter	Value
No. of projections	18
No. of training patterns	5 (Original)
No. of testing patterns	$5 \times 4 = 20$ each
S/N	Variable

Table 29.4 *Performance measure and membership values[a]*

Output of			Performance measure	Membership value
node 1	node 2	node 3		
1.000	0.000	0.000	1.000	1.000
1.000	1.000	0.000	0.500	0.500
1.000	1.000	1.000	0.000	0.000
0.000	1.000	0.000	-0.500	1.000
0.000	1.000	1.000	-1.000	0.500

[a]This is assuming the pattern tested belongs to Class 1, i.e. the output pattern should be (1, 0, 0).

illustrates the effectiveness of this function when used for a neural network with three output nodes.

29.6 Results

In this section, the proposed method is examined and its merits are illustrated. The method is then compared to the method of moments. The example chosen for testing (Figure 29.2) consists of staple remover, stapler, keys, hole punch and tape dispenser. The objects in this example are chosen because they contain similarities and differences among them. The staple remover and the stapler have the same general shape, i.e. the 'V' shape. The hole punch and the tape dispenser have almost the same region of support. However, the keys have a different shape.

The neural network used for classification has the same number of layers, hidden nodes and output nodes in all experiments conducted. It consists of three layers where the number of nodes in the input layer equals the length of the feature vector. The hidden layer consists of 14 nodes. The output layer consists of 5 nodes corresponding to the five output classes.

The singular values are calculated using the subroutine provided by Press *et al.* (1988).

29.6.1 *Feature vector length*

This experiment is conducted to determine the variation of the recognition rate with feature vector length. Changing the length of the feature vector results from changing the angular resolution at which the projections are taken. Changing the angular resolution will affect mostly the recognition of images rotated with angles that are not integer multiples of the angular resolution.

To study this effect, ten images rotated by integer multiples of 10% of the angular resolution are used for testing. The neural network is trained using the feature vectors of the objects in Figure 29.2.

Figure 29.3 and 29.4 show the recognition percentage and the performance measure versus the vector length respectively. As evident, the recognition percentage reached 100% when using six or more projections to contruct the projection-matrix, i.e. an angular resolution of 30° or less. This results in reducing the size of the projection-matrix $\mathbf{P}$ and the matrix $\mathbf{PP}^T$ which is used to calculate the singular values, e.g. to find the singular values of the projection-matrix constructed using six projections, a 6×6 matrix is used. This means a fast feature extraction system and a small neural network.

29.6.2 *Feature vector robustness*

The rotation invariance property is illustrated by this experiment. The length of the feature vector used in this experiment is 18, i.e. angular resolution of 10°. Ten objects of each object of Figure 29.2 are generated by rotating the object by integer multiples of 1° (Figure 29.5). Table 29.5 is a list of the magnitudes of the first seven elements of the 18-length feature vector. The respective variance σ to mean μ percentage $\sigma/\mu\%$, which indicates the percentage of the spread of the values from their corresponding mean for all objects is shown in Table 29.6. The average of $\sigma/\mu\%$ percentages is 3.1%.

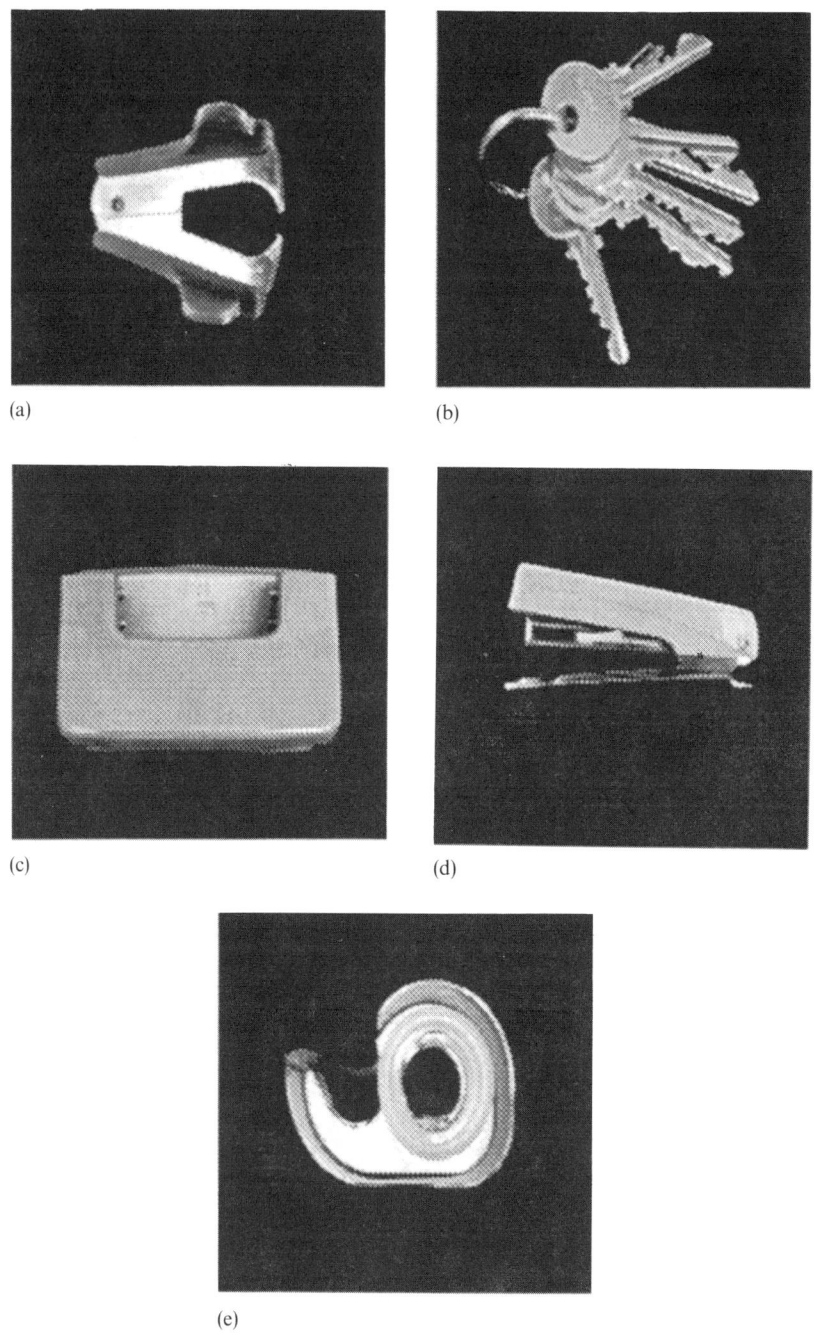

Figure 29.2 *200 × 200 eight-bit images of the five different classes used to test the method. (a) Staple remover; (b) keys; (c) hole punch; (d) stapler; (e) tape dispensor.*

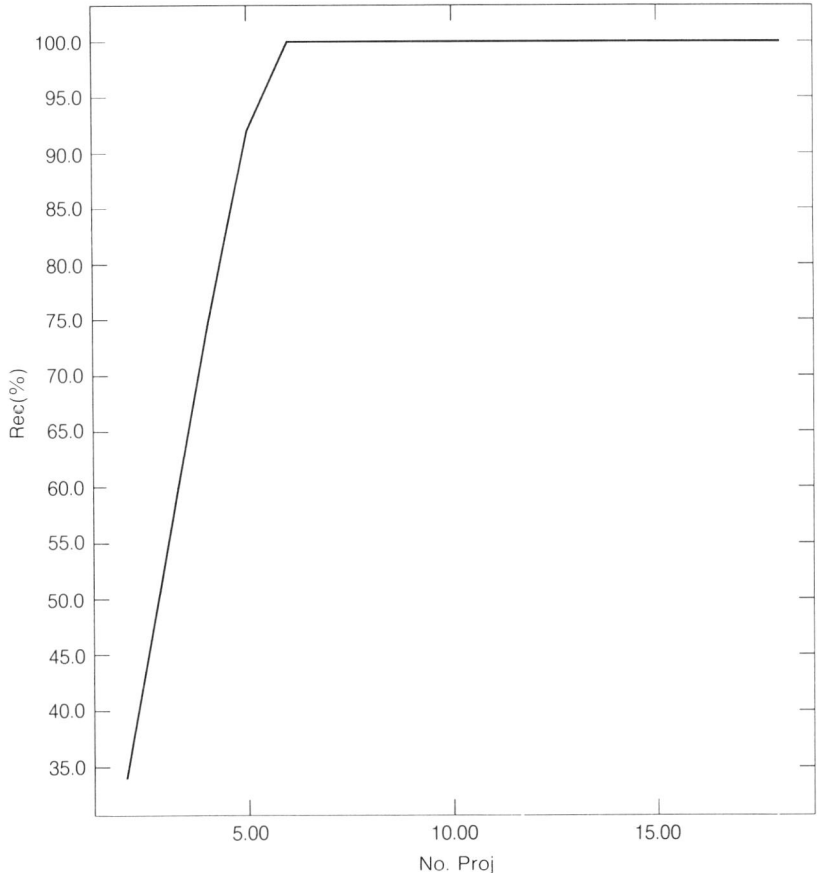

Figure 29.3 *Recognition percentage* versus *number of projections (the feature vector length). As seen, using six projections gives good recognition percentage.*

The rotation angle can be estimated from the shift in the left singular vectors spanning the angle. To illustrate this fact, the left singular vector corresponding to the largest singular value of 0°, 10° and 20° rotated images of the staple remover is shown in Figure 29.6. The translation between each vector of them is one unit, i.e. the angle of rotation is 10°.

The scaling invariance property is illustrated the same way (Tables 29.8 and 29.9). Scaled images (Figure 29.7) with scaling factors of 0.2, 0.4, 0.6, 0.8, 1.0 and 1.2 are used in this experiment. The average of the $\sigma/\mu\%$ percentages is 6.48%.

All the patterns used in this experiment were classified correctly by the neural network used in the previous experiment.

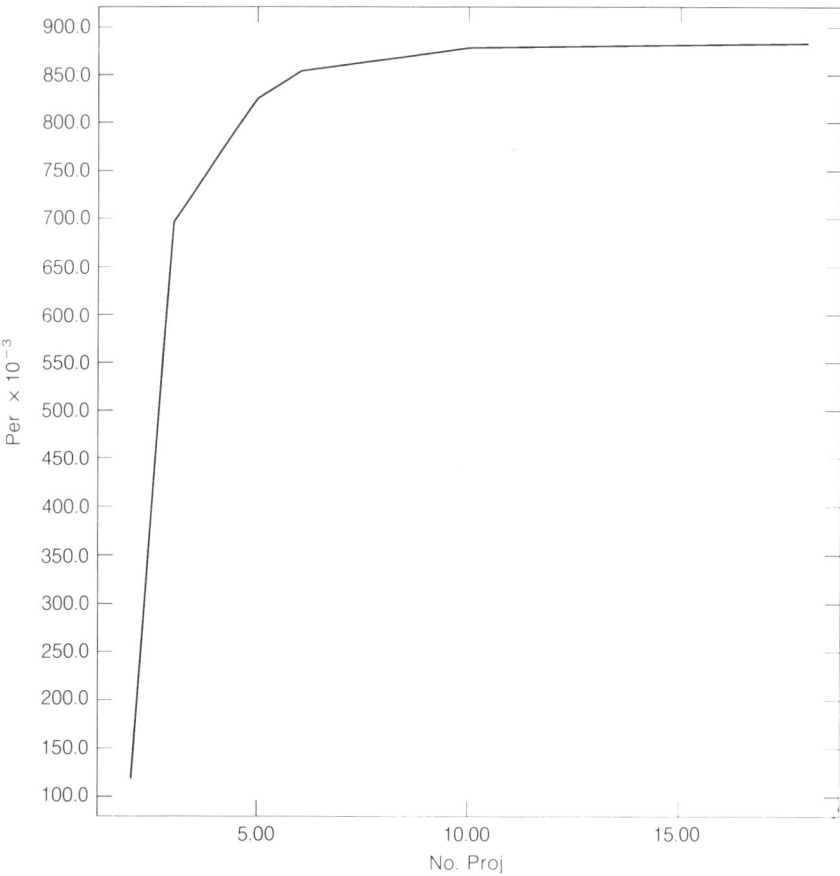

Figure 29.4 *Performance measure* versus *number of projections (the feature vector length). As seen, using six projections gives good performance.*

The scaling factor can be estimated using equation (19). Table 29.7 shows the estimated scaling factor. As evident, the estimation is almost the same as the original.

29.6.3 Effect of white noise

This experiment is conducted to study the effect of white noise on recognition. The feature vector length used in this experiment is 18. In the training phase, only the original non-noisy objects are used. Four transformed objects (Figure 29.8) of each object are used for testing; the original, translated by (10, 10), rotated by 45°, and scaled by a scaling factor of 0.5. White noise with zero

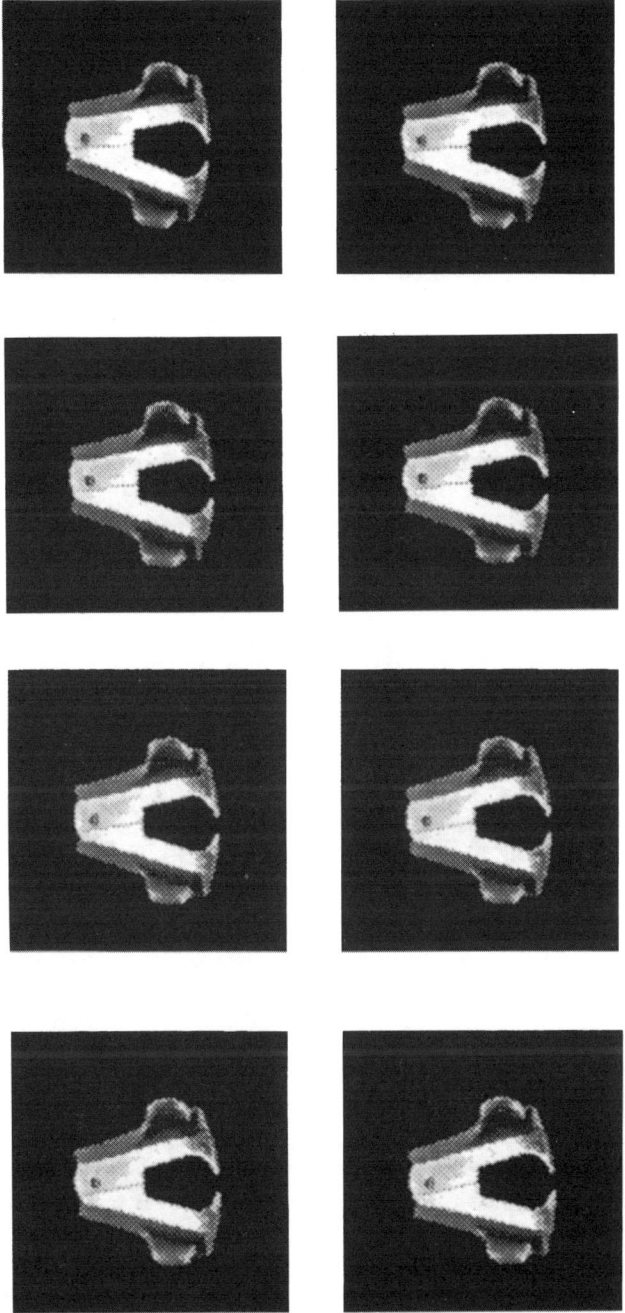

Figure 29.5 *Staple remover images rotated from 0 to 9° with 1° increment to investigate the robustness of the features against rotation.*

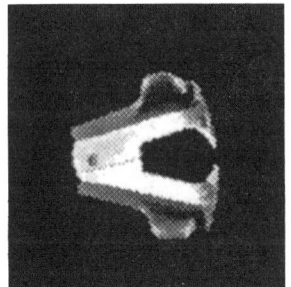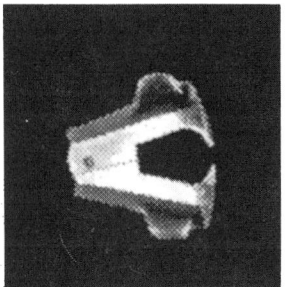

Figure 29.5 *(continued)*

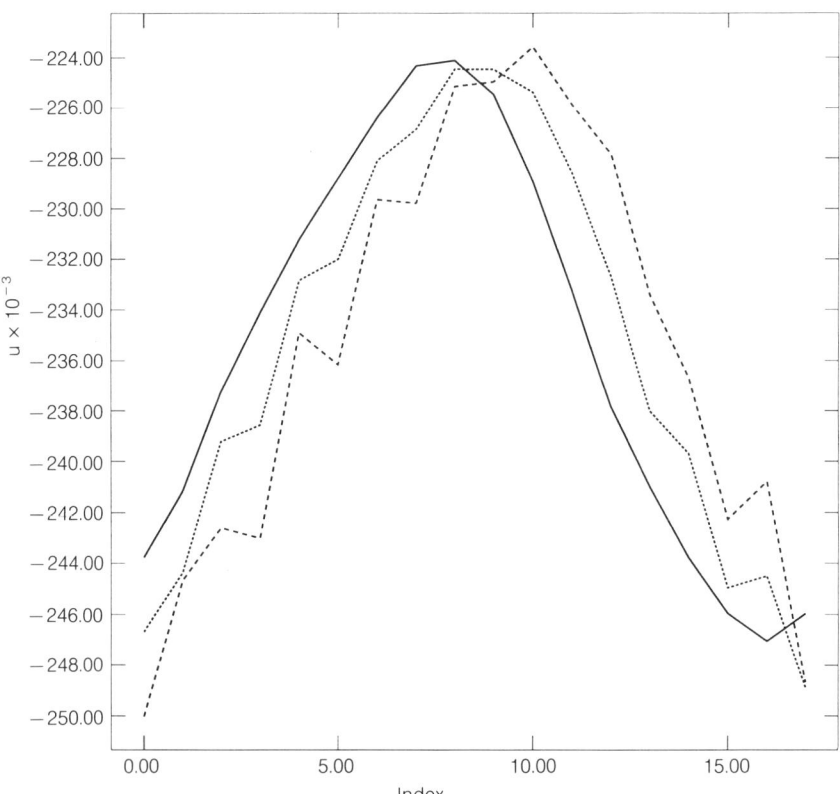

Figure 29.6 *The shift of the first left singular vector due to the rotation of the staple remover by an angle of $0°$ ($-$) $10°$ (- - -) and $20°$ ($--$), respectively. The shift in the left singular vector equals one unit which corresponds to rotation of $10°$.*

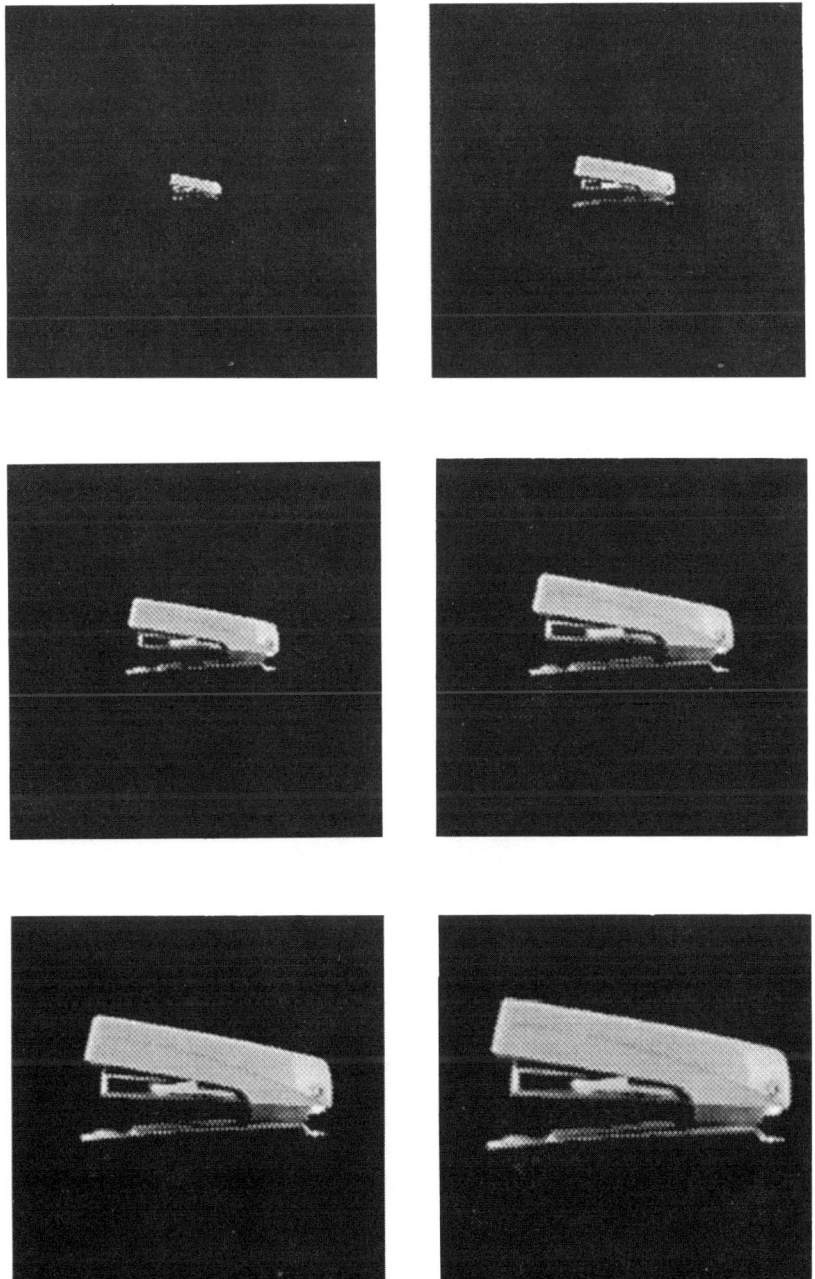

Figure 29.7 *Stapler images scaled from 0.2–1.2 with increments of 0.2 to investigate the robustness of the features against scaling. As seen, the features are robust against scaling.*

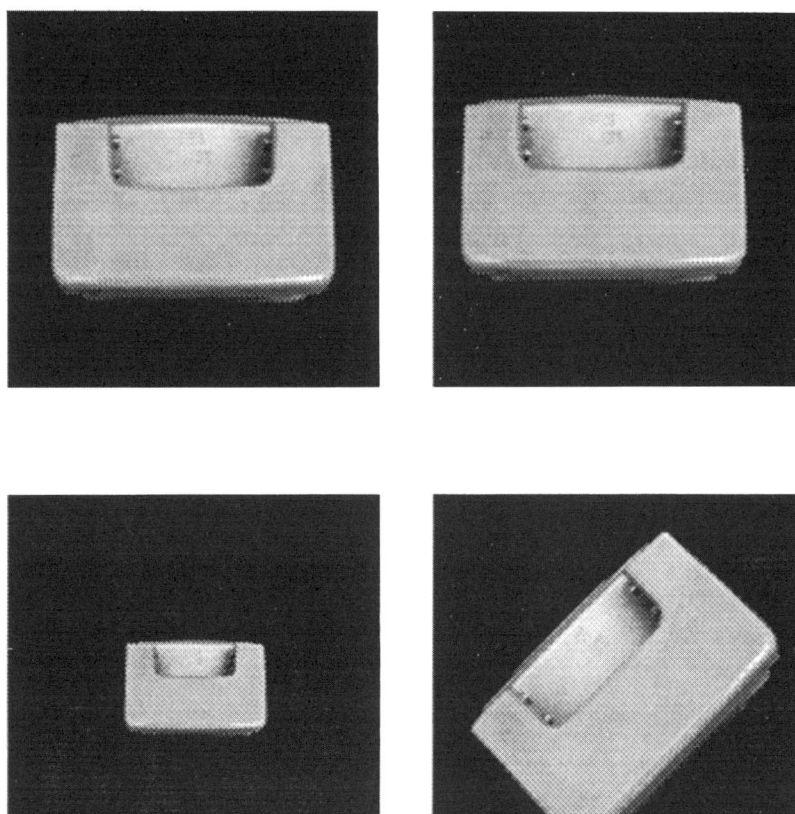

Figure 29.8 *Transformation used to study the white noise effect.*

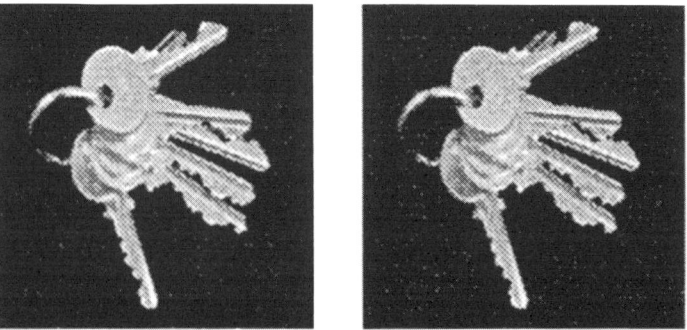

Figure 29.9 *A qualitative illustration for the noise added to the image of the keys when studying the effect of white noise on recognition.*

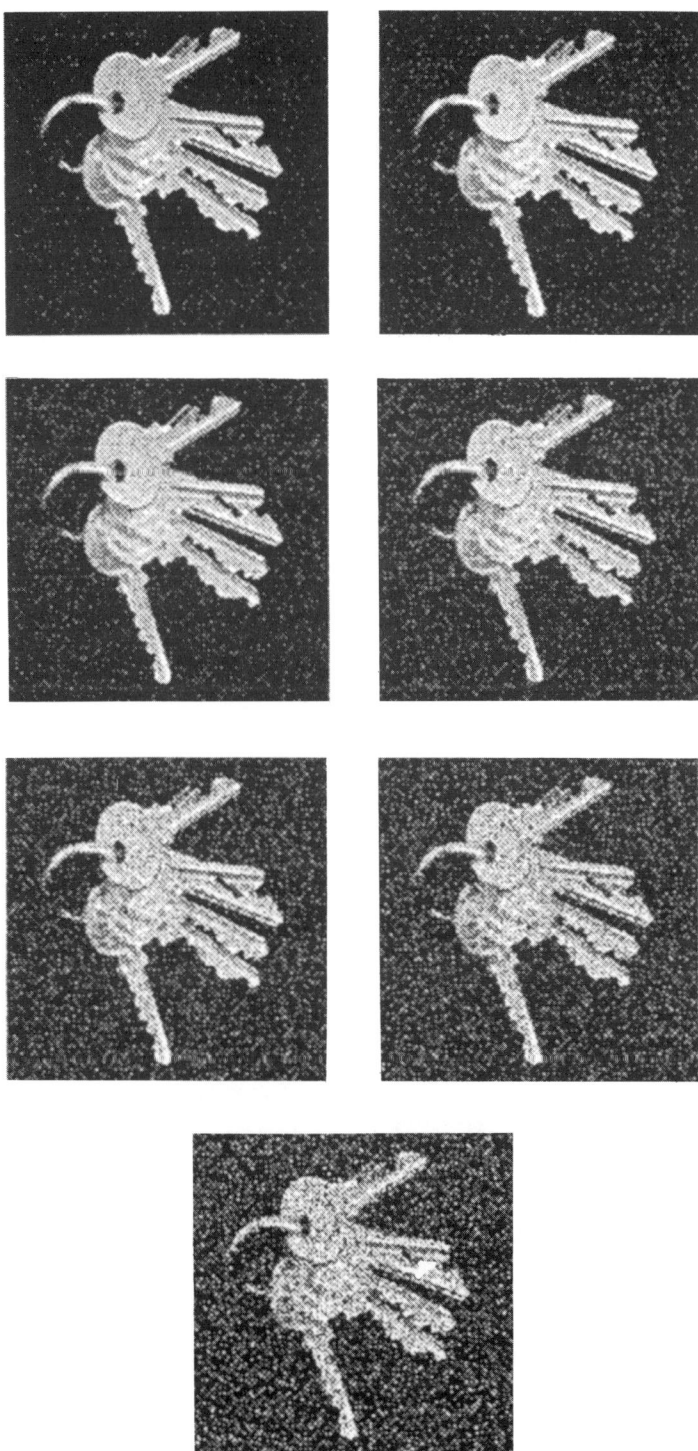

Figure 29.9 (*continued*)

mean was added to each testing image, (Figure 29.9). Recognition percentage and performance measure for each S/N was calculated. Figures 29.10 and 29.11 show the results obtained. Figure 29.12 shows the performance of each transformation done to the objects *versus* noise added.

29.6.4 Comparison with the method of moments

This experiment is conducted to compare the performance of the Radon-based invariant image recognition method with the method of Zernike moments. Moment-based invariant image recognition compares well with the results of other popular invariant feature extraction (Perantonis and Lisboa, 1992). The performance of the Zernike and pseudo-Zernike moments has

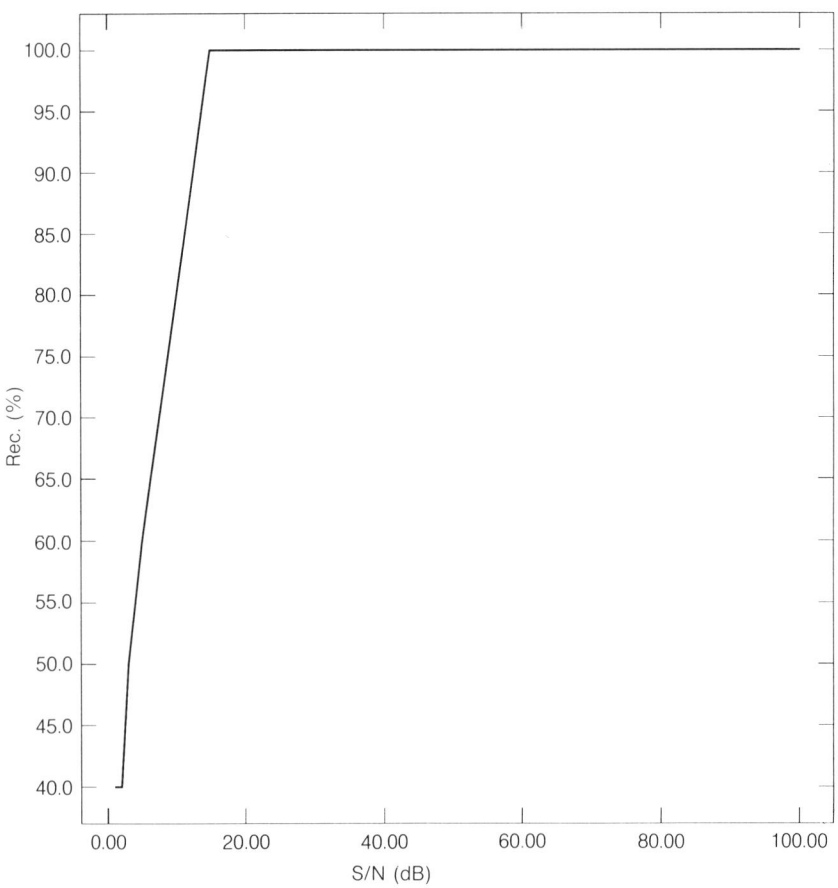

Figure 29.10 *Recognition percentage* versus S/N.

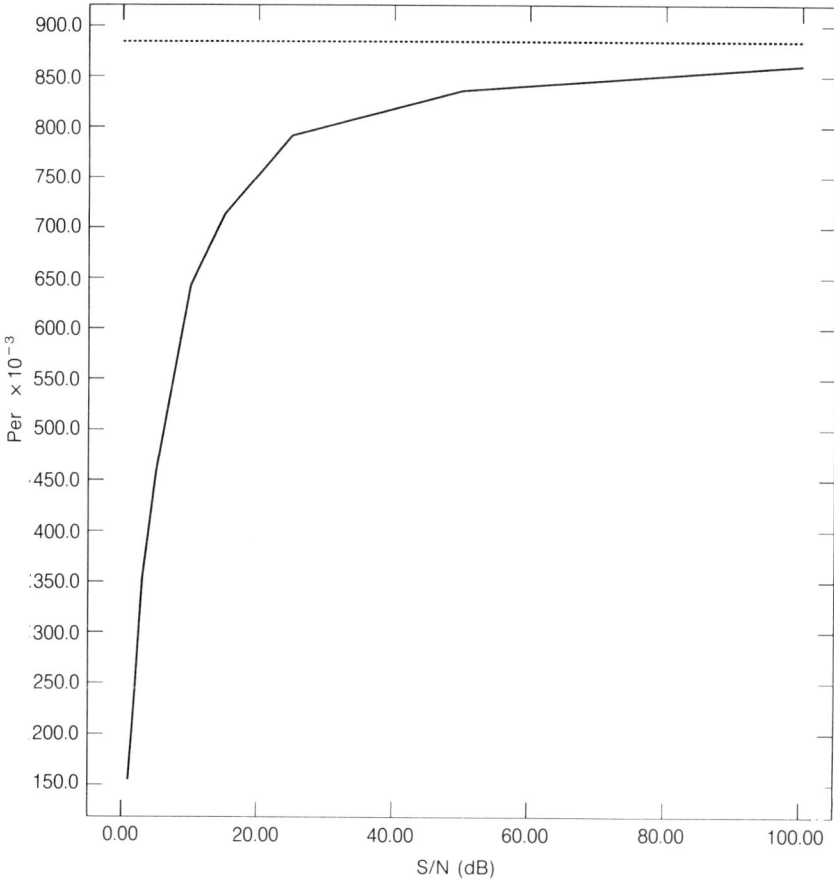

Figure 29.11 *Performamce measure* versus *S/N.* ———: *noisy;* - - -: *non-noisy.*

been shown to be superior to the performance of other types of moments in terms of sensitivity to image noise and information content (Teh and Chin, 1988).

The Zernike moments of order n with respect to l are defined as

$$A_{nl} = \frac{n+1}{\pi} \int_{2\pi} \int_0^\infty [V_{nl}(r, \phi)]^* f(r, \phi) r \, dr \, d\phi \qquad (21)$$

where $n = 0, 1, 2, \ldots, \infty$ and $n - |l| = $ even, $|l| \leqslant n$. The Zernike polynomials are a set of complex-valued functions orthogonal on the unit dis $x^2 + \dot{y}^2 \leqslant 1$. They are defined by

$$V_{nl}(r, \phi) = R_{nl}(r) \, e^{jl\phi} \qquad (22)$$

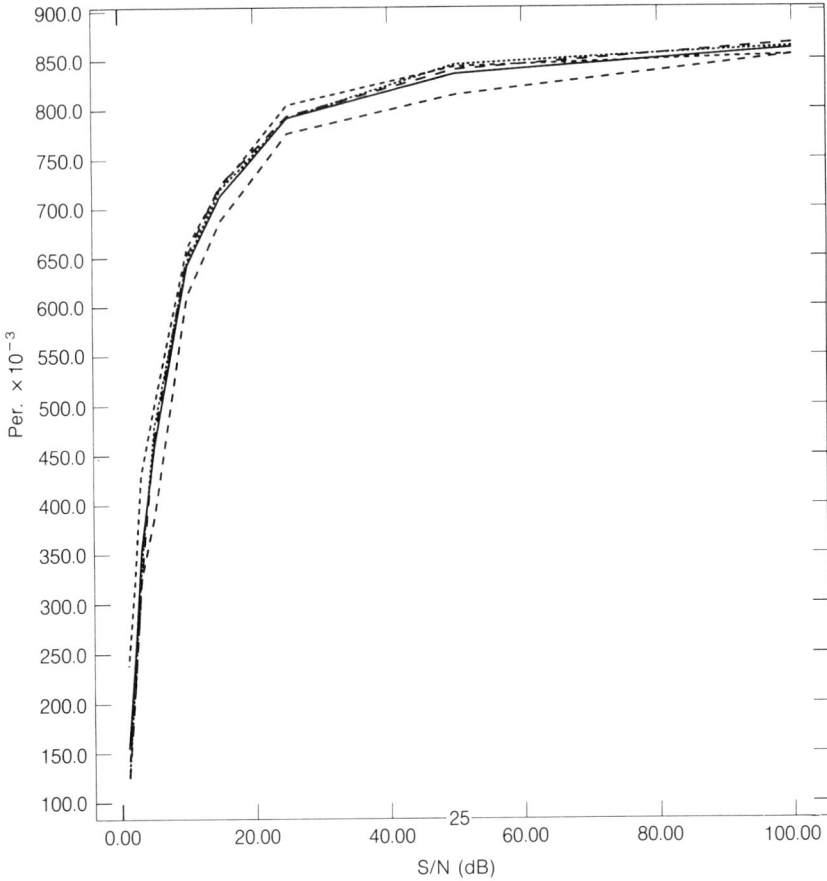

Figure 29.12 *Performance measure versus S/N.* ——: *Total;* · · ·: *original;* - - -: *translated;* - - -: *scaled;* ——: *rotated.*

Table 29.5 *The first seven features of rotated staple remover. As seen, the features are robust aganst rotation*

Angle of rotation	σ_1	σ_2	σ_3	σ_4	σ_5	σ_6	σ_7
0	0.949880	0.253046	0.116033	0.089392	0.062695	0.047311	0.045080
1	0.949954	0.253400	0.115608	0.087676	0.063863	0.048238	0.046302
2	0.949549	0.254868	0.116049	0.088979	0.064080	0.048806	0.045122
3	0.950039	0.253376	0.115791	0.089452	0.064196	0.049605	0.043002
4	0.950269	0.252327	0.114461	0.091734	0.064976	0.051829	0.043843
5	0.950302	0.253028	0.117651	0.090796	0.061883	0.049290	0.042791
6	0.950132	0.254024	0.117760	0.090544	0.061863	0.049779	0.040393
7	0.950280	0.252846	0.119163	0.087849	0.060932	0.050372	0.041152
8	0.950314	0.252748	0.118294	0.088158	0.061528	0.047344	0.041115
9	0.950264	0.252315	0.118293	0.085925	0.062260	0.048379	0.042101

Table 29.6 *Variance to mean ratio (percentage) of all the features of the rotated objects. The ratio is small and by the average it is 3.1%. This table further illustrates the robustness of the feature vector against rotation*

Feature number	Keys	Staple remover	Hole punch	Stapler	Tape dispenser
1	0.016	0.025	0.017	0.079	0.020
2	0.328	0.292	0.031	0.383	0.631
3	0.566	1.229	0.692	1.516	0.713
4	1.557	1.834	1.204	5.107	0.300
5	3.814	2.049	1.580	5.680	2.506
6	2.999	2.691	5.286	6.313	2.429
7	1.392	4.340	7.168	12.720	3.934
8	3.091	5.914	2.261	6.657	2.462
9	3.040	10.920	6.322	5.730	2.732
10	3.783	8.483	4.480	5.705	2.181
11	4.658	7.078	4.461	4.280	4.377
12	4.769	7.213	5.708	6.597	2.717
13	4.833	6.365	5.961	6.935	4.805
14	5.572	6.157	7.513	5.906	2.911
15	3.426	9.868	6.478	6.771	3.886
16	5.083	8.869	6.633	3.636	4.325
17	7.484	8.690	7.602	5.863	5.573
18	9.800	6.164	7.458	5.452	7.813
Average	2.059	3.715	2.903	4.989	1.741

Table 29.7 *The estimated scaling factor[a] factor using equation (19)*

Original scaling factor	Keys	Staple remover	Hole punch	Stapler	Tape dispenser
0.2000	0.1995	0.2020	0.2000	0.2021	0.2006
0.4000	0.4000	0.4003	0.4004	0.4005	0.4005
0.6000	0.5997	0.5997	0.6000	0.6004	0.5998
0.8000	0.8003	0.8007	0.8008	0.8013	0.8007
1.0000	1.0000	1.0000	1.0000	1.0000	1.0000
1.2000	1.1940	1.1972	1.1983	1.1980	1.1978

[a]The scaling factor is determined relative to the objects of Figure 29.2.

Table 29.8 *The first seven features of scaled stapler*

Scaling factor	σ_1	σ_2	σ_3	σ_4	σ_5	σ_6	σ_7
0.2	0.902867	0.363903	0.145755	0.125911	0.062013	0.055039	0.045353
0.4	0.904646	0.358199	0.152912	0.117272	0.074648	0.053142	0.049166
0.6	0.904751	0.357453	0.151978	0.120282	0.076433	0.051824	0.049074
0.8	0.904539	0.355983	0.155194	0.125554	0.075964	0.049724	0.046334
1.0	0.903940	0.355767	0.155259	0.126030	0.077862	0.050962	0.050408
1.2	0.904409	0.357483	0.155013	0.122711	0.076896	0.050097	0.047075

Table 29.9 *Variance to mean percentage of all the features of the scaled objects. The ratio is small and by the average it is 6.5%. This table further illustrates the robustness of the feature vector against scaling*

Feature number	Keys	Staple remover	Hole punch	Stapler	Tape dispenser
1	0.068386	0.032415	0.004781	0.071463	0.056927
2	1.862529	0.931086	0.455430	0.759601	1.870536
3	0.833467	1.028653	0.541184	2.187228	2.571677
4	2.332124	2.138348	3.531025	2.665441	0.923069
5	1.209885	2.517066	2.941441	7.346515	3.177121
6	1.989057	3.809874	2.228511	3.542740	5.660154
7	2.076525	2.244302	1.771226	3.704285	7.833734
8	2.155904	8.808520	10.633659	3.874142	8.478910
9	2.524689	16.365229	12.709072	2.227137	7.728633
10	3.606891	11.691761	11.681385	7.543673	7.570441
11	4.320522	10.603070	12.876406	8.542035	7.945292
12	4.421000	15.615104	4.191956	9.326546	4.276928
13	3.139513	8.984010	12.331057	18.669847	3.594523
14	4.524668	4.823858	5.722368	13.996540	1.712528
15	3.981825	4.570429	16.803171	12.159415	2.830502
16	2.445495	3.401840	18.787466	12.033607	5.861289
17	7.184366	15.953438	12.128682	6.145161	9.295919
18	6.109355	25.314453	17.585051	7.935613	17.050816
19	3.109910	8.261209	7.749619	5.653704	7.645201

where

$$R_{nl}(r) = \sum_{s=0}^{(n-|l|)/2} (-1)^s \frac{(n-s)!}{s!\left(\dfrac{n+|l|}{2}-s\right)!\left(\dfrac{n-|l|}{2}-s\right)!} r^{n-2s} \qquad (23)$$

The image $f(r, \phi)$ can be expanded in terms of the Zernike moments and polynomials over the unit disk by

$$f(r, \phi) = \sum_{n=0}^{\infty} \sum_{\substack{l \\ n-|l|=\text{even} \\ |l| \leqslant n}}^{\infty} A_{nl} V_{nl}(r, \phi). \qquad (24)$$

It can be approximated by limiting the sum to n^*. That is,

$$f(r, \phi) = \sum_{n=0}^{n^*} \sum_{\substack{l \\ n-|l|=\text{even} \\ |l| \leqslant n}}^{\infty} A_{nl} V_{nl}(r, \phi). \qquad (25)$$

Optimal performance is achieved for n^* in the range of 10–12 (Teh and Chin,

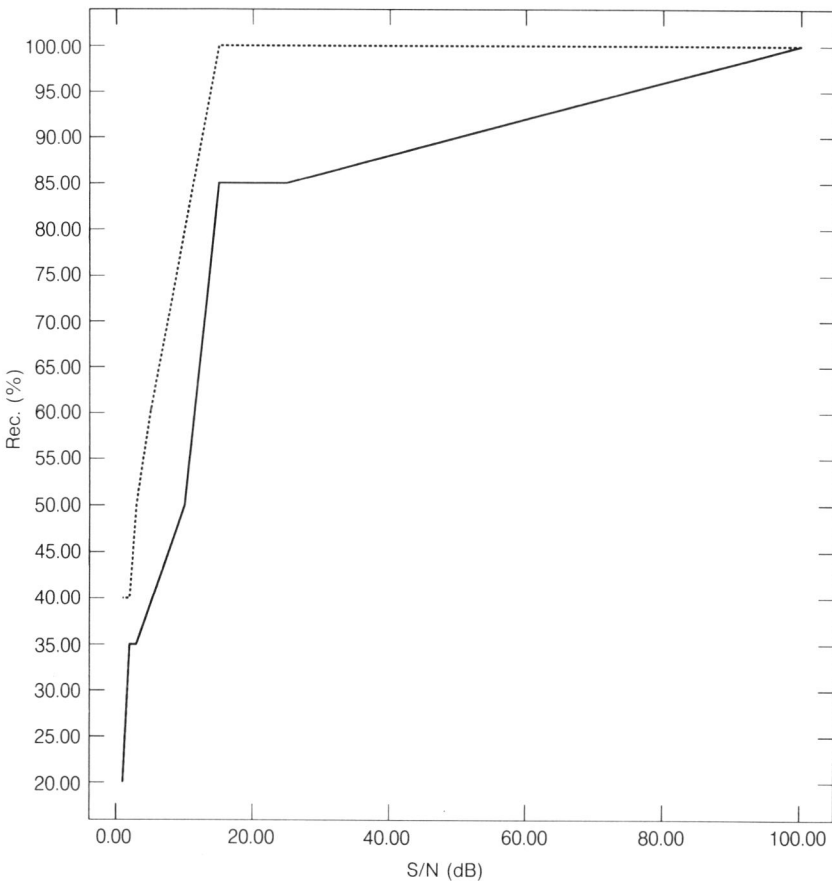

Figure 29.13 *Recognition percentage* versus *S/N for Zernike moments and Radon-based features. As seen, the recognition rate of the projection-based method is better than that of the method of the Zernike moments.* —— *Zernike;* - - - - *Radon-based.*

1988; Perantonis and Lisboa, 1992). In this experiment, we use up to moments of order 11 because it gave the best performance for our example.

The same experiment as the white noise experiment was conducted. The result of this experiment shows that the Radon-based features outperformed the method of Zernike moments (Figures 29.13 and 29.14).

29.7 Conclusions

A discrete Radon transform method for invariant image analysis artificial neural networks has been developed. This method is based on utilizing the projections of the image to achieve invariant features. The singular values of

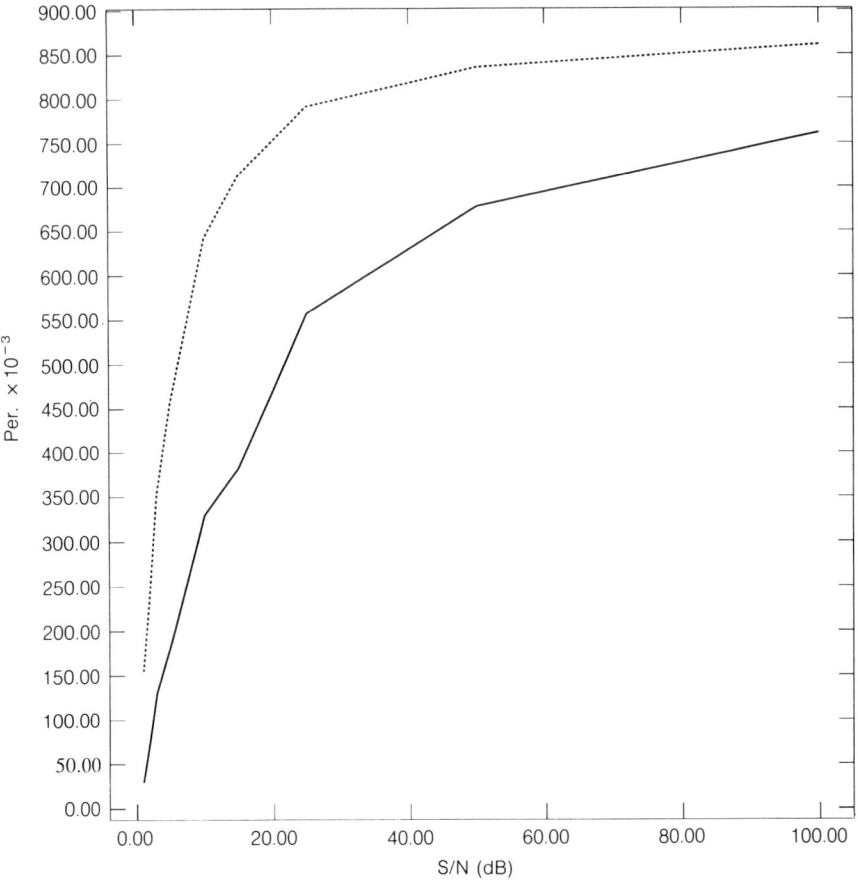

Figure 29.14 *Performance measure* versus *S/N for Zernike moments and Radon-based features. As seen, the performance of the projection-based method is better than that of the method of the Zernike moments.* ⸻ *Zernike;* ---- *Radon-based.*

the projection image, constructed by row-stacking each projection, are used as the invariant features. The feature vector is used as input to a back-propagation neural network followed by a maximum-output-selector to classify the image.

This method has been examined and its merits have been illustrated. It has also been compared with the method of Zernike moments, which is a leading feature extraction method. The proposed method outperformed the method of Zernike moments in terms of recognition percentage, performance measure, sensitivity to image noise, and number of features used.

References

Barnard, E. and Casasent, D. (1991) Invariance and neural nets. *IEEE Transactions on Neural Networks*, **2**(5), September.

Deans, S.R. (1983) *The Radon Transform and Some of its Applications*. Wiley, New York, NY.

Fukumi, M., Omatu, S., Takeda, F. and Kosaka, T. (1992) Rotation-invariant neural pattern recognition system with application to coin recognition. *IEEE Transaction on Neural Networks*, **3**(2), March.

Fukushima, K. and Wake, N. (1991) Handwritten alphanumeric character recognition by the neucognitron. *IEEE Transactions on Neural Networks*, **2**(3), 355–65, May.

Jain, A.K. (1989) *Fundamentals of Digital Image Processing*. Prentice Hall, Englewood Cliffs, NJ.

Khotanzad, A. and Hong, Y.H. (1990) Invariant image recognition by Zernike moments. *IEEE Transactions on Pattern Recognition and Machine Intelligence*, **12**(5), May.

Kollias, S., Stafylopatis, A. and Tirakis, A. (1991) Performance of higher order neural networks in invariant recognition, in *Neural Networks: Advances and Applications* (ed. E. Gelenbe), Elsevier, Amsterdam, pp. 79–108.

Maass, P. (1991) Singular value decompositon for Radon transforms, in *Mathematical Methods in Tomography* (ed. G.T. Herman, A.K. Louis and F. Netterer), *Lecture Notes in Mathematics 1497*, Springer-Verlag, Berlin, pp. 6–14.

Madhvapathy, P.R. (1986) Pattern recognition using simple measures of projections. *Master of Science Thesis*, Colorado State University.

Maxwell, T. and Giles, C.L. (1986) *Transformation Invariance Using High Order Correlation in Neural Net Architectures*. Proc. IEEE International Conference on System, Man and Cybernetics, Atlanta, GA, pp. 627–32.

Mitchell, O.R. and Lutton, S.M. (1978) Segmentation and classification of targets in FLIR imagery. *SPIE Image Understanding Systems & Industrial Applications*, vol. 155, pp. 83–90.

Perantonis, S.J. and Lisboa, P.J.G. (1992) Translation, rotation, and scale invariant pattern recognition by higher-order neural networks and moment classifiers. *IEEE Transactions on Neural Networks*, **3**(2), March.

Pitts, W. and McCulloch, W.S. (1947) How we preceive universals: The perception of auditory and visual forms. *Bull. Math. Biophysics*, **9**, 127–47.

Press, W.H., Flannery, B.P., Teukolsky, S.A. and Vetterling, W.T. (1988) *Numerical Recipes in C, The Art of Scientific Computing*. Cambridge University Press, Cambridge.

Reeves, A.P. and Rostampour A. (1981) Shape of segmented objects using moments. *Proceedings IEEE Computer Society Conference on Pattern Recognition and Image Processing*, pp. 171–4, August.

Sanz, J.L.C., Hinkle, E.B. and Jain, A.K. (1988) *Radon and Projection Transform-based Computer Vision*. Springer-Verlag, Berlin.

Teh, C.H. and Chin, R.T. (1988) On image analysis by the methods of moments. *IEEE Transactions on Pattern Analysis and Machine Intelligence*, **10**(4), July.

Widrow, B., Winter, R.G. and Baxter, R.A. (1988) Layered neural nets for pattern recognition. *IEEE Transactions on Acoustics, Speech, Signal Processing*, **36**(7), 1109–18.

Wong, E. and Steppe, J.A. (1969) Invariant recognition of geometric shapes, in *Methodologies of Pattern Recognition* (ed. S. Watanabe), Academic Press, New York, NY, pp. 535–46.

Zadeh, L.A. (1965) Fuzzy sets. *Information and Control*, **8**, 338–53.

30

Neural network segmentation and recognition of text data on engineering documents

PHILIP GOUIN and CHRISTOPHER SCOFIELD
Nestor, Inc., One Richmond Square, Providence, RI 02906, USA

30.1 Introduction

Vectorization of existing paper engineering documents is a major and challenging phase in the process of implementing a CADAM system. The high cost of manual conversion of data requires the use of automatic or semi-automatic systems to make drawing conversion projects cost effective.

On many documents, large amounts of text data are present that carry critical information relating to the graphical objects on the drawings. Most current automatic character recognition techniques are poorly suited to the task of recognizing the text data present on these drawings. The nature and structure of the text data present on a typical engineering document lead to the difficulties experienced by standard OCR techniques.

The structure of an engineering document is far less constrained than the ordinary 'page' of text that most OCR technologies are designed to operate on. As a consequence, the segmention of the document image (locating and extracting text data) becomes a very significant problem. An example of a typical image segment is shown in Figure 30.1. Text instances are to be discriminated from other objects such as graphics, lines, symbols, specks of noise, etc. Additionally, the text can appear in various styles, sizes and orientations. Perhaps the most difficult aspect of segmentation arises from the fact that characters can be touching each other or any other graphical object, as in Figure 30.2. To address these segmentation problems, we have implemented a segmentation system based on a hierarchical recurrent neural

Artificial Neural Networks for Speech and Vision. Edited by Richard J. Mammone. Published in 1993 by Chapman & Hall, London. ISBN 0 412 54850 X

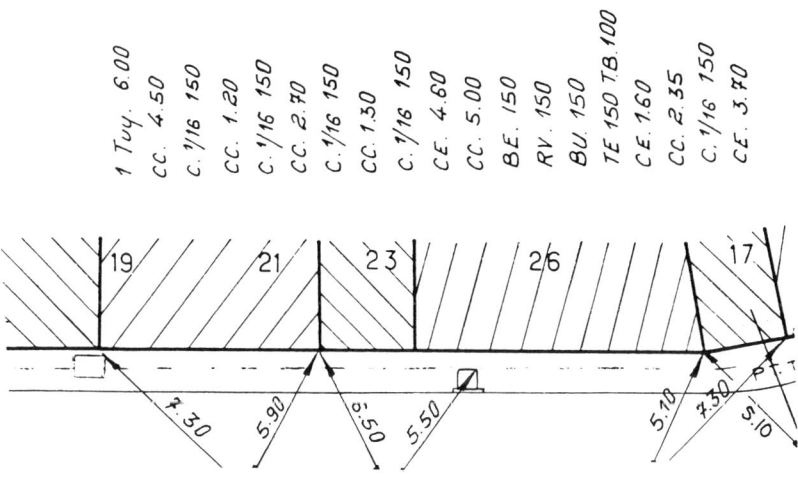

Figure 30.1 *Typical document image segment.*

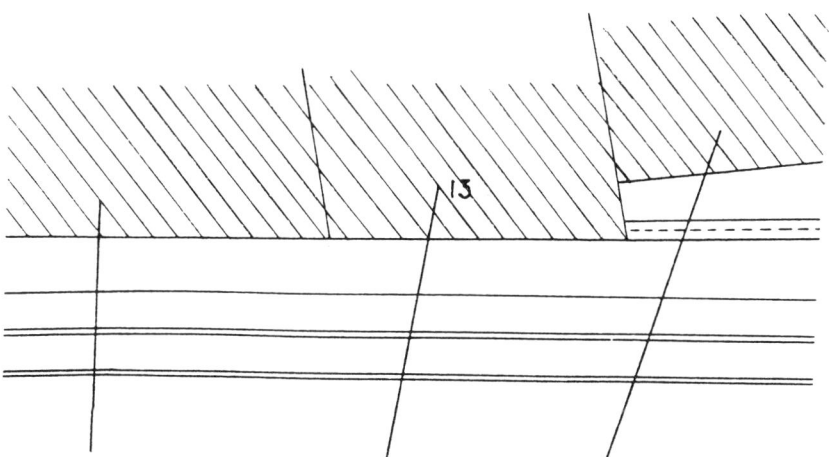

Figure 30.2 *Text instance 'touching' graphical data.*

network structure. Additionally, we have implemented a segmentation 'filter' based on a spatially recurrent neural network. This network uses context information to resolve classification conflicts.

The nature of the text data present on a typical engineering document is a mix of drafted handprint, machine print of various sizes and styles, and a host of special symbols that can be specific to a particular document type. Most current OCR technologies simply cannot robustly handle this mix of text data. We have implemented a neural network classifier that uses three layers of non-adaptive preprocessing followed by a three or four layer gradient descent trained Multi-Layer Perceptron (MLP).

30.2 Segmentation

The goal of segmentation is to isolate and extract all text that may be present on a document image. Because of the unconstrained nature of the structure of the typical engineering document image, commonly used OCR segmentation and isolation techniques are not able to perform this task. We have designed and implemented a three stage segmentation process to perform this task using MLP classification engines.

The first stage of processing uses an MLP that classifies patterns of connected pixels from the document image. The connected pixel patterns are generated by a set of functions that allow a single pass pixel connectivity analysis of the document image with simultaneous feature generation. The functions are based on pixel connectivity algorithms in Cunningham (1981). Processing of a scanned pixel image with these functions produces a list of segmented pixel regions with extracted features for each region. The features are based on first and second order distributions of the pixels in a connected pattern (Hu, 1962). Some of the features used were

area	a	perimeter	p
number of holes	n_h	area of holes	a_h
perimeter of holes	ph		
principal moments	M_1, M_2	moment ratio 1	$\dfrac{M_1 + M_2}{ap}$
moment ratio 2	$\dfrac{M_1 - M_2}{ap}$		

These features form the input layer for a gradient descent MLP. The output layer of the MLP consists of five neurons for each of five distinct classes of patterns. These classes are:

- *Text* (*T*): handprinted or machine printed alpha and numeric text at any location or orientation,
- *Graphics* (*G*): lines or figures that unambiguously comprise the 'drawn' non-text objects,
- *Mixed* (*M*): text touching graphics, but generally of small size,
- *Unknown* (*U*): very large patterns that may or may not be touching text,
- *Noise* (*N*): very small patterns that result from broken lines, specks of dirt, etc.

It should be noted that while these pattern categories have a very specific definition with regard to a particular data set, they are in fact a very generic set of categories that may be extended easily to many other document processing applications.

Two subgroupings of these classes are important to the functionality of the segmentation system. The *T*, *G* and *N* classes form the subgroup of 'terminal' classifications (they cannot be decomposed). The *M* and *U* classes form the subgroup of 'non-terminal' classifications (they can be decomposed into *T*, *G* and *N* subpatterns. The distribution of these classes in a typical map segment (approx. 22 × 28 cm section of a network map) is shown in Figure 30.3. It should be noted that while the *U* category makes up a very small percentage of the total patterns, these patterns are typically quite large and can account for a very large percentage of the 'on' pixels (as much as 40%) in the image. The same is true to a smaller degree for the *M* category. Because these categories may contain hidden or touching text, it is important that their classification accuracy remains high even though the relative frequency of these pattern categories is very low when compared with the other pattern categories. A map segment may have as few as several hundred

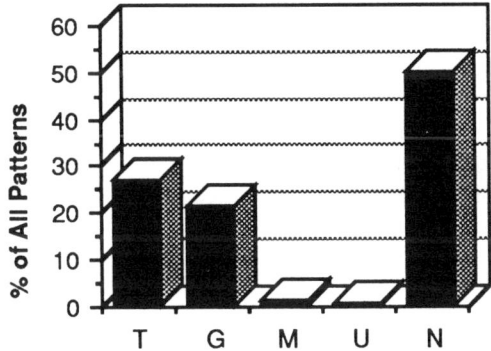

Figure 30.3 *Distribution of pattern categories.*

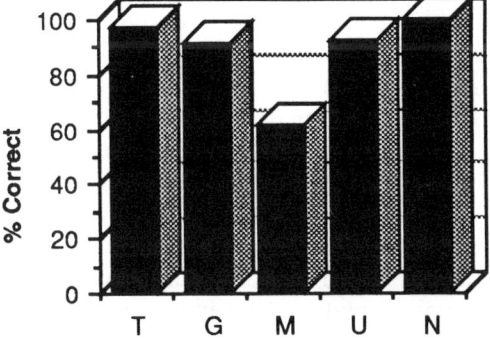

Figure 30.4 *Segmentation ANN accuracy.*

Table 30.1 *Segmentation cross-error table*

Actual	ID as text	ID as graphic	ID as mixed	ID as unknown	ID as noise
Text	3093	66	4	0	4
Graphic	130	2158	8	12	66
Mixed	9	3	19	0	0
Unknown	0	3	0	38	0
Noise	0	4	0	0	6120

patterns, or as many as 1500–2000 patterns. After having been trained on approximately 16 000 patterns, the neural network is able to achieve the classification performance shown in Figure 30.4 on 11 000 unseen patterns.

The breakdown of the errors made in the classification of patterns is shown in the form of a cross-error table in Table 30.1. The diagonal terms in the table represent correct classifications. The off diagonal terms are errors. The type of error is shown by examining the row label followed by the column label. Of particular interest are the text patterns that are erroneously classified as graphic patterns (66 patterns in this test). An analysis of these cases reveal the majority of the misclassifications result from either very small poorly formed text patterns, or long thin text patterns such as i's and 1's that tend to look like line segments (graphic patterns).

Also of interest in the cross-error table is the classification of mixed patterns. Note that most of the misclassifications of mixed patterns are 'called' text. This is a favorable error as it retains the text that is a part of the mixed pattern. If these 'errors' are treated as correct classifications, the performance on mixed patterns rises from 61% to 90%.

30.2.1 *Iterative segmentation*

The second stage of segmentation processing uses a decision tree guided by an MLP classification engine to perform the difficult task of segmenting 'hidden' text, or text touching graphics. Resolution trees have been very effectively applied on a number of machine vision segmentation problems. Conceptually, one starts with the lowest level of resolution possible, and attempts to make a segmentation decision on that level. If the data does not allow an unambiguous decision, branching of the decision tree occurs, and the data is examined at the next higher level of resolution. This approach is most effective if the information is available at lower levels of resolution to rapidly prune the growing decision tree. In this case 1 to 2 orders of magnitude improvement can be realized over an exhaustive search (sliding pattern window) at the highest resolution. Our approach uses an ANN to make the segmentation decision at all resolution branch points. The segmentation is in effect driven by the recognition results of the ANN.

As previously mentioned, the **mixed** and **unknown** classes were specified as 'non-terminal' classifications (they could be decomposed into *T*, *G* and *N* subpatterns). As such, they are ambiguous classifications and are subject to decision tree decomposition that functions as follows. The regions of the image classified as **mixed** or **unknown** by the first stage segmentation network become the root nodes of the decision tree. Each root node covers an area in the input image space determined at its initial classification. Branching of the decision tree is accomplished by splitting this area into four overlapping regions. The subregion overlap is made large enough to enclose the largest **text** patterns typically encountered. This ensures that these patterns will not be split in such a way as to be unrecognizable. Connected pixel groups in each subregion are the successor nodes of each subregion. All successor nodes are analysed by the segmentation ANN. Successor nodes with 'terminal' classifications (**text**, **graphics**, **noise**) become leaf nodes of the tree. Those successor nodes with 'non-terminal' classifications (**mixed**, **unknown**) become new branch points in the tree. Node generation continues until no 'non-terminal' nodes remain to be branched or until a minimum size image area covered by the current branching nodes is reached. The tree expands at first as many new ambiguous patterns are generated. Very quickly, however, the tree begins to prune itself by eliminating **graphics**, **noise**, and **text** nodes of the tree. As the branching reaches the highest resolutions (minimum sized areas to be processed) the overlap region becomes a very high percentage of the area to be processed. This may result in different (text) leaf nodes of the tree covering the same actual text instance. A two dimensional spatial clustering of the final leaf nodes of the tree is used to merge together any such instances.

The same MLP used for the initial segmentation can be used for the decision tree segmentation. Our experimentation with the decision tree segmentation system is very encouraging. We are able to demonstrate a range of capability of extraction of hidden or touching text. With very restrictive control, we are able to extract 20–30% of the hidden or touching text with a very low false alarm (patterns incorrectly identified as text) rate (< 0.25%). With very liberal control, we are be able to extract 95% of the hidden text with only a moderate false alarm rate (3–5%). Figure 30.5 shows an example

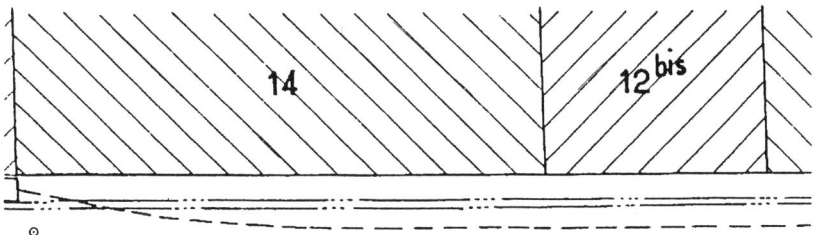

Figure 30.5 *Text instance enmeshed with graphic data.*

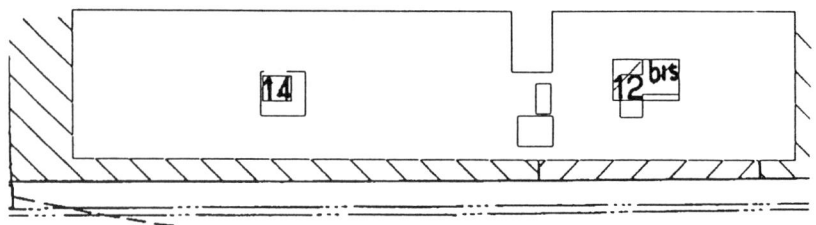

Figure 30.6 *Results using decision tree segmentation.*

image segment with the text enmeshed in a cross hatched pattern. Figure 30.6 shows the segmented text data for the image segment.

30.2.2 *Contextual segmentation*

The third stage of segmentation processing uses the 'context' to address the problem of patterns that are not well enough characterized by their shape to be correctly identified as text. Contextual processing is a powerful tool, and is used by humans at unconscious and conscious levels when performing a segmentation and recognition task. The basic assumption underlying contextual segmentation is that text patterns most often occur in the near proximity of other text patterns. In most document processing applications, this is a fairly safe assumption.

To implement context segmentation, we developed a secondary MLP that would function as a filter on the classifications produced by the first and second stages of segmentation. This secondary MLP uses 'context' information from surrounding patterns as well as the same set of pattern features used for the initial classification of the pattern. The context features are spatially recurrent. They are formed directly from the output activations of the patterns in the vicinity of a pattern that is to be filtered as follows. For all patterns within a radius R of the current pattern:

$$\text{Text Context Feature} = F_T = \sum_{i=1}^{N} A_T(i)^* \, e^{(-\beta * d(i))}$$

where $A_{T(i)}$ is the text activation for the ith pattern, and d is the distance from the ith pattern to the current pattern. β is adjusted to severely attenuate the activation input from patterns beyond twice the width of the average pattern.

In training of the context network the context 'truth set' in the training data was used to create the context features. In this case, all patterns had activations of 1.0 associated with their true class, and 0.0 otherwise. In testing, only the instantiations of pattern classes that would otherwise be discarded (**graphics** and **noise**) are processed by the context network. In these cases, use of the context segmentation network raised the overall performance on true **text** patterns from 97.4% to 98.9% correct.

The overhead involved in the use of the contextual network is only the calculation of the local contextual measures for each blob to be filtered and, in general, is well worth the increased accuracy obtained when employed.

30.3 Character recognition

The feature extraction is performed by three layers of non-adaptive processing. The features correspond to local edge measures derivable either from the 'raw' pixel image, the image medial axis or the character contour. The first layer of processing is the convolution of the image data with a set of 3×3 edge kernels K. The convolution is identical to the processing of the image data by a layer of cells which are selective to various orientations. For image intensities $I(\underline{r}')$ at point $\underline{r}'$ in the pixel image, an activation $x_i^1(\underline{r})$ for edge orientation i is produced in the first plane of cells, at point $\underline{r}$ according to

$$x_i^1(\underline{r}) = \int_r I(\underline{r}')K_i(\underline{r} - \underline{r}')d\underline{r}' \quad \text{for } i = 1, N_K$$

where there are N_K possible edge orientations. The first plane of cells produces a layer of activations with identical spatial coordinates as that of the image. However, N_K cells are located at each point $\underline{r}$ in the cell layer. Figure 30.7 shows a sampling of kernel function $K_i(\underline{r} - \underline{r}'), (i = 1, N_K)$ employed for feature extraction from the character.

The next layer of processing must organize the responses $x_i^1(\underline{r})$ of the first layer. This process may be viewed as a spatial convolution on the activations of the first layer, which produces a second layer of activations $x_i^2(\underline{r})$

$$x_i^2(\underline{r}) = \int_r x_i^1(\underline{r})G(\underline{r} - \underline{r}')d\underline{r}' \quad \text{for } i = 1, N_K.$$

Here the cell receptive fields $G(\underline{r} - \underline{r}')$ are much simpler than those of the

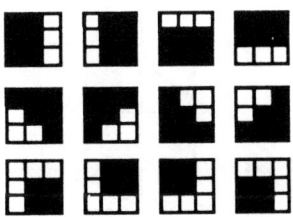

Figure 30.7 *Edge convolution kernels K.*

preceding layer. $G(\underline{r} - \underline{r}')$ simply describes a rectangular window function, with dimensions w_x and w_y, given by

$$G(\underline{r} - \underline{r}') = 1 \quad \text{if } |x - x'| < \frac{w_x}{2} \quad \text{and } |y - y'| < \frac{w_y}{2},$$

$$= 0 \quad \text{otherwise.}$$

Thus the second layer of processing organizes the edge activations from the first layer into 'windows' on the pixel image. The window pattern of receptive fields is shown in Figure 30.8.

The third layer of processing concatenates the second layer activations into a vector f, which serves as input to the MLP. This representation spatially organizes the edge information according to the part of the image in which it occurred. This processing produces a regional estimate of feature frequency

$$H_i(\underline{r}) = \int_{r'} F_i(\underline{r}')G(\underline{r} - \underline{r}')\mathrm{d}\underline{r}'.$$

The neural network must then determine which spatial organization of edges corresponds to which character classes. Feature extraction of this type has been investigated by others for both machine vision and character recognition (Fukushima, 1980; Menon and Heinemann, 1988; Denker *et al.*, 1988; Scofield, 1988).

The adaptive classification network implemented was a three layer feed-forward network. The input layer size varied from 120–240 neurons depending on the output of the feature extraction layers. The activations of the output layer of the classification network were used directly to classify the incoming pattern type. The output layer dimensionality was fixed at 38, for the 26 alphabetic characters (upper and lower cases were matched), the 10 numerics

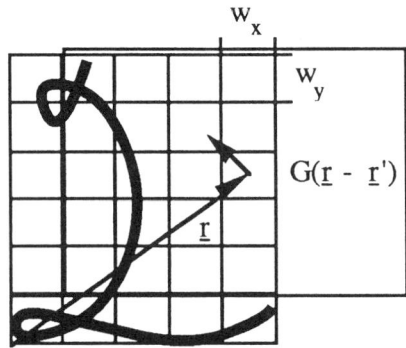

Figure 30.8 *Second layer window processing.*

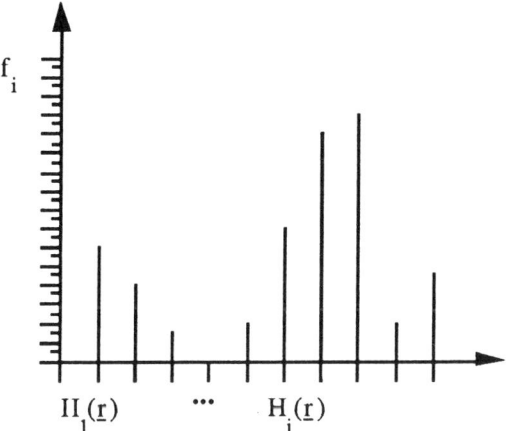

Figure 30.9 *Third layer preprocessing.*

and two special characters ('/' and 'ϕ'). The hidden layer dimensionality (20) was chosen as part of the training regimen to give the best overall network performance with reasonable network training times.

A labeled and verified data set was created from the **water-network** documents. Altogether, approximately 8000 characters, among which alphanumeric characters of varied sizes (ranging from to 3×10 to 50×60 pixels at a resolution of 200 dpi), styles (bloc, handprint, uppercase, lowercase) and orientations (unconstrained) were included. 60% of data were used for training, and 40% for testing.

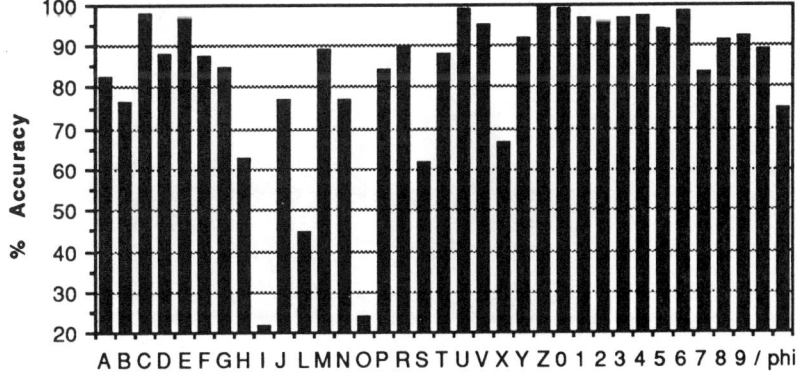

Figure 30.10 *Recognition accuracy.*

Our baseline recognition accuracy on all classes combined with this network memory is 93.85%. The recognition accuracy on a class by class basis is shown in Figure 30.10.

The classes that had the poorest accuracy are shown isolated in Figure 30.11. The bars just to the right of the accuracy bars for each category are the percentages that the category represents in the test data as a whole.

It is clear that the data for these categories represents a relatively small percentage of the overall testing and training data set. As such they are likely to be poorly trained when compared with data that has much higher frequency in the data set. Additionally, it should be noted that these patterns represent many of the ambiguous categories one would expect when training an alpha and numeric memory ('O' and '0', 'I' and 'l', etc.). Table 30.2 presents the

Table 30.2 *Misclassification behavior*

ID	Total Pats	ID as	Frequency	ID as	Frequency
I	28	I	6	1	15
O	25	O	6	0	18
L	38	L	17	1	14
S	52	S	32	5	13
H	8	H	5	4	1
X	9	X	6	2	2
phi	28	phi	21	3	3
B	102	B	78	8	5
J	13	J	10	U	2
N	35	N	27	O	5

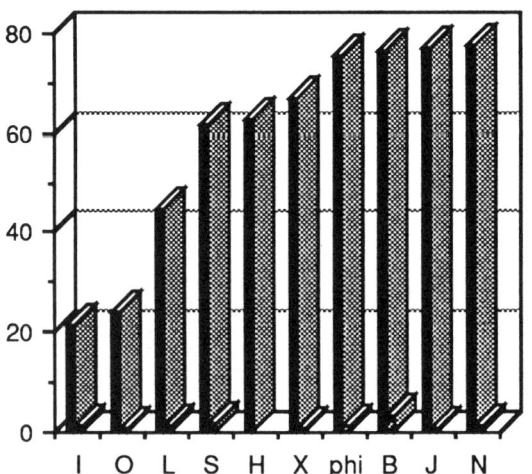

Figure 30.11 *Low accuracy results.*

two most frequently occurring classifications for the patterns of the classes shown in Figure 30.11.

When we look at the actual data being classified in these cases, it is most often unclear what the pattern actually is without the use of contextual information. These errors cannot be trained out and can very likely be removed by the use of a post processor that knows the grammar and semantics of the application.

30.4 Summary

We have developed a novel approach to the segmentation of text data from unconstrained document images using neural networks. Two difficult segmentation problems have been addressed: the segmentation of text touching arbitrary graphical objects (and other text), and the segmentation of noisy, broken data in a cluttered image environment. The neural network guided decision tree classifier developed for segmentation clearly demonstrates the capability to segment text when touching arbitrary graphical objects in the document images. This is a problem that has long defied a general solution. The spatially recurrent neural network used for 'context' aided segmentation demonstrated the capability to enhance the segmentation of noisy, broken and ambiguous data.

References

Cunningham, R. (1981) Segmenting binary images. *Robotics Age*, July/August, pp. 4–19.

Denker, J.S., Gardner, W.R., Graf, H.P., *et al.* (1989) Neural network recognizer for hand-written zip code digits, in *Advances in Neural Information Processing I* (ed. D.S. Touretzky), Morgan Kaufmann, San Mateo, CA, pp. 323–31.

Fukushima, K. (1980) Neocognitron: A self-organizing neural network model for a mechanism of pattern recognition unaffected by shift in position. *Biological Cybernetics*, **36**, 193–202.

Hu, M.-K. (1962) Visual pattern recognition by moment invariant. *IRE Transactions on Information Theory*, **8**, 179–87.

Menon, M.M. and Heinemann, K.G. (1988) Classification of patterns using a self-organizing neural network. *Neural Networks*, **1**(3), 201–15.

Scofield, C.L. (1988) Learning internal representations in the Coulomb energy network. *Proc. IEEE First Int. Conf. on Neural Networks*, San Diego, CA, pp. 271–6.

Index